D1674167

Arabic-Type Books Printed in Wallachia, Istanbul, and Beyond

Early Arabic Printing in the East

Edited by
Ioana Feodorov

Volume 2

Arabic-Type Books Printed in Wallachia, Istanbul, and Beyond

First Volume of Collected Works
of the TYPARABIC Project

Edited by
Radu Dipratu and Samuel Noble

DE GRUYTER

Published in connection with the project TYPARABIC at the Institute for South-East European Studies (ISEES) of the Romanian Academy: http://typarabic.ro/wordpress/en/acasa-english/

This publication is part of a project that has received funding from the European Research Council (ERC) under the Horizon 2020 research and innovation programme (883219-AdG-2019)

European Research Council
Established by the European Commission

ISBN 978-3-11-105780-4
e-ISBN (PDF) 978-3-11-106039-2
e-ISBN (EPUB) 978-3-11-106126-9
ISSN 2751-2797
DOI https://doi.org/10.1515/9783111060392

This work is licensed under the Creative Commons Attribution-NonCommercial-NoDerivatives 4.0 International License. For details go to https://creativecommons.org/licenses/by-nc-nd/4.0/.

Library of Congress Control Number: 2023950571

Bibliographic information published by the Deutsche Nationalbibliothek
The Deutsche Nationalbibliothek lists this publication in the Deutsche Nationalbibliografie; detailed bibliographic data are available on the internet at http://dnb.dnb.de.

© 2024 with the author(s), published by Walter de Gruyter GmbH, Berlin/Boston. This book is published with open access at www.degruyter.com.
Cover image: Front page of the Arabic Gospel printed at Aleppo, 1706.
Collection of the Romanian Academy Library, Bucharest.
Printing and binding: CPI books GmbH, Leck

www.degruyter.com

MIX
Papier | Fördert
gute Waldnutzung
FSC
www.fsc.org
FSC® C083411

Contents

Part 3. **Arabic Liturgical Texts in Printed Form**

Ioana Feodorov

Preface
18th-Century Arabic Printing for the Arab Christians: Most Roads Lead to Istanbul

The first conference of the TYPARABIC project team was hosted by the Library of the Holy Synod in Bucharest on September 5 and 6, 2022. Over the two days, ten core team members and six guests presented the papers published in this volume, the second in the series *Early Arabic Printing in the East* (*EAPE*) dedicated by De Gruyter to the TYPARABIC project developed in Bucharest, at the Institute for South-East European Studies of the Romanian Academy, owing to the Advanced Grant obtained in 2020 from the European Research Council (ERC) in the frame of the Horizon 2020 Grants Program. The final paper is an outcome of recent research by Habib Ibrahim, who presents it to the academic public for the first time. As I am the author of the first volume in the EAPE series, a monograph published with De Gruyter earlier this year,[1] I shall evoke below only a few essential elements of my work, useful to the presentation of the collection of essays contained in this volume.

The TYPARABIC project focuses on the research of a corpus of books printed in the 18th century in the *Arabic language*, with *Arabic type*, for the benefit of the Christians living in Ottoman provinces. Their common feature is that they were printed by Christians outside the confines of Western Europe, in presses founded in the 18th century in areas that were once part of the Byzantine Commonwealth. The corpus that we identified while preparing the project proposal for submission to the ERC included forty titles. Since then, it has been enlarged to forty-six by our increasing knowledge of further editions or reprints of these books. The first two books were printed in Arabic and Greek in Wallachia in 1701–1702, with the financial help of the local prince, Constantin Brâncoveanu, and the best printer of the time, Antim the Iberian.

---

1 I. Feodorov, *Arabic Printing for the Christians in Ottoman Lands. The East-European Connection*, Berlin/Boston, 2023, in Open Access at https://www.degruyter.com/document/doi/10.1515/9783110786996/html

---

This research is part of a project that has received funding from the European Research Council (ERC) under the European Union's Horizon 2020 research and innovation programme (Grant Agreement No. 883219-AdG-2019 – Project TYPARABIC).

∂ Open Access. © 2024 the author(s), published by De Gruyter. (cc) BY-NC-ND This work is licensed under the Creative Commons Attribution-NonCommercial-NoDerivatives 4.0 International License.
https://doi.org/10.1515/9783111060392-203

The diversified nature of the general theme has led us to more topics that are being competently and rigorously surveyed by the TYPARABIC team members, specialists in the history of printing, Ottoman history, book arts, and Christian Arabic literature. We, and myself particularly, are lucky that the excellent researchers whom I invited to join the team have agreed to this. The outcomes of our joint work will be presented to the academic community in open access, as required by the ERC project agreement.

The theme of printing is especially relevant when discussing the birth of a national consciousness in the Middle Eastern provinces of the Ottoman Empire. The role of printing in the cultural and social advancement of Syria in the 18th century was revealed by historians of the last century. First and foremost, the Syrian scholar ʿĪsā Iskandar al-Maʿlūf asserted that the transfer of printing to Greater Syria had significant consequences not only for the national and cultural progress of the Arabic-speaking populations, but also for their access to knowledge and education.[2] According to him, the dissemination of printing and the beginnings of a political press directly contributed to the growth of a national consciousness in the Ottoman lands inhabited by the Arabs and, together with other factors, generated independence movements in present-day Syria and Lebanon.

For Syria, Lebanon, and the Holy Land, the consequences of the first printing ventures in the East – in Wallachia, Aleppo, Khinshāra (Ḍūr al-Shuwayr, Mount Lebanon), Iași in Moldavia, and Beirut – were perceptible until the era of the Arab nationalist Renaissance. Fr Samir Khalil Samir, an erudite scholar of Christian Arabic studies, commented that the Nahḍa, the Arab Renaissance of the 19th century supported by the higher clergy of the Eastern Churches, was not born by chance in Syria, more precisely in the modern and multicultural city of Aleppo, called by the ancient Greeks and Romans Beroea (Βέροια).[3] The mission was then taken over by Lebanon, where the first long-term printing activity took place for more than a century and a half, between 1734 and 1898, at the Monastery of Saint John the Baptist in Khinshāra. In Beirut, over a few decades at the end of the 19th century, twenty-one journals and forty-four magazines were founded, while Lebanese of the diaspora were in the vanguard of the local Arabic language

---

2 ʿĪsā Iskandar al-Maʿlūf, "Maṭbaʿa rūmāniyya al-urthūdhuksiyya alʿarabiyya al-anṭākiyya", al-Niʿma, 3, 1911, p. 55–56.
3 S. K. Samir, S.J., "Les communautés chrétiennes, membres actifs de la société arabe au cours de l'histoire", Proche-Orient Chrétien, 47, 1997, p. 98.

press all over the world: in Egypt, the United States of America, South America, Paris, Nicosia, Cagliari, and Sardinia.[4]

This topic has been discussed from the same perspective by the Lebanese writer Maroun ʿAbboud, in his book *Ruwwād al-Nahḍa al-ḥadītha* (*The Leaders of the Modern Renaissance*, Beirut, 1966), and Albert Hourani, in *Arab Thought in the Liberal Age* (Oxford, 1967). As pertinently expressed on the website of the Bibliothèque nationale de France,

> Le Liban, province ottomane où la communauté chrétienne avait depuis longtemps une forte demande de livres imprimés, devient avec l'Égypte le grand centre d'édition. Le développement de la typographie accompagne les mouvements de renouveau culturel, de modernisation politique, d'ouverture sur l'Occident et d'éveil des indépendances.[5]

Istanbul, a focal point of all research related to Eastern printing between the end of the 15th century and the beginning of the 18th, was chosen as the key topic of the first TYPARABIC conference. Considering that next year the project will advance into a stage where the focus shifts to a careful inventory and detailed description of the book corpus, it seemed natural to start with its historical background, outlining at this early stage the social and political circumstances that caused, or allowed, its existence.

In one way or another, the project evolves in the late Ottoman epoch, when the sultan's authority was slowly decreasing and leaving room for a more modern way of governance for the many peoples that formed this vast empire. It has been said that printing and the wide circulation of modern ideas accompanying it helped nations emerge and peoples define their own future in their own lands – and hands. We thought, therefore, that the first step in addressing the multifaceted core theme of our project was to survey the social and political climate where the first Arabic presses of the Ottoman Empire were founded.

As noted by André Demeerseman in a 1954 article dedicated to Arabic-type presses, Turkey owes printing to Sultan Ahmed III and his grand vizier Ibrahim Pasha. Demeerseman approached the topic as a historian of the political and social circumstances of the Ottoman Empire in the 18th and 19th centuries. In his

---

4 B. Aggoula, "Le livre libanais de 1585 à 1900", in Camille Aboussouan (dir.), *Le livre et le Liban jusqu'à 1900*, Paris, 1982, p. 313.

5 In an unsigned text: "L'imprimé dans le monde arabe", online at: https://essentiels.bnf.fr/fr/livres-et-ecritures/histoire-des-livres-extra-occidentaux/7a29e1a3-e15c-4a49-8f80-2c2ff59ba9bb-livre-en-terres-islam/article/f0cf1f12-37f5-47c9-8259-3ba06b82e2d2-imprimerie-dans-monde-arabe (accessed October 15, 2023).

assessment of the role and influence of printing in the Middle East he took into consideration its potential for bringing down the authority of the Ottoman court.

> La raison qui incita les différents gouvernements à retarder l'introduction de l'imprimerie était le maintien de leur autorité sous sa forme ancienne et ils étaient tout naturellement inclinés à penser que les publications et surtout les journaux n'auraient pas tardé à la battre en brèche. Une censure gouvernementale même très stricte ne leur inspirait, on le conçoit, qu'une confiance très limitée.
>
> C'est très clair pour la *Turquie* où la lutte entre les partisans du régime républicain et ceux du régime monarchiste était ardente. Le sultan 'Abd el Aziz ne voyait aucun intérêt à mettre une arme aussi explosive à la disposition des jeunes Turcs. En réalité, ses craintes portaient sur l'existence de la dynastie elle-même plus encore que vis-à-vis de ce qu'on allait imprimer. Et c'est pourquoi les imprimeurs étrangers jouirent d'une relative tolérance, car les Sultans, sur le plan intérieur, redoutaient naturellement moins l'influence des étrangers que celle des Turcs eux-mêmes.
>
> Et en effet, les imprimeries non musulmanes ont précédé de loin, en Turquie, l'imprimerie turque. [...][6]

This generated a reconsideration of the complex discussions that took place at the Ottoman court and in the intellectual circles of Istanbul about the utility and potential danger that printing for a wide audience entailed. A portrait of the first Ottoman printer, Ibrahim Müteferrika, needs to accompany this recollection of the conditions in which Istanbul became, in his time, the center of Turkish printing in Arabic type. It seemed appropriate to us to consider the needs of Arabic-speaking Christians of the Byzantine-rite Churches who were tenaciously preserving their traditions and culture while living amid a Muslim population.

The present volume is divided into three parts in accordance with the diverse scientific interests of the TYPARABIC team members. Part 1 contains papers devoted to the introduction of printing in the capital of the Ottoman Empire: circumstances, chronology, *pro*s and *con*s, salient figures who helped this adventure begin. Part 2 includes texts that address the European side of the story – early printing in the Romanian Principalities and Central Europe, the collections and study of Arabic incunabula, the first Arabic-type books printed in the East, their circulation and readership, and the historical and philological information their forewords provide. Part 3 addresses topics that belong to the corpus survey that the project team focuses on, with several contributions on the *contents* and *form* of the Eastern-printed books of the 18th century, in Arabic and Greek.

---

6 A. Demeerseman, "Les données de la controverse autour du problème de l'imprimerie (fin)", *IBLA. Revue de l'Institut des Belles Lettres Arabes*, 17, 1954, 66, p. 136.

In these opening pages, I intend to explain concisely why the society, culture and prominent personalities living in 18th-century Istanbul, the Christians' city of Constantinople, are inseparable from any discussion of printing for the Arabic-speaking Christians of the Levant; or, to put it differently, why, when studying printing in the East, Istanbul is the focus of the researchers' attention more than any city inside the borders of the Ottoman Empire.

It may sound unexpected to say that, at one time, Istanbul was a center of printing and the variety of fonts used in its presses rivaled that in Western Europe. The fact that Arabic printing was banned by the Ottoman Court is a legend that several of the colleagues on our team have investigated. In the absence of specific documents issued by the Sublime Porte, testimonies about this ban come from several European travelers to the Empire such as André Thevet, who visited Istanbul around 1549[7] and asserted in his notes written in 1584 that in 1483 Sultan Bayezid II had issued a *hatt-ı şerif* obstructing the establishment of presses, a document renewed in 1515 by his son, Selim I. The penalty for printing books was allegedly nothing less than the execution of the culprit. The ban on printing was also mentioned by Paul Ricaut, who was in Istanbul in 1660, and Giovanni Donado, author of an essay on the literature of the Turks published in 1688. Still, printing was known in the empire's capital soon after Gutenberg's invention became widespread. As the contributors to this volume will explain in more detail, the above-mentioned act issued by the sultan's administration was more likely addressed to Muslims rather than to the *dhimmī*s, a point that the leaders of the Jewish communities residing in Istanbul and other Ottoman cities successfully exploited.[8] Around 1490, Jewish printers arriving from Europe started printing books they declared essential to their community, mostly necessary to religious practices. Between 1493 and 1530, Jewish printers produced in Istanbul more than a hundred books, without having secured an approval from the Ottoman authorities that would survive today, as no such document is preserved.[9] Thus, in 1493, Samuel ben Nahmias and his brother Yosef opened a Hebrew press

---

[7] A. Thevet, *Histoire des plus illustres et savans hommes de leurs siècles*, Paris, 1671, t. II, p. 111.
[8] On the background and development of this story, see D. Glass, G. Roper, "Arabic Book and Newspaper Printing in the Arab World. Part. I: The Printing of Arabic Books in the Arab World", in Hanebutt-Benz, Glass and Roper, *Middle Eastern Languages and the Print Revolution*, p. 177–226; O. Sabev (Orhan Salih), "A Virgin Deserving Paradise or a Whore Deserving Poison: Manuscript Tradition and Printed Books in Ottoman Turkish Society", in J. Miller, L. Kontler (eds.), *Friars, Nobles and Burghers. Sermons, Images and Prints, Studies of Culture and Society in Early-Modern Europe, In Memoriam István György Tóth*, Budapest/New York, 2010, p. 389–409.
[9] See Taisiya Leber's contribution to the present volume.

in Istanbul.[10] A second Hebrew press, brought by Rabbi Eliezer ben Yitzhak Ash-kenazi from Prague, may have been active there in 1563, producing only Hebrew books in Hebrew type.

Armenians were able to print in Istanbul starting in 1567, and their freedom was greater than in other regions where Armenian books were needed, as until the 1866 Ottoman Law of the Press, they were not limited in their choices of authors and works, whether by the government or by Catholic censors. Their experience with printing in the Ottoman capital and dealing with various obstacles to their activity is the reason we have included in the TYPARABIC project an Armenian direction.

The first attempt at printing in Istanbul in Greek, in 1627, is also well-known, as, again, the conference contributors discuss from a fresh perspective. The Pro-testant books brought from Holland to Istanbul by the patriarch Cyril Lukaris (1572–1638) were found inappropriate for his flock and disturbing to the Catho-lic missionaries there. Soon, the imperative for a locally-functioning Greek press became urgent. How this worked out, the authors of several essays included in this volume expertly explain. Suffice it to say that for a while, Greek printers were at work in the Ottoman capital and Greek type and printing tools, even if impor-ted from England, were used to produce books in the Ottoman capital.

By the third decade of the 18th century, when the first Turkish press was opened in the capital of the empire, a large variety of competencies were already at play there, as a reflection of the diversity of linguistic communities and ethnic-ities that Istanbul hosted. One of the theories put forward to explain the source of the Arabic type used by Savary de Brevès in Paris is that he obtained it in Istan-bul around 1600, during his mission there. Arabic type was created by European printers since the early days of the art, possibly the first being Geoffroy Tory, printer of the king of France François I. De Brevès spent twenty-two years in the East, and printing in Arabic was only one of the many skills that he mastered when back in Paris. He first arrived in Istanbul in 1585, and, as this city made a strong impression on him, he resided there as ambassador of France to the Sublime Porte between 1593 and 1605. While in Istanbul, he collected more than one hundred oriental manuscripts, including a *Qāmūs*, an Arabic dictionary in two volumes. His connections there gave rise to conjecture that he ordered local craftsmen to create Arabic type, modelled on the Arabic script of Ottoman manu-scripts.[11] The stronger theory is that he obtained them while serving as an ambas-

---

10 A. Yaari, *Ha-Defus ha-Ivri be-Kushta*, Jerusalem, 1967.
11 G. Duverdier, "De la recherche à l'étude des manuscrits", in Aboussouan (dir.), *Le livre et le Liban jusqu'à 1900*, p. 211.

sador of France in Rome, after 1607. Although this idea was supported by Gérald Duverdier, a librarian at Collège de France and an expert in Oriental printing, the former explanation remains an avenue to further investigate.

The case of Ibrahim Müteferrika was discussed from various perspectives in the first session of our conference. My comments here only address its role in putting Istanbul on the map of the TYPARABIC project. Since we are studying Christian Arabic books, why would an Ottoman press printing Turkish books be of interest to us? Well, this particular press and its founder were the reasons why printing became a topic for passionate discussions in learned circles and at the Sublime Porte. They fueled the dispute between conservatives and modernists, brought supporters of a Western-style society, where knowledge would circulate freely, face to face with traditionalists who preferred their Scriptures to come in manuscript form, as always. The sultan's administration was rather indifferent to the circulation of Western printed material in the vast provinces that it governed. Presses had worked and flourished for centuries in territories ruled or controlled by Catholic and Protestant regimes. But the situation became complicated when the battle between conflicting churches was transferred to Istanbul, where various ambassadors and missionaries promoted divergent interests, also in connection with book-printing. As this imported technology became a reason for dissension in the various divisions of legal authority and confessional leadership, the Sublime Porte was called to have an active role in the approval of the first Turkish press to function in the empire's capital.

Although limited by the approval to print only Turkish lay works, i.e., mostly of a scientific content, and denied the right to print the Qur'an and any other Islamic texts, Müteferrika succeeded in producing seventeen volumes between 1729 and 1742, to which he added a naval chart of the Black Sea of outstanding military value.[12] His strategies, in terms of diplomatic and scholarly support secured from the Istanbul intelligentsia, are worth studying to a deeper extent, as they will help us answer a broader question: how was it possible for Christians to print their liturgical and polemical books in Ottoman-ruled territories?

It is useful to note here that Wahid Gdoura, author of the first Ph.D. thesis and published essay dedicated to printing under the Ottomans, got it all wrong in terms of chronology. He chose as a title *Le Début de l'imprimerie arabe à Istanbul et en Syrie: Évolution de l'Environnement Culturel (1706–1787)*.[13] In fact, the press of Aleppo in Syria came first, opening its series of books in 1706, while in Istanbul

---

12 Printed in 1724–1725. Five copies are preserved worldwide.
13 W. Gdoura, *Le Début de l'imprimerie arabe à Istanbul et en Syrie: Évolution de l'Environnement Culturel (1706–1787)*, Tunis, 1985 (with a second, slightly enlarged Arabic edition).

Ibrahim Müteferrika only started to print in 1729. Between 1706 and 1711, Athanasios Dabbās, in between his two terms as patriarch of the Church of Antioch, printed eleven titles in Aleppo, including liturgical books, homilies and Christian teachings. Nevertheless, due to the scarcity of sources on this topic, Gdoura succeeded in convincing a broad audience that Arabic printing was first achieved in Istanbul.

The Ottoman metropolis was a vast book market where scholars and students from all over the empire came to look for sources to improve their learning and complete their education. If Islamic manuscript texts circulated and were available for purchase in this City of Knowledge, printed books and, remarkably, Christian works were not totally absent from the market. It is in Istanbul that the Romanian Ottomanist Aurel Decei purchased in 1945 a copy of the Book of Hours printed in Bucharest in 1702 by Antim the Iberian and Athanasios Dabbās (now in the collections of the Library of the Romanian Academy). According to a note written on one of the inside covers, the book had belonged to the Greek Catholic Archdiocese of Aleppo, then to the Maronite bishop Germanos Farḥāt. When exactly and how it had reached Istanbul remains a mystery.

The Ottoman capital was also the focus of the Eastern patriarchs' interests, as it was there that most of the laws and regulations that made the Christians' life easy or hard were decided. This was especially the case in the remote provinces ruled by governors who were able to keep a low profile and rule over their *dhimmī* subjects as they pleased. The patriarchs of the Church of Antioch needed the support of influential people at the Ottoman court. Even if the sultan's 'lobby' did not much resemble modern ones, the delicate job of 'lobbying' was not invented in the 20th-century Western world. Thus, Makarios III ibn al-Zaʿīm kept a permanent representative in the capital, who would promptly inform him of the events at court of consequence for the situation of his church. Patriarchs were bound to address the court to receive a firman confirming their election to the See of Antioch, often paid for with large sums of money. Hasan Çolak has surveyed and published letters of Patriarch Sylvester of Antioch held at the Başbakanlık Osmanlı Arşivleri (BOA) in Istanbul containing his pleas and appeals to important people at the sultan's court.

The letters composed by the deacon Mūsā Nawfal Ṭrābulsī, one of the Patriarch Sylvester's disciples and assistants, which are conserved in a file in the library of the Syriac Orthodox Patriarchate of Antioch in Ḥoms (*Ms. nr. 9/22*),[14] provide rich information on the patriarch's journeys to and from Istanbul while

---

14 The manuscript was surveyed in 1968 by Rachid Haddad, who published a commentary on the collection of letters in 2006, in a volume dedicated to Mgr. Joseph Nasrallah.

traveling between the Romanian Principalities and Damascus. The patriarch printed in 1746-1747 at the Monastery of Saint Sava in Iași several books with Arabic type whose origin is still unknown. When this type was worn out, he was unable to obtain a good new set in Iași, and in October 1746 he left for Constantinople, thinking that he could find one there. It is not unlikely that even the first Arabic type-font had been obtained from the Ottoman capital.[15] There, Ibrahim Müteferrika had been printing since 1729, in Turkish with Arabic type, scientific books on geography, language, and state policy. By 1743, he had printed seven titles in 500 to 1,000 copies each. Therefore, his workshop would have had a lot of Arabic type and the knowhow to create new parts. In 1743, Müteferrika retired from the workshop due to poor health, but the printing activity continued. Mūsā's letters refer to Sylvester's efforts to obtain Arabic type in Moldavia and Wallachia, and his departure from Iași to Istanbul for the same purpose. They also reveal the patriarch's efforts to have Arabic type made in the new *metochion* that prince Constantine Mavrocordatos had granted him, the Monastery of Saint Spyridon in Bucharest, where Syrian monks already resided in 1746. The most salient figure in Mūsā Ṭrābulsī's letters is Yūsuf Mark, one of the patriarch's disciples, who reached Bucharest in 1747 and stayed there for nearly three years, until 1750. In a letter to Mūsā, Yūsuf Mark reports that when he reached Bucharest, he found Patriarch Sylvester at the Monastery of Saint Spyridon, busy supervising the manufacture of Arabic type.[16] This is proof enough that the patriarch's quest for Arabic type in Istanbul was not successful.

Mūsā Ṭrābulsī's collection of letters also reveals that Istanbul was a center of scholarly life where Antiochian hierarchs headed when they wished to further their education. Sophronios of Kilis (al-Kilislī)[17] — first, bishop of Acre, then elected patriarch of Jerusalem in 1771, and finally patriarch of Constantinople as Sophronius II, on December 24, 1774 — was aware that good knowledge of ecclesiastical Greek would be an asset in all future posts he would occupy in the church hierarchy. Learning Classical Greek was one of the purposes of the Eastern clerics who left for Constantinople, and later for Bucharest and Iași, aiming to follow the classes of the Princely Academies.[18] It was with the financial help of princes of the Romanian Principalities born in the Fener and the wealthy people of Istanbul

---

15 There is no similarity, as far as we could see, between the Müteferrika and the Beirut type. We still do not know where the Patriarch Sylvester acquired the first set of Arabic type used in Iași.
16 Letter to Mūsā Ṭrābulsī, dated 21 November 1747 (f. 21r).
17 Ca. 1700–1780.
18 In Bucharest after 1694, in Iași after 1707.

that Patriarch Dositheos II Notaras founded schools for Greek and Arabic learning in Jerusalem, Ramla and Kerak.

A new avenue of research has recently been opened in connection with the manufacture of matrices for seals, a prized object that was necessary to all the patriarchs of the churches of the East. Apparently, the best engravers and manufacturers of seals were located – again – in Istanbul. This is especially useful in the examination of the Greek Orthodox (patriarchal?) emblem placed at the end of the Arabic Akathist that I described in my above mentioned work published in 2023,[19] a puzzling book that encloses many a mystery. If Sylvester hunted for Arabic type in the capital of the Ottoman Empire, did he also order there a seal for himself, which he first used in asserting himself as the publisher of the Arabic Akathist preserved in a unique copy, without a title page or colophon?

We should not forget that Istanbul was also the place where rebel princes of the Romanian Principalities were taken by the sultans' emissaries to be punished, replaced, or executed, as was the case with Constantin Brâncoveanu and Antim the Iberian, who were both sentenced in Constantinople (and consecrated as martyr saints by the Romanian Orthodox Church).

It is worth mentioning that interest in printing Christian books existed in Istanbul until late in the 19th century. The library of the Holy Savior Monastery in Şarba (Jūniye), Lebanon holds an Ottoman Turkish version of the New Testament, in 639 pages, printed in Arabic type in Istanbul in 1866.[20] Such cases of an assortment of languages and scripts – not to mention the predictable question of who they were intended for – are too intriguing not to catch the eye of the Ottoman history specialists in our team.

To conclude, Istanbul presents, within the general aim of our project, a cluster of themes connected to the printing presses, their founders, and the general background of the transfer of a Western European technology, through an Eastern European intermediary, all the way to Aleppo, Khinshāra, and Beirut. As the capital of the empire, where the life of all Ottoman subjects and tribute-paying communities was decided, as a milieu for the dispute around the use and misuse of the press, and as host of a somewhat successful printing workshop established in the third decade of the 18th century, Istanbul is worthy of drawing our interest. This volume is dedicated both to the role of Istanbul in this story and the production of the first Arabic-type presses in the East, in terms of contents and book art.

---

19 Feodorov, *Arabic Printing for the Christians in Ottoman Lands*, p. 250–253.
20 Accessible online in the Virtual HMML database (vHMML), project number OBARL 00009.

The ERC conducted a survey during the summer of 2022, asking principal investigators of the projects it finances to fill in a questionnaire about the progress of their team's research and an assessment of the support they receive from the host institution and the team members. The declared intention of the ERC was "to map the breadth and diversity of the research it supports." The final report was released at the end of August 2022 and made available on the ERC website. While defining their aim, the ERC defined *us*, the *grantees*, by declaring that "The ERC funds curiosity-driven research without predetermined thematic priorities." Indeed, we, the TYPARABIC project team, are conducting "curiosity-driven research," as we are driven by curiosity in our research work, with a good chance to achieve ground-breaking results, as the contributors to this volume demonstrate.

Editors' Note

This research is part of a project that has received funding from the European Research Council (ERC) under the European Union's Horizon 2020 research and innovation programme (Grant Agreement No. 883219-AdG-2019 – Project TYPARABIC).

This book is the second volume of the De Gruyter series *Early Arabic Printing in the East* published by members of the TYPARABIC project team in 2023–2026.

All transcriptions from languages other than English follow the Library of Congress system.

Illustrations reproduced from books preserved in the collections of the Library of the Romanian Academy in Bucharest are marked "B.A.R.". We express our gratitude for the approval to publish them.

Illustrations reproduced from books preserved in the collections of the Library of the Holy Synod in Bucharest are marked "B.S.S.". We are grateful to its director, Archim. Policarp Chițulescu, for the approval to print these images.

For all the other illustrations, mention is made of the sources and owner who agreed to their reproduction in the present volume.

The editors thank Ioana Feodorov, Principal Investigator of the TYPARABIC project, and Yulia Petrova, Senior Researcher on the project team, for their thorough review of the final version of the texts included in this book.

We are equally grateful to Andreea Badea for her help in completing the text submitted by the late Dr. Doru Bădără, whose fond memory stays with us.

The De Gruyter team – Aaron Sanborn-Overby, Katrin Hudey, and Teodor Borsa – assisted the editors in the timely progress of this book toward its publication stage. Thank you all for your constant support.

Open Access. © 2024 the author(s), published by De Gruyter. [CC BY-NC-ND] This work is licensed under the Creative Commons Attribution-NonCommercial-NoDerivatives 4.0 International License.
https://doi.org/10.1515/9783111060392-204

Part 1. **Printing in Istanbul, for Istanbul**

Hasan Çolak

İbrahim Müteferrika and the Ottoman Intellectual Culture in the Early 18th Century: a Transcultural Perspective

Why have they not read? Why have they not developed curiosity?
Why have they not wanted to learn? ... In my inheritance,
they will find piles of unsold books. They have not read the ones
that I printed. They have not paid attention to the thing
that I call science. Descartes, Copernicus, Keppler, Galileo
were fairy tales to them... They have not read...
What is this life then? What have I lived for?
What have I achieved?[1]

Written in a stage play in the 1980s, these sentences allude to İbrahim Müteferrika's disappointment with his legacy as a printer on his deathbed. The prized play was written by Jale Baysal, a prominent expert on Müteferrika and printing in Ottoman Turkish. Although she wrote a fictional account of Müteferrika, Baysal relied heavily on her knowledge of the primary and secondary sources on Müteferrika and took care to include pieces of this knowledge into her play.[2] She also gave special importance to presenting Müteferrika with due attention to the qualities that he had both before and after his conversion to Islam. In a similar effort of transcending physical and mental borders, she advised in the introduction that the roles of the people around Müteferrika both in Koloszvár/Cluj and Istanbul should be played by the very same stage actors and actresses.[3] The image of Müteferrika in this play is that of an intellectual fighting for progressive values against a rather rigid intelligentsia and society despite the presence of a handful of individuals in the Ottoman court who tried to help him with his task of estab-

---

1 J. Baysal, *Cennetlik İbrahim Efendi (İbrahim Müteferrika Oyunu)*, Istanbul, 1992, p. 89–90.
2 For a case in which she included a passage from Niyazi Berkes' *Encyclopedia of Islam* article on Müteferrika, see Baysal, *Cennetlik İbrahim Efendi*, p. 24. The said article can be found in N. Berkes, "İbrahim Müteferrika", *The Encyclopaedia of Islam, Second Edition*, vol. III, ed. by B. Lewis, V. L. Ménage, C. Pellat, J. Schacht, Leiden, 1971, p. 996–998.
3 Baysal, *Cennetlik İbrahim Efendi*, p. 3.

This research is part of a project that has received funding from the European Research Council (ERC) under the European Union's Horizon 2020 research and innovation programme (Grant Agreement No. 883219-AdG-2019 – Project TYPARABIC).

∂ Open Access. © 2024, the author(s), published by De Gruyter. (cc) BY-NC-ND This work is licensed under the Creative Commons Attribution-NonCommercial-NoDerivatives 4.0 International License.
https://doi.org/10.1515/9783111060392-001

lishing his printing press. Throughout the play, we see Müteferrika, among his other tasks, writing, commentating, and translating several books, and dealing with many technical and administrative aspects of establishing and maintaining a printing press in Istanbul.

Recent scholarship on İbrahim Müteferrika has shed light on many aspects of this Ottoman printer's life, career, and scholarly and printing activities in the Ottoman Empire, aspects that had been little explored or simply unknown until recent decades.[4] Accordingly, thanks to recent revisionist historiography, the earlier caricature image of an intellectual fighting for progressive values against a rather rigid intelligentsia and society gradually gave way to a more realistic understanding of Müteferrika and his scholarly and printing endeavors. Despite such depth and breadth of scholarship, I believe that there is still a need to delve further into Müteferrika's intellectual entanglements with broader Ottoman intellectual society, one that mirrors the diversity of the Ottoman world. For this purpose, the present paper focuses on some illustrative examples in which a transcultural perspective could help provide a better understanding of both Müteferrika and Ottoman intellectual culture at large. Focusing on Müteferrika as an Ottoman intellectual who was born and raised as a non–Muslim outside the direct influence of the Ottoman scholarly currents, and his own contributions to the larger Ottoman intellectual culture, a broader aim of this paper is to point out the crucial importance of the transcultural aspects of Müteferrika and the intellectual culture surrounding him. This paper maintains that despite his rather exceptional qualities, İbrahim Müteferrika was not alone in his endeavor in generating knowledge across cultural borders. Therefore, it draws on the transcultural networks connected directly and indirectly to him. Accordingly, it highlights the necessity to think beyond the conventional communal borders by highlighting the networks

---

4 *Matbaanın Ön Sözü "Basmacı İbrahim Efendi": Müteferrika Sergisi'21*, Ankara, 2021; Y. Erdem, *Müteferrika'nın İzinde: Kitap ve Matbuat Tarihi Yazıları*, Istanbul, 2021; K. Beydilli, *İki İbrahim: Müteferrika ve Halefi*, Istanbul, 2019; O. Sabev, *Waiting for Müteferrika: Glimpses of Ottoman Print Culture*, Boston, 2018; O. Sabev, *İbrahim Müteferrika ya da İlk Osmanlı Matbaa Serüveni*, Istanbul, 2016 (1st ed. 2006); E. Afyoncu, "İbrahim Müteferrika Hakkında Önemli Bir Vesika", *Türk Kültürü İncelemeleri Dergisi*, 28, 2013, p. 51–56; V. Erginbaş, "Enlightenment in the Ottoman Context: İbrahim Müteferrika and His Intellectual Landscape", in G. Roper (ed.), *Historical Aspects of Printing and Publishing in Languages of the Middle East. Papers from the Symposium at the University of Leipzig, September 2008*, Leiden, 2013, p. 53–100; S. Karahasanoğlu, "Osmanlı Matbaasının Başarısını/Başarısızlığını Yeniden Gözden Geçirmek ya da İbrahim Müteferrika'nın Terekesinin Tespitine Katkı", *Journal of Turkish Studies*, 33/1, 2010, p. 319–328; F. Sarıcaoğlu, C. Yılmaz, *Müteferrika: Basmacı İbrahim Efendi ve Müteferrika Matbaası/Basmacı İbrahim Efendi and the Müteferrika Press*, İstanbul, 2008; E. Afyoncu, "İlk Türk Matbaacısının Kurucusu Hakkında Yeni Bilgiler", *Belleten*, 243, 2001, p. 607–622.

between individuals and institutions that do not immediately pop into our minds when we talk about the Ottoman world of printing. These networks involve individuals such as the Orthodox patriarch of Jerusalem Chrysanthos Notaras, one of the most important Muslim scholars of the 18th century Esad Efendi of Ioannina, the Armenian engraver Mıgırdiç Galatavi, and the Jewish printer Yona Ashkenazi. In working on these individuals and institutions, it also offers a discussion of the major activities related to printing such as copy-editing, translating, commentating, engraving,[5] and broader aspects of printing such as the history of reading and libraries.

In discussing this topic, this paper benefits from the theoretical framework offered by Wolfgang Welsch, notably his conception of transculturality. Welsch maintains that the earlier conception of culture as defined by Herder refers to three major characteristics: social homogenization, ethnic consolidation, and intercultural delimitation. As such, cultures do not interact with each other as if they are islands. Later on, several alternatives have been suggested against Herder's conception of single cultures. While interculturality was aimed at fostering interactions between cultures that occupy different spaces, multiculturalism defined the presence of different cultures that share the same space. Nonetheless, Welsch claimed, for all their positive intentions, these alternatives contain a somewhat similar conception of cultures as homogenous entities. Welsch offers an alternative to these approaches by focusing on the interactions of cultures in several layers. Welsch's conception of transculturality refers to three main characteristics of cultures: their networks with external cultures, their internal differences, and hybridity.[6] Even though Welsch rarely delves into the historical aspects of the term except for his recent book, in which he analyzes certain historical figures through the concept of transculturality,[7] several scholars, includ-

---

5 A. Kabacalı, *Türk Kitap Tarihi*, Part 1. *Başlangıçtan Tanzimat'a Kadar*, Istanbul, 1989; İ. E. Erünsal, *Orta Çağ İslâm Dünyasında Kitap ve Kütüphane*, Istanbul, 2018.
6 For a review of Welsch's criticisms against the Herderian conception of cultures and the alternative concepts of interculturality and multiculturalism, and Welsch's proposal of the concept of transculturality, see W. Welsch, "Transculturality: the changing form of cultures today", *Filozofski Vestnik*, 22/2, 2001, p. 59–86; W. Welsch, "Transculturality – the Puzzling Form of Cultures Today", in M. Featherstone, S. Lash (eds.), *Spaces of Culture: City, Nation, World*, London, 1999, p. 194–213.
7 W. Welsch, *Transkulturalität: Realität – Geschichte – Aufgabe*, Vienna, 2017.

ing some Ottomanists,[8] have incorporated this concept as an analytical grid for explaining historical phenomena.[9]

The three characteristics of transculturality perfectly fit the persona of İbrahim Müteferrika. First, as an intellectual who was in contact with scholarly currents in Europe through his knowledge of several European languages, his networks with external cultures support the idea that he was an exceptional figure in Ottoman intellectual history. Second, despite his conversion to Islam – and even writing an individual tract on Islam[10] – İbrahim Müteferrika's persona probably differed in several ways from other Muslims in the Ottoman Empire, with all their internal differences, which serves his image as an exceptional character. Finally, his hybrid persona, which combines his pre- and post-conversion qualities also strengthen the exceptional nature of his persona in the Ottoman world. While it would be unfair not to recognize Müteferrika's rather exceptional qualities, presenting him as a unique figure in Ottoman intellectual history as we see in the play by Baysal would also be unfair to the people who frequented the same intellectual circles as Müteferrika.

This paper is not the first one to analyze Müteferrika as part of broader Ottoman realities. Nevertheless, there is still a need for a more systematic analysis of both the Müteferrika press and Müteferrika's intellectual network from a transcultural perspective. While the scholarship on the Müteferrika press is careful to mention that there were other presses in the empire owned by Ottoman non–Muslims, until recent decades the possibility of interaction between different presses in the Ottoman Empire had been either little-explored, ignored, or over-ruled rather than actually analyzed as a topic. Baysal, for instance, claimed in her 1968 magnum opus on the books published by the Ottoman Turks, that the print-

---

8 P. Firges, T. P. Graf, "Exploring the contact zone: A critical assessment from the perspective of early modern Euro–Ottoman history", in L. Abu–Er–Rub, C. Brosius, S. Meurer, D. Panagiotopoulos, S. Richter (eds.), *Engaging Transculturality: Concepts, Key Terms, Case Studies*, London/New York, 2019, p. 109–122; R. Murphey, "Ottoman Medicine and Transculturalism from the Sixteenth through the Eighteenth Century", *Bulletin of the History of Medicine*, 66, 1992, p. 376–403.

9 For a few examples, see C. Zhang, *Transculturality and German Discourse in the Age of European Colonialism*, Evanston, 2017; M. Herren, M. Rüesch, C. Sibille, *Transcultural History: Theories, Methods, Sources*, Berlin-Heidelberg, 2012; A. Benessaieh, "Multiculturalism, Interculturality, Transculturality", in A. Benessaieh (ed.), *Amériques Transculturelles – Transcultural Americas*, Ottawa, 2010, p. 11–38; L. Abu–Er–Rub, C. Brosius, S. Meurer, D. Panagiotopoulos, S. Richter (eds.), *Engaging Transculturality: Concepts, Key Terms, Case Studies*, London/New York, 2019.

10 For information on İbrahim Müteferrika's *Risâle-i İslâmiyye*, and the trasliteration of this text (p. 55–139), see H. Necatioğlu, *Matbaacı İbrahim Müteferrika ve Risâle-i İslâmiye (Tenkidli metin)*, Ankara, 1982.

ing houses owned by non-Muslims "did not publish anything in Turkish or about Turkish culture" and "played no role whatsoever" for the Müteferrika press.[11] After drawing on the role of Müteferrika and the Ottoman ambassador Mehmed Said Efendi, and the protection offered by the grand vizier İbrahim Pasha and the sultan Ahmed III, she asserted that the Müteferrika press "was established and developed in complete disconnection from the minority presses."[12]

Recent years have witnessed important developments in the literature on the Müteferrika press and Müteferrika himself. One of the major occupations of this revisionist scholarship is its accent on contextualizing Müteferrika within the broader Ottoman world rather than emphasizing his exceptionality. However, unless we delve into the transcultural aspects of Ottoman intellectual culture, these revisionist works might also suffer from the problems of earlier scholarship.

In a recent piece, Vefa Erginbaş, for instance, draws on the importance of the "environment where he was surrounded by an enlightened elite."[13] In presenting this enlightened circle, he notes that it "was not confined to his friends among the Ottoman intelligentsia"[14] and that it "included Muslim as well as non-Muslim bureaucrats, religious dignitaries, scholars, linguists, commanders, soldiers, and scientists."[15] In his analysis, however, if we exclude the case of Humbaracı Ahmed Pasha/Comte de Bonneval, the Ottoman intellectuals in his circle are presented as if few of them had networks with external cultures, internal differences, or hybridity. All the Ottoman figures in his network appear to be Muslims, all the Christian ones are Europeans and there is no reference to a single non–Muslim Ottoman intellectual. So, this image of Ottoman Muslims and European Christians reminds us of the concept of interculturality in which somewhat homogenous groups from different spaces collaborate with each other. Therefore, Erginbaş reaches the inevitable conclusion of presenting Müteferrika as an exception: "an Ottoman man of the Enlightenment in a unique way."[16]

To return to the play by Baysal quoted at the beginning of this piece, it is necessary to note that it presents Ottoman Muslim men of learning (ulemâ)[17] as being opposed to printing. She narrates the meeting between the young Müteferrika

---

11 J. Baysal, *Osmanlı Türklerinin Bastıkları Kitaplar, 1729–1875*, Istanbul, 2010 (1st ed. 1968), p. 4.

12 Baysal, *Osmanlı Türklerinin Bastıkları Kitaplar*, p. 4.

13 Erginbaş, "Enlightenment in the Ottoman Context", p. 95.

14 Erginbaş, "Enlightenment in the Ottoman Context", p. 84.

15 Erginbaş, "Enlightenment in the Ottoman Context", p. 84.

16 Erginbaş, "Enlightenment in the Ottoman Context", p. 85.

17 For an introductory essay on the ulemâ, see H. A. R. Gibb, H. Bowen, *Islamic society and the West: A study of the impact of Western Civilization in Moslem culture in the Near East*, Vol. I *Islamic Society in the Eighteenth Century*, part II, New York, 1957, p. 81–113.

and the judge (*kadı*) of Istanbul as a conflictual one. The judge, who is depicted as a rather difficult character, is initially happy with Müteferrika. Yet, after interpreting his eagerness for learning as lack of manners, he has Müteferrika lashed and swears at him as "the accursed one who fell from the waist of an infidel!" (*gâvur belinden düşmüş lain!*).[18] Likewise, as Baysal writes in one instance, the French ambassador to the Porte, de Lacroix, tells Müteferrika that "men of religion and the teachers in the *medrese*s" reported to the Ottoman sultan only the potential negative results of printing, a point that Müteferrika confirms.[19]

However, it is well known that the Ottoman *ulemâ* took a very active role in the building and functioning of the printing press.[20] First and foremost, the Ottoman grand mufti Yenişehirli Abdullah Efendi issued a *fetva* in favor of printing "dictionaries and books of logic, philosophy, astronomy, and other high sciences" (*lugat ve mantık ve hikmet ve hey'et ve bunların emsali ulûm-i aliyyede telif olunan kitaplar*).[21] An often-overlooked aspect of this *fetva* is its particular emphasis on copy-editing conducted by competent people. The *fetva* specifies the book to be printed as "a copy-edited book" (*bir musahhah kitap*) and identifies the copy-editors of the text as "a few men of learning who will be appointed with the task of copy-editing the book to be printed" (*birkaç âlim kimesneler sureti nakş olınacak kitabı tashîh için tayin olunup*). As a side note, it must be remarked that after being appointed as the grand mufti by the grand vizier Damat İbrahim Pasha, Yenişehirli Abdullah remained in his post for a long period of time (12.5 years) and was in agreement with the reformist policies of the grand vizier.[22] Likewise, a cursory glance at his *fetva*s on Muslim-non-Muslim interactions also shows his concern for social cohesion.[23] Such concern for social cohesion was probably a key factor for the cohesion between the Ottoman Muslim and non-Muslim men of letters.

---

18 Baysal, *Cennetlik İbrahim Efendi*, p. 49.
19 Baysal, *Cennetlik İbrahim Efendi*, p. 57–58.
20 For a recent evaluation of this theme, see Beydilli, *İki İbrahim: Müteferrika ve Halefi*, p. 15–16. For the role of the *ulemâ* in legitimizing the reforms in the 18th century Ottoman Empire, see M. İpşirli, *Osmanlı İlmiyesi*, İstanbul, 2021, p. 36.
21 Şeyhülislam Yenişehirlî Abdullah Efendi, *Behcetü'l–Fetâvâ*, ed. by S. Kaya, B. Algın, Z. Trabzonlu, A. Erkan, Istanbul, 2011, p. 567–568. On this *fetva*, see also, H. Y. Nuhoğlu, "Müteferrika Matbaasının Kurulması için Verilen Fetvâ Üzerine", *Basım ve Yayıncılığımızın 250. Yılı Bilimsel Toplantısı, 10–11 Aralık 1979, Ankara, Bildiriler*, Ankara, 1980, p. 119–126.
22 M. İpşirli, "Lale Devrinde Yenilikçi Bir Âlim: Şeyhülislam Yenişehirli Abdullah Efendi", in M. Armağan (ed.), *Masaldan Gerçeğe Lale Devri*, Istanbul, 2014, p. 267–277.
23 Şeyhülislam Yenişehirlî Abdullah Efendi, *Behcetü'l–Fetâvâ*, p. 178–186.

To return to the role of the copy-editors (*musahhih*), in the play by Baysal, there is also reference to an unnamed copy-editor. This character is possibly the most interesting person and is depicted in stark contrast to Müteferrika. He is portrayed as an arrogant person who lacks Müteferrika's idealism and threatens him with quitting his job of editing a text in which he found a grammatical problem in Arabic prose.[24] The representation of his indifferent attitude towards the printing press is understandable given the rather negative representation of the Ottoman Muslim men of learning in this play. Only after Müteferrika feeds the arrogance of the copy-editor with sweet words does he calm down and, with a narcissistic smile, says the following words about Müteferrika: "The rascal is a reasonable infidel!" (*Makul keferedir kerata!*).[25]

As the historian of that time Çelebizâde İsmail Âsım informs us, three of these copy-editors came from the *ulemâ* ranks and one was a Mevlevî shaykh: İshak Efendi, Pîrîzâde Sâhib Mehmed Efendi and Esad Efendi, the former judges of Istanbul, Thessaloniki and Galata, and Mûsâ Efendi the shaykh of the Mevlevî tekke in Kasımpaşa.[26]

A closer look at the personae and activities of at least one of these copyeditors, Esad Efendi from Ioannina, shows that he displayed quite similar characteristics to Müteferrika in addition to collaborating with him in printing. He was the judge (*kadı*) of Galata, a teacher (*müderris*) in the prestigious Eyüp Sultan *medrese*, and a prominent man of thinking and letters.[27] He wrote and translated several books in what the Ottomans called *elsine-i selâse*, the three major languages in which Ottoman Muslim scholars wrote: Turkish, Arabic, and Persian. He was also a notable translator and commentator of several texts by Aristotle and his commentators. His interests concentrated on logic, philosophy, astronomy and physics, and he was also a prominent poet of his time. What caused several scholars to regard him as rather an exception, much like in the case of Müteferrika, is the fact that he also knew Greek. His most notable work is *al-Ta'līm al-thālith* which he wrote in Arabic.[28]

---

24 Baysal, *Cennetlik İbrahim Efendi*, p. 76.

25 Baysal, *Cennetlik İbrahim Efendi*, p. 77.

26 Râşid Mehmed Efendi, Çelebizâde İsmaîl Âsım Efendi, *Târîh-i Râşid ve Zeyli*, ed. by A. Özcan, Y. Uğur, B. Çakır, A. Z. İzgöer, Istanbul, 2013, vol. 3, p. 1548.

27 K. Sarıkavak, *XVIII. Yüzyılda Bir Osmanlı Düşünürü, Yanyalı Esad Efendi: Bir Rönesans Denemesi*, Ankara, 1997; B. H. Küçük, "Natural Philosophy and Politics in the Eighteenth Century: Esad of Ioannina and Greek Aristotelianism at the Ottoman Court", *Osmanlı Araştırmaları / The Journal of Ottoman Studies*, 41, 2013, p. 125–158.

28 For the copy handwritten by Esad Efendi himself, see Süleymaniye Yazma Eserler Kütüphanesi, Ragıp Paşa Collection, 824.

This book is a commentary of the first three books of Aristotle's Physics and it is based on Ioannis Kottounios' 17th century Latin commentary on the Physics.[29] In translating the books by Aristotle and Kottounios, Esad Efendi was assisted by a Greek Orthodox intellectual, who was attached to the Patriarchal Academy. So, in great contrast with the copy-editor's attitude to even a convert from Christianity such as Müteferrika in Baysal's play, Esad Efendi in fact collaborated with a Greek Orthodox translator, but there was even more than that.

Esad Efendi was also in correspondence with one of the most influential and notable Orthodox scholars of the time, namely Chrysanthos Notaras, the patriarch of Jerusalem.[30] Just as Müteferrika and Esad Efendi, Notaras knew both Eastern and Western languages and, just like Müteferrika, was presented as a representative of the Ottoman Enlightenment by Erginbaş.[31] One of the most definitive books on Notaras describes him as the "precursor" (*prodromos*) of the Neohellenic Enlightenment.[32] His studies in astronomy were nourished by works written in Greek, Latin and Arabic. One of the manuscripts that he wrote, for instance, shows that he worked on astronomical terminology in Greek through Arabic. Esad Efendi and Chrysanthos Notaras corresponded in Greek and exchanged gifts such as delights (*rahatulhulkum*, which Esad wrote not in Arabic but Greek characters) and fascicles (*ta tzouzia*). Were these fascicles the ones that Chrysanthos Notaras published? Did they have any influence on the materials that Müteferrika published or vice versa? Unfortunately, it is impossible to answer these questions on the basis of the correspondence between them. However, given the depth and breadth of their correspondence, one should not be surprised to see the scholarly exchanges in the realm of printing. We should also remark that the two men also mention other scholars in their correspondence. These include the chief astrologer, an unnamed friend of the chief astrologer, and some other Christians.[33]

---

29 I. Kottounios, *Commentarii lucidissimi in octo libros Aristotelis de physico auditu; una cum quaestionibus*, Venice, 1648. On Kottounios, see G. K. Myaris, "O filosofos tou 17ou aiona Ioannis Kottounios kai i ideologiki prossengisi tou ergou tou", *Peri Istorias*, 4, 2003, p. 183–215.

30 P. Stathi, "O 'sofotatos Esat Efentis' filos kai allilografos tou Chrysanthou Notara", *O Eranistis*, 18, 1986, 57–84.

31 Erginbaş, "Enlightenment in the Ottoman Context", p. 67–82.

32 P. Stathi, *Chrysanthos Notaras Patriarchis Ierosolymon: Prodromos tou Neoellinikou Diafotismou*, Athens, 1999.

33 Stathi, "O 'sofotatos Esat Efentis'". For an analysis of Chrysanthos Notaras' activities in the connected fields of science, theology, and politics with special reference to the Ottoman realities of the time, see H. Çolak, "Bilim, İlahiyat ve Siyasetin Merkezinde Bir Osmanlı Münevveri: Kudüs Patriği Chrysanthos Notaras", *Kebikeç İnsan Bilimleri İçin Kaynak Araştırmaları Dergisi*, 47, 2019, p. 31–56.

Several other Muslim intellectuals around Müteferrika were also in connection with Europe. The first Ottoman ambassador to Europe, Yirmisekiz Mehmet Çelebi, and his son Mehmet Said Efendi, who accompanied his father to Paris and went to Stockholm as the Ottoman ambassador, supported Müteferrika's endeavours in establishing a printing press in Istanbul. Therefore, Müteferrika was not much different in terms of his connections with external cultures beyond the nominal borders of the Ottoman Empire.

One of the Ottoman non-Muslim printers with whom Müteferrika exchanged ideas was Yona ben Ya'akov Ashkenazi, an Ottoman Jew from Poland. Yona's printing house was the most active Jewish printing house in Istanbul. Between 1710 and 1778, Yona, his three sons and grandsons published 188 out of the 210 Jewish books published in Istanbul.[34] We know that Müteferrika quoted his collaboration with Yona in his famous tract on the usefulness of printing. In particular, Müteferrika depicted Yona as someone who was "skilled in the craft of the required tools in (printing) and knowledgeable in the art of printing" (*fenn-i merkum kârhanesinde muktezi edevat ve alât ve mühimmat san'atinde mahir ve san'at-ı basmada ârif ve cümle bisât-ı mühimmeye malik Yona veled nam Yahudi*).[35] As such, Müteferrika requested that Yona be provided with an imperial *berat* that exempts him and his children from taxation in order to recognize his "privilege and honor" (*imtiyaz ve iftihar*).[36] Several European observers refer to a Jew from Poland who had a poor command of Turkish and helped Müteferrika.[37] However, there are also several indications that the two interacted through other media: There was probably an inconsequential attempt by Yona at partnering with the Müteferrika press, and finally, as Müteferrika's inheritance published by Sabev shows, Müteferrika had offered Yona a loan of 1770 aspers.[38]

A major aspect of printing was the engravings and here, we see Müteferrika in collaboration with an Ottoman Armenian, namely Mıgırdiç Galatavî, alongside two Muslims, Ahmed el-Kırımî and İbrahim Tophanevî, whom some scholars associate with none other than İbrahim Müteferrika himself. As his name sug-

---

34 Y. Meral, *İbrahim Müteferrika Öncesi İstanbul'da Yahudi Matbuatı (1493–1729)*, Ankara, 2016, p. 52.

35 The text of this petition by Müteferrika was published in the unpaginated plates in S. N. Gerçek, *Türk Matbaacılığı I: Müteferrika Matbaası*, Istanbul, 1939.

36 Y. Meral, "Yona ben Yakov Aşkenazi ve Matbaacılık Faaliyetleri", in F. M. Emecen, A. Akyıldız, E. S. Gürkan (eds.), *Osmanlı İstanbulu IV: IV. Uluslararası Osmanlı İstanbulu Sempozyumu Bildirileri, 20–22 Mayıs 2016, İstanbul 29 Mayıs Üniversitesi*, Istanbul, 2016, p. 799.

37 For a review of these references, see Meral, "Yona ben Yakov Aşkenazi ve Matbaacılık Faaliyetleri", p. 799–800.

38 Sabev, *İbrahim Müteferrika*, p. 381.

gests, Mıgırdiç was from Galata, across the Golden Horn[39] and as Sabev maintains, he was probably not a permanent employee of the Müteferrika press and collaborated with İbrahim Müteferrika only when there was a need.[40] Therefore, it is very likely that Mıgırdiç also worked for an Armenian printing press in Istanbul. While further research is needed on this topic, one may assume that there was at least some interaction between the Armenian and Muslim printing presses.

The aim of this paper is not to overwhelm the reader with a substantial network of multi-cultural Ottoman intellectuals by emphasizing their communal differences. Instead, it pinpoints cases in which the transcultural networks between these individuals fostered interactions for the process of Müteferrika's printing activities. To return to Wolfgang Welsch's conception of transculturality, we can easily say that Müteferrika was not alone in having the following qualities: 1) networks with external cultures, 2) internal differentiation, and 3) hybridity.

After establishing the similar qualities between Müteferrika and his intellectual circles and the entanglements between these individuals, it would be pertinent to highlight a few points about the circulation of knowledge between them through printed and unprinted media. The *Gazette de France* issued on January 18, 1727 notes that the Ottoman sultan wanted to establish a printing press and İbrahim Müteferrika was entrusted with this task. The newspaper also mentions that if this first project succeeds, the grand vizier Damat İbrahim Pasha would entrust the Ottoman ambassador to Stockholm, Mehmet Said Efendi, with the task of pursuing the same project in the other cities of the empire and "establishing a printing house for works in Greek and Latin characters."[41] While the newspaper does not offer any further information, one should not be surprised by these seemingly two separate projects.

As mentioned above, Esad Efendi of Ioannina, who was a copy-editor in the Müteferrika press, translated a 17th century Latin commentary on Aristotle into Arabic together with a Greek Orthodox intellectual. Several modern scholars have accused Esad Efendi of choosing to translate an outdated book which was not informed of the New Science in Europe. This is epitomized in the very title of the only monograph devoted to him, i.e. "An Attempt at Renaissance" (*Bir Rönesans Denemesi*). Likewise, as the final sentence of this monograph suggests, had Esad chosen another text to translate and comment on, "without doubt, it would not have been necessary to wait for another century to catch up with Western schol-

---

39 T. Hanstein, *A New Print by Müteferrika (?): A Comparative View of Baron's Qibla Finder*, Berlin, 2021, p. 8–10.

40 Sabev, *İbrahim Müteferrika*, p. 177.

41 *Gazette de France* (18 January 1727), p. 26.

arship and technology."[42] However, this text was a neo-Aristotelian response to the New Science and was important not only for the Greek Orthodox but also for Muslim communities. Here it should be noted that the majority of Ottoman Muslim and non-Muslim intellectuals of the time had a somewhat balanced attitude towards the New Science. This is understandable to a certain point, given the catastrophic developments influencing these communities. The execution of the three patriarchs of Constantinople, namely Kyrillos Loukaris (1638), Parthenios II (1650), and Parthenios III (1657), and a grand mufti, namely Feyzullah Efendi (1703), and the trial of Methodios Anthrakitis for charges of heterodoxy in 1723[43] were probably in the memories of the men of letters at the time. Their caution can be seen clearly in the choice of texts to be written, translated, and published.[44] When Chrysanthos Notaras published his *Eisagoge eis ta Geographika kai Sfairika*, for instance, he presented both geocentric and heliocentric systems coexisting with each other.[45] Likewise, in his published works, Müteferrika did not abandon the account of the geocentric system while presenting the heliocentric system. Showing a similar character, practicality was often preferred at the expense of conflict with tradition, values and principles that were deemed as sacred. When Iosipos Moisiodax published his first translation in 1761,[46] for instance, he did not choose the fields of mathematics of physics, but that of moral philosophy, which he "judged ... to be more useful for the needs" of his community.[47] In a similar case of caution, Müteferrika often commented that the new science that he was introducing in his works was not in conflict with the principles of Islamic law.

Such similarities among Ottoman intellectuals irrespective of their communities are also worth noting when it comes to the key works of reference. Yirmisekiz Mehmet Çelebi's account of France, for instance, was translated into Greek a few years after it was written and was a popular reading among the Greek Orthodox

---

42 Sarıkavak, *XVIII. Yüzyılda Bir Osmanlı Düşünürü*, p. 150.

43 K. Sathas, *Neoelliniki Filologia: Viografiai ton en tois grammasi dialampsonton Ellinon apo tis katalyseos tis Vizantinis Autokratorias mechri tis Ellinikis Ethnegersias (1453–1821)*, Athens, 1868, p. 435–437.

44 For a comparative study of Ottoman Muslim and Orthodox intellectuals towards the developments in Western Europe during the 18th century, see R. Murphey, "Westernisation in the eighteenth-century Ottoman empire: how far, how fast?", *Byzantine and Modern Greek Studies*, 23/1, 1999, p. 116 139.

45 C. Notaras, *Eisagogi eis ta Geografika kai Sfairika*, Paris, 1716.

46 I. Moisiodax, *Ithiki Filosofia metafrastheisa ek tou italikou idiomatos*, Venice, 1761–1762 (two volumes).

47 P. Kitromilides, *The Enlightenment as Social Criticism: Iosipos Moisiodax and Greek Culture in the Eighteenth Century*, Princeton, 1992, p. 43.

intelligentsia in the Ottoman Empire.[48] Similarly, Müteferrika's books were also read and, for some researchers, misread, making their way into other manuscripts.[49] Likewise, Evgenios Voulgaris used Müteferrika's works quite extensively when trying to prove to Catherine the Great that the Ottomans could reform their empire and become invincible enemies of Russia again.[50] Finally, the above-mentioned *Eisagoge eis ta Geographika kai Sfairika* published by Chrysanthos Notaras in 1716 was translated into Arabic and remains in manuscript form.[51] While more research is needed for this particular manuscript, on the basis of the first expression on the first page, i.e. the Islamic *basmala* comprising the expression "in the name of Allah, most gracious, most merciful,"[52] we can claim that it was translated by a Muslim and for Muslims.

In addition, a word must be said on the place of printed Christian Arabic books in this picture. In 1939, a pioneer in Turkish printing, Selim Nüzhet Gerçek published the cover page of a Bible in Arabic printed in Aleppo alongside many other books published by non-Muslims in the Ottoman Empire.[53] His presentation of this book contains problems such as not engaging with a discussion of how this book can be contextualized or his misreading of the translator of this manuscript: "Abdullah ibni Fazıl El Fettaki", instead of 'Abdallāh ibn [al-]Faḍl al-Anṭākī.[54] However, his information that the text has 121 folios and 242 pages helps us to identify another copy for the Corpus of Arabic Christian books in the Millet Library in Istanbul. The Arabic Christian book in question is the *Book of the Holy and Pure Gospel or the Resplendently Shining Lamp* (*Kitāb al-Inǧīl al-šarīf al-ṭāhir wa-l-miṣbāḥ al-munīr al-ẓāhir*) published in 1706 by Athanasios Dabbās in Aleppo.[55] The Millet Library copy seems to be located in the Carullah Efendi collec-

48 P. Stathi, "Enas Othomanos Presvis sti Gallia to 18o aiona", *I kath' imas Anatoli*, 5, 2000, p. 135–177.
49 Kalaycıoğulları claims, for instance, that Erzurumlu İbrahim Hakkı misunderstood certain parts of Müteferrika's books and repeated conflicting arguments in the same work. İ. Kalaycıoğulları, *İbrahim Müteferrika ve Yeni Bilim'in Türkiye'ye Girişi*, Istanbul, 2020, p. 92–94.
50 E. G. Atalay, "Rusya'da Bir Osmanlı Rum Âlimi Eugenios Voulgaris ve Ortodoks Kilisesinde Aydınlanma", unpublished MA Thesis, TOBB University of Economics and Technology, Ankara, 2022.
51 Bibliothèque nationale de France, Département des manuscrits, Arabe 2249.
52 Bibliothèque nationale de France, Département des manuscrits, Arabe 2249, p. 2.
53 Gerçek, *Türk Matbaacılığı*, unpaginated plate.
54 Gerçek, *Türk Matbaacılığı*, p. 22–26.
55 For more on this book, see I. Feodorov, *Arabic Printing for the Chistians in Ottoman Lands. The East-European Connection*, Berlin/Boston, 2023, esp. p. 266–267; I. Feodorov, "Beginnings of Arabic printing in Ottoman Syria (1706–1711). The Romanians' part in Athanasius Dabbās's achievements", *ARAM Periodical*, 25/1&2, 2013, p. 242.

tion, as we also see on the cover page in the book by Gerçek. Because the Carullah Efendi collection has been moved from the Millet Library to the Süleymaniye Library, this book has also been moved there, apparently with the same catalogue number.[56] A prominent member of the *ulemâ*, Carullah Veliyyüddin was a notable bibliophile with his collection of more than 2,000 books and his marginalia in these books. The extent of his notes led to the publication of a volume devoted solely to his marginalia, which excludes his books on Christianity.[57] While more research is needed on this particular copy, it is possible that Carullah Efendi acquired it when he was in Aleppo. So, transcultural networks seem to have featured in the circulation of printed Christian Arabic books as well.

Even though the 1706 copy of the *Book of the Holy and Pure Gospel or the Resplendently Shining Lamp* published by Athanasios Dabbās in Aleppo does not contain any marginal notes, an analysis of Christian Arabic texts owned by Muslims has the potential to shed light on transcultural relations in the Ottoman context and to inform us about the readership of these texts. A copy of the *Book of Psalms of David the Prophet* published in 1764 in Khinshāra, currently preserved in Süleymaniye Manuscript Library in Istanbul[58] presents an interesting case in point. In this copy, the first two lines of the first page after the cover page, right before the introduction, appear to have been scratched out. A comparison of this copy with other copies of the same work shows that the "*bi-smi l-āb wa-l-ibn wa-l-rūḥ al-qudus*" ("in the name of the Father, the Son and the Holy Spirit") is missing.[59] It suggests that at least this part of the text was read and scratched out by a Muslim, possibly the owner of the book in the early 1790s whose record of ownership seems to have been written with the same ink.[60]

Finally, the story of unprinted and printed books after their owners died is a point worth mentioning. When a collection is sold off to others, there is a tendency to see this as a negative development. When referring to the death of Nikolaos Kritias, the prominent teacher at the Patriarchal Academy, the author of the most definitive book about this institution, Gritsopoulos, laments that his son sold these books to Jews and grocers in the streets.[61] The grocers mentioned in this episode probably refer to Turkish-speaking Christians from Asia

---

56 Süleymaniye Yazma Eserler Kütüphanesi, Carullah Efendi Collection, 2.
57 B. Açıl (ed.), *Osmanlı Kitap Kültürü: Carullah Efendi Kütüphanesi ve Derkenar Notları*, Istanbul 2021 (1st ed. 2015).
58 Süleymaniye Yazma Eserler Kütüphanesi, Nafiz Paşa Collection, 37.
59 Süleymaniye Yazma Eserler Kütüphanesi, Nafiz Paşa Collection, 37, p. 2.
60 Süleymaniye Yazma Eserler Kütüphanesi, Nafiz Paşa Collection, 37, p. 1.
61 T. A. Gritsopoulos, *Patriarchiki Megali tou Genous Scholi*, Athens, 2004 (1st ed. 1966), vol. I, p. 359.

Minor whom Greek-speaking members of Istanbul's Orthodox community often viewed with contempt. Hence, when Kritias' son sold his father's books, the sale of these books involved not only inter-communal but also intra-communal inter-action through the circulation of books. Of course, one of the biggest problems in the Ottoman intellectual world at the time was the limited number of libraries in Istanbul, as Nicolas Mavrocordatos also mentions in his *Philotheou Parerga*.[62] However, this was also a way for knowledge to circulate across different commu-nities and, possibly, various strata of the same community. Despite frequent ref-erences to İbrahim Müteferrika's unsold copies, Sabev concludes that he was able to sell two thirds of the books that he printed. A substantial number (747) of the rest of the books (3,087),[63] which Baysal characterizes as "piles of unsold books" were actually purchased by a Greek Orthodox buyer. We learn about this incident from a document that Kemal Beydilli published.[64] This was a bookseller[65] by the name of "İstefanaki son of Dimyaki." The fact that he bought a large number of these books shows his confidence that his customers would be able to buy at least some of them. Apparently, he sold these books to a single buyer, another Greek Orthodox by the name of "Panayot son of Kiryako" who lived across from the patriarchate. We know that he was also a publisher and that he also published works in Armenian.[66] Therefore, transcultural interactions appear to have con-tinued even after printers such as İbrahim Müteferrika left behind substantial amounts of unsold books.

In conclusion, the story of İbrahim Müteferrika and the Müteferrika press cannot be understood without regard to other Ottoman Muslim and non-Mus-lim intellectuals who were directly and indirectly connected to the Müteferrika press. Likewise, the interaction between the individuals around Müteferrika show that an extensive understanding of the establishment and maintenance of the Müteferrika Press requires delving into the experiences of the printing houses owned by Ottoman non-Muslims. Similar intellectual attitudes towards the major developments in the Ottoman Empire and Europe appear to have generated

---

62 N. Mavrocordatos, *Les Loisirs de Philothée*, ed. by Jacques Bouchard, Athens/Montreal, 1989, p. 86.

63 We learn about this number thanks to Karahasanoğlu's discovery of the relevant parts of Müteferrika's deed of inheritance. Karahasanoğlu, "Osmanlı Matbaasının Başarısını/ Başarısızlığını Yeniden Gözden Geçirmek", p. 322.

64 Beydilli, *İki İbrahim: Müteferrika ve Halefi*, p. 119, 143.

65 On booksellers in the Ottoman Empire, see İ. E. Erünsal, *Osmanlılarda Sahaflık ve Sahaflar*, Istanbul, 2013.

66 R. F. M. Anhegger, "Hurufumuz Yunanca. Ein Beitrag zur Kenntsniss der karamanisch-türk-ischen Literatur", *Anatolica*, 7, 1979–1980, p. 170.

similar responses among the intellectuals around Müteferrika. As a result, the transculturality in the Ottoman space appears to have caused several interactions between institutions through printed and unprinted media. Evaluating the story of the early Arabic printing for the Arabic–speaking Christians with reference to the broader Ottoman transcultural networks is a task that is worth pursuing during future stages of this project.

Bibliography

Unpublished Sources

Bibliothèque nationale de France, Département des manuscrits, Arabe 2249.
Süleymaniye Yazma Eserler Kütüphanesi, Carullah Efendi Collection, 2.
Süleymaniye Yazma Eserler Kütüphanesi, Nafiz Paşa Collection, 37.
Süleymaniye Yazma Eserler Kütüphanesi, Ragıp Paşa Collection, 824.

Published Sources

Abu-Er-Rub, Laila, Christiane Brosius, Sebastian Meurer, Diamantis Panagiotopoulos, Susan
    Richter (eds.). *Engaging Transculturality: Concepts, Key Terms, Case Studies*.
    London/New York: Routledge, 2019.
Açıl, Berat (ed.). *Osmanlı Kitap Kültürü: Carullah Efendi Kütüphanesi ve Derkenar Notları*.
    Istanbul: İlem, 2021 (1st ed. 2015).
Afyoncu, Erhan. "İbrahim Müteferrika Hakkında Önemli Bir Vesika". *Türk Kültürü İncelemeleri
    Dergisi*, 28, 2013, p. 51–56.
Afyoncu, Erhan. "İlk Türk Matbaacısının Kurucusu Hakkında Yeni Bilgiler". *Belleten*, 243, 2001,
    p. 607–622.
Anhegger, Robert F. M. "Hurufumuz Yunanca. Ein Beitrag zur Kenntsniss der karamanisch-
    türkischen Literatur". *Anatolica*, 7, 1979–1980, p. 157–202.
Baysal, Jale. *Cennetlik İbrahim Efendi (İbrahim Müteferrika Oyunu)*. Istanbul: Cem Yayınevi,
    1992.
Baysal, Jale. *Osmanlı Türklerinin Bastıkları Kitaplar, 1729–1875*. Istanbul: Hiperlink, 2010 (1st ed.
    1968).
Benessaieh, Afef. "Multiculturalism, Interculturality, Transculturality". In Afef Benessaieh (ed.),
    Amériques Transculturelles – Transcultural Americas. Ottawa: University of Ottawa Press,
    2010, p. 11–38.
Berkes, Niyazi. "İbrahim Müteferrika". *The Encyclopaedia of Islam, Second Edition*, vol. III,
    ed. by Bernard Lewis, Victor L. Ménage, Charles Pellat, Joseph Schacht, Leiden: Brill, 1971,
    p. 996–998.
Beydilli, Kemal. *İki İbrahim: Müteferrika ve Halefi*. Istanbul: Kronik, 2019.
Chrysanthos Notaras. *Eisagogi eis ta Geografika kai Sfairika*. Paris, 1716.

Çolak, Hasan. "Bilim, İlahiyat ve Siyasetin Merkezinde Bir Osmanlı Münevveri: Kudüs Patriği Chrysanthos Notaras". *Kebikeç İnsan Bilimleri İçin Kaynak Araştırmaları Dergisi*, 47, 2019, p. 31–56.

Cottunius, Ioannis. *Commentarii lucidissimi in octo libros Aristotelis de physico auditu; una cum quaestionibus*. Venice: Pauli Frambotti, 1648.

Erdem, Yahya. *Müteferrika'nın İzinde: Kitap ve Matbuat Tarihi Yazıları*. Istanbul: Ötüken, 2021.

Erginbaş, Vefa. "Enlightenment in the Ottoman Context: İbrahim Müteferrika and His Intellectual Landscape". In Geoffrey Roper (ed.), *Historical Aspects of Printing and Publishing in Languages of the Middle East. Papers from the Symposium at the University of Leipzig, September 2008*. Leiden: Brill, 2013, p. 53–100.

Erünsal, İsmail E. *Orta Çağ İslâm Dünyasında Kitap ve Kütüphane*. Istanbul: Timaş, 2018.

Erünsal, İsmail E. *Osmanlılarda Sahaflık ve Sahaflar*. Istanbul: Timaş, 2013.

Feodorov, Ioana. "Beginnings of Arabic Printing in Ottoman Syria (1706–1711). The Romanians' Part in Athanasius Dabbās's Achievements". *ARAM Periodical*, 25/1&2, 2013, p. 231–260.

Feodorov, Ioana. *Arabic Printing for the Chistians in Ottoman Lands. The East-European Connection*. Berlin/Boston: De Gruyter, 2023.

Firges, Pascal, Tobias P. Graf. "Exploring the Contact zone: A Critical Assessment from the Perspective of Early Modern Euro-Ottoman History". In Laila Abu-Er-Rub, Christiane Brosius, Sebastian Meurer, Diamantis Panagiotopoulos, Susan Richter (eds.), *Engaging Transculturality: Concepts, Key Terms, Case Studies*. London/New York: Routledge, 2019, p. 109–122.

Gazette de France (18 January 1727).

Genç Atalay, Eda. "Rusya'da Bir Osmanlı Rum Âlimi Eugenios Voulgaris ve Ortodoks Kilisesinde Aydınlanma" (TOBB University of Economics and Technology, Ankara: Unpublished MA Thesis, 2022).

Gerçek, Selim Nüzhet. *Türk Matbaacılığı I: Müteferrika Matbaası*. Istanbul: İstanbul Devlet Basımevi, 1939.

Gibb, H. A. R., Harold Bowen. *Islamic society and the West: A study of the impact of Western Civilization in Moslem culture in the Near East*, Vol. I *Islamic Society in the Eighteenth Century*, Part II. New York: Oxford University Press, 1957.

Gritsopoulos, Tasos A. *Patriarchiki Megali tou Genous Scholi*. Athens: G. Fexi, 2004 (1st ed. 1966).

Hanstein, Thoralf. *A New Print by Müteferrika (?): A Comparative View of Baron's Qibla Finder*. Berlin: EB–Verlag, 2021.

Herren, Madeleine, Martin Rüesch, Christiane Sibille. *Transcultural History: Theories, Methods, Sources*. Berlin/Heidelberg: Springer, 2012.

İpşirli, Mehmet. "Lale Devrinde Yenilikçi Bir Âlim: Şeyhülislam Yenişehirli Abdullah Efendi". Mustafa Armağan (ed.), *Masaldan Gerçeğe Lale Devri*. Istanbul: Timaş, 2014, p. 267–277.

İpşirli, Mehmet. *Osmanlı İlmiyesi*. Istanbul: Kronik, 2021.

Kabacalı, Alpay. *Türk Kitap Tarihi*, Part 1. *Başlangıçtan Tanzimat'a Kadar*. Istanbul: Cem Yayınevi, 1989.

Kalaycıoğulları, İnan. *İbrahim Müteferrika ve Yeni Bilim'in Türkiye'ye Girişi*. Istanbul: Muhayyel, 2020.

Karahasanoğlu, Selim. "Osmanlı Matbaasının Başarısını/Başarısızlığını Yeniden Gözden Geçirmek ya da İbrahim Müteferrika'nın Terekesinin Tespitine Katkı". *Journal of Turkish Studies*, 33/1, 2010, p. 319–328.

Kitromilides, Paschalis. *The Enlightenment as Social Criticism: Iosipos Moisiodax and Greek Culture in the Eighteenth Century*. Princeton, New Jersey: Princeton University Press, 1992.

Küçük, B. Harun. "Early Enlightenment in Istanbul". (University of San Diego, California: Unpublished Ph.D. dissertation, 2012).

Küçük, B. Harun. "Natural Philosophy and Politics in the Eighteenth Century: Esad of Ioannina and Greek Aristotelianism at the Ottoman Court". *Osmanlı Araştırmaları / The Journal of Ottoman Studies*, 41, 2013, p. 125–158.

Matbaanın Ön Sözü "Basmacı İbrahim Efendi": Müteferrika Sergisi'21. Ankara: Cumhurbaşkanlığı Yayınları, 2021.

Meral, Yasin. "Yona ben Yakov Aşkenazi ve Matbaacılık Faaliyetleri". In Feridun M. Emecen, Ali Akyıldız, Emrah Safa Gürkan (eds.), *Osmanlı İstanbulu IV: IV. Uluslararası Osmanlı İstanbulu Sempozyumu Bildirileri, 20–22 Mayıs 2016, İstanbul 29 Mayıs Üniversitesi*. Istanbul: İstanbul 29 Mayıs Üniversitesi Yayınları, 2016, p. 787–808.

Meral, Yasin. *İbrahim Müteferrika Öncesi İstanbul'da Yahudi Matbuatı (1493–1729)*. Ankara: Divan Kitap, 2016.

Moisiodax, Iosipos. *Ithiki Filosofia metafrastheisa ek tou italikou idiomatos*. Venice, 1761–1762, vol. 1–2.

Murphey, Rhoads. "Ottoman Medicine and Transculturalism from the Sixteenth through the Eighteenth Century". *Bulletin of the History of Medicine*, 66, 1992, p. 376–403.

Murphey, Rhoads. "Westernisation in the eighteenth–century Ottoman empire: how far, how fast?" *Byzantine and Modern Greek Studies*, 23/1, 1999, p. 116–139.

Myaris, Georgios K. "O filosofos tou 17ou aiona Ioannis Kottounios kai i ideologiki prossengisi tou ergou tou". *Peri Istorias*, 4, 2003, p. 183–215.

Necatioğlu, Halil. *Matbaacı İbrahim Müteferrika ve Risâle-i İslâmiye (Tenkidli metin)*. Ankara: Elif Matbaacılık, 1982.

Nicolas Mavrocordatos. *Les Loisirs de Philothée*, ed. by Jacques Bouchard. Athens/Montreal: Presses de l'Université de Montréal, 1989.

Nuhoğlu, Hidayet Y. "Müteferrika Matbaasının Kurulması için Verilen Fetvâ Üzerine". *Basım ve Yayıncılığımızın 250. Yılı Bilimsel Toplantısı, 10–11 Aralık 1979, Ankara, Bildiriler*. Ankara: Türk Kütüphaneciler Derneği, 1980, p. 119–126.

Râşid Mehmed Efendi, Çelebizâde İsmaîl Âsım Efendi. *Târîh-i Râşid ve Zeyli*, ed. by Abdülkadir Özcan, Yunus Uğur, Baki Çakır, Ahmet Zeki İzgöer. Istanbul: Klasik, 2013, vol. 3.

Sabev, Orlin. *İbrahim Müteferrika ya da İlk Osmanlı Matbaa Serüveni*. Istanbul: Yeditepe, 2016 (1st ed. 2006).

Sabev, Orlin. *Waiting for Müteferrika: Glimpses of Ottoman Print Culture*. Boston: Academic Studies Press, 2018.

Sarıcaoğlu, Fikret, Coşkun Yılmaz. *Müteferrika: Basmacı İbrahim Efendi ve Müteferrika Matbaası/Basmacı İbrahim Efendi and the Müteferrika Press*. Istanbul: Esen Ofset, 2008.

Sarıkavak, Kazım. *XVIII. Yüzyılda Bir Osmanlı Düşünürü, Yanyalı Esad Efendi: Bir Rönesans Denemesi*. Ankara: Kültür Bakanlığı Yayınları, 1997.

Sathas, Konstantinos. *Neoelliniki Filologia: Viografiai ton en tois grammasi dialampsonton Ellinon apo tis katalyseos tis Vizantinis Autokratorias mechri tis Ellinikis Ethnegersias (1453–1821)*. Athens: Typografia ton Teknon Andreou Koromila, 1868.

Şeyhülislam Yenişehirli Abdullah Efendi. *Behcetü'l–Fetâvâ*, ed. by Süleyman Kaya, Betül Algın, Zeynep Trabzonlu, Asuman Erkan. Istanbul: Klasik, 2011.

Stathi, Pinelopi. "Enas Othomanos Presvis sti Gallia to 18o aiona". *I kath' imas Anatoli*, 5, 2000, p. 135–177.

Stathi, Pinelopi. "O 'sofotatos Esat Efentis' filos kai allilografos tou Chrysanthou Notara". *O Eranistis*, 18, 1986, p. 57–84.

Stathi, Pinelopi. *Chrysanthos Notaras Patriarchis Ierosolymon: Prodromos tou Neoellinikou Diafotismou*. Athens: Syndesmos ton en Athinais Megaloscholiton, 1999.

Welsch, Wolfgang. "Transculturality – the Puzzling Form of Cultures Today". In Mike Featherstone, Scott Lash (eds.), *Spaces of Culture: City, Nation, World*. London: Sage, 1999, p. 194–213.

Welsch, Wolfgang. "Transculturality: the changing form of cultures today". *Filozofski Vestnik*, 22/2, 2001, p. 59–86.

Welsch, Wolfgang. *Transkulturalität: Realität – Geschichte – Aufgabe*. Vienna: New Academic Press, 2017.

Zhang, Chunjie. *Transculturality and German Discourse in the Age of European Colonialism*. Evanston: Northwestern University Press, 2017.

Orlin Sabev

The Müteferrika Press: Obstacles, Circumvention, and Repercussion According to Contemporary German Sources (1727–1741)

Print culture became quite developed in Europe by the 18th century and European literati who had been accustomed to it for over three centuries were very curious about the endorsement of printing by the Ottoman ruling class. It happened only in 1727 when a sultan's decree was given to Said Agha (d. 1761) and Ibrahim Müteferrika (d. 1747) in order to allow them to run a printing house in Constantinople and to print secular Turkish texts in Arabic script. Said Agha and his father, the high-ranking Ottoman statesman Yirmisekiz Mehmet Çelebi (d. 1732), were sent as extraordinary envoys to Paris in 1720–1721 in order to learn more about French cultural and technological achievements. The other partner, Ibrahim Müteferrika, was a Transylvanian-born renegade and convert to Islam who served at the Ottoman court. While Said Agha mainly provided financial support, Ibrahim Müteferrika was the real initiator and mover of the printing enterprise. Their first book, the renowned Arabic-Turkish dictionary of Vankulu appeared in two volumes in 1729, and the printing house operated until early 1747, when Müteferrika died as the only owner of the printshop (Said Agha left the partnership in late 1732).[1]

The Müteferrika press, as this printshop is usually referred to in historiography, sparked curiosity in the European Republic of Letters. European literati were curious about the assumed obstacles that its founders had to overcome, Ibrahim Müteferrika's non-Ottoman and non-Muslim origin, as well as its printing agenda. Because of the strong diplomatic relations and cultural interaction between France and the Ottoman Empire (the two countries made efforts to establish an anti-Habsburg coalition) French literati were the most interested in uncovering any information about the Müteferrika press. Contemporaneous

---

1 See O. Sabev, *Waiting for Müteferrika: Glimpses of Ottoman Print Culture*, Boston, 2018; O. Sabev, *İbrahim Müteferrika ya da İlk Osmanlı Matbaa Serüveni (1726-1746): Yeniden Değerlendirme*, Istanbul, 2016 (fourth edition).

This research is part of a project that has received funding from the European Research Council (ERC) under the European Union's Horizon 2020 research and innovation programme (Grant Agreement No. 883219-AdG-2019 – Project TYPARABIC).

∂ Open Access. © 2024, the author(s), published by De Gruyter. [CC) BY-NC-ND] This work is licensed under the Creative Commons Attribution-NonCommercial-NoDerivatives 4.0 International License.
https://doi.org/10.1515/9783111060392-002

French sources suggest that Ottoman Turkish printing was introduced in spite of Islamic conservatism and restrictions and express the hope that the newly established press would benefit the Republic of Letters by publishing valuable manuscripts that had presumably been preserved in the sultan's seraglio. In fact, these sources, which are explored by Henri Omont[2] and Jonathan Haddad,[3] are neither abundant in terms of number nor comprehensive in terms of content. The earliest one is a report dating from November 19, 1726, and published first in the French newspaper *Gazette de France* on January 18, 1727.[4] The same information was republished with minor reductions in the January 1727 issue of the *Mercure de France*,[5] the February 1727 issue of the *Journal de Savants* (in Paris),[6] as well as in the 81st volume (April 1727) of the Amsterdam edition of the same journal.[7]

Here I am going to focus on the information about the Müteferrika press published in contemporaneous German newspapers, periodicals and books.[8] As will be shown, part of this information was derived from the abovementioned French sources. Some of the German sources in question have been only partly used in the scholarly works of Franz Babinger,[9] Kemal Beydilli, Fikret Sarıcaoğlu, Coşkun Yılmaz[10] and Paul Babinski.[11]

---

2 H. Omont, "Documents sur l'imprimerie à Constantinople au XVIIIᵉ siècle", *Revue des bibliothèques*, 5, 1895, p. 185–200, 228–236.

3 J. Haddad, *Imagining Turkish Literature: Between the French Republic of Letters and the Ottoman Empire*, University of California, Berkely, 2016 (unpublished Ph.D. thesis); J. Haddad, "People Before Print: *Gens de Lettres*, the Ottoman Printing Press, and the Search for Turkish Literature", *Mediterranean Studies*, 2, 2017, p. 189–228.

4 *Gazzete de France*, 3, January 18, 1727, p. 25–26; this report is partly quoted in: Omont, "Documents sur l'imprimerie à Constantinople", p. 186.

5 *Mercure de France*, January 1727, p. 122.

6 *Journal de Sçavans* (Paris edition), February 1727, p. 121.

7 *Journal de Sçavans* (Amsterdam edition), 81, April 1727, p. 550–551; this report is partly quoted in: B. Tezcan, "İbrâhîm Müteferrika ve Risâle-i İslâmiyye", *Kitaplara Vakfedilen Bir Ömre Tuhfe: İsmail E. Erünsal'a Armağan*, ed. by H. Aynur, B. Aydın, M. B. Ülker, vol. 1, Istanbul, 2014, p. 547.

8 I would like to express my gratitude to Thoralf Hanstein and Carsten-Michael Walbiner for drawing my attention to some of these publications.

9 F. Babinger, *Stambuler Buchwesen im 18. Jahrhundert*, Leipzig, 1919, p. 11.

10 F. Sarıcaoğlu, C. Yılmaz, *Müteferrika: Basmacı İbrahim Efendi ve Müteferrika Matbaası/ Basmacı İbrahim Efendi and the Müteferrika Press*, Istanbul, 2008, p. 37, 115 (footnote 12).

11 P. Babinski, *World Literature in Practice: The Orientalist's Manuscript Between the Ottoman Empire and Germany*, Princeton University, 2020, p. 389 (unpublished Ph.D. thesis).

1. Contemporary German Sources about the Müteferrika Press

Between 1727 and 1741 many German newspapers, periodicals and books reported about the opening and the operation of the Müteferrika press. The earliest publications were just German translations of earlier French ones, and in the course of time the authors of books tended to copy and paste fully or partly the reports published in the newspapers, as well as to compile information that was already available in previously published or other accessible sources.

1.1 Neue Zeitungen von gelehrten Sachen and Mercurii Relation, 1727

It seems that the Leipzig newspaper *Neue Zeitungen von gelehrten Sachen* was the earliest German source to provide news about the opening of the Müteferrika press. On February 6, 1727, it published in German translation[12] – without mentioning the original source – the report released a bit earlier in the *Gazette de France* on January 18, 1727. Soon after – on February 15, 1727 – the Munich-based German weekly newspaper *Mercurii Relation* published in its Saturday supplement (*Sambstägige Extra-Zeitungen*) a slightly different German translation of the same French publication.[13] Some months later – on July 13, 1727 – the *Neue Zeitungen von gelehrten Sachen* published another report on the opening of this press in Constantinople. The second report is shorter but contains new information.[14] In the following years, the two German newspapers continued to provide up-to-date information about the output of the Müteferrika press.

1.2 Der europäische Postilion, 1728

The German series *Der europäische Postilion: oder Begebenheiten, so sich in Europa bin und wieder zu Wasser und zu Land zugetragen* (*The European Postilion: or Incidents that have Occurred in Europe Now and Then on Water and on Land*)

---

12 *Neue Zeitungen von gelehrten Sachen*, 11, 6 February 1727, p. 113–114.
13 *Mercurii Relation, oder wochentliche Ordinari Zeitungen von underschidlichen Orthen*, 7, February 15, 1727, *Sambstägige Extra-Zeitungen*, p. 4–5.
14 *Neue Zeitungen von gelehrten Sachen*, 61, 31 July 1727, p. 609; this information is referred to in Sarıcaoğlu, Yılmaz, *Müteferrika: Basmacı İbrahim Efendi*, p. 37, 115 (footnote 12).

published in 1728 a short report about the introduction of Ottoman Turkish printing in Constantinople.[15]

1.3 Johann Heinrich Gottfried Ernesti, 1733

The second edition of Johann Heinrich Gottfried Ernesti's printing handbook *Die wol-eingerichtete Buchdruckerey* (*The Well-established Printshop*), published in Nuremberg in 1733, contains four pages entitled "Reliable information from the Turkish printing house established in Constantinople in 1728 AD" ("*Zuverlässige Nachricht von der in Constantinopel A. C. 1728 angelegten Türkischen Buchdruckerey*"), describing the introduction of the art of printing by the Ottoman authorities.[16] Since Ernesti himself was a printer, he was particularly interested in the technical aspects of the establishment and operation of the Müteferrika press.

1.4 Andreas Lazarus von Imhof, 1735

The chronicle or the universal history *Des Neu-eröffneten historischen Bilder-Saals* (*The Newly Opened Historical Picture Hall*) by the German historian Andreas Lazarus von Imhof (1656–1704) is another German book that contains paragraphs dealing with the Müteferrika press. Between 1692 and 1704, the year of his death, Imhof managed to publish five volumes of his massive work. However, because of the enormous popularity of the series twelve more volumes (seventeen volumes in total), describing historical events after his death, were published by 1782. The chronicle is also renowned for being illustrated with thousands of copper engravings that attract not only scholarly but wider interest.[17] The first part of the ninth volume, including accounts of the events that happened between 1723 and 1733, was printed twice, in 1735 and 1740, by Christian von Loss (1697–1770) and Andreas Heinrich Beyer (d. 1752) who received printing privileges in Dresden on October 3, 1732.[18] On pages 834 and 835 in both editions there is a brief account of the introduction of Ottoman Turkish printing in Constantinople, entitled "Turkish

---

15 *Der europäische Postilion: oder Begebenheiten, so sich in Europa hin und wieder zu Wasser und zu Land zugetragen*, vol. 1, Part 2, Augsburg, 1728, p. 631–632.

16 J. H. G. Ernesti, *Die wol-eingerichtete Buchdruckerey*, Nuremberg, 1733.

17 See https://de.wikipedia.org/wiki/Neueröffneter_Historischer_Bildersaal (Retrieved 5 August 2022).

18 A. L. von Imhof, *Des Neu-Eröffneten Historischen Bilder-Saals*, vol. 9, Part 1, Nuremberg, 1735, 1740.

printing press that has now really come into being". On the top of page 835 there is an engraving depicting the Müteferrika press. This is the same engraving that the renowned Turkish researcher of Ottoman printing history Yahya Erdem published in 2011.[19]

1.5 Kundmann and Bachstrom, 1737

One can find a compilation of the same information already available in the abovementioned newspapers and books in another German book printed in 1737, namely *Rariora naturae et artis* (*Rarities of Nature and Art*) by Johann Christian Kundmann (1684–1751),[20] which is extensively referenced by Franz Babinger.[21] Besides the compiled information, Kundmann adds what he was told by Johann Friedrich Bachstrom (1686–1742), who spent some time in Constantinople in 1728 and 1729. Kundmann also gives detailed description of the output of the Müteferrika press between 1729 and 1734.[22]

1.6 Heinrich Scholz, 1741

One may find a compilation of the same information, derived from the above newspapers and books, in the fifth paragraph of Heinrich Scholz's short essay on *Bibliothecae arabicae de typographiis arabicis* (*Arabic Books printed with Arabic Script*) printed in Hamburg in 1741.[23] In the sixth paragraph he provides a brief description of Müteferrika's output between 1729 and 1737.[24]

---

19 Y. Erdem. "Müteferrika Matbaasının Erken Dönemde Yapılmış Bilinmeyen Bir Resmi", *Müteferrika*, 39, 2011, p. 222; Yahya Erdem points out the he came accross this engraving in a German book printed in the 1750s. On the other hand, he admits that he did not write down its title because of his "negligence" (*gaflet eseri*, in the author's words). Having in mind the shape of the commas within the text to which this engraving is attached, it seems that Erdem published the engraving appearing in the 1735 edition. In this regard, Erdem might have been confused in saying that his source dates from the 1750s. Nonetheless, Erdem's discovery is very important since for the first time ever a scholarly study draws attention to a contemporary image of the Müteferrika press.
20 J. C. Kundmann, *Rariora Naturae et Artis Item in re Medica, Oder Seltenheiten der Natur und Kunst*, Breslau/Leipzig, 1737.
21 Babinger, *Stambuler Buchwesen im 18. Jahrhundert*, p. 11.
22 Kundmann, *Rariora Naturae et Artis*, column 718–728.
23 H. Scholz, *Bibliothecae Arabicae de Typographiis Arabicis*, Hamburg, 1741, p. 11–13.
24 Scholz, *Bibliothecae Arabicae de Typographiis Arabicis*, p. 13–16.

2. Müteferrika's Socinian Origin

The abovementioned report from Constantinople, dated November 19, 1726 and released on January 18, 1727 by the French newspaper *Gazette de France* (reprinted also by the Amsterdam edition of *Journal des Savants* in April 1727) that had been translated into German and published by the *Neue Zeitungen von gelehrten Sachen* and the *Mercurii Relation* in February 1727 reads as follows:

> From Constantinople, November 19, 1727
> The Grand Signior is establishing here a printing house, in the Arabic and Turkish languages, the management of which he has entrusted to Zair-Aga,[25] son of Mehemet Effendi, grand treasurer of the empire, and formerly ambassador extraordinary of his Highness to the Court of France: the typefaces have been cast, and everything is ready for this new establishment. It is not yet known what the first work to be published will be, but the Grand Vizier has promised to make available all the manuscripts of the court and Zair-Aga, intending to publish first those things which are least known to the scholars, is to take the advice of a renegade monk who has been here for some time and who has a great reputation for literature. Zair-Aga also proposes, if this first establishment is successful, to make others in the principal cities of the empire, and to have in the capital a printing office for Greek and Latin works: he is going to have engraved in the near future a collection of maps which he has brought from Paris, most of them by the late Sir de L'Isle,[26] after which he will publish those which have been drawn up by the Arabs and by the Persians.[27]

With the exception of Ernesti's book, the contemporaneous German sources repeat more or less this information but add the claim that Ibrahim Müteferrika was Socinian by denomination. On July 31, 1727, the *Neue Zeitungen von gelehrten Sachen* reported the opening of the Müteferrika press in Constantinople, pointing out the following:

> Constantinople: It is not yet known when the plan to set up a printing house in this city will be started. However, one has learned for sure that one of the two founders was a disgraced

---

25 Said Agha.
26 Guillaume de l'Isle (1675–1726).
27 *Gazzete de France*, 3, 18 January 1727, p. 25–26; Cf. *Journal de Sçavans* (Amsterdam edition), 81, April 1727, p. 550–551; Omont, "Documents sur l'imprimerie à Constantinople", p. 186; it is believed that the originals of some maps that Ibrahim Müteferrika printed later on – the maps of the Black Sea (1137/1724-1725) and of Iran (1142/1729) – were brought by Said Agha from Paris, see: C. Yılmaz, "Müteferrika Matbaasının Kurucu Kadrosu", *Matbaanın Ön Sözü "Basmacı İbrahim Efendi": Müteferrika Sergisi'21*, Ankara, 2021, p. 35.

monk, a Socinian[28] from Transylvania, who became a Turk. The other chief is Zaide Aga,[29] son of Mehemed Effendi, former ambassador to the French court.[30]

Imhof's chronicle of 1735 explains that Müteferrika was "a disgraced Socinian, Jacobin from Transylvania".[31] One can find the same information in Kundmann's book. He relates the following:

> Since Zair Aga had knowledge, he opted to have those books printed first which are least known among the learned. He attracted an apostate monk who had been staying for some time in Constantinople and who was in great demand for his knowledge of the literature there. He was supposed to have been a Socinian from Transylvania who had become a Turk (although it was later learned that he was not an apostate monk).[32]

One must keep in mind that these sources were written by persons who presumably never knew Ibrahim Müteferrika in person. Kundmann also narrates what he was told by Johann Friedrich Bachstrom, who was an eyewitness of the newly-opened printshop. Bachstrom rejects the rumours that Ibrahim Müteferrika was an "apostate monk" or a "Socinian from Transylvania," claiming that he was merely "a Hungarian renegade."[33] As a matter of fact, Bachstrom's claim is only partly correct. Ibrahim Müteferrika wrote in 1710 a treatise in Ottoman Turkish without a title, but usually referred to by researchers as *Risâle-i İslâmiye* (*Treatise on Islam*). He relates that he was born in Kolozsvár (today, Cluj-Napoca in Romania), the principal city of Transylvania, and studied in a theological college in order to become a Protestant minister.[34] As will be discussed further on, some scholars assume that Müteferrika belonged to the Unitarian Church that embraced the Socinian doctrine of the Polish Reformed Church.[35] What Bachstrom might have had in mind was probably the fact that Müteferrika was of Hungarian, and not Polish, Socinian origin (since many Socinian Poles took refuge in Transylvania).

---

28 "*Socinianer*" in the original text.
29 Said Agha.
30 *Neue Zeitungen von gelehrten Sachen*, 61, July 31, 1727, p. 609.
31 Imhof, *Des Neu-Eröffneten Historischen Bilder-Saals*, vol. 9, Part 1, p. 834–835.
32 Kundmann, *Rariora Naturae et Artis*, column 712.
33 Kundmann, *Rariora Naturae et Artis*, column 713.
34 See H. Necatioğlu, *Matbaacı İbrâhîm-i Müteferrika ve Risâle-i İslâmiye*, Ankara, 1982, p. 55–56.
35 See E. M. Wilbur, *A History of Unitarianism*, vol. 2, Cambridge, MA, 1952, p. 121–122; I. Feodorov, *Dimitrie Cantemir, Salvation of the Sage and Ruin of the Sinful World*, Leiden, 2016, p. 23–24; I would like to express my gratitude to Ioana Feodorov for drawing my attention to her publication.

In the same treatise Müteferrika also claims that while studying and living in Kolozsvár he had attained insight into Muhammad's prophethood.[36] On the basis of this claim Niyazi Berkes concludes that Müteferrika was Unitarian. According to Berkes, although the treatise condemns the Catholic Church and claims that it will be defeated by Islam, it seems that it was written to suggest a direct link between Müteferrika's previous denomination and his conversion to Islam.[37]

Baki Tezcan's scrutinous study of the *Treatise on Islam* shows that Müteferrika does not mention at all that his pre-Ottoman denomination was directly linked to Unitarianism. In contrast to Berkes, who claims that in his treatise Müteferrika refers to the Unitarian scholar Servetus (d. 1553)'s Latin translation of the Bible, Tezcan convincingly points out that Müteferrika refers to another Latin translation of the Bible, published in Amsterdam in 1639 with a preface written by André Rivet (d. 1651), who was a Calvinist theologian at Leiden University. Tezcan stresses that in writing this treatise Müteferrika's main preoccupation was to prove that Muhammad's prophethood was predicted in the Bible, rather than to take part in the theological controversy between Catholicism, Calvinism and Unitarianism concerning the Holy Trinity.[38] Tezcan also questions Gérald Duverdier's misleading interpretation of Charles de Peyssonnel's account of his meeting with Müteferrika. Charles de Peyssonnel, who served as secretary to the French ambassador in Constantinople, the Marquis de Villeneuve (between 1728 and 1741), was assigned to the Grand Vizier Yeğen Mehmet Pasha (1737–1739) as a military observer during the 1736–1739 war between the Habsburgs and the Ottomans. He met Ibrahim Müteferrika in the grand vizier's camp near Sofia in 1738,[39] and in one of his letters, dated May 12, 1738, he wrote that Müteferrika was a former Protestant minister (*"jadis minister"*).[40] According to Tezcan, however, Duverdier added in brackets to Peyssonnel's account the word "Unitarian" (*"unitarien"*) thus following the general notion about Müteferrika's former denomination assumed by Niyazi Berkes.[41] Tezcan's suspicion has recently been con-

---

36 Necatioğlu, *Matbaacı İbrâhîm-i Müteferrika ve Risâle-i İslâmiye*, p. 13–14, 57–58.

37 N. Berkes, "İlk Türk Matbaası Kurucusunun Dinî ve Fikrî Kimliği", *Belleten*, 104, 1962, p. 715–737; Berkes, "İbrahim Müteferrika", *The Encyclopaedia of Islam, Second edition*, vol. III, ed. by B. Lewis, V. L. Ménage, C. Pellat, J. Schacht, Leiden, 1971, p. 996–998.

38 Tezcan, "İbrâhîm Müteferrika ve Risâle-i İslâmiyye", p. 515–545.

39 Haddad, "People Before Print", p. 189.

40 G. Duverdier, "Savary De Brèves et İbrahim Müteferrika: Deux drogmans culturels à l'origine de l'imprimerie Turque", *Bulletin du bibliophile*, 3, 1987, p. 322–359; Haddad, "People Before Print", p. 212.

41 Tezcan, "İbrâhîm Müteferrika ve Risâle-i İslâmiyye", p. 545–546.

firmed by Jonathan Haddad's study of Peyssonnel's correspondence.[42] Finally, Tezcan touches upon the abovementioned German newspaper *Neue Zeitungen von gelehrten Sachen*'s issue dating from July 31, 1727, according to which Müteferrika was formerly a Socinian. Tezcan points out that besides such claims there were also other claims according to which Müteferrika was a Franciscan friar, a Calvinist minister or simply "a renegade monk" (as referred to in the *Journal de Savants* and other sources).[43]

3. Obstacles to Müteferrika's Printing Activity

According to published and unpublished Ottoman documentation, in 1726 Ibrahim Müteferrika wrote a treatise entitled *Er-Risaletü'l-müsemmâ bi-Vesîletü't-tıbâa* (*The Utility of Printing*) in order to convince the Ottoman authorities of the reasonableness of his undertaking. In it, Ibrahim makes the case for the useful-ness of a printing enterprise exposing its eventual benefits to the Muslims and to the future of the Ottoman state.[44] Later on, Müteferrika submitted to the Grand Vizier Nevşehirlî Damat Ibrahim Pasha (1662–1730) an application for an offi-cial permit to run a printing house.[45] In this application, he reveals his inten-tion to print dictionaries as well as books in the field of astronomy, medicine, arithmetic, geometry, geography. He writes that he had been attempting to print for eight years through the help of the Constantinople-based Jewish printer and letter-maker Yona and the facilities of his printing house. Ibrahim also adds that for two years he had enjoyed the financial support of Said Agha. He applies not only for an official permit, but also for financial aid from the state. Along with the application, Müteferrika presented a few specimen pages from the Arabic-Turkish dictionary of Vankulu, asking for a permit to print 500 copies of it.[46]

---

42 Haddad, *Imagining Turkish Literature*, p. 54 (footnote 50); Haddad, "People Before Print", p. 224 (footnote 26).

43 Tezcan, "İbrâhîm Müteferrika ve Risâle-i İslâmiyye", p. 546–548; Cf. Haddad, "People Before Print", p. 209.

44 The text is presented in transcribed form in T. Kut, F. Türe, *Yazmadan Basmaya: Müteferrika, Mühendishane, Üsküdar*, Istanbul, 1996, p. 34; translation in English is provided in: C. M. Murphy, "Appendix: Ottoman Imperial Documents Relating to the History of Books and Printing", in G. N. Atiyeh (ed.), *The Book in the Islamic World. The Written Word and Communication in the Middle East*, Albany, 1995, p. 286–292; for the French translation, see: Omont, "Documents sur l'imprimerie à Constantinople", p. 193–200.

45 İ. Sungu, "İlk Türk Matbaasına dair Yeni Vesikalar", *Hayat*, 73, 1928, p. 11–13.

46 See H. R. Ertuğ, *Basın ve Yayın Hareketleri Tarihi*, İstanbul, 1970, p. 96–101.

The grand vizier approved the application,[47] then the Grand Mufti Yenişe-hirlî Abdullah Efendi (d. 1743) issued an official religious opinion (*fetva*) admitting that printing technology is a useful way to multiply written materials,[48] and finally the Sultan Ahmed III (r. 1703-1730) signed a special decree (*ferman*), dated *evâsıt-ı Zilkade* 1139/the beginning of July 1727, giving Said Agha and Ibrahim Müteferrika an official permit to run the printing house. Four former high-level religious officials were appointed as proofreaders.[49]

The Ottoman authorities reached a compromise solution in that case, since the printing house was allowed to print books on secular matters only, while the crowded army of manuscript copyists was left undisturbed to duplicate manuscripts that were predominantly on religious matters. The abovementioned German sources contain some new details and claims about the possible obstacles that Ibrahim Müteferrika and his partner had to overcome or subvene in order to get official permission for their printing enterprise.

In its issue of May 8, 1728 *Mercurii Relation* communicated a report from Vienna dated April 24, 1728. It conveyed that it had "received a sheet from the newly established printing house in Constantinople, which is widely admired for the purity of the paper and the letters." It also points out that the grand mufti and his clerics "have shown how it is not only dangerous for the teachings of their prophet, but also how the state can derive no benefit from the mission of the scribes, who make a living from copying." According to the report the grand vizier succeeded in neutralizing the grand mufti's opposition.[50]

The same report from Vienna is communicated with different wording in the 1728 issue of *Der europäische Postilion* as follows:

---

47 Sungu, "İlk Türk Matbaasına dair Yeni Vesikalar", p. 11; S. N. Gerçek, *Türk Matbaacılığı*, Part 1. *Müteferrika Matbaası*, Istanbul, 1939, p. 52–57; the text is presented in transcribed form in: A. Refik, *Hicrî Onikinci Asır'da İstanbul Hayatı (1100-1200) [Onikinci Asr-ı Hicrî'de İstanbul Hayatı (1689-1785)]*, Istanbul, 1988, p. 91–94.

48 The text is presented in transcribed form in: A. Şen, *İbrahim Müteferrika ve Usûlü'l-hikem fî Nizâmi'l-ümem*, Ankara, 1995, p. 56; comments on the text are available in: H. Y. Nuhoğlu, "Müteferrika Matbaasının Kurulması için Verilen Fetvâ Üzerine", in *Basım ve Yayıncılığımızın 250. Yılı Bilimsel Toplantısı, 10-11 Aralık 1979, Ankara, Bildiriler*, Ankara, 1980, p. 119–126.

49 *Tercümetü'ş-şiḥaḥ-ı Cevherî [Lugat-ı Vankulu]*, Istanbul, 1141 [1729], p. [4]; the text is presented in transcribed form in: Refik, *Hicrî Onikinci Asır'da İstanbul Hayatı*, p. 89–91; Şen, *İbrahim Müteferrika ve Usûlü'l-hikem fî Nizâmi'l-ümem*, p. 57–59; translation in English is provided in: Murphy, "Appendix", p. 284–285; French translation is provided in: Omont, "Documents sur l'imprimerie à Constantinople", p. 190–192.

50 *Mercurii Relation*, 19, May 8, 1728, p. 2.

> The mufti has sought to ban this [printing enterprise] in every possible way, and has stipulated that [the introduction of] this innovation would not only be detrimental to the teachings of the Prophet, but also to the state itself, because a great many scribes, who until now had earned their living by copying, would become a burden to the state for lack of food. But the grand vizier, who was the most active in this excellent work, reacted to these attitudes very sensibly and finally succeeded.[51]

A bit later, on 17 July 1728 *Mercurii Relation* conveyed from Constantinople a report dating from May 12, 1728. It represents in the same way the grand mufti's initial opposition to printing but specifies that the grand vizier succeeded to neutralize him by threatening to remove him from office. According to the report. the printers of the Müteferrika press

> have presented samples in Greek, Arabic and Turkish to the nobles of the great sultan, who have accepted them very well, despite the threats of the mufti, who is very bitter against this innovation and considers such an establishment of a printing press to be a special punishment, which is just as detrimental to the Turkish subjects as the other one [the plague], which still makes great ravages here and elsewhere. It is said, however, that the grand vizier threatened the mufti to depose him if he did not refrain from speaking this.[52]

In the second edition of Johann Ernesti's printing handbook, published in 1733, the grand mufti's initial opposition to printing and its neutralization by the grand vizier is told in the following more elaborate way:

> It is true that the grand vizier, who is the main cause and director of the whole work, initially had a great deal of objection from the Turkish chief priest, or mufti, who considered this innovation to be a severe scourge of God, which was not only very dangerous because of the teachings of its Prophet Mahomet, but was also more harmful and detrimental to the subjects of the grand sultan than any plague. In Constantinople, as well as in the whole Ottoman Empire, a million people have been fed up with writing, who, in the case of such an innovation, would come into conflict with each other and thus become a terrible burden for the great sultan. The grand vizier, however, who had a far greater insight into the whole matter, as well as greater power and prestige, succeeded with his excellent proposal, neutralized the unfounded objections of the mufti, and thus appealed to the time that would show the clear success of this useful arrangement.[53]

One can find a confirmation of the claim that the grand mufti was initially opposite to the idea of introducing printing in French sources as well. For instance, on

---

51 *Der europäische Postilion*, p. 631–632.
52 *Mercurii Relation*, 28, July 17, 1728, p. 1–2.
53 Ernesti, *Die wol-eingerichtete Buchdruckerey*.

November 26, 1729 the *Gazette de France* published a report from Venice, dated November 4, 1729. It relates that the grand mufti was no longer opposed to the printing enterprise and that the grand vizier had given some European ministers of foreign affairs a copy of the first books printed by the Müteferrika press.[54] The same information is republished in the first volume of the December 1729 issue of the *Mercure de France*.[55]

Imhof's chronicle of 1735 follows Ernesti's claim by pointing out that Ottoman Turkish printing had been hitherto prevented by the grand mufti due to two reasons, namely the fear that printing would be dangerous to religion and to many thousands of copyists who made their living from manuscript copying. However, the grand vizier was opposed to that attitude and supported Said Agha and the "disgraced Socinian, Jacobin from Transylvania" (that is, Ibrahim Müteferrika) in their endeavor to run a printing press.[56]

Kundmann's narration which compiles the information available in the previously published German sources, adds new details. According to him it was the French ambassador Marquis de Villeneuve's suggestion to open a printing house:

> At the same time, he [the grand vizier] was struck by the thought that a learned society should be founded in Constantinople and directed by some learned French people. Through this society these studies would become better known to the Turks. He therefore conferred with the French ambassador Mons. de Villeneuve, who held the opinion that the whole thing would be impracticable unless a printing press is set up.[57]

Kundmann points out that Said Agha and Ibrahim Müteferrika had been granted permission "to print books written in the local language, except those pertaining to the Mahometan religion".[58] Kundmann correctly notes that four experienced and capable correctors had been appointed to correct the texts that would be printed and that Müteferrika "composed a treatise on the benefits and various advantages which the Turks could expect from the establishment of a new printing press in Constantinople".[59] Kundmann stresses also that the newly-opened printing house caused some nuisance and anxiety among the numerous manuscript copyists by claiming that "more than 6,000 people in Constantinople alone

---

54 *Gazette de France*, November 26, 1729, p. 578; Omont, "Documents sur l'imprimerie à Constantinople", p. 188.
55 *Mercure de France*, vol. 1, December 1729, p. 2915–2916; this report is partly quoted in: Haddad, *Imagining Turkish Literature*, p. 41, 48; Haddad, "People Before Print", p. 202–203.
56 Imhof, *Des Neu-Eröffneten Historischen Bilder-Saals*, vol. 9, Part 1, p. 834–835.
57 Kundmann, *Rariora Naturae et Artis*, columns 711 and 712.
58 Kundmann, *Rariora Naturae et Artis*, column 715.
59 Kundmann, *Rariora Naturae et Artis*, column 716.

have lived from copying books".[60] According to Kundmann the so-called Patrona Halil rebellion in September 1730 that dismissed the grand vizier and the sultan from their offices did not affect the printing house since new sultan and the new grand mufti[61] encouraged its activity by issuing "express orders".[62] Indeed, the new Sultan Mahmud I (1730–1754) has issued a new *ferman* allowing the Müteferrika press to continue to work.[63]

Having in mind the German sources cited above, the impression remains that the official opening of the Müteferrika press had to overcome some obstacles set by the alleged opponents of the printing press like the scribes, the manuscript copyists and the men of religion.

17th-century western travellers also claim that the resistance of the copyists and calligraphers and the obstacles set by the religious officials were the main reasons for the lack of Ottoman Turkish printing. In his book on the Ottoman Empire, published in 1668, Paul Rycaut claims that printing was absolutely prohibited because it could develop learning and thus become a threat for the tyrannical Ottoman rule, as well as depriving the numerous scribes of their livelihood.[64] In his book on Turkish literature, printed in 1688, Giovanni Battista Donado asserts that the Ottoman sultans had banned printing in order to maintain the manuscript copyists' means of subsistence and that the Turks considered printing technology a Christian invention.[65] On the other hand, Count de Marsigli, who spent eleven months in Istanbul in 1679–1680 and visited the Ottoman capital once again in 1692, relates in a book on the military state of the empire, printed in 1732, that the Turks do not print their books not because of any prohibition, but because of the concern about the livelihood of the numerous copyists and calligraphers.[66]

60 Kundmann, *Rariora Naturae et Artis*, column 716.
61 Mirzazâde Şeyh Mehmet Efendi (1730–1731).
62 Kundmann, *Rariora Naturae et Artis*, column 717–718.
63 Yılmaz, "Müteferrika Matbaasının Kurucu Kadrosu", p. 41.
64 P. Rycaut, *The Present State of the Ottoman Empire*, London, 1668, p. 32.
65 G. B. Donado, *Osservationi fatte della letteratura de Turchi*, Venice, 1688, p. 43; Cf. Babinger, *Stambuler Buchwesen im 18. Jahrhundert*, p. 8.
66 C. di Marsigli, *Stato Militare dell'Impero Ottomanno Incremento e Decremento del Medesimo/ L'Etat militaire de l'Empire Ottoman, ses progrès et sa décadence*, The Hague/Amsterdam, 1732, p. 40; for more on this topic, see K. A. Schwartz, "Did Ottoman Sultans Ban Print?", *Book History*, 20, 2017, p. 1–39.

4. The Location, Equipment, and Staff of the Müteferrika Press

One can see on the engraving published in Imhof's chronicle and illustrating the operation of Müteferrika's printshop two presses, a type case and six workers. All of them are depicted with turbans and caftans, thus leaving no room for hesitation that the picture represents an Oriental, that is, Muslim or Ottoman/Turkish printshop. The very fact that a special engraving had been prepared for the paragraph relating the opening of the first printing press in the Muslim world to be run by a Muslim (albeit a convert and former Christian) is indicative for the immense interest it caused among its European counterparts. There are many well-known engravings depicting the art of book printing that had developed in Europe as early as the 15th century. Such imagery representing printing presses, printers and printshops started appearing by the close of the same century in books and plates dealing with the inventions of the time. Ernesti's handbook is also furnished with a similar engraving.

One may raise the question, however, whether the engraving appearing in Imhof's chronicle represents the actual situation in this particular printshop or whether it was prepared just in order to provide a general notion about it. Since the engraver is unknown and one may rightfully assume that he himself was not an eyewitness of the operation of this printshop, the second option seems more plausible.

In the issue dated July 17, 1728 *Mercurii Relation* transmits a report from Constantinople dating from May 12, 1728, containing the following news:

> The printing press established by the grand vizier in the seraglio has almost reached perfection. There are 36 young apprentices working in it, under the direction of eight masters, most of whom are learned Greeks, but who have knowledge of the local [language].[67]

In addition, in its issue dated September 4, 1728 *Mercurii Relation* releases the following report from Vienna:

> The Turkish consul[68] here has purchased many Oriental manuscripts at a high price in order to send them to the grand vizier to be presented [to him]. He has sent some typesetters, who

---

67 *Mercurii Relation*, 28, July 17, 1728, p. 1.
68 Kazancızade Ömer Ağa served as an Ottoman consul (*şehbender*) in Vienna between 1726 and 1732, see H. Wurm, "Entstehung und Aufhebung des osmanischen Generalkonsulats in Wien (1726–1732): Eine Relation Heinrich von Penklers aus dem Jahr 1761", *Mitteilungen des Österreichischen Staatsarchivs*, 42, 1992, p. 152–187.

are to be used in the new printing house in Constantinople. It is believed that similar print-shops will also be established in other cities of the Ottoman Empire.[69]

Ernesti's handbook of 1733 repeats this information and adds something more related to the origin of the types:

> Various credible reports testify to this, as a true certainty, such as that 36 young apprentices, led by Greeks well-versed in this art, were working on their printing presses set up in the seraglio, and had already achieved a fair degree of perfection...
> The Turkish consul at Vienna bought many Oriental manuscripts at a high price and sent them to the grand vizier to be presented [to him]. He also sent a good and suitable typesetter to Constantinople, although he is of the Protestant religion. Six Turks were sent from Constantinople to Leiden to cast and produce 40 to 50 centners[70] of Turkish letters so that there would be no shortage of them for printing.[71]

Imhof's chronicle repeats that Said Agha and Ibrahim Müteferrika disposed with a staff consisting of "eight masters and 36 boys, mostly Greeks". It also claims that 40 to 50 centners of "Turkish types" were brought from Holland.[72]
Kundmann adds the following details:

> He [Zair Aga] first had Arabic and Turkish letters cast; but as these did not last, six Turks were sent to Vienna, where the Turkish consul sent them to the kaiser.[73] He sent them to Leiden in Holland to have 40 to 50 centners of Arabic and Turkish letters made there, so that they could enforce the work quite extensively ... The Turkish agha [consul] in Vienna commissioned journeymen book printers and scribes and sent them to Constantinople, where eight master printers, most of them learned Greeks and perfectly versed in the language of the country, and 36 apprentices were at work in the seraglio, where the printing press had been established. So that in the beginning of the 1729 year they were already able to present a specimen of their art to the grand vizier.[74]

Kundmann also retells Bachstrom's account that the printshop was not located in the seraglio but in a private house. According to Bachstrom, Ibrahim Müteferrika "bought a bad press from an Armenian book printer; however, he then had two presses that came from France. And since there have already been in Constantinople various Jewish book printers for many years, he got from them some Jews, who

---

69 *Mercurii Relation*, 35, September 4, 1728, p. 4.
70 Since one German centner (*Zentner*) was equal to 50 kg, the total weight mentioned here must have been equal to 2–2,5 tons.
71 Ernesti, *Die wol-eingerichtete Buchdruckerey*.
72 Imhof, *Des Neu-Eröffneten Historischen Bilder-Saals*, vol. 9, Part 1, p. 834–835.
73 Charles VI (r. 1711–1740).
74 Kundmann, *Rariora Naturae et Artis*, columns 711–712.

cast the types. [Then] he began to print the abovementioned work [the *Vankulu* dictionary] and happily published it in folio in two volumes." Bachstrom brought to Kundmann several specimen pages of this newly printed book showing its good typographical quality.[75] Further on Kundmann provides some brief information about the output of the printshop until 1734, mentioning that Rashid's chronicle is "under press" (it actually appeared in 1741).[76]

One may find out the same information as provided in Ernesti's, Imhof's and Kundmann's books, in Heinrich Scholz's short essay on *Bibliothecae arabicae de typographiis arabicis* (*Arabic Books printed in Arabic Script*) printed in Hamburg in 1741.[77]

The information provided by Bachstrom, who obviously had personal impressions from Müteferrika's printshop while residing in Constantinople in 1728–1729,[78] should be more reliable and trustworthy. He points out that the printshop was located not in the seraglio, as the initial European notion was, but in a private house. Indeed, Müteferrika set up the press in his own house. According to Bachstrom, the printshop started its operation with "a bad press" purchased from an Armenian printer, but later on two presses were brought from France. If his information is correct, in 1729 the Müteferrika press worked with two fully functional presses as one can see depicted on the abovementioned engraving in Imhof's chronicle, depicting its operation in 1727–1728. Unfortunately, Bachstrom does not provide any information, at least in Kundmann's reference, about the staff that worked in the printshop.

Nevertheless, there are other eyewitnesses that provide relevant yet discrepant information. B. A. Mistakidis refers to information provided by Lorck, according to which Said Agha ordered Arabic types to be cast in Istanbul.[79] This confirms Kundmann's narrative. Giambattista Toderini (1728–1799), who spent four and a half years in Constantinople between 1781 and 1786 and wrote three volumes on Turkish literature, was also convinced that the types were prepared in the Ottoman capital.[80]

---

75 Kundmann, *Rariora Naturae et Artis*, column 712–714; Cf. Babinski, *World Literature in Practice*, p. 389.
76 Kundmann, *Rariora Naturae et Artis*, column 719–728.
77 Scholz, *Bibliothecae Arabicae de Typographiis Arabicis*, p. 11–12.
78 Paul Babinski assumes that Bachstrom "appears to have worked with Müteferrika in the new press," see Babinski, *World Literature in Practice*, p. 388–389.
79 B. A. Mystakidis, "Hükümet-i Osmaniye Tarafından İlk Tesis Olunan Matbaa ve Bunun Neşriyatı", *Tarih-i Osmanî Encümeni Mecmuası*, 5, 1326 [1910], p. 326.
80 G. Toderini, *De la Littérature des Turcs*, ed. by Abbé de Cournand, vol. 3, Paris, 1789, p. 212–219; G. Toderini, *İbrahim Müteferrika Matbaası ve Türk Matbaacılığı*, ed. by Ş. Rado, Istanbul, 1990, p. 24.

Nesimi Asım, who does not provide any source, claims that the types were cast by a local Armenian named Arapoğlu.[81] Some other authors also maintain the opinion that an Armenian letter-maker cast the letters.[82] According to a quite later account dating from 1776 and written by the interpreter at the time at the French Foreign Office, LeGrand, the necessary equipment was brought from the Leiden in the Netherlands.[83] This is what Ernesti, Imfof's chronicle and Kundmann also claim.

The claim that the Arabic letters used in the Mütteferika press were cast in the Netherlands might be a result of a misunderstanding, since according to other, more reliable sources Ibrahim Mütteferika did not ask for Arabic, but rather for Latin types to be provided from Holland or France in order to be able to print in 1730 with both Arabic and Latin letters the *Grammaire turque ou Méthode courte & facile pour apprende la langue turque* by Jean-Baptiste Daniel Holdermann (1694–1730), a French Jesuit missionary in Constantinople. According to a report dating from October 4, 1728 by the Dutch ambassador Cornelis Calkoen (in office between 1727 and 1744) "the Turkish director [of the printshop] has written to Holland to get Latin type as a *Grammar and Lexicon Turco Latinum* will be printed here, to serve as an instruction [book] in the Latin language for the Turks, for which the Jesuit father has set up a college with the permission of the [Sublime] Porte in Constantinople."[84] Such a college, called the *École des jeunes de langue*, was indeed established in Constantinople in 1670, but its aim was not to train "Turks" but French youths to become dragomans of the Turkish, Arabic and Persian languages. Holdermann's handbook was intended to provide basic knowledge of Turkish grammar for Francophones living or studying in the Ottoman Empire.[85] According to a letter by the French ambassador at the time, Marquis de Villeneuve (in office between 1728 and 1741), dated March 2, 1730, Müteferrika asked that a French typeface be made for him as a "royal gift", providing several Arabic fonts to keep their size and proportion.[86] Holdermann himself, however, claimed

---

81 N. Asım [Yazıksız], "Türk Matbaacılığı", *Türk Tarih Encümeni Mecmuası* (new series), 2, 1929, p. 46–48. In fact Arapoğlu Bogos and his sons cast new types in 1817 for the state printing house in Constantinople, Devlet Arşivleri– Istanbul (BOA), Cevdet-Maarif, 120/5983.

82 Ertuğ, *Basın ve Yayın Hareketleri Tarihi*, p. 103.

83 Omont, "Documents sur l'imprimerie à Constantinople", p. 229; Cf. O. Ersoy, *Türkiye'ye Matbaanın Girişi ve İlk Basılan Eserler*, Ankara, 1959, p. 34.

84 National Archive of the Netherlands, NL HaNA_1.02.20_25_0002 (https://www.nationaa-larchief.nl/onderzoeken/archief/1.02.20/invnr/25/file/NL-HaNA_1.02.20_25_0017) (accessed January 8, 2023); I would like to express my gratitude to Dr. Thoralf Hanstein for drawing my attention to this document.

85 See Sabev, *İbrahim Müteferrika ya da İlk Osmanlı Matbaa Serüveni*, p. 215–216.

86 Omont, "Documents sur l'imprimerie à Constantinople", p. 188–189.

that the French letters were cast by people who did not speak French.[87] Babinger, quoting the year 1729's issue 192 (p. 93) of the *Neue Zeitungen von gelehrten
Sachen*, claims that this grammar book was "the first French work printed in Constantinople and with letters cast there."[88] However, the quoted number and page
do not contain such information.[89] Babinger might have had in mind the same
year's issue 52 (December 22, 1729, p. 937), in which it is said that "so far various
works have been published in the newly established printing house here, and
they are also in the process of acquiring French letters in order to print a history of
Europe in the same language, because most of the distinguished Muslim men are
well versed in them."[90] However, this information does not support Babinger's
claim that the "French" letters were cast in Constantinople. It is also uncertain
whether any types – be they Arabic or Latin – were brought from France, the
Netherlands or elsewhere.

As for the number of the presses in Müteferrika's printshop, according to
Jean-Baptiste Holdermann, who personally observed the process of printing his
grammar handbook in 1730, there were four presses for printing books and two
more for geographical maps.[91]

A report from Genoa, dated March 15, 1731 and published in the Saturday
supplement (*Sambstägige Extra-Zeitungen*) of *Mercurii Relation*'s April 14, 1731
issue, confirms Holdermann's information. The report also claims that the size of
the French letters that had been specially cast for the printing of Holdermann's
grammar handbook was equal to the "Turkish" letters, as was the Müteferrika's
abovementioned request to the French ambassador. The report is also noteworthy
for its claim that there were six "Turks" working in the printshop. Whether coincidental or not, this number matches exactly the number of figures depicted in the
engraving printed in Imhof's chronicle. The report reads as follows:

---

87 Omont, "Nouveaux documents sur l'imprimerie à Constantinople", p. 6.
88 Babinger, *Stambuler Buchwesen im 18. Jahrhundert*, p. 14; here Babinger also points out that
Müteferrika did not ask the sultan for permission to print this book since it was printed at the
request of the French people living in Constantinople. It seems that non-Muslim subjects of the
Ottoman sultan did not need his permission to print whatever book they needed for their own
community. To the best of my knowledge, such permission is neither printed in any non-Muslim
book printed in the Ottoman domains, nor preserved in the Ottoman archive.
89 https://zs.thulb.uni-jena.de/rsc/viewer/jportal_derivate_00245940/dt_zs_1071_jg1729_00889.
tif?logicalDiv=jportal_jparticle_00495918&q=1729 (accessed January 8, 2023).
90 *Neue Zeitungen von gelehrten Sachen*, 52, December 22, 1729, p. 937; https://zs.thulb.uni-
jena.de/rsc/viewer/jportal_derivate_00245940/dt_zs_1071_jg1729_00993.tif?logicalDiv=jportal_
jparticle_00495964&q=1729 (accessed January 8, 2023).
91 H. Omont, "Nouveaux documents sur l'imprimerie à Constantinple au XVIIIᵉ siècle", *Revue
des bibliothèques*, 33, 1926, p. 10.

Genoa, March 15

There are six presses in the printing house, namely four for books and two for maps, and six Turks work on the composition of Turkish books. A certain clergyman and missionary [Holdermann] has also induced Ibrahim Effendi to have books printed for the use of the French, or free people, for which he has had the matrices and French letters cast for him, together with other Turkish letters proportioned with the French letters. The 200,000 Turkish letters consist of three different sizes. It is hoped that Roman letters will be cast for the other prints.[92]

The claim of the abovementioned German sources that eight masters, "most of whom are/were learned Greeks," and 36 young apprentices worked in the Müteferrika press needs to be confirmed by other sources too. There are different accounts of the origin of the employed printers. The French sources tend to exaggerate the role of France in the foundation of the Ottoman printing press by highlighting the role of Said Agha.[93] Some of them claim that it began to operate with printers brought from France.[94] According to Ernesti's handbook, "shortly afterwards, many Frenchmen came by water from Marseilles to Constantinople, who were prescribed to these printers."[95] However, it seems that he meant here that French printers went to Constantinople in order to help the printing of Holdermann's handbook at the Müteferrika press. Ernesti also mentions that "more and more improvements have been made to this office, and the Dutch Jews are said to have contributed to it in no small measure."[96] The Swedish ambassador to Constantinople, Edvard Carleson (1704–1767), who visited the printshop and sent specimens of its output to the Swedish court in 1735, points out that Ibrahim Müteferrika immediately set to work, as he had at his disposal printers and typesetters brought from Germany.[97] According to another eyewitness, César de Saussure (1705–1783), who was a Swiss nobleman in the service of Prince Ferenc

---

92 *Mercurii Relation*, 6, April 14, 1731, *Sambstägige Extra-Zeitungen*, p. 4; Almost the same information could be found in *Bibliothèque raisonnée des ouvrages des savans de l'Europe*, 6/1, January, February and March 1731, p. 237; see also: T. Hanstein, *A New Print by Müteferrika? A Comparative View of Baron's Qibla Finder*, Berlin, 2021, p. 8.

93 Haddad, "People Before Print", p. 201–202, 206–207.

94 R. Zaïmova, "Quelques traits de l'Européanisation culturelle dans l'Empire Ottoman au début du XVIIIᵉ siècle", *Centre(s) et périphérie(s): Les lumières de Belfast à Beijing/Centre(s) and Margins. Enlightenment from Belfast to Beijing*, ed. by M. C. Skuncke, Paris, 2003, p. 77.

95 Ernesti, *Die wol-eingerichtete Buchdruckerey*.

96 Ernesti, *Die wol-eingerichtete Buchdruckerey*; Cf. Babinger, *Stambuler Buchwesen im 18. Jahrhundert*, p. 11.

97 E. Carleson, *İbrahim Müteferrika Basımevi ve Bastığı İlk Eserler/Ibrahim Müteferrika's Printing House and Its First Printed Books*, ed. by M. Akbulut, Ankara, 1979, p. 9.

Rákóczi II (1676–1735), the printers, engravers and letter-makers were brought from Vienna.[98] This is what Ernesti and then Kundmann (after Ernesti) claimed.

Fatma M. Göçek notes that the Müteferrika press was the only and the most important technological consequence of the 1720–1721 Ottoman embassy to France, and that it came into being due to the presence of experienced printers working in the non-Muslim printshops at the Ottoman capital.[99] Adil Şen also emphasizes that Müteferrika benefited from the experience of Jewish, Armenian-Gregorian and Eastern Orthodox (Greek) printing traditions already existing in the empire, and criticizes Jale Baysal, who is convinced that the Ottoman printing house was founded and developed completely independently from the "minority" printers.[100] Şen recalls what Müteferrika wrote in his petition to the grand vizier, according to which he prepared the first proofs of the *Vankulu* dictionary with the help of the experienced Jewish printer and typographer Yona, who was one of the prominent representatives of the non-Muslim printing in the Ottoman Empire.[101] Holdermann also notes that Müteferrika was assisted by the Jewish typographer Yona, who prepared the typefaces.[102] An interesting observation by Michel Fourmont (d. 1746), librarian at the Royal Library in Paris and lecturer at Collège de France, is contained in a letter of his dated March 26, 1729 and sent to Jean-Frédéric Phélypeaux, known as the Count de Maurepas (1701–1781). He writes that he visited the printing house, whose activity was quite difficult due to its founders' inexperience in the art of printing. Fourmont also adds that since one of the two partners, Said Agha, was assigned as a state servant (*nazır*), the printing house was actually relying on the other partner, Ibrahim Müteferrika. and his hard work, as well as on the work of the letter-maker and typesetter who was "a poor Polish Jew," barely speaking Turkish.[103] This Jewish printer, Yona (d. 1745), was son of Ya'akov Ashkenazi from Vilnius and owned a printing house

---

98 *Lettres de Turquie (1730-1739) et Notices (1740) de César de Saussure*, ed. by C. de Thály, Budapest, 1909, p. 94.

99 F. M. Göçek, *East Encounters West: France and the Ottoman Empire in the Eighteenth Century*, New York/Oxford, 1987, p. 80–81.

100 Şen, *İbrahim Müteferrika ve Usûlü'l-hikem fî Nizâmi'l-ümem*, p. 61–62 (footnote 113). Cf. J. Baysal, *Müteferrika'dan Birinci Meşrutiyete kadar Osmanlı Türklerinin Bastıkları Kitaplar*, Istanbul, 1968, p. 3.

101 Şen, *İbrahim Müteferrika ve Usûlü'l-hikem Fî Nizâmi'l-ümem*, p. 61–62.

102 Omont, "Nouveaux documents sur l'imprimerie à Constantinople", p. 8–9.

103 H. Omont, *Missions archéologiques Françaises en Orient au XVIIᵉ et XVIIIᵉ siècles*, vol. 2, Paris, 1902, p. 543; Mystakidis, "Hükümet-i Osmaniye Tarafından İlk Tesis Olunan Matbaa", p. 325–326; Haddad, "People Before Print", p. 208–209.

in Istanbul, founded in 1711.[104] Said Agha's inability to be fully engaged with the printing enterprise caused him to leave it in late 1732 and Müteferrika continued to run the printshop as the only officially recognized owner.[105]

The abovementioned Swedish ambassador, Edvard Carleson, remarks in his report of July 1735 that "during the last riots [the so-called Patrona Halil rebellion of 1730] all the German workers [in the printshop] fled" the country and therefore Ibrahim Müteferrika continued to work with "his five sons" who quickly became accustomed to the art of printing.[106] Müteferrika did not actually have five sons and what Carleson seems to have had in mind was the five workers employed in the printshop. Their names appear in Müteferrika's probate inventory, prepared upon his death in early 1747. According to this inventory, Müteferrika owed monthly wages to the following workers: Mehmet Çelebi, another Mehmet son of Ali, Ahmet son of Osman, another Ahmet son of Mehmet and Hafız Abdülkerim Efendi. The inventory also mentions a debt to be paid off to a Jewish letter-maker (*hurufatçı*).[107] The name of the latter is not indicated but one can assume that he was one of the abovementioned Yona's sons who ran his printshop after his death in 1745.[108] The names of the two engravers, Ahmet al-Kırımî and Mıgırdiç Galatavî, who undersigned some of the graphic images and maps in Katip Çelebi's geographical work *Cihannümâ* (*Mirror of the World*), printed by Müteferrika in 1730, are also not mentioned in probate inventory. Like Yona, they might have been employed on a part-time basis to produce certain visual appendices.

To sum up, before his death in early 1747 Müteferrika employed five Muslim/ Turkish printers who worked for him on a full-time basis, and three other part-time contractors: a Jewish letter-maker and typesetter (Yona) and two map-makers of Muslim/Turkish (Ahmet al-Kırımî) and Armenian origin (Mıgırdiç Galatavî). Müteferrika had five full-time and three part-time workers, eight in total. It is a matter of speculation whether it is coincidental that this number matches the number of eight senior printers mentioned in *Mercurii Relation* (1728), in Imhof's chronicle (1735) and Kundmann's narrative (1737). Nevertheless, as the above-

---

104 A. Galante, *Histoire des Juifs de Turquie*, vol. 2, Istanbul, s. a., p. 90; Ersoy, *Türkiye'ye Matbaanın Girişi*, p. 35; Y. Meral, *İbrahim Müteferrika Öncesi İstanbul'da Yahudi Matbuatı (Matbaalar, İlmî Hayat ve Dinî Literatür), 1493-1729*, Ankara, 2016, p. 49–55.
105 Refik, *Hicrî Onikinci Asır'da İstanbul Hayatı*, p. 123–125; E. Afyoncu, "Yirmisekiz Çelebizâde Mehmed Said Paşa (ö. 1761)", in *Matbaanın Ön Sözü "Basmacı İbrahim Efendi": Müteferrika Sergisi'21*, Ankara, 2021, p. 46.
106 Carleson, *İbrahim Müteferrika Basımevi ve Bastığı İlk Eserler*, p. 12.
107 Sabev, *İbrahim Müteferrika ya da İlk Osmanlı Matbaa Serüveni*, p. 381.
108 Meral, *İbrahim Müteferrika Öncesi İstanbul'da Yahudi Matbuatı*, p. 50.

mentioned sources imply, in the very beginning the number of workers and their origins might have been different.

One may assume that in the beginning of the printing enterprise the number of printers employed was larger than later on because its initial stage required more investment and human labor. Ottoman documents dating from late 1727 reveal that "every day fifteen pairs of bread loaves should be given on the account of the [imperial] kitchen to the workers employed at the printshop where Ibrahim Efendi began printing the *Vankulu* dictionary with [movable] type until it is finished."[109] One may assume that the mentioned number of "fifteen pairs of bread loaves" could indicate a number of fifteen persons involved in the printing of the dictionary, each of them having received a pair of bread loaves on a daily basis until the work was done. It also makes sense that foreign printers along with imported equipment had been used initially, and over the course of time local Muslim/Turkish printers were trained to continue the enterprise.

5. Conclusions

The introduction of Ottoman Turkish printing in the 1720s sparked serious curiosity among European literati who had for centuries expressed their wonder at the lack of such printing activity. They tried to explain this lack assuming that the conservative Muslim society was not eager to adopt western technologies and that the Ottoman rulers protected the livelihoods of the numerous manuscript copyists. Once printing was endorsed by Ottoman officials, the European Republic of Letters expressed its great expectations for its future output, hoping that many ancient manuscripts, presumably preserved in the sultan's seraglio, would also be printed and thus made accessible for a wider reading public. The French literati were perhaps the first to inform western societies about the introduction of printing by the Ottoman ruling class. They were followed by German learned circles, which also published short or detailed reports about the newly opened Ottoman Turkish press in Constantinople. German authors borrowed information from the previously published French newspapers and journals, on the one hand, and added new details, on the other. They openly stressed the grand mufti's initial unwillingness to allow printing among the Muslims and his subsequent backtrack as a result of the grand vizier's threat. Although no Ottoman source openly discusses this obstacle, one may easily read it between the lines of the application for a privilege to print submitted by Müteferrika in 1726. He declared

---

109 Sungu, "İlk Türk Matbaasına dair Yeni Vesikalar", p. 14.

that he would print only books on secular subject matter and this intention of his might have been based on his unspoken attempt circumvent the obvious obstacles related to Muslim bias and/or anxiety about the printing of religious books.

The German sources are curious about Ibrahim Müteferrika's pre-Muslim denomination, claiming that he was Socinian (hence Unitarian). This claim might only be speculation based on the German authors' desire to neglect the French (and maybe Catholic) role in the introduction of Ottoman Turkish printing. They also highlight the role of the Habsburgs (France's rivals at the time) in this process by pointing out that the printing equipment and staff were provided from Vienna and the Netherlands (then its southern part was under the rule of the Austrian branch of the Habsburg family[110]).

The German sources also provide the only known visual representation of the Müteferrika press (Fig. 1). If one assumes that it represents the actual situation in the printshop by featuring six figures, including Ibrahim Müteferrika himself and his five full-time workers, then their Oriental appearance (caftans and turbans) might imply that even in the very beginning they were not foreigners, as the European sources suggest, but Muslims/Turks. On the other hand, since this engraving is supposed to be just an illustration that could spark the reader's imagination, the Oriental appearance of the depicted figures might simply be an artistic approach to highlight the Oriental character of the newly opened printing press in Constantinople. Whatever the case may be, this engraving has sparked not only the imagination of the readers in the time of its publication but also the imagination of today's scholars of the history of Ottoman printing.

110 See Hugh Dunthorne, "Flanders and Holland in the Eighteenth Century", *State Papers Online, The Eighteenth Century 1714-1782*, Cengage Learning EMEA Ltd, 2015; https://www.gale.com/intl/essays/hugh-dunthorne-flanders-holland-eighteenth-century (accessed on December 15, 2022).

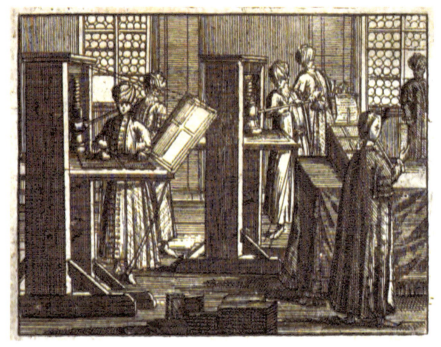

Fig. 1: Engraving depicting the Müteferrika Press in Constantinople (Andreas Lazarus von Imhof, *Des Neu-eröffneten historischen Bilder-Saals*, vol. 9, part 1, Nuremberg: Johann Leonhard Buggel and Johann Andreas Seitz, 1735, p. 835).

Bibliography

Unpublished Sources

National Archive of the Netherlands, NL-HaNA_1.02.20_25_0002.
Devlet Arşivleri – Istanbul (BOA), Cevdet-Maarif, 120/5983.

Published Sources

Afyoncu, Erhan. "Yirmisekiz Çelebizâde Mehmed Said Paşa (ö. 1761)". In *Matbaanın Ön Sözü "Basmacı Ibrahim Efendi": Müteferrika Sergisi'21*. Ankara: Cumhurbaşkanlığı Millet Kütüphanesi, 2021, p. 46–48.

Asım [Yazıksız], Nesimi. "Türk Matbaacılığı". *Türk Tarih Encümeni Mecmuası* (new series), 2, 1929, p. 46–48.

Babinger, Franz. *Stambuler Buchwesen im 18. Jahrhundert*. Leipzig: Breitkopf und Haertel, 1919.

Babinski, Paul. *World Literature in Practice: The Orientalist's Manuscript Between the Ottoman Empire and Germany*. Princeton: Princeton University, 2020 (unpublished Ph.D. thesis).

Baysal, Jale. *Müteferrika'dan Birinci Meşrutiyete kadar Osmanlı Türklerinin Bastıkları Kitaplar*. Istanbul: Edebiyat Fakültesi, 1968.

Berkes, Niyazi. "Ibrāhīm Müteferriķa". In *The Encyclopaedia of Islam, Second Edition*, vol. III, ed. By Bernard Lewis, Victor-Louis Ménage, Charles Pellat, Joseph Schacht. Leiden: Brill, 1971, p. 996–998.

Berkes, Niyazi. "İlk Türk Matbaası Kurucusunun Dinî ve Fikrî Kimliği". *Belleten*, 104, 1962, p. 715–737.

Bibliothèque raisonnée des ouvrages des savans de l'Europe, 6/1, January, February and March 1731.

Carleson, Edvard. *Ibrahim Müteferrika Basımevi ve Bastığı İlk Eserler/Ibrahim Müteferrika's Printing House and Its First Printed Books*, ed. by Mustafa Akbulut. Ankara: Türk Kütüphaneciler Deneği, 1979.

Der europäische Postilion: oder Begebenheiten, so sich in Europa hin und wieder zu Wasser und zu Land zugetragen, vol. 1, Part 2. Augsburg: Andreas Maschenbauer and Witibund Erben, 1728.

Donado, Giovanni Battista. *Osservationi fatte della letteratura de Turchi*. Venice: Andrea Poletti, 1688.

Dunthorne, Hugh. "Flanders and Holland in the Eighteenth Century". *State Papers Online, The Eighteenth Century 1714-1782*, Cengage Learning EMEA Ltd, 2015; https://www.gale.com/intl/essays/hugh-dunthorne-flanders-holland-eighteenth-century (accessed on 15 December 2022).

Duverdier, Gérald. "Savary De Brèves et Ibrahim Müteferrika: Deux drogmans culturels à l'origine de l'imprimerie Turque". *Bulletin du bibliophile*, 3, 1987, p. 322–359.

Erdem, Yahya. "Müteferrika Matbaasının Erken Dönemde Yapılmış Bilinmeyen Bir Resmi". *Müteferrika*, 39, 2011, p. 221–224.

Ernesti, Johann Heinrich Gottfried. *Die wol-eingerichtete Buchdruckerey*. Nuremberg: Johann Andreas Endters Erben, 1733.

Ersoy, Osman. *Türkiye'ye Matbaanın Girişi ve İlk Basılan Eserler*. Ankara: Ankara Üniversitesi Dil ve Tarih-Coğrafya Fakültesi, 1959.

Ertuğ, Hasan R. *Basın ve Yayın Hareketleri Tarihi*. Istanbul: Yenilik Basımevi, 1970.

Feodorov, Ioana. *Dimitrie Cantemir, Salvation of the Sage and Ruin of the Sinful World*. Leiden: Brill, 2016.

Galante, Abraham. *Histoire des Juifs de Turquie*, vol. 2. Istanbul: Isis Press, s. a.

Gazzete de France, 3, January 18, 1727.

Gerçek, Selim Nüzhet. *Türk Matbaacılığı*, Part 1. *Müteferrika Matbaası*. Istanbul: Maarif Vekaleti, 1939.

Göçek, Fatma Müge. *East Encounters West: France and the Ottoman Empire in the Eighteenth Century*. New York/Oxford: Oxford University Press, 1987.

Haddad, Jonathan. "People Before Print: *Gens de Lettres*, the Ottoman Printing Press, and the Search for Turkish Literature". *Mediterranean Studies*, 2, 2017, p. 189–228.

Haddad, Jonathan. *Imagining Turkish Literature: Between the French Republic of Letters and the Ottoman Empire*. Berkely: University of California, 2016 (unpublished Ph.D. thesis).

Hanstein, Thoralf. *A New Print by Müteferrika? A Comparative View of Baron's Qibla Finder*. Berlin: EB-Verlag, 2021.

History of Transylvania, ed. by Béla Köpeczi. Budapest: Akadémiai kiadó, 1989.

Imhof, Andreas Lazarus von. *Des Neu-Eröffneten Historischen Bilder-Saals*, vol. 9, Part 1. Nürnberg: Johann Leonhard Buggel and Johann Andreas Seitz, 1735, 1740.

Journal de Sçavans (Amsterdam edition), 81, April 1727,

Journal de Sçavans (Paris edition), February 1727.

Kundmann, Johann Christian. *Rariora Naturae et Artis Item in re Medica, Oder Seltenheiten der Natur und Kunst*. Breslau/Leipzig: Ben Michael Hubert, 1737.

Kut, Turgut, Fatma Türe *Yazmadan Basmaya: Müteferrika, Mühendishane, Üsküdar*, Istanbul: Yapı ve Kredi Bankası Yayınları, 1996.

Lettres de Turquie (1730-1739) et Notices (1740) de César de Saussure, ed. by Coloman de Thály. Budapest: Académie hongroise des sciences, 1909.

Marsigli, Signore Conte di. *Stato Militare dell'Impero Ottomanno Incremento e Decremento del Medesimo/L'Etat militaire de l'Empire Ottoman, ses progrès et sa décadence*. The Hague/Amsterdam: Pietro Gosse et al., 1732.

Meral, Yasin. *Ibrahim Müteferrika Öncesi İstanbul'da Yahudi Matbuatı (Matbaalar, İlmî Hayat ve Dinî Literatür), 1493-1729*. Ankara: Divan Kitap, 2016.

Mercure de France, January 1727; December 1729.

Mercurii Relation, oder wochentliche Ordinari Zeitungen von underschidlichen Orthen, 7, February 15, 1727; 19, May 8, 1728; 28, July 17, 1728; 35, September 4, 1728; 6, April 14, 1731.

Murphy, Cristopher M. "Appendix: Ottoman Imperial Documents Relating to the History of Books and Printing". In George N. Atiyeh (ed.), *The Book in the Islamic World. The Written Word and Communication in the Middle East*. Albany: State of New York University Press, 1995, p. 283–292.

Mystakidis, B. A. "Hükümet-i Osmaniye Tarafından İlk Tesis Olunan Matbaa ve Bunun Neşriyatı". *Tarih-i Osmanî Encümeni Mecmuası*, 5, 1326 [1910], p. 322–328.

Necatioğlu, Halil. *Matbaacı İbrâhîm-i Müteferrika ve Risâle-i İslâmiye*. Ankara: Elif Matbaacılık, 1982.

Neue Zeitungen von gelehrten Sachen, 11, February 6, 1727; 61, July 31, 1727.

Nuhoğlu, Hidayet Y. "Müteferrika Matbaasının Kurulması için Verilen Fetvâ Üzerine". In *Basım ve Yayıncılığımızın 250. Yılı Bilimsel Toplantısı, 10-11 Aralık 1979, Ankara, Bildiriler*. Ankara: Türk Kütüphaneciler Derneği, 1980, p. 119–126.

Omont, Henri. "Documents sur l'imprimerie à Constantinople au XVIIIᵉ siècle". *Revue des bibliothèques*, 5, 1895, p. 185–200, 228–236.

Omont, Henri. "Nouveaux documents sur l'imprimerie à Constantinple au XVIIIᵉ siècle". *Revue des bibliothèques*, 33, 1926, p. 1–10.

Omont, Henri. *Missions archéologiques Françaises en Orient au XVIIᵉ et XVIIIᵉ siècles*, vol. 2. Paris: Imprimerie nationale, 1902.

Refik, Ahmed. *Hicrî Onikinci Asır'da İstanbul Hayatı (1100-1200) [Onikinci Asr-ı Hicrî'de İstanbul Hayatı (1689-1785)]*. Istanbul: Enderun Kitapevi, 1988.

Rycaut, Paul. *The Present State of the Ottoman Empire*. London: John Starkey and Henry Brome, 1668.

Sabev, Orlin. *Ibrahim Müteferrika ya da İlk Osmanlı Matbaa Serüveni (1726-1746): Yeniden Değerlendirme*. Istanbul: Yeditepe Yayınevi, 2016 (fourth edition).

Sabev, Orlin. *Waiting for Müteferrika: Glimpses of Ottoman Print Culture*. Boston: Academic Studies Press, 2018.

Sarıcaoğlu, Fikret, Coşkun Yılmaz. *Müteferrika: Basmacı Ibrahim Efendi ve Müteferrika Matbaası/Basmacı Ibrahim Efendi and the Müteferrika Press*. Istanbul: Esen Ofset, 2008.

Scholz, Henrici. *Bibliothecae Arabicae de Typographiis Arabicis*. Hamburg: Literris Phil. Ludov. Scromeri, 1741.

Şen, Adil. *Ibrahim Müteferrika ve Usûlü'l-hikem fî Nizâmi'l-ümem*. Ankara: Diyanet Vakfı Yayınları, 1995.

Sungu, İhsan. "İlk Türk Matbaasına dair Yeni Vesikalar". *Hayat*, 73, 1928, p. 9–15.

Tercümetü'ş-şiḥaḥ-ı Cevherî [Lugat-ı Vankulu]. Istanbul: Dârü't-tıbâti'l-mâʿmûre, 1141 [1729].

Schwartz, Kathryn A. "Did Ottoman Sultans Ban Print?". *Book History*, 20, 2017, p. 1–39.

Tezcan, Baki. "İbrâhîm Müteferrika ve Risâle-i İslâmiyye". *Kitaplara Vakfedilen Bir Ömre Tuhfe: İsmail E. Erünsal'a Armağan*, ed. by Hatice Aynur, Bilgin Aydın and Mustafa Birol Ülker, vol. 1. Istanbul: Ülke Armağan, 2014.

Toderini, Giambattista. *De la Littérature des Turcs*, ed. by Abbé de Cournand, vol. 3. Paris: Poinçot, 1789.

Toderini, Giambattista. *İbrahim Müteferrika Matbaası ve Türk Matbaacılığı*, ed. by Şevket Rado. Istanbul: Şevket Rado, 1990.

Wilbur, Earl Morse. *A History of Unitarianism*, vol. 2. Cambridge, MA.: Harvard University Press, 1952.

Wurm, Heidrun. "Entstehung und Aufhebung des osmanischen Generalkonsulats in Wien (1726–1732): Eine Relation Heinrich von Penklers aus dem Jahr 1761". *Mitteilungen des Österreichischen Staatsarchivs*, 42, 1992, p. 152–187.

Yılmaz, Coşkun. "Müteferrika Matbaasının Kurucu Kadrosu". In *Matbaanın Ön Sözü "Basmacı Ibrahim Efendi": Müteferrika Sergisi'21*. Ankara: Cumhurbaşkanlığı Millet Kütüphanesi, 2021, p. 34–42.

Zaïmova, Raia. "Quelques traits de l'Européanisation culturelle dans l'Empire Ottoman au début du XVIIIᵉ siècle". In M.-C. Skuncke (ed.), *Centre(s) et périphérie(s): Les lumières de Belfast à Beijing/Centre(s) and Margins: Enlightenment from Belfast to Beijing*. Paris: Honoré Champion, 2003, p. 71–79.

https://de.wikipedia.org/wiki/Neueröffneter_Historischer_Bildersaal (accessed August 5, 2022).

Radu Dipratu
Ottoman Endorsements of Printing in 18th-Century Istanbul

The topic of this chapter was inspired by an article on the opposite subject. That is, the banning of printing in the Ottoman Empire. Most readers are probably intrigued from the very beginning by the title of Kathryn Schwartz's 2017 article, "Did Ottoman Sultans Ban Print?", because the answer seems obvious: of course they banned print, right? This seems to be one of those facts that are even often stated in academic works without even requiring a citation: "it is well known that Ottoman sultans banned print". It seems, however, that this was not the case. According to Schwartz's very convincing enquiry, there is no documentary evidence to support this claim. The often-cited bans of Bayezid II and Selim I are nowhere to be found, and the earliest mention of such a banning *ferman* – or imperial edict – seems to have come from the famous French traveller and cosmographer André Thevet, in 1584.[1] From then on, different statements were made concerning what exactly these two *ferman*s banned: printing altogether, printing with Arabic type, the printing of religious materials?

On the other hand, some authors claim that Bayezid II actually approved printing, though not for the general population of the Empire, let alone for Muslims, but only for a specific non-Muslim group: the Jews recently arrived from Spain.[2] As with the fabled ban, documentary evidence of sultanic warrants favouring print for the Jewish communities in this early period is likewise missing.[3] As for the other two non-Muslim communities that established their own printing houses in

---

1 K.A. Schwartz, "Did Ottoman Sultans Ban Print?", *Book History*, 20, 2017, p. 6–7, 12–15. Schwartz's conclusions are widely supported by specialists in the field. See, for example, O. Sabev, *Waiting for Müteferrika: Glimpses of Ottoman Print Culture*, Boston, 2018, p. 13–15.
2 G. Oman, "Maṭbaʿa in the Arab World", in C.E. Bosworth, E. van Donzel, W.P. Heinrichs, Ch. Pellat (eds.), *The Encyclopaedia of Islam, Second Edition*, vol. VI, Leiden, 1991, p. 795; H.Y. Nuhoğlu, "Müteferrika's Printing Press: Some Observations", in K. Çiçek (ed.), *The Great Ottoman Civilization. Volume 3: Philosophy, Science and Institutions*, Ankara, 2000, p. 83.
3 Nil Palabıyık suggested that there may have been a single *ferman* through which Bayezid II allowed the Jews to print and at the same time forbade any printing of Islamic books. N. Pektaş (Palabıyık), "The Beginnings of Printing in the Ottoman Capital: Book Production and Circulation

---

This research is part of a project that has received funding from the European Research Council (ERC) under the European Union's Horizon 2020 research and innovation programme (Grant Agreement No. 883219-AdG-2019 – Project TYPARABIC).

∂ Open Access. © 2024, the author(s), published by De Gruyter. [CC BY-NC-ND] This work is licensed under the Creative Commons Attribution-NonCommercial-NoDerivatives 4.0 International License.
https://doi.org/10.1515/9783111060392-003

the sixteenth and seventeenth centuries, namely the Armenians and Greeks, the state-of-the-art does not seem to discuss, with the same vigour, at least, whether the imperial authorities formulated any bans or approvals.

Thus emerged the topic for this chapter: while indeed it seems pointless to further search for the elusive prohibitive *fermans*, researching how Ottoman-Muslim authorities endorsed print proved to be much more valuable. This exposition will, of course, discuss imperial decrees, but also other types of documents and literary compositions. It will focus on the early 18th century and the opening of the Müteferrika press, just a few years after the first Arabic books for Christians began to be printed in Wallachia and Syria. Müteferrika's first published volume, *Lugat-ı Vankulu*, a Turkish translation prepared by Vankulu Efendi of Abu Naṣr al-Jawharī's (d. 1003) classic Arabic dictionary,[4] contained in its preface several pieces of literature endorsing the newly-established printing endeavour.

This chapter's main contention is that the many endorsements added to *Lugat-ı Vankulu* were produced not to counter a pre-existing sultanic ban, but a strong religious resentment. Although this idea was accepted in the past, more recent re-evaluations of the reasons behind the late adoption of printing in the Ottoman Empire tend to disregard the religious element, focusing instead on social and economic arguments, especially on a strong tie to manuscript culture and opposition from scribes.

A couple of examples best illustrate this shift. In the second edition of the *Encyclopaedia of Islam* entry on the history of the printing press in Turkey, Günay Alpay Kut states that because Müteferrika "feared religious opposition" he submitted a petition to the grand vizier and sought further authorization from the sultan and grand mufti (*şeyhülislâm*).[5] On the other hand, in the splendidly-illustrated recent volume dedicated to the life and works of Ibrahim Müteferrika, authors Fikret Sarıcaoğlu and Coşkun Yılmaz maintain that "the generally accepted view is that the social, political and psychological conditions were not suitable at an earlier date" for printing to be established. In addition, they add:

in Early Modern Constantinople", *Osmanlı Bilimi Araştırmaları*, 16, 2015, p. 13, n. 38. See also Taisiya Leber's chapter in this present volume.

4 *Tercümetü'ş-Şiḥaḥ-ı Cevherî* [*Lugat-ı Vankulu*], Istanbul, 1141 [1729].

5 G.A. Kut, "Maṭbaʿa in Turkey", in C.E. Bosworth, E. van Donzel, W.P. Heinrichs and Ch. Pellat (eds.), *The Encyclopaedia of Islam, Second Edition*, vol. VI, Leiden, 1991, p. 800. On the other hand, in an earlier volume of the same reference work, Berkes maintained that Müteferrika "met no opposition from the 'religious institution'. The alleged opposition to the opening of the printing press does not seem to have been motivated by religion but rather by the economic interests of copyists and calligraphers": N. Berkes, "Ibrāhīm Müteferriḳa", in B. Lewis, V. L. Ménage, C. Pellat, J. Schacht (eds.), *The Encyclopaedia of Islam, Second Edition*, vol. III, Leiden, 1971, p. 997.

that the religious sector could be an obstacle to the enterprise of printing [...] was proved to be totally without foundation. The number of those who insisted on this mistaken thinking and those who felt the need to argue gradually decreased. [...] The irony here is that if Basmacı Ibrahim Efendi and Neveşehirli Damad Ibrahim Pasha had lived in an earlier era the Ottoman state would not have lagged behind in this field.[6]

Going along with this counterfactual argument, one can wonder if Müteferrika and Nevşehirlî Ibrahim Pasha would have been able to open the press just a few decades earlier, during the peak of the *kadızâdelî* movement and its profound opposition to innovation (*bid'at*).[7] For Sarıcaoğlu and Yılmaz, the endorsements of sixteen religious officials present on Müteferrika's first printed volume prove that there were no concerns regarding printing coming from the religious milieu.[8] This chapter will argue that the exact opposite is more probable.

The earliest text known to have discussed printed books in the Ottoman Empire is a *ferman* issued by Sultan Murad III in 1588.[9] It was meant to protect two foreign merchants who were importing from Europe (*Firengistân*) among other goods, "some esteemed Arabic, Persian, and Turkish printed books and treatises" (*bazı meta ve Arabî ve Fârsî ve Türkî basma bazı mu'teber kitaplar ve risâleler getirüb*). Such protection was required because apparently some locals had forcibly opened the merchants' cargo and taken their goods, including these books, without paying. "What are you doing with these Arabic and Persian books?" asked the seemingly bewildered locals.[10]

---

6 F. Sarıcaoğlu, C. Yılmaz, *Müteferrika: Basmacı İbrahim Efendi ve Müteferrika Matbaası*, Istanbul, 2008, p. 149, 153.

7 For this religious conservative movement see M. C. Zilfi, "The *Kadizadelis*: Discordant Revivalism in Seventeenth-Century Istanbul", *Journal of Near Eastern Studies*, 45, 1986, p. 251–269 and E. E. Tuşalp Atiyas, "The 'Sunna-Minded' Trend", in M. Sariyannis, *A History of Ottoman Political Thought up to the Early Nineteenth Century*, with a chapter by E. Ekin Tuşalp Atiyas, Leiden/Boston, 2019, p. 233–278.

8 The same conclusion, based on the grand mufti's favourable *fetva* is shared by S. Reese, "Introduction", in S. Reese (ed.), *Manuscript and Print in the Islamic Tradition*, Berlin/Boston, 2022, p. 1–2.

9 This *ferman*, one of the first ever printed Turkish texts, was included at the end of the Arabic version of Euclid's *Elements*, attributed to al-Ṭūsī (*Kitāb taḥrīr uṣul li-Uqlīdis min ta'līf Khōja Naṣīr al-Dīn al-Ṭūsī*), coming out of the Medici press in Rome, in 1594. For this early Arabic European printing house see A. Tinto, *La Tipografia Medicea Orientale*, Lucca, 1987; Pektaş (Palabıyık), "The Beginnings", p. 5–6, 11–12; Sabev, *Waiting for Müteferrika*, p. 72. For a facsimile and translit-eration of the *ferman* see T. Kut, F. Türe (eds.), *Yazmadan Basmaya: Müteferrika, Mühendishane*, *Üsküdar*, Istanbul, 1996, p. 16; English translation in C. M. Murphy, "Appendix: Ottoman Imperial Documents Relating to the History of Books and Printing", in G. N. Atiyeh (ed.), *The Book in the Islamic World. The Written Word and Communication in the Middle East*, Albany, 1995, p. 283.

10 *fuzulî yüklerin yıkub denklerin bozub içinden beğendükleri akmişe ve sair emtia kısmını akçesüz ve cüz-i beha ile cebren alub ve siz Arabî ve Fârsî kitaplar neyler deyü cemi kitaplarını*

This situation appears to have been widespread and not specific to one commercial center since the *ferman* was a collective one, addressed to all secular and religious officials (namely, *sancakbeyi*s, *kapudan paşa*s and *kadı*s) across the Ottoman Empire, and not those of a certain place. In fact, its diplomatic parts very much resemble those of a *yol fermanı* (travel permit) issued for foreigners coming to the Ottoman Empire.[11] Therefore, this document should be seen more as an import license with books just happening to be among the merchandise brought by the two Europeans to the Well Protected Domains to be sold.[12]

The *ferman* does not actually make any comment about printing. It neither endorses nor bans the action, but simply sanctions the sale of printed books, without mentioning the reason behind the locals' indignation towards them. However, it is hard to believe that dissatisfaction regarding the aesthetic quality of the Arabic typeface produced in Europe was the driving factor behind the locals' embezzling the book shipment. This seems to contradict the more recent state-of-the-art which argues that the main deterrent in establishing printing presses in Muslim societies was that printed books offered poor aesthetics when compared to manuscripts.[13] The locals mentioned in Murad III's *ferman* seemed very interested in taking those printed books, though not for the purpose or in the manner intended by their sellers. In other words, the two European merchants encountered problems not because of the appearance of their books, but because of their contents. It is very possible that their cargo contained not only scientific books, like that of Euclid, to which this *ferman* was attached, but also Qurans published in the West.

---

ellerinden alub bahasın vermiyüb. All translations present in this chapter, when not signalled otherwise, are my own.

11 For such a road permit see R. Dipratu, *Regulating Non-Muslim Communities in the Seventeenth-Century Ottoman Empire: Catholics and Capitulations*, London/New York, 2022, p. 147–148.

12 The closing lines of the *ferman* indicate that, besides the Sharia, the two merchants were under the protection of the capitulations (*şer-i şerife ve ahidname-i hümâyuna muhalif asla ve kat'a kimesne dahl u tecavüz etdirmiyesiz*), meaning that they were subjects of a European sovereign who received commercial privileges from the Porte or at least declared themselves as such, traveling under his banner. Their names appear to be Italian (*Branton ve Orasiu veled Bandini*), though this does not necessarily mean that they were subjects of Venice, the only Italian polity to have valid capitulations during this period.

13 T. Nemeth, "Overlooked: The Role of Craft in the Adoption of Typography in the Muslim Middle East", in S. Reese (ed.), *Manuscript and Print in the Islamic Tradition*, Berlin/Boston, 2022, p. 41: "Despite numerous accounts from various parts of the Arabic script world that describe the rejection of print based on aesthetic grounds, it is yet to be accepted as a key factor in the disinterest of the Muslim world in typography."

Furthermore, arguments pertaining to the aesthetic quality of printed Arabic books often ignore the very existence of Arabic print in the Ottoman Empire before Müteferrika's endeavour: the books printed for the Arabic-speaking Christians of Greater Syria. Christian Arabs lived in the same manuscript-driven society as Muslims, yet it seems that they had no such aesthetic problems in adopting printed liturgical books. Financial arguments are equally not convincing.[14] It is true that Christian Arabs benefited from the financial support of Orthodox princes in Wallachia and Moldavia, and later that of Catholic and Protestant missions, but Müteferrika also relied on capital other than his own, namely that of his business partner, Said Çelebi, but he also asked for and obtained state support.[15] In any case, it seems unsound to presume that Ottoman Arab Christians were in a better financial position than their Muslim counterparts to run a printing house. Therefore, the only trait which seems to differentiate the attitude of the two groups remains the religious one. This argument is further substantiated by the fact that the first printed books for Christian Arabs were religious ones, whereas Müteferrika explicitly mentions that he would not print religious texts, as detailed further in this chapter.

The next official documents issued by the Muslim authorities of the empire to discuss print appeared almost a century and a half later, in the wake of Müteferrika's printing enterprise.

The pages coming before the proper text of *Lugat-ı Vankulu*, the first volume to come out of the Müteferrika press in early 1729, contain valuable documentary evidence for this present enquiry. The documents in question are: Ibrahim Müteferrika's petition (*arz-ı hal*) approved by Grand Vizier Nevşehirlî Damat Ibrahim Pasha; a *ferman* of Sultan Ahmed III, containing a favourable *fetva* from *şeyhü-lislâm* Yenişehirlî Abdullah Efendi; the *fetva* itself, printed separately; sixteen *takariz* (sg. *takriz*) or recommendations penned by various religious officials; and finally Müteferrika's treatise on "The means of printing" (*Vesîletü't-tıbâa*).[16]

Müteferrika was, of course, the paramount endorser of printing. Both in his petition and treatise he presented some of the main benefits of printing, such as in education, the preservation of ancient works which otherwise might be

---

14 Nemeth, "Overlooked", p. 36–37 indeed discusses the Christian Arabic presses of Syria and Lebanon but argues that their situation is not comparable to the Muslims' since they were top-down initiatives, serving propagandistic and not commercial interests.

15 Sabev, *Waiting for Müteferrika*, p. 40.

16 Except for the *takariz*, all documents are transliterated in Kut, Türe, *Yazmadan Basmaya*, p. 30–35 and in Sarıcaoğlu, Yılmaz, *Müteferrika*, p. 353–362. For translations of Müteferrika's treatise and Ahmed III's *ferman* see H. Omont, *Documents sur l'imprimerie a Constantinople au XVIIIe siècle*, Paris, 1895, p. 10–21 and Murphy, "Appendix", p. 284–292.

lost, technical advantages over manuscripts, accessibility and availability, ease
of compiling indexes and so on. I will not insist here on Müteferrika's exposition because they have been discussed in countless other studies.[17] However, it is
important to highlight that the *ferman* and *fetva* adopted the ideas presented by
Müteferrika in his treatise, some even verbatim, and thus endorsed his endeavour on account of the practical benefits of printing, stressing that this production
method had the advantage of producing many copies with little effort and in a
short amount of time.

Because errors could have very well been disseminated just as easily, these
two official documents stressed that the printing process was to be supervised by
several proof-readers and the *ferman* even nominated them: Ebûishakzâde İshak
Efendi (former *kadı* of Istanbul), Pîrîzâde Mehmet Sâhib Efendi (former *kadı* of
Thessaloniki), Yanyalî Esad Efendi (former *kadı* of Galata) and Safî Musa el-Mevlevî (current shaykh of the Kasımpaşa Mevlevi lodge). Since all four designated
proof-readers were members of the *ulemâ*, one would be very much tempted to
perceive a religious interference in the printing process of works on virtually any
other topic than religion. However, this is not true, at least not entirely. Far from
being narrow-minded dogmatists, these four were highly trained intellectuals,
with expertise in linguistics and philosophy, among other things, and who did
not shun scholarly contacts with non-Muslims.[18] One may argue that a court historian or astronomer, for example, could also have been nominated as a proofreader, but there is no evidence to indicate that these four individuals were
anything less than competent to do the job they had been given. As such, while
their appointment cannot be considered a pure act of religious censorship, it also
cannot be completely ruled out, since the *ulemâ* proof-readers could potentially

---

17 S. Reichmuth, "Islamic Reformist Discourse in the Tulip Period (1718-1730): Ibrahim
Müteferriqa and His Arguments for Printings", in A. Çaksu (ed.), *International Congress on
Learning and Education in the Ottoman World, Istanbul, 12–15 April 1999. Proceedings*, Istanbul,
2001, p. 149–161; M. van den Boogert, "The Sultan's Answer to the Medici Press? Ibrahim
Müteferrika's Printing House in Istanbul", in A. Hamilton, M. van den Boogert, B. Westerweel
(eds.), *The Republic of Letters and the Levant*, Leiden/Boston, 2005, p. 270–279; J. R. Osborn,
Letters of Light. Arabic Script in Calligraphy, Print, and Digital Design, Cambridge/London, 2017,
p. 113–116.
18 For more information on Esad Efendi from Ioannina see Hasan Çolak's chapter in this present
volume. For the other three proof-readers see M. N. Doğan, "İshak Efendi, Ebûishakzâde", in
TDV İslâm Ansiklopedisi, vol. 22, Istanbul, 2000, p. 530–531; T. Özcan, "Pîrîzâde Mehmed Sâhib
Efendi", in *TDV İslâm Ansiklopedisi*, vol. 34, Istanbul, 2007, p. 288–290; A. Mete, "İstanbul'da
Trabluslu Bir Şeyh Efendi: Safî Musa el-Mevlevî (ö. 1157/1744)", in A. H. Furat, N. K. Yorulmaz,
O. S. Arı (eds.), *Sahn-ı Semân'dan Dârülfünûn'a Osmanlı'da İlim ve Fikir Dünyası (Âlimler,
Müesseseler ve Fikrî Eserler) - XVIII. Yüzyıl*, vol. 2, Istanbul, 2018, p. 249–261.

guarantee that texts coming out of the Müteferrika press would not only be free of errors but also of religious matters. However, there are other signs indicating more clearly that religious concerns against printing were indeed present.

As mentioned above, Müteferrika already announced the crucial printing restriction on religious topics in his treatise, and it was likewise adopted and emphasized in the sultan's and grand mufti's documents. Müteferrika stated in *Vesîletü't-tıbâa* that he would only print books pertaining to the secular sciences, explicitly mentioning dictionaries and works on history, medicine, philosophy, astronomy, geography and topography (*lugat ve tarih ve tıp ve fünun-ı hikmet ve hey'et ve ana tabi coğrafya ve mesâlik-i memâlik*). Texts on Islamic jurisprudence, commentaries, traditions of the Prophet, and theology (*fıkıh ve tefsir ve hadis ve kelâm*) would be excluded (*maada*) from printing. Nothing was said about printing the Quran itself. Considering these statements, one must surely address the elephant in the room: if no religious opposition was expected, then why would Müteferrika bother to declare this exclusion, repeated also in the *ferman* and, more importantly, in the *fetva*? Moreover, were not the benefits of printing presented by Müteferrika applicable also to students of theology and Islamic law, and would it not contribute to the dissemination of knowledge in these fields? Müteferrika's inclusion of his treatise on the benefits of print, along with its statement that no religious texts would be published on half of the volumes produced by his printing press is a clear indication that some sort of opposition continued to be feared.[19]

An innovation, especially one coming from the West, was prone to encounter opposition from the more conservative elements of Ottoman society.[20] However, in the most popular translations of Müteferrika's tract and Ahmed III's warrant, used by almost all modern scholars in the field, printing appears several times as "this Western activity" or "this innovative Western technique".[21] Then again, defining something as being "Western" – which in Ottoman Turkish would have

---

19 V. Erginbaş, "Enlightenment in the Ottoman Context: İbrahim Müteferrika and his Intellectual Landscape", in G. Roper (ed.), *Historical Aspects of Printing and Publishing in Languages of the Middle East. Papers from the Third Symposium on the History of Printing and Publishing in the Languages and Countries of the Middle East, University of Leipzig, September 2008*, Leiden/Boston, 2014, p. 70.

20 The problem with printing being a Western innovation is discussed by G. Duverdier, "İlk Türk Basımevinin Kuruluşunda İki Kültür Elçisi: Savary de Brèves ile İbrahim Müteferrika", *Belleten*, 56, 1992, p. 303–304.

21 Murphy, "Appendix", p. 291, 292. The following exposition wishes to highlight the need of re-checking the original texts concerning printing in the early-modern Ottoman Empire and by no means discredits Murphy's crucial translation effort.

been designated through the term *frenk* – may not have been exactly positive. One would have most certainly not expected to endorse a novel enterprise through such a term. Notwithstanding, Müteferrika did not describe printing as being *frenk*. It turns out that the translated phrase "Western activity" was, in the original language, *sanat-ı garip*, that is "a strange art", and the "Western technique" was, in fact, *fen-i mergup*, i.e. "a desirable science". The author of these translations most likely confused *garip* with *garp*[22] and *mergup* with *mağrip* – the latter term indeed being used by Müteferrika when referring to the unsuitable aspect of Arabic books printed in Western Europe. While presenting the benefits of printing and its usefulness for Muslims, in general, and for the development of the Ottoman Empire, in particular, Müteferrika could not have insisted on its Western-European origins.

Ahmed III's *ferman* presents a couple of features which, although not exceptional, indicate that the subject discussed was a delicate one. The first element is the phrase *mucibince amel oluna* ("let it be done accordingly"), which represents the *hatt-ı şerif* ("noble writing"), also known as *hatt-ı hümâyun* ("imperial writing"). This would have been the only element written by the sultan himself, left of the imperial monogram or tughra, sometimes in a lavishly decorated rectangle, whereas the rest of the document would have been written by scribes in the imperial chancery. *Ferman*s dealing only with the most important or delicate topics would have required the sultan's *hatt-ı hümâyun*.[23] Müteferrika chose to print this element above the main text with a clearly distinct *sulus*-type script, larger and more elegant than the *nesih* type used everywhere else in the volume.[24] Thus, he reproduced a manuscript feature with differentiated script into his printed version of the *ferman*, signaling to readers that this venture was

---

22 Although the two terms are actually related, both stemming from the Arabic root *gh-r-b*: H. Wehr, *A Dictionary of Modern Written Arabic*, ed. by J. M. Cowan, third edition, Ithaca, 1976, p. 668–669; E. M. Badawi, M. A. Haleem, *Arabic-English Dictionary of Quranic usage*, Leiden/Boston, 2008, p. 661–662. I am grateful to Hasan Çolak for bringing this information to my attention.

23 On *hatt-ı hümâyun*s, also known as *hatt-ı şerif*s see M. S. Kütükoğlu, *Osmanlı Belgelerinin Dili (Diplomatik)*, Istanbul, 1994, p. 172–183.

24 Another way in which Müteferrika's press departed from the Ottoman manuscript tradition was the uniform use of the *nesih* script across many different literary genres, whereas Ottoman scribes customarily employed different scripts for different types of texts, such as *divanî* for imperial edicts, or *nastalik* for *fetva*s. J. R. Osborn, "The Ottoman System of Scripts and the Müteferrika Press", in S. Reese (ed.), *Manuscript and Print in the Islamic Tradition*, Berlin/Boston, 2022, p. 77.

personally approved by the sultan, who otherwise had nothing to do with the document's production.

The second notable element of the *ferman* was its citation of a *fetva*, or legal opinion, issued by grand mufti Yenişehirlî Abdullah Efendi. Although *fetva* rulings were not mandatory, quoting a favourable one certainly gave more weight to the *ferman*, much like the sultan's handwritten *hatt-ı hümâyun*. That an imperial edict was grounded on a legal opinion likewise indicated that this was a delicate matter since more trifling subjects did not require such measures. Müteferrika certainly took all the necessary precautions when requesting approval from both the sultan and the mufti.

It appears esceptional that the *fetva* was printed again separately, even though its contents were already included in the *ferman*. While *ferman*s containing a mufti's legal opinion are certainly not uncommon,[25] this is a rare case in which a stand-alone *fetva* is found alongside the *ferman* it is quoted in and must be a strong piece of evidence that Müteferrika sought extra guarantees in face of a potential opposition grounded on religious terms. Nevertheless, the endorsements did not stop with these two documents.

The presence of no less than sixteen *takariz* in the first printed edition of *Lugat-ı Vankulu* is a remarkable feature. Studies on Ottoman *takriz* writing are few and far between, with authors such as Christine Woodhead and Guy Burak producing a couple of recent articles. In Ottoman context, a *takriz* (pl. *takariz*) was a sort of recommendation sought by an aspiring writer from an established intellectual, often a senior member of the *ulemâ* or the imperial bureaucracy. The presence of a *takriz* at the beginning of a piece of literature not only endorsed it but also signalled a patronage relationship between the endorser and the aspiring writer. Moreover, the *takriz* was something of a literary genre of its own: its author tried his best to showcase his literary prowess in a few elegant phrases while praising the work.[26]

---

25 For a somewhat contemporary case from 1714 see Ahmed III's *ferman* for the deposition of Constantin Brâncoveanu, the voivode of Wallachia, which likewise contained şeyhülislâm Mahmut Efendi's favourable *fetva*: V. Veliman, *Relaţiile româno-otomane (1711-1821). Documente turceşti*, Bucharest, 1984, p. 85–88. Another earlier example involved the renovation of the Catholic Church of St. Francis in Galata, approved by Sultan Mehmed IV through a *ferman* containing the favourable *fetva* of şeyhülislâm Minkârîzâde Yahyâ Efendi· R Dipratu, "'I Shall Not Take Their Churches and Turn Them into Mosques': The Legal Status of Catholic Churches in Ottoman Galata as Prescribed by the ʿahdnâmes", in V. R. de Obaldía, C. Monge (eds.), *Latin Catholicism in Ottoman Istanbul: Properties, People & Missions*, Istanbul, 2022, p. 26–27, 32–33.

26 C. Woodhead, "Puff and Patronage: Ottoman *Takrîż*-writing and Literary Recommendation in the 17th Century", in Ç. Balim-Harding, C. Imber (eds.), *The Balance of Truth. Essays in Honour*

What first strikes the eye upon comparing Woodhead and Burak's *takariz* samples with those found in *Lugat-ı Vankulu* is the sheer numbers. For Woodhead, the six *takariz* included in her study led her to conclude that the aspiring author "was trying particularly hard to gain attention".[27] Imagine the amount of attention Müteferrika wanted to attract with his sixteen *takariz*!

Besides numbers, the identities of the authors of these *takariz* are particularly important. It must be mentioned from the beginning that all of them were members of the *ulemâ*, and none were bureaucrats, members of the *kalemiye*. One might have expected that the endorsement of a vizier or some other high-ranking bureaucrat would also find its way amongst the many *takariz* of the *ulemâ* to support Müteferrika's novel enterprise. Admittedly, *ulemâ* were sought to write *takariz* because they often possessed the best literary skills, but the complete absence of any secular official can be another clue pointing out which sector was most concerned with the printing press.

The first one on the list of *takariz* authors, as if his *fetva* did not suffice, was the *şeyhülislâm* himself, Yenişehirlî Abdullah Efendi. Next were the current military judges (*kazasker*) of Rumelia and Anatolia, the highest legal and religious authorities of the Empire apart from the mufti. Then there was the judge (*kadı*) of Istanbul, the imperial preacher (*imâm-ı şehriyâr*) and the *nakîbüleşraf* (an official who supervised the well-being of the *şerif*s, that is the descendants of the Prophet Muhammad). The ten remaining signatories were either former military judges or former judges of Istanbul. The presence of these later individuals who were registered with their former position raises a critical question: why would Müteferrika bother to obtain endorsements from former officials if he already had the backing of all the current major ones? The answer lies in the fact that far from being permanent, the duration of these offices was in fact quite short. At the beginning of the 18th century, *kadı*s and *kazasker*s would often be in office for just several months, a year or two at most. Müteferrika was well aware that the power of his endorsers was only temporary, and he therefore wanted to future-proof his enterprise. Even grand muftis were in office for comparable short periods, although Yenişehirlî Abdullah Efendi's twelve-year term made him stand out from amongst

---

of Professor Geoffrey Lewis, Istanbul, 2004, p. 396–397; G. Burak, "Reflections on Censorship, Canonization and the Ottoman Practices of *Takriz* and *Imza*", revised version of "Sansür, kanonizasyon ve Osmanlı imzâ-takrîz pratikleri üzerine düşünceler", in H. Aynur et al. (eds.), *Eski Türk Edebiyatı Çalışmaları X: Eski Metinlere Yeni Bağlamlar: Osmanlı Edebiyatı Çalışmalarında Yeni Yönelimler*, Istanbul, 2015, p. 96–117.

27 Woodhead, "Puff and Patronage", p. 397.

his peers.[28] Moreover, recent incidents had proved that sultans could just as easily be deposed.

Müteferrika was most likely no stranger to the events of the so-called "Edirne Incident" (*Edirne Vak'ası*) of 1703 which saw the deposition of Sultan Mustafa II and the gruesome killing of then-*şeyhülislâm* Feyzullah Efendi at the hands of a rebellious mob.[29] Having the approval of the current sultan and grand mufti simply did not guarantee that the first Ottoman printing press would be secured for years to come. Whereas obtaining endorsements from Ottoman heirs-apparent (*şehzâde*) was out of the question, Müteferrika could instead appeal to high-ranking *ulemâ* who had the potential to become future *şeyhülislâm*s, military judges or Istanbul judges. And it appears that he had a good hand in choosing his endorsers.

Only a year and a half after his first volume was printed, Müteferrika's most powerful supporters were brought down during Patrona Halil's rebellion. Sultan Ahmed III and *şeyhülislâm* Abdullah Efendi were deposed, while grand vizier Nevşehirlî Damat İbrahim Pasha was killed.[30] Although his most influential backers were either deposed or killed, Müteferrika continued his publishing activity not least because he had already secured the endorsements of those coming to power in late 1730 and after. The table below shows the offices mentioned by the *takariz* authors and the ones that they held after Patrona Halil's rebellion.

Tab. 1: Signatories of *takariz* on *Lugat-ı Vankulu*[31].

No.	Name	Position given in the takariz	Position held after the rebellion of 1730
1	Yenişehirlî Abdullah Efendi	current *şeyhülislâm*	None: exiled, died in 1743.
2	Damadzâde Ebülhayr Ahmet Efendi	former *kazasker* of Rumelia	*şeyhülislâm* (1732–3).
3	Mirzazâde Şeyh Mehmet Efendi	former *kazasker* of Rumelia	*şeyhülislâm* (1730–1).

---

28 A. Altunsu, *Osmanli Şeyülislâmları*, Ankara, 1972, p. 117–118; M. İpşirli, "Abdullah Efendi, Yenişehirli", in *TDV İslâm Ansiklopedisi*, vol. 1, Istanbul, 1988, p. 100–101.

29 The events are amply described and analysed in R. Abou El-Haj, *The 1703 Rebellion and the Structure of Ottoman Politics*, Leiden, 1984.

30 M. Aktepe, *Patrona İsiyam (1730)*, Istanbul, 1958; R. W. Olson, "The Esnaf and the Patrona Halil Rebelion of 1730: A Realignment in Ottoman Politics?", *Journal of the Economic and Social History of the Orient*, 17/3, 1974, p. 329–344.

31 The information on the identities of the signatories was compiled from Altunsu, *Osmanlı Şeyülislâmları*; *TDV İslâm Ansiklopedisi* and M. Süreyya, *Sicill-i Osmanî*, ed. by N. Akbayar, S. A. Kahraman, Istanbul, 1996.

Tab. 1: Signatories of *takariz* on *Lugat-ı Vankulu* (continued).

No.	Name	Position given in the takariz	Position held after the rebellion of 1730
4	Paşmakçızâde Abdullah Efendi	former *kazasker* of Rumelia	*şeyhülislâm* (1731–2).
5	Feyzullah b. Yahyâ Efendi	former *kazasker* of Rumelia	None: exiled, died in 1747.
6	Seyyid Mehmet Zeynelâbidîn Efendi	current *kazasker* of Rumelia	*şeyhülislâm* (1746–8)
7	Topkapılî Sâlih Efendi	former *kazasker* of Anatolia	None: died in December 1730.
8	Dürrî Mehmet Efendi	former *kazasker* of Anatolia	*şeyhülislâm* (1734–6)
9	Biraderzâde Mustafa Efendi	current *kazasker* of Anatolia	*kazasker* of Rumelia (1734)
10	Mirzazâde Sâlim Mehmet Emin Efendi	former *kadı* of Istanbul	*kazasker of* Anatolia (1730) and Rumelia (1733); *kadı of* Mecca (1736) and Damascus (1738).
11	Ebûishakzâde İshak Efendi	former *kadı* of İstanbul	*şeyhülislâm* (1733–4).
12	Arabzâde Bâhir Abdurrahman Efendi	current imperial preacher	First exiled, afterwards *kazasker* of Anatolia (1738) and Rumelia (1745).
13	Vardarî Şeyhzâde Mehmet Efendi	former *kadı* of İstanbul	again *kadı* of İstanbul (late 1730), then *kazasker* of Anatolia (1732).
14	Esseyyid Zeynelâbidîn b. Seyyid Ali	current *nakibül'-eşraf*	*kazasker* of Anatolia (1732) and Rumelia (1737; 1743).
15	Zülâlî Hasan Efendi	current *kadı* of İstanbul	*kazasker* of Anatolia (1730)
16	İshakzâde Nûr Mehmet Efendi	former *kadı* of İstanbul	None: died in April 1730, before the rebellion began.

The five consecutive grand muftis appointed after the rebellion of 1730, and a total of six out of nine grand muftis holding office until Müteferrika's death in

1747 had signed *takariz* on *Lugat-ı Vankulu*. Moreover, two of the four proof-readers, Ebûishakzâde İshak Efendi and Pîrîzâde Mehmet Sahîb Efendi also became grand muftis in this era, while the former was among the *takariz* signatories, too. Most of the remaining signatories went on to occupy other important positions in the state administration and therefore it was highly probable that at any given moment at least one of the two *kazasker* offices would be occupied by an endorser of Müteferrika's press. In this way, the juridical and religious elites were guaranteed to be favourable during the two remaining decades of Müteferrika's life, thanks to the *takariz* included along with the first printed volume. Moreover, the printing press also received further sultanic backing in early 1732, when the new sultan, Mahmud I, renewed the *ferman* originally issued by Ahmed III back in 1727.[32]

Nevertheless, *Lugat-ı Vankulu* was not the only volume coming out of Müteferrika's press to include such forms of endorsement. The second book to be published, Kâtip Çelebi's history of maritime wars, *Tuhfetü'l-Kibâr fî Esfâri'l-Bihâr*, also included in its preface four *takariz* from the *şeyhülislâm*, the current *kazaskers* of Rumelia and Anatolia, and that of a former *kazasker* of Rumelia.[33] However, while reading their signatures, one will be surprised to encounter the names of some well-known officials such as *şeyhülislâm* Bolevî Mustafa Efendi or *kazasker* Seyyid Mehmet Emin Efendi who were in office in the 1650s, some seventy years before the first printed edition of this volume. It then becomes obvious that these *takariz* were not produced in Müteferrika's time, but when *Tuhfetü'l-Kibâr* first came out of Kâtip Çelebi's hands, or very shortly after, in 1657.

And this brings us to probably the most crucial aspect of the *takariz* included in *Lugat-ı Vankulu*, and which sets them apart from others. Normally, *takariz* were included in the volume for which they were written. For example, the *takariz* printed with *Tuhfetü'l-Kibâr* were produced for *Tuhfetü'l-Kibâr*. However, the *takariz* printed with *Lugat-ı Vankulu* were not produced for *Lugat-ı Vankulu*, but for İbrahim Müteferrika's own treatise on the usefulness of printing. They did not endorse, praise, or recommend al-Jawhari's dictionary, nor Vankulu Efendi's translation, but Müteferrika's exposition and the art of printing itself. Hence, unlike the proof-readers, whose skills were put to good use for revising texts within their competence, these *ulemâ* were only required here to comment on the treatise, not the book itself. Their *takariz* would stand as proof that the highest

---

32 Kut, "Maṭbaʿa in Turkey", p. 800.
33 Kâtip Çelebi, *Tuhfetü'l-Kibâr fî Esfâri'l-Bihâr*, Istanbul, 1141 [1729], no pagination; for a transliterated version of these endorsements see the recent edition by İ. Bostan, Ankara, 2018, p. 69–70.

religious authorities of the empire supported the establishment of the printing press in Istanbul.

Nevertheless, the support of these particular *ulemâ* does not mean that the entire religious milieu shared their views. After all, *şeyhülislâm* Abdullah Efendi is nowadays considered to be not just a regular scholar but a representative of the progressive and reformist movement of the early 18th century.[34] It is possible that other former *şeyhülislâms*, *kazaskers* or *kadıs* of Istanbul were not so enthusiastic about Müteferrika opening up his printing press. If there was a general consensus, why would anyone have bothered to go to such lengths to show that printing was a valid pursuit?

Before concluding, I would like to point out yet another fact about the sixteen *takariz*, that may very well be yet an additional clue as to their intended purpose: they were written in Arabic. Christine Woodhead's and Guy Burak's samples, as well as the *takariz* for *Tuhfetü'l-Kibâr* were all written in Ottoman Turkish. Müteferrika's *takariz*, being written in Arabic, might indicate that their intended targets were precisely members of the *ulemâ*, who were more likely to be trained and sensible to Arabic literature. Perhaps, they were precisely aimed at those clerics who were against the establishment of a printing press.

If, however, all of the evidence presented so far seems circumstantial, one should return to Müteferrika's own words concerning the endorsements of the *ulemâ*, found in his *Vesîletü't-tıbâa*:

> When commencing production, the endorsement and opinion containing [the mufti's] noble will, as well as the endorsements emanating from the religious scholars and other virtuous men are necessary so that it will be evident under any circumstances that [the printed book] is conformable to the Sharia. The opinion and endorsements will also be written in the preface of the book and will be present in all of the bound volumes, making them more desirable to the audience.[35]

Müteferrika clearly states that the purpose of all the endorsements was to declare that printing was valid under Islamic law and would thus secure buyers. He, therefore, believed that there were potential readers who would have refrained from purchasing his printed volumes if not sanctioned by the *ulemâ*. And while he did indeed address the aesthetics of published books he did not comment

---

34 Erginbaş, "Enlightenment", p. 86.
35 *husulüne mübaşeretde izn-i şeriflerin mutazammın takriz ve işaret-i aliyeleri ihsan ve sudûr-ı ulemâ ve sair fuzalâdan dahi takriz olunmak şayestedir ta kim her halde şer-i mübine mutabık olup ol işaret ve takariz dahi sadr-ı kitapda mestûr ve cümle-i mücelledâtda mevcut olup rağabat-ı nâs müzdadına bâis ola.*

anything about the other frequently-invoked impediment for the establishment of an Arabic-type printing press, the resistance of scribes and calligraphers.

Imperial endorsements for the printing enterprise continued to be present on the books put out by Müteferrika and his successors. Ahmed III's *ferman* of 1727, apart from Mahmud I's renewal of 1732, would also be confirmed by Osman III in 1755, and printed along with the second edition of *Lugat-ı Vankulu*, published a year later.[36] These two later decrees did not bring any new elements to the first one, except for updating the names of current sultans and grand muftis. However, a unique feature had appeared back in 1729, when Müteferrika printed his third book, a translation of Krusinski's *History* of the fall of the Safavid dynasty in Iran.[37] After the introduction, readers would find another *arz-ı hal* for the printing of this particular volume, along with an approving *ferman*. The sultanic warrant, however, was not given in full, but only in a summarized version highlighting the public benefit (*nefi-i âm*) that came along with the dissemination of knowledge through printed words (*intişar-ı menafiçün basma hutut ile*).[38]

Furthermore, beginning with the *History* of Mehmet Râşid, published by Müteferrika in 1741, an "imperial covenant" (*ahd-i hümâyun*) would be included in a decorated cartouche, on the first or last page of any given volume. Unlike the *ferman*s or other forms of endorsements, these *ahd-i hümâyun* simply evoked the sultan, grand mufti and grand vizier who were in office at the date of publication, without any comments concerning printing or the published book.[39] They would become a standard element of future Ottoman printing presses, appearing in books well into the late 18th century.[40]

*****

To conclude, one may tend to forget that the early modern Ottoman Empire, with all its impressive bureaucratic apparatus, was still heavily dependent upon customary practices. Not every activity had to be regulated through written acts and so Ottoman sultans did not need to formally ban print through *ferman*s. Introdu-

---

36 Kut, Türe, *Yazmadan Basmaya*, p. 71.

37 Judasz Tadeusz Krusinski, *Târih-i Seyyâh der Beyân-ı Zuhûr-ı Ağvâniyân ve Sebeb-i İnhidâm-ı Binâ'i Devlet-i Şahân-ı Safeviyân*, Istanbul, 1142 [1729].

38 Kut, Türe, *Yazmadan Basmaya*, p. 41; Sarıcaoğlu, Yılmaz, *Müteferrika*, p. 208.

39 Kut, Türe, *Yazmadan Basmaya*, p. 62; Sarıcaoğlu, Yılmaz, *Müteferrika*, p. 187.

40 Kut, Türe, *Yazmadan Basmaya*, p. 67, 70, 73, 76, 78, 80, 85.

cing it, however, to a still conservative Ottoman-Muslim audience required approvals and endorsements from the highest levels.

Printing was an innovation. Moreover, it was a European innovation and could not have been initiated without any serious debate, especially when it had the potential to interfere with religious beliefs. There was a certain inertia dictating that old, established customs were good, while innovations were treated with suspicion, at best. In Vefa Erginbaş's words, "intellectuals such as İbrahim Müteferrika struggled to find ways to incorporate new ideas into a society that took comfort in keeping up with tradition."[41] As such, Müteferrika cautiously stressed in his treatise that he would not print religious and legal texts but only those pertaining to the secular sciences. Some years later, when he wrote the introduction to the printed edition of another work by Kâtip Çelebi, the geographical opus *Cihannüma*, Müteferrika was careful to explain that debates over the heliocentric and geocentric arrangements of the heavenly bodies were purely scientific and had nothing to do with religious convictions.[42] Copernican astronomy could indeed be a controversial topic amongst the more conservative elements of Ottoman society.[43]

This chapter has exposed some of the measures taken by Müteferrika in order to secure his printing activities for the foreseeable future. One cannot doubt that some of the most prominent religious figures of the time were favourable to and even endorsed Müteferrika's printing venture. Nevertheless, there is convincing evidence, such as the very need for so many written approvals from the highest religious authorities of the empire, which indicate a still prevailing anxiety that printing could interfere with religious issues. On the other hand, the long list of *ulemâ* endorsers most likely guaranteed the survival of the printing press even after Patrona Halil's Rebellion of 1730, which brought down Muteferrika's chief patrons.

---

41 Erginbaş, "Elightenment", p. 63

42 B. H. Küçük, "Ibrahim Müteferrika's Copernican Rethoric", in S. Franse, N. Hodson, K. A. E. Enenkel (eds.), *Translating Early Modern Science*, Leiden/Boston, 2017, p. 258–285.

43 C. Orhonlu, "The Geography of Wallachia Written by a Turkish Politician", *Revue des Études Sud-Est Européennes*, 13/3, 1975, p. 448.

Bibliography

Abou El-Haj, Rifa'at. *The 1703 Rebellion and the Structure of Ottoman Politics*. Leiden: Nederlands Instituut voor het Nabije Oosten, 1984.

Aktepe, Münir. *Patrona İsiyanı (1730)*. Istanbul: Edebiyat Fakültesi Basımevi, 1958.

Altunsu, Abdülkadir. *Osmanli Şeyülislâmları*. Ankara: Ayyıldız Matbaası, 1972.

Badawi, Elsaid M., Muhammad Abdel Haleem. *Arabic-English Dictionary of Quranic usage*. Leiden/Boston: Brill, 2008.

Berkes, Niyazi. "Ibrāhīm Müteferriḳa". In Bernard Lewis, Victor-Louis Ménage, Charles Pellat, Joseph Schacht (eds.), *The Encyclopaedia of Islam, Second Edition*, vol. III. Leiden: Brill, 1971, p. 996–998.

Boogert, Maurits van den. "The Sultan's Answer to the Medici Press? Ibrahim Müteferrika's Printing House in Istanbul". In Alastair Hamilton, Maurits van den Boogert, Bart Westerweel (eds.), *The Republic of Letters and the Levant*. Leiden/Boston: Brill, 2005, p. 265–291.

Burak, Guy. "Reflections on Censorship, Canonization and the Ottoman Practices of Takriz and Imza", revised version of "Sansür, kanonizasyon ve Osmanlı imzâ-takrîz pratikleri üzerine düşünceler". In Hatice Aynur et al. (eds.), *Eski Türk Edebiyatı Çalışmaları X: Eski Metinlere Yeni Bağlamlar: Osmanlı Edebiyatı Çalışmalarında Yeni Yönelimler*. Istanbul: Klasik Yayınları, 2015, p. 96–117.

Dipratu, Radu. "'I Shall Not Take Their Churches and Turn Them Into Mosques': The Legal Status of Catholic Churches in Ottoman Galata as Prescribed by the *'ahdnāmes*". In Vanessa R. de Obaldía, Claudio Monge (eds.), *Latin Catholicism in Ottoman Istanbul: Properties, People & Missions*. Istanbul: The Isis Press, 2022, p. 17–33.

Dipratu, Radu. *Regulating Non-Muslim Communities in the Seventeenth-Century Ottoman Empire: Catholics and Capitulations*. London/New York: Routledge, 2022.

Doğan, Muhammet Nur. "İshak Efendi, Ebûishakzâde". In *TDV İslâm Ansiklopedisi*, vol. 22. Istanbul: TDV İslâm Ansiklopedisi Genel Müdürlüğü, 2000, p. 530–531.

Duverdier, Gérald. "İlk Türk Basımevinin Kuruluşunda İki Kültür Elçisi: Savary de Brèves ile İbrahim Müteferrika". *Belleten*, 56, 1992, p. 275–305.

Erginbaş, Vefa. "Enlightenment in the Ottoman Context: İbrahim Müteferrika and his Intellectual Landscape", in Geoffrey Roper (ed.), *Historical Aspects of Printing and Publishing in Languages of the Middle East. Papers from the Third Symposium on the History of Printing and Publishing in the Languages and Countries of the Middle East, University of Leipzig, September 2008*. Leiden/Boston: Brill, 2014, p. 53–100.

İpşirli, Mehmet. "Abdullah Efendi, Yenişehirli". In *TDV İslâm Ansiklopedisi*, vol. 1. Istanbul: TDV İslâm Ansiklopedisi Genel Müdürlüğü, 1988, p. 100–101.

Kâtip Çelebi. *Tuhfetü'l-Kibâr fî Esfâri'l-Bihâr*. Istanbul: Dârü't-tıbâti'l-mâʿmûre, 1141 [1729]; ed. by İdris Bostan. Ankara: Türkiye Bilimler Akademisi, 2018.

Krusinski, Judasz Tadeusz. *Târih-i Seyyâh der Beyân-ı Zuhûr-ı Ağvâniyân ve Sebeb-i İnhidâm-ı Binâ'i Devlet-i Şahân-ı Safeviyân*. Istanbul: Dârü't-tıbâti'l-mâʿmûre, 1142 [1729].

Kut, Günay Alpay. "Maṭbaʿa in Turkey". In Clifford Edmund Bosworth, Emeri van Donzel, Wolfhart P. Heinrichs, Charles Pellat (eds.), *The Encyclopaedia of Islam, Second Edition*, vol. VI. Leiden: Brill, 1991, p. 799–803.

Kut, Turgut, Fatma Türe. *Yazmadan Basmaya: Müteferrika, Mühendishane, Üsküdar*. Istanbul: Yapı Kredi Kültür Müzesi, 1996.

Küçük, B. Harun. "Ibrahim Müteferrika's Copernican Rethoric". In Sietske Franse, Niall Hodson, Karl A.E. Enenkel (eds.), *Translating Early Modern Science*. Leiden/Boston: Brill, 2017, p. 258–285.

Kütükoğlu, Mübahat S. *Osmanlı Belgelerinin Dili (Diplomatik)*. Istanbul: Kubbealtı Akademisi Kültür ve San'at Vakfı, 1994.

Mete, Ayşegül. "İstanbul'da Trabluslu Bir Şeyh Efendi: Safî Musa el-Mevlevî (ö. 1157/1744)". In Ahmet Hamdi Furat, Nilüfer Kalkan Yorulmaz, Osman Sacid Arı (eds.), *Sahn-ı Semân'dan Dârülfünûn'a Osmanlı'da İlim ve Fikir Dünyası (Âlimler, Müesseseler ve Fikrî Eserler) - XVIII. Yüzyıl*, vol. 2. Istanbul: Zeytinburnu Belediyesi Kültür Yayınları, 2018, p. 249–261.

Murphy, Cristopher M. "Appendix: Ottoman Imperial Documents Relating to the History of Books and Printing". In George N. Atiyeh (ed.), *The Book in the Islamic World. The Written Word and Communication in the Middle East*. Albany: State of New York University Press, 1995, p. 283–292.

Nemeth, Titus. "Overlooked: The Role of Craft in the Adoption of Typography in the Muslim Middle East". In Scott Reese (ed.), *Manuscript and Print in the Islamic Tradition*. Berlin/Boston: De Gruyter, 2022, p. 21–60.

Nuhoğlu, Hidayet Y. "Müteferrika's Printing Press: Some Observations". In Kemal Çiçek (ed.), *The Great Ottoman Civilization. Volume 3: Philosophy, Science and Institutions*. Ankara: Yeni Türkiye, 2000, p. 83–90.

Olson, Robert W. "The Esnaf and the Patrona Halil Rebelion of 1730: A Realignment in Ottoman Politics?". *Journal of the Economic and Social History of the Orient*, 17/ 3, 1974, p. 329–344.

Oman, G. "Maṭba'a in the Arab World". In Clifford Edmund Bosworth, Emeri van Donzel, Wolfhart P. Heinrichs, Charles Pellat (eds.), *The Encyclopaedia of Islam, Second Edition*, vol. VI. Leiden: Brill, 1991, p. 795–799.

Omont, Henri. *Documents sur l'imprimerie à Constantinople au XVIIIe siècle*. Paris: Émile Bouillon, 1895.

Orhonlu, Cengiz. "The Geography of Wallachia Written by a Turkish Politician". *Revue des Études Sud-Est Européennes*, 13/3, 1975, p. 447–452.

Osborn, J.R. *Letters of Light. Arabic Script in Calligraphy, Print, and Digital Design*. Cambridge/London: Harvard University Press, 2017.

Osborn, J.R. "The Ottoman System of Scripts and the Müteferrika Press". In Scott Reese (ed.), *Manuscript and Print in the Islamic Tradition*. Berlin/Boston: De Gruyter, 2022, p. 61–88.

Özcan, Tahsin. "Pîrîzâde Mehmed Sâhib Efendi". In *TDV İslâm Ansiklopedisi*, vol. 34, Istanbul: 2007, TDV İslâm Ansiklopedisi Genel Müdürlüğü, p. 288–290.

Pektaş (Palabıyık), Nil. "The Beginnings of Printing in the Ottoman Capital: Book Production and Circulation in Early Modern Constantinople". *Osmanlı Bilimi Araştırmaları*, 16, 2015, p. 3–32.

Reese, Scott. "Introduction". In Scott Reese (ed.), *Manuscript and Print in the Islamic Tradition*. Berlin/Boston: De Gruyter, 2022, p. 1–16.

Reichmuth, Stefan. "Islamic Reformist Discourse in the Tulip Period (1718-1730): Ibrahim Müteferriqa and His Arguments for Printings". In Ali Çaksu (ed.), *International Congress on Learning and Education in the Ottoman World, Istanbul, 12–15 April 1999. Proceedings*. Istanbul: Research Centre for Islamic History, Art and Culture, 2001, p. 149–161.

Sabev, Orlin. *Waiting for Müteferrika: Glimpses of Ottoman Print Culture*. Boston: Academic Studies Press, 2018.

Sarıcaoğlu, Fikret, Coşkun Yılmaz. *Müteferrika: Basmacı İbrahim Efendi ve Müteferrika Matbaası*. Istanbul: Esen Ofset, 2008.

Schwartz, Kathryn A. "Did Ottoman Sultans Ban Print?". *Book History*, 20, 2017, p. 1–39.

Süreyya, Mehmed. *Sicill-i Osmanî*, 6 vols., ed. by Nuri Akbayar, Seyit Ali Kahraman. Istanbul: Türkiye Ekonomik ve Toplumsal Tarih Vakfı, 1996.

Tercümetü'ş-şiḥaḥ-ı Cevherî [Lugat-ı Vankulu], Istanbul: Dârü't-tıbâti'l-mâʿmûre, 1141 [1729].

Tinto, Alberto. *La Tipografia Medicea Orientale*. Lucca: Maria Pacini Fazzi, 1987.

Tuşalp Atiyas, Ekin E. "The 'Sunna-Minded' Trend". In M. Sariyannis, *A History of Ottoman Political Thought up to the Early Nineteenth Century*, with a chapter by E. Ekin Tuşalp Atiyas. Leiden/Boston: Brill, 2019, p. 233–278.

Veliman, Valeriu. *Relaţiile româno-otomane (1711–1821). Documente turceşti*. Bucharest: Direcţia generală a arhivelor statului, 1984.

Wehr, Hans. *A Dictionary of Modern Written Arabic*, ed. by J. Milton Cowan, third edition. Ithaca: Spoken Languages Services, 1976, p. 668–669.

Woodhead, Christine. "Puff and Patronage: Ottoman *Taḳrīẓ*-writing and Literary Recommendation in the 17th Century". In Çigdem Balim-Harding, Colin Imber (eds.), *The Balance of Truth. Essays in Honour of Professor Geoffrey Lewis*. Istanbul: The Isis Press, 2004, p. 395–406.

Zilfi, Madeline C. "The *Kadizadeli*s: Discordant Revivalism in Seventeenth-Century Istanbul". *Journal of Near Eastern Studies*, 45, 1986, p. 251–269.

Taisiya Leber

Hebrew Printing in Early Modern Istanbul: Between Mobility and Stability

Sephardic Jews became pioneers of book printing in the Ottoman Empire and in the whole Middle East, as their first printing press started its activity around 1493 in Istanbul. Hebrew printing remained the most stable and successful printing enterprise in the Ottoman Empire during the whole pre-modern and even most of the modern period. This stability and success of Hebrew printing in Istanbul is a rare phenomenon in comparison to attempts by South Slavs, Armenians and Greeks to establish their printing presses in the Ottoman Empire, all of which had a rather short life and did not leave a large mark in the history of book printing in the Middle East. Apart from its stability, Hebrew printing in Istanbul was also characterized by the factor of the high mobility of Jewish printers, who were immigrants themselves and often brought their equipment from abroad, sometimes remaining mobile in the Ottoman Empire as they moved from Istanbul to other cities, taking their printing tools with them.

1. Hebrew Printing in the Ottoman Empire: *Pro et Contra*

There is no evidence that the Ottoman authorities had any objections against Hebrew printing in Istanbul or in other places in the Ottoman Empire. Most researchers suppose that Jews were given a particular license, a *ferman* from Sultan Bayezid II (r. 1481–1512), authorizing Hebrew printing in the Ottoman Empire.[1] The reasons for these presumptions are twofold. As the Ottoman Empire is known for having not been particularly welcoming to print culture, the fact that the Jews initiated a printing press at the end of the 15th century means that they had to be allowed to do so and also that they could hope for a consistent ability to operate only with a license in their pocket. Furthermore, Jews were well known

---

1 J. R. Hacker, "Authors, Readers, and Printers of Sixteenth-Century Hebrew Books in the Ottoman Empire", in P. Pearlstein et al. (eds.), *Perspectives on the Hebraic Book*. Washington D.C., 2012, p. 18; N. Pektaş, *The First Greek Press in Constantinople (1625–1628)*. Unpublished Ph.D. Dissertation. University of London, London, 2014, p. 19.

Funded by the Deutsche Forschungsgemeinschaft (DFG, German Research Foundation) – project number PA 736/9–1, within the framework of the SPP 1981 Transottomanica (313079038).

∂ Open Access. © 2024, the author(s), published by De Gruyter. [(cc) BY-NC-ND] This work is licensed under the Creative Commons Attribution-NonCommercial-NoDerivatives 4.0 International License.
https://doi.org/10.1515/9783111060392-004

for their printing activities in the Ottoman Empire even beyond their community, e.g. among European travelers. According to Pierre Belon's (1517–1564) accounts, Jews printed not only in Hebrew, but also in other languages, though they were prohibited from printing in Arabic or Turkish.[2] These factors led researchers to suggest that Ottoman authorities gave the Jews written permission to print in Hebrew, which also included an item banning them from printing in any languages connected with Muslim tradition.[3] As no documents are extant today that would confirm the theory of an Ottoman license for Jewish printing or any written legal prohibition against Jews printing in Arabic script, the question can be asked whether such documents really existed in the early modern period. Was there a *ferman* or license that was issued by the Ottoman authorities at the end of the 15th century permitting Jews to establish a printing press in Istanbul? Did such licenses need to be confirmed or renewed periodically? As far as the author can judge, in the prefaces of the books, no such documents are mentioned, which makes me wonder if such a license for Jews was actually necessary. It seems to me that as there was no ban on printing itself in the Ottoman Empire, there was also no need to give someone an official privilege or permission for printing, as long as it did not conflict with the interests of the Ottoman state or its religion. It seems especially unnecessary in the case of an autonomous community that did not show interest in printing any other books than the ones that were needed by the Jewish community itself. Additionally, it is strange that no documents have been found by researchers so far. As far as I know, there is also no evidence of the existence of such written permissions for Christian printers, Armenians, or Greeks and their printing presses in Istanbul. Only in the context of the Greek printing press of the 17th century in Istanbul was it mentioned by Thomas Roe (a British diplomat) in his *Negotiations* that he had obtained some kind of a printing license for Nikodemos Metaxas,[4] a Greek printer from London who wanted to

---

2 "Les Juifs qui ont esté chassez d' Espagne et du Portugal ont si bien augmenté leur Judaism en Turquie, qu'ils ont presque traduict toutes sortes de livres en leur language hébraique et maintenant ils ont mis impression à Constantinople, sans aucuns poincts. Ils y impriment aussi en Espagnol, Italien, Latin, Grec, et Alman; mais ils n'impriment point en Turc ni en Arabe; car il ne leur est pas parmis", cf. P. Belon du Mans, *Les observations de plusieurs singularites et choses mémorables touvées en Grèce, Asie, Judée, etc.*, Paris, 1555, III, ch. 13, p. 145. Here according to: Hacker, "Authors, Readers, and Printers", p. 51, rem. 20.
3 Hacker, "Authors, Readers, and Printers", p. 18; Hacker, "Introduction", in J. Hacker, A. Haberman (eds.), *The Alphabet of Ben Sira: Facsimile of 1519 Edition*. London, 1997, p. 18; M. Heller, *Further Studies in the Making of Early Modern Hebrew Book*. Leiden/Boston, 2013, p. 81, ft.5.
4 Th. Roe, *The negotiations of Sir Thomas Roe, in his Embassy to the Ottoman Porte, from the Year 1621 to 1628 Inclusive*, London, 1740, p. 761.

establish a press together with Patriarch Kyrillos Loukaris in Istanbul. But again, there is no real proof that a written document containing permission for Metaxas to begin printing activities in Istanbul ever existed. It can also be taken into consideration that Western travelers and diplomats were acquainted in their home countries with established printing industries that were actually under the state control, where licenses were needed and books were censored by authorities;[5] these authors possibly ascribed similar policies to the Ottoman situation. Hence, it must be stressed that Jews were able to print in the Ottoman Empire from the end of the 15th century onwards and that there is no evidence that the Ottoman authorities had any issues with Hebrew printing in the premodern period.

What was the reason for Jews to initiate book printing in Istanbul at the end of the 15th century? What do we know about *pro* and *contra* from the Jewish perspective on the issue of printing in the Ottoman Empire? It is important to say that the first Jewish printers were Sephardic refugees from Spain who started a press shortly after their arrival in Istanbul. Their main motive seems closely connected with the nature of their expulsion – among other losses that they had experienced was that of numerous books, in particular manuscripts, that were left behind on the way to the Ottoman Empire. I would like to quote one of the prefaces to the edition of the Torah with Rashi's Commentary, which was printed in Istanbul in 1506:

> Since that day, when God confused the languages of the earth by the sudden and bitter expulsion from Spain...books were also abandoned in the trauma of destruction and the confusion of sudden change, for the constant afflictions have left us an empty shell...and because of troubles of the times and the lack of books, people have neglected the education of their children. So that even if they have the Chumash (Pentateuch) they lack the Targum and if they find that, then they lack the commentaries. May their hearts inspire them to spread knowledge of the Torah in Israel...and to replace some of the numerous works which were destroyed.[6]

This introduction reminds its readers of the losses and injuries that the Jewish inhabitants of Spain experienced after they were forced to leave their homeland in 1492. The printers and editors expressed their vocation and inclination to provide necessary editions to replace the lost ones in their struggle to preserve Jewish religious knowledge and support religious learning in the new Ottoman environ-

5 On this topic see, for example, the contributions in the following volume: N. Lamal, J. Cumby, H. J. Helmers (eds.), *Print and Power in Early Modern Europe (1500 – 1800)*, Leiden/Boston, 2021.
6 Quoted in English from Y. Ben-Na'eh, *Hebrew Printing Houses in the Ottoman Empire. Jewish Journalism and Printing Houses in the Ottoman Empire and Modern Turkey*, Istanbul, 2001, p. 79; A. Yaari, *Ha-Defus ha-Ivri be-Kushta*, Jerusalem, 1967, p. 18, 59–60.

ment. Moreover, the above-mentioned quote also explains the future program of Hebrew printing with its particular focus on "basic" sacred and religious books and compendiums, the main mission of printing being to preserve Jewish religious tradition and support religious learning in the Ottoman Empire.

Given that Sephardic printing houses had already met with success in Italy and Spain, it seemed to be a logical decision for Jews to begin printing in the Ottoman Empire, using the skills and tools that they brought from abroad. For example, it is known about the first Jewish printers in Istanbul, David and Samuel ben Nahmias, that they originated from one of the most distinguished Jewish families in Spain, who had already been associated there with printing presses. According to the research of Adri Offenberg, they brought their printing tools from Naples to Istanbul. The first Hebrew printed book was called *Arba'ah Turim* [Four Rows/Columns]. It appeared in 1493 in Istanbul.[7] The title of this legal book refers to the four rows of jewels on the High Priest's breastplate (Exodus 28:17). This is a legal code, which, containing a systematic analysis and summary of Jewish laws in France, Spain and Germany, settled various controversial issues surrounding halakhic rulings. The colophon of this book contains a sort of apology for printing that is worth quoting here.

> We saw the excellence of this work and its great value in preference to other codes and that it is splendidly fitting and we made the effort to spread learning in Israel through the craftsmen Rabbi David ben Nahmias and his brother Samuel, may their reward be complete... And I have done my best to make it as perfect as possible by removing all errors imaginable; I, an insignificant man among thousands, Elia, son of Benjamin ha-Levi, may his soul rest in paradise. And truly, it is in the nature of this work that has come about through copying from one hand to another, that none can stand free from error, but thanks to an effort within the limits of things possible, a comparative perfection has been achieved.[8]

As we see, this text was composed by a professional proofreader, Elias ha-Levi, who was possibly a Romaniote Jew (of Byzantine origin) and who collaborated with the Sephardic brothers Nahmias on this edition of this legal code. It shows

---

7 A. K. Offenberg, "The Printing History of the Constantinople Hebrew Incunable of 1493. A Mediterranean Voyage of Discovery", *The British Library Journal*, 22/2, 1996, p. 221–235; Hacker, "Introduction", p. 20; Hacker, "Authors, Printers, and Readers", p. 22–24; Ben-Na'eh, *Hebrew Printing Houses*, p. 79.

8 Quoted in English from Offenberg, "The Printing History of the Constantinople Hebrew Incunable of 1493", p. 232–233; Yaari, *Hebrew Printing at Constantinople*, p. 59. On this edition, see also Y. Meral, "Osmanlı İstanbulu'nda Yahudi Matbaası ve Basılan Bazı Önemli Eserler", in F. M. Emecen, A. Akyıldız, E. Safa Gürkan (eds.), *Osmanlı İstanbulu*. Vol. 2. Istanbul, 2014, p. 456–459.

the importance of printing for spreading knowledge among Ottoman Jews and praises the quality of printed books in comparison to manuscripts. So, from the Jewish perspective, printing was definitely very useful for preserving Jewish books and scholarly tradition. Still, this kind of apology of printing also shows that there were critical voices regarding printed books as well in the Jewish community. It is interesting that both passages from the earliest printed books are somewhat similar to the contents of the *ferman* that was issued by the sultan Ahmed III in 1727 granting permission for Ibrahim Müteferrika's printing activities and so serving as a license for the first Ottoman Muslim printing press to be established in Istanbul.

> However, with the passing of days and with the years going by as the Chingizids created chaotic disturbances and Hulâgu rose to power, and with resplendent Andalusia in the hands of the Europeans, and with the convulsions of wars, killing and destruction, most literary works have disappeared with their authors. Therefore, today in the Muslim lands the dictionaries of Cevheri and Van Kulu in the Arabic language and books of history and copies of scientific works which were burned are rare. Also, people did not give proper care and attention, and lacked concern about copying, so works were not carefully copied. These rare books are an inspiration to students of the arts and sciences and to seekers of knowledge [...] Books produced by printing cause several thousand volumes to be produced from a single volume, all of which are accurate copies. With little effort there is great return, making this a desirable activity to pursue.[9]

Similar to Hebrew prefaces, this passage contains complaints about losses of books because of the destruction of cities (e.g. of Spain in the framework of the so-called *Reconquista*), about the resulting negative impact on education due to the lack of some important books, and about bad handwritten copies and the superior quality of printing production. So, we have here, although more than 100 years later, the same topoi that have the task of persuading the (this time Muslim) community about the particular value of book printing.

There is no evidence as to whether there were serious opponents of printing among the Jews of the Ottoman Empire. It seems that Jewish religious authorities approved this manner of multiplying texts and books in print, making them accessible for bigger audiences. Rabbis were interested in printing their own books and themselves decided freely if they wanted to have their works published in some prestigious publishing house in Venice or Amsterdam, or in the Ottoman

---

9 C. M. Murphy, "Appendix: Ottoman Imperial Documents Relating to the History of Books and Printing", in G. N. Atiyeh (ed.), *The Book in the Islamic World. The Written Word and Communication in the Middle East*, Albany, 1995, p. 284.

Empire.[10] However, one attempt to introduce internal censorship by Jewish religious authorities in the Ottoman Empire is known. In Thessaloniki, as in various European cities during the early modern period,[11] rabbis made a decision in 1529 to control printing and issue individual approval for books in order for them to be printed on that city's Hebrew press. Leading religious scholars – representatives of seven Jewish communities – were to decide whether the works were worthy of publishing. Printers were not allowed to print without the permission of the rabbis, and Jews were prohibited from reading books printed without such an approval by rabbis.[12] It seems that this move by Jewish religious authorities to get involved and control the publishing activities of their coreligionists did not please Jewish printers. It was possibly the reason why a famous Jewish printer of Italian origin, Gershom Soncino, decided to leave Thessaloniki in 1529 and continue his printing activities in Istanbul instead.[13]

2. Hebrew Printing in Istanbul: Periodization and Peculiarities

Researchers observe seven stages in the periodization of book printing in Istanbul.[14] The first stage begins with the legal code printed by the brothers Nahmias in 1493 and lasts until 1530. In this period printers produced at least 120 titles. Some of these were major works, while others were small tractates.[15] The second period was between 1530 and 1553; the first half of this period was marked by the activities of the Soncino family after Gershom Soncino's arrival in Istanbul.[16] The third period (1560–1598) was considered the most productive in the history of Hebrew printing in Istanbul. At least one hundred and twenty titles are known to have been published there in this period.[17] Especially active as printers in Istan-

---

10 Hacker, "Authors, Printers, and Readers", p. 37, 40.
11 On the issue of Jewish censorship, see: J. Hacker, "Sixteenth-Century Jewish Internal Censorship", in J. Hacker, A. Shear (eds.), *The Hebrew Book in Early Modern Italy*, Philadelphia, 2011, p. 109–120 as well as Y. Meral, "Erken Dönem İbrani Matbaacılığında Haham Onayları ve Cemaat İçi Sansür", *Dini Araştırmalar*, 18/47, 2015, p. 96–118.
12 More detailed here: Meral, "Erken Dönem İbrani Matbaacılığında", p. 99.
13 Hacker, "Sixteenth-Century Jewish Internal Censorship", p. 110.
14 See, Ben-Na'eh, *Hebrew Printing Houses*, p. 79–85.
15 Hacker, "Introduction", p. 28; Ben-Na'eh, *Hebrew Printing Houses*, p. 79.
16 Ben-Na'eh, *Hebrew Printing Houses*, p. 80. On the titles printed by Soncino family, see: A. Freimann, "Die Soncinaten-Drucke in Salonichi und Constantinopel (1526–1547)", *Zeitschrift für hebräische Bibliographie*, 1, 1905, p. 21–25.
17 Ben-Na'eh, *Hebrew Printing Houses*, p. 80–81.

bul were the brothers Shlomo and Yosef Ya'abetz, who printed almost sixty titles, including fifteen tractates of the Babylonian Talmud.[18] After Reyna Nasi's press ceased its activity after the death of its female patron in 1599, Hebrew printing was disrupted in the Ottoman capital for several decades – the longest break in Jewish printing production that occurred during the early modern period. Only in 1639 was a new printing press established in Istanbul by a former Marrano (forced convert), Shlomo ben David Franko, who had acquired his extensive skills in Spain. This fourth period lasted until 1695, and it did not produce more than twenty-eight titles in almost five decades.[19] The fifth period is dated 1710–1808, and the final two periods lasted from 1808 until 1940, which lays beyond the chronological framework of this paper.

As we see from previous examples, the main goal of the Hebrew printing enterprise was to provide the Jewish community – or to be more precise, the Sephardic, Ashkenazic, Romaniot and Karaite communities[20] – with necessary religious and legal books in order to preserve the Jewish scholarly heritage. Most researchers doubt that printing in the Ottoman Empire was really profitable.[21] A sponsor was needed for every volume, and there was hardly more than one printing press functioning at a time in Istanbul. It is known from the sources that books were sometimes sold or distributed at the synagogues on Shabbat, but there is no evidence of bigger profits from the book market. Among the difficulties for printers in Istanbul remained the lack of printing equipment, including type, which needed to be imported from other countries, as well as the need to import paper e.g. from Italy.[22]

Another important motive for printing was meticulously proven by Minna Rozen in her chapter on the social role of book printing in Istanbul. In numerous examples of prefaces from the 17th – 18th centuries she demonstrated that Jewish printers or their sponsors often felt motivated by their family situation – first and foremost, they wanted to preserve the memory of their whole family.[23] Some Hebrew books were dedicated to the father or even mother of the author or

---

18 Hacker, "Authors, Readers and Printers", p. 24.

19 Ben-Na'eh, *Hebrew Printing Houses*, p. 82.

20 On the diversity of Jewish communities in the Ottoman Empire see, for example, S. Härtel, "A Question of Competition? How to Deal with Inner-Jewish Diversity in Cities of the Ottoman Empire at the Turn of the 16th Century", *Hamsa. Journal of Judaic and Islamic Studies*, 8, 2022, p. 1–22.

21 Hacker, "Introduction", p. 28–29.

22 Hacker, "Introduction", p. 30.

23 M. Rozen, *Studies in the History of Istanbul Jewry. A Journey through Civilization*, Turnhout, 2015, p. 260.

publisher.[24] In other cases, especially when the persons were childless or did not have male heirs, they expressed their concern about this in the prefaces and tried to replace their offspring with printed books.[25]

3. Languages and Letters of Printing

Jewish printing production in the Ottoman Empire was very successful, as Jews published in the 16th century alone more than 460 titles; 280 of them were printed in Istanbul. Most of these books were printed in Hebrew, and only seven percent in Ladino (30), Greek (two, for former Byzantine, Romaniote Jews[26]) or Persian (one).[27] There is currently no material evidence known regarding whether Jews in Constantinople and other Ottoman cities printed in other characters than Hebrew. However, there are at least two reports by European travelers from the 16th century that Jews used to also print in other languages than Hebrew, yet not in Turkish or Arabic. Although technically it should have been possible to also print in Greek or Latin characters, there is no evidence apart from rare travelers' accounts[28] that Jews printed any books in other than Hebrew characters. Only in the second half of the 17th century were the first books in Latin letters printed by Jews: Avraham Gabbai printed two books in Judeo-Spanish with Latin lettering in Izmir in 1659 (a second edition of two books by Menashe ben Yisrael).[29]

---

24 Rozen, *Studies in the History of Istanbul Jewry*, p. 272.
25 Rozen, *Studies in the History of Istanbul Jewry*, p. 262, 264, 267.
26 One of them is the famous edition of the Torah with translations into Judeo-Spanish and Greek that was published in Istanbul by Eliezer Soncino in 1547. On the Greek edition of it, see: J. Krivoruchko, "The Constantinople Pentateuch within the Context of Septuagint Studies", in M. K.H. Peters (ed.), *XIII Congress of the International Organization for Septuagint and Cognate Studies Ljubljana 2007*, Atlanta, 2008, p. 255–276.
27 Hacker, "Authors, Readers, and Printers", p. 20–21.
28 Pierre Belon (1517–1564) and Kryštof Harant (1564–1612) wrote about Jews printing in Constantinople in numerous languages. See, Belon du Mans, *Les observations de plusieurs singularites*, III, ch. 13, p. 181; K. Harant z Polžic, *Cesta do Země Svaté a do Egypta*, Prague, 1855, Vol. 2, p. 47.
29 In 1663 Avraham Gabbai also printed Sir Paul Rycaut's Capitulations in English with Latin characters. He also apologised in his preface for technical problems with some letters like "w", cf. P. Rycaut, *The Capitulations and Articles etc.*, Istanbul, 1663, p. 8. The Dominican father Jean-Michel Vansleb said about Jewish printer Avraham ben Yedida Gabbai (1674/5): "Un Juif nommé Gabai et qui est aujourdhuy Truchement de M. Augustin Spinola, Résident pour la Rép. de Gennes à Cple [Constantinople] a une imprimerie et les matrices pour faire des caractères des langues Sclavonique, Armenienne, Hebraïque, Grecque, et Latine; il a fait imprimer plusieurs ouvrages dans ces trois derniers Langues." (quoted after Hacker, "Authors, Printers, and

4. Hebrew Printing beyond Istanbul

Istanbul played an absolutely central role for Hebrew printing in the Ottoman Empire. Only there was it so continuous, functioning consistently with only short breaks. Those breaks in printing in Istanbul were mostly connected with the death of one printer or one family of printers before they could be succeeded by members of other families. Thessaloniki became the second important center of Hebrew printing. The first phase of printing here lasted between 1512 and 1530. The press issued more than 30 titles in over a decade.[30] The above-mentioned departure of Gershom Soncino and his son Eliezer from Thessaloniki to Constantinople left the city without a press. The second phase of printing in Thessaloniki was more long-term: the press operated from 1559 until 1628.[31] Nearly all of the Jewish printing shops in Istanbul and Thessaloniki were run by immigrant Jewish printers who arrived from Spain and Italy (Sephardim) or the Polish-Lithuanian Commonwealth and Prague (Ashkenazim), and so on. But the owner of such a shop would usually employ proofreaders, editors, compositors, etc. from local (Romaniote or Sephardic) Jewry. Still, Istanbul and Thessaloniki were not the only centers of Hebrew book printing; there were also attempts at organizing printing shops in other cities and towns of the Ottoman Empire. Early printed books provide evidence about the existence of these alternative centers of Hebrew printing. Of note is a Hebrew printing press in the city of Safed (Tzfat), one of four Holy Cities of Judaism. It was Eliezer ben Itzhak Ashkenazi who initiated printing in Safed in 1577. Himself an Ashkenazic Jew from Lublin (Polish-Lithuanian Commonwealth), he moved with his son first to Constantinople, where he continued his activities as a printer before he decided to move closer to Jerusalem and start his own printing press in Safed. Eliezer brought printing tools to Safed and established the first local printing press. Together with another printer named Abraham Ashkenazi, they printed their first book, *Lekhah Tov*, in 1577 ("Good Doctrine", a commentary on the book of Esther by Yom Tov ben Moses Zahalon, 1558–1638). Eliezer printed several more kabbalistic-homiletic books before he left Safed in 1579; then Eliezer found himself again printing in Constantinople. However, several years later, in 1587, Eliezer went back to Safed and printed three

---

Readers", p. 51–52, rem. 23). But as already stated before, there is no proof that Gabbai had printed in other characters than Hebrew and Latin.

30 Heller, *Further Studies in the Making of the Early Hebrew Book*, p. 81.

31 A further two phases on printing in Thessaloniki are dated to 1705–1840 and 1840–1941. Ben-Na'eh, *Hebrew Printing Houses*, p. 89–92.

more books there.[32] Among the reasons why an experienced printer like Eliezer Ashkenazi chose the city of Safed for printing was possibly the wish to avoid the major competition among printers and booksellers in Istanbul. But certainly, the pious motive of printing books in the holy city also stimulated Eliezer, who possibly saw a chance for profit by bringing books from Safed to other pious Jews.[33]

In the city of Edirne (Adrianople) a Hebrew printing press was founded by brothers Shlomo and Yosef Ya'abetz, printers from Thessaloniki, in 1554. According to Marvin Heller, it was primarily the plague that forced the brothers Ya'abetz to flee Thessaloniki and relocate to Edirne, where they printed four titles during their brief stay.[34] Among the books they printed in Edirne was a historical chronicle entitled *Shevet Yehudah* by Shlomo ben Verga, which included a collection of polemics with Christians and a long list of persecutions of the Jews. This chronicle was later republished many times e.g. in Thessaloniki (1570), and in Yiddish in Kraków (1570).[35] By 1555/56, as the plague had abated, the brothers Ya'abetz left Edirne. Shlomo went to Istanbul, where he established a new press that was active for several decades to come, whereas Yosef returned to Thesssaloniki, where he resumed printing until 1572.[36] Then he joined Shlomo in Istanbul, where they would publish more than forty books together.[37]

One of the members of the already-mentioned Soncino family – Gershom Soncino – established a printing press in Cairo, which was active from 1557 until 1562.[38] At least two Hebrew titles are known from the Cairo press – *Pitron haLomot* ("Interpretation of Dreams", 1557), and *Refuot haTalmud* ("Prescriptions of the Talmud", 1562). Their fragments were discovered in the *geniza* (storage place) of the old Synagogue of Cairo.[39] Attempts were also made to establish Hebrew presses in the 17th century in Damascus (1605). More is known about the print-

---

32 M. J. Heller, "Early Hebrew Printing From Lublin to Safed. The Journeys of Eliezer ben Isaac Ashkenazi", in M. H. Heller, *Studies in The Making of the Early Hebrew Book*, Leiden/Boston, 2008, p. 116–117.

33 Heller, "Early Hebrew Printing From Lublin to Safed"; T. Leber, "The Early History of Printing in the Ottoman Empire through the Prism of Mobility", *Diyâr*, 2/1, 2021, p. 65.

34 Heller, *Further Studies in the Making of the Early Hebrew Book*, p. 82.

35 More than twenty-seven editions of this chronicle are known until the 20th century. See: Heller, *Further Studies in the Making of the Early Hebrew Book*, p. 84.

36 C. Harris, *The Way Jews Lived. Five Hundred Years of Printed Words and Images*. Jefferson,NC/London, 2009, p. 48.

37 Heller, *Further Studies in the Making of the Early Hebrew Book*, p. 89.

38 Harris, *The Way Jews Lived. Five Hundred Years of Printed Words and Images*, p. 24.

39 D. Rowland-Smith, "The Beginnings of Hebrew Printing in Egypt", *British Library Journal*, 15, 1989, p. 16–22, p. 16; Ben Na'eh, *Hebrew Printing Houses*, p. 80; Leber, "The Early History of Printing", p. 66.

ing press in the city of Izmir (Smyrna) that was set up in 1657 by Avraham ben Yedida Gabbai, which functioned until at least 1675.[40] His father had already been a founder of the first Hebrew press in Livorno; he supported his son with the necessary equipment for starting his own press in Izmir.[41] Marvin Heller speaks of two distinct periods in the printing activities by Avraham ben Gabbai in Izmir, the first from 1657 through 1660, and the second from 1671 until 1675. During the first period Gabbai published nine Hebrew and two Judeo-Spanish works; in the second period he printed seven further titles.[42] These two smaller Judeo-Spanish books – *Esperanza de Israel* by Menasseh ben Israel and *Apología por la Noble Nación de los Judios*, attributed to Eduard Nicholas[43] – are particularly important as the very first books printed in the Ottoman Empire in Latin letters. It is also the first example of Hebrew printing houses publishing books not in Hebrew letters. Avraham ben Gabbai did not print only in Izmir; he is also known for printing books in Istanbul in the 1660s. After he finally left Izmir in 1675, he went to Thessaloniki and established his printing press there.[44] Another famous printer – Yona ben Ya'akov Ashkenazi (d. 1745) – came to Izmir from Istanbul in 1728 and set up a Hebrew press there. It was active until 1739; in this time more than thirty Hebrew books appeared in Izmir.[45]

One of the clues to understanding these numerous centers of printing is the high mobility of Jewish printers, who not only came from different countries to the Ottoman Empire, but were also ready to establish their presses in different areas of the empire. The reason was often competition with the main current-ly-active family of printers in Istanbul or Thessaloniki. These initiatives in the Ottoman provinces did not succeed so well as in the capital because of book market problems, a lack of available tools and lesser demand from the Jewish reading audience. But these examples also demonstrate how important the aspect of mobility for Hebrew printing in the Ottoman Empire was – we are talking about mobile printers who brought their skills and often their tools from abroad into the Ottoman Empire; they relied on locals in their undertaking and thus contributed

---

40 In the 18th and 19th centuries there were also Hebrew printing presses in Izmir, in the period between 1728 and 1767 as well as between 1838 and 1920.

41 Heller, *Further Studies in the Making of the Early Hebrew Book*, p. 104.

42 Heller, *Further Studies in the Making of the Early Hebrew Book*, p. 104.

43 The description of both books see here: Heller, *Further Studies in the Making of the Early Hebrew Book*, p. 114.

44 Heller, *Further Studies in the Making of the Early Hebrew Book*, p. 115.

45 Y. Meral, "Yona ben Ya'kov Aşkenazi ve Matbaacılık Faaliyetleri (1710-1778)", in F. M. Emecen, A. Akyıldız, E. Safa Gürkan (eds.), *Osmanlı İstanbulu*, Vol. IV, Istanbul, 2016, p. 792.

to a very stable environment for printing in Istanbul, which provided the Jewish community with printed books over decades and centuries.

5. A Mobile Jewish Printer *en route* from Kraków to Istanbul

As the previous examples have shown, among the Jewish printers in Istanbul, most were immigrants themselves or one generation distant from the immigration to the Ottoman Empire. Some of them remained mobile in the empire itself, moving from Istanbul to Thessaloniki or other smaller cities in order to establish printing presses there. This short case study provides a mobile biography of another Jewish printer who came from the Polish-Lithuanian Commonwealth to the Ottoman Empire in order to continue his printing activities there.

Samuel Helicz originated from a famous family of printers in Kraków. He and his brothers started the first Hebrew printing press in Kraków together in 1530. It seems, however, that they were not very successful with the distribution of books in Hebrew. Later, the brothers started printing in Yiddish. At some point we know that the Helicz brothers converted to Catholicism (possibly in 1537) and took Christian names.[46] This meant a break with the Jewish community of the city and the end of printing in Hebrew. Samuel Helicz made a decision to move to Istanbul. His brother Paul remained an active Catholic in Kraków and prepared an edition of the New Testament in Yiddish (translated or more accurately stated, transliterated, according to the translation of the Bible by Martin Luther, 1540) as well as a dictionary of Yiddish for Christians. Samuel reconverted to Judaism in Istanbul, and he retook his old name and came back to printing in the sacral language, Hebrew. He printed his first book, the Pentateuch, in 1551. In the colophon he expresses his regrets about this earlier decision of changing religion. Three books from his printing house in Istanbul are known (the last one from 1553).[47] In this case of a migrating printer, we can be sure that his decision to move to the Ottoman Empire was connected with his religious interests – it seemed to be a better place for re-converting, a more tolerant place for Jews, but it was also a chance to come back from the vernacular language of Ashkenazim (Yiddish) to the sacred language of Judaism, Hebrew. In this sense, Istanbul was a place where Hebrew books could be printed and distributed, where Jews were educated and religious enough to be interested in such editions.

---

46 K. Pilarczyk, *Leksykon drukarzy ksiąg hebrajskich w Polsce. Z bibliografią polonojudaików w językach żydowskich (XVI–XVIII wiek)*, Kraków, 2004, p. 67–70, 136.
47 Ben Na'eh, *Hebrew Printing Houses*, p. 80.

6. Aspects of Interreligious Relations in Print

As many Jewish inhabitants had had to flee from Christian countries before they settled in the Ottoman Empire, it seems important to pose a question on the relationship between Jews and Muslims as well as that between Jews and Christians in this context, on the basis of printed texts. It is important that no books containing critiques of Islam were printed by Jews in the Ottoman Empire. It does not seem surprising in the face of the censorship that Jews had to keep in mind during their activities under Muslim rule. It can also be stated that the Jewry's interaction with Muslim culture in the Ottoman Empire in general remained very limited and did not have much impact on Jewish culture during the premodern period.[48] Still, Hebrew printed books could also be used to demonstrate loyalty towards the Ottoman sultan and the new environment, which welcomed Jews after they were expelled by Christians. Worth mentioning, for example, is a part of the colophon of the first Hebrew book printed in Istanbul *Arba'ah Turim* (1493): "Friday 4 Tevet of the year five thousand two hundred and fifty-four, here in the large city of Constantinople, at the time of the great Mohammedan King Sultan Bayezid's reign, may he live and may the Lord help him and may He enhance his royal rule. Amen."[49] The mention of the sultan's name and the blessing of his rule deserve particular attention as a demonstration of loyalty, acknowledgement and appreciation by the new Sephardic subjects of their Muslim ("Mohammedan") ruler. Hence, Jewish printing in Constantinople also served to glorify the Ottoman ruler Sultan Bayezid II, preserving his memory among his Jewish subjects, too.[50]

It is not surprising that Jewish interreligious polemics in the Ottoman Empire were directed against Christians. On the one hand, disputes with Christians had constituted a widespread genre in the European context since the Middle Ages. But unlike in the Ottoman Empire, such anti-Christian polemics could not be printed in any European cities because of censorship. History of forced conversions of Jews in Southern and Western Europe, inquisitions and also fear of the popularity of Christian ideas among Jews were among the motives for composing and printing some anti-Christian texts. On the other hand, such polemics also served the new framework and environment of various Jewish communities in the Ottoman Empire who had to maintain the confessional border between Judaism

---

48 D. B. Ruderman, *Early Modern Jewry: A New Cultural History*, Princeton/Oxford, 2010, p. 123.
49 Offenberg, "The Printing History of the Constantinople Hebrew Incunable of 1493", p. 232–233.
50 On the subject of Jewish attraction and allegiance to the Ottoman state, see, for example, A. Levi, *The Sephardim in the Ottoman Empire*, Princeton, N.J., 1992, p. 19–21.

on the one side and other religious groups on the other. Here, the lens of the confessionalization processes in the Ottoman Empire[51] seems particularly helpful.

An important example of Jewish polemics with representatives of Christianity is a Sephardic treatise by an anonymous author that was published in Thessaloniki in 1595 under the title of *Fuente Clara* ("Clear Fountain").[52] The treatise in Judeo-Spanish was definitely written by a Sephardic Jew, possibly a former *converso*, who used to study philosophy and medicine at a Southwestern or Western European university. The author was obviously very well acquainted with the main texts and teachings of the Catholic Church and its doctrines, but he also knew about the existence of different Protestant denominations.[53] The book is written as a detailed compendium of arguments on all doctrines of the Christian faith (on the Holy Spirit, veneration of Jesus as son of God and Messiah, absolution through Christ's resurrection, the virginity of Mary, transubstantiation, etc.) as well as numerous Christian arguments against Judaism. One of the aims of this treatise was to persuade Jews to remain faithful to Judaism, to prevent Jews from (at least voluntary) conversions. It is obvious that the *Fuente Clara* was very successful among Jewish readers, as it was reprinted in 1740 in Constantinople, this time at the printing house of Yona ben Ya'akov Ashkenazi.[54] Yona ben Ya'akov Ashkenazi himself originated from the city of Zaliztsi in what is today Ukraine; the subject of Christian proselytism seemed to bother him during his long and successful career in Istanbul and Izmir, where he printed altogether more than 125 books. In the preface to the Judeo-Spanish Pentateuch (Constantinople, 1739) he formulated a polemical passage against Christians, criticizing Christians for their animosity towards Judaism and their own religious mistakes:

> And in the whole Law, only the name of Israel is mentioned, and no other nation, even though Christians say that God abandoned us and took them instead, saying that we had sinned. But we can easily respond to them: they could say such things if God had achieved something by taking better people instead of us. But this is not so, as we see that those who say that God abandoned us and took them instead are much worse sinners who do not perform a single commandment of the Law (in particular, the commandment of circumcision or rules and injunctions of the Law which God told them to perform). So why would

---

51 See the newest volume on peculiarities of confessionalization in the Ottoman Empire: T. Krstić, D. Terzioğlu (eds.), *Entangled Confessionalizations? Dialogic Perspectives on the Politics of Piety and Community-Building in the Ottoman Empire, 15th – 18th Centuries*, Piscataway, 2022.
52 P. Romeu, *Fuente clara (Salónica, 1595). Un converso sefardí a la defensa del judaísmo y a la búsqueda de su propia fe*, Barcelona, 2007.
53 O. Borovaya, *The Beginnings of Ladino Literature. Moses Almosnino and His Readers*, Bloomington, 2017, p. 45.
54 Borovaya, *The Beginnings of Ladino Literature*, p. 227.

God, who knows the future, abandon us without gaining anything? And knowing that this is not so but that they found themselves in power because of our sins, they are wondering why the Master of the Universe left them in exile for so long despite their having such a holy law; and thus [...] they say that he abandoned us.[55]

According to Olga Borovaya, beyond the publication of the anti-Christian polemics in the 18th century, the Jews of Istanbul were not so much concerned about real Christian proselytism in the Ottoman Empire, but rather feared European Christian influence through culture and literature, through translations of fiction accessible at the book market in the Ottoman Empire.[56]

It seems reasonable at this point to mention that on the Christian side in the Ottoman Empire, among Orthodox Greeks, anti-Jewish texts were also composed and widespread in printed form. One of the first books that was printed at the already-mentioned Greek printing press in Istanbul in 1627 was a treatise against Jews, which was written by the Patriarch Cyril Lukaris. Lukaris dedicated the treatise "Against the Jews" to the noble Cypriot Georgios Pargas with the remark: "for everyday use in his dialogues with his Jewish friends."[57] The tone of the writing is critical towards Judaism, with the usual accusations of Jewish errors and sins, their blindness, as they and their theologians failed to recognize Jesus as Messiah and the Trinity.[58] Here we can also speak of tendencies for confessionalization among Orthodox Christians in the Ottoman Empire, which included conscious opposition to other religions and denominations, among whom Jews were usually the first target.

7. Female Patronage of Book Printing and the Issue of Female Readership

The dedicated patronage and charity of Jewish notables played a crucial role in the relative success of the Hebrew presses. Without private sponsorship by wealthy individuals of the Hebrew press in general and specific editions in particular, Hebrew printing would not have survived for so long. Also, female patrons were active in supporting book printing and the spread of Jewish learning — one

---

55 Quoted in English from Borovaya, *The Beginnings of Ladino Literature*, p. 226–227.

56 Borovaya, *The Beginnings of Ladino Literature*, p. 227.

57 É. Legrand, *Bibliographie hellénique ou description raisonnée des ouvrages publiés par des Grecs au dix-septième siècle*, Vol. 1. Paris, 1894, no. 166, p. 234–237.

58 Legrand 166 (from Houghton Library), F. 1, 2, 15 etc. I am very thankful to Nil Palabıyık for providing me a digital copy of this early printed book.

of them was the famous *kira* Esther Handali, the widow of Elias Handali, who sponsored the printing of the astronomer and mathematician Avraham Zacuto's genealogical chronicle *Sefer ha-Yuhasin* that was published by Samuel Shalom and printed at the Ya'abetz press in Constantinople in 1566 (and later reprinted in Kraków in 1581, Amsterdam in 1717, etc.). In the introduction to the book, it is stressed that Esther had spent her entire fortune on charity.[59]

Another Jewish noble woman, Reyna Nasi, a daughter of Portuguese Marranos (forced converts from Judaism to Christianity), came from Western Europe to Ottoman Constantinople in the middle of the 16th century, where she re-converted to Judaism and married Yosef Nasi, the future Duke of Naxos. Yosef Nasi already possessed an impressive library in Constantinople, which he placed at the disposal of Jewish scholars, some of whom he particularly encouraged and motivated to write and edit treatises. He possibly also planned to establish a printing house, but never succeeded.[60] Together with his aunt, Gracia Nasi, Yosef financially supported the press that belonged to the brothers Ya'abetz.[61] After Yosef Nasi's death in 1579, a big part of his property was confiscated by the Ottoman authorities. His childless widow Reyna Nasi could barely save her own dowry of 90,000 ducats, which she later used to found and run her printing house.[62] According to Yasin Meral, Reyna Nasi had more income after Nasi's death than was recorded at the time and usually counted by researchers, as she continued to receive payment from Nasi's companions.[63] It is interesting that Reyna Nasi did not set up her printing press immediately after her husband's death in 1579, but waited for almost thirteen years to execute her plan. It was most probably the fact that until the 1590s, the Hebrew press of the brothers Ya'abetz was very active in Istanbul and there was no demand for establishing a further press as long as there was enough printed production for Jews in Istanbul.[64] Reyna Nasi

---

59 Yaari, *Hebrew Printing at Constantinople*, p. 113; N. Palabıyık (Pektaş), "The Beginnings of Printing in the Ottoman Capital: Book Production and Circulation in Early Modern Istanbul", *Osmanlı Bilimi Araştırmaları*, 16/2, 2015, p. 15; M. Rozen, *History of the Jewish Community in Istanbul. The Formative Years, 1453–1566*, Leiden/Boston, 2010, p. 206.

60 M.A. Levy, *Don Joseph Nasi, Herzog von Naxos, seine Familie und zwei judische Diplomaten seiner Zeit. Eine Biographie nach neuen Quellen dargestellt*, Wrocław, 1859, p. 28, 56.

61 Y. Meral, "Nasi-Mendes Ailesi ve İstanbul'da Reyna Nasi Matbaası", in E. Demirli et al. (eds.), *Sahn-ı Semân'dan Dârülfünûn'a Osmanlı'da İlim ve Fikir Dünyası (Âlimler, Müesseseler ve Fikrî Eserler) - XVI. Yüzyıl*, Istanbul, 2017, p. 187.

62 Levy, *Don Joseph Nasi*, p. 29, 102; P. Grunebaum-Ballin, *Joseph Naci duc de Naxos*, Paris, 1968, p. 166.

63 Meral, "Nasi-Mendes Ailesi", p. 186–187.

64 Meral, "Nasi-Mendes Ailesi", p. 187, 190.

set up a printing press in the Belvedere Palace, on the outskirts of Istanbul, in the place called Ortaköy in 1592, as the Ya'abetz's press was no longer in service. This area later became an important center of Jewish learning in Istanbul. The press was operated by Yosef ben Yitzhak Ashkeloni, who produced seven titles between 1593 and 1597. For this purpose, type letters were fashioned into new forms.[65] Dona Reyna is mentioned on title pages of the books as "…the illustrious lady […] widow of the Duke, Minister and great leader in Israel Don Yosef Nasi, of blessed memory…"[66] After 1597, the printing house was moved to the near suburb of Kuruçeşme, where eight further books were printed within a two-year period.[67] Foremost among the fifteen works published by Reyna's printing house were books of commentary printed in Hebrew. One part of the Talmud was printed (the *Ketuboth* treatise with its commentaries is preserved to this day). *Iggeret Schmuel*, a commentary on the Book of Ruth by Samuel di Uzeda, which states: "Printed in the publishing house and with the type font of the noble lady of noble lineage Reyna, widow of the Duke and Prince in Israel Don Yosef Nasi, by Yosef ben Isaac Ashkeloni".[68] One book in Judeo-Spanish (Ladino) was also printed in Reyna's press — *Libro intitulado yihus hatzadikim*, a Ladino translation of a work on holy places in the Land of Israel with explanations about where Jewish *tzadikim* (righteous people) are buried (*qui trata en mostar el lugar, unde estan enterados los tzadikim en Eretz Israel*).[69] This edition was probably destined for the use of those intending to go on pilgrimage to the Holy Land (*ziyara*).[70] Unlike Hebrew books from Reyna's printing press that could be read by all educated members of Jewish communities in the Ottoman Empire and beyond, this *Libro intitulado* addressed only Sephardic Jews, who were able to read in Ladino, but unlike the Hebrew ones, the *Libro intitulado* as a treatise in vernacular language could also be accessible for ex-converts or even Jewish women. Thus one might assume that Reyna's own origin and gender provided a particular motivation for her as a patroness to have this Ladino book printed. The press near Constantinople ceased activity after Reyna's death in 1599, which left the Jewish community without a means to print for several decades until 1639.

---

65 Ben-Na'eh, *Hebrew Printing Houses*, p. 81; Meral, "Nasi-Mendes Ailesi", p. 187.
66 Ben-Na'eh, *Hebrew Printing Houses*, p. 81.
67 Ben-Na'eh, *Hebrew Printing Houses*, p. 81; Yaari, *Hebrew Printing at Constantinople*, p 139–147.
68 Yaari, *Hebrew Printing at Constantinople*, p. 143.
69 Yaari, *Hebrew Printing at Constantinople*, p. 140–142; R. Simon, "The Contribution of Hebrew Printing Houses and Printers in Istanbul to Ladino Culture and Scholarship", *Judaica Librarianship*, 16/17, 2011, p. 129.
70 Ben-Na'eh, *Hebrew Printing Houses*, p. 81.

8. Conclusions: Between Mobility and Stability

The aim of this chapter was to address the history of successful Hebrew printing in the early modern Istanbul focusing on both prisms – mobility and stability of Hebrew printing. The insight into the Sephardic origins of Hebrew printing, the high mobility of printers and the necessity of importing printing equipment, paper and printing skills from abroad makes this permanent connection between mobility and stability visible. The main use of the sacred language of Hebrew made possible the consolidation of members of various Jewish communities with different spoken languages on the basis of the religious and legal books in print, but it also supported religious learning in vernacular languages, first of all Judeo-Spanish. Although Istanbul remained the most important center of Hebrew printing, as the examples demonstrate, cities such as Thessaloniki and, to a lesser degree, Izmir and Safed, also played a role in the history of Jewish printing. Among the texts that were published there were also examples of anti-Christian polemics, which could only be printed outside of European censorship. These polemics aimed to protect Jewish people from Christian proselytism and conversions, to draw the borders of Jewish religion and consciousness, and to support the process of confessionalization in the framework of Judaism. The success of Hebrew printing would not have been possible without the support of private benefactors, among whom were also noble women, who fostered printing as a way to widely spread Jewish religious culture and learning among the Ottoman Jewry.

Bibliography

Belon du Mans, Pierre. *Les observations de plusieurs singularites et choses mémorables trouvées en Grèce, Asie, Judée, etc.* Vol. 3. Paris: Chez Guillaume Cavellat, 1555.

Ben-Na'eh, Yaron. *Hebrew Printing Houses in the Ottoman Empire. Jewish Journalism and Printing Houses in the Ottoman Empire and Modern Turkey*, ed. by Gad Nassi. Istanbul: The Isis Press, 2001.

Borovaya, Olga. *The Beginnings of Ladino Literature. Moses Almosnino and His Readers.* Bloomington: Indiana University Press, 2017.

Freimann, Aron. "Die Soncinaten-Drucke in Salonichi und Constantinopel (1526–1547)". *Zeitschrift für hebräische Bibliographie*, 1, 1905, p. 21–25.

Grunebaum-Ballin, Paul. *Joseph Naci duc de Naxos*. Paris: Mouton, 1968.

Hacker, Joseph. "Introduction". In Joseph Hacker, Avraham Haberman (eds.), *The Alphabet of Ben Sira: Facsimile of 1519 Edition*. London: Valmadonna Trust Library, 1997, p. 17–37.

Hacker, Joseph R. "Sixteenth-Century Jewish Internal Censorship". In Joseph R. Hacker, Adam Shear (eds.), *The Hebrew Book in Early Modern Italy*. Philadelphia: University of Pennsylvania Press, 2011, p. 109–120.

Hacker, Joseph R. "Authors, Readers, and Printers of Sixteenth-Century Hebrew Books in the Ottoman Empire". In Peggy Pearlstein et al. (eds.), *Perspectives on the Hebraic Book*. Washington: Library of Congress, 2012, p. 16–63.

Harant z Polžic, Kristof. *Cesta do Země Svaté a do Egypta*. Vol. 2. Prague: V Komissi u Františka Řivnáče, 1855.

Harris, Constance. *The Way Jews Lived. Five Hundred Years of Printed Words and Images*. Jefferson/London: McFarland & Company, Inc., Publishers, 2009.

Härtel, Susanne. "A Question of Competition? How to Deal with Inner-Jewish Diversity in Cities of the Ottoman Empire at the Turn of the 16th Century". *Hamsa. Journal of Judaic and Islamic Studies,* 8, 2022, p. 1–22.

Heller, Marvin J. "Early Hebrew Printing From Lublin to Safed. The Journeys of Eliezer ben Isaac Ashkenazi." In Marvin J. Heller, *Studies in The Making of the Early Hebrew Book*. Leiden/ Boston: Brill, 2008, p. 106–120.

Heller, Marvin J. *Further Studies in the Making of Early Modern Hebrew Book*. Leiden/Boston: Brill, 2013.

Krivoruchko, Julia. "The Constantinople Pentateuch within the Context of Septuagint Studies". In Melvin K.H. Peters (ed.), *XIII Congress of the International Organization for Septuagint and Cognate Studies Ljubljana 2007*. Atlanta: Society of Biblical Literature, 2008, p. 255–276.

Krstić, Tijana, Derin Terzioğlu (eds.). *Entangled Confessionalizations? Dialogic Perspectives on the Politics of Piety and Community-Building in the Ottoman Empire, 15th – 18th Centuries*. Piscataway: Gorgias Press, 2022.

Lamal, Nina, Jamie Cumby, Helmer J. Helmers (eds.). *Print and Power in Early Modern Europe (1500 – 1800)*. Leiden/Boston: Brill, 2021.

Leber, Taisiya. "The Early History of Printing in the Ottoman Empire through the Prism of Mobility". *Diyâr*, 2/1, 2021, p. 59–82.

Legrand, Émile. *Bibliographie hellénique ou description raisonnée des ouvrages publiés par des Grecs au dix-septième siècle*. Vol. 1. Paris: Culture et civilisation, 1894.

Levi, Avigdor. *The Sephardim in the Ottoman Empire*. Princeton: Darwin Press, 1992.

Levy, Moritz Abraham. *Don Joseph Nasi, Herzog von Naxos, seine Familie und zwei judische Diplomaten seiner Zeit. Eine Biographie nach neuen Quellen dargestellt.* Wrocław: Schletter, 1859.

Meral, Yasin. "Osmanlı İstanbulu'nda Yahudi Matbaası ve Basılan Bazı Önemli Eserler". In Feridun M. Emecen, Ali Akyıldız, Emrah Safa Gürkan (eds.), *Osmanlı İstanbulu*. Vol. 2. Istanbul: İstanbul Büyükşehir Belediyesi Kültür A.Ş., 2014, p. 455–469.

Meral, Yasin. "Erken Dönem İbrani Matbaacılığında Haham Onayları ve Cemaat İçi Sansür". *Dini Araştırmalar*, 18/47, 2015, p. 96–118.

Meral, Yasin. "Yona ben Ya'kov Aşkenazi ve Matbaacılık Faaliyetleri (1710-1778)." In Feridun M. Emecen, Ali Akyıldız, Emrah Safa Gürkan (eds.), *Osmanlı İstanbulu*. Vol. IV, Istanbul: İstanbul Büyükşehir Belediyesi Kültür A.Ş., 2016, p. 787–808.

Meral, Yasin. "Nasi-Mendes Ailesi ve İstanbul'da Reyna Nasi Matbaası." In Ekrem Demirli et al. (eds.), *Sahn-ı Semân'dan Dârülfünûn'a Osmanlı'da İlim ve Fikir Dünyası (Âlimler, Müesseseler ve Fikrî Eserler) - XVI. Yüzyıl*. Istanbul: Zeytinburnu Belediyesi Kültür Yayınları, 2017, p. 177–190.

Murphy, Cristopher M. "Appendix: Ottoman Imperial Documents Relating to the History of Books and Printing". In George N. Atiyeh (ed.), *The Book in the Islamic World. The Written Word and Communication in the Middle East*. Albany: State of New York University Press, 1995, p. 283–292.

Palabıyık (Pektaş), Nil. *The First Greek Press in Constantinople (1625–1628)*. Unpublished Ph.D. Thesis, University of London, London, 2014.

Palabıyık (Pektaş), Nil. "The Beginnings of Printing in the Ottoman Capital: Book Production and Circulation in Early Modern Istanbul". *Osmanlı Bilimi Araştırmaları*, 16/2, 2015, p. 3–32.

Pilarczyk, Krzysztof. *Leksykon drukarzy ksiąg hebrajskich w Polsce. Z bibliografią polono-judaików w językach żydowskich (XVI–XVIII wiek)*. Kraków: Wydawn. Antykwa, 2004.

Rycaut, Paul. *The Capitulations and Articles etc*. Istanbul: Abraham Gabai chaf nahat, 1663.

Roe, Thomas. *The negotiations of Sir Thomas Roe, in His Embassy to the Ottoman Porte, from the Year 1621 to 1628 Inclusive*. London: Samuel Richardson, 1740.

Romeu, Pilar. *Fuente clara (Salónica, 1595). Un converso sefardí a la defensa del judaísmo y a la búsqueda de su propia fe*. Barcelona: Tirocinio, 2007.

Rowland-Smith, Diana. "The Beginnings of Hebrew Printing in Egypt". *British Library Journal*, 15, 1989, p. 16–22.

Rozen, Minna. *History of the Jewish Community in Istanbul. The Formative Years, 1453–1566*. Leiden/Boston: Brill, 2010.

Rozen, Minna. *Studies in the History of Istanbul Jewry. A Journey through Civilization*. Turnhout: Brepols, 2015.

Ruderman, David B. *Early Modern Jewry: A New Cultural History*. Princeton/Oxford: Princeton University Press, 2010.

Simon, Rachel. "The Contribution of Hebrew Printing Houses and Printers in Istanbul to Ladino Culture and Scholarship". *Judaica Librarianship*, 16/17, 2011, p. 125–135.

Yaari, Abraham, *Ha-Defus ha-Ivri be-Kushta*. Jerusalem: The Magnes Press, 1967.

Ovidiu Olar

'Libertà et licenza… di stampare mille heræsie et schismi:' The Propaganda Fide and the Greek Printing Press at Constantinople (1627–1628)

In 1631, Monsignor Francesco Ingoli, the Secretary of the Sacred Congregation for the Propagation of the Faith (*Propaganda Fide*) mapped the Roman missionary activities that his dicastery officially coordinated. Written in the form of five letters addressed to the Capuchin friar and Apostolic missionary Valeriano Magni and entitled *Report on the Four Parts of the World* (*Relazione delle Quattro Parti del Mondo*), the account was lengthy, thoroughly documented, and insightful. Its first four instalments covered Europe, Asia, Africa and America, while the last chapter focused on "the things done in Rome for the propagation of the Faith" and presented the organizational efforts made by the Pope and his proxies to counter heresies, schism, "Mahometanism", idolatry, sectarianism and atheism.[1]

The *Report* was self-serving. On the one hand, Ingoli showcased the most important results in order to prove that despite being only nine years old and in spite of its rather miniature size, the Propaganda Fide was a global institution of unparalleled efficiency.[2] On the other hand, the indefatigable secretary constantly drew the attention of his correspondent – a seasoned missionary belonging to a prestigious order with a strong missionary thrust[3] – and of the potential

---

1 F. Ingoli, *Relazione delle Quattro Parti del Mondo*, ed. by F. Tosi, Vatican City, 1999. The manuscript is conserved in the State Archive of Rome (Archivio di Stato di Roma – *Archivio Santacroce* 85).
2 G. Pizzorusso, *Governare le missioni, conoscere il mondo nel XVII secolo. La Congregazione pontificia de Propaganda Fide*, Viterbo, 2018; Pizzorusso, *Propaganda fide I. La congregazione pontificia e la giurisdizione sulle missioni*, Rome, 2022.
3 Magni's role in the restoration of Catholicism in Bohemia was recently addressed by A. di Napoli, *Valeriano Magni da Milano e la riforma ecclesiastica in Boemia attraverso la corrispondenza della Congregazione de Propaganda Fide (1626–1651)*, Milan, 2015. See also H. Louthan, "Mediating Confessions in Central Europe: The Ecumenical Activity of Valerian Magni, 1586–1661", *Journal of Ecclesiatical History*, 55/ 4, 2004, p. 681–699; A. Catalano, "La politica della curia romana in Boemia dalla strategia del nunzio Carlo Carafa a quella del cappuccino Valeriano Magni", in R. Bösel, G. Klingenstein, A. Koller (eds.), *Kaiserhof – Papsthof (16.–18. Jahrhundert)*, Vienna, 2006, p. 105–121. For Capuchin missionary activities, see N. Papaïliaki, *Aspects de la mission catholique auprès des Grecs de l'Empire ottoman. Archives grecques inédites des Capucins de Paris (XVIIe–XVIIIe siècles)*, Paris – EPHE, 2009 (unpublished Ph.D. thesis); Papaïliaki-Gamelon, "Conflits et coexistences: les relations des missionaires capucins français avec les

🔓 Open Access. © 2024, the author(s), published by De Gruyter. [CC] BY-NC-ND This work is licensed under the Creative Commons Attribution-NonCommercial-NoDerivatives 4.0 International License.
https://doi.org/10.1515/9783111060392-005

readers to possible adjustments that the Congregation could make in order to boost the promotion of the faith. Yet self-interest notwithstanding, the result was impressive: conjuring a wide range of sources, Ingoli depicted a papal agency with a universal vocation.

The Propaganda's objectives, as listed in the *Report*, were ambitious. But adapting them to reality did not go as smoothly as advertised.[4] Rome's centralizing initiatives encountered the opposition of the Portuguese and Spanish kings, the creation of a papal missionary agency displeased the Society of Jesus, keen to preserve its independence, and the Propaganda's jurisdiction over doctrinal issues triggered a series of conflicts with the Holy Office. The management of remote missions was haunted by personnel and logistic troubles. And to top it all off, defending the faithful in non-Catholic environments, returning schismatics and heretics to unity, and propagating the faith in non-Christian lands were no small feat, as it meant dealing with rapidly changing, complex religious and political contexts.

The case of the patriarch of Constantinople Kyrillos Lukaris (d. 1638) is indicative for the Propaganda's potential and limits in a hostile milieu. Suspected of heresy, Lukaris appeared early on the Congregation's radar. Already in 1624, the head of the Greek College in Rome, Andrea Eudaimoioannes, one of the Propaganda's experts, composed an "Instruction" on the patriarch, to be sent to an undisclosed recipient.[5] The same year, the "Instruction" addressed by the Holy See's Secretariat of State to Bernardino Spada, the papal nuncio to France, included recommendations concerning Lukaris, which emanated from the Propaganda.[6] Spada was informed that the patriarch of Constantinople was "a Cal-

---

ecclésiastiques et les laïcs grecs au XVIIe siècle," in *Concurrences en mission. Propagandes, conflits, coexistences, XVIe–XXIe siècle. Actes du 31e Colloque du CRÉDIC tenu à Brive-la-Gaillarde (Corrèze, France) du 30 août au 3 septembre 2010*, ed. by S. Eyezo'o, J.-F. Zorn, Paris, 2011, p. 65–78; G. Santarelli, "Missioni e missionari", in V. Criscuolo (ed.), *I Cappuccini. Fonti documentarie e narrative del primo secolo (1525–1619)*, Rome, 2020, p. 911–975.

4 As noted by C. Windler, "Ambiguous Belongings: How Catholic Missionaries in Persia and the Roman Curia Dealt with *Communicatio in Sacris*", in R. Po-chia Hsia (ed.), *A Companion to Early Modern Catholic Global Missions*, Leiden/Boston, 2018, p. 231: "the Congregation for the Propagation of the Faith in the 17th and 18th centuries hardly qualifies as a success story."

5 Vatican City, Archivio Storico de Propaganda Fide (APF) – *Istruttioni diverse degl'anni 1623 sino al 1638*, f. 53r–54r. See also S. Giordano, "Il mondo di Propaganda Fide nelle istruzioni di Francesco Ingoli (1623–1648)", in G. Braun (ed.), *Diplomatische Wissenskulturen der Frühen Neuzeit. Erfahrungsräume und Orte der Wissensproduktioned*, Berlin, 2018, p. 217. For the Cretanborn Eudaimoioannes, see J. Krajcar, "The Greek College in the Years of Unrest (1604–1630)," *OCP 32*, 1/1966, p. 23–31.

6 APF – *Istruzioni 1623–1638*, f. 54r–56r. See Giordano, "Il mondo di Propaganda Fide", p. 221–222, 225.

vinist heretic who spread Calvin's heresy in the Eastern Church".[7] At the direct request of the Propaganda, the French ambassador to the Ottoman Porte had him deposed and replaced with a candidate sympathetic to the Roman Church, but Lukaris regained his position with the help of the Dutch resident. Fearing "a horrible persecution of the catholic Church", as well as a wave of Calvinist bishops and metropolitans set to take advantage of a flock "buried in ignorance because of Turkish tyranny", the Congregation asked the nuncio to convince King Louis XIII to back Lukaris' rival, support the project of a Capuchin mission to Constantinople, and protect the Levantine Catholics.[8]

The Propaganda's negative stance towards Lukaris increased in the years to follow. In 1630, for example, the nuncio to France Alessandro Bichi was instructed to advocate the patriarch's removal from the throne by all means necessary.[9] By offering an informed glimpse of the workings of the Congregation, Ingoli's *Report on the Four Parts of the World* allows us to better grasp the rational underpinning this relentless hostility. In the following pages I will take a closer look at Ingoli's depiction of Lukaris, which the 1631 *Report* was ready to make public.[10] Corroborating it with archival materials, I will argue that the founding of a Greek printing press at Constantinople in the summer of 1627 played a major role in shaping the Propaganda's policies with regards to Lukaris.[11]

The opening of the first Greek press in the Ottoman Empire generated great interest among scholars. Valuable studies have been dedicated to its founder (Nikodimos Metaxas), its patron (Lukaris), its supporters and its adversaries.[12]

---

7 "*Eretico calvinista che andava spargendo l'eresia di Calvino nella Chiesa Orientale*": A. Leman, *Recueil des instructions générales aux nonces ordinaires de France de 1624 à 1634*, Lille/Paris, 1920, p. 68.

8 Leman, *Recueil*, p. 68–70.

9 APF – *Istruzioni 1623–1638*, f. 155v–56r. See Giordano, "Il mondo di Propaganda Fide", p. 225.

10 The General Congregation held on June 13, 1633 discussed the publication of the *Report*, but the work was not printed: F. Tosi, "La memoria perduta di Propaganda Fide", in Ingoli, *Relazione*, VII–XLI, p. XXVIII–XXX.

11 I expand here a hypothesis proposed in O. Olar, *La Boutique de Théophile. Les relations du patriarche de Constantinople Kyrillos Loukaris (1570–1638) avec la Réforme*, Paris, 2019, p. 145–182.

12 The most important contribution to the subject is that of L. Augliera, *Libri politica religione nel Levante del Seicento. La tipografia di Nicodemo Metaxas primo editore di testi greci nell'Oriente ortodosso*, Venice, 1996 [Greek version: *Biblia politikē thrēskeia stēn Anatolē ton 17o aiōna. To typographeio tou Nikodēmou Metaxa prōtou ekdotē Hellēnikōn keimenōn stēn orthodoxē Anatolē*, trans. Stathis Birtachas, Athens, 2006]. The list of recent studies on the topic includes N. Pektaş (Palabıyık), *The First Greek Printing Press in Constantinople (1625–1628)*. Unpublished Ph.D. Dissertation, University of London, London, 2014; Palabıyık, "An Early Case of the Printer's Self-Censorship in Constantinople", *The Library*, 16/4, 2015, p. 381–404; Palabıyık, "Redundant

Despite the sustained interest, however, historians still struggle to untangle the complicated web of truths, half-truths, lies and deceit surrounding the failed "adventure." Since the Propaganda Fide was one of the major actors interested in the event, deconstructing its aggressive attitude towards Lukaris and the first Greek printing press of Constantinople will undoubtedly shed additional light on this dark but spectacular corner of early modern European confessional history.[13]

1. A Universal Congregation

The *Report on the Four Parts of the World* bestows upon Lukaris the dubious honor of being the greatest of the evils afflicting Greek Christianity, in Constantinople, Greece and the Levant. As if the Greek errors were not enough, the patriarch "had drank the venom of Calvin's heresy," trying to infect the whole East.[14] Maintaining a close relationship with the English and Dutch diplomatic representatives to the Porte, he had sent several monks to study in England in order to disseminate better upon return the heretical ideas acquired there. Although the Greeks were stubbornly attached to their beliefs and bad rites, they were also ignorant and susceptible to being seduced by the corrupt scholars. Traces of good doctrine and relics of the true religion could still be found among the schismatics, but they were in serious danger of extinction.[15]

Presses and Recycled Woodcuts: The Journey of Printing Materials from London to Constantinople in the Seventeenth Century", *The Papers of the Bibliographical Society of America*, 110/3, 2016, p. 273–298; Palabıyık, "A Public Debate on Cyril of Alexandria's Views on the Procession of the Holy Spirit in Seventeenth-Century Constantinople: The Jesuit Reaction to Nicodemos Metaxas's Greek Editions", *International Journal of the Classical Tradition*, 27/3, 2020, p. 427–448.

13 Important literature has been produced on the topic: T. I. Papadopoulos, "Biblia Katholikōn kai biblia Orthodoxōn", *O Eranistēs*, 19, 1993, p. 36–65; Papadopoulos, "Agnōsta erga Hellēnōn hypo ekdosē", in K. Sp. Staikos, T. E. Sklavenitis (eds), *To entypo hellēniko biblio 15os–19os aiōnas. Praktika diethnous synedriou Delphoi, 16–20 Maiou 2001*, Athens, 2004, p. 291–308; V. Tsakiris, "O rolos tou typographeiou tou Loukarē stēn idrysē tou Hellēnikou typographeiou tēs Propaganda Fide", *O Eranistēs*, 27, 2009, p. 53–67.

14 "*E 'l maggior male fra molti, e grandi, che vi sono, è forse quello, che può cagionare non solo colà, ma in tutto il Levante il presente Patriarca Scismatico, per nome Cirillo, di natione Candiotto, il quale, non contento de gli errori Greci, ha bevuto il veleno dell'heresia di Calvino, e cerca di infettarne la chiesa Greca, e con essa tutto l'Oriente*": Ingoli, *Relazione*, 71.

15 "*Si teme a gran ragione, che alla fine non seducano i popoli, e non guastino, et estinguano que' semi di buona dottrina, e quelle reliquie di vera religione, che hoggi ne' Greci, etiando Scismatici, rimangono*": Ingoli, *Relazione*, 72.

In order to mitigate the risk, the Propaganda decided to send to the capital of the Ottoman Empire a titular bishop who was a suffragan of the Latin patriarch of Constantinople, namely Livio Gigli, newly appointed archbishop of Edessa. Residing in the cosmopolitan Pera neighborhood, the suffragan could tend to the spiritual needs of both Latins and Greeks.[16] He could also remind Lukaris of the illicit nature of his power: since the conquest of Constantinople by the crusaders in 1204, the legitimate patriarch was the Latin one. Therefore, the real holder of the see was not Lukaris, but Ascanio Gesualdo, the archbishop of Bari.[17]

The Propaganda also championed the establishment of a Capuchin mission to Constantinople, which was meant to assist the Latin-rite Christians of Pera.[18] Nevertheless, Lukaris retaliated. He could not prevent the arrival of the Capuchins in July 1626.[19] He did, however, secure, albeit for a brief period of time, the confinement and expulsion of the Jesuits in early 1628.[20] In agreement with the leaders of the Latin-rite community, who feared the diminishment of their revenues, and with Ottoman officials, either weary of political consequences or corruptible, he drove Gigli out of the capital. Then, enlisting the help of the *qaimaqam* Receb Pasha and of several ambassadors to the Sublime Porte, including the English one, he forced the suffragan to move from Chios to Candia and from Candia to

---

16 C. A. Frazee, *Catholics and Sultans: The Church and the Ottoman Empire 1453–1923*, Cambridge, 1983, p. 94–95. For the office of (Latin) patriarchal vicar, see Georg Hofmann, SJ, *Il Vicariato Apostolico di Costantinopoli*, Rome, 1935.

17 S. Feci, "Gesualdo Ascanio", *DBI*, 53, 1999, p. 492–495.

18 "*Intanto per soccorso di Pera, se ben v'erano altri religiosi Dominicani, Franciscani, e Gesuiti, la Sacra Congregatione vi ha introdotti li Padri Cappuccini, e fatta loro havere la Chiesa di S. Giorgio di Pera, là dove col buono esempio, e le humili maniere di trattare, che tengono, operano gran frutto*": Ingoli, *Relazione*, p. 73. In addition to the official mission, that is, helping the Latin-rite community, the (French) Capuchins were supposed to counter Jesuit influence in the missionary field, enhance centralization, and promote the papal and French take on missionary policy in Eastern Mediterranean: Pizzorusso, "Reti informative e strategie politiche tra la Francia, Roma e le missioni cattoliche nell'impero ottomano agli inizi del XVII secolo," in G. Motta (ed.), *I Turchi, il Mediterraneo e l'Europa*, Milan, 1998, p. 212–231.

19 The plan to send Capuchin missionaries to Constantinople and the Levant, advocated by Pacifique de Provins, had been approved by the Propaganda in January 1623 (APF – Acta 3, f. 27), but postponed due to internal conflicts: M. Binasco, *Viaggiatori e missionari nel Seicento. Pacifique de Provins fra Levante, Acadia e Guyana (1622–1648)*, Novi Ligure, 2006, p. 27–31.

20 Ingoli, *Relazione*, p. 73–74. For the Jesuit mission, see A. Ruiu, "Conflicting Visions of the Jesuit Missions to the Ottoman Empire, 1609–1628", *Journal of Jesuit Studies*, 1, 2014, p. 260–80; Ruiu, "Missionaries and French Subjects: The Jesuits in the Ottoman Empire", in R. Po-chia Hsia (ed.), *A Companion to Early Modern Catholic Global Missions*, Leiden/Boston, 2018, p. 181–204.

his native Naxos.[21] For this type of shady business to succeed, reflected Ingoli bitterly, one needed the assistance of foreign diplomatic representatives or money.[22]

Moreover, Lukaris, a Cretan by birth and therefore a Venetian subject, attempted to "spread his venom" across Venice's maritime empire by means of "some pestiferous books printed in England and Constantinople in order to infect the whole East."[23] The plan was blocked with the help of Francesco Molin, governor general of the Realm of Candia, but the danger was far from being over.[24]

In the footsteps of Augustine, Ingoli depicted the preservation and propagation of the one and only true, Catholic, Apostolic, Roman faith as a conflict between the City of God (*città di Dio*) and the Earthly City (*città del Mondo*).[25] Fueled by political goals and assisted by agents such as Lukaris, the latter had the upper hand in the realm of "Turkish barbary", which ruined completely a once-prosperous part of Europe.[26] Yet there were still ways to fortify the former: revival of the canonical visitations, such as the ones conducted by Pietro Masarecchio (Pjetër Mazrreku), papal visitor for Bulgaria, Serbia, Bosnia and Ottoman Hungary, in 1623–1624, and by Luca Stella, archbishop of Candia in the Ionian islands, in 1625;[27] foundation of schools, such as the one in Nafplio (Morea),

---

21 Ingoli, *Relazione*, p. 72–73. For the involvement of Sir Thomas Roe, see Kew, The National Archives – *State Papers* 97/13, f. 74 (Loukaris to Roe – Constantinople, 22 March 1627).

22 "*Questa sorte di affari, che possono aver congionta alcuna ragione di stato, non si sostentano alla Porta, se non con l'autorità de' Ministri di Principi, o co' denari*": Ingoli, *Relazione*, p. 73.

23 "*Ma perciò che Cirillo Patriarca vorrebbe spargere il suo veleno là dove, per esser lui Candiotto, si persuade che sia per esser più facilmente ricevuto; havendo inviato colà alcuni pestiferi libri stampati in Inghilterra, et in Costantinopoli con proponimento d'infettarne tutto l'Oriente, si è fatta opera, che col braccio del S.ᵉ Francesco Molini Providitor Generale in quel regno ne sia impedita la distributione, sì come n'è stata vietata la stampa da i Turchi medesimi*": Ingoli, *Relazione*, p. 74.

24 Augliera, *Libri politica religione*, p. 86–87.

25 "*Ma a questa santa oper[a], che si dee veramente affermare, essere un'ampliatione della città di Dio, non si può esprimere, quanto da per tutto si opponga la città del Mondo; onde, se non fossero li rispetti politici, si potrebbe anche in queste parti sperare di fare col divino aiuto un profitto grandissimo*": Ingoli, *Relazione*, p. 74.

26 According to Ingoli, the ruin was inevitable: "*tanto può la barbarie Turchesca, al cui intollerabile dominio sono sottoposte*" [these regions] (Ingoli, *Relazione*, p. 68).

27 Ingoli, *Relazione*, p. 66, 69, 77–78. Documents concerning Masarecchio's visitation of the "four realms under Turkish doimnion" (APF – *Visite e Collegi* 1, 56-82) were published by K. Draganović, "Izvješće apostolskog vizitatora Petra Masarechija o prilikama katol(ičkog) naroda u Bugarskoj, Srbiji, Srijemu, Slavoniji i Bosni g. 1623. I 1624", *Starine*, 39, 1948, p. 1–48; see also M. Jačov, *Spisi kongregacije za propagandu vere u Rimu o Srbima*, vol. I *(1622–1644)*, Belgrade, 1986, p. 12–18. For Masarecchio's "Short discourse on the Albanian nation" (APF – *Scritture originali riferite nelle Congregazioni Generali*, 263, 271–74), see P. Bartl (ed.), *Albania Sacra. Geistliche Visitationsberichte aus Albanien*, vol. III *Diözese Sappa*, Wiesbaden, 2014,

which was operated by two alumni of the Greek College in Rome;[28] establishment of missions in major cities, such as Edirne, Sofia, Nafplio and Thessaloniki;[29] investigation of the Athonite and Sinaite monastic communities, who repeatedly professed allegiance to the pope while requesting Rome's financial support;[30] and reconstruction of the Latin episcopal network in the Aegean Islands.[31]

All these ways led to Rome, as the last chapter of the *Report* clearly underlined.[32] The propagation of the faith had always been a matter of major importance and had constantly attracted papal attention. Yet the recent progress of heresies and of Islam required a different approach to the conversion of infidels, one based less on money and goods (which Ingoli rejected as missionary instruments), and more on better "human tools": suitable people who could engage in doctrinal debates, speak the language of the targeted audience and translate sacred texts.[33]

With regard to these people – Cardinals, bishops, and missionaries –, Pope Gregory XV founded the Propaganda (1622), whose configuration and modus operandi Ingoli described in detail.[34] Once founded, the Congregation did its best to recruit and train new "Apostles", investing in the extant seminaries and colleges,

---

p. 114–118; I. Zamputti (ed.), *Dokumente për historinë e Shqipërisë (1623–1653)*, St. Gallen-Prishtina, 2015, p. 67–72. Masarecchio's visitation and its consequences have been thoroughly studied by A. Molnár, *Le Saint-Siège, Raguse et les missions catholiques de la Hongrie ottomane 1572–1647*, Rome/Budapest, 2007, p. 192–98.

28 Ingoli, *Relazione*, p. 71.

29 Ingoli, *Relazione*, p. 74.

30 Ingoli, *Relazione*, p. 74, 104. Nikolaos Rossi, an alumnus of the Greek College in Rome, was indeed sent to Mount Athos, in 1635: G. Hofmann, *Rom und der Athos. Briefwechsel zwischen dem Missionar auf dem Athos Nikolaus Rossi und der Kongregation de Propaganda Fide*, Rome, 1954. Hofmann also studied Rome's contacts with Athos and Sinai: *Athos e Roma*, Rome, 1925; *Rom und Athosklöster*, Rome, 1926; *Sinai und Rom*, Rome, 1927.

31 Ingoli, *Relazione*, p. 74–77. For details, see Hofmann, *Vescovadi cattolici della Grecia*, vol. I. *Chios*, Rome, 1934; vol. II. *Tinos*, Rome, 1936; vol. III. *Syros*, Rome, 1937; vol. IV. *Naxos*, Rome, 1938; vol. V. *Thera (Santorino)*, Rome, 1941. The same was valid for Cyprus: Ingoli, *Relazione*, p. 91.

32 Ingoli, *Relazione*, p. 271–289.

33 "*Dunque conchiuderemo esser quattro gl'istrumenti humani per operare la conversione già detta; l'uno principale io dico le persone, e gl'altri quasi accessori, e come strumenti del primo cioè le dottrine, le lingue e le scritture:*" Ingoli, *Relazione*, p. 271.

34 Ingoli, *Relazione*, p. 271–277. The Congregation's founding documents are published in J. Metzler (ed.), *Sacræ Congregationis de Propaganda Fide memoria rerum: 350 anni a servizio delle missioni, 1622–1972*, vol. III/2, Rome/Freiburg/Vienna, 1976), p. 655 (January 6, 1622), 662–664 (June 22, 1622).

such as the San Paolo College (1613), and opening new ones, such as the Urban College, also known as the College of the Propaganda (1627).[35]

The curriculum included the study of doctrines – the second tool –, deemed instrumental in the conversion and salvation of Christian heretics and schismatics, Jews, Muslims, "gentiles" and various sects. Scholastic theology was of little use in such cases: informed polemical training fared better.[36] And this led automatically to the third tool – the study of languages: in order to refute and persuade, one needed to find a common linguistic ground.[37]

For Ingoli, there were two types of languages: the literary (*letterale*) and the demotic (*volgari*). The first category included the languages, into which the Scriptures had been translated in full or partly from days of old (Hebrew, Greek, Latin, Chaldean, Syriac, Arabic, and Illyrian); Latin, Illyrian, and Arabic were still in use and therefore useful for missionary purposes.[38] The second category comprised the spoken languages, in all their diversity (in Europe, the most important ones were Italian, French, Spanish, German, "Slavic" and vernacular Greek).[39] Their knowledge was vital for preaching and propagating the faith across the world, which induced

---

35 Ingoli, *Relazione*, p. 278–279. The Urban College was seen as a model for all future colleges: G. Pizzorusso, "I satelliti di Propaganda Fide: il Collegio Urbano e la Tipografia Poliglotta. Note di ricerca su due istituzioni culturali romane nel XVII secolo", *Mélanges de l'École Française de Rome. Italie et Méditerranée*, 116/2, 2004, p. 471–298; Pizzorusso, "Note sul carattere sovranazionale / multinazionale del Collegio Urbano di Propaganda Fide", in A. Boccolini, M. Sanfilippo, P. Tuso (eds.), *I collegi per stranieri a/e Roma nell'età moderna* I. *Cinque-Settecento*, Viterbo, 2023, p. 183–195.

36 Ingoli, *Relazione*, p. 279–281.

37 *"E quindi me ne passo al terzo necessario mezzo per propagar la fede, che sono le lingue, non potendosi trattare co' popoli se nella lingua loro propria, o in altra da loro intesa non si favella"*: Ingoli, *Relazione*, p. 281. As observed by Aurélien Girard, "Teaching and Learning Arabic in Early Modern Rome: Shaping a Missionary Language," in J. Loop, A. Hamilton, C. Burnett (eds.), *The Teaching and Learning of Arabic in Early Modern Europe*, Leiden/Boston, 2017, p. 202: "the study of the languages encouraged by the Propaganda was inextricably linked to the missionary activity". See also Pizzorusso, "Le lingue a Roma: studio e pratica nei collegi missionari nella prima età moderna", *Rivista storica italiana*, 132/1, 2020, p. 248–271; Girard, "Le Collège maronite de Rome et les langues au tournant des XVIᵉ et XVIIᵉ siècles: éducation des chrétiens orientaux, science orientaliste et apologétique catholique", *Rivista storica italiana*, 132/1, 2020, p. 272–299.

38 *"Oltre all'Hebrea, ch'è la radice et l'origine d'ogni altra, veggiamo la scrittura voltata nella Greca, Latina, Caldea, Siriaca, Arabica et Illirica, delle quali per l'uso del parlare sono più necessarie dell'altre la Latina, l'Illirica, l'Arabica"*: Ingoli, *Relazione*, p. 281–282. Illyrian (*"la quale è una medesima cosa con la Schiava"*) designates the early modern Croatian Church Slavonic.

39 *"Nell'Europa oltre all'Italiana, Francese e Spagnola, che servono in molte provincie, importano molto la Tedesca, e la Schiava, e la Greca volgare"*: Ingoli, *Relazione*, p. 283. "Slavic" seems to designate the spoken, pre-standardized early modern Croatian.

the Propaganda to promote their teaching and learning. Illyrian, for example, was taught in the Italian Illyrian colleges, while Arabic was taught mainly in the Roman Franciscan convent of San Pietro in Montorio, but also in Florence and Malta.[40]

In order to facilitate this difficult process, the Propaganda decided to assemble and print grammars and vocabularies of the world's most popular vernaculars, such as the Georgian – Italian dictionary compiled by Stefano Paolini (1629) and the Arabic grammar by the Franciscan Tommaso da Novara, Custos of Holy Land (1631). Some editorial plans came slowly to fruition and others never materialized: the *Coptic or Egyptian Forerunner* by the Jesuit polymath Athanasius Kircher, which included a Coptic grammar, was only published in 1636, while the Italian – (demotic) Greek vocabulary by the Jesuit missionary Girolamo Germano, published in 1622, was never reprinted. However, the delays and failures were not for want of trying.[41]

2. A Polyglot Printing Press

Printing was, in fact, the last major tool on Ingoli's list: it compensated for the "defect of memory" of potential converts and was remarkably efficient, reaching audiences near and remote, present and future.[42] Consequently, the *Report* pre-

---

40 Ingoli, *Relazione*, p. 282. Ingoli mentions three lectors of Arabic, all Franciscans: Tommaso da Novara, Lorenzo Lammari and Francesco da Malta. For details, see Pizzorusso, "Tra cultura e missione. La congregazione de Propaganda Fide e le scuole di lingua araba nel XVII secolo," in A. Romano (ed.), *Rome et la science moderne entre Renaissance et Lumières*, Rome, 2009, p. 121–152; Pizzorusso, "La preparazione linguistica e controversistica dei missionari per l'Oriente islamico: scuole, testi, insegnanti a Roma e in Italia", in B. Heyberger, M. García-Arenal, E. Colombo, P. Vismara (eds.), *L'Islam visto da Occidente. Cultura e religione del Seicento europeo di fronte all'Islam*, Milan, 2009, p. 253–288; Girard, "Des manuels de langue entre mission et érudition orientaliste au XVIIᵉ siècle: les grammaires de l'arabe des Caracciolini", in I. Fosi, G. Pizzorusso (eds.), *L'Ordine dei Chierici Regolari Minori (Caracciolini): religione e cultura in età postridentina. Atti del Convegno (Chieti, 11–12 aprile 2008)*, Casoria, 2010, p. 279–295; Girard, "Teaching and Learning Arabic".

41 Ingoli, *Relazione*, p. 286–287. For the Arabic grammar, see J. Guardi, "Tommaso Obicini", in D. Thomas, J. Chesworth (eds.), *Christian-Muslim Relations: A Bibliographical History*, vol. IX. *Western and Southern Europe (1600–1700)*, Leiden/Boston, 2017, p. 743–748. The foundation of the Propaganda also boosted interest in the 1613 Arabic translation of Bellarmine's Doctrina Christiana and the 1620 Institutiones linguæ arabicæ by Francesco Martellotto: C. M. Grafinger, "Bildungspolitische Funktion der Biblioteca Apostolica Vaticana zu Beginn des 17. Jahrhunderts: ihre Bedeutung für die Franziskaner in der Orientmission," *Collectanea Franciscana*, 61/3-4, 1991, p. 587–604.

42 "[La scrittura] per due cagioni fa di mestieri, l'una per supplire il diffetto della memoria di coloro, che presenti ascoltano gl'insegnamenti de Missionarij, l'altra per comunicare li medesimi

sented in detail the activity of the printing press founded "with great expense and princely spirit" for missionary purposes in Rome, in 1626.[43]

Apart from dictionaries and grammars of didactic use, the examples provided by Ingoli included catechisms, polemical works (*libri dogmatici*), edifying texts (*libri spirituali*), and translations of sacred texts (*libri sacri*, that is, the Holy Liturgy and Scripture) in a variety of languages and original scripts.[44] The first category was represented by the *Christian Doctrine* of Robert Bellarmine SJ (translated into several languages). The "spiritual" works were embodied by the *Guide for Sinners* of Louis de Granada OP (in vernacular Greek).[45] The last category was illustrated by the project of an Arabic translation of the Bible, a monumental missionary tool that was only completed in 1671–1673.[46] Conversely, the polemical section took the lion's share: the *Report* showcased five titles related to the Council of Ferrara – Florence (one in Armenian – printed for the Propaganda before the founding of the Propaganda printing press –, one bilingual – printed for the Propaganda in Paris –, one in Latin, one in literary Greek, and one in vernacular Greek), two anti-Protestant works (in Latin), and an anti-Islamic *Apology for Christianity*.[47]

---

insegnamenti non solo a i presenti ascoltanti, ma anche a i lontani, e non solo a i viventi, ma a i posteri": Ingoli, *Relazione*, p. 283.

43 "*Ha dunque la Sacra Congregatione con ispesa grande, et animo regio instituita una stampa in Roma con caratteri di tutte le principali lingue antiche, e moderne, che per le Missioni sono necessarie, e di mano in mano la va accrescendo*": Ingoli, *Relazione*, p. 284. For the press, see Willi Henkel, "The Polyglot Printing-office of the Congregation", in *Sacræ Congregationis de Propaganda Fide memoria rerum*, vol. I/1, Rome/Freiburg/Vienna, 1971), p. 335–350; Henkel, "Die Druckerei der Propaganda Fide im Dienste der Glaubensverbreitung", *Communicatio Socialis*, 9/2, 1976, p. 105–117; 9/3, 1976, p. 217–231.

44 Ingoli listed these categories during a meeting of Propaganda's "special commission" (*Congregatio Particularis*) in November 1642: W. Henkel, "Francesco Ingoli, erster Sekretär der Propaganda Fide, über Druckerpresse und Mission (I)", *Communicatio Socialis*, 3/1, 1970, p. 63–64.

45 Ingoli, *Relazione*, p. 285. *Guía de pecadores* was translated into "Romaic," that is, vernacular Greek (*metaglōttismenē eis rhōmaikēn glōssan*) by the Jesuit Andrea Rendi of Chios (*Hodēgia tōn hamartōlōn* 1628): É. Legrand, *Bibliographie hellénique ou description raisonnée des ouvrages publiés par des Grecs au dix-septième siècle*, vol. I, Paris,1894, p. 260–261 (No. 182).

46 Ingoli, *Relazione*, p. 286. For the *Biblia Sacra Arabica*, the Propaganda's bilingual Arabic-Latin edition of 1671–1673, see P. Féghali, "The Holy Books in Arabic: The example of the Propaganda Fide Edition", in S. Binay, S. Leder (eds.), *Translating the Bible into Arabic: Historical, Text-Critical and Literary Aspects*, Beirut, 2012, p. 35–52.

47 Ingoli, *Relazione*, p. 114–115, 285–286. *Apologia pro Christiana Religione* polemicized with the Safavid scholar Aḥmad b. Zayn al-ʿĀbidīn. Translated into Arabic, it was republished in 1637, together with the Latin original. The *Apology*'s author, Filippo Guadagnoli, a member of the order

The two anti-Protestant tracts were directed against Lukaris. The first rejected both in demotic Greek and Latin the "seventy blasphemies" (11 concerned the Eucharist, 12 – the Bible, 17 –Purgatory, 24 – the pope, 6 – other issues) contained in the "false catechism" published in Wittenberg in 1622 by Zacharias Gerganos, who has been ever since considered by the Propaganda as Lutheran and a proxy of the patriarch of Constantinople.[48] The second rebutted a "Calvinist" *Confession of faith* printed in Latin, French and German in 1629, which circulated under the name of Lukaris.[49] Both confutations of these "wicked books" were written by the Rome-based Latin Archbishop of Iconium Ioannis Matthaeos Caryophilis, a Crete-born Catholic educated at the pontifical Greek College of St Athanasios (†1633).[50]

---

of Clerics Regular Minor (Caracciolini), was also involved in the making of *Biblia Sacra Arabica*: A. Tiburcio, "Filippo Guadagnoli", in *Christian-Muslim Relations*, vol. IX, p. 749–755.

48 I. M. Caryophilis, *Elenchos tēs pseudochristianikēs katēchēseōs Zachariou tou Gerganou apo tēn Artēn / Refutatio Pseudochristianæ Catechesis editæ a Zacharia Gergano Græco*, Rome, 1631; the book included a "Lament for the misfortunes of unfortunate Hellas" (*Monōdia epi tais symphorais tēs dystychous Hellados*), in political verse. See Legrand, *Bibliographie hellénique*, vol. I, p. 285–288 (No. 208); A. Argyriou, "Zacharie Gerganos et Jean-Matthieu Caryophyllos: un cas typique d'aliénation de la pensée orthodoxe dans la première moitié du XVIIᵉ siècle", in *Communications grecques présentées au VIᵉ Congrès international des études du Sud-Est européen, Sofia, 30 août – 5 septembre 1989*, Athens, 1990, p. 183–192.

49 I. M. Caryophilis, *Censura confessionis fidei, seu potius perfidiæ Calvinianæ, quæ nomine Cyrilli Patriarchæ Constantinopolitani edita circumfertur*, Rome, 1631. See Legrand, *Bibliographie hellénique*, vol. I, 288–289 (No. 209).

50 "*E perché un certo Gergano da Itaca ha publicato un catechismo in lingua Greca volgare che tutte l'heresie di Lutero abbraccia, et ancora sotto nome di Cirillo Patriarca presente di Costantinopoli si vede stampata una professione di fede in lingua Latina, Francese e Tedesca, che contiene il calvinismo; perciò sono stati amendue questi pessimi libri dal medesimo Mons.ᵉ Carcofilo in lingua Latina, e Greca volgare confutati, e nella nostra stamperia stampati*": Ingoli, *Relazione*, p. 285. For Caryophilis, see Z. N. Tsirpanlis, *To Hellēniko Kollegio tēs Rōmēs kai oi mathētes tou (1576–1700). Symbolē stē meletē tēs morphōtikēs politikēs tou Batikanou*, Thessaloniki, 1980, p. 289–92 (No. 60); G. Podskalsky, *Griechische Theologie in der Zeit der Türkenherrschaft (1453–1821). Die Orthodoxie im Spannungsfeld der nachreformatorischen Konfessionen des Westens*, Munich, 1988, p. 181–83 (Greek version: *Hē Hellēnikē theologia epi Tourkokratias 1453–1821. Hē Orthodoxia stē sphaira eporroēs tōn Dutikōn Dogmatōn meta tē Metarrythmisē*, trans. G. D. Metallinos, Athens, 2005, p. 241–243).

Tab. 1: Works printed by the Propaganda mentioned in Ingoli's Report (*Quinta lettera delle cose fatte in Roma*)[51].

Pope Eugenius' 1439 Bull of Union with the Armenians	Armenian (1623)
Robert Bellarmine's "small" Christian Doctrine	Armenian (1623) Illyrian (Glagolitic alphabet 1628) Vernacular Greek (1628) Illyrian (Cyrillic alphabet 1629)
Robert Bellarmine's "long" Christian Doctrine	Illyrian (Latin alphabet 1627) Italian & Armenian (1630)
Caryophilis' Confutation of Kabasilas' treatise On the Primacy of the Pope	Greek & Latin (1626)
Acts of the Council of Florence	Literary Greek (1628)
Explanation of the 1439 Decree of Union, attributed to Georgios-Gennadios Scholarios	Vernacular Greek (1628)
Louis of Granada's Guide for Sinners	Vernacular Greek (1628)
Georgian Dictionary	Georgian & Italian (1629)
Caryophilis' Rejection of Gerganos' Catechism	Vernacular Greek & Latin (1631)
Caryophilis' Refutation of Lukaris' Confession of Faith	Latin (1631)
Filippo Guadagnoli's Apology for Christianity	Latin with Arabic (1631)
Tommaso da Novara's Arabic Grammar	Latin with Arabic (1631)

Lukaris' *Confession* caused boisterous reactions all over Europe and the Propaganda invested a lot of effort in countering its effects. In 1632, for example, it pub-

51 The first catalogue of the Propaganda's printing press, compiled by Giovanni Domenico Verusio, its superintendent, lists 80 volumes in a variety of languages: *Elenchus librorum Sive Typis, sive impensis Sacræ Congregationis de Fide propaganda impressorum, qui modo in eiusdem Sacræ Congregationis Typographico reperiuntur*, Rome, 1639. For the Greek books, see Z. N. Tsirpanlis, "I libri greci pubblicati dalla 'Sacra Congregatio de Propaganda Fide' (XVII sec.) (Contributo allo studio dell'umanesimo religioso)", *Balkan Studies*, 15/2, 1974, p. 204–224 (Greek version: "Hoi hellēnikes ekdoseis tēs 'Sacra Congregatio de Propaganda Fide' (17os ai.) (Symbolē stē meletē tou thrēskeutikou oumanismou)", *Parnassos*, 16, 1974, p. 508–532); I. Korinthios, "Hoi hellēnikes ekdoseis tou Typographeiou tēs Propaganda Fide", *Parnassos*, 19, 1977, p. 247–262.

lished Caryophilis' refutation in demotic and literary Greek respectively; since the readers may have been wary of a Catholic Greek, the volume in demotic did not mention the name of the author.[52] However, the *Confession* only fueled the Propaganda's ire: what triggered it was the setting up of a Greek printing press in Constantinople, under the patronage of Lukaris, in June 1627.

Built from scratch in London by the Kefalonian-born Nikodimos Metaxas, the printing press had been active for a couple of months before being confiscated by the Ottoman authorities, in January 1628. To the Propaganda's distress, however, Metaxas had managed to bring to Constantinople several crates of books printed in London, in 1624–1625 and (perhaps) Kefalonia, in 1627.[53]

> *In questi giorni passati più che un mese venne un'altra peste. Un monacho greco dall'isola di Cephalonia sottoposta ai Venetiani di casa richa e principale, se ne porti de là, e andò in Inghilterra, dove studiò et haveva stampato gli antichi errori degli scismatici, e d'alcuni moderni, portò quà 24 casse piene di libri simili, e la stampa ancora, per stampare di novo: cosa che mai venne in tutta Grecia: hora sta con l'Ambasciator d'Inghilterra...*[54]

In 1626, Caryophilis published a *Confutation* of one of the incriminated texts, namely Neilos Kabasilas' treatise *On the Primacy of the Pope*. According to Ingoli, the volume, which has been subsidized by the Cardinal prefect of the Propaganda himself, proved very useful in Aleppo.[55] Yet the threat posed by a Constantinopolitan Greek printing press controlled by Lukaris could no longer be ignored.

---

52 Demotic Greek: *Katakrisis tēs homologies tēs pisteōs, malista tēs kakopistias tōn Kalbinistōn, hopou etypōthēken eis onoma Kyrillou Patriarchou Kōnstantinoupoleōs*, Rome, 1632; Caryophilis himself requested that his name is not mentioned: Tsirpanlis, "I libri greci", p. 212–213 (note 9). Literary Greek: *Apodokimasia kai katakrisis tēs ep' onomati Kyrillou Patriarchou Kōnstantinoupoleōs ekdotheisēs homologies tēs pisteōs, eitoun apistias tōn Kalbinistōn hē syn-ēptai, kai hē tōn anathematismōn par' autou dē tou Kyrillou palai ekphōnēthentōn aporripsis*, Rome, 1632 (it was reprinted by the Propaganda in 1671). See Legrand, *Bibliographie hellénique*, vol. I, p. 304–305 (No. 216), 305–06 (No. 217); Legrand, *Bibliographie hellénique ou description raisonnée des ouvrages publiés par des Grecs au dix-septième siècle*, vol. II, Paris, 1894, p. 265 (No. 497).

53 Except for the *Book called Confirmation of Truth* (*Biblion tou orthou logou, bebaiōsis kalou-menon*), which was recently signaled in the Iakovatios Library in Lixouri (Kefalonia), all other volumes are present in the Library of the Romanian Academy and the Library of the Holy Synod of the Romanian Orthodox Church (both in Bucharest).

54 APF – SOCG 270, f. 177r, 179r (Canachio Rossi to Ingoli –September 10, 1627).

55 "*Et è ben certo, che 'l solo libro scritto da Mons.ʳᵉ Carcofilio sopradetto per confutar Nilo stam-pato a spese del Sig.ʳᵉ Card.ˡᵉ Ludovisi in Francia, ha operato gran frutto in Aleppo nel render capaci della verità Cattolica gl'intendenti*", Ingoli, *Relazione*, p. 286. For the *Antirrhēsis pros Neilon ton Thessalonikēs peri tēs arches tou Papa / Confutatio Nili Thessalonicensis de primatu Papæ*, Paris, 1626, see Legrand, *Bibliographie hellénique*, vol. I, p. 216–218 (No. 155).

Tab. 2: Works printed for or by Nikodimos Metaxas (1624–1628)[56].

Gregorios Palamas' Apodictic Treatises on the Procession of the Holy Spirit (Fig. 1); Georgios-Gennadios Scholarios' First Treatise on the Procession of the Holy Spirit (Fig. 2); Dialogue between a Greek and a Latin or an Orthodox and a Latin (ascribed to Maximos Margounios but actually compiled by Georgios Moschabar) (Fig. 3).	London: William Jones 1624
Meletios Pigas' (Four) Letters against the Primacy of the Pope (Fig. 4); Georgios Koressios' Dispute with a Certain Monk (Fig. 5); Neilos Kabasilas (two texts, including a treatise against the primacy of the Pope) (Fig. 6); An Anti-Latin Anonymous Dialogue between a Greek and a Cardinal; Barlaam of Calabria's Treatise against the Primacy of the Pope; an Anonymous Treatise against the Purgatory (actually, the work of Mark of Ephesus and Bessarion of Nicaea); Gabriel Seviros' First Part of a Polemical Trilogy Directed against Antonio Possevino, SJ (Fig. 7).	London: Eliot's Court Press 1624
Theophilos Korydaleos' on Epistolary Types; Aphthonios' Preliminary Exercises; Korydaleos' Explanation of Rhetoric.	London: William Stansby 1625
Book called Confirmation of Truth (the canonization dossier of Saint Gerasimos the New), which includes a Brief Exposition of the Orthodox Faith.	Omala Monastery in Kefalonia 1627
Lukaris' Brief Treatise Against the Jews, preceded by Margounios' (Seven) Sermons.	Kefalonia (Lukaris' treatise) & Constantinople (the rest), 1627

Such innovation, warned the papal agents, posed a threat to the nation and the Church, because "all the wicked, pervert and ignorant Greek monks, false messiahs and fake prophets had the freedom and permission to print a thousand heresies and schisms."[57] Lukaris unlawfully canonized unworthy saints, such as Gerasimos "the New" of Kefalonia. He printed anti-Latin books in order to sway

---

56 I adopted the chronology proposed by Letterio Augliera; however, I did not include in the list works that may have been printed in Kefalonia – "*un libretto picciolo di 150 carte*" containing "*diversi laudi alla Beata Vergine*", "*uno picciolo che erano alcuni versi della messa*", and some small catechism –, because no copy survived (Augliera, *Libri politica religione*, p. 159, 207–208, 210).

57 The arrival of the printing press "*sarà la totale ruina della nostra povera natione, perche haveranno adesso libertà et licenza tutti i maligni, perversi, et ignoranti calogeri græci pseudochristi et pseudoprofetæ di stampare mille heræsie et schismi*": APF – SOCG 270, f. 238–239 (Gieremia Barbarigo, "Arcivescovo græco di Paronexia", to Cardinal Ludovisi – August 7, 1627).

the "poor souls of the simple Greeks" from the "true way of the Catholic faith."[58] He intended to introduce "new dogmas and heresies, schisms and errors."[59] In short, "this new Antipope and Antichrist" had to be deposed for the Oriental Church to change (ironically, the accuser used the verb *riformare* in order to designate the anticipated aim).[60] Consequently, the Propaganda suspended the ongoing negotiations for church union with Lukaris and amplified its efforts to depose the patriarch.

The alumni of the pontifical Greek College spearheaded the attack. Since Metaxas' Greek printing press published a plethora of anti-Latin tracts, the Propaganda decided to publish – preferably in vernacular Greek[61] – pro-Unionist texts. Ingoli's *Report* mentions two such works: a bilingual Greek-Latin edition of the *Acts* of the Council of Florence and related materials, which may date from 1626, and the translation in vernacular Greek of an *Explanation* of the Florentine Decree of Union allegedly written by Scholarios, dated 1628.[62] Involved in

---

58 "*Tutto con intentione di slontanare le povere anime de' semplici græci dalla vera strada della fede catholica*": APF – SOCG 270, f. 238–239.

59 "*Questo nostro Patriarcha... machina con mille modi et pretende di estirpar la fede catholica da cuori de' semplici græci della nostra misera natione, et introdurre novi dogmi et hæresie, scismi, et errori*": APF – SOCG 270, f. 237, 240 (Barbarigo to Pietro Arcudi – August 12, 1627).

60 "*Il Patriarcha bisogna che sia privato del Patriarchato, se volia che la chiesa orientale si riformi*", APF – SOCG 270, f. 236 (Barbarigo to Ingoli – 8 August 1627); "*Stà et minaccia grandissima ruina, alla natione, et à tutto Oriente, se non si leva dal mezzo questo novo Antipapa et Antichristo*", APF – SOCG 270, f. 237, 240.

61 Papadopoulos, "Biblia", p. 41–42 (note 10); Papadopoulos, "Agnōsta erga Hellēnōn", p. 293 (note 7).

62 Ingoli, *Relazione*, p. 285. Printed by Stefano Paolini, *Hē hagia kai oikoumenikē en Phlōrentia Synodos tomos prōtos / Sancta generalis Florentina Synodus. Tomus primus* and *Tēs hagias kai oikoumenikēs en Phlōrentia Synodou tomos deuteros / Sanctæ generalis Florentinæ Synodi. Tomus secundus* are not dated: Legrand, *Bibliographie hellénique*, vol. I, p. 265–266 (No. 187). For 1626, see I. Herklotz, "The Academia Basiliana. Greek Theology, Ecclesiastical History and the Union of Churches in Barberini Rome", in L. Mochi Onori, S.Schütze, F. Solinas (eds.), *I Barberini e la cultura europea del Seicento. Atti del Convegno internazionale Palazzo Barberini alle Quatro Fontane, 7–11 dicembre 2004*, Rome, 2007, p. 152 (note 54). The 1639 *Elenchus librorum* indicate Caryophilis as translator into Latin. As for the *Hermēneia tōn pente kephalaiōn, hopou periechei hē apophasis tēs hagias kai oikoumenikēs Synodou tēs Phlorentias, kamōmenē eusebōs palaiothen, Kai metaglōttismenē eis to idiōtikon milēma dia koinēn ōpheleian. Hē hopoia ēton hellēnika typōmenē pseudōs eis to onoma Gennadiou Patriarchou / Explanatio quinque capitum definitionis S. generalis Florentinæ Synodi, Iam olim piè conscripta, Nunc verò ad communem Græcorum utilitatem vernaculo eorum sermone donata. Falso antea Gennadio Patriarchæ adscripta*, Rome, 1628, both the 1639 *Elenchus librorum* and Ingoli cited Caryophilis as translator into simple Greek. See also Legrand, *Bibliographie hellénique*, vol. I, p. 259–260 (No. 181).

both projects as editor and translator, Caryophilis might have also authored an *Account* of the Council of Florence, in vernacular Greek.[63]

In the following years, other authors joined the fight and the number of books increased. As convincingly argued by Vasileios Tsakiris, Lukaris' enterprise functioned as catalyst for the Propaganda.[64]

3. Conclusions

Lukaris was not the Calvinist his adversaries wanted him to be. Many of his adversaries – Barbarigo, for example[65] – had personal, interested motives to slander him. Gerganos was neither Lutheran nor an avatar of the patriarch.[66] None of the texts published by Metaxas were "heretical," despite the fact that some of them followed Protestant models: for example, in the case of the *Brief Exposition of the Orthodox Faith*, the editor reprinted a 1570 Genevan edition by Théodore de Bèze. But the Patriarch's projects clashed with the Roman ones.

Ingoli had a clear view on the Propaganda's "methods and ways to disseminate faith," which as enduring first secretary he meticulously shaped from 1622 to 1649.[67] Within this system, the printing press played a key role: publishing

---

63 *Diēgēsis peri tēs hagias kai oikoumenikēs Synodou tēs Phlorentias pros ekeinous hopou tēn sykophantousi me pollen pseudologian*, Rome, 1628. The *Account* is anonymous: Legrand, *Bibliographie hellénique*, vol. I, p. 264–265 (No. 186).

64 Tsakiris, "Ho rolos tou typographeiou". See also Tsirpanlis, "I libri greci"; Papadopoulos, "Biblia"; V. Tsakiris, *Die gedruckten griechischen Beichtbücher zur Zeit der Türkenherrschaft. Ihr kirchen politischer Entstehungszusammenhang und ihre Quellen*, Berlin, 2009.

65 E. Gara, O. Olar, "Confession-Building and Authority: The Great Church and the Ottoman State in the First Half of the 17th Century", in T. Krstić, D. Terzioğlu (eds.), *Entangled Confessionalizations? Dialogic Perspectives on the Politics of Piety and Community-Building in the Ottoman Empire, 15th–18th Centuries*, Piscataway, 2022, p. 179–180.

66 N. Pissis, "Zacharias Gerganos in Wittenberg: New Findings and Considerations," in K. Sarris, N. Pissis, M. Pechlivanos (eds.), *Confessionalization and/as Knowledge Transfer in the Greek Orthodox Church*, Wiesbaden, 2021, p. 47–77.

67 "Mezzi e vie della Congregazione de Propaganda Fide per la propagazione della fede" is the title of a report written ca. 1640 (APF – *Congregazioni Particolari* 3, f. 248r–49v): J.Metzler, "Mezzi e modi per l'evangelizzazione dei popoli secondo Francesco Ingoli", *Pontificia Universitas Urbaniana. Annales*, 341, 1967-1968, p. 38–50; W. Henkel, "Francesco Ingoli, erster Sekretär der Propaganda Fide, über Druckerpresse und Mission (II)", *Communicatio Socialis*, 3/2, 1970, p. 170–171. For Ingoli's career and impact, see N. Kowalski, "Il testamento di Monsignor Ingoli, primo segretario della Sacra Congregazione 'de Propaganda Fide'", *Neue Zeitschrift für Missionsgeschichte*, 19/1963, p. 272–283; J. Metzler, "Francesco Ingoli, der erste Sekretär der Kongregation (1578–1649)," in *Sacræ Congregationis de Propaganda Fide memoria rerum*, vol. I/1,

the right books equaled fighting the "darkness of ignorance."[68] Therefore, Ingoli defended it repeatedly: it was costly – the amassing of 23 complete printing sets for 23 languages had cost 18000 scudi and the monthly budget, regarded as insufficient, was 100 scudi[69] –, but it was a crucial missionary tool. In November 1642 and February 1644, he criticized the decision of Pope Paul V to discontinue the activity of the Vatican printing press: the edition of the church councils curated by Bellarmino should have been followed by the edition of the Greek Fathers of the Church. Instead, corrupt patristic editions had been printed in England and were disseminated in Greece together with other wicked books by Lukaris, the heretical Constantinopolitan patriarch.[70] Lukaris' successor, Kyrillos II Kontaris confiscated and burned several copies of such works printed in England, many of them found among the possessions of his predecessor, but the real solution was to edit the Church Fathers in Rome.[71]

The challenge to preserve the printing press went hand in hand with the struggle for monopoly: the Propaganda wanted to control printing in Oriental languages. In 1628, it blocked projects for printing presses operated by Capuchins in Constantinople and Lebanon, despite the excellent collaboration with the order (the Capuchin Père Joseph de Paris, prefect for all French Capuchin missions, actually invoked as an argument the need to counter Lukaris' editorial plans).[72]

Although Ingoli's *Report* considered him illegitimate and restricted his authority to Constantinople, Greece and the Islands, Lukaris was by title an "ecumenical" patriarch. His church had rejected the provisions of the Council

---

p. 197–243 (Italian version: Ingoli, *Relazione*, p. 291–332); Tosi, "La memoria perduta". For an overview, see Pizzorusso, "Francesco Ingoli", in *DBI*, 62, 2004, p. 388–391.

68 Ingoli, *Relazione*, p. 286. Books and reading were increasingly important for the economy of redemption: B. Heyberger, "Livres et pratique de la lecture chez les chrétiens (Syrie, Liban) XVIIe–XVIIIe siècles", *Revue des Mondes Musulmans et de la Méditerranée*, 87–88, 1999, p. 209–223.

69 Henkel, "Francesco Ingoli (II)", p. 161, 166–167, 170–171. An income of 100 scudi a year was "reasonable"; Caravaggio received 1½ scudi for the *Boy Bitten by a Lizzard* and 1000 scudi for the *Adoration of the Shepherds* and the *Raising of Lazarus* in Messina: R. E. Spear, "Scrambling for Scudi: Notes on Painters' Earnings in Early Baroque Rome", *The Art Bulletin*, 85/2, 2003, p. 312–313.

70 Henkel, "Francesco Ingoli (I)", p. 64; Henkel, "Francesco Ingoli (II)", p. 163–164. For the *Editio Romana* of the Church Councils, printed in 1608–1612, see F. Malasevic, *Inventing the Council Inside the Apostolic Library: The Organization of Curial Erudition in Late Cinquecento Rome*, Berlin, 2021, p. 178–189.

71 Henkel, "Francesco Ingoli (II)", p. 164–165, 168.

72 APF – *Acta* 6 (1628-1629), f. 11v; L. Dedouvres, *Le père Joseph polémiste. Ses premiers écrits (1623–1626)*, Paris, 1895, p. 447; Henkel, "The Polyglot Printing-office", p. 338.

of Ferrara-Florence in 1483-1484, so he did not feel compelled to abide by them. In fact, he considered Rome's constant intrusions in the name of the true faith to be dangerous. And he had his own ideas with regard to the salvation of his flock.

Printing in Greek in Constantinople was one of them. By means of a polemical approach, which had the additional advantage of avoiding a conflict with Venice over the printing of liturgical texts, it showed that the "Greeks" were neither heretics, nor schismatics: they were orthodox. When the plan fell short, alternative options, namely England and Muscovy, were taken into consideration. The Muscovite project failed and the books printed in England only reached Constantinople after Lukaris' execution by the Ottomans in 1638. Still, the fight over books is illustrative of the importance ascribed to the printing press for confession-building: both Lukaris and the Propaganda considered it more effective than, say, a confession of Faith. After all, it shed light into the abyss of ignorance.

This research was funded by the European Research Council under the European Union's Horizon 2020 research and innovation program (ORTHPOL project; grant agreement no. 950287).

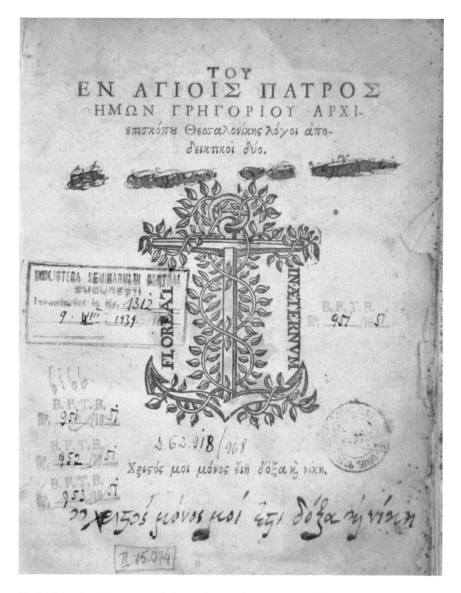

Fig. 1: Gregorios Palamas, *Apodictic Treatises on the Procession of the Holy Spirit*, London: William Jones, 1624 (B.S.S.).

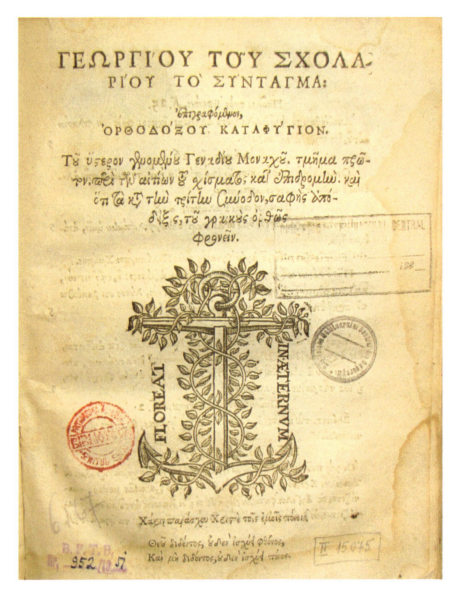

Fig. 2: Georgios-Gennadios Scholarios' first *Treatise on the Procession of the Holy Spirit*, London: William Jones, 1624 (B.S.S.).

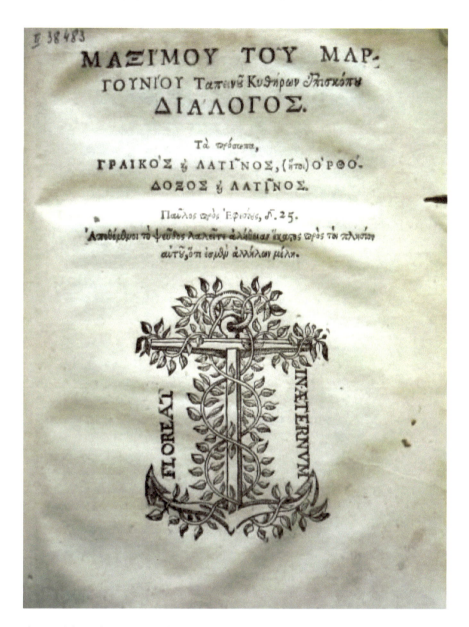

Fig. 3: *Dialogue between a Greek and a Latin or an Orthodox and a Latin* ascribed to Maximos Margounios, London: William Jones, 1624 (B.A.R.).

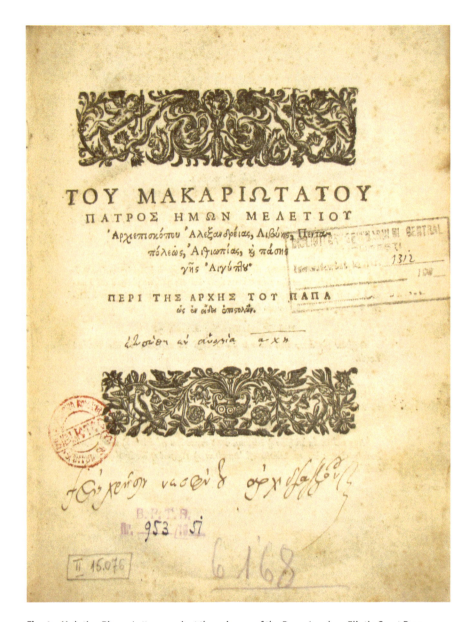

Fig. 4: Meletios Pigas, *Letters against the primacy of the Pope*, London: Eliot's Court Press 1624 (B.S.S.).

Fig. 5: Georgios Koressios, *Dispute with a certain monk*, London: Eliot's Court Press 1624 (B.S.S.).

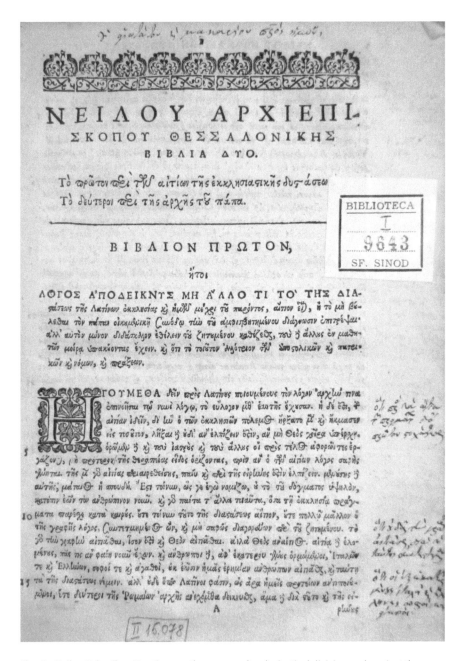

Fig. 6: Neilos Kabasilas, *Treatises on the causes of ecclesiastical division and against the primacy of the Pope*, London: Eliot's Court Press 1624, (B.S.S.).

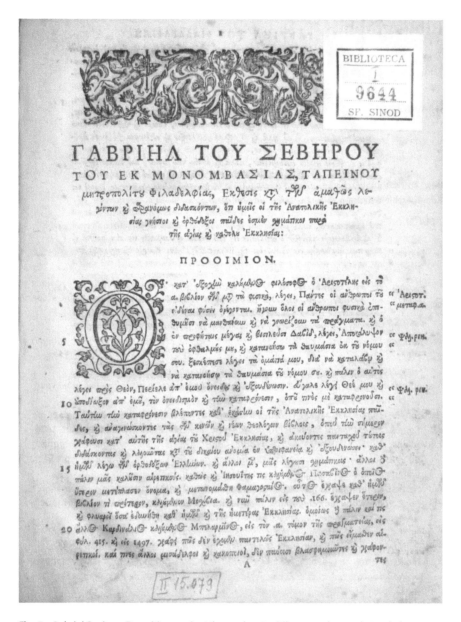

Fig. 7: Gabriel Seviros, *Exposition against those who stupidly say and wrongly teach that we, the genuine and orthodox children of the Oriental Church, are in fact schismatics outside the Holy and Whole Church*, London: Eliot's Court Press 1624, (B.S.S.).

Bibliography

Primary Sources

Unpublished

Vatican City, Archivio Storico de Propaganda Fide (APF) – *Acta* 3 (1622–1625), *Acta* 6
(1628–1629); *Congregazioni Particolari* 3; *Istruttioni diverse degl'anni 1623 sino al 1638*;
Scritture Originali riferite nelle Congregazioni Generali (SOCG) 263, 270; *Visite e Collegi* 1.
Kew, The National Archives – *State Papers* 97/13.
Rome, Archivio di Stato di Roma – *Archivio Santacroce* 85.

Published

Albania Sacra. Geistliche Visitationsberichte aus Albanien, vol. III. *Diözese Sappa*, edited by
Peter Bartl. Wiesbaden: Harrassowitz, 2014.
*Biblia Sacra Arabica Sacræ Congregationis de Propaganda fide jussu edita. Additis è regione
Bibliis Latinis Vulgatis*, vol. I–III. Rome: Typis Sacræ Congregationis de Propaganda Fide,
1671.
(Bull of Union with the Armenians.) *Concordia Armenorum cum S.R. Eccl. Et declaratio
articulorum septem, novæ legis Sacramenta, pleraque alia concernentium. Sub Eugenio
Papa IV. in Concilio Florentino anno 1439. facta. Iussu S.D.N. Gregorij 15. & Sac. Congre-
gationis de Propaganda Fide impressa*. Rome: Stefano Paolini, 1623.
(Canonization of St. Gerasimos the New.) Βιβλίον τοῦ ὀρθοῦ λόγου, βεβαίωσις καλούμενον
[Kefalonia (Omala Monastery): Nikodimos Metaxas, 1627].
Caryophilis, Ioannis Matthaeos. *Antirrhēsis pros Neilon ton Thessalonikēs peri tēs arches tou
Papa / Confutatio Nili Thessalonicensis de primatu Papæ*. Paris: Adrian Taupinart, 1626.
Caryophilis, Ioannis Matthaeos. *Censura confessionis fidei, seu potius perfidiæ Calvinianæ,
quæ nomine Cyrilli Patriarchæ Constantinopolitani edita circumfertur*. Rome: Typis Sacræ
Congregationis de Propaganda Fide, 1631 (reprinted in 1671).
Caryophilis, Ioannis Matthaeos. *Elenchos tēs pseudochristianikēs katēchēseōs Zachariou
tou Gerganou apo tēn Artēn / Refutatio Pseudochristianæ Catechesis editæ a Zacharia
Gergano Græco*. Rome: Typis Sacræ Congregationis de Propaganda Fide, 1631.
Caryophilis, Ioannis Matthaeos. *Apodokimasia kai katakrisis tēs ep' onomati Kyrillou
Patriarchou Kōnstantinoupoleōs ekdotheisēs homologies tēs pisteōs, eitoun apistias
tōn Kalbinistōn hē synēptai, kai hē tōn anathematismōn par' autou dē tou Kyrillou palai
ekphōnēthentōn aporripsis*. Rome: Typis Sacræ Congregationis de Propaganda Fide, 1632
(reprinted in 1671).
Caryophilis, Ioannis Matthaeos. *Katakrisis tēs homologies tēs pisteōs, malista tēs kakopistias
tōn Kalbinistōn, hopou etypōthēken eis onoma Kyrillou Patriarchou Kōnstantinoupoleōs*.
Rome: Typis Sacræ Congregationis de Propaganda Fide, 1632.
(Council of Florence.) *Diēgēsis peri tēs hagias kai oikoumenikēs Synodou tēs Phlorentias pros
ekeinous hopou tēn sykophantousi me pollen pseudologian*. Rome: Typis Sacræ Congregationis de Propaganda Fide, 1628.

(Council of Florence.) *Hermēneia tōn pente kephalaiōn, hopou periechei hē apophasis tēs hagias kai oikoumenikēs Synodou tēs Phlorentias, kamōmenē eusebōs palaiothen, Kai metaglōttismenē eis to idiōtikon milēma dia koinēn ōpheleian. Hē hopoia* ēton *hellēnika typōmenē pseudōs eis to onoma Gennadiou Patriarchou / Explanatio quinque capitum definitionis S. generalis Florentinæ Synodi, Iam olim piè conscripta, Nunc verò ad communem Græcorum utilitatem vernaculo eorum sermone donata. Falso antea Gennadio Patriarchæ adscripta.* Rome: Typis Sacræ Congregationis de Propaganda Fide, 1628.

(Council of Florence.) *Hē hagia kai oikoumenikē en Phlōrentia Synodos tomos prōtos / Sancta generalis Florentina Synodus. Tomus primus.* Rome: Stefano Paolini [1626]; *Hē hagia kai oikoumenikē en Phlōrentia Synodos tomos deuteros / Sanctæ generalis Florentinæ Synodi. Tomus secundus.* Rome: Stefano Paolini [1626].

Dittionario giorgiano e italiano composto da Stefano Paolini con l'aiuto del M.R.P.D. Niceforo Irbachi Giorgiano, Monaco di S. Basilio. Ad uso de' missionarii della Sagra Congregatione de Propaganda Fide. Rome: Stefano Paolini, 1629.

Dokumente për historinë e Shqipërisë (1623–1653), edited by Injac Zamputti. Sankt Gallen: Albanisches Institut & Prishtina: Faik Konica, 2015.

Draganović, Krunoslav. "Izvješće apostolskog vizitatora Petra Masarechija o prilikama katol(ičkog) naroda u Bugarskoj, Srbiji, Srijemu, Slavoniji i Bosni g. 1623. i 1624". *Starine* 39, 1948, p. 1–48.

Granada, Luis de. *Hodēgia tōn hamartōlōn tou patros Aloysiou tou Granata metaglōttismenē eis rhōmaikēn glōssan. Dia meson tou patros Andreou tou Rhentiou tou Chiou. Ek tēs syntrophias tou Iēsou.* Rome: Stampa della Sacra Congregazione de Propaganda Fide, 1628.

Guadagnoli, Filippo. *Apologia pro Christiana Religione... respondetur ad objectiones Ahmed filii Zin Alabedin, Persæ Asphahensis, contentas in Libro inscripto Politor speculi.* Rome: Typis Sacræ Congregationis de Propaganda Fide, 1631 (reprinted in 1637 with an Arabic translation).

Hofmann, SJ, Georg. *Athos e Roma.* Rome: PIOS, 1925.

Hofmann, SJ, Georg. *Rom und Athosklöster.* Rome: PIOS, 1926.

Hofmann, SJ, Georg. *Sinai und Rom.* Rome: PIOS, 1927.

Hofmann, SJ, Georg. *Il Vicariato Apostolico di Costantinopoli.* Rome: PIOS, 1935.

Hofmann, SJ, Georg. *Vescovadi cattolici della Grecia,* vol. I. *Chios.* Rome: PIOS, 1934; vol. II. *Tinos.* Rome: PIOS, 1936; vol. III. *Syros.* Rome: PIOS, 1937; vol. IV. *Naxos.* Rome: PIOS, 1938; vol. V. *Thera (Santorino).* Rome: PIOS, 1941.

Hofmann, SJ, Georg. *Rom und der Athos. Briefwechsel zwischen dem Missionar auf dem Athos Nikolaus Rossi und der Kongregation de Propaganda Fide.* Rome: PIOS, 1954.

Ingoli, Francesco. *Relazione delle Quattro Parti del Mondo,* edited by Fabio Tosi. Vatican City: Urbaniana University Press, 1999.

Jačov, Marko. *Spisi kongregacije za propagandu vere u Rimu o Srbima,* vol. I *(1622–1644).* Belgrade: Srpska Akademija Nauka i Imetnosti, 1986.

Korydaleos, Theophilos. *Ekthesis peri epistolikōn typōn en hē prosetethēsan kai Aphthoniou progymnasmata kai hetera Ekthesis peri Rhētorikēs.* London: William Stansby, 1625.

Lukaris, Kyrillos. *Tou makariōtatou kai sophōtatou patros hēmōn Papa kai Patriarchou Alexandreias, ta nun de oikoumenikou Kōnstantinoupoleōs Kyrillou syntomos pragmateia kata Ioudaiōn en haplē dialektō pros Geōrgion ton Pargan.* [Kefalonia & Constantinople: Nikodimos Metaxas, 1627.]

Novara, Tommaso da. *Grammatica arabica al-Ajurrūmīya Agrumia appellata. Cum versione Latina, ac dilucida expositione.* Rome: Typis Sacræ Congregationis de Propaganda Fide, 1631.

Palamas, Gregorios, Georgios-Gennadios Scholarios and Maximos Margounios. *Tou en hagiois patros hēmōn Grēgoriou archiepiskopou Thessalonikēs logoi apodeiktikoi duo / Geōrgiou tou Scholariou to Syntagma: epigraphomenon Orthodoxou kataphygion. Tou hysteron genomenou Gennadiou monachou. Tmēma proton. Peri tou aition tou schimatos kat' epidromēn. Kai hoti ta kata tēn tritēn Synodon, saphēs apodeixis, tous Graikous orthōs phronein / Maximou tou Margouniou tapeinou Kythērōn episkopou Dialogos. Ta prosōpa, Graikos kai Latinos (ētoi) Orthodoxos kai Latinos.* [London: William Jones 1624.]

Pigas, Meletios, Georgios Koressios, Neilos Kabasilas, Barlaam of Calabria, Gabriel Seviros and two anonymous authors. *Tou makariōtatou patros hēmōn Meletiou archiepiskopou Alexandreias, Libyēs, Pentapoleōs, Aithiopias, kai pasēs gēs Aigyptou peri tēs arches tou Papa hōs en eidei epistolōn / Kyriou Geōrgiou Koressiou tou Chiou Dialexis meta tinos tōn Frarōn / Neilou archiepiskopou Thessalonikēs biblia duo. To proton peri tōn aition tēs ekklēsiastikēs dystaseōs. To deuteron peri tēs arches tou Papa / Gabriēl tou Sebērou tou ek Monombasias, tapeinou mētropolitiou Philadelphias, Ekthesis kata tōn amathōs legontōn kai paranomōs didaskontōn, hoti hēmeis hoi tēs Anatolikēs Ekklēsias gnēsioi kai orthodoxoi paides semen schēmatikoi para tēs hagias kai katholou Ekklēsias.* [London: Eliot's Court Press 1624.]

Verusio, Giovanni Domenico. *Elenchus librorum Sive Typis, sive impensis Sacræ Congregationis de Fide propaganda impressorum, qui modo in eiusdem Sacræ Congregationis Typographico reperiuntur.* Rome: Typis Sacræ Congregationis de Propaganda Fide, 1639.

Secondary Sources

Argyriou, Astérios. "Zacharie Gerganos et Jean-Matthieu Caryophyllos: un cas typique d'aliénation de la pensée orthodoxe dans la première moitié du XVIIᵉ siècle". In *Communications grecques présentées au VIᵉ Congrès international des études du Sud-Est européen, Sofia, 30 août – 5 septembre 1989.* Athens: Comité national grec des études du Sud-Est européen – Centre d'études du Sud-Est européen, 1990, p. 183–192.

Augliera, Lettero. *Libri politica religione nel Levante del Seicento. La tipografia di Nicodemo Metaxas primo editore di testi greci nell'Oriente ortodosso.* Venice: Istituto Veneto di scienze, lettere ed arti, 1996 [Greek version: *Biblia politikē thrēskeia stēn Anatolē ton 17o aiōna. To typographeio tou Nikodēmou Metaxa prōtou ekdotē Hellēnikōn keimenōn stēn orthodoxē Anatolē,* trans. Stathis Birtachas. Athens: Topikē Enōsē Dēmōn kai Koinotētōn Kephalonias kai Ithakēs, 2006].

Binasco, Matteo. *Viaggiatori e missionari nel Seicento. Pacifique de Provins fra Levante, Acadia e Guyana (1622–1648).* Novi Ligure: Città del Silenzio, 2006.

Catalano, Alessandro. "La politica della curia romana in Boemia dalla strategia del nunzio Carlo Carafa a quella del cappuccino Valeriano Magni". In Richard Bösel, Grete Klingenstein, Alexander Koller (eds.), *Kaiserhof – Papsthof (16.–18. Jahrhundert).* Vienna: ÖAW, 2006, p. 105–121.

Dedouvres, Louis. *Le père Joseph polémiste. Ses premiers écrits (1623–1626).* Paris: Alphonse Picard & Fils, 1895.

Feci, Simona. "Gesualdo Ascanio". In *Dizionario Biografico degli Italiani (DBI)* 53, 1999, p. 492–495.

Féghali, Paul. "The Holy Books in Arabic: The example of the Propaganda Fide Edition". In Sara Binay, Stefan Leder (eds.), *Translating the Bible into Arabic: Historical, Text-Critical and Literary Aspects*. Beirut: Orient Institut Beirut, 2012, p. 35–52.

Frazee, Charles A. *Catholics and Sultans: The Church and the Ottoman Empire 1453–1923*. Cambridge: Cambridge University Press, 1983.

Gara, Eleni, Ovidiu Olar. "Confession-Building and Authority: The Great Church and the Ottoman State in the First Half of the 17th Century". In Tijana Krstić , Derin Terzioğlu (eds.), *Entangled Confessionalizations? Dialogic Perspectives on the Politics of Piety and Community-Building in the Ottoman Empire, 15th–18th Centuries*. Piscataway, NJ: Gorgias Press, 2022, p. 159–214.

Giordano, Silvano. "Il mondo di Propaganda Fide nelle istruzioni di Francesco Ingoli (1623–1648)". In Guido Braun (ed.), *Diplomatische Wissenskulturen der Frühen Neuzeit. Erfahrungsräume und Orte der Wissensproduktioned*, Berlin/Boston: De Gruyter, 2018, p. 215–324.

Girard, Aurélien. "Des manuels de langue entre mission et érudition orientaliste au XVIIe siècle: les grammaires de l'arabe des Caracciolini". In Irene Fosi, Giovanni Pizzorusso (eds.), *L'Ordine dei Chierici Regolari Minori (Caracciolini): religione e cultura in età postridentina. Atti del Convegno (Chieti, 11–12 aprile 2008)*. Casoria: Loffredo, 2010, p. 279–295.

Girard, Aurélien. "Le Collège maronite de Rome et les langues au tournant des XVIe et XVIIe siècles: éducation des chrétiens orientaux, science orientaliste et apologétique catholique". *Rivista storica italiana*, 132/1, 2020, p. 272–299.

Girard, Aurélien. "Teaching and Learning Arabic in Early Modern Rome: Shaping a Missionary Language". In Jan Loop, Alastair Hamilton, Charles Burnett (eds.), *The Teaching and Learning of Arabic in Early Modern Europe*. Leiden/Boston: Brill, 2017, p. 189–212.

Grafinger, Christine Maria. "Bildungspolitische Funktion der Biblioteca Apostolica Vaticana zu Beginn des 17. Jahrhunderts: ihre Bedeutung für die Franziskaner in der Orientmission", *Collectanea Franciscana*, 61/3-4, 1991, p. 587–604.

Guardi, Jolanda. "Tommaso Obicini". In David Thomas, John Chesworth (eds.), *Christian-Muslim Relations: A Bibliographical History*, vol. IX. *Western and Southern Europe (1600–1700)*. Leiden/Boston: Brill, 2017, p. 743–748.

Henkel, Willi. "Francesco Ingoli, erster Sekretär der Propaganda Fide, über Druckerpresse und Mission (I-II)". *Communicatio Socialis*, 3, 1970, p. 60–72, 160–173.

Henkel, Willi. "The Polyglot Printing-office of the Congregation". In Josef Metzler (ed.). *Sacræ Congregationis de Propaganda Fide memoria rerum: 350 anni a servizio delle missioni, 1622–1972*, vol. I/1. Rome/Freiburg/Vienna: Herder, 1971, p. 335–350.

Henkel, Willi. "Die Druckerei der Propaganda Fide im Dienste der Glaubensverbreitung". *Communicatio Socialis*, 9, 1976, p. 105–117, 217–231.

Herklotz, Ingo. "The Academia Basiliana. Greek Theology, Ecclesiastical History and the Union of Churches in Barberini Rome". In Lorenza Mochi Onori, Sebastian Schütze, Francesco Solinas (eds.), *I Barberini e la cultura europea del Seicento. Atti del Convegno internazionale Palazzo Barberini alle Quatro Fontane, 7–11 dicembre 2004*. Rome: De Luca, 2007, p. 147–154.

Heyberger, Bernard. "Livres et pratique de la lecture chez les chrétiens (Syrie, Liban) XVIIe–XVIIIe siècles". *Revue des Mondes Musulmans et de la Méditerranée* 87–88, 1999, p. 209–223.

Korinthios, Ioannis. "Hoi hellēnikes ekdoseis tou Typographeiou tēs Propaganda Fide". *Parnassos*, 19, 1977, p. 247–262.

Kowalski, Nicola. "Il testamento di Monsignor Ingoli, primo segretario della Sacra Congregazione 'de Propaganda Fide'". *Neue Zeitschrift* für *Missionsgeschichte*, 19, 1963, p. 272–283.

Krajcar, J. "The Greek College in the Years of Unrest (1604–1630)". *Orientalia Christianba Periodica*, 32/1, 1966, p. 5–38.

Legrand, Émile. *Bibliographie hellénique ou description raisonnée des ouvrages publiés par des Grecs au dix-septième siècle*, vol. I–II. Paris: Alphonse Picard & Fils, 1894.

Leman, Auguste. *Recueil des instructions générales aux nonces ordinaires de France de 1624 à 1634*. Lille: René Giard/Paris: Édouard Champion, 1920.

Louthan, Howard. "Mediating Confessions in Central Europe: The Ecumenical Activity of Valerian Magni, 1586–1661". *Journal of Ecclesiatical History*, 55/4, 2004, p. 681–699.

Malasevic, Filip. *Inventing the Council Inside the Apostolic Library: The Organization of Curial Erudition in Late Cinquecento Rome*. Berlin: De Gruyter Saur, 2021.

Metzler Josef (ed.). *Sacræ Congregationis de Propaganda Fide memoria rerum: 350 anni a servizio delle missioni, 1622–1972*, vol. I/1. Rome/Freiburg/Vienna: Herder, 1971; vol. III/2. Rome/Freiburg/Vienna: Herder, 1976.

Metzler, Josef. "Francesco Ingoli, der erste Sekretär der Kongregation (1578–1649)". In Josef Metzler (ed.). *Sacræ Congregationis de Propaganda Fide memoria rerum: 350 anni a servizio delle missioni, 1622–1972*, vol. I/1. Rome/Freiburg/Vienna: Herder, 1971, p. 197–243 [Italian version: Francesco Ingoli, *Relazione delle Quattro Parti del Mondo*, edited by Fabio Tosi. Vatican City: Urbaniana University Press, 1999, p. 291–332].

Metzler, Josef. "Mezzi e modi per l'evangelizzazione dei popoli secondo Francesco Ingoli". *Pontificia Universitas Urbaniana. Annales*, 341, 1967–1968, p. 38–50.

Molnár, Antal. *Le Saint-Siège, Raguse et les missions catholiques de la Hongrie ottomane 1572–1647*. Rome/Budapest: Accademia d'Ungheria – Bibliothèque Nationale de Hongrie / Société pour l'Encyclopédie de l'Histoire de l'Église en Hongrie, 2007.

Napoli, Alfredo di. *Valeriano Magni da Milano e la riforma ecclesiastica in Boemia attraverso la corrispondenza della Congregazione de Propaganda Fide (1626–1651)*. Milan: Biblioteca Francescana, 2015.

Olar, Ovidiu–Victor, *La Boutique de Théophile. Les relations du patriarche de Constantinople Kyrillos Loukaris (1570–1638) avec la Réforme*. Paris: EHESS – Centre d'études byzantines et néo-helléniques, 2019.

Palabıyık, Nil. "An Early Case of the Printer's Self-Censorship in Constantinople." *The Library*, 16/4, 2015, p. 381–404.

Palabıyık, Nil. "Redundant Presses and Recycled Woodcuts: The Journey of Printing Materials from London to Constantinople in the Seventeenth Century". *The Papers of the Bibliographical Society of America*, 110/3, 2016, p. 273–298.

Palabıyık, Nil. "A Public Debate on Cyril of Alexandria's Views on the Procession of the Holy Spirit in Seventeenth-Century Constantinople: The Jesuit Reaction to Nicodemos Metaxas's Greek Editions". *International Journal of the Classical Tradition*, 27/3, 2020, 427–448.

Papadopoulos, Thomas I., "Biblia Katholikōn kai biblia Orthodoxōn". *O Eranistēs*, 19, 1993, p. 36–65.

Papadopoulos, Thomas I. "Agnōsta erga Hellēnōn hypo ekdosē," in Konstantinos Sp. Staikos, Triantaphyllos E. Sklavenitis (eds.), *To entypo hellēniko biblio 15os–19os aiōnas. Praktika diethnous synedriou Delphoi, 16–20 Maiou 2001*. Athens: Κότινος, 2004, p. 291–308.

Papaïliaki, Niki. *Aspects de la mission catholique auprès des Grecs de l'Empire ottoman. Archives grecques inédites des Capucins de Paris (XVIIe–XVIIIe siècles)*. Paris: EPHE, 2009 (unpublished Ph.D. Thesis).

Papaïliaki-Gamelon, Niki. "Conflits et coexistences: les relations des missionaires capucins français avec les ecclésiastiques et les laïcs grecs au XVIIe siècle," in *Concurrences en mission. Propagandes, conflits, coexistences, XVIe–XXIe siècle. Actes du 31e Colloque du CRÉDIC tenu à Brive-la-Gaillarde (Corrèze, France) du 30 août au 3 septembre 2010*, ed. by Salvador Eyezo'o, Jean-François Zorn. Paris: Karthala, 2011, pp. 65–78.

Pektaş (Palabıyık), Nil Ozlem. *The First Greek Printing Press in Constantinople (1625–1628)* [Ph.D. Thesis]. Royal Holloway – University of London, 2014.

Pissis, Nikolas. "Zacharias Gerganos in Wittenberg: New Findings and Considerations". In Kostas Sarris, Nikolas Pissis, Miltos Pechlivanos (eds.), *Confessionalization and/ as Knowledge Transfer in the Greek Orthodox Church*. Wiesbaden: Harrassowitz, 2021, p. 47–77.

Pizzorusso, Giovanni. "Reti informative e strategie politiche tra la Francia, Roma e le missioni cattoliche nell'impero ottomano agli inizi del XVII secolo". In Giovanna Motta (ed.), *I Turchi, il Mediterraneo e l'Europa*. Milan: FrancoAngeli, 1998, p. 212–231.

Pizzorusso, Giovanni. "Francesco Ingoli". In *Dizionario Biografico degli Italiani* (*DBI*), 62, 2004, p. 388–391.

Pizzorusso, Giovanni. "I satelliti di Propaganda Fide: il Collegio Urbano e la Tipografia Poliglotta. Note di ricerca su due istituzioni culturali romane nel XVII secolo". *Mélanges de l'École Française de Rome. Italie et Méditerranée* 116/2, 2004, p. 471–498.

Pizzorusso, Giovanni. "La preparazione linguistica e controversistica dei missionari per l'Oriente islamico: scuole, testi, insegnanti a Roma e in Italia". In Bernard Heyberger, Mercedes García-Arenal, Emanuele Colombo, Paola Vismara (eds.), *L'Islam visto da Occidente. Cultura e religione del Seicento europeo di fronte all'Islam*. Milan: Marietti, 2009, p. 253–288.

Pizzorusso, Giovanni. "Tra cultura e missione. La congregazione de Propaganda Fide e le scuole di lingua araba nel XVII secolo". In Antonella Romano (ed.), *Rome et la science moderne entre Renaissance et Lumières*. Rome: École française de Rome, 2009, p. 121–152.

Pizzorusso, Giovanni. *Governare le missioni, conoscere il mondo nel XVII secolo. La Congregazione pontificia de Propaganda Fide*. Viterbo: Sette città, 2018.

Pizzorusso, Giovanni. "Le lingue a Roma: studio e pratica nei collegi missionari nella prima età moderna". *Rivista storica italiana* 132/1, 2020, p. 248–271.

Pizzorusso, Giovanni. "Note sul carattere sovranazionale / multinazionale del Collegio Urbano di Propaganda Fide". In Alessandro Boccolini, Matteo Sanfilippo, Péter Tusor (eds.), *I collegi per stranieri a/e Roma nell'età moderna*, vol. I. *Cinque-Settecento*. Viterbo: Sette città, 2023, p. 183–195.

Pizzorusso, Giovanni. *Propaganda fide*, vol. I. *La congregazione pontificia e la giurisdizione sulle missioni*. Rome: Edizioni di Storia e Letteratura, 2022.

Podskalsky, Gerhard. *Griechische Theologie in der Zeit der Türkenherrschaft (1453–1821). Die Orthodoxie im Spannungsfeld der nachreformatorischen Konfessionen des Westens*. Munich: C.H. Beck, 1988 [Greek version: Η Ελληνική θεολογία επί Τουρκοκρατίας 1453–1821. Η Ορθοδοξία στη σφαίρα επιρροής των Δυτικών Δογμάτων μετά τη Μεταρρύθμιση, trans. Georgios D. Metallinos. Athens: ΜΙΕΤ, 2005].

Ruiu, Adina. "Conflicting Visions of the Jesuit Missions to the Ottoman Empire, 1609–1628". *Journal of Jesuit Studies*, 1, 2014, p. 260–280.

Ruiu, Adina. "Missionaries and French Subjects: The Jesuits in the Ottoman Empire". In Ronnie Po-chia Hsia (ed.), *A Companion to Early Modern Catholic Global Missions*. Leiden/Boston: Brill, 2018, 181–204.

Santarelli, Giuseppe. "Missioni e missionari". In Vincenzo Criscuolo (ed.), *I Cappuccini. Fonti documentarie e narrative del primo secolo (1525–1619)*. Rome: Istituto Storico dei Cappuccini, 2020, p. 911–975.

Spear, Richard E. "Scrambling for Scudi: Notes on Painters' Earnings in Early Baroque Rome". *The Art Bulletin*, 85/2, 2003, p. 310–320.

Tiburcio, Alberto. "Filippo Guadagnoli". In David Thomas, John Chesworth (eds.), *Christian-Muslim Relations: A Bibliographical History*, vol. IX. *Western and Southern Europe (1600–1700)*. Leiden/Boston: Brill, 2017, p. 749–755.

Tosi, Fabio. "La memoria perduta di Propaganda Fide," in Francesco Ingoli, *Relazione delle Quattro Parti del Mondo*, edited by Fabio Tosi. Vatican City: Urbaniana University Press, 1999, p. VII–XLI.

Tsakiris, Vasileios. "Ho rolos tou typographeiou tou Loukarē stēn idrysē tou Hellēnikou typographeiou tēs Propaganda Fide". *O Eranistēs* 27, 2009, 53–67.

Tsakiris, Vasileios. *Die gedruckten griechischen Beichtbücher zur Zeit der Türkenherrschaft. Ihr kirchen politischer Entstehungszusammenhang und ihre Quellen*. Berlin: De Gruyter, 2009.

Tsirpanlis, Zacharias N. "I libri greci pubblicati dalla 'Sacra Congregatio de Propaganda Fide' (XVII sec.) (Contributo allo studio dell'umanesimo religioso)". *Balkan Studies* 15/2, 1974, p. 204–224 [Greek version: " Hoi hellēnikes ekdoseis tēs 'Sacra Congregatio de Propaganda Fide' (17os ai.) (Symbolē stē meletē tou thrēskeutikou oumanismou)". *Parnassos* 16, 1974, p. 508–532].

Tsirpanlis, Zacharias N. *To Hellēniko Kollegio tēs Rōmēs kai oi mathētes tou (1576-1700). Symbolē stē meletē tēs morphōtikēs politikēs tou Batikanou*. Thessaloniki: Patriarchikon Idruma Paterikōn Meletōn, 1980.

Windler, Christian. "Ambiguous Belongings: How Catholic Missionaries in Persia and the Roman Curia Dealt with *Communicatio in Sacris*". In Ronnie Po-chia Hsia (ed.), *A Companion to Early Modern Catholic Global Missions*. Leiden/Boston: Brill, 2018, p. 205–234.

Part 2. **Beyond Istanbul: The Printed-Book Culture
in Central and South-Eastern Europe**

Doru Bădără (†)

The Beginning of Printing and Print Culture in the Romanian Principalities

The printing press was introduced in the Romanian Principalities in 1508, at a time when Church Slavonic served as the liturgical and administrative language. Both Slavonic and the vernacular language, Romanian, employed the Cyrillic script.

Slavonic was the language of the first printed books, especially liturgical books, which formed the majority of printed works during the first two centuries of printing. Cyrillic script continued to be used for nearly one and a half centuries after Romanian became the official liturgical, literary and administrative language.

The first printed work, in November 1508, was, *Liturghierul*, a Slavonic *Book of the Divine Liturgies* (Fig. 1).[1] It was printed by the Montenegrin hieromonk Macarie (Makarios), who had already printed five books before the year 1500, when he took refuge in Wallachia. The book is a small in-4° consisting of 128 unnumbered pages decorated with headpieces and ornate initials. Although the exact location of the first center of printing in Romania remains unknown, two possible locations were suggested: the Dealu Monastery near Târgoviște, or the Bistrița Monastery in Oltenia (Lesser Wallachia). Even though the source of the type is not known, a resemblance between Macarie's initials and those used in Moldavian manuscripts has been noticed. Also, books printed in Wallachia in the 16th century have no title page or page numbers.

In 1510 Macarie also printed a Slavonic Octoechos, *Octoih* (in-4°, [200] pp., with one woodcut, headpieces, and ornate initials),[2] and a Slavonic *Tetraevangheliar* (*The Four Gospels*), in 1512 (in-4°, [290] pp., with intricate initials and headpieces).[3]

The first precisely identified center of printing in the Romanian Principalities was Târgoviște, where another monk by the name of Macarie, an apprentice of Dimitrie Liubavici (Dimitrije Ljubović), printed a Slavonic *Molitvenic* (*Prayer Book*) in 1545, using Liubavici's type.[4] The latter also printed an *Apostol* (*Acts of*

---

1 I. Bianu, N. Hodoș, *Bibliografia Românească Veche 1508-1830*, tom. I: fasc. I (1508–1588), Bucharest, 1898, p. 1–8, nr. 1.
2 Bianu, Hodoș, *Bibliografia*, I, p. 9, nr. 2.
3 Bianu, Hodoș, *Bibliografia*, I, p. 9–21, nr. 3.
4 Bianu, Hodoș, *Bibliografia*, I, p. 23–29, nr. 4.

∂ Open Access. © 2024, the author(s), published by De Gruyter. [CC BY-NC-ND] This work is licensed under the Creative Commons Attribution-NonCommercial-NoDerivatives 4.0 International License.
https://doi.org/10.1515/9783111060392-006

the *Apostles and Epistles*) in Târgoviște, in 1547.[5] The edition had two different print runs, commissioned individually by the voivods of Wallachia and Moldavia, and emblazoned with the respective crests of the two principalities. Liubavici's type is different from that of the hieromonk Macarie, and the former's initials clearly reflect Venetian influences.[6]

The Deacon Coresi learned the art of printing from Liubavici. He printed a Slavonic *Triod-Penticostar*[7] (*Triodion*) in Târgoviște in 1550 – the last book to be printed in this city in the 16th century.

Bucharest became a center of printing in 1582, when a *Tetraevangheliar* was printed at the nearby Monastery of Plumbuita. The colophon, which includes the hieromonk Lavrentie's statement regarding the hard work involved in the creation of the type, a process which stretched over an entire decade, provides the first piece of information about the conception and manufacturing of type in the Romanian Principalities.[8]

From the start, the printing work in the Romanian Principalities had a close relationship with South-Eastern European printing. Macarie and Liubavici, who had both studied the art of printing in Venice, brought a Southern Slavic influence. The *Four Gospels* (*Tetraevangheliar*) printed in Wallachia in 1512 served as a model for many subsequent editions printed in South-Eastern Europe, both in terms of content and visual elements. Examples of later editions influenced by the Wallachian *Tetraevangheliar* include the 1537 edition of Rujan and the 1552 edition of Belgrade.

The first book printed in *Romanian*, in Cyrillic type, was *Catehismul* (*The Catechism*).[9] It was printed in 1544 in Sibiu, in the magistrates' printing press, by Filip Moldoveanul, the local governor's Romanian translator.[10] It was commissioned by the Saxons of the city in an effort to disseminate the ideas of the Reformation among the Romanian population. As no copies of this book have survived, its existence is only attested by contemporary documents.

5 Bianu, Hodoș, *Bibliografia*, I, p. 29–31, nr. 5.
6 M. Tomescu, *Istoria cărții românești de la începuturi până la 1918*, Bucharest, 1968, p. 67.
7 Bianu, Hodoș, *Bibliografia*, I, p. 31–43, nr. 9.
8 L. Demény, "Tiparul bucureștean în secolul al XVI-lea", in L. Demény, L. A. Demény, *Carte, tipar și societate la romani în secolul al XVI-lea*, Bucharest, 1986, p. 113.
9 Bianu, Hodoș, *Bibliografia*, I, p. 21–23, nr. 5.
10 Demény, "Où en est-on dans le recherche concernant les débuts de l'imprimerie en langue Roumaine?," *Revue des études sud-est européennes*, 8/2, 1970, p. 241–267.

The earliest book printed in Romanian that has survived is a Slavonic and Romanian *Four Gospels* printed in Cyrillic type in Sibiu by Filip Moldoveanul in 1551 or 1553.[11]

Printing came to a halt in the Romanian Principalities in 1583, until 1635, and, unfortunately, no examples of the type used in the 16th century have survived. It resumed during the period of relative stability during the reigns of Matei Basarab in Wallachia and Vasile Lupu in Moldavia. Thus, printing equipment and master printers came over from Ukraine, with the assistance of Petru Movilă (Petro Mohyla), the metropolitan of Kyiv and Halych.

Matei Basarab wished to establish a printing press, but his initial negotiations with Rafael Levaković, the owner of a Cyrillic press in Rome, were unsuccessful. The prince then dispatched Meletie Macedoneanul to Kyiv in order to acquire a printing press and typographical material on his behalf. The acquisition of the press is mentioned in the preface of the Slavonic *Molitvelnic*,[12] the first book printed using this equipment, in 1635 in Câmpulung. The prince's new press had five varieties of type and was operated by experienced printers led by Timotei Alexandrovich Verbitsky, who had previously overseen the Pechersk Lavra press in Kyiv, while the typesetter was Ivan Glebkovich. Verbitsky was succeeded by Ivan Kunotovich, the former head of the Orthodox Brotherhood press in L'viv, mentioned in the Slavonic *Antologion* printed in Câmpulung in 1643.[13]

Vasile Lupu also succeeded in acquiring a printing press with the assistance of Petru Movilă. Overseen by Sofronie Poceatsky, the former rector of the Orthodox Academy of Kyiv and head of the Kyiv press, the Moldavian workshop was placed in Iași, at the Monastery of the Three Holy Hierarchs. The first work printed here, in 1643, was *Carte românească de învățătură* (*Romanian Instruction Book*), an anthology of sermons translated into Romanian by the Metropolitan Varlaam (Fig. 2).[14] Liturgical books in Slavonic were printed both for the benefit of local churches and to support Orthodox Christians in the Ottoman Empire. The new press in Iași attracted local and South-Eastern European apprentices, some – refugees in the Romanian Principalities: Dobre, Proca Stanciu from Râmnic, Tudor Dumitrovici – a Serb from Râmnic, Ștefan from Ohrid (Macedonia), Radu and Preda Stancevici.

---

11 Tomescu, *Istoria cărții*, p. 45.
12 Bianu, Hodoș, *Bibliografia*, I, p. 103–104, nr. 35.
13 Tomescu, *Istoria cărții*, p. 67.
14 Bianu, Hodoș, *Bibliografia*, I, p. 137–143, nr. 45.

The type imported to the Romanian Principalities copied the Cyrillic semi-uncial and the tilt towards the left – a Russian feature similar to that used by Orthodox presses in Ukraine and Poland.

During this period, the number of books printed in the vernacular began to rise. They include the first legislative codices in Romanian: *Pravila* (Govora, 1640),[15] *Carte românească de învățătură* (Iași, 1646),[16] and *Îndreptarea legii* (Târgoviște, 1652).[17]

The first polemical book, written in Romanian by the Metropolitan Varlaam, was printed in Iași in 1645: *Carte ce se cheamă răspunsul împotriva Catihismului calvinesc* (*Arguments against the Calvinist Catechism*).[18]

After a two-decades interruption, printing resumed in Bucharest, once the printed book had proved its fundamental contribution to the establishment of the vernacular as the liturgical language and its utility beyond the spiritual sphere. Thus, the Metropolitan Varlaam established a new press in Bucharest, under the aegis of the Metropolitan See. The first book, printed here in 1678 with new Cyrillic type influenced by Ukrainian Orthodox models, was a Romanian translation of Ioaniky Galeatovsky's *Cheia înțelesului* (*The Key to Understanding*).[19] The same type was used at the metropolitan press until 1683.

After two earlier attempts (one in 1709 and one in 1715, the latter using the type of Antim Ivireanul, "the Iberian", presented below), the metropolitan press resumed its operations in 1728, using new Cyrillic and Greek types. It continued to function until the 19th century.

In Iași, printing continued through the efforts of the Metropolitan Dosoftei, a major translator and supporter of the vernacular as a liturgical language. The books printed in this period included a Romanian *Liturghier* (*Book of the Divine Liturgies*), printed in 1679,[20] and a Slavonic and Romanian *Psaltire* (*Psalter*), printed in 1680.[21] These works were printed using old type, which was supplemented by type acquired from Poland. The results were rather modest. Nevertheless, but these two attempts demonstrate an interest in printing several books before new type and equipment could arrive from Russia.

According to an inventory preserved in the archives of the Patriarchate of Moscow, the typographical equipment dispatched to Iași in Moldavia on Decem-

15 Bianu, Hodoș, *Bibliografia*, I, p. 108–114, nr. 39.
16 Bianu, Hodoș, *Bibliografia*, I, p. 156–158, nr. 50.
17 Bianu, Hodoș, *Bibliografia*, I, p. 190–203, nr. 61.
18 Bianu, Hodoș, *Bibliografia*, I, p. 150–152, nr. 48.
19 Bianu, Hodoș, *Bibliografia*, I, p. 217–222, nr. 68.
20 Bianu, Hodoș, *Bibliografia*, I, p. 222–225, nr. 69.
21 Bianu, Hodoș, *Bibliografia*, I, p. 226–230, nr. 70.

ber 16, 1679, included a printing press, printing frames, several tools, type, and punches.[22] The metal type came in three sizes. The poor quality of the type and the fact that matrices had not been included, contrary to Metropolitan Dosoftei's express instructions, explain why the office closed few years laters. The first book printed at Dosoftei's press was a *Molitvenic* in 1681 (Fig. 3),[23] while the last was volume four of *Viața sfinților* (*Lives of the Saints*, 1686).[24]

Some of the printers who worked in this office included the monk Mitrofan (who printed six books in Iași between 1680 and 1585) and his apprentices – Andrei, Nicolae, and Ursu.

Starting in 1697, the princely press commenced its operation in Iași. It had access to new Cyrillic and Greek type, employed in the printing of Dimitrie Cantemir's seminal work *Divanul sau Gâlceva înțeleptului cu lumea* (*The Divan or the Quarrel of the Wise Man with the World*).[25]

Mitrofan, by then bishop of Huși, was summoned to Bucharest by Șerban Cantacuzenos and entrusted with the management of the princely press. During Mitrofan's office, the press acquired new Cyrillic type of exceptional quality. Due to the austere beauty and flawless proportions of these type pieces, the printed works produced there display an elegant design, with properly aligned rows and straight letters. Mitrofan employed this same type to print the first complete Romanian translation of the Bible in 1688.[26]

The princely press continued to function until 1704, using Cyrillic and Greek types, and then intermittently, in 1714, and from 1745 to 1746.

After Mitrofan became bishop of Buzău, he established a new press by means of a princely grant. The first book he printed in Buzău, *Pravoslavnica mărturisire* (*The Orthodox Witness*, 1691),[27] employed the same type used by the princely press in Bucharest. The following book, *Mineiu* (*Menaion*),[28] a work in twelve volumes, was printed using a different type created by Mitrofan "with [his] own two hands."

The press of the Diocese of Buzău ceased its activity in 1704 and was inactive until the middle of the 18th century. Between 1743 and 1747, and again in 1767 and 1768, it produced a further eight books in Romanian, Greek, and Slavonic.

---

22 N. Codrescu, *Uricariu cuprinzătoriu de hrisoave, firmanuri și alte acte ale Moldovei din suta XIV-a până la a XIX-a*, Part III, Iași, 1853, p. 102–104.
23 Bianu, Hodoș, *Bibliografia*, I, p. 237–240, nr. 73.
24 Bianu, Hodoș, *Bibliografia*, I, p. 321–324, nr. 92.
25 Bianu, Hodoș, *Bibliografia*, I, p. 365–369, nr. 111.
26 D. Bădără, *Tiparul românesc la sfârșitul secolului al XVII-lea și începutul secolului al XVIII-lea*, Brăila, 1998, p. 62.
27 Bianu, Hodoș, *Bibliografia*, I, p. 321–324, nr. 92.
28 Bianu, Hodoș, *Bibliografia*, I, p. 365–369, nr. 111.

During his 23-year printing career (1680–1702), Mitrofan printed eighteen books and established three presses.

Antim the Iberian (Ivireanul), who had worked as a printer at the princely press in Bucharest, opened a press at the Snagov Monastery following his appointment as its abbot. The workshop, established with financial support from Constantin Brâncoveanu, the prince of Wallachia, initially used type borrowed from the princely press. Afterwards, it procured its own type.

The books printed at Snagov were for the most part liturgical and theological texts produced for the benefit of Orthodox Christians in the Ottoman Empire. Between 1696 and 1701, fourteen books were printed in Romanian, Greek, Slavonic, and Arabic.

Having been elected bishop of Râmnic, in 1705, Antim established a press in the bishop's residence in Râmnicu Vâlcea. Using Cyrillic and Greek type from the Snagov press, he printed nine works in several languages (Romanian, Greek, or Romanian and Slavonic) between 1705 and 1707.

A new press was later established at Râmnicu Vâlcea under the aegis of the Bishopric. It produced 118 books between 1724 and 1819. During the first part of this period, the entire corpus of liturgical books, including prayer books and hymnals, was printed here *in Romanian*.

In 1708, following his election as metropolitan of Wallachia, Antim the Iberian moved to Târgoviște, bringing his typographical equipment along from Râmnic. Between 1708 and 1715, this press produced twenty-one books in Romanian, Greek and Slavonic.

In 1725, the metropolitan press in Iași resumed its operations. Between 1778 and 1794, it was leased to Mihai Strilbițki, a printer and engraver whose work, done in association with his son, Policarp, was undoubtedly interesting and valuable. However, the Metropolitan Iacob Stamate decided to revive the metropolitan press and acquired several type sets – Latin, Cyrillic, Greek, and civil Russian script. The press experienced a period of intense activity until just after 1830.

The princely press in Iași did not resume its operations immediately. In order to alleviate the scarcity of liturgical texts in the Diocese of Rădăuți, the prince Constantine Mavrocordatos decreed that a press be established there. This press, which was active between 1744 and 1746, produced Romanian books exclusively. Based on information supplied by the *Ceaslov* (*Book of Hours*) published in 1745,[29] the printing was done by the master Grigore Stan Brașovean. The Cyrillic type was

---

29 Bianu, Hodoș, *Bibliografia*, tom. II, Bucharest, 1910, p. 85, nr. 241.

transferred to the metropolitan press in Iași after 1752, following the election of the bishop of Rădăuți, Iacob Putneanul, to the Metropolitan See of Moldavia.[30]

As an insufficient number of books were published at this time, Constantine Mavrocordatos granted a princely privilege consisting of tax exemptions and stipends to Duca Sotiriovici of Thassos, who consequently established a press in Iași. This press produced fourteen books in Romanian and Greek between 1743 and 1752, using Cyrillic and Greek type.

Mihai Strilbițki was able to obtain his own typographical material before his contract with the Bishopric expired. His press operated, alternatively, in Iași, Dubăsari, 1791–1794, and Movilău, 1796–1800. During this period, until the expiration of his lease, Strilbițki worked both in his own press and in the rented one. After 1800, he donated part of his typographical equipment to the Neamț Monastery, where a new press started operating in 1807.[31] In addition to Strilbițki's donated equipment, the press used imported type, which had been acquired with the assistance of the metropolitan of Iași. The Neamț Monastery press became one of the most prestigious in the Romanian Principalities at the beginning of the 19th century, producing a series of high-quality books and training skilled master printers who later carried out their own work across the country. One of the most important works printed there was the monumental Gospel (*Evanghelie*) of 1821.[32]

The escalating demand for printed books in the Romanian Principalities during this time is evidenced by new attempts by private printers to secure the lease of princely or ecclesiastical presses. Thus, in 1819, the brothers Gheorghe and Nicolae Dimitrievici, members of the Athanasievici family, a renowned family of printers who operated in Râmnicu Vâlcea from the second half of the 18th century on,[33] rented part of the type and equipment belonging to the episcopal press in Râmnic.

1. Periodicals and Newspapers

The first periodicals published in the Romanian Principalities in the 18th century were calendars.

A calendar published in Iași in 1785, *Calendar pe 112 ani* (*A Calendar for 112 Years*),[34] was printed with cursive Cyrilic type cast specifically for the printing

---

30 Tomescu, *Istoria cărții*, p. 99.
31 Tomescu, *Istoria cărții*, p. 120.
32 I. Bianu, D. Simonescu, *Bibliografia*, tom. III, fasc. III–VIII, Bucharest, 1936, p. 380, nr. 1120.
33 Tomescu, *Istoria cărții,* p. 101.
34 Bianu, Hodoș, *Bibliografia*, II, p. 301, nr. 484.

of Romanian texts. This is demonstrated by the fact that some of the characters employed by this script were not used in the Russian alphabet of the time. The volume is illustrated with engravings by Mihai and Policarp Strilbiţchi.

The first *Calendar* printed in Bucharest was published in 1794. While no copies have survived, the existence of this edition is documented by a second edition published in 1795, where it was stated that it was printed for the second time.[35]

At the beginning of the 19th century, several periodicals were being published abroad in Romanian. One such publication was *Biblioteca românească* (*The Romanian Library*), a periodical printed in Cyrillic script at Buda, which appeared irregularly from 1821 until 1834 under the supervision of Zaharia Carcalechi. In addition, seven issues of the newspaper *Fama Lipschi pentru Daţia* were published in 1827 in Leipzig. The newspaper was financed by Dinicu Golescu[36] and edited by I. M. C. Rosetti and Anastasie Lascăr.

The first newspaper published in the Romanian Principalities was *Courier de Moldavie* which was edited in Iaşi, in 1790, by the Russian army commander. At the time, during the Russo-Turkish War (1787–1791), Moldavia was under Russian occupation.

The first newspaper printed in Bucharest was *Curierul Românesc* edited by Ion Heliade Rădulescu.[37] At first, it appeared regularly between April 8, 1829, and April 19, 1848.[38] Later, it appeared for a few months between November 29 and December 13, 1859. In Iaşi, *Albina Românească*, edited by Gheorghe Asachi,[39] appeared intermittently between June 1, 1829[40] and November 24, 1858.

Between 1829–1847, the number of periodicals published in Wallachia and Moldavia rose to thirty-seven and included cultural journals (*Curier de ambele sexe* and *Dacia literară*), historical journals (*Arhiva românească* and *Magazin istoric pentru Dacia*), and commercial publications (*Mercur* and *Jurnal comercial al portului Brăila*).[41]

---

35 Bianu, Hodoş, *Bibliografia*, II, p. 374, nr. 585.

36 Constantin (Dinicu) Radovici Golescu (1777–1830), was a Wallachian man of letters, member of a family of boyars, famous for his travel notes and journalism.

37 Ion Heliade Rădulescu (1802–1872) was a Wallachian scholar, poet, essayist, and literature writer, a newspaper editor, and a politician.

38 Bianu, Simonescu, *Bibliografia*, III, p. 625, nr. 1418.

39 Born in Herţa, in the north of Moldavia (today, a city in Ukraine), Gheorghe Asachi (1788–1869) was a Romanian educator, writer and newspaper editor, and a forerunner of the generation that initiated the Revolution of 1848 in the Romanian Principalities.

40 Bianu, Simonescu, *Bibliografia*, III, p. 613, nr. 1409.

41 Tomescu, *Istoria cărţii*, p. 132.

2. Cartographic Material

Harta administrativă cu tăbliță statistică a Principatului Valahiei (*The Administrative Map of the Principality of Wallachia, with a Statistical Table*, 1833), drawn by Bergenheim and Galițin and lithographed in Bucharest by I. Eliad and R. T. Biliț, was the first map printed in the Romanian Principalities.

In 1848, in Iași, P. Antoni printed *Harta Moldovei vechi* (*The Map of Old Moldavia*) at *Institutul tipografic "Albina"* (The "Albina" Press).

Starting in 1843, Carol Bergheanu used geodesic and topographic instruments for the creation of maps and charts.

In 1850, in Iași, the lithographic press of P. Miller & Parteni produced *Harta generală a Moldovei cu învecinatele țeri* (*The General Map of Moldavia with Its Neighboring Countries*).

Harta generală a Moldovei (*The General Map of Moldavia*), created in 1853 by the first Romanian cartographic engineer, F. Filipescu-Dubău, was published by Parteni-Miller in Iași.

"Depozitul de război" ("The Military Warehouse"), which later became "Institutul topografic militar" (The Military Topographic Institute) was established in 1873. It specialized in the creation of high-precision maps.

3. Illustrations

The Slavonic *Octoih* (*Oktoechos*) of 1508 included the first engraving printed in the Romanian Principalities – a woodcut representing the Saints Joseph, Theophrastus, and John against a church background.[42]

Until the beginning of the 19th century, illustrations produced in the Romanian Principalities consisted of woodcut prints, most of which had religious themes.

The first full-page illustrations were twelve woodcuts representing scenes from the New Testament, which adorned the pages of *Triodul – Penticostar* printed in Târgoviște in 1550.[43]

The Slavonic *Liturghier* printed at the Dealu Monastery in 1646 included a woodcut portraying the first secular figures – prince Matei Basarab and his wife, Elena, along with Ioan, the abbot of the Dealu Monastery.

---

42 A. Andreescu, *Arta cărții: cartea românească veche*, Bucharest, 2002, p. 17.
43 Andreescu, *Arta cărții*, p. 23.

In the first part of the 17th century, the woodcut prints included in the most richly illustrated books of the time (*Cartea românească de învățătură*, Iași, 1642, and *Îndreptarea legii*, Târgoviște, 1652) were the work of the engravers Ilia, Theodor Tișevici, and Petru Teodor.[44] While displaying a clear Russian influence, their engravings also included distinct local techniques and features. Among the engravers active during the second half of the 17th century were Damaschin Gherbest, Antim the Iberian, Dimitrios, Ursul Zugravul, and Ivan Bakov.

Woodcut engravings continued to be used during the 18th century. They included both new works and reprints of older ones. Around this time, the first metal engravings were imported. The first such engraving is a map of the Holy Mount included in *Proschinatarul Sfântului Munte* (*The Proskinitarion of the Holy Mount*, Snagov, 1701). *Pravilă de rugăciune pentru sfinții sârbești* (*Prayer Order for the Serbian Saints*, Râmnic, 1761),[45] also included thirteen copper engravings – the work of Hristofor Zhefarovich from Karlowitz.

Several Romanian printers produced or acquired *intaglio* plates during this period, but these were generally used for printing *antimensia*.

The first etching, depicting the four Evangelists, was produced in Iași by Dimitrie Kontoleu and included in the *Chiriacodromion* printed in 1816.[46]

Starting with the third decade of the 19th century, lithography was used for the illustration of almanacs and calendars and the production of printing stamps or molds. In the beginning, the images were drawn on the surface of a smooth lithographic stone and printed in Vienna or Paris.

Among Romanian lithographers were Gheorghe Asachi and Dimitrie Pappasoglu. A lithograph depicting Alexander I the Good of Moldavia and his wife, attributed to Asachi, bears the following stamp: "Institutul Albinei Romane. A[gha] G. Asaki, Jassy, 1828." A lithographic portrait of Saint Stephen the Great, the great prince of Moldavia, drawn and produced by Ion Müller, mentions the first lithography workshop in Iași – "Tipo-litografia Institutului Albinei."

In Bucharest, lithography was practised by several artists: D. Pappasoglu, A. Chladek, C. Lecca, I. Negulici, and Carol Popp de Szathmary. Their works were printed in Paris and Vienna, as well as in local presses.

---

44 Andreescu, *Arta cărții*, p. 58–64.
45 Bianu, Simonescu, *Bibliografia*, III, p. 157, nr. 327.
46 Bianu, Simonescu, *Bibliografia*, III, p. 163–164, nr. 926.

4. The Beginning and Evolution of Printing in Non-Latin Characters

4.1 Greek Type

The first Greek type reached the Romanian Principalities in the 17th century, thanks to the efforts of the Metropolitan Petru Movilă. This type was used in the printing of *Decretul Patriarhului Partenie* (*Patriarch Partenie's Decree*, Iași, 1642), a document which marked the end of the Council of Iași held that year.[47]

In 1680, the first Greek press opened in Iași. It belonged to the Orthodox Church: thus, the Church was able to shape and direct its editorial policies. At the time, Greek books printed in Italy were subjected to severe censorship, which prevented the publication of Orthodox texts dedicated to polemical theology.

The press was established by Patriarch Dositheos Notaras with the financial support of the Moldavian ruling prince, Gheorghe Duca. In *Istoria patriarhilor Ierusalimului* (*History of the Patriarchs of Jerusalem*, Bucharest, 1715),[48] the Patriarch states that he had ordered Greek type from Iași in 1680. The type was designed and manufactured by the monk Mitrofan. The first book printed with this type was *Întâmpinare în contra primatului Papei* (*Argument Against the Primacy of the Pope*, 1682), written by Nektarios, the patriarch of Jerusalem.[49] The press, which operated in several monasteries under the aegis of the Patriarchate of Jerusalem (the Cetățuia Monastery and Saint Sabbas Monastery in Iași), remained under patriarchal control. This press operated between 1682 and 1715. A Greek and Romanian Gospel was printed at Bucharest in 1693 (Fig. 4). Out of ten books, seven addressed topics of polemical theology. The printers who worked in this press included Mitrofan, Constantin (in 1715), Dionisie Monahul (in 1698), Ieremia Marcovici (in 1714 and 1715), and Dumitru Pădure, (1692–1694).

The princely presses that possessed Greek typographical material included:
- Iași (1698): The Greek type employed here was different from the one used by the Cetățuia Monastery press. It was used for the printing of the Greek text in Dimitrie Cantemir's previously mentioned *Divanul sau Gâlceva înțeleptului cu lumea sau giudețul sufletului cu trupul*.[50]
- Bucharest: This type was cast by Mitrofan, at prince Constantin Brâncoveanu's request. Starting in 1690, with the work of Meletios Syrigos *Argument Against*

---

47 Bianu, Hodoș, *Bibliografia*, I, p. 119, nr. 41.
48 Bianu, Hodoș, *Bibliografia*, I, p. 501–508, nr. 175.
49 Bianu, Hodoș, *Bibliografia*, I, p. 251–258, nr. 75.
50 Bianu, Hodoș, *Bibliografia*, I, p. 355–365, nr. 110.

the Catholic Principles and Cyril Lukaris' Theses,[51] and until 1714, the press produced eighteen books fully or partially in Greek.
- the Snagov Monastery: between 1697 and 1701, the Snagov press produced six Greek books. The most impressive of these books were the work of Ioannes Karyophylles and Maxim of Peloponnese.

Antim the Iberian also established his own press at the Snagov Monastery. In 1701, he printed John Comnene's work *Proschinatarul Sf. Munte* (*The Proskinitarion of the Holy Mount [Athos]*).[52]

Antim the Iberian's Greek type was subsequently used by the press of the Metropolitan See of Bucharest, where Antim worked between 1701 and 1705.

During Antim's ecclesiastical office, the same type was used by the presses of the Bishopric of Râmnic (1705–1707), where three Greek books were printed during this time, and the Metropolitan See of Târgoviște (1709–1715), where six Greek books were printed (Fig. 5).

Greek books continued to be printed during the 18th century by newly endowed or refurbished diocesan presses. The metropolitan press in Bucharest printed eight books partially in Greek. The metropolitan press in Iași also occasionally printed Greek texts, while the Bishopric presses in Buzău and Râmnicu Vâlcea produced eight works partially in Greek.

Additionally, the Metropolitan Antim established a press at Mănăstirea Tuturor Sfinților (All Saints' Monastery), now known as the Monastery of Antim, where he printed two Greek books.

In order to ensure the editorial autonomy of the Patriarchate of Jerusalem, the princes of the Romanian Principalities established new presses at the patriarchs' request. These presses were placed under the Patriarchate's direct control.

Constantin Brâncoveanu, with Antim the Iberian's assistance, founded a Greek press in Bucharest (1709–1713), which was subsequently placed under the administration of the Patriarchate of Jerusalem. The first book printed there was *Istoria Patriarhilor Ierusalimului* (1715).[53] The press and its owner are mentioned on the title page of the 1741 *Liturghier* (*Book of the Divine Liturgies*).[54]

At the request of Patriarch Ephrem II of Jerusalem, the Prince Alexandru Scarlat Ghika's financially supported the estabslihment of a new Greek press in Bucharest, which operated between 1767 and 1769. During this period, the press

51 Bianu, Hodoș, *Bibliografia*, I, p. 298–315, nr. 90.
52 Bianu, Hodoș, *Bibliografia*, I, p. 422–423, nr. 129.
53 Bianu, Hodoș, *Bibliografia*, p. 501–508, nr. 175.
54 Bianu, Hodoș, *Bibliografia*, II, p. 55, nr. 220.

produced five Greek books, as well as one book in *karamanlidika* (Turkish in Greek characters), *Christian Teachings* (1768).[55]

Greek books were also produced in private presses.

In 1783, the brothers Nicolae and Ioan Lazaru, from Ioannina, were granted a privilege by Prince Nicolae Caragea, which allowed them to open a press in Bucharest. The press, which operated between 1783–1784 and 1789, published four Greek books.

Between 1813 and 1821, a Greek press in Iași produced nineteen books. It is likely that the venture benefited from prince Scarlat Ghika's support, whose patronage is mentioned in the first book printed there.

In 1817, Constantin Caracaș, Răducanu Clinceanu and Dumitrache Toplicean obtained a twenty-year privilege, signed by prince Ioan Caragea, which allowed them to open a new press in Bucharest and granted them the exclusive right to print Greek books in the Principality of Wallachia. Between 1817 and 1821, their press produced ten Greek books.[56]

In Iași, Duca Sotiriu from Thassos printed Greek books intermittently (1752). Another press, founded by the priest Mihail together with Gheorghe Hagi Dimu of Trikka, published one Greek book in 1786.

4.2 Arabic

Around 1700, Athanasios III Dabbās, a former patriarch of Antioch, metropolitan of Aleppo at the time, requested prince Constantin Brâncoveanu's assistance in printing liturgical books in Arabic. Brâncoveanu financed the casting of the first Arabic type produced in Eastern Europe. The type was cut at the Snagov Monastery by Antim the Iberian. This venture is mentioned in Patriarch Athanasios's preface to the Greek and Arabic *Book of the Divine Liturgies/Liturgikon*, Snagov, 1701,[57] printed with Brâncoveanu's financial assistance for the benefit of the Arabic-speaking Christians in the Ottoman Empire.[58]

The Arabic type was transferred to the princely press in Bucharest once Antim was elected metropolitan of Wallachia. Antim printed there a Greek and Arabic

---

55 Bianu, Hodoș, *Bibliografia*, III, p. 184–188, nr. 360.
56 Simoncscu, "Din activitatea tipografică a Bucureștilor (1678–1830)", *Bucureștii Vechi. Buletinul Societății istorico-arheologice „Bucureștii-Vechi"*, I–IV, 1935, p. 131–132.
57 Bianu, Hodoș, *Bibliografia*, I, p. 423, nr. 130.
58 Ioana Feodorov, *Arabic Printing for the Christians in Ottoman Lands. The East-European Connection*, Berlin/Boston, 2023, especially p. 143–186.

Horologion/Book of the Hours in 1702.[59] Later, the Arabic type was presented by Constantin Brâncoveanu to the Church of Antioch and taken to Aleppo by the metropolitan Athanasios Dabbās.[60]

During some of the more difficult periods for Orthodox Christians in the Ottoman Empire, Sylvester I, the patriarch of the Church of Antioch (1724–1766), received support from the Romanian Principalities for the printing of Arabic books.[61]

In order to meet the cultural and spiritual needs of the period, three of the six books printed in the Romanian Principalities were works of polemical theology.

In Iaşi, four Arabic books were produced at the Saint Sabbas Monastery, with the assistance of Arabic typesetters – the deacon George of Aleppo and the monk Michael of Kūrat al-Dhahab (Lebanon), both of whom were part of Patriarch Sylvester's circle. Other works included, in 1745, a reedition of the 1701 Greek and Arabic *Book of the Divine Liturgies*, financed by John Mavrocordatos; in 1746, a miscellany comprising polemical writings about the primacy of the pope, composed by the Patriarch Nektarios of Jerusalem and Eustratios Argentis and translated from Greek by Mas'ad Nashw, a monk from Cairo; the acts of three Holy Synods of Constantinople addressing the Catholic "inventions" and the Latins' disruptive missionary activities in Syria, and another work by Eustratios Argentis, *The Lord's Supper*.

In Bucharest, at the Monastery of Saint Spyridon, a metochion of the Church of Antioch since 1746, an Arabic Psalter was printed in 1747, and several other titles that are little know and studied so far.[62]

4.3 Georgian

The *khutzuri* characters created by the Transylvanian master Kis Miklós in 1686 in Amsterdam at the request of King Artsil did not reach Georgia.

The casting of the first Georgian type in the Romanian Principalities was also accomplished with prince Constantin Brâncoveanu's support. The first Georgian book, the Gospels, was printed in Tbilisi in 1709 by one of Antim the Iberian's apprentices, the Romanian printer Mihail Ştefan, also known as Iştvanovici.[63]

---

59 Feodorov, *Arabic Printing for the Christians in Ottoman Lands*, p. 256–260, Fig. 17.
60 Feodorov, *Arabic Printing for the Christians in Ottoman Lands*, especially p. 143–186, Fig. 19–37.
61 Feodorov, *Arabic Printing for the Christians in Ottoman Lands*, p. 227–233, Fig. 38–42.
62 Feodorov, *Arabic Printing for the Christians in Ottoman Lands*, p. 233.
63 Bianu, Hodoş, *Bibliografia*, I, p. 543–550, nr. 157.

The title page of the Georgian *Book of the Divine Liturgies* printed in Tbilisi in 1710 with the same type includes King Vakhtang's statement that he had hired "a Wallachian printer" – a reference to Mihail Iştvanovici.[64]

Two copies of the Tbilisi Gospel printed in 1709, currently held at the Romanian Academy Library, are inscribed with Antim the Iberian's dedications to Constantin Brâncoveanu. In these, Antim expresses his gratitude for the prince's support for the manufacturing of Georgian type.

This information confirms the fact that Antim, who was of Georgian origin and well-acquainted with the Georgian alphabet, was the creator of this first set of Georgian type, which he manufactured in Wallachia most likely between 1706 and 1708. Antim, as shown above, had already manufactured Arabic and Greek type.

The press established by Mihail Iştvanovici in Tbilisi was well-equipped, as demonstrated by the ten books he printed using his own type.[65]

5. The Beginning and Evolution of Printed Music Works

The first music work printed in the Romanian Principalities was the *Anastasimatar* of Peter of Ephesus, in psaltic notation (Bucharest, 1820).[66] Peter of Ephesus came in 1816 to Bucharest, where he established a music school near the Şelari Church of Saint Nicholas. With the financial support of the great ban Grigore Băleanu, he started designing and manufacturing musical type in 1817. The preface of the *Anastasimatar* mentions that the note types were cast by the master goldsmith Serafim Christodulos.

In 1820, Peter of Ephesus printed Petru Lambadarie's *Brief Doxology Book* at his "newly established press", This was a more carefully printed work.[67] The imperfect note type cast by the first goldsmith were likely recast by Ştefan D., a master goldsmith from Litotip, who signed the preface along with Peter of Ephesus and Hagi Teodosie Sterghios from Naousa.

In 1827, Peter of Ephesus's type was purchased by the metropolitan press in Bucharest and used by the Hieromonk Macarie to print in 1827 *Tomul al doilea al Antologhionului* (*The Second Volume of the Antologion*), the first book printed in

---

64 Bianu, Hodoş, *Bibliografia*, I, p. 483–484, nr. 161.
65 N. Iorga, *Istoria literaturii române în secolul al XVIII-lea (1688-1821)*, I, Bucharest, 1969, p. 338.
66 Bianu, Simonescu, *Bibliografia*, III, p. 351–356, nr. 1092.
67 Bianu, Simonescu, *Bibliografia*, III, p. 358–361, nr. 1095.

the Romanian Principalities to include the Romanian text of Orthodox chants, printed in Cyrillic characters.[68]

In 1843, Anton Pann established a press devoted to printing liturgical music. Anton Pann's *Versuri musicești* (*Musical Verses*), published in 1830, also employed Cyrillic characters and psaltic notation.[69]

This summary of the printing activities in the Romanian Principalities is only meant to concisely present the interest of the local leaders of the Church, scholars and printers to provide to the Romanian Orthodox clergy and believers the necessary printed books for church services as well as for everyday prayer and spiritual life. This effort started quite early, at the beginning of the 16th century, and covered the entire century, progressing in the 17th–18th century towards an uninterrupted printing activity and a consistent number of books produced in many languages and scripts for a wide Orthodox public living in territories that covered most of the post-Byzantine world.

---

[68] Bianu, Simonescu, *Bibliografia*, III, p. 539–541, nr. 1316.
[69] Bianu, Simonescu, *Bibliografia*, III, p. 698–699, nr. 1492.

Fig. 1: Slavonic Book of the Divine Liturgies, Dealu Monastery, 1508 (B.S.S.).

Fig. 2: Varlaam, *Carte românească de învățătură* (*Romanian Instruction Book*), Iași, 1643 (B.S.S.).

Fig. 3: Molitvenic, Iași, 1681 (B.S.S.).

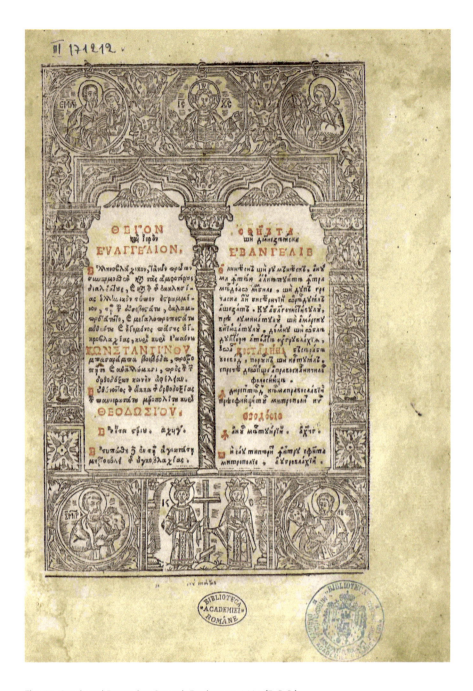

Fig. 4: Greek and Romanian Gospel, Bucharest, 1693 (B.S.S.).

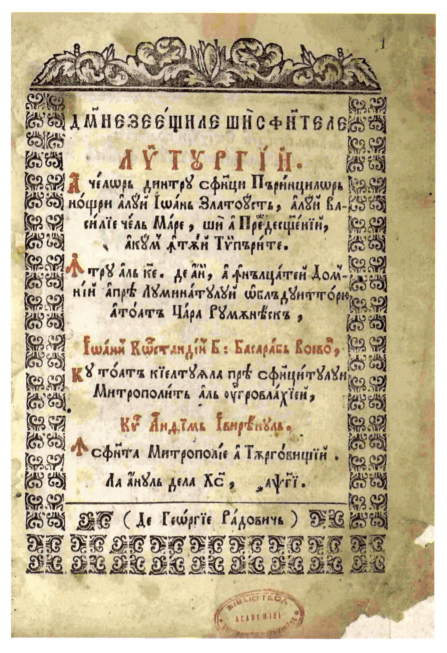

Fig. 3: Book of the Divine Liturgies, Târgoviște, 1713 (B.S.S.).

Bibliography

Andreescu, Ana. *Arta cărţii. Cartea românească veche. 1508–1700*. Bucharest: Univers Enciclopedic, 2002.

Bădără, Doru. *Tiparul românesc la sfârşitul secolului al XVII-lea si începutul secolului al XVIII-lea*. Brăila: Editura Istros a Muzeului Brăilei "Carol I", 1998.

Bianu, Ioan, Nerva Hodoş, Dan Simionescu. *Bibliografia românească veche 1508–1830*, 4 vols. Bucharest: Atelierele grafice Socec & Co, 1903–1944.

Codrescu, Teodor. *Uricariu cuprinzătoriu de hrisoave, firmanuri şi alte acte ale Moldovei din suta XIV-a până la a XIX-a,* Part III. Iaşi: Editura Buciumului Român, 1853.

Demény, Ludovic. "Où en est on dans la recherche concernant les débuts de l'imprimerie en langue roumaine?". *Revue des études sud-est européennes*, 8/2 (1970), p. 241–268.

Demény, Ludovic. "Tiparul bucureştean în secolul al XVI-lea". In Ludovic Demény, Lidia A. Demény, *Carte, tipar şi societate la români în secolul al XVI-lea*. Bucharest: Kriterion, 1986, p. 106–127.

Feodorov, Ioana. *Arabic Printing for the Christians in Ottoman Lands. The East-European Connection*. Berlin/Boston: De Gruyter, 2023.

Iorga, Nicolae. *Istoria literaturii române în secolul al XVIII-lea (1688–1821)*, vol. I. Bucharest, 1969.

Simonescu, Dan. "Din activitatea tipografică a Bucureştilor, (1678–1830)". *Bucureştiul Vechi*, 1–4, 1930–1934, p. 118–135.

Tomescu, Mircea. *Istoria cărţii româneşti de la* începuturi *până la 1918*. Bucharest: Editura Ştiinţifică, 1968.

Vera Tchentsova

La naissance du portrait dans l'espace orthodoxe : Représenter l'auteur dans les livres grecs du début du XVIIIe siècle

« …[même] dans les typographies de toute l'Italie jamais rien de meilleur n'a été fait… »
Métrophane Grègoras à Chrysanthe Notaras, à propos de *l'Histoire* de Dosithée de Jérusalem, 1720[1]

Les premières typographies à même de publier des livres en grec apparurent en Occident, et notamment à Venise où résidait une population orthodoxe grecque considérable.[2] Au XVIIe siècle, le relai fut pris par les pays roumains où, grâce au soutien des princes locaux, des imprimeries produisirent pour la première fois dans le monde orthodoxe des livres en grec.[3] Évidemment, ces premières imprimeries roumaines furent influencées par la longue tradition de l'art typographique d'Europe occidentale. Deux acteurs clés du développement de l'imprimerie orthodoxe, et pas seulement en grec, furent le patriarche Dosithée de Jérusalem (1669–1707), et son neveu et successeur Chrysanthe Notaras

---

1 G. P. Kournoutos, « He Dodekavivlos tou Dositheou eis ten tupographian tou Voukourestiou », *Theologia*, 24, 1953, p. 266.
2 E. Layton, *The Sixteenth Century Greek Book in Italy. Printers and Publishers for the Greek World*, Venice, 1994 ; G. S. Ploumides, « Protase gia ten kategoriopoiese tes eikonographeses ton leitourgikon ekdoseos Venetias », *Epeirotika khronika*, 39, 2005, p. 9–49 ; H. Kilpatrick, « From Venice to Aleppo : Early Printing of Scripture in the Orthodox World », *Chronos. Revue d'histoire de l'Université de Balamand*, 30, 2014, p. 35–61.
3 A. E. Karathanases, *Oi Ellenes logioi ste Vlakhia (1670–1714). Sumvole ste melete tes elle-nikes pneumatikes kineses stis paradounavies egemonies kata ten prophanariotike periodo*, Thessalonique, 1982, p. 158–172 ; F. Marineskou, M. Rafailă, « To helleniko entupo ste Roumania (1642–1918) », *To Entupo helleniko vivlio. 15os-19os aionas. Praktika tou diethnous sunedriou. Delphoí, 16-20 Maiou 2001*, Athènes, 2004, p. 265–278 ; M. Ţipău, *Orthodoxe suneidese kai ethnike tautoteta sta Valkania (1700–1821)*, Thessalonique, 2015, p. 11–19.

Cet article fait partie du projet financé par le Conseil Européen de la Recherche (ERC) dans le cadre du projet de recherche et innovation Horizon 2020 de l'Union Européenne (Grant Agreement No. 883219-AdG-2019 – Project TYPARABIC).
Je tiens à remercier chaleureusement pour leur aide Alina Năchescu (Oxford), Benjamin Guichard (Paris), Natalia Bondar (Kiev), Ioana Feodorov (Bucarest), Cecilia Angeletti et Matteo Vacchini (Milan), ainsi que Vivien Prigent (Paris ; Rome) pour la relecture du texte.

∂ Open Access. © 2024, the author(s), published by De Gruyter. (cc) BY-NC-ND This work is licensed under the Creative Commons Attribution-NonCommercial-NoDerivatives 4.0 International License.
https://doi.org/10.1515/9783111060392-007

(1707–1731).[4] Ces deux hiérarques étaient liés à certains cercles intellectuels occidentaux qui comptaient dans leurs rangs des imprimeurs, notamment vénitiens et parisiens. Le souci d'apologie de la foi orthodoxe et de diffusion de textes polémiques dans le contexte des antagonismes religieux du temps[5] n'empêchait nullement la collaboration avec les typographes catholiques ou protestants. Les liens avec ces spécialistes occidentaux, permirent aux éditeurs orthodoxes d'adopter les techniques les plus nouvelles pour la publication de leurs livres. Et parmi ces nouveautés, on doit citer l'insertion de portraits gravés des auteurs.[6]

---

4 Kh. M. Loparev, « Ierusalimskiĭ patriarkh Khrisanf (1707–1731) i ego otnoshenie k Rossii », dans P. S. Uvarova, M. N. Speranskiĭ (éds.), *Trudy Vos'mogo arkheologicheskogo s"ezda v Moskve, 1890*, t. 2, Moscou, 1895, p. 20–27 ; A. Palmieri, *Dositeo patriarca greco di Gerusalemme (1641–1707)*, Florence, 1909, p. 46–93 ; I. V. Durǎ, *Ho Dositheos Hierosolumon kai he prosphora autou eis tas Rhoumanikas khoras kai ten ekklesian auton*, Athènes, 1977, p. 237–256 ; G. Podskalsky, *Griechische Theologie in der Zeit der Türkenherrschaft (1453–1821). Die Orthodoxie im Spannungsfeld der nachreformatorischen Konfessionen des Westens*, Munich, 1988, p. 282–294, 317–319 ; P. M. Kitromilides, *Neoellenikos Diaphotismos. Oi politikes kai koinonikes idees*, Athènes, 1996, p. 21–82 ; P. Stathi, *Chrysanthos Notaras, Patriarkhes Hierosolumon. Prodromos tou Neoellenikou Diaphotismou*, Athènes, 1999, p. 242–247 ; Kl.-P. Todt, « Dositheos II. von Jerusalem », dans C. G. Conticello, V. Conticello (éds.), *La Théologie Byzantine et sa tradition*, vol. II (XIIIᵉ–XIXᵉ s.), Turnhout, 2002, p. 659–720 ; K. Sarris, « O Chrysanthos Notaras kai e ekdose tes Dodekavivlou tou Dositheou Hierosolumon : mia periptose analethous khronologias ekdoses (1715 / c. 1722) », *Mnemon*, 27, 2005, p. 27–52 ; M. Bernatskiĭ, « Dosifeĭ II Notara, patriarkh Ierusalimskiĭ », *Pravoslavnaia ėntsiklopediia*, t. 16, Moscou, 2007, p. 71–77 ; N. Miladinova, *The Panoplia Dogmatike by Euthymios Zygadenos. A Study on the First Edition Published in Greek in 1710*, Leyde/Boston, 2014, p. 38–43 ; A. Pippidi, « The Enlightenment and Orthodox Culture in the Romanian Principalities », dans P. M. Kitromilides (éds.), *Enlightenment and Religion in the Orthodox World*, Oxford, 2016, p. 157–174 ; Țipău, *Orthodoxe suneidese*, p. 60–62 ; H. Çolak, « Bilim, İlahiyat ve Siyasetin Merkezinde Bir Osmanlı Münevveri : Kudüs Patriği Chrysanthos Notaras », *Kebikeç*, 47, 2019, p. 31–56 ; V. Kontouma, « Vestiges de la bibliothèque de Dosithée II de Jérusalem au Métochion du Saint-Sépulcre à Constantinople », *Les bibliothèques grecques dans l'Empire Ottoman*, Turnhout, 2020, p. 259–273.
5 Sur les efforts déployés par les deux patriarches pour renforcer leur Église et lutter pour la pureté de la doctrine orthodoxe, voir (avec bibliographie à jour) V. Kontouma, « La Confession de foi de Dosithée de Jérusalem : les versions de 1672 et de 1690 », dir. par M.-H. Blanchet, F. Gabriel, *L'Union à l'épreuve du formulaire. Professions de foi entre Églises d'Orient et d'Occident (XIIIᵉ–XVIIIᵉ siècle)*, Leuven/Paris/Bristol, 2016, p. 341–372 ; I.-A. Tudorie, « The Eucharistic Controversy between the 'Orthodox' Dositheos II of Jerusalem and the 'Calvinist' Ioannis Karyofyllis (1689–1697) », dans K. Sarris, N. Pissis, M. Pechlivanos (éds.), *Confessionalization and/as Knowledge Transfer in the Greek Orthodox Church*, Wiesbaden, 2021, p. 273–327.
6 Sur la rencontre des chrétiens orientaux avec le « monde d'images » occidental, voir C. Walbiner, « 'Images Painted with Such Exalted Skill as to Ravish the Senses...' : Pictures in the Eyes of Christian Arab Travellers of the 17th and 18th Centuries », dans B. Heyberger, S. Naef (éds.), *La multiplication des images en pays d'Islam : De l'estampe à la télévision (17ᵉ–21ᵉ siècle). Actes du colloque « Images : fonctions et langages. L'incursion de l'image moderne dans l'Orient musulman et sa périphérie », Istanbul, Université du Bosphore (Boğaziçi Üniversitesi), 25–27 mars 1999*, Würzburg, 2016, p. 15–25 ;

Au XVIIe siècle, en Europe occidentale, les livres présentent en effet de plus en plus souvent des portraits pleine page en frontispice, réalisés communément à l'eau-forte.[7] Cette technique de gravure par oxydation du métal permettait des effets graphiques plus fins, et notamment des ombrages plus nuancés, qui rapprochaient la gravure du dessin. Les portraits gagnèrent ainsi en réalisme et expressivité. Les gravures exécutées d'après des peintures ou des dessins comportent fréquemment la signature du graveur ou cette dernière accompagnée de celle de l'artiste lorsqu'il s'agissait de personnes différentes.

Parmi les premiers exemples connus d'adoption de cette évolution en terre orthodoxe, on trouve le portrait du patriarche Dosithée de Jérusalem, intégré en frontispice dans un livre publié en Valachie, à Bucarest. (Fig. 1) Une image magnifique du pontife, coiffé de la mitre, drapé dans ses vêtements liturgiques et trônant sur la chaire patriarcale, introduit son grand 'œuvre, *L'Histoire des patriarches de Jérusalem* (*in folio*, format du papier : 384 x 276 mm ; format du champ occupé par l'impression de l'image : 335 x 224 mm).[8] Le livre fut publié grâce aux soins du successeur du patriarche, son neveu Chrysanthe, par deux imprimeurs, le hiéromoine Métrophane Grègoras de Dodone, en Epire, et le

---

B. Heyberger, « De l'image religieuse à l'image profane? L'essor de l'image chez les chrétiens de Syrie et du Liban (XVIIe – XIXe siècle) », dans Hetberger, Naef (éds.), *La multiplication des images en pays d'Islam*, p. 26–43.

7 A. Calabi, *La gravure italienne au XVIIIe siècle*, Paris, 1931, p. 1–19.

8 Dosithée de Jérusalem, *Historia peri ton en Hierosolumois patriarkheusanton*, Bucarest, 1715 [1722]. Voir les descriptions de l'édition dans É. Legrand, *Bibliographie hellénique ou description raisonnée des ouvrages publiés par des Grecs au dix-huitième siècle*, t. 1, Paris, 1918, p. 120–122, n. 97, pl. ; I. Bianu, N. Hodoş, *Bibliografia Românească veche, 1508–1830*, t. 1, Bucarest, 1903, p. 501–508, n. 175 ; Th. I. Papadopoulos, *Hellenike vivliographia (1466 ci.–1800)*, t. 1 : *Alphavetike kai khronologike anakatataxis*, Athènes, 1984, p. 331, n. 4442 ; Todt, « Dositheos II. von Jerusalem », p. 679–680 ; *Antim Ivireanul. Opera tipografică*, éd. Arhim. Policarp (Chiţulescu), D. Bădără, I. M. Croitoru, G. Dumitrescu, I. Feodorov, Bucarest, 2016, p. 209–211 ; O.-L. Dimitriu, *Ilustraţia cărţii româneşti vechi din secolul al XVIII-lea în colecţiile Bibliotecii Academiei Române. Gravura, vol. 1 : Ţara Românească*, Bucarest, 2023, p. 24–25, 96–99.

9 P. Synodinos, « Metrophanes Gregoras », *Epeirotika khronika*, 1–2, 1927, p. 302–303 ; Kournoutos, « He *Dodekavivlos* tou Dositheou », p. 259–273 ; Sarris, « O Chrysanthos Notaras », p. 28–38 ; D. Lupu, « Tipografi bucureşteni : popa Stoica Iacovici (1715–1749) şi familia sa », *Bucureşti. Materiale de istorie şi muzeografie*, vol. XXV, 2011, p. 240–258 ; Miladinova, *The Panoplia Dogmatike*, p. 61–66, 75–76 ; Dzh. N. Ramazanova, « 'Istoriia ierusalimskikh patriarkhov' Dosifeia v russkoĭ kul'ture XVIII XIX vv. », *Rossiia i Khristianskiĭ Vostok*, t. IV–V, Moscou, 2015, p. 440–441 ; E. Chiaburu, « 'Cazul' tipografului Stoica Iacovici (1715–1749). Clarificări noi », *Istorie şi cultură. In honorem academician Andrei Eşanu*, Chişinău, 2018, p. 428–439.

10 Kournoutos, « He *Dodekavivlos* tou Dositheou », p. 263–273 ; Stathi, *Chrysanthos Notaras*, p. 244–245 ; Sarris, « O Chrysanthos Notaras », p. 32–52 ; K. Sarris, « 'Diorthonontas' ten

prêtre Stoica Iacovici.[9] Bien qu'il ait été publié vers 1722, quinze ans après le décès de Dosithée, la page de titre de l'ouvrage porte la date de 1715.[10]

Le portrait de Dosithée inséré dans le livre de Bucarest influença probablement les éditeurs d'Europe occidentale qui souhaitèrent ultérieurement embellir tel ou tel ouvrage d'une représentation de patriarche orthodoxe. Citons le premier volume de l'édition des œuvres de Théodoret de Cyr, publié à Halle en 1768 par Eugénios Voulgaris : l'ouvrage comprend une dédicace au patriarche œcuménique Samuel Ier Hangerli (1763–1768, 1773–1774), ainsi qu'un portrait de patriarche[11] gravé par l'artiste allemand Gottlieb August Liebe de Leipzig (« Liebe fec: Lipsiae »).[12] Le même modèle fut utilisé pour représenter le patriarche Éphrem II de Jérusalem (1766–1770) par un autre graveur allemand actif à Leipzig, Johann Michael Stock (1770).[13] Il était également utilisé à Venise : en 1790, une édition de l'*acolouthia* commémorant le saint martyr Séraphin († 1601) intégra un portrait visiblement influencé par celui de Dosithée de Jérusalem, mais qui fonda pourtant la tradition iconographique de cet archevêque de Fanari et Neochori.[14] Enfin, le psautier en arabe publié à Vienne en 1792 offre l'image du patriarche Anthime de Jérusalem (1788–1808), vraisemblablement inspirée elle aussi de celle de Dosithée.[15]

---

akolouthia khronon : ta ikhni tou Chrysanthou Notara sten ekdosi tes *Istorias* tou Dositheou Hierosolumon (Voukouresti, 1722) », *Elenkhos ideon kai logokrisia apo tis aparkhes tes ellenikes tupographias mekhri to Suntagma tou 1844. Praktika sunedriou, Leukosia, 18–20 Noembriou 2015*, Athènes, 2018, p. 193–215 ; Ramazanova, « 'Istoriia ierusalimskikh patriarkhov' Dosifeia », p. 435–458. La correspondance concernant les travaux typographiques en Valachie dans les années 1714–1720 a été publiée dans E. de Hurmuzaki, *Documente privitoare la Istoria Românilor*, vol. 14. *Documente grecești privitoare la istoria Românilor*, pt. 3 (c. 1560–c. 1820), éd. N. Iorga, Bucarest, 1936, p. 115–123, 137–139, 143–145 ; Kournoutos, « He *Dodekavivlos* tou Dositheou », p. 265–272. Dans les années 1720, le patriarche Chrysanthe voyagea beaucoup, séjournant notamment à Jérusalem. Le livre fut-il imprimé à Bucarest pendant son absence ? Ou doit-on approfondir la réflexion sur la date de l'*Histoire* de Dosithée ? Voir A. Papadopoulos-Kerameus, *Hierosolumitike vivliotheke*, t. 4, Bruxelles, 1963, n. 237, p. 201–202.

11 Theodoritos, episkopos Kurou, *Ta Sozomena, hellenisti hama kai romaisti ekdothenta*, t. 1, Halle, 1768.

12 M. Huber, *Catalogue raisonné du cabinet d'estampes de feu Monsieur Winckler*, t. 1 : *L'école allemande*, Leipzig, [1801], p. 532.

13 Vienne, Österreichische Nationalbibliothek, *Ephraim II., Patriarch von Jerusalem*. https:// data.onb.ac.at/rep/BAG_7495690 (accès le 11.11.2022). Le portrait est publié dans *Isaak tou Surou ta Eurethenta asketika*, Leipzig, 1770.

14 *Akolouthia tou hagiou Hieromartyros Serapheim, arkhiepiskopou Phanariou kai Neokhoriou, tou thaumatourgou*, Enetiesi, 1790.

15 *Kitāb tafsīr al-zabūr al-ilāhī al-sharīf ta'līf... Anthīmūs baṭriyark madīnat Ūrshalīm*, Fiḥyinā [Vienne], 1792. Cf. : G. Roper, « Arabic Biblical and Liturgical Texts Printed in Europe in the

Le portrait de Dosithée dans *L'Histoire des patriarches de Jérusalem* présente une inscription en grec comportant sa titulature abrégée « Dosithée, par la grâce de Dieu patriarche de la Ville Sainte de Jérusalem » (Δοσίθεος ἐλέῳ Θεοῦ πατριάρχης τῆς Ἁγίας Πόλεως Ἱερουσαλήμ). Dans le coin inférieur droit sont visibles en outre les initiales « AF » en monogramme. On retrouve ces mêmes initiales sur le portrait de Chrysanthe Notaras publié dans son *Introduction à la géographie et sphèrologie*, édité à Paris en 1716 (format du papier : 375 x 255 mm ; format du champ occupé par l'impression de l'image : 299 x 202 mm).[16] (Fig. 2) Ce portrait s'accompagne de l'inscription « Chrysanthe Notaras, archimandrite du trône patriarchal de Jérusalem » (Χρύσανθος Νοταρᾶς Πελοποννήσιος, ὁ τοῦ πατριαρχικοῦ θρόνου τῶν Ἱεροσολύμων ἀρχιμανδρίτης). Un second portrait de Chrysanthe, observable dans l'*Histoire des Lieux Saints*, ne porte pas de signature mais présente de tels similitudes avec le précédent qu'on le doit très probablement au même artiste ou qu'il servit de modèle.[17] La représentation de Dosithée est véritablement la figuration en majesté d'un pontife orthodoxe, tandis que celui de Chrysanthe le montre sous les traits d'un savant astronome, muni d'un globe et d'une boussole à la manière des savants occidentaux.[18] Dans les deux cas, on note la similitude des polices de caractères employées pour les inscriptions.

16th–18th Centuries », dans A. Berciu, R. Pop, J. Rotaru (éds.), *Lucrările Simpozionului Internaţional : Cartea. România. Europa. Ediţia a II-a – Biblioteca Metropolitană Bucureşti, 20–24 septembrie 2009 : 550 de ani de la prima atestare documentară a oraşului Bucureşti*, Bucarest, 2010, p. 180 ; Roper, « The Vienna Arabic Psalter of 1792 and the Role of Typography in European-Arab Relations », dans J. Frimmel, M. Wögerbauer (éds.), *European-Arab Relations in the 18th Century and Earlier. Kommunikation und Information im 18. Jahrhundert : das Beispiel der Habsburgermonarchie*, Wiesbaden, 2009, p. 77–89 ; Heyberger, « De l'image religieuse à l'image profane ? », p. 36.

16 Chrysanthos Notaras. *Eisagoge eis ta geographika kai sphairika*. Paris, 1716, deuxième édition : Venise, 1718. Description : Legrand, *Bibliographie hellénique*, t. 1, p. 137–140, n. 107, pl. ; Papadopoulos, *Hellenike vivliographia*, t. 1, p. 330, n. 4431–4432. Sur les livres édités par Chrysanthe Notaras et sur ses projets scientifiques, voir Kournoutos, « He *Dodekabiblos tou Dositheou* », p. 258–261 ; Stathi, *Chrysanthos Notaras*, p. 89–90 ; Dzh. N. Ramazanova, « Èkzempliary sochineniĭ ierusalimskogo patriarkha Khrisanfa Notara v sobranii Muzeia knigi RGB », *Vivliofika : Istoriia knigi i izuchenie knizhnykh pamiatnikov*, t. 2, Moscou, 2011, p. 168–175 ; V. Kontouma, « The Archimandrite and the Astronomer. The Visit of Chrysanthos Notaras to Giovanni Domenico Cassini : a New Approach », dans K. Sarris, N. Pissis, M. Pechlivanos (éds.), *Confessionalization and/as Knowledge Transfer in the Greek Orthodox Church*, Wiesbaden, 2021, p. 234–272 ; G. Aujac, « Chrysanthos Notaras et les systèmes du monde », *Pallas. Revue d'études antiques. Palladio Magistro. Mélanges Jean Soubiran*, Toulouse, 2002, p. 75–88.

17 Chrysanthos Notaras. *Historia, kai perigraphe tes Hagias Ges, kaì tes Hagías Poleos Hierousalem*, Venise, 1728.

18 Kontouma, « The Archimandrite and the Astronomer », p. 240.

Chrysanthe succéda à son oncle Dosithée sur la chaire de Jérusalem à la mort de ce dernier en 1707. L'inscription visible sur le portrait de l'édition de 1716 ne correspondait donc pas au statut de Chrysanthe au moment de la publication. Le texte de l'ouvrage présente la même inexactitude, désignant l'auteur comme « prêtre et archimandrite » alors même que le livre fut publié près de dix ans après l'élection de Chrysanthe à la chaire de son oncle. L'*Introduction* est dédicacée à Scarlat Mavrocordate, fils né en 1701 du prince Nicolas Mavrocordate, « souverain et voïvode de Hongrovalachie » lorsque parut le livre (1715–1716, 1719–1730). On ignore les raisons qui déterminèrent le choix de ne désigner en 1716 le « très savant » auteur, alors patriarche, que comme « prêtre et archimandrite ». Certains auteurs supposent que le texte du livre et le portrait étaient finalisés avant l'élection patriarcale de Chrysanthe mais que, pour une raison ou pour une autre, l'édition en fut pendant longtemps repoussée.[19]

Autre bizarrerie du livre de Chrysanthe, le lieu d'édition indiqué sur la page de titre. Habituellement, les éditeurs spécifiaient toujours leurs noms en plus du lieu d'impression. Or, dans le cas de l'*Introduction à la géographie et sphèrologie*, le nom de l'éditeur est absent, le lieu d'édition étant seul indiqué : Paris, sans autres précisions.[20] Cette prétendue publication à Paris relève sans doute moins de la réalité que d'une forme d'affectation :[21] la deuxième édition du livre sortit de la typographie vénitienne d'Antonio Bortoli seulement deux ans plus tard, en 1718.[22] L'édition de 1716 comprenait une carte du monde réalisée, selon l'inscription qu'elle porte, en 1700 à Padoue par « le prêtre Chrysanthe » lui-même.[23] Cette même édition présentait par ailleurs une épigramme sur le socle supportant

---

19 Ramazanova « Ėkzempliary sochineniĭ », p. 171 ; Kontouma, « The Archimandrite and the Astronomer », p. 240.

20 Ces collaborations des hiérarques de Jérusalem avec les éditeurs parisiens ne doivent pas étonner. Les décisions du Concile de l'Église orthodoxe réuni à Bethleem et à Jérusalem en 1672 furent précisément publiées en grec avec une traduction latine à Paris : *Synodus Bethlehemitica adversus Calvinistas hæreticos*, Paris, 1676 ; *Synodus Jerosolymitana, adversus Calvinistas haereticos*, Paris, 1678.

21 Kontouma, « The Archimandrite and the Astronomer », p. 262, n. 118.

22 Legrand, *Bibliographie hellénique*, t. 1, p. 151–152, n. 122 ; Stathi, *Chrysanthos Notaras*, p. 99–103, 201–204. Le seul exemplaire de l'édition de 1718 connu d'É. Legrand appartenait à la bibliothèque de l'École évangélique de Smyrne. La photographie de la page de titre de cette édition rare est publiée dans Stathi, *Chrysanthos Notaras*, p. 168.

23 Ramazanova, « Ėkzempliary sochineniĭ », p. 172 ; Kontouma, « The Archimandrite and the Astronomer », p. 250–262. Sur les sources occidentales de cette carte, voir E. Livieratos, Ch. Boutoura, M. Pazarli, N. Ploutoglou, A. Tsorlini, « The Very First Printed Map in Greek, a Derived Map from Dutch Cartography : Chrysanthos Notaras' World Map (1700) vs Jan Luyts' World Map (1692) », *e-Perimetron*, 6 (3), 2011, p. 200–218.

le portrait de Chrysanthe. Le poème était l'œuvre d'un Crétois nommé Nikolaos Vouvoulios, médecin et philosophe ayant étudié à Padoue, connu également pour des épigrammes sur ces deux compatriotes, Gérasime Vlachos et Nikolaos Comnenos Papadopoulos, lesquels résidaient également à Venise et Padoue.[24] Tout indique donc que l'édition fut préparée en réalité à Venise et Padoue, où Chrysanthe avait étudié trois ans durant, plutôt qu'à Paris où il ne fit qu'un court séjour au printemps 1700.[25]

Le secret de l'apparition de Paris en lieu et place de Venise comme lieu de la première édition du livre de Chrysanthe semble devoir être cherché dans les difficultés rencontrées par le typographe pour obtenir le droit d'éditer le livre.[26] Antonio Bortoli, dont le nom figure sur la deuxième édition du livre du 1718, avait acheté en 1707 la typographie de Nicolas Saros après la mort de ce dernier à la condition expresse d'en conserver le nom sur les pages de titre. La concurrence sur le marché vénitien du livre était très forte et il était nécessaire par ailleurs d'obtenir le « privilège », c'est-à-dire l'autorisation de publier un ouvrage. Pour cette raison, sans doute, Antonio Bortoli publia certains ouvrages avec la marque de Saros, dont les fils étaient ses associés, tandis que d'autres portaient sa propre marque.[27] L'édition de 1718, réalisée à Venise « con licenza de' superiori, e pri-

---

24 A. Papadopoulos-Bretos, *Neoellenike philologia*, t. 2, Athènes, 1857, p. 247 ; Legrand, *Bibliographie hellénique*, t. 1, p. 138 ; Karathanases, *Oi Ellenes logioi*, p. 63 ; Stathi, *Chrysanthos Notaras*, p. 91.

25 Stathi, *Chrysanthos Notaras*, p. 82–91 ; Kontouma, « The Archimandrite and the Astronomer », p. 233–238. Hasan Çolak préfère envisager que le livre ait pu être imprimé à Vienne : Çolak, « Bilim », p. 47, ann. 54.

26 De telles fausses adresses d'imprimeries ne sont pas rares à l'époque car elles permettaient de produire des « contrefaçons » en contournant l'obligation d'obtenir le « privilège » autorisant la publication, ou encore d'éditer des livres prohibés. Voir, par exemple, les nombreux cas recensés en Italie et en France dans M. Parenti, *Dizionario dei luoghi di stampa falsi, inventati o supposti*, Firenze, 1951, p. 7–11 (l'ouvrage de Chrysanthe Notaras est absent du dictionnaire) ; H. Boyer, « Une fausse marque typographique », *Archives du bibliophile*, 1, 1858, p. 83–84 ; G. Brunet, *Imprimeurs imaginaires et libraires supposés. Étude bibliographique suivie de recherches sur quelques ouvrages imprimés avec des indications fictives de lieux ou avec des dates singulières*, Paris, 1866, p. 1–12 ; E. Droz, « Fausses adresses typographiques », *Bibliothèque d'Humanisme et Renaissance*, 23 (1), 1961, p.138–152 ; t. 23 (2), 1961, p. 379–394 ; D. Coq, « Les livres anciens : formats, cahiers, signatures, page de titre, fausses adresses, colophon et toutes ces sortes de choses », *Apprendre à gérer des collections patrimoniales en bibliothèque*, Villeurbanne, 2012, p. 71. Je remercie Jean-Claude Waquet pour ces références bibliographiques.

27 G. Ploumidis, « Tre tipografie di libri greci : Salicata, Saro e Bortoli », *Ateneo Veneto*, n. s., 9 (1–2), 2071, p. 246–250 ; G. Ploumidis, « Stampando greco a Venezia », *Crkvene studije, Niš / Church Studies, Nis*, 15, 2018, p. 210. La marque de Saros se trouve sur l'édition des « didascalies » réalisée à Venise en 1724 par Chrysanthe, toujours mentionné comme « prêtre et archimandrite »

vilegio », fut identique, selon Émile Legrand, à celle de « Paris ».[28] Néanmoins, ce deuxième tirage fut probablement plus restreint que le premier dont on a conservé plusieurs exemplaires. On pourrait également envisager que la mention de Paris comme lieu officiel d'édition ait pu découler d'un choix délibéré de Chrysanthe. En terre roumaine, celui-ci se trouvait dans une situation délicate à cause du conflit entre Venise et l'Empire ottoman (1714–1718) et peut-être préféra-t-il alors attribuer à son ouvrage une origine française en raison de l'alliance ancienne entre Paris et Constantinople.

Le patriarche Chrysanthe, responsable de l'édition de l'*Introduction* et de celle de l'*Histoire des patriarches de Jérusalem* de son oncle, poursuivait les travaux lancés par son prédécesseur en Valachie grâce au soutien constant et généreux du prince Constantin Brâncoveanu (1688–1714). L'exécution de ce bienfaiteur par les autorités ottomanes en 1714 mit en péril le financement de ses entreprises éditoriales. En outre, le successeur du souverain, Ştefan II Cantacuzène (1675–1716), fut également exécuté en juin 1716, tandis que le célèbre imprimeur Antim Ivireanul, métropolite de Hongrovalachie (1708–1716), était déposé de sa chaire et tué sur le chemin de l'exil la même année.[29] La modification de la date de publication de l'*Histoire* de Dosithée reflète sans doute cette instabilité politique en Valachie.[30] Ce n'est qu'à partir des années 1720, selon Constantin Sarris, que la situation se calma, ce qui aura permis à Chrysanthe d'achever la publication du manuscrit du patriarche Dosithée, sortie probablement en 1722, ainsi que de poursuivre les travaux d'édition d'autres livres.[31]

Ces problèmes politiques poussèrent Chrysanthe à rechercher des collaborations à l'étranger. Le recours à Antonio Bortoli ne dut sans doute rien au hasard, ce typographe ayant déjà des liens avec la Valachie : en 1712, il avait publié pour le compte de Constantin Brâncoveanu une réédition du dictionnaire de la langue grecque de Guarino Favorino imprimé pour la première fois à Bâle en 1538. Le livre était dédicacé au prince, protecteur et mécène du patriarche Dosithée et de son successeur Chrysanthe.[32] Le frontispice de cette édition était embelli d'un portrait

---

du patriarcat de Jérusalem : Chrysanthos Notaras, *Didaskalia ophelimos peri metanoias, kaì exomologeseos*, Venise, 1724.

28 Legrand, *Bibliographie hellénique*, t. 1, p. 151–152.

29 Sur le sort des typographies en Pays roumains, voir Kournoutos, « He *Dodekabiblos* tou Dositheou », p. 262–264.

30 Sarris, « O Chrysanthos Notaras », p. 32, 37–52.

31 Sarris, « O Chrysanthos Notaras », p. 46.

32 Guarino Favorino [Varinus Phavorinus]. *To mega lexikon, e ho thesauros pases tes Hellenikes glosses*. Venise, 1712. À propos de cette édition, voir L. Augliera, « Hellenes kai hellenika biblia sta epistemonika kaì philologika periodika tes Benetias tou 18-ou aiona », *To Entupo helleniko*

de Constantin Brâncoveanu par le graveur Alessandro Dalla Via (« Alexander á Via sculp. Venet. ») qui travaillait pour Bortoli. Plus tard, en 1718, le même graveur contribua à la réalisation d'un autre portrait d'après une image du célèbre artiste vénitien Pietro Uberti (1671– c. 1762).[33] L'image est placée entre les pages 192 et 193 de l'*Istoria delle moderne rivoluzioni della Valachia* par Antonmaria Del Chiaro, publiée dans l'imprimerie Bortoli en 1718.[34] Le souverain y était représenté avec ses quatre fils, Constantin, Ştefan, Radu et Matei, et le portrait précédait le récit de leur exécution à Constantinople en 1714 en présence du sultan. La similitude du portrait intégré dans l'*Istoria delle moderne rivoluzioni* avec celui du diction- naire de Guarino Favorino amène à supposer que, là aussi, Alessandro Dalla Via travailla d'après un modèle fourni par Uberti.

On l'a vu, les noms de l'artiste et du graveur vénitiens qui réalisèrent les portraits du prince Constantin Brâncoveanu sont connus. En revanche, l'iden- tité de l'artiste qui exécuta les portraits présents dans les éditions commandées par Chrysanthe n'a jamais été élucidée bien que ces images aient été publiées par Émile Legrand, qui souligna l'existence des initiales de l'artiste, dès 1918.[35] Au XVIIIᵉ siècle, les graveurs vénitiens étaient célèbres et leur production très diffusée, contribuant à la conquête du marché du livre européen par les produc- tions de la Sérénissime.[36] Ainsi, puisque diverses indications nous ont permis de proposer que l'*Introduction à la géographie et sphèrologie* ait été éditée d'emblée à Venise, on pourrait sans doute à raison chercher dans cette ville l'artiste qui se dissimule derrière les initiales AF. En outre, les similitudes de composition des portraits de Chrysanthe et du prince Constantin Brâncoveanu, le partage de cer- tains éléments ornementaux (par exemple les motifs décoratifs des vêtements), le style commun des inscriptions portant les noms et titres des personnages, per- mettent d'envisager qu'ils aient été produits dans le même cercle.

L'étude du milieu artistique vénitien révèle une famille d'artistes et graveurs du nom de Faldoni, originaire de la région d'Asolo, ville proche de Venise, dont

---

biblio. 15os-19os aionas. Praktika tou diethnous sunedriou. Delphoi, 16-20 Maiou 2001, Athènes, 2004, p. 255–257.

33 V. Donaggio, « Alessandro Dalla Via : un contributo all'arte incisoria veneta tra XVII e XVIII secolo », *Arte in Friuli – Arte a Trieste*, 36, 2017, p. 108.

34 A. Del Chiaro, *Istoria delle moderne rivoluzioni della Valachia*, Venise, 1718. Plus tard, en 1742, le même éditeur publia d'autres textes sur l'histoire des princes roumains ; G. S. Ploumides, « Ta en Padoue palaia hellenika vivlia (Biblioteca Universitaria – Biblioteca Civica) », *Thesaurismata*, 5, 1968, p. 224–225, ill. 15.

35 Legrand, *Bibliographie hellénique*, t. 1, p. 122, 138.

36 G. Morazzoni, *Il libro illustrato veneziano del Settecento*, Milan, 1943, p. 55–76 ; *Il libro illustra- to italiano. Secoli XVII–XVIII*, éd. par E. C. Pirani, Rome ; Milan, 1956, p. 10.

certains membres signaient leurs œuvres d'initiales AF qui servaient en quelque sorte de « marque d'entreprise familiale ».[37] Au XVIIIᵉ siècle, le plus célèbre artiste de cette famille était Giovanni Antonio (Gianantonio) Faldoni (1689–1770).[38] Représentant de l'école vénitienne de gravure, il était surtout connu pour ses portraits à l'eau-forte.[39] Il signait ses œuvres de diverses manières, indiquant parfois le nom « Antonio Faldoni » ou simplement « Faldonus », ou encore deux ou trois initiales.[40] Les premières œuvres attribuées à ce graveur furent le portrait du procurateur de Saint-Marc Giovanni Emo, exécuté d'après un dessin d'Angelo Trevisani en 1723, et, en 1724–1726, les gravures d'après les œuvres du Parmigianino que commanda A. M. Zanetti (également originaire de la région d'Asolo).[41] Ce même éditeur demanda également à Faldoni de graver diverses

---

37 F. Brulliot, *Dictionnaire des monogrammes, marques figurées, lettres initiales, noms abrégés etc. avec lesquels les peintres, dessinateurs, graveurs et sculpteurs ont désigné leurs noms*, t. 1, Munich, 1832, p. 43, n. 317 ; G. Duplessis, H. Bouchot, *Dictionnaire des marques et monogrammes de graveurs*, Paris, 1886, p. 13 ; O. Ris-Paquot, *Dictionnaire encyclopédique des marques et monogrammes, chiffres, lettres initiales, signes figuratifs, etc., etc. contenant 12.156 marques*, t. 1 : A-I, Paris, [s. d.], p. 23, n. 515–516, cf. n. 505 ; p. 25, n. 541–543.

38 A. Ravà, « Faldoni, Giovanni Antonio », dans U. Thieme, F. Becker (éds.), *Allgemeines Lexikon der Bildenden Künstler von der Antike bis zur Gegenwart*, Bd. 11, Leipzig, 1915, p. 227 ; G. Lorenzetti, « Un dilettante incisore veneziano del XVIII secolo. Anton Maria Zanetti di Gerolamo », *Miscellanea di Storia Veneta della R. Deputazione di Storia Patria*, serie III, vol. XII, Venise, 1917, p. 34, 53–55, 67, 69 ; G. Moschini, *Dell'incisione in Venezia. Memoria di Giannantonio Moschini*, Venise, 1924, p. 88–90 ; *Aspetti dell'incisione veneziana nel Settecento. Catalogo della mostra*, éd. par G. Dillon, R. Da Tos, Venise, 1976, p. 40 ; L. Comacchio, *Giovanni Antonio Faldoni incisore Asolano (1689–1770)*, Castelfranco Veneto, 1976 ; *Da Carlevarijs ai Tiepolo. Incisori veneti e friulani del Settecento. Catalogo della mostra*, éd. par D. Succi, Venise, 1983, p. 161–165, n. 178–184 ; L. Dal Poz, « La memoria incisa. Interventi di tutela del Fondo storico dell'Accademia di Belle Arti di Venezia », dans A. G. Cassani (éd.), *Annuario dell'Accademia di belle arti di Venezia. Che cos'è scenografia ? Lo spazio dello sguardo dal teatro alla città*, Venise, 2012, p. 494, 499.

39 L. M. di. Sannazaro, *Catalogo di una raccolta di stampe antiche*, vol. 2, Milan, 1824, p. 372–373; *Da Carlevarijs ai Tiepolo*, p. 161 ; S. Boorsch, *Venetian Prints and Books in the Age of Tiepolo. The Metropolitan Museum of Arts*, New York, 1997, p. 6–8, 38–39, fig. 5, cat. 67–70, 82 ; *Tiepolo, Piazzetta, Novelli. L'incanto del libro illustrato nel Settecento veneto. Catalogo della mostra (Padova 22 novembre 2012 – 7 aprile 2013)*, éd. par V. C. Donvito, D. Ton, Padoue, 2012, p. 426–427.

40 *Tiepolo, Piazzetta, Novelli*, p. 426–429, n. VIII.10–13.

41 *Raccolta di varie stampe e chiaroscuro tratte da disegni originali di Francesco Mazzuola detto il Parmigiano e d'altri insigni autori da Anton Maria Zanetti q. m. Gir. che gli istessi disegni possiede*, Venise, 1749 ; *Varii disegni inventati dal celebre Francesco Mazzuola detto Il Parmigianino tratti dalla Raccolta Zanettiana, incisi in rame da Antonio Faldoni e novamente pubblicati*, Venise, 1786. Voir R. Gallo, *L'incisione nel '700 a Venezia e a Bassano*, Venise, 1941, p. 20–22 ; Comacchio, *Giovanni Antonio Faldoni*, p. 11, 15 ; Ch. Gauna, « I Rembrandt di Anton Maria Zanetti e le 'edizioni' di stampe a Venezia : tra tecnica e stile », *Saggi e Memorie di storia dell'arte*, 36, 2012, p. 189–234.

représentations de statues antiques publiées dans un catalogue en 1740–1743[42] (signé : « G. Ant. Faldoni sculp[sit] »).[43] En 1724, Faldoni exécuta le portrait d'un collègue vénitien, artiste du nom de Marco Ricci de Belluno, le signant « AFaldoni Ven. Sculp. 1724 ».[44] L'atlas botanique de Gian Girolamo Zanichelli, publié par Antonio Bortoli en 1735, fut également décoré par les soins de Faldoni d'un portrait du procurateur de Saint-Marc Andrea Da Lezze, auquel le livre était dédié. Il signa en cette occasion « AFaldoni delineauit, et sculpsit ».[45] Ultérieurement, Faldoni collabora à la préparation d'un magnifique ouvrage dédié aux intérieurs d'un palais florentin et glorifiant l'empereur François Ier Étienne du Saint-Empire, également grand-duc de Toscane (1737–1765), signant « Antonio Faldoni Inta. ».[46] La signature en monogramme AF, identique à celles présentes sur les portraits de Dosithée et Chrysanthe, s'observe sur le portrait du cardinal Niccolò Albergati (1373–1443), canonisé par le pape Benoît XIV en 1744.[47] (Fig. 3)

Faldoni collabora avec divers éditeurs, dont Antonio Bortoli, qui lui commandaient des gravures sur des sujets très variés pour illustrer livres ou albums d'images. Rien d'étonnant donc à ce que l'on retrouve dans un autre ouvrage

---

42 A. M. Zanetti, *Delle antiche statue greche e romane, che nell'antisala della Libreria di San Marco, e in altri luoghi publici di Venezia si trovano*, vol. 1–2, Venise, 1740–1743. Voir sur cette édition, C. Crosera, « Anton Maria di Girolamo Zanetti (1680–1767), Anton Maria di Alessandro Zanetti (1706-1778) », *Tiepolo, Piazzetta, Novelli*, p. 390–395, n. VIII.1.

43 À propos des autres variantes de signature de l'époque de la collaboration de l'artiste avec Zanetti, voir Lorenzetti, « Un dilettante incisore », p. 126–131. Portrait de Zanetti, gravé par Faldoni : Boorsch, *Venetian Prints*, p. 6, fig. 5. Pour les listes et les exemples des œuvres de l'artiste et son style, voir Comacchio, *Giovanni Antonio Faldoni*, p. 19–34 ; D. Succi, *La Serenissima nello specchio di rame. Splendore di una civiltà figurativa del Settecento. L'opera completa dei grandi maestri veneti*, vol. 1, Castelfranco Veneto, 2013, p. 21, 145, 148, 450–451, 453, 455.

44 Boorsch, *Venetian Prints*, p. 38, n. 67 ; *Tiepolo, Piazzetta, Novelli*, p. 428.

45 G. G. Zannichelli, *Istoria delle piante che nascono ne'lidi intorno a Venezia*, Venise, 1735. Voir C. Skordoulis, G. Katsiampoura, E. Nicolaidis, « The Scientific Culture in Eighteenth to Nineteenth Century Greek Speaking Communities : Experiments and Textbooks », dans P. Heering, R. Wittje (éds.), *Learning by Doing: Experiments and Instruments in the History of Science Teaching*, Stuttgart, 2011, p. 3–18.

46 *Pitture del salone imperiale del palazzo di Firenze, si aggiungono le pitture del salone e cortile delle imperiali ville della Petraia e del Poggio a Caiano, opere di vari celebri pittori fiorentini in tavole XXVI, date ora la prima volta in luce*, Florence, 1766, n. IV, V.

47 Londres, Wellcome Collection. Reference: 6691i (Public domain) https://wellcomecollection.org/works/nq2qslic8 (acces 21.12.2022). Ce cardinal était célèbre pour avoir ouvert le concile de Florence qui vit promulguer l'Union entre les Églises catholique et orthodoxe : E. Pásztor, « Albergati, Niccolò », Dizionario biografico degli Italiani, Rome, 1960, p. 619–621 ; R. Parmeggiani, *Il vescovo e il capitolo : il cardinale Niccolò Albergati e i canonici di S. Pietro di Bologna (1417-1443). Un'inedita visita pastorale alla cattedrale (1437)*, Bologne, 2009, p. 3–79.

publié par ce typographe en 1720 un portrait à l'eau-forte réalisé par le même artiste et signé par le même monogramme AF dans le coin inférieur gauche. Il embellit une publication des « enseignements » sur le Carême du savant évêque de Kernikè (Kernitza) et Kalavryta, Hélie Miniatis (format du papier : 225 x 165 mm ; format du champ occupé par l'impression de l'image : 190 x 130 mm).[48] (Fig. 4) L'inscription qui accompagne le portrait indique l'âge de la mort du hiérarque : « Hélie Miniatis de Céphalonie, [évêque] de Kernikè et Kalabryta au Péloponnèse, âgé de 45 ans, 1714 » (Ἠλίας Μηνιάτης Κεφαληνιεὺς ὁ Κερνίκης καὶ Καλαβρύτων ἐν Πελοποννήσῳ ἐπίσκοπος ἐτῶν ΜΕʹ, ΑΨΙΔʹ).[49] La date d'exécution du portrait est inconnue mais il est probable que cette eau-forte fut réalisée peu ou prou en même temps que l'édition (1720), c'est-à-dire après la mort du personnage représenté.

Les portraits de Chrysanthe Notaras, d'Hélie Mignatis et de Dosithée de Jérusalem comptent donc au nombre des tous premiers travaux de Faldoni, œuvres qu'il exécuta pour l'imprimerie de Bortoli ou pour les projets éditoriaux de Chrysanthe Notaras, liés à cette imprimerie. (Fig. 5) Curieusement, ils sont devenus les œuvres les plus célèbres, et les plus diffusées, de cet artiste, alors même que les admirateurs de ces portraits en ignoraient jusqu'à aujourd'hui l'attribution.

Il n'est pas impossible que les dates des eaux-fortes qu'exécuta Faldoni pour Chrysanthe Notaras aient pu différer de celles portées sur les pages de titre des éditions qu'elles décorent. Il est en effet significatif que certains exemplaires de la première édition de l'*Introduction* de Chrysanthe ne contiennent pas son portrait. À la Bibliothèque d'État de Russie à Moscou, l'un des deux exemplaires

---

48 Helias Meniates, *Didakhai eis ten Hagian kai Megalen Tessarakosten kai eis allas episemous heortas*. Venise, 1720 (rééditions en 1727, 1738, 1755, 1763). Voir Legrand, *Bibliographie hellénique*, t. 1, p. 162–163, n. 128 ; p. 205–205, n. 172 ; p. 268–269, n. 254 ; p. 440, n. 450 ; t. 2, Paris, 1928, p. 13, n. 586. Sur Hélie Miniatis, voir G. Podskalsky, *Griechische Theologie*, p. 319–323 ; IU. A. Kazachkov, « Iliia (Min'latis) », *Pravoslavnaia èntsiklopediia*, t. 22, Moscou, 2009, p. 284–285.

49 Il n'est pas impossible que dans la réalisation du portrait de Hélie Miniatis l'artiste se soit inspiré de celui de Mélèce Typaldos, métropolite de Philadelphie († 1713), gravé en 1690 par Aniello Porzio d'après un tableau de Sebastiano Bombelli : https://www.pinterest.it/pin/758645499721337589/ (accès le 11.12.2022). La date du décès de Miniatis est spécifiée aussi dans l'inscription que porte la copie de son portrait réalisée pour des cercles russes où circulaient ses œuvres, très appréciées (https://www.hermitagemuseum.org/wps/portal/hermitage/digital-collection/04.+engraving/1509727 [accès le 10.12.2022]). Sur les traductions des œuvres de Miniatis en langues slaves : Dzh. N. Ramazanova, « Russkie spiski perevodnykh sochineniĭ Ilii Miniatisa (Miniatiia) v XVIII v. », *Vestnik RGGU*, 4(37), ser. « Istoriia. Filologiia. Kul'turologiia. Vostokovedenie », 2018, p. 117–123 ; Dzh. N. Ramazanova, « Grecheskiĭ istoriko-dogmaticheskiĭ traktat Ilii Miniatisa i ego serbskie perevodchiki XVIII veka », *Slověne*, 7 (2), 2018, p. 134–178.

de l'édition de 1716 est dépourvu de portrait d'auteur ;[50] il en va de même pour l'exemplaire de la Bibliothèque Casanatense à Rome (B XI 46).[51] L'*Histoire* du patriarche Dosithée n'est pas davantage toujours illustrée de son portrait. L'image est ainsi absente des exemplaires de la Bodleian Library (N 2.2,3 Th.), de la bibliothèque du Queen's College (Upper Library, 9. E. 21–22) d'Oxford et de la Bibliothèque Apostolique du Vaticane (Hist Riserva. I. 50). En revanche, les portraits du patriarche Dosithée en frontispice se trouvent dans les exemplaires de Christ Church (Special Collections WT. 3. 24, venu de la bibliothèque de l'archevêque de Canterbury William Wake [1657–1737]),[52] dans trois exemplaires de la Bibliothèque de l'Académie roumaine CRV 175 (Unicat/inv. 960 ; doublet 1/inv. 961 et 2/inv. 962), dans un exemplaire de la Bibliothèque du Saint Synode de l'Église orthodoxe roumaine,[53] ainsi que dans un exemplaire de la Bibliothèque universitaire des langues et civilisations orientales à Paris (Res Mon Fol 426 ; l'ancienne cote Q.I.32, t. 1).[54] Dans un exemplaire de la Bibliothèque Apostolique du Vaticane (Hist R. G. Oriente. S. 21, t. 1), le portrait est présent bien qu'en très mauvaise état de conservation.[55]

Dans deux exemplaires, l'un de la Bibliothèque de l'Académie roumaine (CRV 175 doublet 3 /inv. 963) et l'autre de la Bibliothèque du Saint Synode de l'Église orthodoxe roumaine, le portrait de Dosithée fut inséré après la page 182.[56]

---

50 *Russian Travellers to the Greek World (12ᵗʰ – First Half of the 19ᵗʰ Centuries), Exhibition Catalogue*, Moscou, 1995, p. 103; Ramazanova, « Ėkzempliary sochineniĭ », p. 173.

51 Les portraits de Chrysanthe sont présents dans les exemplaires de la Bibliothèque Braidense de Milan (8. 02.H. 0015) et de la Bibliothèque Marciana à Venise (deux exemplaires : D 070D 038 et D 234D 030).

52 Sur la collection de William Wake, voir A. Nachescu, « East-West Connections in the Wake Archive », *Christ Church Library Newsletter*, 12 (1), 2020, p. 32–39. Que le livre ait appartenu à l'archevêque fait penser à la correspondance entre Chrysanthe et William Wake dans le cadre des négociations entre orthodoxes et anglicans : Stathi, *Chrysanthos Notaras*, p. 150.

53 L'exemplaire de la Bibliothèque des Augustins de l'Assomption à Kadi-Keuï, actuellement à la Bibliothèque de l'Institut catholique à Paris (Réserve. R III 11), ne comporte ni frontispice, ni page de titre. Il n'est donc pas possible de préciser si le livre présentait originellement le portrait. L'exemplaire de Bibliothèque de l'Académie roumaine (CRV 175 doublet 4 /inv. 964), qui transita par les bibliothèques du métropolite Andrei Szeptycki de Lviv et du métropolite moldave Iosif Naniescu, est incomplet et dépourvu de toute une partie du livre.

54 L'exemplaire de la BULAC appartenait au patriarche de Constantinople, Païsios II Kioumourtzoglou (1726–1732, 1740–1743, 1744–1748, 1751–1752) : sa signature se trouve à la p. 6 du livre.

55 *Libri romeni antichi e moderni a Roma, nella Biblioteca Apostolica Vaticana (sec. XVII–XIX). Catalogo / Carte românească veche și modernă la Roma, în Biblioteca Apostolică vaticană (sec. XVII–XIX). Catalog*, éd. A. E. Tatay, B. Andriescu, Cité du Vatican, 2020, p. 366.

56 *Antim Ivireanul*, p. 210–211.

Il prend donc place après le sommaire détaillé de l'*Histoire* qui occupe les pages 1–182 et avant le premier livre de l'ouvrage du patriarche Dosithée qui dispose de la nouvelle pagination. Le portrait se trouve donc à l'articulation des deux parties du livre, une variante dont on pourrait sans doute trouver encore d'autres témoins. Les exemplaires dépourvus de portraits ne sont donc pas nécessairement « défectueux », leur frontispice perdu, mais furent sans doute simplement reliés et diffusés avant que Chrysanthe ait reçu les eaux-fortes commandés à Venise. Il est également possible qu'une version moins luxueuse, privée de cette illustration de grande qualité, ait été souhaitée par les éditeurs.

D'autres « irrégularités » et variantes de l'édition de l'*Histoire* peuvent également être repérées. L'exemplaire CRV 175 « Unicat » /inv. 960 de la Bibliothèque de l'Académie roumaine et un exemplaire de la Bibliothèque d'État de Russie[57] contiennent, outre le portrait, deux textes en slavon : une page de titre en traduction (p. 2 : verso de la page de titre grecque) et une adresse (datée d'octobre 1715, p. 14–15) à Stéphane Iavorski, métropolite de Riazan et Mourom, *locum tenens* en absence du patriarche de Moscou (1701–1721),[58] pour obtenir son soutien au

---

57 Bianu, Hodoş, *Bibliografia Românească veche*, p. 507–508 ; Ramazanova, « 'Istoriia ierusa-limskikh patriarkhov' Dosifeia », c. 439, 441–446.

58 Sur Stéphane Iavorski, voir A. V. Ivanov, *A Spiritual Revolution. The Impact of Reformation and Enlightenment in Orthodox Russia*, Madison, WI, 2020, p. 31–40, 82–84. À l'époque du patriarche Dosithée de Jérusalem, les liens de ce siège avec Stéphane Iavorski furent tendus. Voir, par exemple, une lettre de Dosithée à Iavorski écrite en 1701 : É. Legrand, Bibliothèque grecque vulgaire, t. 1, Paris, 1880, p. 40–43. Cf. : N. F. Kapterev, *Sobranie sochineniĭ*, Moscou, 2008, t. 1, p. 580–582 ; t. 2, p. 233–245 ; Palmieri, *Dositeo*, p. 40–42. Le texte adressé à Stéphane Iavorski le mentionne seulement comme métropolite et non comme suppléant du patriarche moscovite. L'édition de l'*Histoire* datant des alentours de l'année 1722 (malgré la date présente sur la page du titre), on notera qu'à cette époque Iavorski avait non seulement perdu sa charge de *locum tenens* du patriarche mais également entrepris de lutter contre le *Règlement spirituel*. Ce *Règlement*, rédigé personnellement par le tsar Pierre le Grand, entra en vigueur en Russie à partir de l'hiver 1721, abolissant le patriarcat moscovite en le remplaçant par « le Très Saint Synode Gouvernant ». Iavorski exprima l'opinion que les nouvelles « autocéphalies » (telles que Moscou) devaient être abolies pour restaurer les prérogatives du patriarcat œcuménique. Selon lui, seul le rétablissement de la prééminence traditionnelle des patriarches de Constantinople sur l'Église russe pouvait permettre au Saint Synode de gouverner en accord avec les canons. Voir V. M. Zhivov, *Iz tserkovnoĭ istorii vremën Petra Velikogo : issledovaniia i materialy*, Moscou, 2004, p. 71–76, 245–265 ; Ivanov, *A Spiritual Revolution*, p. 83. Sur la *Régulation*, voir J. Cracraft, *The Petrine Revolution in Russian Culture*, Cambridge MA/Londres, 2004, p. 174–184. L'idée de Iavorski déplut au tsar qui obtint des patriarches orientaux l'approbation de sa version du *Règlement*. Cependant, cette tentative de Iavorski pour faire réintégrer à « l'ex-patriarcat de Moscou » le giron de l'Église orientale fut bien accueillie par Chrysanthe et le rétablissement de leurs relations se manifesta par la lettre du patriarche de Jérusalem, inclue dans le texte de l'*His-*

projet de traduction du livre. L'adresse à Iavorski en complétait une première qui présentait aux quatre « grands » patriarches orientaux et aux membres du clergé orthodoxe l'œuvre de Dosithée de Jérusalem (p. 3–6). Ces variations de contenu d'exemplaires conçus parfois spécialement pour un destinataire précis montrent comment les éditeurs adaptaient les ouvrages aux nécessités du moment, les décorant d'images ou ajoutant des pages supplémentaires.

Si la date exacte de réalisation des deux portraits de Dosithée et Chrysanthe demeure inconnue, il ne semble pas que l'artiste ait pu les exécuter à partir de modèles vivants, ce qui vaut également pour celui de l'évêque Hélie Miniatis. La carrière du jeune Faldoni ne commença pas réellement avant les années 1720. Les eaux-fortes des deux portraits des hiérarques orthodoxes de Jérusalem comptèrent donc parmi ses premières œuvres, probablement exécutées lorsque Chrysanthe entreprit de rechercher un éditeur hors de Bucarest après la crise politique des années 1714–1715.[59] Quand Dosithée décéda à Constantinople, Faldoni n'avait que 17 ans et en l'absence de toute connaissance de son sujet, il donna au patriarche des traits très réguliers, presqu'impersonnels, à la différence de ce qu'il affectionnait pour les portraits d'individus qu'il put connaître.

Chrysanthe parcourut les pays européens, faisant ses études à Venise et Padoue et séjournant à Paris. Faldoni s'y forma lui-même à la gravure mais à l'époque des voyages de Chrysanthe, l'artiste était encore trop jeune pour avoir pu rencontrer le futur patriarche de Jérusalem.[60] L'artiste, qui ne pouvait observer directement son modèle, s'en remit sans doute là aussi largement à son imagination.[61] Ainsi,

---

toire. Le métropolite ne vit toutefois ni l'introduction définitive du système synodal, ni la publication de l'*Histoire*, puisqu'il décéda en novembre 1722. Sur les relations difficiles du patriarche Chrysanthe et de son patron, le prince Constantin Brâncoveanu, avec la Russie dans les années 1711–1720, voir Kapterev, *Sobranie sochineniĭ*, t. 2, p. 265–276. Les projets d'organisation d'une typographie grecque à Moscou, formulés dans les années 1690, étaient alors depuis longtemps oubliés : Kapterev, *Sobranie sochineniĭ*, t. 1, p. 586–598, t. 2, p. 200–202. L'exemplaire CRV 175 doublet 3 / inv. 963 de la Bibliothèque de l'Académie roumaine présente une page de titre slavonne mais ne comporte pas l'adresse de Chrysanthe à Stéphane Iavorski. Cet exemplaire était-il destiné à un autre « lecteur slavophone » que ce métropolite ?

59 Il a été impossible de trouver confirmation des commandes par Chrysanthe Notaras de gravures ou d'autres éléments décoratifs pour la typographie à Bucarest ; il est néanmoins assuré que l'élite de la principauté entretenait les liens avec le marché vénitien du livre. Voir par exemple, E. de Hurmuzaki, *Documente privitoare la Istoria Românilor*, vol. 14 : *Documente greceşti privitoare la istoria Românilor*, pt. 2 (1716–1777), éd. N. Iorga, Bucarest, 1917, p. 887–888.

60 Moschini, *Dell'incisione in Venezia*, p. 88 ; *Da Carlevarijs ai Tiepolo*, p. 161.

61 Le portrait du cardinal Niccolò Albergati, réalisé par Faldoni (sans doute à l'occasion de sa canonisation en 1744), ne ressemble pas au portrait du cardinal qu'effectua Jan van Eyck dans les années 1430. La ressemblance n'était donc pas à l'époque une considération prioritaire pour

nous nous retrouvons à nouveau devant la nécessité d'expliquer les raisons pour lesquels Chrysanthe Notaras décida de ne pas se désigner comme « patriarche » sur son portrait, préférant se présenter aux futurs lecteurs de l'*Introduction à la géographie et sphèrologie* comme simple « prêtre et archimandrite ».

L'artiste improvisa donc les traits du patriarche Dosithée et de son neveu Chrysanthe mais la chose n'était guère problématique car la ressemblance physique n'était pas le souci principal des éditeurs d'ouvrages adressés aux orthodoxes et les « portraits » étaient même facilement interchangeables. On le réalisera en s'intéressant à l'édition des œuvres de Théodoret de Cyr publiée à Halle par Eugénios Voulgaris. Chacun des quatre volumes était dédié à l'un des patriarches orientaux : le premier volume constituait un hommage au patriarche Samuel Ier de Constantinople, le deuxième au patriarche Cyprien Ier d'Alexandrie (1766–1783), le troisième au patriarche Daniel Ier d'Antioche (1767–1791), le quatrième au patriarche Sophrone V de Jérusalem (1770–1775).[62] Le portrait patriarcal placé dans le premier volume devait apparaître aux éventuels lecteurs comme celui du patriarche de Constantinople à qui le volume était dédicacé. Toutefois, l'*épigonation* du patriarche porte une image de la Résurrection du Christ, symbole du patriarcat de Jérusalem, détail que l'on retrouve sur le portrait du patriarche Dosithée. On peut donc supposer que l'artiste souhaitait initialement représenter un patriarche de la Ville Sainte (Éphrem II ?). Ce fut donc simplement la décision de l'éditeur de placer ce portrait dans le premier volume des œuvres de Théodoret de Cyr qui « transforma » l'image en « portrait du patriarche de Constantinople ».

Bien qu'ils se soient inspirés des modes « occidentales » en intégrant des portraits d'auteurs dans les livres, les éditeurs souhaitaient avant tout disposer de la représentation d'un « hiérarque orthodoxe idéal », ou d'un savant représentant du clergé, dont la fidélité aux traits d'un individu spécifique n'avait guère d'importance. C'est ainsi qu'un artiste de l'école vénitienne de gravure conçut un portrait de patriarche qui devait ultérieurement servir de modèle, restant jusqu'à aujourd'hui l'archétype de l'iconographie d'un pontife orthodoxe.

Les contacts que Chrysanthe tissa avec les milieux artistiques liés aux typographies vénitiennes ne furent pas seulement mis à profit pour la réalisation de

---

ce genre d'œuvre. Sur la question parallèle de la « ressemblance » des portraits de sultans ottomans, voir H. G. Majer, « Zur Ikonographie der osmanischen Sultane », dans M. Kraatz, J. Meyer zur Capellen, D. Seckel (éds.), *Das Bildnis in der Kunst des Orients*, Stuttgart, 1990, p. 99–128.
62 Theodoritos, episkopos Kurou. *Ta Sozomena*, t. 1–5, 1768–1775. Dans le troisième volume de la même édition, on trouve en frontispice une représentation de Théodoret de Cyr qui reproduit l'image de ce théologien publiée dès le XVIe siècle : A. Thevet, *Les vrais pourtraits et vies des hommes illustres grecz, latins, et payens, recueilliz de leurs tableaux, livres, medailles antiques et modernes*, Paris, 1584, p. 20.

son propre portrait et de celui de son oncle Dosithée. En feuilletant l'*Histoire des patriarches de Jérusalem* qu'il fit publier à Bucarest, on remarque d'emblée que cette édition présente davantage d'éléments typographiques ornementaux que dans celles commandées en terre roumaine par le patriarche Dosithée lui-même. Neuf types de lettrines de styles divers, les bandeaux situés en tête de la première page de chaque livre, ainsi que plusieurs vignettes offrent des similitudes marquées avec ceux observables dans certains livres sortis de la typographie de Bortoli (Fig. 1). Par exemple, les couillards en fleurs séparant les textes dans l'*Histoire* sont identiques à ceux utilisés dans de nombreux livres de la typographie vénitienne de Nicolas Saros et de son successeur Antonio Bortoli. Des parallèles proches des culs-de-lampe en forme de mascaron ou en rhombe fleuri se retrouvent toutefois dans des ouvrages de pays divers : il n'est pas impossible que le patriarche en ait rapporté les matrices de ses voyages ou ait commandé leur gravure d'après les modèles qu'il trouvait dans des livres.[63] Les ressemblances les plus marquées s'observent avec l'édition vénitienne des « enseignements » de Hélie Miniatis publiée pour la première fois en 1720, laquelle fut presque contemporaine des livres préparés par Chrysanthe Notaras. On peut ainsi supposer que divers éléments décoratifs de l'*Histoire* de Dosithée et du livre de Miniatis furent réalisés par le même artiste. On soulignera donc que certains d'entre eux présentent des similitudes avec le décor floral du portrait de Dosithée de Jérusalem. Cette observation permet d'envisager qu'un certain nombre de lettrines, ainsi qu'un bandeau fleuri utilisé pour ouvrir chaque « livre » de l'œuvre du patriarche, aient pu être également réalisés par Faldoni. Quoiqu'il en soit, la longue collaboration de Chrysanthe Notaras avec les typographes européens, et notamment Antonio Bortoli, exerça une influence marquante et durable sur la culture visuelle de l'art typographique du monde orthodoxe au siècle des Lumières.

---

63 Voir, par exemple, L. Daneau, *Confirmatio verae et orthodoxae doctrinae.* Genève, 1585, p. 5, 45 ; A. Barlet, N. Charles, *Le vray et methodique cours de la physique resolutiue, vulgairement dite chymie,* Paris, 1653, p. 102 ; *Journal de ce qui s'est fait pour la réception du Roy dans sa ville de Metz, le 4 aoust 1744,* Metz, 1744, p. 58. On trouve également des images très proches dans les éditions faites en terres ukrainiennes : Ioannikij Galiatovskij, *Kazanija, pridannye do knigi Kljuch razumeniia,* Kiev, 1660, fol. 197 v, 240 v ; 67 r. (seconde numérotation) ; *Ukrainskie knigi kirillovskoĭ pechati XVI-XVIII vv. Katalog izdaniĭ, khraniaschihsia v Gosudarstvennoĭ biblioteke SSSR imeni V. I. Lenina,* vol. 1 : *1574 g. – I polovina XVII v.,* éd. T. N. Kameneva, A. A. Gouseva, Moscou, 1976 [1977], no. 279, 300, 331, 341, 345. Pour l'utilisation de mêmes éléments décoratifs dans certains livres publiés ultérieurement en pays roumains, voir Dimitriu, *Ilustraţia cărţii româneşti vechi,* vol. 1, p. 99, 107, 207, 211.

Fig. 1: Le Patriarche Dosithée de Jérusalem, *Historia peri ton en Hierosolumois patriarkheusanton*, Bucarest : epistatountos te typographia Stoika hiereos tou Iakobitze, 1715 [1722], frontispice (BULAC).

Fig. 2: Chrysanthos Notaras, *Eisagoge eis ta geographika kai sphairika*, Paris : s. n., 1716, frontispice (Public domain, accès 21.12.2022).

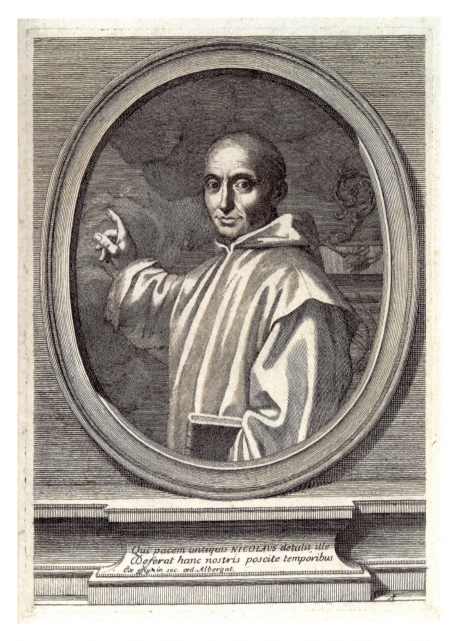

Fig. 3: Portrait du cardinal Niccolò Albergati. Londres, Wellcome Collection. Reference: 6691i (Public domain, https://wellcomecollection.org/works/nq2qshc8, accès 21.12.2022).

Fig. 4: Helias Mcniates, *Didakhai eis ten Hagian kai Megalen Tessarakosten kai eis allas episemous heortas*, Venise : para Antonio to Bortoli, 1720, frontispice.

Fig. 5: Initiales de Giovanni Antonio (Gianantonio) Faldoni sur les eau-fortes (fragments).

Fig. 6: Dosithée de Jérusalem, *Historia*. Lettrines.

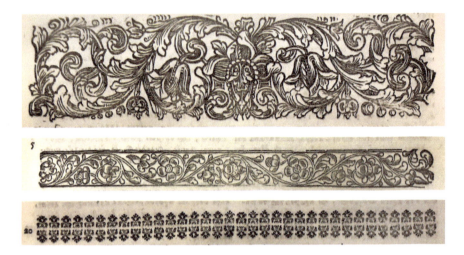

Fig. 7: Dosithée de Jérusalem, *Historia*. Éléments de décor.

Fig. 8: Dosithée de Jérusalem, *Historia*. Éléments de décor.

Bibliographie

Akolouthia tou hagiou Hieromarturos Serapheim, arkhiepiskopou Phanariou kai Neokhoriou, tou thaumatourgou. Enetiesi : Para Nikolao Glukei, 1790.

Anthimos. *Kitāb tafsīr al-zabūr al-ilāhī al-sharīf ta'līf... Anthīmūs baṭriyark madīnat Ūrshalīm.* Vienne, 1792.

Antim Ivireanul. Opera tipografică, éd. par Arhim. Policarp (Chiţulescu), Doru Bădără, Ion Marian Croitoru, Gabriela Dumitrescu, Ioana Feodorov. Bucarest : Editura Institutului Cultural Român, 2016.

Aspetti dell'incisione veneziana nel Settecento. Catalogo della mostra, éd. par Gianvittorio Dillon, Renzo Da Tos. Venise : Tip. commerciale, 1976.

Augliera, Letterio. « Hellenes kai hellenika biblia sta epistemonika kaì philologika periodika tes Benetias tou 18-ou aiona ». *To Entupo helleniko biblio. 15os-19os aionas. Praktika tou diethnous sunedriou. Delphoi, 16–20 Maiou 2001.* Athènes : Kotinos, 2004, p. 245–263.

Aujac, Germaine. « Chrysanthos Notaras et les systèmes du monde ». *Pallas. Revue d'études antiques. Palladio Magistro. Mélanges Jean Soubiran.* Toulouse, 2002, p. 75–88.

Barlet, Annibal, Charles Noël. *Le vray et methodique cours de la physique resolutiue, vulgairement dite chymie.* Paris : chez N. Charles, 1653.

Bernatskiĭ, Mikhail M. « Dosifeĭ II Notara, patriarkh Ierusalimskiĭ ». *Pravoslavnaia èntsiklopediia*, t. 16. Moscou : Pravoslavnaia èntsiklopediia, 2007, p. 71–77.

Bianu, Ioan, Hodoş Nerva. *Bibliografia Românească veche, 1508–1830*, t. 1. Bucarest : Socec, 1903.

Boorsch, Suzanne. *Venetian Prints and Books in the Age of Tiepolo. The Metropolitan Museum of Arts.* New York : Metropolitan Museum of Art, 1997.

Boyer, Hippolyte. « Une fausse marque typographique ». *Archives du bibliophile*, I, 1858, p. 83–84.

Brulliot, François. *Dictionnaire des monogrammes, marques figurées, lettres initiales, noms abrégés etc. avec lesquels les peintres, dessinateurs, graveurs et sculpteurs ont désigné leurs noms*, t. 1. Munich : Institut littéraire artistique de la librairie J.-C. Cotta, 1832.

Brunet, [Pierre-]Gustave. *Imprimeurs imaginaires et libraires supposés. Étude bibliographique suivie de recherches sur quelques ouvrages imprimés avec des indications fictives de lieux ou avec des dates singulières.* Paris : Librairie Tross, 1866.

Calabi, Augusto. *La gravure italienne au XVIIIe siècle.* Paris : Van Oest, 1931.

Chiaburu, Elena. « 'Cazul' tipografului Stoica Iacovici (1715–1749). Clarificări noi ». *Istorie şi cultură. In honorem academician Andrei Eşanu.* Chişinău : Institutul de Istorie, 2018, p. 428–439.

Çolak, Hasan. « Bilim, İlahiyat ve Siyasetin Merkezinde Bir Osmanlı Münevveri : Kudüs Patriği Chrysanthos Notaras ». *Kebikeç*, 47, 2019, p. 31–56.

Comacchio, Luigi. *Giovanni Antonio Faldoni incisore asolano (1689–1770).* Castelfranco Veneto : Tecnoprint, 1976.

Coq, Dominique. *Les livres anciens : formats, cahiers, signatures, page de titre, fausses adresses, colophon et toutes ces sortes de choses, Apprendre à gérer des collections patrimoniales en bibliothèque.* Villeurbanne : Presses de l'Enssib, 2012 (La Boîte à outils, 26), p. 70–79.

Cracraft, James. *The Petrine Revolution in Russian Culture.* Cambridge, MA/Londres : The Belknap Press of Harvard University Press, 2004.

Crosera, Claudia. « Anton Maria di Girolamo Zanetti (1680–1767), Anton Maria di Alessandro Zanetti (1706–1778) (VIII.1) ». Dans Vincenza Cinzia Donvito, Denis Ton (éds.), *Tiepolo, Piazzetta, Novelli. L'incanto del libro illustrato nel Settecento veneto. Catalogo della mostra (Padova 22 novembre 2012 – 7 aprile 2013)*. Padoue : Antiga Edizioni, 2012, p. 390–395.

Da Carlevarijs ai Tiepolo. Incisori veneti e friulani del Settecento. Catalogo della mostra, éd. par Dario Succi. Venise : Albrizzi editore, 1983.

Dal Poz, Lorena. « La memoria incisa. Interventi di tutela del Fondo storico dell'Accademia di Belle Arti di Venezia ». Dans Alberto Giorgio Cassani (éd.), *Annuario Accademia di belle arti di Venezia. Che cos'è scenografia? Lo spazio dello sguardo dal teatro alla città*. Venise, 2012, p. 489–503.

Daneau, Lambert (Danoeus Lambertus). *Confirmatio verae et orthodoxae doctrinae*. Genève : Apud Eustathium Vignon, 1585.

Del Chiaro, Antonmaria. *Istoria delle moderne rivoluzioni della Valachia*. Venise : Antonio Bortoli, 1718.

Dimitriu, Oana-Lucia. *Ilustraţia cărţii româneşti vechi din secolul al XVIII-lea în colecţiile Bibliotecii Academiei Române. Gravura, vol. 1 : Ţara Românească*. Bucarest : Editura Academiei Române, 2023.

Donaggio, Vanessa. « Alessandro Dalla Via : un contributo all'arte incisoria veneta tra XVII e XVIII secolo ». *Arte in Friuli – Arte a Trieste* 36, 2017, p. 47–131.

Donvito, Vincenza Cinzia, Denis Ton (éds.) *Tiepolo, Piazzetta, Novelli. L'incanto del libro illustrato nel Settecento veneto. Catalogo della mostra (Padova, 22 novembre 2012 – 7 aprile 2013)*. Padoue : Antiga Edizioni, 2012.

Dosithée de Jérusalem. *Historia peri ton en Hierosolumois patriarkheusanton*. Bucarest : epistatountos te tupographia Stoika hiereos tou Iakobitze, 1715 [1722].

Droz, Eugénie. « Fausses adresses typographiques ». *Bibliothèque d'Humanisme et Renaissance*. Paris : Librairie Droz, 1961, t. 23 (1), p.138–152 ; t. 23 (2), p. 379–394.

Duplessis, Georges, Bouchot Henri. *Dictionnaire des marques et monogrammes de graveurs*. Paris : Librairie de l'art – Jules Rouam, 1886.

Dură, Ioan V. *Ho Dositheos Hierosolumon kai he prosphora autou eis tas Rhoumanikas khoras kai ten ekklesian auton*. Athènes : [s. n.], 1977.

Favorino, Guarino [Varinus Phavorinus]. *To mega lexikon, e ho thesauros pases tes Hellenikes glosses*. Venise : En te tupographia Antoniou tou Bortoli, 1712.

Galiatovskiĭ, Ioannikiĭ. *Kazaniia, pridannye do knigi Kliuch razumeniia*. Kiev : Tipografiia Pecherskoĭ lavry, 1660.

Gallo, Rodolfo. *L'incisione nel '700 a Venezia e a Bassano*. Venise : Libreria Serenissima Depositaria, 1941.

Gauna, Chiara. « I Rembrandt di Anton Maria Zanetti e le "edizioni" di stampe a Venezia: tra tecnica e stile ». *Saggi e Memorie di storia dell'arte* 36, 2012, p. 189–234. https://www.royalacademy.org.uk/art-artists/name/giovanni-antonio-faldoni (accès le 29.04.2019).

Heyberger, Bernard. « De l'image religieuse à l'image profane? L'essor de l'image chez les chrétiens de Syrie et du Liban (XVIIe – XIXe siècle) ». Dans Bernard Heyberger, Silvia Naef (éds.), *La multiplication des images en pays d'Islam : De l'estampe à la télévision (17e–21e siècle). Actes du colloque « Images : fonctions et langages. L'incursion de l'image moderne dans l'Orient musulman et sa périphérie », Istanbul, Université du Bosphore (Boğaziçi Üniversitesi), 25–27 mars 1999*. Würzburg : Ergon-Verlag, 2016 (Istanbuler Texte und Studien, 2), p. 26–43.

Huber, Michel. *Catalogue raisonné du cabinet d'estampes de feu Monsieur Winckler, t. 1 : L'école allemande*. Leipzig : Breitkopf et Härtel, [1801].

Hurmuzaki, Eudoxiu de. *Documente privitoare la Istoria Românilor*. Vol. 14 : *Documente greceşti privitoare la istoria Românilor*, éd. Nicolae Iorga, pt. 2–3. Bucarest : Socece & Co, 1917–1936.

Il libro illustrato italiano. Secoli XVII–XVIII, éd. par Emma C. Pirani. Rome/Milan : Ed. d'Arte Bestetti, 1956.

Isaak tou Surou. *Ta Eurethenta asketika*, Leipzig : En te Tup. tou Breitkopf, 1770.

Ivanov, Andrey V. *A Spiritual Revolution. The Impact of Reformation and Enlightenment in Orthodox Russia*. Madison, WI : The University of Wisconsin Press, 2020.

Journal de ce qui s'est fait pour la réception du Roy dans sa ville de Metz, le 4 aoust 1744. Metz : Veuve de Pierre Collignon, 1744.

Kapterev, Nikolaĭ F. *Sobranie sochineniĭ*, t. 2. Moscou : Dar″, 2008.

Karathanases, Athanasios E. *Oi Ellenes logioi ste Vlakhia (1670–1714). Sumvole ste melete tes ellenikes pneumatikes kineses stis paradounavies egemonies kata ten prophanariotike periodo*. Thessalonique : Aphoi Kuriakide, 1982.

Kameneva, T. N., A. A. Guseva (éds). *Ukrainskie knigi kirillovskoĭ pechati XVI–XVIII vv. Katalog izdaniĭ, khraniashchikhsia v Gosudarstvennoĭ biblioteke SSSR imeni V. I. Lenina*, vol. 1 : *1574 g. – I polovina XVII v*. Moscou : GBL, 1976 [1977].

Kazachkov, IU. A., « Iliia (Min'iatis) », *Pravoslavnaia ėntsiklopediia*, t. 22, Moscou, 2009, p. 284–285..

Kilpatrick, Hilary. « From Venice to Aleppo: Early Printing of Scripture in the Orthodox World ». *Chronos. Revue d'histoire de l'Université de Balamand*, 30, 2014, p. 35–61.

Kitromilides, Paskhalis M. *Neoellenikos Diaphotismos. Oi politikes kai koinonikes idees*. Athènes : MIET, 1996.

Kontouma, Vassa. « La Confession de foi de Dosithée de Jérusalem : les version de 1672 et de 1690 ». Dans Marie-Hélène Blanchet, Frédéric Gabriel (éds.), *L'Union à l'épreuve du formulaire. Professions de foi entre Églises d'Orient et d'Occident (XIIIᵉ–XVIIIᵉ siècle)*. Leuven/Paris/Bristol : Peeters, 2016 (Centre de recherche d'histoire et civilisation de Byzance. Monographies, 51), p. 341–372.

Kontouma, Vassa. « Vestiges de la bibliothèque de Dosithée II de Jérusalem au Métochion du Saint-Sépulcre à Constantinople ». *Les bibliothèques grecques dans l'Empire Ottoman*. Turnhout : Brepols, 2020 (Bibliologia 54), p. 259–289.

Kontouma, Vassa. « The Archimandrite and the Astronomer. The Visit of Chrysanthos Notaras to Giovanni Domenico Cassini: a New Approach ». Dans Kostas Sarris, Nikolas Pissis, Miltos Pechlivanos (éds.), *Confessionalization and / as Knowledge Transfer in the Greek Orthodox Church*. Wiesbaden : Harrassowitz Verlag, 2021 (Episteme in Bewegung, 23), p. 233–272.

Kournoutos, Georgios P. « He *Dodekavivlos* tou Dositheou eis ten tupographian tou Voukourestiou ». *Theologia* 24, 1953, p. 250–273.

Layton, Evro. *The Sixteenth Century Greek Book in Italy. Printers and Publishers for the Greek World*. Venise : Istituto Ellenico di Studi Bizantini e Postbizantini di Venezia, 1994 (Library of the Hellenic Institute of Byzantine and Post-Byzantine Studies, 16).

Legrand, Émile. *Bibliothèque grecque vulgaire*, t. 1. Paris : Maisonneuve, 1880.

Legrand, Émile. *Bibliographie hellénique ou description raisonnée des ouvrages publiés par des Grecs au dix-huitième siècle*, t. 1–2. Paris : Garnier frères, 1918 ; Paris : Belles Lettres, 1928.

Livieratos, Evangelos, Boutoura Chryssoula, Pazarli Maria, Ploutoglou Nopi, Tsorlini Angeliki. « The Very First Printed Map in Greek, a Derived Map from Dutch Cartography: Chrysanthos Notaras' World Map (1700) vs Jan Luyts' World Map (1692) ». *e-Perimetron*, 6 (3), 2011, p. 200–218.

Loparev, Khrisanf M. « Ierusalimskiĭ patriarkh Khrisanf (1707–1731) i ego otnoshenie k Rossii ». Dans P. S. Uvarova, M. N. Speranskiĭ (éds.), *Trudy Vos'mogo arkheologicheskogo s"ezda v Moskve, 1890*, t. 2. Moscou : Tovarishchestvo tipografii A. I. Mamontova, 1895, p. 20–27.

Lorenzetti, Giulio. « Un dilettante incisore veneziano del XVIII secolo. Anton Maria Zanetti di Gerolamo ». *Miscellanea di Storia Veneta della R. Deputazione di Storia Patria*, serie III, 12, 1917, p. 3–147.

Lupu, Daniela. « Tipografi bucureşteni : popa Stoica Iacovici (1715–1749) şi familia sa ». *Bucureşti. Materiale de istorie şi muzeografie*, 25, 2011, p. 240–258.

Majer, Hans Georg. « Zur Ikonographie der osmanischen Sultane ». Dans Martin Kraatz, Jürg Meyer zur Capellen, Dietrich Seckel (éds.), *Das Bildnis in der Kunst des Orients*. Stuttgart : Franz Steiner Verlag, 1990, p. 99–128.

Marineskou, Florin, Rafailă Maria. « To helleniko entupo ste Roumania (1642–1918) ». *To Entupo helleniko vivlio. 15os-19os aionas. Praktika tou diethnous sunedriou. Delphoí, 16–20 Maiou 2001*. Athènes : Kotinos, 2004, p. 265–278.

Meniates, Helias. *Didakhai eis ten Hagian kai Megalen Tessarakosten kai eis allas episemous heortas*. Venise : para Antonio to Bortoli, 1720.

Miladinova, Nadia. *The Panoplia Dogmatike by Euthymios Zygadenos. A Study on the First Edition Published in Greek in 1710*. Leyde/Boston : Brill, 2014 (Texts and Studies in Eastern Christianity, 4).

Morazzoni, Giuseppe. *Il libro illustrato veneziano del Settecento*. Milan : Hoepli, 1943.

Moschini, Giannantonio. *Dell'incisione in Venezia*. Venise : Zanetti, 1924.

Năchescu, Alina. « East-West Connections in the Wake Archive ». *Christ Church Library Newsletter*, 12 (1), 2020, p. 32–39.

Notaras, Chrysanthos. *Eisagoge eis ta geographika kai sphairika*. Paris : s. n., 1716 (deuxième édition : Venise, par'Antonio to Vortoli, 1718).

Notaras, Chrysanthos. *Didaskalia ophelimos peri metanoias, kaì exomologeseos*. Venise : para Nikolao to Saro, 1724.

Notaras, Chrysanthos. *Historia, kai perigraphe tes Hagias Ges, kaì tes Hagías Poleos Hierousalem*. Venise : para Antonio to Vortoli, 1728.

Palmieri, Aurelio. *Dositeo patriarca greco di Gerusalemme (1641–1707)*. Florence : Libreria editrice fiorentina, 1909.

Papadopoulos, Thomas I. *Hellenike vivliographia (1466 ci.–1800), t. 1 : Alphavetike kai khronologike anakatataxis*. Athènes : Grapheion Demosieumaton tes Akademias Athenon, 1984.

Papadopoulos-Bretos, Andreas. *Neoellenike philologia*, t. 2. Athènes : Vilaras – Lioumes, 1857.

Papadopoulos-Kerameus, Athanasios. *Hierosolumitike vivliotheke*, t. 4. Bruxelles : Culture et civilisation, 1963.

Parenti, Marino. *Dizionario dei luoghi di stampa falsi, inventati o supposti*. Florence : Sansoni, 1951.

Parmeggiani, Riccardo. *Il vescovo e il capitolo: il cardinale Niccolò Albergati e i canonici di S. Pietro di Bologna (1417–1443). Un'inedita visita pastorale alla cattedrale (1437)*. Bologne : Deputazione di storia patria, 2009 (Documenti e studi, 39).

Pásztor, Edith. « Albergati, Niccolò ». *Dizionario biografico degli Italiani*. Rome : Istituto della Enciclopedia italiana, 1960, p. 619–621.

Pippidi, Andrei. « The Enlightenment and Orthodox culture in the Romanian principalities ». Dans Paschalis M. Kitromilides (éd.), *Enlightenment and Religion in the Orthodox World*. Oxford : Voltaire Foundation, 2016, p. 157–174.

Pitture del salone imperiale del palazzo di Firenze, si aggiungono le pitture del salone e cortile delle imperiali ville della Petraia e del Poggio a Caiano, opere di vari celebri pittori fiorentini in tavole XXVI, date ora la prima volta in luce. Florence : Giuseppe Bouchard in Mercato Nuovo, 1766.

Ploumides, Georgios S. « Ta en Padoue palaia hellenika vivlia (Biblioteca Universitaria – Biblioteca Civica) ». *Thesaurismata*, 5, 1968, p. 204–249.

Ploumides, Georgios S. « Protase gia ten kategoriopoiese tes eikonographeses ton leitourgikon ekdoseos Venetias ». *Epeirotika khronika* 39, 2005, p. 9–49.

Ploumidis, Giorgio S. « Tre tipografie di libri greci : Salicata, Saro e Bortoli ». *Ateneo Veneto*, n. s., 9 (1–2), 2017, p. 245–251.

Ploumidis, Georgios. « Stampando greco a Venezia ». *Crkvene studije, Niš / Church Studies, Nis* 15, 2018, p. 205–316.

Podskalsky, Gerhard. *Griechische Theologie in der Zeit der Türkenherrschaft (1453–1821). Die Orthodoxie im Spannungsfeld der nachreformatorischen Konfessionen des Westens*. Munich : Beck, 1988.

Raccolta di varie stampe e chiaroscuro tratte da disegni originali di Francesco Mazzuola detto il Parmigiano e d'altri insigni autori da Anton Maria Zanetti q. m. Gir. che gli istessi disegni possiede. Venise : s. n., 1749.

Ramazanova, Dzhamilia N. « Êkzempliary sochineniĭ ierusalimskogo patriarkha Khrisanfa Notara v sobranii Muzeia knigi RGB ». *Vivliofika : Istoriia knigi i izuchenie knizhnykh pamiatnikov*, t. 2. Moscou : Pashkov dom, 2011, p. 166–186.

Ramazanova, Dzhamilia N. « 'Istoriia ierusalimskikh patriarkhov' Dosifeia v russkoĭ kul'ture XVIII-XIX vv. ». *Rossiia i Khristianskiĭ Vostok* IV–V. Moscou : Indrik, 2015, p. 435–458.

Ramazanova, Dzhamilia N. « Grecheskiĭ istoriko-dogmaticheskiĭ traktat Ilii Miniatisa i ego serbskie perevodchiki XVIII veka ». *Slověne*, 7 (2), 2018, p. 134–178.

Ramazanova, Dzhamilia N. « Russkie spiski perevodnykh sochineniĭ Ilii Miniatisa (Miniatiia) v XVIII v. ». *Vestnik RGGU* 4(37), ser. « Istoriia. Filologiia. Kul'turologiia. Vostokovedenie », 2018, p. 117–123.

Ravà, Aldo. « Faldoni, Giovanni Antonio ». Dans Ulrich Thieme, Felix Becker (éds.), *Allgemeines Lexikon der Bildenden Künstler von der Antike bis zur Gegenwart*, t. 11. Leipzig : Seemann, 1915, p. 227.

Ris-Paquot, Oscar-Edmond. *Dictionnaire encyclopédique des marques et monogrammes, chiffres, lettres initiales, signes figuratifs, etc., etc. contenant 12.156 marques*, t. 1 : A-I. Paris : H. Laurens, [1893].

Roper, Geoffrey. « The Vienna Arabic Psalter of 1792 and the Role of Typography in European-Arab Relations ». Dans Johannes Frimmel, Michael Wögerbauer (éds.), *European-Arab Relations in the 18th Century and Earlier. Kommunikation und Information im 18. Jahrhundert : das Beispiel der Habsburgermonarchie*. Wiesbaden : Harrassowitz, 2009, p. 77–89.

Roper, Geoffrey. « Arabic Biblical and Liturgical Texts Printed in Europe in the 16th–18th Centuries ». Dans Adina Berciu, Rodica Pop, Julieta Rotaru (éds.), *Lucrările Simpozionului Internaţional: Cartea. România. Europa. Ediţia a II-a – Biblioteca Metropolitană Bucureşti,*

*20–24 septembrie 2009: 550 de ani de la prima atestare documentară a oraşului
    Bucureşti.* Bucarest : Editura Biblioteca Bucureştilor, 2010, p. 174–186.
*Russian Travellers to the Greek World (12ᵗʰ – First Half of the 19ᵗʰ Centuries). Exhibition
    Catalogue.* Moscou : Indrik, 1995.
Sannazaro, Luigi Malaspina, di. *Catalogo di una raccolta di stampe antiche*, vol. 1. Milan :
    Bernardoni, 1824.
Sarris, Kostas. « O Chrysanthos Notaras kai e ekdose tes Dodekavivlou tou Dositheou
    Hierosolumon : mia periptose analethous khronologias ekdoses (1715 / c. 1722) ».
    Mnemon, 27, 2005, p. 27–53.
Sarris, Kostas. « 'Diorthonontas' ten akolouthia khronon : ta ikhni tou Chrysanthou Notara sten
    ekdosi tes *Istorias* tou Dositheou Hierosolumon (Voukouresti, 1722) ». *Elenkhos ideon
    kai logokrisia apo tis aparkhes tes ellenikes tupographias mekhri to Suntagma tou 1844.
    Praktika sunedriou, Leukosia, 18–20 Noembriou 2015.* Athènes : E.I.E., 2018, p. 193–215.
Skordoulis, Constantine, Katsiampoura Gianna, Nicolaidis Efthymios. « The Scientific Culture
    in Eighteenth to Nineteenth Century Greek Speaking Communities : Experiments and
    Textbooks ». Dans Peter Heering, Roland Wittje (éds.), *Learning by Doing: Experiments and
    Instruments in the History of Science Teaching.* Stuttgart : Franz Steiner, 2011, p. 3–18.
Stathi, Penelope. *Chrysanthos Notaras, Patriarkhes Hierosolumon. Prodromos tou
    Neoellenikou Diaphotismou.* Athènes : Sundesmos ton en Athenais Megaloskholiton, 1999
    (Analekta tes Kath'Hemas Anatoles, 6).
Succi, Dario. *La Serenissima nello specchio di rame. Splendore di una civiltà figurativa del
    Settecento. L'opera completa dei grandi maestri veneti*, vol. 1. Castelfranco Veneto :
    Cecchetto prior Alto Antiquariato, 2013.
Synodinos, Polykarpos. « Metrophanes Gregoras ». *Epeirotika khronika* 1–2, 1927, p. 302–303.
Synodus Bethlehemitica adversus Calvinistas hæreticos. Paris : apud viduam Edmundi Martini,
    1676.
Synodus Jerosolymitana, adversus Calvinistas haereticos. Paris : apud viduam Edmundi
    Martini, 1678.
Tatay, Anca Elisabeta, Bogdan Andriescu (éds.). *Libri romeni antichi e moderni a Roma, nella
    Biblioteca Apostolica Vaticana (sec. XVII–XIX). Catalogo / Carte românească veche şi
    modernă la Roma, în Biblioteca Apostolică vaticană (sec. XVII–XIX). Catalog.* Cité du
    Vatican : Biblioteca Apostolica Vaticana, 2020.
Theodoritos, episkopos Kurou. *Ta Sozomena, hellenisti hama kai romaisti ekdothenta... hupo
    Eugeniou diakonou tou Voulgareos*, t. 1–5. Halle : En to tupographeio tou Orphano-
    tropeiou, 1768–1775.
Thevet, André. *Les vrais pourtraits et vies des hommes illustres grecz, latins, et payens,
    recueilliz de leurs tableaux, livres, medailles antiques et modernes.* Paris : par la veuve J.
    Kervert et Guillaume Chaudière, 1584.
Țipău, Mihai. *Orthodoxe suneidese kai ethnike tautoteta sta Valkania (1700–1821).* Thessa-
    lonique : Epikentro, 2015.
Todt, Klaus-Peter. « Dositheos II. von Jerusalem ». Dans Carmelo Giuseppe Conticello, Vassa
    Conticello (éds.), *La Théologie Byzantine et sa tradition*, vol. II : XIIIᵉ–XIXᵉ s. Turnhout :
    Brepols, 2002, p. 659–720.
Tudorie, Ionuț-Alexandru. « The Eucharistic Controversy between the 'Orthodox' Dositheos II
    of Jerusalem and the 'Calvinist' Ioannis Karyofyllis (1689–1697) ». Dans Kostas Sarris,
    Nikolas Pissis, Miltos Pechlivanos (éds.), *Confessionalization and/as Knowledge Transfer*

in the Greek Orthodox Church. Wiesbaden : Harrassowitz Verlag, 2021 (Episteme in Bewegung, 23), p. 273–327.

Varii disegni inventati dal celebre Francesco Mazzuola detto Il Parmigianino tratti dalla Raccolta Zanettiana, incisi in rame da Antonio Faldoni e novamente pubblicati. Venise : s. n., 1786.

Walbiner, Carsten. « 'Images Painted with Such Exalted Skill as to Ravish the Senses...': Pictures in the Eyes of Christian Arab Travellers of the 17th and 18th Centuries ». Dans Bernard Heyberger, Silvia Naef (éds.), *La multiplication des images en pays d'Islam : De l'estampe à la télévision (17e–21e siècle). Actes du colloque « Images : fonctions et langages. L'incursion de l'image moderne dans l'Orient musulman et sa périphérie », Istanbul, Université du Bosphore (Boğaziçi Üniversitesi), 25–27 mars 1999*. Würzburg : Ergon-Verlag, 2016 (Istanbuler Texte und Studien, 2), p. 15–25.

Zanetti, Anton Maria. *Delle antiche statue greche e romane, che nell'antisala della Libreria di San Marco e in altri luoghi publici di Venezia si trovano*, vol. 1–2. Venise : s. n., 1740–1743.

Zannichelli, Gian Girolamo. *Istoria delle piante che nascono ne'lidi intorno a Venezia*. Venise : Antonio Bortoli, 1735.

Zhivov, Viktor M. *Iz tserkovnoĭ istorii vremën Petra Velikogo : issledovaniia i materialy*. Moscou : Novoe literaturnoe obozrenie, 2004.

Mihai Țipău

Arabic Books Printed in Wallachia and Moldavia and their Phanariot Readers

For anyone not familiar with Romanian historical writing, the word "Phanariot" needs at least some explanation. A few dictionaries of the English language do provide a short, often repetitive, definition and alternative spellings but usually that is not enough for a thorough understanding of its meaning.[1]

First of all, we should state that "Phanariot" as a word and as a meaning is a modern construction, pretty much as "Byzantine" was used by later scholars to define the identity of the Christian Eastern Roman Empire. Therefore, some caution in its use and some explanations are always welcome. In this paper, "Phanariot" is used in a conventional way to define the Greek Orthodox elite of Constantinople, a group that also provided the rulers of the Romanian Principalities during most of the 18th century and the first decades of the 19th century. The limits of this definition must be stated as well. Members of this group were not all ethnically Greek and, more importantly, the ethnic component of their group identity must not be understood in modern terms during this timeframe. The neighborhood of Phanar (the "lighthouse" district), or Diplophanarion in older sources, was home to the most important institution of the Orthodox Christians, the Patriarchate of Constantinople.[2] However, during the 18th century, the Greek

---

1 See for example https://www.merriam-webster.com/dictionary/Phanariot, accessed December 10, 2022; Britannica, The Editors of Encyclopaedia, "Phanariote", *Encyclopedia Britannica*, https://www.britannica.com/ topic/Phanariote (accessed December 10, 2022). One of the first mentions of the term "Phanariote" is in M.-Ph. Zallony, *Essai sur les Fanariotes où l'on voit les causes primitives de leur élévation aux hospodariats de la Valachie et de la Moldavie, leur mode d'administration, et les causes principales de leur chute ; suivi de quelques réflexions sur l'état actuel de la Grèce*, Marseille, 1824. The book was translated in English in 1826 and it also provided the fundaments for the negative meaning of the term. For older occurrences of the term Φαναριώτης see J. Bouchard, "Perception des Phanariotes avant et après Zallony", *Cahiers balkaniques* [Online], 42 (2014), http://journals.openedition.org/ceb/4935 (accessed December 10, 2022).
2 The bibliography on the Phanariots in Romanian, Greek, but also in French, English, German or Turkish for the past two centuries is extensive and even a short survey would surpass by far the aims of this paper. For an attempt of a bibliographical survey on the topic of Phanariot princes up to 2008 see M. Țipău, *Domnii fanarioți în Țările Române 1711–1821. Mică enciclopedie*, Bucharest, 2008, p. 151–154

This research is part of a project that has received funding from the European Research Council (ERC) under the European Union's Horizon 2020 research and innovation programme (Grant Agreement No. 883219-AdG-2019 – Project TYPARABIC).

∂ Open Access. © 2024, the author(s), published by De Gruyter. (cc) BY-NC-ND This work is licensed under the Creative Commons Attribution-NonCommercial-NoDerivatives 4.0 International License. https://doi.org/10.1515/9783111060392-008

aristocracy of Constantinople was not based exclusively in Phanar and many of the richest families had mansions in the suburbs on the shores of the Bosphorus.

As for the princely families, those who provided at least a "bey" or ruling prince in Wallachia or Moldavia, they were a much smaller group within the broader circles of Constantinopolitan aristocracy. They had close relationships with each other but conflicts also arose when power games were involved. The highest Ottoman rank for a Christian was that of Grand Dragoman (*baş tercü-manı*), not merely a translator, but someone virtually responsible for most of the foreign affairs of the empire. Being eligible for an even greater position, that of ruling prince in the semiautonomous Wallachia or Moldavia, usually meant that one should have first held the office of Great Interpreter. For such a position, knowledge of foreign languages, both Western and Oriental, was an important prerequisite. The present paper will endeavor to provide some additional data to clarify the question of the knowledge of oriental languages among the Phanariot elite and especially the ruling princes of Wallachia and Moldavia. It is logical to presume that these individuals had some degree of knowledge of spoken Ottoman Turkish and the ability to read and understand official Ottoman documents. The sources presented here suggest however that they studied Arabic as well, sometimes from an early age, and they even prepared written material in Greek in order to help others to learn the language.

The Arabic books printed in Wallachia and Moldavia in the first and the fifth decade of the 18th century are part of a unique cultural achievement. In the early 1800s, the leading French oriental scholar Silvestre de Sacy was puzzled by these books and made inquiries about the size of the Arabic-speaking community in the Romanian Principalities.[3] Of course, there was virtually no such community in the two countries. The initiative belonged to two high-ranking hierarchs of the Orthodox Church and was facilitated by the active support of the state and the Church in the principalities.

The initiator of the first series of Arabic books printed in Bucharest in 1701–1702 was Athanasios Dabbas.[4] Although he is often referred to as patriarch of Antioch, at the time he was only former patriarch and metropolitan of Aleppo,

---

3 See the 1812 exchange of letters of Silvestre de Sacy with J. Ledoulx, vice consul of France in Bucharest in T. Holban, "Tipografii și cărți armenești (sic) în Țările Românești", *Arhiva. Revistă de istorie, filologie și cultură românească*, 43, 1936, p. 111–115. The letters are kept in the Institut de France in Paris.

4 For a survey of the typographical activity of Athanasios Dabbas in Wallachia see I. Feodorov, *Arabic Printing for the Christians in Ottoman Lands. The East European Connection*, Berlin/Boston, 2023, p. 255–263. Feodorov, "Livres arabes chrétiens imprimés avec l'aide des Principautés Roumaines au début du XVIIIe siècle. Répertoire commenté", *Chronos*, 34, 2016, p. 14–18.

following an agreement with his rival Cyril ibn al-Za'īm.[5] Athanasios enjoyed the support of the ruling Prince Constantine Brâncoveanu and that of a skillful and indefatigable Georgian-born monk and typographer, soon to become metropolitan of Ungro-Wallachia, Anthimos the Iberian. Anthimos' skills went beyond the typographical activity and it is possible that the Arabic typesets for the books printed in Wallachia were engraved by him.[6]

In 1745–1747 Patriarch Silvestros of Antioch successfully renewed the book printing projects of Athanasios in both Moldavia and Wallachia with the support of their ruling princes John and Constantine Mavrocordatos.[7] At the same time in Wallachia an ongoing project of publishing Romanian translations of all the liturgical books was in progress, supervised by the metropolitan of Ungro-Wallachia Neophytos of Crete.[8] Some influence of the Romanian project might be possible since Silvestros' books were entirely in Arabic and no longer bilingual (Arabic and Greek) as some of those published by Athanasios had been. Even these books published in 1701–1702 had not all been entirely bilingual, providing Greek versions only for some of the texts.

There is no available information about the number of copies of the Arabic books printed in Wallachia and Moldavia. Based on the existing data for other titles and on technical limitations such as the degree of wear on the typographical plates, it may be surmised that the print run for each book was around several hundred and perhaps up to 1,500 copies. Other limitations on the print runs, such as the cost and availability of paper, are not applicable, given the official support of the ruling princes and the scale of the printing activity in the Romanian lands in the 18th century. In contrast, good printing paper was not readily available in the Middle East when the Patriarch Silvestros tried to relocate his printing activity to Beirut. Therefore, he was forced to enlist the help of the Greek community in Venice in order to obtain the necessary stockpiles of good-quality Western paper.[9]

Why are the print runs relevant? Is the relatively small number of copies preserved today indicative of smaller than usual print runs? Not necessarily. Several

---

5 I. Feodorov, "The Romanian Contribution to Arabic Printing", in E. Siupiur, Z. Mihail (eds.), *Impact de l'imprimerie et rayonnement intellectuel des Pays Roumains*, Bucharest, 2009 p. 42.

6 Feodorov, *Arabic Printing for the Christians in Ottoman Lands*, p. 256.

7 Feodorov, *Arabic Printing for the Christians in Ottoman Lands*, p. 285–295. Feodorov, "Livres arabes chrétiens", p. 28–35. I. Feodorov, "The Arabic Book of the Divine Liturgies Printed in 1745 în Iași by Patriarch Sylvester of Antioch", *Scrinium*, 16/1, 2020, p. 1–19.

8 On Neophytos of Crete, metropolitan of Ungro-Wallachia see M. Țipău, "Mitropolitul Ungrovlahiei Neofit I Cretanul", in *Șerban Cantacuzino, Antim Ivireanul și Neofit Cretanul – Promotori ai limbii române în cult*, Bucharest, 2013, p. 223–272.

9 G. Hēlioupoleos, "Epistolai tou patriarchou Antiocheias Silvestrou", *Hellēnika*, 8, 1935, p. 244.

other factors may be involved. Of all the copies of the Arabic books printed in Wallachia and Moldavia some never left the Romanian lands. Even if the bulk of the books was intended to be shipped to today's Syria and Lebanon, there is a logical explanation for the copies left behind. It is possible that they even belonged to different categories. Some of them were most likely presentation copies sent to the ruling prince, members of his family and notable scholars of the time. Others might belong to a sort of legal deposit before its time, perhaps intended to enrich the collections of the few emerging libraries in Wallachia. The study of some of these and other copies confirms these suppositions and provides even more surprising data about their readers and owners. A small number of books remained perhaps in the metochia of the Patriarchate of Antioch in Wallachia and Moldavia for the use of the Arab-speaking clergy. It should be noted that Silvestros of Antioch gave the monastery of Saint Sabbas in Moldavia a set of Greek *Menologia* printed in Venice.[10]

The Arabic books printed in the Romanian Principalities have been studied for more than two centuries by a number of distinguished scholars. Their work is now made available and widely known by the TYPARABIC project.[11] The aim of this paper is not to present the already known information about these books but to study some aspects concerning their audience.

At first glance, this issue may seem minor, as things seem clear. They are for the most part liturgical books, while the rest contain polemical and canonical texts published by Silvestros. Therefore, the liturgical books were intended for use in the churches of the Arabic-speaking areas of the Patriarchate of Antioch and maybe in some areas of the Patriarchate of Jerusalem. In this respect, we might refer to a joint Arabic edition published in 1711 by the Patriarchs Athanasios of Antioch and Chrysanthos of Jerusalem of the *Sermons* of Athanasios II of Jerusalem and of *Sermons* of Saint John Chrysostom.[12] In this case, the intended

---

10 I. Gheorghiţă, "Tipografia arabă din Mănăstirea Sf. Sava şi venirea lui Silvestru patriarhul Antiohiei la Iaşi", *Mitropolia Moldovei şi Sucevei*, 24/5–6, 1958, p. 422–423; Gh. Diaconu, "Relaţiile Patriarhiei din Antiohia cu Ţările Române şi închinarea Mănăstirii Sfântul Nicolae Domnesc Popăuţi" (I), *Teologie şi viaţă*, 26 (92)/9–12, 2016, p. 153, 175, 181; L. Diaconu, *Mănăstirea "Sfântul Nicolae Domnesc" din Popăuţi. Importantă ctitorie a Moldovei închinată Patriarhiei din Antiohia*, vol. II, *Mănăstirea "Sfântul Nicolae domnesc" Popăuţi în perioada 1750–2018*, Iaşi, 2018, p. 24–26; P. Chiţulescu, "Patriarhul Silvestru al Antiohiei şi dania sa de carte către mănăstirea Sfântul Sava din Iaşi. O reevaluare necesară", in Mariana Lazăr (coord. ed.), *Mărturii de istorie şi cultură românească*, I, Bucharest, 2022, p. 53–64.
11 For the TYPARABIC project, its goals and its achievements, see the project's website: http://typarabic.ro/wordpress/en/acasa-english/ (accessed December 10, 2022).
12 Feodorov, *Arabic Printing for the Christians in Ottoman Lands*, p. 276–277.

audience was perhaps the Arabic-speaking Orthodox Christians in both patriarchal jurisdictions. In the foreword of the *Book of Hours* published in 1702 Athanasios clearly states that the books were sponsored by Constantine Brâncoveanu in order to be distributed for free to the churches in the Arabic-speaking areas.

Nevertheless, a closer inspection of the question reveals that there were also other categories of potential readers or owners of the Arabic books printed in the Romanian lands. These audiences were often unintended or overlooked by the publishers themselves.

Two of the Arabic books now preserved in the Library of the Romanian Academy in Bucharest followed a more complex journey. Today bound together, both of them were published in Iași by Silvestros of Antioch and contain polemical treatises against Latin practices.[13] The book bears a stamp indicating that it belonged to the Church of San Pietro in Vincoli in Rome,[14] famous for the statue of Moses by Michelangelo. How these copies found their way to the library of a Roman church is not yet very clear, but their presence in a Roman Catholic environment reveals yet another potential audience, albeit unintended, for the Arabic books published by Silvestros. It is almost certain that such polemical books were collected by Roman emissaries in order to better understand the critics and to provide an appropriate answer to them in their own polemical publications.

Most of the copies of the Arabic books preserved today in Romania are in good or even excellent condition, not showing signs of use. This is not an unexpected fact. These books are most likely the copies intended to be treasured in local, mainly monastic libraries, not only as curiosities but also as typographical achievements. Some copies were perhaps intended as models for future editions.

---

13 The book was a gift of Cyrile Charon (Korolevskij) to the Library of the Romanian Academy see I. Feodorov, "Arabic Printed Books in the Library of the Romanian Academy of Bucharest", *MELA Notes*, 94, 2021, p. 84. See also Feodorov, *Arabic Printing for the Christians in Ottoman Lands*, p. 292.

14 Feodorov, "Arabic Printed Books", ill. p. 96. Feodorov, *Arabic Printing for the Christians in Ottoman Lands*, p. 294. The text on the stamp is "Bibliothecae S. Petri ad Vincula". There is no doubt that the book belonged to the library of the convent of San Pietro in Vincoli in Rome, also known as "Biblioteca del Convento dei Chierici Regolari Lateranensi di Roma". Its collections were merged with those of other libraries in the "Biblioteca Nazionale Centrale Vittorio Emanuele II" in Rome. The stamp is identical with known stamps of the library of San Pietro in Vincoli. See for comparison https://archiviopossessori.it/archivio/1217-biblioteca-del-convento-di-san-pietro-vincoli (accessed December 10, 2022) (on a book in "Biblioteca Nazionale Centrale Vittorio Emanuele II", MISC.A.4.10). See also M. Venier, "Librerie dei conventi riuniti nella Vittorio Emanuele", p. 31, https://www2.bodleian.ox.ac.uk/__data/assets/pdf_file/0019/122185/Marina-Venier,-Monastic-Libraries-now-in-Rome,-National-Central-Library.pdf (accessed December 10, 2022).

In fact, Silvestros' *Book of Divine Liturgies* published in Iaşi in 1745 reprints the Arabic text of Athanasios' edition of 1701, leaving aside the Greek version.[15]

The research of the handwritten notes on some Arabic books printed in Wallachia offered an excellent opportunity to understand who their owners and their readers were.

The first is a copy of the *Book of Divine Liturgies* published in 1701 by Athanasius of Antioch kept in the Library of the Romanian Academy in Bucharest.[16] The book has on its title page no less than three handwritten notes containing highly important historical data and it is connected with key political figures in Wallachia and Moldavia.[17]

The first note, written in Romanian, states that the book in Greek and Arabic published by the former patriarch of Antioch Athanasios with the help of Prince Constantine Brâncoveanu was offered to Constantine Cantacuzenos and now belonged to him. Cantacuzenos was Brâncoveanu's uncle and a well-known scholar and Hellenist, and also the owner of an important library:[18]

> Aceste *Leturghii* greceşti şi hărăpeşti, fiind aici Sfinţia sa Părintele proin Antiohias şi rugându pre măria sa Costandin vodă de le-au dat în tipariu datuse-au şi dumnealui lui jupan Costandin C[antacuzino] biv vel stol(nic). Aceasta carea acum să chiamă că iaste den cărţile dumnealui.
>
> These Greek and Arabic *Liturgies*, when His Holiness Father former [patriarch] of Antioch was here and he asked His Highness Constantine voivode to print them, they were given also to *jupan*[19] Constantine C[antacuzenus] former great *stolnic*[20]. This is it, [so] this [book] is considered now as part of his books.

The next note, in chronological order, dated June 1723 and this time written in Greek, mentions that the book was one of those offered by the Prince Nicolas Alexander to the monastery of Văcăreşti:

15 Feodorov, "The Arabic Book of the Divine Liturgies", p. 1–19.
16 Library of the Romanian Academy, Bucharest CRV 130, II 171117.
17 I. Feodorov, *Tipar pentru creştinii arabi. Antim Ivireanul, Atanasie Dabbās şi Silvestru al Antiohiei*, Brăila, 2016, p. 156. A pdf version of this copy of the book published by Athanasius is available online: http://aleph23.biblacad.ro:8991/exlibris/aleph/a23_1/apache_media/VR4I-EGC HMQ2RSJYPEP7RRPV6XRDVS6.pdf (accessed December 10, 2022).
18 For Constantine Cantacuzenos, the *stolnic*, see V. Cândea, *Stolnicul între contemporani*, Bucharest, 2014, passim.
19 From the Slavic "županŭ", here with the meaning of "Sir".
20 The great "Stolnic" was the holder of an important court office in Wallachia and Moldavia. The "stolnic" was initially the person in charge of the ruling princes' table.

Καὶ τόδε τῶν ἀφιερωθέντων τῇ σεβασμίᾳ αὐθεντικῇ μονῇ τῆς Παναγίας Τριάδος τοῦ Βακαρεστίου παρὰ τοῦ ὑψηλοτάτου καὶ εὐσεβεστάτου αὐθέντου καὶ ἡγεμόνος πάσης Οὐγγροβλαχίας κ(υρίο)υ κ(υρίο)υ Ἰω(άννου) Νικολαου Ἀλεξάνδρου βοεβ(όδα) 1723 μηνὶ Ἰουνίῳ.

This one is also from those [books] dedicated to the respected princely Monastery of the All-Holy Trinity in Văcăreşti by the highest and most pious lord and prince sir sir John Nicolas Alexander voivode 1723 in the month of June.

The hospodar was none other than Nicolas Mavrocordatos, one of the most culti-vated Greek scholars of his time and a passionate collector of books. The Văcăreşti monastery, near Bucharest, was his foundation and also had a very rich library.

It is easy to suppose that the book was found by Mavrocordatos, appointed ruler of Wallachia in 1716, after the fall from power of the Cantacuzenos family. Once again the particular interest that this book received from a highly educated member of the Phanariot elite is remarkable.

Nicolas Mavrocordatos was not, however, the last Phanariot ruler to read the book. A third note, written in Greek and dated January 24, 1777, mentions that the book was donated to the Frumoasa Monastery by Gregory Ghikas. The mon-astery was located in Iaşi in Moldavia and the note's author was none other than Gregory Ghikas III, another famous and educated Phanariot prince and former great interpreter. There is no doubt that the note is in his handwriting, as it is formulated in the first person:

"Καὶ τόδε ἀφιέρωται παρ' ἐμοῦ, ἐν τῇ μονῇ τοῦ ἐν Φρωμόσα μοναστηρίου ͵αψοζ Ἰανουαρίου κδ'. Γρηγόριος Γκίκας".

This [book] is also dedicated by me to the convent in the Fromosa [= Frumoasa] monastery. 1777, January 24. Gregory Ghikas.

In addition, on another page of the book, the small seal of the same prince fea-turing the coat of arms of both Wallachia and Moldavia is applied in ink above some notes in Greek in the same handwriting. The seal, bearing the year 1775, is the same as the seal on some of the official documents issued during Ghikas' second reign in Moldavia.

It is not clear how the book was brought from Wallachia to Moldavia. If Gregory Ghikas took it from Bucharest during his Wallachian reign (1767–1769) he must have taken it with him in his captivity in Russia.[21]

---

21 Gregory Ghikas III was twice appointed ruling prince of Moldavia (1764–1767 and 1714–1777) and once ruling prince of Wallachia (1768–1769). See Ţipău, *Domnii fanarioţi în Ţările Române*, p. 75–78.

The book's history does not end here. In the late 19th century it came into possession of the Şaraga Brothers,[22] famous antique book dealers of Iaşi, whose stamp is applied on the same title page. From the Şaragas' bookstore it was purchased for the library of the Romanian Academy.

It may be argued that the above-mentioned book was a singular case and the Phanariots' interest in it was an exception. However, another discovery in Greece this time confirms the interest of yet another famous Phanariot in the Arabic books printed in Wallachia.

In the collections of the Library of the University of Thessaloniki there is a copy of the *Book of Hours* published in Arabic in Bucharest in 1702. No information on the provenance is recorded, but the book bears the stamp of the Fund of the Exchangeable Communal and Public Benefit Proprieties,[23] an institution established with the aim, among others, of collecting and distributing the cultural artefacts of the communities subjected to the population exchange between Greece and Turkey. The book was therefore preserved until 1924 somewhere in Eastern Thrace or Asia Minor. Sometime after 1934, the book entered the collections of the library of the University of Thessaloniki. The book but not the edition was correctly identified by the librarians as a *Book of Hours* and they also attempted a description from the first page with Greek text, the one with the coat of arms of Wallachia.[24]

A Greek note on the third page of the Arabic *Book of Hours* records the name of a previous owner "Ek tōn tou Kōnstantinou Maurokordatou hyiou N. V." ("Ἐκ τῶν τοῦ Κωνσταντίνου Μαυροκορδάτου υἱοῦ N. B.", "From those of Constantine Mavrocordatos son of N. V." The last two initials must be read "Nicolas Voevodas"), leaving no doubt that Constantine was the future prince of Wallachia and Moldavia and one of the most famous Phanariot rulers of the Romanian lands.[25] Constantine Mavrocordatos was born in 1711[26] and the lack of any princely titles suggests that the note was written before 1730, during his formative years. As there was plenty of reading material in Greek in the library of the Mavrocordatos family, Constantine's interest in this particular book was likely because of the

---

22 Their stamp applied on the first and the last printed page of the book reads: "Fraţii Şaraga, library – antiquari, Jaşi" On the history of the Şaraga family, antique book and stamp dealers and medal minters see I. Massoff, *Strădania a cinci generaţii*, Bucharest, 1941, passim.

23 In Greek "Tameion Antallaximōn Koinōtikōn kai Koinophelōn Periousiōn".

24 The book is available online at the Digital Library of the Aristotle University of Thessaloniki https://digital.lib.auth.gr/record/137084 (accessed December 10, 2022).

25 On Constantine Mavrocordatos see F. Constantiniu, *Constantin Mavrocordat reformatorul*, Bucharest, 2015.

26 Ţipău, *Domnii fanarioţi în Ţările Române*, p. 112.

Arabic text. As part of the Phanariot elite he was supposed to learn Arabic among other languages and the *Book of Hours* was sometimes used at the time by young students to improve their reading skills for other languages too.

Another copy of the same edition of the Greek and Arabic *Book of Hours* published by Athanasios in 1702 has other interesting handwritten notes.[27] The first note, written in Romanian in 1703, records that Theodosios (Theodosie), metropolitan of Ungro-Wallachia, gave the book as a gift to the Monastery of Tismana.

> Această sfântă carte ce să chiamă *Orologiu* hărăpesc dar iaste de kyr Theodosiie mitroppolitul Ungrovlahiei Sfintei Mănăstiri Tismeanei, unde iaste hramul Uspenee B(ogorodi)ţăi ca să se afle acolo. Ap(rilie) Adam leat 7211.
>
> This holy book that it is called in Arabic *Horologion* is a gift from kyr Theodosios metropolitan of Ungro-Wallachia to the Holy Monastery of Tismana, dedicated to the the Dormition of the Mother of God, in order to be there. April, [the year] from Adam 7211.

The information is valuable as it confirms the supposition that a number of copies of the Arabic books were made available for the Romanian upper clergy and dignitaries.

The book remained in the library of Tismana Monastery as can be inferred from the latter handwritten notes. One of them, dated September 19th, 1712, is of particular interest, as it records a previously unknown historical fact. Its author, "Nikephoros the Protosyncellos", wrote about his exile at the monastery, during the reign of Constantine Brâncoveanu, after the accusations brought against him by Dionysios, metropolitan of Tarnovo, that he was conspiring to take over his Metropolitan See. The protosyncellos was forcibly taken from Tarnovo by the Turks, a certain Haci Ahmet from the same city being involved in these events. Nikephoros' subsequent actions are not recorded, and it is unknown how long he remained in Tismana.

The note reads as follows:

> 1712 Σεπτεμβρίου 19. Εἰς τὸν καιρῶν (correct καιρὸν) τοῦ εὐσεβεστάτου καὶ ἐκλαμπροτάτου Ἰω[άννου] Κωνσταντίνου βοεβόδα ἅς εἶναι πολήχρονος (correct πολύχρονος) μᾶς ἔστειλεν ἐδῶ εἰς τὸ Ἅγιον Μοναστήριον μετὰ σύρτηρη ἐστόντας νὰ πηστεύση (correct πιστεύσει) τὸν τερλὸν Τουρνόβου Διονύσιον πῶς ἐπήγα νὰ τοῦ πάρω τὴν ἐπαρχίαν, καὶ ἔτζη ἔστειλεν καὶ μὲ ἔκλεψεν μάλον μὲ ἐπαράδωσεν ὁ Χατζὴ Ἀχμέτης ἀπὸ το Τούρνοβον. Καὶ τὰ κακὰ ὅπου ἔπαθα, τόσον ἀπὸ τὸν Τουρνόβου, ὅσον καὶ ἀπὸ τοὺς Τούρκους τὶς νὰ τὰ διηγήσεται, ὁ Θ(εὸ)ς νὰ μὲ γλη[τώσ]ει (correct γλυτώσει) ἐμένα καὶ κάθε Χριστιανῶν (sic). Ὁ Πρωτοσύγγελος Νικηφόρος.

---

27 The book is available online at https://books.google.ro/books?id=uO1lAAAAcAAJ (accessed December 10, 2022).

September 19th, 1712. In the time of the most pious and most resplendent John Constantine voivode, may his years be many, we were sent here to the Holy Monastery by force, believing the mad Dionysios of Tarnovo that I was about to take his eparchy, and this way he sent and he stole me, or rather I was surrendered by Haci Ahmet from Tarnovo. And [from] the bad things that happened to me both from [the metropolitan] of Tarnovo and from the Turks (who could narrate them?), may God spare me and every Christian. Nikephoros the Protosyncellos.

Some of the rest of the notes in the Arabic *Book of Hours* were written more than a decade later by a certain "Nicodim Eclesiarh" of Tismana who wrote his name and position in Romanian and Latin in 1727 during the period of Austrian rule in Oltenia. He is perhaps the same as the "Nicodemus egum[enus]. Tismanensis" who signed a petition of the Romanian boyars at about the same time.[28] From the Monastery of Tismana, the book made its way to a western library, probably the Imperial Library in Vienna (today the National Library of Austria, Österreichische Nationalbibliothek). A note in Latin on the title page may suggest that the book was removed from Tismana already in the 18th century, perhaps before the end of Austrian rule in Oltenia (1739).

It is interesting to mention another princely owner of an Arabic book, Rodolphus (i. e. Radu) Cantacuzenos.[29] Although not a Phanariot in the usual sense of the word, Radu was the son of Stephanus Cantacuzenos, ruling prince of Wallachia between 1714 and 1716. His signature and the date August 5, 1713 can be found in a *Book of Psalms* printed in Aleppo in 1706 by Athanasios Dabbas with the support of Constantine Brâncoveanu.[30] The book was in the Royal Library in Dresden by 1744. It is likely that Radu Cantacuzenos brought the book with him to Central Europe during his exile.[31]

---

28 Eudoxiu de Hurmuzaki, *Documente privitoare la istoria românilor*, vol. VI *1700–1750*, Bucharest, 1878, p. 317–318. See also N. Dobrescu, *Istoria Bisericii române din Oltenia în timpul ocupaţiunii austriace (1716–1739)*, Bucharest, 1906, p. 70, 199.
29 I wish to thank Carsten Walbiner for bringing to my attention this information and providing me with the bibliographical references.
30 [J. Chr. Götze], *Die Merkwürdigkeiten der Königlichen Bibliothek zu Dresden. Ausführlich beschreiben, und mit Anmerkungen erläutert. Die erste Sammlung*, Dresden, 1744, p. 203–204. The book is preserved today in the Sächsische Landesbibliothek – Staats- und Universitätsbibliothek in Dresden (Shelf-mark: Biblia.1243). See https://katalog.slub-dresden.de/en/id/0-1523854235 (accessed at December 10, 2022).
31 On Radu Cantacuzenos see N. Iorga, "Radu Cantacuzino", *Academia Română. Memoriile Secţiunii Istorice*, Seria III, Tom XIII, 1933, p. 149–158. O. Olar, "Un aventurier al Luminilor. Prinţul Radu Cantacuzino (1699–1761) şi Ordinul constantinian al Sfântului Gheorghe", in R. G. Păun, O. Cristea (eds.), *Istoria: utopie, amintire şi proiect de viitor. Studii de istorie oferite Profesorului Andrei Pippidi*, Iaşi, 2013, p. 153–166.

There is also another recent discovery that I have already mentioned in a previous paper[32] which shows in the most definite manner the interest of the Phanariot princes for the Arabic language. A manuscript of a Greek grammar of the Arabic language surfaced in 2016 in a sale of an important international auction house. The manuscript was previously owned by the Antiquariat Inlibris, Gilhofer Nfg in Vienna, Austria.

The manuscript was lot 118 of the auction "Travel, Atlases, Maps and Natural History" at the Sotheby's in London and it was sold at the price of £4,375 on November 15, 2016. According to the description provided by the auction house, its size is in folio (308 x 190 mm.) and it comprises the title page and 107 folios numbered in Arabic.

The title mentions as the author of the book Constantine Racovitzas, prince of Wallachia, previously not known to have had philological interests:[33]

Σύντομος εἰσαγωγὴ τῆς ἀραβικῆς γλῶσσης, συντεθεῖσα παρὰ τοῦ ὑψηλοτάτου, καὶ εὐσεβεστάτου αὐθέντου καὶ ἡγεμόνος πάσης Οὐγγροβλαχίας κυρίου κυρίου Ἰωάννου Κωνσταντίνου Μιχαὴλ Ῥακοβίτζα βοεβόδα, 1758 κατὰ μῆνα Δεκέμβριον.
Short introduction to the Arabic language, composed by the highest, most pious lord and prince of all Ungro-Wallachia kyr kyr John Constantine Michael Racovitzas voivode, 1758, in the month of December.[34]

In the description provided by the auction house the date of the manuscript is 1754, and the whole text is considered to be an autograph of the author (a hypothesis that doesn't seem to be supported by the rendering of the title and could be proved only by comparison with other texts in Racovitzas' own handwriting).

In 1758 Constantine Racovitzas was probably in Constantinople, during a time when it is conceivable that a lack of public duties allowed him to dedicate himself to philological activities. Previously he had twice held the office of ruling prince of Moldavia (1749–1753 and 1756–1757) and once that of Wallachia (1753–1756). It is interesting to note that in the manuscript the author's title is that of ruling prince of Ungro-Wallachia (i.e. Wallachia), a position he would obtain for a second time in 1763. The year on the title page of the manuscript presents some degree of paleographical difficulty and can be read either as 1754 or as 1758. If the

---

32 M. Ţipău, *Istoriografia greco-română. Stadiul cercetării și perspective*, in A. Timotin (ed.), *Dinamici sociale și transferuri culturale în sud-estul european (secolele al XVI-lea – al XIX-lea)*, Bucharest, 2019, p. 307.

33 On Constantine Racovitzas (Constantin Racoviţă Cehan) see Ţipău, *Domnii fanarioți în Ţările Române*, p. 211–261.

34 http://www.sothebys.com/en/auctions/ecatalogue/2016/travel-atlases-maps-natural-histo ry-l16405/lot.118.html (accessed October 24, 2017).

first version is correct, then Racovitzas' princely title of ruling prince of Wallachia is appropriate for that particular timeframe.

A manuscript with a similar title, *Syntomos eisagōgē tēs aravikēs glōsēs*, but without stating the author's name is kept in the library of the Orthodox Patriarchate of Jerusalem, in the collection Timiou Stavrou (Τιμίου Σταυροῦ), number 20. The 154 folios manuscript was chronologically placed by Alexandros Papadopoulos Kerameus in the 19th century,[35] the paleographical features of the text however, favor most likely an 18th-century date for the manuscript. [36]

A summary comparison of the few pages presented by Sotheby's with the anonymous Arabic grammar with Greek explanation in the Jerusalem manuscript shows without a doubt that it is one and the same text. In this case, the Phanariots not only studied Arabic but were actively involved in composing useful study material for others.

It is clear that Phanariot interest in the books published by Athanasios of Antioch was centered on the Arabic and not on the Greek text, as Greek books were readily available and even printed in large numbers in early 18th-century Wallachia.[37] On the contrary, a printed book with Arabic text was difficult to obtain even in Constantinople. Such a book, if available, would make a good learning auxiliary for anyone interested in studying Arabic and the bilingual text made it even more useful for this purpose.

The information presented here may be a good starting point for a more detailed study of the Arabic books printed in the Romanian Principalities in their historical context.

---

35 A. Papadopoulos – Kerameus, *Hierosolymitikē Vivliothēkē ētoi Katalogos tōn en tais vivliothēkes tou Hagiōtatou Apostolikou te kai Katholikou Orthodoxou Patriarchikou Thronou tōn Hierosolymōn kai Pasēs Palaistinēs apokeimenōn hellēnikōn kōdikōn*, vol. 3, Saint Petersburg, 1897, p. 49, nr. 20.

36 A digital copy of the microfilm of this manuscript is available on the website of the Library of Congress: https://www.loc.gov/item/00279395451-jo (accessed October 24, 2017). See also K. W. Klark (ed.), *Checklist of Manuscripts in the Greek and Armenian Patriarchates in Jerusalem microfilmed for the Library of Congress, 1949–50*, Washington, 1953, p. 13.

37 A comprehensive history of the Greek printing presses in Wallachia and Moldavia is yet to be written. For published material on this topic see C. Erbiceanu, *Bibliografia Greacă sau cărţile greceşti imprimate în Principatele Române în epoca fanariotă şi dedicate domnitorilor şi boierilor români. Studii literare*, Bucharest, 1903 (2nd edition ed. M. Ţipău, Bucharest, 2020). D. V. Oikonomidēs, "Ta en Moldavia hellēnika typographeia kai ai ekdoseis autōn (1642–1821)", *Athēna*, 75, 1974–1975, p. 259–301. Oikonomidēs, "Ta en Vlachia hellēnika typographeia kai ai ekdoseis autōn (1690–1821)", *Athēna*, 76, 1977, p. 59–102. C. Papacostea–Danielopolu, L. Démeny, *Carte şi tipar în societatea românească şi Sud-Est europeană (secolele XVII–XIX)*, Bucharest, 1985, p. 145–195.

Bibliography

Bouchard, Jacques. "Perception des Phanariots avant et après Zallony". *Cahiers balkaniques* [Online], 42 (2014): http://journals.openedition.org/ceb/4935 (accessed December 10, 2022).

Britannica, The Editors of Encyclopaedia. "Phanariot". *Encyclopedia Britannica*, https://www. britannica.com/topic/Phanariot (accessed December 10, 2022).

Cândea, Virgil. *Stolnicul între contemporani*. Bucharest: Idaco, 2014 (2nd edition).

Chiṭulescu, Archim. Policarp. "Patriarhul Silvestru al Antiohiei şi dania sa de carte către mănăstirea Sfântul Sava din Iaşi. O reevaluare necesară". In Mariana Lazăr (coord. ed.), *Mărturii de istorie şi cultură românească. I*. Bucharest: Muzeul Naţional Cotroceni, 2022, p. 53-64.

Constantiniu, Florin. *Constantin Mavrocordat reformatorul*. Bucharest: Editura Enciclopedică, 2015 (2nd edition).

Diaconu, Gheorghe. "Relaţiile Patriarhiei din Antiohia cu Ţările Române şi închinarea Mănăstirii Sfântul Nicolae Domnesc Popăuţi" (I). *Teologie şi viaţă*, 26 (92), 2016, 9–12, p. 150–191.

Diaconu Luca. *Mănăstirea "Sfântul Nicolae Domnesc" din Popăuţi. Importantă ctitorie a Moldovei închinată Patriarhiei din Antiohia*, vol. II, *Mănăstirea "Sfântul Nicolae domnesc" Popăuţi în perioada 1750–2018*. Iaşi: Doxologia, 2018.

Dobrescu, Nicolae. *Istoria Bisericii române din Oltenia în timpul ocupaţiunii austriace (1716–1739)*. Bucharest: Ediţia Academiei Române, 1906.

Erbiceanu, Constantin. *Bibliografia Greacă sau cărţile greceşti imprimate în Principatele Române în epoca fanariotă şi dedicate domnitorilor şi boierilor români. Studii literare*. Bucharest: Tipografia Cărţilor Bisericeşti, 1903 (2nd ed. by Mihai Ţipău, Bucharest: Editura Enciclopedică, 2020).

Feodorov, Ioana. "The Romanian Contribution to Arabic Printing". In Elena Siupiur, Zamfira Mihail (eds.), *Impact de l'imprimerie et rayonnement intellectuel des Pays Roumains*. Bucharest: Editura Biblioteca Bucureştilor, 2009, p. 41–61.

Feodorov, Ioana. "Livres arabes chrétiens imprimés avec l'aide des Principautés Roumaines au début du XVIIIe siècle. Répertoire commenté". *Chronos*, 34, 2016, p. 7–49.

Feodorov, Ioana. *Tipar pentru creştinii arabi. Antim Ivireanul, Atanasie Dabbās şi Silvestru al Antiohiei*. Brăila: Editura Istros a Muzeului Brăilei "Carol I", 2016.

Feodorov, Ioana. "The Arabic Book of the Divine Liturgies Printed in 1745 in Iaşi by Patriarch Sylvester of Antioch". *Scrinium. Revue de patrologie, d'hagiographie critique et d'histoire ecclésiastique*, 16/1, 2020, p. 1–19.

Feodorov, Ioana. "Arabic Printed Books in the Library of the Romanian Academy of Bucharest". *MELA Notes*, 94, 2021, p. 69–99.

Feodorov, Ioana. *Arabic Printing for the Christians in Ottoman Lands. The East-European Connection*. Berlin/Boston: De Gruyter, 2023.

Gheorghiṭă, Ilie. "Tipografia arabă din Mănăstirea Sf. Sava şi venirea lui Silvestru patriarhul Antiohiei la Iaşi". *Mitropolia Moldovei şi Sucevei*, 26/5–6, 1958, p. 418–423.

[Götze, Johann Christian]. *Die Merkwürdigkeiten der Königlichen Bibliothek zu Dresden. Ausführlich beschreiben, und mit Anmerkungen erläutert. Die erste Sammlung*. Dresden: George Conrad Walther, 1744.

Holban, T. "Tipografii şi cărţi armeneşti (sic) în Ţările Româneşti". *Arhiva. Revistă de istorie, filologie şi cultură românească*, 43, 1936, p. 111–115.

Hurmuzaki, Eudoxiu de. *Documente privitoare la istoria românilor*, vol. VI *1700–1750*. Bucharest: Socecŭ, Sander & Teclu, 1878.

Hēlioupoleos, Gennadios. "Epistolai tou patriarchou Antiocheias Silvestrou". *Hellēnika*, 8, 1935, p. 239–245.

Iorga, Nicolae. "Radu Cantacuzino". *Academia Română. Memoriile Secțiunii Istorice*. Seria III, Tom XIII, 1933, p. 149–158.

Klark, Kenneth W. (ed.). *Checklist of Manuscripts in the Greek and Armenian Patriarchates in Jerusalem microfilmed for the Library of Congress, 1949–50*. Washington, 1953.

Massoff, I. *Strădania a cinci generații*. Bucharest: Biblioteca evreească, 1941.

Oikonomidēs, Dēmētrios V. "Ta en Moldavia hellēnika typographeia kai ai ekdoseis autōn (1642–1821)". *Athēna*, 75, 1974–1975, p. 259–301.

Oikonomidēs, Dēmētrios V. "Ta en Vlachia hellēnika typographeia kai ai ekdoseis autōn (1690–1821)". *Athēna*, 76, 1977, p. 59–102.

Olar, Ovidiu. "Un aventurier al Luminilor. Prințul Radu Cantacuzino (1699–1761) și Ordinul constantinian al Sfântului Gheorghe". In Radu G. Păun, Ovidiu Cristea (eds.), *Istoria: utopie, amintire și proiect de viitor. Studii de istorie oferite Profesorului Andrei Pippidi*. Iași: Editura Universității "Alexandru Ioan Cuza", 2013, p. 153–166.

Papacostea-Danielopolu, Cornelia, Lidia Démeny. *Carte și tipar în societatea românească și Sud-Est europeană (secolele XVII–XIX)*. Bucharest: Editura Eminescu, 1985.

Țipău, Mihai. *Domnii fanarioți în Țările Române 1711–1821. Mică enciclopedie*. Foreword by Prof. Dr. Paschalis M. Kitromilides. Bucharest: Omonia Publishig House, 2008 (2nd edition).

Țipău, Mihai. *Istoriografia greco-română. Stadiul cercetării și perspective*. In Andrei Timotin (ed.), *Dinamici sociale și transferuri culturale în sud-estul european (secolele al XVI-lea – al XIX-lea)*. Bucharest: Editura Academiei Române, 2019, p. 298–308.

Țipău, Mihai. "Mitropolitul Ungrovlahiei Neofit I Cretanul". In *Șerban Cantacuzino, Antim Ivireanul și Neofit Cretanul – Promotori ai limbii române în cult*. Bucharest: Editura Cuvântul Vieții, 2013, p. 223–272.

Papadopoulos – Kerameus, Alexandros. *Hierosolymitikē Vivliothēkē ētoi Katalogos tōn en tais vivliothēkes tou Hagiōtatou Apostolikou te kai Katholikou Orthodoxou Patriarchikou Thronou tōn Hierosolymōn kai Pasēs Palaistinēs apokeimenōn hellēnikōn kōdikōn*, vol. 3. Saint Petersburg, 1897.

Venier, M[arina]. "Librerie dei conventi riuniti nella Vittorio Emanuele", p. 31, https://www2.bodleian.ox.ac.uk/__data/assets/pdf_file/0019/122185/Marina-Venier,-Monastic-Libraries-now-in-Rome,-National-Central-Library.pdf (accessed December 10, 2022).

Zallony, Marc-Philippe. *Essai sur les Fanariotes où l'on voit les causes primitives de leur élévation aux hospodariats de la Valachie et de la Moldavie, leur mode d'administration, et les causes principales de leur chute ; suivi de quelques réflexions sur l'état actuel de la Grèce*. Marseille, 1824.

Carsten Walbiner

The Collection, Perception and Study of Arabic Incunabula from the Near East in Europe (17th – early 19th Centuries)

1. Introduction

The aim of this paper is to establish how the knowledge and possession of material printed in the Arab world developed between 1610 and 1810 in Europe. The objects of investigation are books printed during this period in the Arabic language (in Arabic and Syriac script). The time frame is not chosen randomly: it is marked by the appearance of the first book that was ever printed in the Arab lands in Arabic (1610 in Quzḥayyā, Lebanon in Garshūnī, i.e. in Syriac script) and the publication of the first scholarly catalogue describing prints in Arabic (von Schnurrer's *Bibliotheca arabica*; Halle [Saale], Germany, 1811).

Before starting with the investigation proper, it might be useful to make a quantitative assessment to clarify how many items, i.e. printed books, we actually speak about. During the period in question five, mostly only short-lived, printing shops existed in the Arab world. The following overview contains the places, the duration of operations and the number of titles produced:[1]

- Quzḥayyā, Lebanon (1610 / 1809 – [1810]): 2 titles
- Aleppo (1706–1711): 8 titles
- al-Shuwayr, Lebanon (1734–[1810]): 25 titles
- Beirut (1751–?): 3 titles
- Mār Mūsā al-Duwwār, Lebanon (1789–?): 4 titles

All in all, 42 titles appeared from these presses, an insignificant amount compared with European book production.[2]

---

1 For a full list see the table at the end of this chapter in the section dealing with von Schnurrer's catalogue.

2 In just the first 50 years following Gutenberg's invention of printing with moveable type, there existed in Europe ca. 1,100 printing shops in 255 places which produced around 30,000 titles amounting to 15 million copies (F. Funke, *Buchkunde. Die historische Entwicklung des Buches von der Keilschrift bis zur Gegenwart*, Wiesbaden, 2006, p. 112–113). In the following centuries book production exploded and created an even wider gap between printing in East and West which the East was never able to close.

ðﾠOpen Access. © 2024, the author(s), published by De Gruyter. (cc) BY-NC-ND This work is licensed under the Creative Commons Attribution-NonCommercial-NoDerivatives 4.0 International License. https://doi.org/10.1515/9783111060392-009

2. European Acquisitions and Studies of Early Prints from the Arab World

How and when did knowledge about these prints arrive in Europe? The answer might be surprising: Partly very quickly, not to say immediately. This shall be illustrated by two examples:

The first book in Arabic which ever appeared in the Arab world, the Quzḥayyā Psalter of 1610,[3] was already purchased by a German traveler in the year of its publication or one year later. The book bears an interesting remark by its first European owner: "*In memoriam itineris Syriaci Psalterium hoc Arabico Chaldaicum excusum in monte Libano a fratribus Maronitis comparavi ibidem loco[rum] ab Archiepiscopo Edeniensi 2 piaster. Tob. Adami.*"[4] (In commemoration of the Syrian journey, I procured this Chaldean Arabic Psalter, forged [printed] by the Maronite brothers on Mount Lebanon, there from the archbishop of Ehden [for] two piasters. Tob. Adami.) Tobias Emmanuel Adami (1581–1643) was a German jurist and philosopher who had accompanied a German nobleman on a journey through the Eastern Mediterranean, including Syria and Palestine. The book later became part of the library of the preacher and bibliophile Adam Rudolph Solger (1693–1777) of Nuremberg which was acquired in 1766 by the Municipality of Nuremberg,[5] where it is kept until today at the Municipal Library.[6] And another German traveler – Henning von Steinberg (1584–1639) – received in 1612 a copy of the Quzḥayyā psalter as a present from the Maronite patriarch whom he met "in monasterio prope Cedros," in all likelihood the Monastery of Our Lady of Qannūbīn, which served as the patriarchal seat.[7]

---

3 On this book see J. Moukarzel, "Le Psautier syriaque-garchouni édité à Qozhaya en 1610. Enjeux historiques et presentation du livre", *Mélanges de l'Université Saint-Joseph*, 63, 2010–2011, p. 511–566.

4 F. Babinger, "Ein vergessener maronitischer Psalterdruck auf der Nürnberger Stadtbücherei", *Zeitschrift für die Alttestamentliche Wissenschaft*, 43, 1925, p. 275.

5 Cf. https://www.nuernberg.de/internet/stadtbibliothek/privatbibliotheken.html (accessed October 23, 2022).

6 Stadtbibliothek Nürnberg, Solg. Ms. 21.21. For a brief description of this copy see C. Walbiner, "*Ktobō d-mazmūrē d-Dawūd malkō wa-nbīyō* (Book of the Psalms of the King and Prophet David)", in K. Kreiser (ed.), *The Beginnings of Printing in the Near and Middle East: Jews, Christians, Muslims*, Wiesbaden, 2001, p. 22–23.

7 Ch. Boveland, "Souvenir aus dem Libanongebirge. Ein syrisch-arabischer Psalter von 1610", blog of Herzog August Bibliothek Wolfenbüttel, posted on 4 July 2023 (https://www.hab.de/souvenir-aus-dem-libanongebirge/). The book is nowadays kept at the Herzog August Bibliothek in Wolfenbüttel, Germany (shelf mark: Bibel-S. 4° 227). A digitized version is accessible at http://diglib.hab.de/drucke/bibel-s-4f-227/start.htm (accessed October 23, 2022).

Also, the first product of the printing shop at al-Shuwayr published in 1734 made it to Europe surprisingly quickly. The copy of the book nowadays kept at the State Library in Munich[8] bears an inscription which states that the famous French traveler Jean de la Roque (1661–1745) had received it from Syria in August 1735.[9] The same inscription informs us that in September of the same year, de la Roque had already sent it to Christophe Maunier, a nobleman of Aleppine origin and an "authority" on the East, to get his opinion. It is not known how this book finally came to Munich, but this is not relevant. Two facts are important. These Oriental prints, or at least some of them, made their way quickly to Europe where they were noted by the scholarly community and became – as we will soon show – partly objects of investigation and study.

But information about, let only the physical copies of, the products of the presses in the East did not always travel that fast. When, in 1709, the French bibliographer Jacques Lelong (1665–1721) published his *Bibliotheca Sacra*, an index of all the publications of the Christian Holy Scriptures,[10] he had no idea of the Arabic Gospels and the Psalms which had appeared in 1706 in Aleppo,[11] but he makes reference to the Quzḥayyā Psalter,[12] and information on the Aleppo publications was added to an extended re-edition of his work which appeared post-humously in 1723.[13]

To avoid a misunderstanding: these Oriental prints were true rarities and knowledge of their existence, let alone of their concrete content, remained partial and very limited. To give a few examples: *An extract of several letters relating the great charity and usefulness of printing the New Testament and Psalter in the Arabic language; for the benefit of the poor Christians in Palestine, Syria, Mesopotamia,*

---

8 Bayerische Staatsbibliothek München, 4° A .or. 1352. For a brief description of this copy, see C. Walbiner, "Juan Eusebio Nieremberg: *Mīzān al-zamān wa-qisṭās abadiyyyat al-insān* (The scales of time and the measure of man's eternity)", in K. Kreiser (ed.), *The Beginnings of Printing in the Near and Middle East: Jews, Christians, Muslims*, Wiesbaden, 2001, p. 26–27.

9 Bayerische Staatsbibliothek München, 4° A .or. 1352, last page.

10 The work appeared in 1709 in three separate editions in Paris, Antwerp and Leipzig. In what follows, I refer to the one published in Leipzig: I. Le Long, *Bibliotheca sacra seu syllabus omnium ferme sacrae scripturae editionum ac versionum secundum seriem linguarum quibus vulgatae sunt notis historicis et criticis illustratus adiunctis praestantissimis Codd. Msc.*, 2 parts in one volume, Leipzig, 1709.

11 They are not mentioned in a chronological list of prints of Biblical texts under the year 1706 (cf. Le Long, *Bibliotheca sacra*, part 2, p. 559).

12 Le Long, *Biblia sacra*, part 1, p. 193–194.

13 I. Le Long, *Bibliotheca sacra in binos syllabos distincta quorum prior qui jam tertio auctior prodit, omnes sive textus sacri sive versionum ejusdem quâvis lingua expressarum editiones; nec non præstantiores MSS codices, cum notis historicis & criticis exhibet*, vol. 1, Paris, 1723, p. 125–126.

Arabia, Egypt and other Eastern countries: with a proposal for executing so good an undertaking, published in London in 1721, opens with "An extract of a letter from Mr. Salomon Negri, Native of Damascus in Syria, dated March 28, 1720. To a member of the Society at London for Promoting Christian Knowledge."[14] In his treatment of "the few printed copies still extant, either of the whole New Testament, or of part of it,"[15] Negri (1665–1727) only refers to a couple of European editions.[16] It seems that he was ignorant of the Aleppo prints and believed that the setting up of a press in the East would not be possible because "the constitution of the Country allows of no printing."[17] Later Negri obviously became acquainted with the Aleppo prints and in 1725 published a revision of the Aleppo Psalter of 1706, calling himself a "disciple" (*tilmīdh*) of its initiator, Athanasius Dabbās (1647–1724), whom he praises loudly in the introduction of the re-edition.[18]

The first volume of the catalogue of the Oriental manuscripts at the Vatican Library, published in 1719, reveals that its author, the famous Joseph Simon Assemani (Yūsif Simʿān al-Simʿānī, 1687–1768), had good knowledge of the products of the Aleppo printing house, a couple of which he had purchased during his acquisition journeys to the East.[19] But he was ignorant of the Quzḥayyā Psalter or at least makes no reference to it. And also his nephew Stephan Evodius Assemani (Isṭifān ʿAwwād al-Simʿānī, 1711–1782), who speaks about this work in his catalogue of the of the Oriental manuscripts of the Medicean-Laurentian library in Florence (1742), clearly did not have a copy available but relied either on his memory or second-hand information.[20] Thus, Solger was right in calling this print a true rarity and comparing it with regard to its availability to manuscripts.[21]

And this was also true for the other books printed in the East. The well-known German scholar Johann David Michaelis says in his introduction to the New Testament (first edition published in 1750) that in 1700 "an Arabic Bible" had been

---

14 *An extract of several letters*, p. 3–9.
15 *An extract of several letters*, p. 4.
16 *An extract of several letters*, p. 4–5.
17 *An extract of several letters*, p. 5.
18 Cf. S. A. Frantsouzoff, "Les psautiers arabes imprimés dans les bibliothèques de Saint-Petersbourg", in P. Chiṭulescu, I. Feodorov (eds.), *Culture manuscrite et imprimé dans et pour l'Europe du Sud-Est*, Brăila, 2020, p. 198–199, 205–206 (fig. 5 & 6).
19 J. S. Assemanus, *Bibliotheca orientalis Clementino-Vaticana*, vol. 1. Rome, 1719, p. 631; on Assemani's acquisition of manuscripts and books in the East see briefly H. Kaufhold, "Die Rechtsliteratur in der 'Bibliotheca Orientalis'", *Parole de l'Orient*, 47, 2021, p. 48.
20 St. E. Assemanus, *Bibliothecae Mediceae Laurentianae et Palatinae Codicum MSS. Orientalium Catalogus*, Florence, 1742, p. 7–72.
21 A. R. Solger, *Bibliotheca sive supellex librorum impressorum*, vol. 1, Nuremberg, 1760, p. 214.

printed in Bucharest and the "Arabic Gospels" in 1706 in Aleppo, but that he only knows about this from Le Long[22] and Helladius[23] (i.e., from secondary sources).[24] And he makes the following request: "Whoever would like to do critical research a service, is hereby asked to provide me with them and to give at the same time information whether they are printed based on manuscripts and whether they have been changed by the editors or were left as contained in the original."[25] This plea was still part of the fourth – and as I can see – last edition of Michaelis's work published in 1788.[26]

The references to the prints from the East to be found in Western publications were mostly nothing else than short bibliographical notes, often not derived from an inspection of the work itself but taken from secondary sources. In a little thesis on Arabic typography published in 1741 in Latin in Uppsala, the part dealing with book-printing in Syria is based on three books from al-Shuwayr and so remained of course – due to the inadequate material base – insufficient.[27] But the treatise shows that there was some scholarly interest in works printed in the East.

Regarding a more thorough treatment of these early Oriental prints, there is only one noteworthy example, a brief philological-theological study of the Quzḥayyā Psalter by the German scholar Johann Christoph Döderlein (1745–1792), published in 1778 as part of a treatise on the Arabic Psalters.[28] The author worked with the copy available at the Municipal Library of Nuremberg.[29]

The Quzḥayyā Psalter was the Oriental print which received by far the most attention in Europe. The following chronology lists the most important stages of acquisition and perception of this work.

- 1610 or 1611: A copy is purchased by a German traveler, brought to Germany, and becomes part of a private library.

---

22 See above footnote 13.

23 The Greek scholar Alexander Helladius (1686–?) refers briefly to the printing activities of "the patriarch of Antioch in Bucharest" without providing any details (cf. A. Helladius, *Status praesens Ecclesiae Graecae: in quo etiam causae exponuntur cur graeci moderni Novi Testamenti editiones in graeco-barbara lingua factas acceptare recusant*, no place and publisher, 1714, p. 17–18).

24 J. D. Michaelis, *Einleitung in die göttlichen Schriften des Neuen Bundes*, Göttingen, 1765 (2nd edition), p. 209.

25 Michaelis, *Einleitung*, p. 209–210.

26 Michaelis, *Einleitung*, 4th edition, Göttingen, 1788, p. 454–455.

27 H. Scholtz, *Specimen I. Bibliothecae Arabicae de typographia arabicis*, Hamburg, 1741, p. 9–10.

28 J. Ch. Döderlein, "Von arabischen Psaltern. Ein Beytrag zu einer Einleitung ins A. Test.", in *Repertorium für Biblische und Morgenländische Litteratur*, part 2, Leipzig, 1778, p. 151–179 (the Quzḥayyā Psalter is dealt with on p. 156–170).

29 Döderlein, "Von arabischen Psaltern", p. 157.

- 1612: The German traveler Henning von Steinberg receives a copy as a gift from the Maronite patriarch.
- 1633: The first known reference to the work in a European publication: Leon Allatius, *Apes urbanae sive de viris illustribus qui ab Anno MDCXXX per totum MDCXXXII Romae adfuerunt, ac typis aliquid evulgarunt* ("Urban bees, or about the illustrious men who were present in Rome from the year 1630 through the year 1632, and published something in print"), Rome, 1633.[30]
- 1709: The Psalter is mentioned in *Bibliotheca Sacra* by Le Long, a major reference book. (The information provided goes beyond what is said by Allatius and reveals that a copy of the work was inspected, though whether by Le Long or someone else is not clear.)
- 1742: The catalogue of the Oriental manuscripts of the Medicean-Laurentian Library in Florence, established by Stephanus Evodius Assemani, contains some dubious information on the Psalter and dates it to 1585.
- 1760: The existence of the copy in Nuremberg is made publicly known through a catalogue of the library of the by-then owner, Adam Rudolph Solger.
- 1766: The acquisition of Solger's library by the city of Nuremberg for the Municipal Library makes the work accessible for interested readers.
- 1778: The Quzḥayyā Psalter of Nuremberg Library is dealt with in some detail by Johann Christoph Döderlein in a treatise on Arabic Psalters.
- 1780ff.: Döderlein's study is exploited for other works – most notably Johann Gottfried Eichhorn's *Einleitung ins Alte Testament* ("Introduction into the Old Testament")[31] – and remains even in the 19th century a main source on the Quzḥayyā Psalter.[32]
- 1811: Christian Friedrich von Schnurrer examines another copy of the Psalter and in his *Bibliotheca arabica* makes a few corrections and additions to Döderlein's description.[33]

With von Schnurrer, we seem to be already at the end of this paper. But before depicting von Schnurrer's achievements for the establishment of a scholarly bibliography of Arabic prints, there shall be a brief excursion into the role travelers played in the collection of the books printed in the East and knowledge about the places where they were produced.

---

30 Allatius briefly mentions Sergius Risius (Sarkīs al-Rizzī, 1572–1638), the Maronite archbishop of Damascus, as the initiator of the 1610 edition of the Psalms (p. 233).

31 Vol. 1. Leipzig, 1780, p. 515–519.

32 See, for instance, H. Cotton, *A Typographical Gazetteer*, Oxford, 1831, p. 144 (indirectly via A. G. Masch. *Bibliotheca Sacra post Jacobi Le Long et C. F. Boerneri iterates curas*, vol. 2. Halle [Saale], 1781, p. 121).

33 See below footnote 76.

The importance of travelers for the transfer of printed books from the East to Europe had already been briefly highlighted by the examples of Adami and Assemani. The journeys which resulted in the acquisition of prints and information on the presses were of different kinds. Sometimes – like in the case of Adami – the purchase of prints was an accidental side effect, while Assemani's sojourn in the East aimed explicitly at the collection of manuscripts and books. Such journeys and "missions" did not only lead to the acquisition of printed books but resulted also in gaining information on the history and operation of these printing shops, especially that at al-Shuwayr, the only one which could develop a lasting existence.

The first European to publish an eyewitness report on an Eastern printing shop was the German Protestant theologian Stephan Schultz (1714–1776), who travelled between 1752 and 1756 in the Ottoman Empire.[34] In September 1755 he visited the monastery of al-Shuwayr, where he saw the printing press[35] and purchased a few of its publications.[36] The inventory of Schultz's legacy in books contains the Psalms,[37] Nieremberg's *Mīzān al-zamān* (1734)[38] and Segneri's penitential manual entitled in Arabic *Murshid al-khāṭī* (1747).[39] Additionally, two works which are only classified as "Arabic books"[40] might also be prints.

---

34 On Schultz and his journey see D. Haas, "Von Halle in den Orient. Stephan Schultz auf Reisen im Osmanischen Reich in den Jahren 1752 bis 1756", in A. Schröder-Kahnt, C. Veltmann (eds.), *Durch die Welt im Auftrag des Herrn. Reisen von Pietisten im 18. Jahrhundert*, Halle (Saale), 2018, p. 67–79.

35 St. Schultz (ed.), *Fernere Nachricht von der zum Heil der Juden errichteten Anstalt, nebst den Auszügen aus den Tagebüchern der reisenden Mitarbeiter*, part 7, Halle, 1769, p. 131–132. (The volume contains extracts from Schultz's travel journal for the year 1755). See also a similar report in St. Schultz, *Der Leitungen des Höchsten nach seinem Rath auf den Reisen durch Europa, Asia und Africa*, part 5, Halle (Saale), 1775, p. 452.

36 Schultz, *Fernere Nachricht*, p. 133.

37 The year of publication is not mentioned. Before Schultz's visit, the Psalms had appeared three times (1735, 1739, and 1753).

38 The acquisition of the Psalms and *Mīzān al-zamān* is also mentioned in Schultz's memoirs (Schultz, *Die Leitungen des Höchsten*, p. 452).

39 *Verzeichnis derer Bücher und einer sehr starken Anzahl und Sammlung der neuesten theologischen, juristischen, medicinischen und philosophischen Disputationen, welche der sel. Hr. M. und Oberdiaconus Stephan Schultze hinterlassen, so den 26sten May 1777. und folgende Tage ... In dem Diaconathause bey der St. Ulrichskirche, gegen baare Bezahlung an den Meistbiethenden durch Auction verlassen werden soll*, Halle (Saale), 1777, p. 23 (no 72), p. 73 (no 3), p. 74 (no 10). I am very grateful to Daniel Haas of Hamburg who has provided me with that reference and other information on Schultz.

40 *Verzeichnis derer Bücher*, p. 34 (no. 340), p. 75 (no. 21.2).

Until the middle of the 19th century, the most influential and often quoted source on printing in the Arab world was derived from a travelogue of the French philosopher and proponent of the Enlightenment, Constantin François Volney (1757–1820). Between 1783 and 1785 Volney visited Syria, Lebanon, Palestine and Egypt. In his travel report[41] he makes extensive reference to the printing shop at the monastery of al-Shuwayr where he stayed for a while to learn Arabic. An account of the history of the press and its current state[42] is followed by a "Catalogue des Livres imprimés au Couvent de Mar-hanna-el-Chouair, dans la montagne des Druzes" which comprises thirteen titles.[43] In a chapter on the arts, sciences and ignorance of the Orientals ("Des Arts, des Sciences & de l'Ignorance") Volney also makes some general considerations about the importance and the impact of printing ("considerations sur l'importance & les effets de l'Imprimerie").[44] Its absence is in his opinion key for the "scarcity of books" ("*la rareté des livres*") in the East, which is in turn a decisive cause for "the general ignorance of the Orientals" ("*l'ignorance general des Orientaux*").[45] Whether Volney acquired any publications of the printing shop at al-Shuwayr has still to be established.

As for the influence that Volney's account of the al-Shuwayr press exercised for decades, it might suffice to mention that Carl Ritter (1779–1859), the founding father of modern university geography, used it as his major source of information for the description of the press in his famous *Geography of Asia*.[46]

The traveler to whom we owe the most, in terms of collecting Oriental prints for the period under investigation, as well as for information on the printing shops where they were produced, is the German Ulrich Jasper Seetzen (1767–1811). In 1803, Seetzen came to the Arab lands to prepare himself for an exploration mission into inner Africa. His first station was Aleppo, where he stayed for one and a half years, learning Arabic and getting acquainted with life in the Orient.[47] Having been equipped by the Archduke of Saxe-Gotha-Altenburg with funds to acquire manuscripts, books and other artefacts for an "Oriental Museum", in Aleppo Seetzen began to collect information on the printing shops of the Arab

---

41 C.-F. Volney, *Voyage en Syrie et en Égypte pendant les anneés 1783, 1784, et 1785*, 2 vols, Paris, 1787.

42 Volney, *Voyage en Syrie et en Égypte*, vol. 2, p. 174–181.

43 Volney, *Voyage en Syrie et en Égypte*, p. 180–181.

44 Volney, *Voyage en Syrie et en Égypte*, p. 412–417.

45 Volney, *Voyage en Syrie et en Égypte*, p. 410.

46 C. Ritter, *Die Erdkunde von Asien*, vol. VIII/2: Die Sinai-Halbinsel, Palästina und Syrien, part 3: Syrien, Berlin, 1854, p. 766–768.

47 On Seetzen's sojourn in Aleppo, see C. Walbiner, "Ulrich Jasper Seetzen [in Aleppo (1803–1805)]", in N. Cooke, V. Daubney (eds.), *Every Traveller Needs a Compass. Travel and Collecting in Egypt and the Near East*, Oxford, 2015, p. 197–204.

East – past and present – and also purchased all the printed books he could get hold of. The sources of his knowledge about the different presses were mainly his local interlocutors – the Greek Orthodox metropolitan for the printing shop of Aleppo,[48] "Stephán Conti", a "Frank" residing in Aleppo who had seen the printing press of Quzḥayyā being used[49] or the bookbinder "Schemmáss Jakúb" for a dubious printing shop that had allegedly been established approximately twelve years earlier in the Greek Orthodox monastery of Jerusalem.[50] Seetzen gained further information by inspecting the prints produced in Aleppo, al-Shuwayr and Beirut to which he had access in Aleppo.[51]

Much to his regret, however, Seetzen was not able – "despite all efforts" – to establish a "complete collection of the Arabic works printed in Aleppo, Beirut and Mount Lebanon [i.e. al-Shuwayr], although those already procured will be a great rarity in Germany."[52] He furthermore laments that he couldn't get an "authentic complete list" of the publications of al-Shuwayr[53] and that he had not yet seen any products from the press at Quzḥayyā.[54]

Despite his limited access to the books thus far printed in Greater Syria, at the end of his stay in Aleppo Seetzen published an article which includes the up to then best account of the history of printing in the Arab world.[55]

In the further course of his travels, Seetzen had the opportunity to visit the two presses in Lebanon operating during his sojourn in the region; descriptions of them are to be found in his diary.[56] A catalogue of the "Oriental manuscripts and printed works, artefacts and natural products" acquired for the Oriental collection in Gotha and prepared by Seetzen himself in 1810 lists for the category

---

48 U. J. Seetzen, *Tagebuch des Aufenthalts in Aleppo 1803–1805*, Hildesheim/Zürich/New York, 2011, p. 210–211.
49 Seetzen, *Tagebuch*, p. 244–245.
50 Seetzen, *Tagebuch*, p. 254. From the titles of the two works that are listed as having been printed there it becomes clear that reference is made to books which had been printed by the patriarch of Jerusalem in Vienna for distribution in the East.
51 Seetzen, *Tagebuch*, p. 200, 211 (Aleppo); 41, 200 (al-Shuwayr); 211 (Beirut).
52 Seetzen, *Tagebuch*, p. 210.
53 Seetzen, *Tagebuch*, p. 211.
54 Seetzen, *Tagebuch*, p. 245. Seetzen was, by the way, also not aware of the Psalms printed in Quzḥayyā in 1610 which had obviously fallen totally into oblivion in the East at the time of his sojourn.
55 U. J. Seetzen, "Nachricht von den in der Levante befindlichen Buchdruckereyen", *Intelligenzblatt der Jenaischen Allgemeinen Literatur-Zeitung*, 76 (13 July 1805), coll. 641–654.
56 F. Kruse (ed.), *Ulrich Jasper Seetzen's Reisen durch Syrien, Palästina, die Transjordan-Länder, Arabia Petraea und Unter-Aegypten*, vol. 1, Berlin, 1854, p. 175, 177 (Quzḥayyā); p. 251–253 (al-Shuwayr).

"Oriental printed works" 26 publications.[57] Ten of these entries refer to publications from the printing shops of Lebanon: eight from al-Shuwayr (nos. 1–8), "Chudmet Kúddos ríttbet el Muárrny" printed at the Maronite Monastery of Mār Mūsā [al-Duwwār] in 1789 (no. 18), and "two prayers printed in Garshūnī at the new Syriac press in the Maronite monastery Quzḥayyā at [Mount] Lebanon" (no 19).[58] It is strange that the prints from the presses in Aleppo and Beirut and some publications from al-Shuwayr also acquired by Seetzen[59] do not appear in his 1810 catalogue. They are still partly traceable in the holdings of Gotha Research Library.[60] The above-mentioned Maronite missal printed in 1789 at the monastery of Mār Mūsā al-Duwwār, Lebanon, which was recently rediscovered at Gotha Research Library, deserves special attention.[61] Worldwide, it is the only product from this printing shop available for scholarly investigation.

Travelers coming to Europe from the Ottoman Empire also contributed to making prints from the East known and available in the West. One interesting example is to be found at the Saxonian State Library in Dresden, which holds a copy of the Book of Psalms printed in Aleppo in 1706. It bears an owner's statement made on August 5, 1713 in Târgoviște by the Romanian Prince Radu Cantacuzenos (1699–1761),[62] who was a pretender to the throne of Wallachia but spent

---

57 U. J. Seetzen, *Verzeichnis der für die orientalische Sammlung in Gotha zu Damask, Jerusalem u.s.w. angekauften orientalischen Manuscripte und gedruckten Werke, Kunst- und Naturprodukte u.s.w*, Leipzig, 1810, p. 16–17.

58 Seetzen, *Verzeichnis der für die orientalische Sammlung*, p. 16–17.

59 See, for instance, Kruse (ed.), *Ulrich Jasper Seetzen's Reisen*, p. 210.

60 M. Hasenmüller, "Ulrich Jasper Seetzen als Sammler orientalischer Handschriften", in D. Haberland (ed.), *Der Orientreisende Ulrich Jasper Seetzen und die Wissenschaften*, Oldenburg, 2019, p. 459–576, at 468–469. A complete overview of Seetzen's acquisition of printed works is still a desideratum (ibid., p. 469). The importance of Seetzen's acquisitions becomes obvious when comparing figures. While the Bavarian State Library in Munich, one of the major holders of Oriental prints in Germany, in 1957 owned only four 18th century publications from the printing shop of al-Shuwayr (cf. H. Bojer, "Einiges über die arabische Druckschriftensammlung der Bayerischen Staatsbibliothek", in H. Franke [ed.], *Orientalisches aus Münchener Bibliotheken und Sammlungen*, Wiesbaden, 1957, p. 78), the Gotha Research Library holds – due to Seetzen's purchases – at least ten.

61 *Kitāb khidmat al-quddās ḥasaba rutbat al-kanīsa al-suryānīya al-mārūniyya al-muqaddasa*, [Dayr] Mārī Mūsā al-ḥabashī [al-Duwwār], 1798 (Forschungsbibliothek Gotha, Theol. 8° 00314b/03; https://dhb.thulb.uni-jena.de/receive/ufb_cbu_00042073).

62 [J. Ch. Götze,] *Die Merckwürdigkeiten der Königlichen Bibliothek zu Dreßden, ausführlich beschrieben, und mit Anmerkungen erläutert*, Die erste Sammlung, Dresden, 1744, p. 203–204, no 219. The work is until today kept under the signature Biblia. 1243 at the Saxonian Sate Library in Dresden (message dated September 12, 2022, from Kerstin Vogl, whom I would like to thank for this and other information; cf. https://katalog.slub-dresden.de/id/0-1523854235).

most of his life in exile in Europe. Although the editor of the catalogue of the Royal Library in Dresden assumes that the book could have been war booty,[63] it is more likely that it was brought to Dresden by Cantacuzenos, who visited the Saxonian capital several times, demonstrably in 1727 and 1740.[64]

3. Von Schnurrer's *Bibliotheca Arabica*

By the early 19th century, it was possible to establish a quite complete overview of the works that had been printed up to that time in the East. In 1811 the German scholar Christian Friedrich von Schnurrer (1742–1822) published a bibliographical reference work which aimed at providing information on all works published in Arabic to date.[65] It also contains references to most of the publications produced in the five printing shops of the Arab world as can be learnt from the following overview.

Tab. 1: Quzḥayyā (1610 / ca. 1809–[1810])[66] [Garshūnī].

Year	Title / Content	Re-editions (until 1810)	Von Schnurrer
1610	The Psalms (Syriac/Arabic)		319
1809	Kitāb al-shabīya (The Maronite Breviary)		---

---

63 [Götze,] *Die Merckwürdigkeiten*, p. 204.
64 Cf. N. Iorga, "Radu Cantacuzino", *Analele Academiei Române (Memoriile Secţiunii Istorice),* Seria III, 13, 1932–1933, p. 152; R. Albu-Comănescu, "The Constantinian Order of the Cantacuzene family", in G. S. Sainty, *The Constantinian Order of Saint George: and the Angeli, Farnese and Bourbon Families Which Governed it,* Madrid, 2018, p. 511. I am extremely grateful to Mihai Ţipău of Bucharest who referred me to these sources and provided me with further valuable information on Cantacuzenos.
65 Ch. F. von Schnurrer, *Bibliotheca arabica,* Halle (Saale), 1811.
66 Moukarzel, "Le Psautier syriaque-garchouni édité à Qozhaya en 1610"; R. El Ghobry, *The Second Printing Press of Quzḥayyā Monastery. History of the Press and Descriptive Catalogue of its Imprints,* unpublished MA thesis, Université Saint-Esprit de Kaslik, 2018.

Tab. 2: Aleppo (1706–1711)[67].

Year	Title / Content	Re-editions	Von Schnurrer
1706	al-Zabūr (The Psalms)	1709	339, ---
1706	al-Injīl (The Gospels)	1708	340/341, ---
1707	al-Durr al-muntakhab (Homilies of John Chrysostom)		267
1708	al-Nubū'āt (The Prophetologion)		268
1708	al-Rasā'il (The Epistolary)		---
1711	Kitāb al-mawā'iẓ al-sharīf (Homilies of Athanasius of Jerusalem)		270
1711	al-Mu'azzī (The Octoechos/ Paraclet-ice)		269
1711	Risāla wajīza (Treatise on Confession)		271

Tab. 3: Al-Shuwayr (1734–[1810])[68].

Year	Title / Content	Re-editions (until 1810)	Von Schnurrer
1734	Mizān al-zamān		282
1735	al-Zabūr (The Psalms)	1739, 1753, 1764, 1770, 1780, 1797, 1809	347, 348, 356, 358, 359, 361,[69] ---, ---
1736	Ta'ammulāt rūḥīya		284
1738	al-Murshid al-masīḥī		287
1739[70]	Iḥtiqār abāṭīl al-'ālam, vol. 1		--- [cf. p. 289]

---

67 W. Gdoura, *Le début de l'imprimerie arabe à Istanbul et en Syrie: evolution de l'environment culturel (1706–1787)*, Tunis, 1985, p. 138–153.

68 Y. Ṣfayr, *Maṭba'at al-Shuwayr, al-maṭba'a a al-'arabīya al-ūlá (1733–1899). Fihris al-maṭbū'āt al-mufaṣṣal*, unpublished MA thesis, Université Saint-Esprit de Kaslik, 2019–2020.

69 Von Schnurrer dates the 6th edition erroneously to 1789 which was corrected by de Sacy in his review of *Bibliotheca arabica* (S. de Sacy, *Notice de l'ouvrage intitulé : Bibliotheca Arabica : auctam nunc atque integram editit D. Christianus Fridericus de Schnurer, etc*, no publisher and year, p. 26).

70 Based on a remark by Assemani, von Schnurrer mentions for 1739 an Arabic edition of Thomas à Kempis's "The imitation of Christ" exercised by 'Abdallāh Zākhir "in monte Libano", i. e. in al-Shuwayr (von Schnurrer, Bibliotheca arabica, p. 292, no 290), but this is obviously a mistake as no trace of such a publication has come to light so far.

Tab. 3: Al-Shuwayr (1734–[1810]) (continued).

Year	Title / Content	Re-editions (until 1810)	Von Schnurrer
1740	Iḥtiqār abāṭīl al-ʿālam, vol. 4		293
1747	Murshid al-khāṭī	1794	295, 313
1753	Tafsīr sabʿat mazmūrāt		296
1756	Mukhtaṣar al-taʿlīm al-masīḥī	1807	297; ---
1756	Aʿmāl al-rusul wa-l-rasāʾil	1770, 1792	---, ---, ---
1760	Murshid al-kāhin		298
1764	al-Burhān al-ṣarīḥ		---
1767	al-Ukṭū[ʾ]īkhūs (The Octoechos)	1784	300, ---
1768	Īḍāḥ al-taʿlīm al-masīḥī		---
1769	Taʾammulāt jahannam al-murīʿa		301
1772	Qūt al-nafs		304
1775	al-Nubūʾāt (The Prophetologion)		305
1776	al-Injīl (The Gospels)		330
1779	al-Ūrūlūjiyūn/ al-Sawāʿī (The Horologion)	1787, 1805	---, 309, ---
1788	al-Majmaʿ al-lubnānī		310
1797	Qaṭf al-azhār		---
1802	Sharḥ al-taʿlīm		---
1804	Irshād ilá muʿallimī al-iʿtirāf		---
1810	al-Majmaʿ al-anṭākī		---

Tab. 4: Beirut (1751–?)[71].

Year	Title / Content	Re-editions	Von Schnurrer
1751	The Psalms	1752	354, ---
????	The Horologion		354
????	The Liturgikon		354

---

71 Gdoura, *Le début de l'imprimerie arabe*, p. 180–185.

Tab. 5: Al-Duwwār (1789–?)[72] [Garshūnī].

Year	Title / Content	Re-editions	Von Schnurrer
1785 (?)	??? (The Diakonikon)		---
1789	Khidmat al-quddās (Missal)		---
1789	al-Shaḥīma (Shḥīme) (The Maronite Breviary)		---
????	al-Rasā'il (The Epistolary)		---

In his brief introduction[73] von Schnurrer does not say much about how he gathered his information, but he obviously used a vast network of contacts, the exploitation of which was facilitated by his friendly manner and collegial attitude. Thus, the abovementioned Döderlein obtained from him a partial copy of a Psalter kept at the British Library,[74] while von Schnurrer used, for instance, a copy of the Quzḥayyā Psalter from the private library of a friend.[75] One of von Schnurrer's most important sources of information was the famous French Orientalist Silvestre de Sacy (1758–1738), with whom he had studied in Paris and to whom he dedicated the *Bibliotheca arabica*. De Sacy wrote a comprehensive review of von Schnurrer's bibliography[76] in which he praises the description of 22 works as especially detailed and useful.[77] Among them are also four publications from the presses of the East: The Book of Prophecies (al-Shuwayr, 1775);[78] The acts of the Maronite "Lebanese Synod" (al-Shuwayr, 1788)[79] and the Psalters printed in Quzḥayyā (1610)[80] and Aleppo (1706),[81] respectively.

4. Final Remarks

We still owe much to the European pioneers of collecting and studying Arabic prints from the Middle East, most notably Christian Friedrich von Schnurrer and

---

72 J. Nasrallah, *L'imprimerie au Liban*, Harissa, 1948, p. 65–66.
73 Von Schnurrer, *Bibliotheca arabica*, p. V–XII.
74 Döderlein, "Von arabischen Psaltern", p. 157.
75 Von Schnurrer, *Bibliotheca arabica*, p. 351.
76 See above footnote 69 (offprint from *Magasin Encyclopédique* 1814, tome 1, p. 183–211).
77 De Sacy, *Notice*, p. 6–7.
78 De Sacy, *Notice*, p. 6 (cf. von Schnurrer, *Bibliotheca arabica*, no. 305, p. 298–301).
79 De Sacy, *Notice*, p. 6 (cf. von Schnurrer, *Bibliotheca arabica*, no. 310, p. 309–320).
80 De Sacy, *Notice*, p. 6 (cf. von Schnurrer, *Bibliotheca arabica*, no. 319, p. 351–354).
81 De Sacy, *Notice*, p. 6 (cf. von Schnurrer, *Bibliotheca arabica*, no. 339, p. 371–374).

Ulrich Jasper Seetzen. That both are still valuable sources is due to the serious-ness of their approaches but is also a very telling proof of the scholarly neglect the subject has been and still is suffering from. Hopefully TYPARABIC will be a successful effort to improve our knowledge about the incunabula of the East, alt-hough it can only be a small step towards a comprehensive scientific catalogue of (early) Arabic prints. That such a bibliography has not been established might be due to the limited role book-printing played in the Arab world. Compared with global developments it remained and remains marginal.

Bibliography

Albu-Comănescu, Radu. "The Constantinian Order of the Cantacuzene family". In Guy Stair Sainty, *The Constantinian Order of Saint George: and the Angeli, Farnese and Bourbon Families Which Governed It*. Madrid: Agencia Estatal Boletín Oficial del Estado, 2018, p. 509–520.

Allatius, Leon. *Apes urbanae sive de viris illustribus qui ab Anno MDCXXX per totum MDCXXXII Romae adfuerunt, ac typis aliquid evulgarunt*. Rome: Ludouicus Grignanus, 1633.

An extract of several letters relating the great charity and usefulness of printing the New Testament and Psalter in the Arabic language; for the benefit of the poor Christians in Palestine, Syria, Mesopotamia, Arabia, Egypt and other Eastern countries: with a proposal for executing so good an undertaking. London: J. Downing, 1721.

Assemanus, Joseph Simonius. *Bibliotheca orientalis Clementino-Vaticana*, vol. 1. Rome: Typis Sacrae Congregationis de Proganda Fide, 1719.

Assemanus, Stepahnus Evodius. *Bibliothecae Mediceae Laurentianae et Palatinae Codicum MSS. Orientalium Catalogus*. Florence: Typographia Albiziniana, 1742.

Babinger, Franz. "Ein vergessener maronitischer Psalterdruck auf der Nürnberger Stadtbücherei". *Zeitschrift für die Alttestamentliche Wissenschaft*, 43, 1925, p. 275.

Bojer, Hermann. "Einiges über die arabische Druckschriftensammlung der Bayerischen Staatsbibliothek". In Herbert Franke (ed.), *Orientalisches aus Münchener Bibliotheken und Sammlungen*. Wiesbaden: Steiner, 1957, p. 77–87.

Boveland, Christoph. "Souvenir aus dem Libanongebirge. Ein syrisch-arabischer Psalter von 1610", blog of Herzog August Bibliothek Wolfenbüttel, posted 4 July 2023 (https://www.hab.de/souvenir-aus-dem-libanongebirge/).

Cotton, Henry. *A Typographical Gazetteer*. Oxford: University Press, 1831.

De Sacy, Silvestre. *Notice de l'ouvrage intitulé : Bibliotheca Arabica : auctam nunc atque integram editit D. Christianus Fridericus de Schnurer, etc.* n. p.; n. y. (offprint from *Magasin Encyclopédique* 1814, tome 1, p. 183–211).

Döderlein, Joh. Christoph. "Von arabischen Psaltern. Ein Beytrag zu einer Einleitung ins A. Test.". In *Repertorium für Biblische und Morgenländische Litteratur*, part 2. Leipzig: Weidmanns Erben und Reich, 1778, p. 151–179.

Eichhorn, Gottfried. *Einleitung ins Alte Testament*, vol. 1. Leipzig: Weidmanns Erben und Reich, 1780.

El Ghobry, Rana. *The Second Printing Press of Quzḥayyā Monastery. History of the Press and Descriptive Catalogue of its Imprints*. Unpublished MA thesis: Université Saint-Esprit de Kaslik, 2018.

Frantsouzoff, Serge A. "Les psautiers arabes imprimés dans les bibliothèques de Saint-Petersbourg". In Policarp Chiţulescu, Ioana Feodorov (eds.), *Culture manuscrite et imprimé dans et pour l'Europe du Sud-Est*. Brăila: Editura Istros a Muzeului Brăilei "Carol I", 2020, p. 197–214.

Funke, Fritz. *Buchkunde. Die historische Entwicklung des Buches von der Keilschrift bis zur Gegenwart*. Wiesbaden: VMA, 2006.

Gdoura, Wahid. *Le début de l'imprimerie arabe à Istanbul et en Syrie: evolution de l'environment culturel (1706–1787)*. Tunis: Université de Tunis, Institut Supérieur de Documentation, 1985.

[Götze, Johann Christian.] *Die Merckwürdigkeiten der Königlichen Bibliothek zu Dreßden, ausführlich beschrieben, und mit Anmerkungen erläutert*, Die erste Sammlung. Dresden: George Conrad Walther, 1744.

Haas, Daniel. "Von Halle in den Orient. Stephan Schultz auf Reisen im Osmanischen Reich in den Jahren 1752 bis 1756". In Anne Schröder-Kahnt, Claus Veltmann (eds.), *Durch die Welt im Auftrag des Herrn. Reisen von Pietisten im 18. Jahrhundert*. Halle (Saale): Verlag der Franckeschen Stiftungen, 2018, p. 67–79.

Hasenmüller, Monika. "Ulrich Jasper Seetzen als Sammler orientalischer Handschriften". In Detlef Haberland (ed.), *Der Orientreisende Ulrich Jasper Seetzen und die Wissenschaften*. Oldenburg: Isensee, 2019, p. 459–576.

Helladius, Alexander. *Status praesens Ecclesiae Graecae: in quo etiam causae exponuntur cur graeci moderni Novi Testamenti editiones in graeco-barbara lingua factas acceptare recusant*. n. p.: no publisher, 1714.

Iorga, Nicolae. "Radu Cantacuzino". *Analele Academiei Române* (Memoriile Secţiunii Istorice), Seria III, 13, 1932–1933, p. 149–158.

Kaufhold, Hubert. "Die Rechtsliteratur in der 'Bibliotheca Orientalis'". *Parole de l'Orient*, 47, 2021, p. 43–71.

Kruse, Fr. (ed.). *Ulrich Jasper Seetzen's Reisen durch Syrien, Palästina, die Transjordan-Länder, Arabia Petraea und Unter-Aegypten*, vol. 1. Berlin: Reimer, 1854.

Le Long, Iacob. *Bibliotheca sacra seu syllabus omnium ferme sacrae scripturae editionum ac versionum secundum seriem linguarum quibus vulgatae sunt notis historicis et criticis illustratus adiunctis praestantissimis Codd. Msc.*, 2 parts in one volume. Leipzig: Joh. Ludov. Gleditsch, 1709.

Le Long, Iacob. *Bibliotheca sacra in binos syllabos distincta quorum prior qui jam tertio auctior prodit, omnes sive textus sacri sive versionum ejusdem quâvis lingua expressarum editiones; nec non præstantiores MSS codices, cum notis historicis & criticis exhibet*, 2 vols. Paris: F. Montalant, 1723.

Masch, Andreas Gottlieb. *Bibliotheca Sacra post Jacobi Le Long et C. F. Boerneri iterates curas*, vol. 2. Halle (Saale): Johann Jakob Gebauer, 1781.

Michaelis, Johann David. *Einleitung in die göttlichen Schriften des Neuen Bundes*. Göttingen: Verlag der Witwe Vandenhoek, 1765 (2nd edition); Göttingen: Verlag der Vandenhoek-Ruprechtschen Buchhandlung, 1788 (4th edition).

Moukarzel, Joseph. "Le Psautier syriaque-garchouni édité à Qozhaya en 1610. Enjeux historiques et presentation du livre". *Mélanges de l'Université Saint-Joseph* 63, 2010–2011, p. 511–566.

Nasrallah, Joseph. *L'imprimerie au Liban*. Harissa: Imprimerie de Saint Paul, 1948.

Ritter, Carl. *Die Erdkunde von Asien*, vol. VIII/2: Die Sinai-Halbinsel, Palästina und Syrien, part 3: Syrien. Berlin: Reimer, 1854.

Scholtz, Henrici. *Specimen I. Bibliothecae Arabicae de typographis arabicis*. Hamburg: Ludov. Stromer, 1741.

Schultz, Stephan. *Der Leitungen des Höchsten nach seinem Rath auf den Reisen durch Europa, Asia und Africa*, part 5. Halle (Salle): Carl Hermann Hemmerde, 1775.

Schultz, Stephan (ed.). *Fernere Nachricht von der zum Heil der Juden errichteten Anstalt, nebst den Auszügen aus den Tagebüchern der reisenden Mitarbeiter*, part 7. Halle (Salle): no publisher, 1769.

Seetzen, U. J. "Nachricht von den in der Levante befindlichen Buchdruckereyen". *Intelligenzblatt der Jenaischen Allgemeinen Literatur-Zeitung*, Numero 76 (13 July 1805), coll. 641–654.

Seetzen, U. J. *Verzeichnis der für die orientalische Sammlung in Gotha zu Damask, Jerusalem u.s.w. angekauften orientalischen Manuscripte und gedruckten Werke, Kunst- und Naturprodukte u.s.w.* Leipzig: Breitkopf & Härtel, 1810.

Şfayr, Yūsif. *Maṭbaʻat al-Shuwayr, al-maṭbaʻa al-ʻarabīya al-ūlá (1733–1899). Fihris al-maṭbūʻāt al-mufaṣṣal*. Unpublished MA thesis: Université Saint-Esprit de Kaslik, 2019–2020.

Solger, Adamus Rudolphus. *Bibliotheca sive supellex librorum impressorum*, vol. 1. Nuremberg: Endter, 1760.

Verzeichnis derer Bücher und einer sehr starken Anzahl und Sammlung der neuesten theologischen, juristischen, medicinischen und philosophischen Disputationen, welche der sel. Hr. M. und Oberdiaconus Stephan Schultze hinterlassen, so den 26sten May 1777. und folgende Tage ... in dem Diaconathause bey der St. Ulrichskirche, gegen baare Bezahlung an den Meistbiethenden durch Auction verlassen werden soll. Halle (Saale): Hundt, 1777.

Volney, C.-F. *Voyage en Syrie et en Égypte pendant les anneés 1783, 1784, et 1785*, 2 vols. Paris: Volland & Desenne, 1787.

Von Schnurrer, Christian Friedrich. *Bibliotheca arabica*. Halle (Salle): I. C. Hendel, 1811.

Walbiner, Carsten. "Juan Eusebio Nieremberg: *Mīzān al-zamān wa-qisṭās abadiyyat al-insān* (*The scales of time and the measure of man's eternity*)". In Klaus Kreiser (ed.), *The Beginnings of Printing in the Near and Middle East: Jews, Christians, Muslims*. Wiesbaden: Harrassowitz, 2001, p. 26–27.

Walbiner, Carsten. "*Ktobō d-mazmūrē d-Dawūd malkō wa-nbīyō* ('Book of the Psalms of the King and Prophet David')". In Klaus Kreiser (ed.), *The Beginnings of Printing in the Near and Middle East: Jews, Christians, Muslims*. Wiesbaden: Harrassowitz, 2001, p. 22–23.

Walbiner, Carsten. "Ulrich Jasper Seetzen [in Aleppo (1803–1805)]". In Neil Cooke, Vanessa Daubney (eds.), *Every Traveller Needs a Compass. Travel and Collecting in Egypt and the Near East*. Oxford: Oxbow Books, 2015, p. 197–204.

Part 3. **Arabic Liturgical Texts in Printed Form**

.

Archim. Policarp Chițulescu

Analyse comparative du texte gréco-arabe du Hiératikon imprimé à Snagov en 1701

L'importance de la liturgie dans la vie de l'Eglise, l'Eucharistie étant le centre de cette vie, a déterminé bien d'historiens et de liturgistes de l'Eglise d'aborder ce sujet, dans une perspective plutôt théologique et spirituelle. Suivant une perspective comparative, nous souhaitons aborder les textes du Hiératikon édité en 1701, en grec et arabe, à Snagov, un monastère orthodoxe près de Bucarest.

Figurant aujourd'hui dans la liste des livres rares et précieux, ce Hiératikon peut très bien être considéré comme une œuvre d'art typographique, notamment du fait de sa présentation graphique. Il convient de noter l'influence qu'a eue Anthime l'Ibérien - un Géorgien érudit, fin connaisseur du grec et du roumain, établi vers la fin du XVIIe siècle en Valachie - sur le Hiératikon gréco-arabe de 1701 (fig. 1).

Anthime l'Ibérien a traduit et publié en roumain le Hiératikon et l'Euchologe en 1706 (fig. 2) à Ramnic (Valachie) à partir de l'édition grecque de l'Euchologe publié à Venise en 1691 (fig.3), qu'il mentionne dans cette première édition roumaine de 1706.[1] Les ressemblances entre les deux éditions du Hiératikon, c'est-à-dire sa version gréco-arabe de 1701 et sa version roumaine de 1706, attestent de l'influence majeure d'Anthime. Un autre aspect doit également mériter toute notre attention. Si les Roumains célébraient la liturgie en slavon – les rubriques et textes de prières étant traduites parfois du slavon – un premier changement s'est opéré à partir de la seconde moitié du XVIIe siècle. Et cela pour une raison très simple : l'influence catholique sur la pensée et la réforme liturgique de Pierre Moghila a provoqué une certaine méfiance à l'égard des éditions slaves des livres d'offices, notamment des liturgies, lorsqu'ils commençaient à être massivement traduits en roumain.

---

1 L'Euchologe édité à Râmnic en 1706 en roumain par Anthime l'Ibérien qui était alors évêque de Ramnic, incluait les sept Saints Sacrements donc aussi les liturgies et les autres offices nécessaires à l'existence de l'homme. Toujours par les soins d'Anthime l'Ibérien, en tant que métropolite de Valachie, l'Euchologe de 1706 connut une seconde édition en 1713, à Târgoviște ; cette fois-ci, le Hiératikon fut édité séparément de l'Euchologe. Le Hiératikon contenait les trois liturgies byzantines et l'Euchologe les autres six Saints Sacrements ainsi que d'autres hiérurgies.

Cet article fait partie du projet financé par le Conseil Européen de la Recherche (ERC) dans le cadre du projet de recherche et innovation Horizon 2020 de l'Union Européenne (Grant Agreement No. 883219-AdG-2019 – Project TYPARABIC).

∂ Open Access. © 2024, the author(s), published by De Gruyter. (cc) BY-NC-ND This work is licensed under the Creative Commons Attribution-NonCommercial-NoDerivatives 4.0 International License. https://doi.org/10.1515/9783111060392-010

Pour les versions en roumain, on tenait principalement compte des éditions grecques des livres de culte qui se trouvaient en abondance dans les Principautés roumaines. Il convient de mentionner qu'un important nombre de livres parus en grec à Venise, à Vienne ou à Leipzig étaient financés par les princes des Principautés roumaines.[2]

Dans ses études, l'érudit orientaliste Cyrille Charon a abordé également les livres liturgiques parus dans différents endroits du monde pour les chrétiens arabophones, dont aussi le Hiératikon gréco-arabe de Snagov.[3] Ses remarques au sujet de ce livre ont une importance particulière, Charon étant le premier spécialiste à l'avoir analysé de manière adéquate.[4]

Même si Cyrille Charon a dressé comme conclusion que le texte arabe de cette première édition du Hiératikon de 1701 proviendrait de la version de Mélèce Karma, restée à l'état de manuscrit et qui a circulé comme telle,[5] il ne réussit pas à identifier de manière correcte la source du texte grec qui avait considérablement influencé le texte arabe, tel que nous allons le montrer ci-après.

Cela était dû au fait qu'il ne savait pas que le typographe-éditeur du Hiératikon de 1701, Anthime l'Ibérien, n'était pas un simple ouvrier, mais un polyglotte versé dans la traduction des textes liturgiques. Ce fait est en mesure de répondre à bien des incertitudes de Charon à propos du texte grec et surtout à propos de la présence dans le texte arabe de certaines influences étrangères à la tradition liturgique arabe, donc inexistantes dans la version arabe de Mélèce Karma.

---

2 P. Chițulescu, « Livres imprimés à Venise aux XVIIe et aux XVIIIe siècles avec la contribution des Pays Roumains », dans *Culture manuscrite et imprimée dans et pour l'Europe du Sud-Est*, éd. archim. P. Chițulescu, I. Feodorov, Brăila, 2020, p. 13–41.

3 C. P. Charon, *Histoire des Patriarcats Melkites (Alexandrie, Antioche, Jérusalem) depuis le schisme monophysite du sixième siècle jusqu'à nos jours, t. III. Les institutions. Liturgie, Hiérarchie, Statistique, Organisation, Listes épiscopales*, Rome/Paris, fasc. I-II, 1909–1911, p. 55–72.

4 Nous analyserons ces remarques à la fin de cette étude.

5 Mélèce Karma était un hiérarque né en 1572 à Hama, en Syrie. Il entra dans les ordres au monastère de S. Sabbas, près de Jérusalem, devenant en 1612 métropolite d'Alep et en 1634 patriarche de l'Antioche sous le nom d'Euthyme II et mourant une année plus tard, en 1635. Il s'est occupé de la traduction des livres liturgiques orthodoxes du grec en arabe, langue parlée par la plupart des habitants de l'actuelle Syrie et du Liban. Au sujet de son activité de traduction des livres de culte du grec en arabe, voir l'étude avec la bibliographie actualisée à : Ch. Nassif, « La révision liturgique du métropolite melkite d'Alep Malâtyûs Karma et les réformes liturgiques dans les pays d'Europe de l'Est au XVIIe siècle », dans *Europe in Arabic Sources: "The Travels of Macarius", Patriarch of Antioch*, éd. Y. Petrova, I. Feodorov, Kiev, 2016, p. 117–134 et C. A. Pancenko, *Arab Orthodox Christians under the Ottomans : 1516–1831*, Jordanville, NY, 2016, p. 373–374. À la page 374, C. Pancenko fait une remarque très juste : Mélèce Karma s'est efforcé d'intégrer les Arabes orthodoxes dans la sphère culturelle byzantine.

L'importance du Hiératikon de 1701 allait devenir d'autant plus grande que ce livre, grâce à son tirage significatif, s'est répandu très vite parmi les prêtres arabophones.

Ainsi, s'est fixée dans les églises orthodoxes arabophones une variante de la liturgie, adaptée en Valachie, en particulier s'agissant des rubriques qui concernent l'ensemble des gestes que le prêtre doit accomplir durant la célébration de l'office divin.

Il convient de mentionner ici le rôle du patriarche Athanase Dabbas qui, non seulement a accepté mais a également encouragé ce ralliement aux offices de tradition grecque ainsi que l'uniformisation des indications typiconales, les susdites rubriques. Ce phénomène d'introduction de la langue vernaculaire dans les offices liturgiques d'après le modèle des livres byzantins était en plein essor aux Principautés roumaines, son artisan étant justement Anthime l'Ibérien. En ce sens, il faut considérer avec prudence les affirmations de Cyrille Charon au sujet de l'influence slavo-russe sur le texte du Hiératikon de 1701,[6] car les influences sont plutôt gréco-roumaines, puisque le texte gréco-arabe et celui roumain ont la même source grecque, avec certaines interventions du traducteur en roumain, Anthime l'Ibérien.

Cette première édition arabe et grecque du Hiératikon orthodoxe constitua un événement majeur, le livre étant utilisé par Rome aussi, en vue d'une réédition ultérieure destinée aux gréco-catholiques. Mais ce que l'on ignore c'est que la seconde édition du Hiératikon arabe fut imprimée toujours par les Roumains, cette fois-ci en Moldavie, à Jassy, en 1745 (fig. 4), ce que même les orientalistes liturgistes ont perdu de vue.[7] Dans la présente étude, nous allons prendre en considération cette édition aussi.

A la fin du XVIIe siècle et le début du XVIIIe, l'activité typographique en Valachie prit un essor spectaculaire grâce à la présence providentielle du génie que fut Anthime l'Ibérien[8] pour son époque. Cette personnalité qui traverse et unifie plusieurs parties du monde et dont la biographie ne cesse de révéler de nouveaux

---

6 Charon, *Histoire des Patriarcats Melkites*, p. 62, 63, 66, 71 etc. Affirmations reprises sans arguments par d'autres chercheurs aussi.

7 Un exemplaire de cet imprimé rare fut découvert par Ioana Feodorov entre les couvertures d'un manuscrit, à Balamand, au Liban. Voir I. Feodorov, « The Arabic Book of the Divine Liturgies Printed in 1745 in Jassy by Patriarch Sylvester of Antioch », *Scrinium*, 16, 2020, p. 158–176. Un autre exemplaire enregistré comme le manuscrit no. 4 se trouve en Syrie, en l'église paroissiale de la ville de Muḥradah. Voir https://www.vhmml.org/readingRoom (Hill Museum & Manuscript Library (HMML), Collegeville, Minnesota, EUA).

8 Voir la plus récente monographie de son activité typographique avec la bibliographie aférente : P. Chiṭulescu (éd.), *Antim Ivireanul - Opera tipografică*, Bucarest, 2016.

détails inédits, naquit vers la moitié du XVIIe siècle en Géorgie, cette terre bénie entourée de plusieurs empires, où le Caucase rencontre la Mer Noire. Il paraît que le jeune André (selon son nom de baptême) avait été fait esclave par des envahisseurs et racheté avec de l'argent provenu de la trésorerie du Saint Sépulcre par l'érudit patriarche Dosithée de Jérusalem.

C'est cet hiérarque qui allait officier la prise d'habit monastique de l'ancien esclave géorgien en l'église du Saint Sépulcre, lui donnant le nom d'Anthime. Ayant décelé ses capacités artistiques et sa polyglossie, le patriarche Dosithée envoya Anthime en Moldavie, au monastère de Cetățuia, auprès de l'évêque érudit Mitrophane, pour qu'il apprenne le métier de typographe. C'est par l'évêque Mitrophane que le patriarche Dosithée, initiateur d'une ample action de sauvegarde de l'Orthodoxie, a mis en fonction la première typographie d'écriture grecque des Principautés roumaines. De Moldavie, Anthime fut appelé à Bucarest, probablement autour de l'an 1690, par le prince Constantin Brancoveanu, le grand bienfaiteur de l'Orient orthodoxe, pour éditer des livres aux frais de l'Etat.

Là, Anthime devint higoumène du monastère de Snagov, près de Bucarest, où, entre 1695–1701, il publia 14 titres de livres liturgiques et polémiques en roumain, slavon, arabe et grec, destinés à raffermir l'Orthodoxie dans le contexte de la turcocratie.

Toujours à Snagov, Anthime fonda sa propre typographie, en 1701.[9] De là, il allait partir à Bucarest où il continua à imprimer des livres à la typographie de la cour voïvodale. En 1705, il fut élu évêque de Ramnic, où il fonda une nouvelle typographie, éditant dans les années 1705– 1707, 3 ouvrages en roumain, 3 en grec et 3 bilingues : en roumain et slavon. Élu en 1708 métropolite de la Valachie, Anthime s'installa à Targoviste, siège de la métropole et ancienne capitale du pays. Il y ouvrit une typographie où allaient paraître encore 21 titres en roumain, grec et slavon. Pour la première fois, les principaux livres de culte en roumain sont parus à l'initiative d'Anthime l'Ibérien dans une traduction meilleure que les versions antérieures, ce qui contribua de manière décisive au processus d'introduction du roumain dans le culte de l'Eglise qui, dans les Principautés roumaines, ne se déroulait que dans les langues considérées comme "sacrées" : le slavon et le grec.

Il est à mentionner que la langue roumaine n'avait été utilisée jusqu'alors que dans les recueils d'homélies et les rubriques des livres de culte, c'est-à-dire dans les textes non-liturgiques.

---

9 D. Bădără, « Vademecum de istoria tiparului și cărții din Țara Românească și Moldova, 1508–1830 », *Analele Brăilei*, 19, 2019, p. 256.

Les livres imprimés par Anthime vont contribuer au développement du langage liturgique et de la langue roumaine littéraire, cultivant la conscience de l'unité nationale, de l'unité de langue et de foi de Roumains vivant dans des provinces qui faisaient parties d'empires différents (la Valachie, la Moldavie et la Transylvanie).

Vers l'année 1715, Anthime ouvrit une typographie au monastère édifié par lui à Bucarest et consacré à « Tous les Saints », monastère qui allait porter son nom, Anthime. C'est là qu'il fonda une des premières bibliothèques publiques de la capitale. À l'aide du prince Constantin Brancoveanu, Anthime envoya des installations typographiques et des maîtres imprimeurs en Géorgie, à Alep, en Transylvanie, pour aider les chrétiens orthodoxes persécutés et dépourvus des moyens nécessaires à éditer des livres d'offices.

Les ouvrages qui se rattachent au nom d'Anthime sont au nombre de 67, en plusieurs langues, la liste étant provisoire, puisqu'on découvre encore de nouveaux ouvrages édités par lui.

Anthime l'Ibérien est décrit comme un excellent théologien, prédicateur, traducteur polyglotte, typographe, fondateur de typographies, éditeur, auteur de préfaces et donateur de livres, doté par ailleurs d'un remarquable sens artistique. Devenu incommode pour le pouvoir séculier de l'Etat, il fut tué en 1716.

En 1992, l'Église orthodoxe roumaine le canonisa et établit comme date de sa commémoration le 27 septembre.

Si l'on revient au début de l'activité typographique déroulée par Anthime au monastère de Snagov (monastère qu'il avait réorganisé),[10] il est important de mentionner que les ouvrages réalisés dans ce monastère ont conduit le prince Constantin Brancoveanu à considérer Anthime comme un maître de l'art typographique.

De même, ces ouvrages ont constitué une source d'espérance pour tous les hiérarques grecs apologètes de l'Orthodoxie, qui allaient venir en Valachie pour y faire imprimer des livres interdits dans l'espace contrôlé par la censure papale.

Imprimer en Valachie un livre dans une langue difficile comme l'arabe, avec un autre alphabet que l'alphabet grec ou cyrillique déjà utilisés dans la typographie de Snagov depuis 1695 et 1696) fut l'occasion pour Saint Anthime l'Ibérien de témoigner son profond attachement aux chrétiens arabes. De même, l'impression d'un tel livre constitua un grand défi et une certaine preuve de courage.

Sa sensibilité à l'égard des chrétiens arabes - dont il connaissait les difficultés à Jérusalem - motivait une telle démarche. Cette dernière n'aurait pu aboutir sans son talent d'artiste typographe capable de surmonter tous les obstacles techniques et

---

10 Policarp Chițulescu, « Etat de l'art des livres et objets sacrés ayant appartenu à Saint Anthime d'Ivir », *Museikon*, 2, 2018, p. 105–116.

linguistiques. Cette impulsion à la faveur d'une impression des livres pour les chrétiens arabophones, fut influencée certes, par la présence du patriarche d'Antioche Athanase Dabbas, en 1700, à la cour du prince Constantin Brancoveanu, et par la décision du prince qui releva le défi de financer ce projet complexe qui frôlait l'impossible.

Nous soulignons dès le début qu'Anthime a réussi d'imprimer deux livres bilingues, en grec et en arabe: un Hiératikon, en 1701, à Snagov, et un Horologion, en 1702, à Bucarest. Les deux livres ont été préfacés par le patriarche d'Antioche Athanase Dabbas.

Dans la préface en grec et en arabe du Hiératikon imprimé en 1701, adressée au prince de Valachie Constantin Brancoveanu, le patriarche Athanase souligne qu'il est « accouru des confins de la terre, de la cité de Dieu Antioche, en toute hâte, vers la bienheureuse cité de Bucarest, car il avait entendu de si loin parler des brillantes vertus du prince Constantin Brancoveanu qui attiraient les gens comme l'aimant attire le fer ».

Le hiérarque antiochien, en grande difficulté avec son clergé à cause du manque de livres liturgiques en langue arabe et du prix trop élevé des manuscrits, eut le courage de demander de l'aide au prince Brancoveanu, ce dernier n'hésitant pas à faire preuve de générosité. La réalisation d'une telle oeuvre de traduction se fondait ainsi, selon les dires du Patriarche antiochien : « sur la grande bienveillance et la disposition du prince d'édifier des églises, des monastères et des écoles en Valachie et surtout sur sa disponibilité d'accorder des aides généreuses aux autres sièges apostoliques et à tous les chrétiens trouvés en difficulté. »

Toutefois, l'argent seul ne pouvait pas résoudre ce problème, il y avait besoin de typographes avisés et de bons connaisseurs de l'arabe, afin de pouvoir projeter et mouler comme il se doit les caractères qui allaient être mis en page et sous presse. Les caractères arabes confectionnés à la typographie d'Anthime l'Ibérien de Snagov sont si réussis, si élégants et si clairs qu'ils rivalisent avec n'importe quelle démarche similaire des grandes typographies occidentales. Le patriarche Athanase affirme lui-même dans la seconde préface bilingue en grec et en arabe adressée aux prêtres orthodoxes arabes, qu'Anthime savait très bien faire les caractères arabes et tout ce qui était nécessaire pour imprimer un livre.[11] Anthime le typographe s'excusait lui-même dans la langue des destinataires du livre, l'arabe, en disant qu'il avait dû travailler dans une langue qu'il ne connaissait pas auparavant.[12] Et pourtant, le projet a été couronné de succès.

---

11 I. Bianu, Hodoș, *Bibliografia românească veche*, vol. I (1508–1716), Bucarest, 1903, p. 432.
12 I. Feodorov, *Tipar pentru creștinii arabi. Antim Ivireanul, Atanasie Dabbas și Silvestru al Antiohiei*, Brăila, 2016, p. 275.

Le processus d'édition a été surveillé avec grande attention par le maître typographe Anthime et corrigé avec soin par le patriarche Athanase lui-même, comme il l'affirme dans la même préface adressée à ses prêtres.[13] Puisque la présence du patriarche antiochien Athanase à Bucarest, en 1700, fut attestée deux fois,[14] elle peut être corrélée avec la préparation du Hiératikon pour l'impression, qui allait être mise au point au premier mois de 1701.

Le titre du livre est le suivant :

> « Le livre des trois Divines Liturgies, avec d'autres [écrits] nécessaires aux offices orthodoxes,[15] nouvellement imprimé maintenant[16] en grec et en arabe, à la demande et par les soins de Sa Béatitude Kiriou Kir Athanase le patriarche d'Antioche, aux frais du pieux et glorieux prince régnant sur tout le pays de l'Oungrovalachie, Ioan Constantin Basarab Voïvode, au temps de Sa Béatitude le Métropolite du susdit pays le Seigneur Théodose, au monastère de Notre Dame la Mère de Dieu, nommé Snagov, en l'année chrétienne mille sept cents et un, par la main du hiéromoine Anthime,[17] d'origine géorgienne. »

Le titre arabe du Hiératikon de 1701 :

كتاب القداسات الثلاثه الالهيه * مع بعض احتياجات اخر ضروريه للصلوات الارتوذكسيه * قد طبع الان حديثا
في اللغة اليونانيه والعربيه * بالتماس ومشارفة الاب الطوباني كيريو كير اثناسيوس البطريرك الانطاكي سابقا *
بمصرف السيد الامجد الرفيع الشان * مقلد حكم جميع بلاد ونكروفلاخيا * كير كير يوانو قسطنطين بسارابا
ويوضا المكرم في تقليد رياسة كهنوت الاب المطران الكلّى الغبطه كير ثاوضوسيوس للبلاد المذكوره اعلا في دير
سيدتنا والدة الاله المكنا بسيناغوفو * في سنة الف وسبعمايه واوحده[18] مسيحيه بيد الكاهن في المتوحدين انتيموس
الكرجي الاصل[19]

Le texte du livre est imprimé en rouge et noir, placé sur deux colonnes, le texte en arabe étant prépondérant, certaines rubriques du Typikon et parties de l'office étant en grec ; chaque page présente la réclame à gauche en bas. Les titres généraux sont donnés en arabe, tandis que la colonne titre est en grec et ce, jusqu'à la fin du texte. Le livre n'a pas de table des matières.

---

13 Bianu, Hodoş, *Bibliografia românească veche*, vol. I, p. 432.

14 I. Feodorov, *Arabic Printing for the Christians in Ottoman Lands. The East-European Connection*, Berlin/Boston, 2023, p. 139.

15 Dans le texte arabe : *prières*.

16 Au sens de : *pour la première fois*.

17 Dans le texte arabe : *prêtre parmi les moines*.

18 *Sic*. Corr., واوحده.

19 La plus récente description du livre dans une forme corrigée et complétée a été réalisée par I. Feodorov, *Arabic Printing for the Christians in Ottoman Lands*, p. 256–260, et par Archim. P. Chiţulescu (éd.), *Antim Ivireanul, Opera tipografică*, p. 88–96.

Le livre présente un inventaire significatif de décorations xylographiques : culs-de-lampe, frontispices et xylogravures en pleine page, mais nous ne les décrivons pas puisque ce n'est pas le but de la présente recherche.

Étant donné que tous les chercheurs jusqu'à présent ont reproduit de manière erronée la pagination du livre, nous la précisons à cette occasion : 14 feuilles non-numérotées, 96 pages numérotées plus 253 pages numérotées, donc un total de 14 feuilles plus 349 pages organisées en deux parties.

La première partie (14 feuilles non-numérotées + p. 1–96) comprend : Vêpres, Matines, et Prothèse, services divins précédant la Sainte Liturgie : *Kitāb ṣalāt al-aghribnīyāt wa-tartīb afāshīn al-saḥrīyāt wa-khidhmat asrār al-quddās li-iḥtiyāj al-kāhin wa-l-shammās ta'līf Yūḥannā Fam al-Dhahab wa-l-qiddīs al-kabīr Bāsīliyūs wa-l-Brūyijiyāsmānā al-mansūb ilā al-qiddīs Ghrīghūriyūs.*

La seconde partie, avec sa propre numérotation (p. 1–253), comprend les trois liturgies byzantines en usage dans l'Église orthodoxe c'est à dire celles de Saint Jean Chrysostome, Saint Basile le Grand et celle des Dons Présanctifiés, dite de Saint Grégoire le Dialogue, la prière de préparation à la communion avec la Sainte Eucharistie et quelques autres textes.

Le texte grec a été placé sur des colonnes parallèles au texte arabe, de manière qu'ils correspondent. Les lettres grecques étant bien plus petites qu'en arabe, l'inconvénient fut facilement solutionné, le texte grec étant disséminé sur la page pour éviter un décalage des textes.

Le texte de la Prothèse (gr. *Próthesis* ; ar. *tartīb al-dhabīḥa al-muqaddasa*) est imprimé exclusivement en arabe, et comme aucun prêtre ne peut célébrer la Divine Liturgie sans célébrer la Prothèse, nous concluons que le Hiératikon bilingue de 1701 n'était destiné qu'aux prêtres arabophones. À l'appui de cette conclusion vient aussi le fait que la partie qui concerne la préparation à la Communion (gr. *Metalēpsis* ; ar. *ṭaqs ṣalāt al-Maṭālibsīs*) est elle aussi seulement en arabe (p. 206–239). On sait que tant le diacre que l'évêque et le prêtre, comme tout chrétien d'ailleurs, ont le devoir de lire avant de communier ces prières de préparation, afin de devenir conscients de la venue réelle du Christ, réellement présent par Son corps et Son sang, dans l'Eucharistie. La présence du Polychronium pour le patriarche d'Antioche, qui se prononçait dans le cadre de la Divine Liturgie, semble également confirmer notre thèse. D'ailleurs, le patriarche Athanase Dabbas dit dans sa préface adressée au prince Constantin Brancoveanu qu'il était de coutume pour les prêtres d'Orient de prononcer les ecphonèses[20] en grec lors des offices, surtout lors de la Divine Liturgie, tandis que les autres prières étaient évidemment récitées en arabe. De même, on peut observer que dans le texte arabe apparaissent parfois

---

20 Répliques à haute voix qui constituent la fin d'une une prière récitée à voix basse.

des mots grecs en caractères grecs, outre les termes arabes calqués d'après le grec, mais écrits en alphabet arabe.[21] Le patriarche Athanase s'est montré profondément reconnaissant au prince Constantin Brancoveanu et à Anthime l'Ibérien non seulement d'avoir imprimé le Hiératikon en arabe, mais aussi d'avoir assumé la difficile opération de mettre le texte grec et le texte arabe en colonnes parallèles, considérant justement l'habitude des prêtres arabes de célébrer de manière bilingue. Cette oeuvre facilitait la célébration des offices aux *prêtres helléno-arabes*,[22] le Patriarche se référant certes aux Arabes qui étaient aussi hellénophones.

Le fait qu'un livre liturgique destiné presqu'exclusivement aux célébrants arabophones de l'autel fut imprimé avec un texte bilingue, grec et arabe, signifie que bien d'entre eux connaissaient aussi le grec, ce qui témoigne d'une bonne formation intellectuelle de ces prêtres. Cela est confirmé aussi par l'habitude, qui s'est conservée jusqu'à nos jours dans le monde arabe chrétien, de réciter certains textes à haute voix en grec aussi. Le texte bilingue aidait certes à une meilleure compréhension du texte liturgique proprement-dit.

Les caractères grecs du Hiératikon gréco-arabe de 1701 sont plus beaux, disonsnous, d'une qualité supérieure, rehaussés par un découpage plus précis, plus clair, avec moins de ligatures que celui utilisé à Snagov dans les imprimés grecs antérieurs, notamment l'Anthologion de 1697 (fig. 5), œuvre de grandes dimensions qui a 985 pages, imprimées en caractères minuscules. Mais nous avons remarqué les mêmes imperfections et les mêmes erreurs que dans l'édition de l'Anthologion de 1697.[23] Cela nous révèle qu'Anthime avait déjà le texte de la liturgie en grec mis en page et utilisé en 1697 à l'Anthologion et qu'il le reprit en 1701 en perfectionnant les caractères et en développant les rubriques du Typikon selon l'édition vénitienne de l'Euchologe de 1691.

D'où savons-nous quelle édition grecque de la liturgie a utilisé Saint Anthime l'Ibérien pour ses imprimés et ses traductions ?

C'est lui-même qui affirme avoir utilisé l'édition grecque de l'Euchologe imprimé à Venise en 1691, dans le colophon de l'édition roumaine traduite et imprimée par lui à Ramnic, en 1706, sous le même titre d'*Euchologe*. Par comparaison, nous avons constaté que le texte vénitien de 1691 se retrouve tant dans l'Anthologion de Snagov

---

21 Au sujet du vocabulaire liturgique orthodoxe calqué en arabe d'après le grec, voir Y. Petrova, « The Developement of the Christian Vocabulary in Arabic », *Romano-Arabica*, 20, 2020, p. 259–269, notamment p. 264–266.

22 Bianu et Hodoş, *Bibliografia Românească Veche*, vol. I, p. 429.

23 Nous faisons référence au texte de liturgie inclus dans l'Anthologion de Snagov, 1697, dans la partie finale du livre, aux p. 12–34.

1697, que dans le Hiératikon gréco-arabe de 1701, et en version roumaine, dans l'Euchologe de Ramnic imprimé en 1706.

Le Hiératikon gréco-arabe était déjà imprimé en janvier 1701, au monastère de Snagov, près de Bucarest. Donc, tout au long de l'année 1700, on a travaillé à l'exécution des matrices, au moulage des caractères arabes et à la mise en page du texte gréco-arabe. On doit compter aussi les quelques mois nécessaires à l'impression du texte sur des feuilles de papier, ultérieurement reliées en cahiers à couvertures de cuir. Le texte grec fut corrigé par Ignace le Phytien de Chaldée, tel que nous renseigne le colophon.

La typographie de Snagov travaillait en parallèle à plusieurs livres, puisque dans l'intervalle 1700–1701 a paru un très beau Psautier en grec, de grand format, et dans cette même période on y préparait pour la presse l'*Eortologion* de Sebastos de Trébizonde (paru en juin 1701) et le *Proskinitaire du Saint Mont Athos*, de Jean Comnène (paru après le Hiératikon gréco-arabe). C'est toujours en 1700 que fut imprimé en roumain un petit recueil de sentences morales intitulé *Floarea darurilor* (« La Fleur des dons »), traduit du grec. Ces livres travaillés et imprimés au même moment où l'on travaillait sur le Hiératikon gréco-arabe nous montrent que la typographie de Snagov disposait de plusieurs équipes de maîtres et de typographes et que plusieurs presses typographiques imprimaient simultanément des livres en plusieurs langues.

Pour la présente étude, nous avons analysé neuf exemplaires du Hiératikon gréco-arabe de 1701, dont : cinq trouvés à Bucarest (quatre à la Bibliothèque de l'Académie Roumaine – BAR et un à la Bibliothèque Nationale de Roumanie-BNaR), et les quatre autres, comme suit : un à Saint-Pétersbourg[24] (l'Institut de Manuscrits Orientaux), un au Vatican (Biblioteca Apostolica Vaticana), un à Kaslik (Université Saint-Esprit), et le neuvième au monastère de Vatopedi au Mont Athos. Ainsi, nous avons pu observer qu'il y a des différences entre les exemplaires et constater qu'il y a des exemplaires de type A/initiaux (fig. 6) et de type B/corrigés (fig. 7). Rappelons que le Hiératikon gréco-arabe comporte deux parties :

I. Les p. 1–95[25] contiennent l'office de la Vigile qui commence par l'office des Vêpres, fait signalé en grec dans le colonne-titre *Akolouthia tou Esperinou* tandis que le titre arabe est plus généreux et plus explicite en ce qui concerne le contenu du livre : *Kitāb ṣalāt al-aghribnīyāt wa-tartīb afāshīn al-saḥrīyāt wa-khidhmat asrār al-quddās li-iḥtiyāj al-kāhin wa-l-shammās ta'līf Yūḥannā Fam al-Dhahab wa-l-qiddīs al-kabīr Bāsīliyūs wa-l-Brūyijiyāsmānā al-mansūb ilā al-qiddīs Ghrīghūriyūs.*

---

24 S. A. Frantsuzov, « Pervaia arabografichnaia kniga, napechatannaia v mire islama, v sobranii Instituta vostochnykh rukopiseĭ RAN », *Vestnik PSTGU. Seriia III: Filologiia*, 61, 2019, p. 104–122.
25 A la page 96 il y a une gravure avec l'icône de S. Jean Chrysostome.

II. Les p. 1–253 contiennent les trois Liturgies et d'autres prières. Cette partie commence par la Divine Liturgie de St. Jean Chrysostome qui est signalée en grec dans le colonne-titre *he Theia Leitourgeia tou Chrysostomou*, tandis que le titre arabe est plus somptueux, avec de grandes lettres : *Khidmat al-quddās al-ilāhī li-abī-nā al-jalīl fī al-qiddīsīn Yūḥannā Fam al-Dhahab.*

Les exemplaires de type A (BAR, BnaR, Vatican, Saint-Pétersbourg, Kaslik, Vatopedi.) contiennent, dans la IIe partie, des erreurs de pagination et d'impression :

a. P. 89 (noté par erreur 99) : au début de la Liturgie de Saint Basile le Grand, l'incipit arabe *Mubāraka* (fr. *bénie*) est partiellement couvert et entouré d'un cadre ornemental. L'ornement est identique à celui de la majuscule initiale (lettrine) en grec et il est composé de modules typographiques disposés en forme de carré.

b. La page 94 est notée comme 84.

c. La page 212 est notée comme 221 (σβι΄) au lieu de 212 (σιβ΄).

d. La page 229 est notée comme 239.

Les exemplaires de type B (BAR) ont dans la IIe partie des erreurs de pagination dans la numérotation grecque, mais en échange les erreurs d'impression ont été remédiées :

a. A la page 89, au début de la Liturgie de Saint Basile le Grand, on observe que pour rendre visible le mot initial (l'incipit) en arabe, l'ornement a été réduit, simplifié. Donc l'erreur typographique a été corrigée, mais en ajoutant une nouvelle erreur de pagination. Le nouvel ornement qui entoure l'incipit arabe est disposé toujours en forme de carré et est constitué d'une rangée de fleurs séparées par des petites feuilles.

b. P. 103 les initiales rouges ont été replacées pour rendre le texte grec lisible.

c. La page 94 figure comme 84.

d. La page 212 figure comme 221 (σβι΄) au lieu de 212 (σιβ΄).

e. La page 229 porte le numéro 239.

Nous supposons qu'un nombre important d'exemplaires de la version A avaient déjà été imprimés et qu'ils étaient déjà distribués, puisque sur 9 exemplaires, seulement deux contiennent la correction graphique, tandis que les erreurs de pagination n'ont pas été remarquées. Les deux exemplaires « corrigés » sont conservés à Bucarest, à la Bibliothèque de l'Académie.

Le papier utilisé pour le Hiératikon de 1701 est de provenance vénitienne et porte en filigrane trois croissants de lune décroissants, symbole fréquemment rencontré au sein des livres roumains du XVIIe siècle et du début du XVIIIe.

Le chroniqueur roumain Radu Popescu (cca. 1665-1729), bon connaisseur des milieux intellectuels et qui avait accès aux informations du monde orthodoxe, notait que : « Le premier livre aux caractères arabes suscita de l'étonnement et de la joie au pays d'Antioche. »[26] Pourquoi cette joie ? Parce que c'était le premier livre arabe orthodoxe du monde qui venait d'être imprimé, le premier Hiératikon arabe orthodoxe, qui pouvait désormais être facilement accessible au clergé orthodoxe, car jusqu'alors, la plupart des livres orthodoxes étant des manuscrits, ils étaient extrêmement rares, coûteux et difficiles à se procurer, comme se plaignait le patriarche Athanase Dabbas lui-même. Cette apparition éditoriale spectaculaire, considérée presque comme un miracle, suivie par l'Horologion gréco-arabe imprimé à Bucarest en 1702, constituait en même temps le début d'un intense effort des hiérarques antiochiens de sauvegarder leur foi face au prosélytisme papal latin.

Dans notre approche préliminaire des deux textes parallèles en grec et en arabe du Hiératikon gréco-arabe de 1701, nous avons commencé par étudier notamment les rubriques du Typikon, c'est-à-dire les indications pour le clergé visant le déroulement de l'office divin. Mais dans cette étude comparative nous ne pouvons pas faire abstraction des éditions de la liturgie ayant un lien avec Anthime l'Ibérien (l'Euchologe grec, Venise, 1691, utilisé pour le texte abrégé des liturgies qu'il avait incluses dans l'Anthologion grec imprimé à Snagov en 1697 et dans la version roumaine de l'Euchologe paru à Ramnic en 1706), comme nous ne pouvons non plus ignorer le Hiératikon arabe édité à Jassy en 1745[27] par le patriarche Sylvestre d'Antioche.[28]

De même, nous avons pris en considération le Hiératikon manuscrit gréco-arabe 1049[29] conservé au monastère de Vatopedi au Mont Athos.[30] Ce manuscrit présente une importance spéciale car il contient le Hiératikon dans la version arabe due au renommé traducteur de textes liturgiques Mélèce Karma. En plus, il porte la signature du patriarche de l'Antioche Macaire III qui l'avait utilisé à son tour.[31]

---

26 Radu Popescu, *Istoriile domnilor Țării Românești*, éd. Constantin Grecescu, Bucarest, 1959, p. 273–274.

27 Voir note 5.

28 Nous adressons nos remerciements à Mme dr. Yulia Petrova et à M. Nicholas Bishara pour l'aide accordée dans l'analyse du texte arabe trouvé dans les ouvrages mentionnés dans la présente étude.

29 Le manuscrit a été décrit par Nassif, « Le Liturgicon arabe de Vatopédi, (Mont Athos, Vatopédi 1049) », *Chronos*, 42, 2021, p. 57–82. Nous avons étudié nous mêmes ce manuscrit l'été de 2022 et nous remercions Mme dr. Yulia Petrova et dr. Charbel Nassif pour l'aide accordée dans cette étude.

30 Nous continuerons de citer ce manuscrit : Vatopédi 1049.

31 Voir note 5.

En ce qui suit, nous allons présenter une sélection de situations : rapproche-ments et différences entre le texte grec et le texte arabe de 1701,[32] rapprochements entre le texte gréco-arabe de 1701, la traduction de Mélèce Karma (Vatopedi 1049), le prototype vénitien de 1691 et la version roumaine.

Ainsi, dans les Hiératikons orthodoxes, à la prière de la Litie, d'habitude on fait référence au saint patron du monastère/du paroisse, mais dans dans le 1701 (p. 27) on a :

a. en grec, la référence au saint patron du monastère (*Hagiou tes mones*) et

b. en arabe, la référence au saint du jour (*wa-l-qiddīs (fulān) allādhī nukmilu tidkāra-hu al-ān*)

Dans un autre cas « le saint patron et le saint du jour » – éd. 1706 (p. 188), est nommé en 1701, en grec, le « saint du monastère », *Hagiou tes mones* tandis qu'en arabe il est nommé aussi le « saint de l'église ou du saint lieu »: *Khatm al-ṣalawāt fī al-a'yād al-sayyidīya*.

Parce que le texte arabe préfère se référer à une communauté paroissiale, laïque, l'exemple suivant en confirme encore une fois l'idée. Ainsi, on a dans l'ec-ténie de l'office de la Litie:

a. en grec: « Pour ce monastère » (*ten hagian monen tauten*) et

b. en arabe: « Pour cette sainte ville » *(hādhihi al-madīna al-muqaddasa).*

1. À l'indication concernant les bénéfices du pain béni dans l'office de la Litie, le texte arabe, à la différence du texte grec, ajoute que « pour ceux qui prennent avec foi ce pain », il « apaise la fièvre et (délivre) de tous les maux » (p. 38) : *Wa-ammā al-khubz al-mubārak fa-lahu manāfi' jamma yurīḥu min al-ḥummā wa-min sā'ir al-aswā' li-l-ladhīn yatanāwalūna min-hu bi-amāna.* Cette explication supplémentaire se retrouve aussi dans le manuscrit Vatopedi 1049 (f. 16v).

1. Analyse des Liturgies

1. La Grande Ecténie dans la liturgie de S. Jean Chrysostome inclut en grec et en arabe la prière « pour l'empereur et pour son triomphe contre ses ennemis » (p. 4): gr. *hyper ton eusebestaton, kai theophylakton Basileon hemon, pantos tou Palatiou, kai tou stratopedou auton*; ar. *min ajl mulūki-nā al-ḥasanīn al-'ibāda al-maḥfūẓīn min Allāh wa-jamī' balāṭi-him wa-ajnādi-him* tandis que l'édition grecque Venise de1691 (p. 34) ne l'a pas, à la différence seulement

---

32 Par la suite, les éditions des livres seront nommées par l'année de leur parution. Ainsi : 1691-Euchologe, Venise, 1691; 1697-Anthologion, Snagov, 1697; 1701-Hiératikon, Snagov, 1701; 1706-Euchologe, Râmnic, 1706; 1745- Hiératikon, Jassy, 1745.

de celle de Vatopedi 1049 (f. 39ᵛ) et de la version roumaine d'Anthime de 1706 (p. 54). On constate donc un rapprochement entre ces textes.

2. Les indications montrant comment le prêtre lit l'Evangile, comment le diacre tient son orarion avec les doigts sont identiques en 1701 (p. 17), 1691 (p. 35), 1706 (p. 55).

3. Les rubriques du Typikon pour la Petite Entrée (la sortie avec l'Evangile) est identique en 1701 (p. 11), 1691 (p. 36), tandis qu'en 1706 (p. 57) il prévoit plusieurs indications, comme la sortie du prêtre précédé par deux chandeliers portés par le sacristain etc. Le terme « d'entrée » a été calqué en arabe *īṣūdun* d'après le grec *eisodios* 1701 (p. 11).

4. A la récitation de l'ecphonèse « Car tu es Saint, ô notre Dieu, et nous Te rendons gloire, Père, Fils et saint Esprit », les rubriques du Typikon prévoient que le prêtre bénisse le diacre sur la tête. Il est le même en 1691 (p. 37), 1701 (p. 14), 1706 (p. 58).
La prière du diacre en grec « Kyrie soson tous eusebeis (Seigneur, sauve les fidèles) » est identique en 1701 (p. 15), 1691 (p. 37), mais a été omise dans l'édition roumaine de 1706 (p. 58). En arabe apparaît *ya Rabb khalliṣ al-malik* (« Seigneur, sauve l'empereur ») comme dans Vatopedi 1049 aussi (f. 43v).

5. Dans le Crédo, l'édition 1701 dans les deux langues, Vatopedi 1049 et toutes les autres éditions dont il fut ici question - 1691, 1706 et 1745 – disent: « que tous les gens qui sont dans l'église récitent le Crédo ». Dans Vatopedi 1049 (f. 53ᵛ) et les éditions 1701 et 1745 en arabe, les gens prononcent le Crédo au pluriel: *Nu'minu bi-Ilāh wāḥid:* « Nous croyons en un seul Dieu », et non au singulier: « Je crois en un seul Dieu comme en grec Pisteuo eis hena theon » ... et comme en roumain: *Cred într-Unul Dumnezeu.*

6. L'ecphonèse: *L'hymne triomphale*...et l'Anaphore sont identiques en 1701 (p. 48–50) et 1691 (p. 46).
Dans l'ecphonèse: « Ce qui est à Toi, le tenant de Toi, nous Te **l'offrons** en tout et pour tout », le terme grec *prosphérontes* (1701 - p. 51) est comme à Snagov (1697), tandis qu'en 1691 c'est *prospheronton* (p. 47). Il y a donc un rapprochement entre le texte grec de 1701 et celui imprimé par Anthime auparavant, en 1697.

7. Concernant le tropaire de la IIIᵉ Heure qui se récite avant l'épiclèse : il n'y en a que le début en 1691, tandis qu'en 1701 il figure dans les deux langues, et en 1706 il est reproduit intégralement. Dans l'édition moderne orthodoxe du Hiératikon arabe (Beyrouth, 2000), ce tropaire ne figure plus.

8. La prière d'après l'épiclèse : « Nous te supplions encore : souviens Toi, Seigneur, de notre empereur, de toute sa cour et ses soldats » est identique en 1691 (p. 48); 1701 (p. 57–58); 1706 (p. 84).

9. Après la prière de l'épiclèse suit le texte : « *pour Saint Jean Baptiste...* » : en 1701, gr./ar. à la pages 56–58 et où le chantre répond « Pour tous et pour toutes/

kai panton kai pason » comme en roumain, dans l'édition d'Anthime de 1706 (p. 84), mais cette réponse est absente des éditions grecques de 1691 et 1697.

10. Dans l'édition gréco-arabe, dans la prière d'après l'épiclèse : « Pour Saint Jean Baptiste... » immédiatement après les saints Apôtres apparaît le nom du Saint Archidiacre Etienne, chose inhabituelle dans les Hiératikons. Vatopedi 1049 n'en fait pas mention non plus.

11. Le Polychronium d'après l'épiclèse, après que le prêtre ait dit : « D'abord sou-viens-Toi Seigneur de notre Archevêque » en cette édition 1701, est spécifique au patriarche d'Antioche, dont le titre complet d'archipasteur orthodoxe de l'Antioche et de tout l'Orient, était peu connu (p. 59), et c'est pour cette raison que nous le reproduisons ici :

Τοῦ μακαριωτάτου καὶ ἁγιωτάτου, πατέρος πατέρων, ποιμένος ποιμένων, ἀρχιερέως ἀρχιερέων, τρίτου καὶ δεκάτου τῶν ἀποστόλων, πατροὸς ἡμῶν καὶ πατριάρχου, τῆς μαγάλης θεουπόλεως Ἀντιοχείας καὶ πάσης Ἀνατολῆς, πολλὰ τὰ ἔτη.

(فلان) القديس الطوباني اب الابا ورييس الروسا وراعي الرعاه ثالث الاثني عشر الرسل الاطهار بطريرك مدينة الله العظما انطاكيه وساير المشرق

« A Sa Béatitude et Très Saint, le Père des Pères, Le Pasteur des Pasteurs, L'Évêque des Évêques, le treizième apôtre, Notre Père et Patriarche de la très grande ville de Dieu Antioche et de tout l'Orient, longue vie. »

La position du Polychronium après l'épiclèse est suggérée également par l'édition 1691 (p. 49).

12. Le Hiératikon de 1701 présente en grec et en arabe (p. 60–61) un Polychronium nominal, bref, pour les patriarches apostoliques orientaux : de Constanti-nople, d'Alexandrie et de Jérusalem, ce qui révèle que c'est le patriarche qui a commandé l'impression de cette édition du Hiératikon. Nous mentionnons que ce Polychronium est identique dans Vatopedi 1049 (f. 58v) et dans le Hié-ratikon arabe imprimé à Jassy en 1745, commandé lui aussi par un patriarche d'Antioche, Sylvestre.

13. A la p. 60 du Hiératikon de 1701, après avoir mentionné le hiérarque du lieu, suit une prière qui ne figure pas dans les éditions de 1691 et 1706, ni dans le Hiératikon arabe moderne. Cette prière évoque tout le clergé, hiéromoines, prêtres, hiérodiacres, diacres, moines, ainsi que les bienfaiteurs de l'Eglise et elle se trouve dans la traduction de Mélèce Karma, Vatopedi 1049 (f. 58v). On la récite aujourd'hui à Constantinople lors de la Grande Entrée avec les saintes espèces. C'est là qu'on voit peut-être l'intervention–surveillance du patriarche Athanase, qui a inclut une note spécifique dans le texte grec aussi. Une particularité du Hiératikon de 1701 c'est que tant en grec qu'en arabe, à la prière *Souviens-Toi, Seigneur*, où l'on mentionne les bienfaiteurs de l'église, en général, ici est mentionné nominalement *Ioannou Konstantinou Boebonda*

(Brancoveanu) *kai ton peri auton* avec toute sa lignée. Le nom du prince en arabe *Yūwānū Qusṭanṭīn fūyfūḍā wa-wāliday-hi* (p. 61) a été calqué d'après le grec. Le geste représente, certes, un acte de reconnaissance envers le patron financier de l'édition. La situation ne se répète pas au Hiératikon arabe de Jassy, 1745, où le nom du donateur, le prince Jean Maurocordato, ne figure pas.

14. Les recommandations pour la Divine Liturgie des Présanctifiés de l'édition 1701 (p. 157–165) sont reproduites à l'identique d'après l'édition vénitienne de 1691 (p. 79–81).

15. L'édition 1701 (p. 177) inclut des explications détaillées sur la manière de célébrer la Petite Entrée à la Liturgie des Présanctifiés, explications qui manquent aux éditions de 1691 (p. 84) et 1706 (p. 168), peut-être s'agit-il d'une autre intervention du patriarche Athanase.

16. L'éd. 1701 prévoit pour la préparation des célébrants à l'élévation du Saint Agneau les rubriques du Typikon identiques à celui de 1691, et de même sont identiques la prière et les rubriques du Typikon pour la consommation des Saints Dons (1701 - p. 203 et 1691 - p. 89).

17. La clôture de l'office et la distribution de l'antidoron sont identiques en 1701 (p. 204), 1691 (p. 89) et 1706 (p. 184).

Après le texte de la Liturgie des Présanctifiés est placé le chapitre *Apolyseis tes holes hebdomados* c'est-à-dire les formules de clôture des offices pour les jours de la semaine, de lundi jusqu'à samedi. Ce chapitre avec les *Apolyseis* quotidiennes ne se retrouve qu'en 1701 en arabe (p. 240–243), en roumain 1706 (p. 188) et de nouveau en arabe en 1745[33] (f. 68.) Étant donné qu'Anthime a traduit le texte de la liturgie du grec en roumain et l'a publié en 1706, en utilisant l'édition vénitienne de 1691 qui n'inclut pas ce chapitre, on peut supposer qu'il soit intervenu dans l'édition gréco-arabe de 1701 avec cette adjonction qui ne se retrouve que dans l'édition roumaine, ultérieure à celle gréco-arabe. L'édition de 1701 contient des rubriques du Typikon plus développées de ces *Apolyseis* quotidiennes par rapport à l'édition roumaine de 1706.

18. *Hai apolyseis ton despotikon heorton / Khatm al-ṣalawāt fī al-a'yād al-sayyidīya* (les formules de clôture des offices pour les Fêtes royales) sont identiques : 1691 (p. 464–465); 1701 (p. 244); 1706 (p. 185–188).

19. La prière de la bénédiction de la colybe :

---

33 Nous mentionnons que l'exemplaire du Hiératikon édité en arabe, à Iasi en 1745, étudié par nous, n'est pas complet mais présente des complètements manuscrits puisque le début et la fin manquent. Ainsi, nous supposons que ce chapitre cité par nous et qui figure à la page 68, bien que manuscrit, ait été copié d'après un autre exemplaire, complet celui-ci. Voir également note 19.

a. En éd. 1701 est placée à la fin des liturgies, après le chapitre *Hai apolyseis* (p. 250–252), avec une explication en majuscules, seulement en arabe :

« Que tous les chrétiens orthodoxes sachent que lors des Grandes Fêtes et celles des Martyrs (Saints) on apporte de la colybe à l'église pour être bénie par les [saints] commémorés. Nous avons placé ici cette prière pour que l'on s'en serve aux pays arabes pour l'aide et la bénédiction de ceux qui le souhaitent. »

اعلم ان جميع المسيحيين ابنا الروم بيقدموا في الاعياد المميزة واعياد الشهدا سليقه في الكنايس لاجل اخد البركه بواسطة صاحب التدكار وهذا الافشين نوضع هاهنا لكي يستعملوه ايضا في البلاد العربيه لاجل المنفعه والبركه الحاصله منه لمن اراد

b. En 1706, cette prière se trouve tout juste après la liturgie de Saint Jean Chrysostome (p. 102), sans explications supplémentaires.

c. L'édition de 1691 la place au chapitre *Prières pour diverses nécessités* (p. 273

d. Le Vatopedi 1049 ne contient pas cette prière.

En conclusion de notre analyse, nous voulons discuter les observations appartenant au renommé orientaliste français Cyrille Charon au sujet du texte du Hiératikon gréco-arabe de 1701, puisqu'il fut le seul chercheur à avoir étudié attentivement le texte de 1701.

L'affirmation que le Hiératikon 1701 fut imprimé avec « peu de soin »[34] est exagérée. Il faut tenir compte, d'une part, du fait que les typographes roumains n'étaient pas des connaisseurs de la langue arabe, fait souligné par Anthime lui-même dans le colophon du Hiératikon ; d'autre part, le texte arabe de la liturgie n'était pas très bien fixé dans la pratique liturgique. Cette initiative fut un véritable acte de courage jamais assumé par personne jusqu'alors, ni même par Rome qui n'avait pu satisfaire un tel besoin, notamment pour les gréco-catholiques, alors qu'en Occident étaient édités des dizaines de titres en arabe, sauf le Hiératikon, pourtant nécessaire à la vie liturgique des fidèles. Une erreur dans la présentation du texte de la liturgie aurait créé de grands troubles au sein du clergé et des communautés chrétiennes de l'Orient, déjà en proie aux conflits et aux divisions.

A l'office de la Prothèse, en 1701, Charon considère étrange qu'à la Xe parcelle (en fait, celle pour les vivants) soient mentionnés en plus les prêtres et les fidèles et à la XIe (pour les morts) soient mentionnés les fondateurs qui ont édifié l'église respective.[35] Mais cette pratique figure également dans le Hiératikon grec vénitien de 1691 et dans celui roumain de 1706. C'est exactement ce que l'on trouve à Vatopedi 1049 aussi (f. 36r).

---

34 Charon, *Histoire des Patriarcats Melkites*, p. 61.
35 Charon, *Histoire des Patriarcats Melkites*, p. 61.

L'emploi du terme archevêque pour le hiérarque du lieu est également inhabituel chez les Arabes, étant donné que ce titre, comme dit Charon, n'est attribué qu'au Patriarche œcuménique de Constantinople.[36] Or, tant le texte grec de 1691 que celui roumain de 1706 désignent le hiérarque du lieu par ce titre d'archevêque. En plus, chez les Roumains, le métropolite du pays était également archevêque. Cela atteste un plus grand rapprochement du texte arabe et de celui grec-byzantin.

Les ecphonèses des trois premières antiennes sont placées après les prières des antiennes comme dans le culte slavo-russe d'aujourd'hui[37] (sic), dit Charon. En fait, c'est la place qu'occupe l'ecphonèse en 1691 et en 1706, son rôle étant justement celui de clore la prière de l'antienne et non l'ecténie. Donc, placer l'ecphonèse avant la prière d'une antienne comme elle apparaît dans la version arabe de la liturgie, n'était pas correcte et cela fut corrigé en 1701. D'ailleurs, à Vatopedi 1049 la grande ecténie s'achevait par l'ecphonèse suivie par la prière (f. 41r). Tandis qu'au deuxième antiphone c'est comme en 1701 : l'ecphonèse est située après la prière (f. 42r).

Avant la lecture de l'Apôtre, dans la version slavo-russe le prêtre dit : Paix à tous ! ce qui en 1701 manque.[38] Mais, en 1691 et 1706, comme en 1701, on ne retrouve plus cette formule, qui manque également à Vatopedi 1049 (f. 44v).

Lors de la communion des prêtres dans le sanctuaire, on prononçait, avant qu'ils communient, trois prières, comme dans la tradition slavo-russe, dit Charon.[39] Cette pratique, que l'on retrouve dans le Hiératikon grec de 1691 et dans celui roumain de 1706, n'est pas de tradition slavo-russe, mais byzantine. On constate de nouveau une adoption du rituel liturgique constantinopolitain pour l'espace arabe aussi. D'ailleurs, Vatopedi 1049 contient intégralement toutes les trois prières (f. 62v), exactement comme en 1701 (dont le texte grec n'en mentionne que l'incipit).

Nous remarquons aussi des différences qui ont persisté en 1701 (p. 72–74) par rapport à l'édition grecque de 1691. Lors de la communion, le prêtre donne au diacre une parcelle du Saint Corps et ensuite en prend une pour lui-même. Charon considère que c'est une tradition melkite et slavo-russe et il est possible que ce soit ainsi, puisque nous avons vu qu'en 1691 (p. 51) de même qu'en 1706 (p. 93–94) c'est l'inverse. C'est le prêtre qui prend le premier une parcelle sainte et communie, puis il en donne aussi une au diacre.

---

36 Charon, *Histoire des Patriarcats Melkites*, p. 62.
37 Charon, *Histoire des Patriarcats Melkites*, p. 62.
38 Charon, *Histoire des Patriarcats Melkites*, p. 63.
39 Charon, *Histoire des Patriarcats Melkites*, p. 66.

Vatopedi 1049 note que le prêtre doit prendre le premier le Saint Corps et puis en donner au diacre (ff. 62–63v), il paraît qu'ici Athanase se fût éloigné de la version de Mélèce Karma (Vatopedi 1049) et de 1691. Qu'Athanase n'ait pas suivi à la lettre la version arabe de Karma résulte aussi de la situation suivante : en 1701, après avoir mis les saintes parcelles dans le calice, le diacre sort devant les portes saintes et dit : « Approchez-vous avec crainte de Dieu, foi et charité ! » (p. 77); à Vatopedi 1049 n'apparaît pas le mot « charité » (f. 64r).

Si lors de la mise des parcelles dans le Saint Calice, les tropaires sont absents tout comme la formule pour la communion des fidèles,[40] nous ajoutons qu'ils ne figurent non plus ni dans les textes de 1691, 1706 et de Vatopedi 1049 (f. 63v).

Charon dit qu'après le transfert du calice à la prothèse, lorsque la communion des fidèles s'est achevée, la tradition slavo-russe indique la prière : « Que nos lèvres s'emplissent de ta louange, Seigneur » mais cette dernière est absente de 1701[41] donc Charon lui-même montre que 1701 ne respecte pas la tradition slavo-russe, mais la prière respective ne figure ni dans l'édition grecque de 1691, et apparaît en échange dans l'édition roumaine de 1706.

Nous, Roumains, ne pouvons pas éluder tout à fait la tradition slave, si la prière en question appartient vraiment à cette tradition. Une autre particularité de 1701 que Charon met en lumière est un fait bien curieux :[42] dans l'édition 1701, à la fin de la liturgie, le prêtre sort devant les portes saintes et s'incline, en disant diverses prières. Cela ne figure ni en 1691 ni en 1706. Il est clair qu'il s'agit là d'une pratique spécifiquement arabe, conservée dans l'édition de 1701. Cette indication liturgique pourrait être même une adjonction faite par le patriarche Athanase Dabbas, car elle manque aussi dans la version de Mélèce Karma (Vatopedi 1049).

Charon considérait que Athanase Dabbas avait utilisé pour l'édition bilingue de 1701 le texte grec de l'Euchologe édité à Venise en 1663.[43] Nous ne savons pas pourquoi Charon eût-t-il identifié cette édition, car jusqu'en 1701 sont parues plusieurs encore. Nous avons montré que l'édition de 1691 est la plus proche de celle de 1701, d'autant plus qu'Anthime l'Ibérien l'avait à sa portée puisque c'est toujours lui qui s'occupait de la traduction des liturgies en roumain.

À la liturgie des Présanctifiés, l'édition 1701 omet les textes des stichères et des lectures bibliques et débute directement par l'explication des rubriques de cet office.[44] En 1691, ces textes se trouvent avant l'explication des rubriques (p. 73–79),

---

40 Charon, *Histoire des Patriarcats Melkites*, p. 66.
41 Charon, *Histoire des Patriarcats Melkites*, p. 66.
42 Charon, *Histoire des Patriarcats Melkites*, p. 67.
43 Charon, *Histoire des Patriarcats Melkites*, p. 71.
44 Charon, *Histoire des Patriarcats Melkites*, p. 71.

et dans l'édition roumaine de 1706, l'explication des rubriques est suivie par des stichères et des lectures bibliques dans le cas où l'on ne disposait pas d'un Triode (p. 158). Nous considérons que 1701 les a omis par économie d'espace.

Compte tenu de tous ces arguments et des nombreux exemples présentés dans cette étude, l'affirmation de Charon selon laquelle: « l'édition d'Athanase serait tributaire à la recension slavo-russe qui dérive de celle faite par les soins du patriarche de Moscou Nikon, en 1656 »,[45] ne paraît plus justifiée.

Le Hiératikon de 1701 se retrouve dans toute la chrétienté et pas seulement dans le monde chrétien arabophone.[46] N'oublions pas qu'il n'y a que les prêtres arabophones qui puissent s'en servir, puisque des parties essentielles et indispensables à la célébration de la liturgie ne sont qu'en arabe. L'usure des exemplaires connus et mentionnés par nous atteste clairement leur emploi intense par des prêtres arabes. Charon relate plusieurs tentatives de réédition faites par les catholiques. Ceux-ci ont réussi à éditer l'Euchologe (c'est-à-dire l'ensemble des offices concernant les Sept Sacrements, donc aussi la Sainte Liturgie) à Rome, en 1738 et 1754[47] plutôt en grec qu'en arabe, ce qui rend compte de la difficulté d'une telle démarche.

Une commission réunie à l'ordre du pape Benoît XIVe envisageait de publier une nouvelle édition du Hiératikon de 1701.[48] L'exemplaire de cette édition de 1701 avec les modifications nécessaires pour correspondre au culte gréco-catholique se trouve de nos jours encore à la bibliothèque de Pontificio collegio greco di Sant'Atanasio, à Rome.[49] Ce projet des catholiques ne devait se réaliser qu'en 1839, lorsque parut la liturgie en arabe et ce n'est qu'en 1843 que le patriarche

---

45 Charon, *Histoire des Patriarcats Melkites*, p. 71.

46 Nicholas Bishara a effectué une recherche visant la circulation dans le monde des livres d'Anthime l'Ibére à partir de l'ouvrage de V. Cândea, *Mărturii românești peste hotare*, nouvelle série, soignée par Ioana Feodorov (avec Andrei Timotin), Bucarest et Brăila, 2010-2018: I. Albania-Etiopia, II. Finlanda-Grecia, III. India-Olanda, IV. Polonia-Rusia, V. Serbia-Turcia, VI.1. Ucraina-Vatican, VI.2. Ungaria. Ainsi, selon cette recherche, aujourd'hui il y a des exemplaires de ces livres en: Autriche, Vienne, Österreichische Nationalbibliothek; Égypte, Alexandrie, Patriarcheio Alexandreias, Livyīs, Pentapoleōs, Aithiopias kai Pasīs Afrikīs; Grèce, Athènes, Gennadeios Vivliothīkī; Liban, Dūr El-Shuweyr, Deir Mār Yuḥannā; Syrie, Damasc, al-Baṭriyarkiyya al-Anṭākiyya li-l-Rūm al-'Urtūduks bi-Dimashq; Syrie, Ṣaydnāyā, Dayr Sayyidat Ṣaydnāyā al-Baṭriyarkiyy; Vatican, Biblioteca Apostolica Vaticana; Bzummār, Couvent Notre Dame de Bzummār, Liban; Institut français d'études byzantines, Paris, France; Ṣarba, Église du Sauveur (Ordre Basilien Alépin), Sarba, Liban; Séminaire Sainte-Anne de Jérusalem. À ces exemplaires s'ajoutent d'autres encore, mentionnés dans ce texte, dont quelques-uns découverts par nous.

47 Charon, *Histoire des Patriarcats Melkites*, p. 72–73.

48 Charon, *Histoire des Patriarcats Melkites*, p. 73.

49 Information reçue de Vera Tchentsova, que nous remercions.

gréco-catholique Maxime III Mazloûm « prescrivit de laisser de côté le liturgicon valaque : *'al qondâq, al flâkhî.* »[50] Cela nous montre que l'édition de Snagov, de 1701, avait été utilisée en égale mesure par les orthodoxes et par les grecs-catholiques.

Les orthodoxes ont réussi à rééditer les liturgies de 1701 à Jassy, en 1745, à l'initiative du patriarche Sylvestre d'Antioche et aux frais du prince de Moldavie Jean Maurocordato, comme nous l'avons déjà dit, puis, toujours au milieu du XVIIIe siècle, il semblerait que fut publiée à Beyrouth même une nouvelle édition, aujourd'hui inconnue, au monastère de S. Georges.[51] En tout cas, une réédition du Hiératikon arabe par les orthodoxes n'eut lieu qu'en 1860, à Jérusalem.[52]

2. Conclusions récapitulatives

1. Anthime a imprimé à Snagov, en 1697, dans le livre intitulé *Anthologion*, le texte grec des Divines Liturgies, sans des rubriques (indications typiconales). Il avait pris ce texte de l'édition grecque de l'Euchologe imprimé à Venise en 1691. C'est de cette même édition vénitienne qu'il allait prendre le texte, mais cette fois-ci avec les rubriques pour le Hiératikon gréco-arabe de 1701, en utilisant, selon ses dires, la même édition vénitienne pour la version roumaine parue à Ramnic, en 1706.
2. L'existence d'exemplaires corrigés du Hiératikon de 1701 nous indique le fait que le livre avait eu au moins deux tirages et, en même temps, semble indiquer la préoccupation du typographe Anthime à faire de son mieux pour la réalisation d'un tel ouvrage.
3. Dans le Hiératikon de 1701, le texte grec est en parallèle au texte arabe. L'existence de certaines différences dans le texte grec de 1701 par rapport au prototype grec de 1691 peut indiquer l'intervention du patriarche Athanase Dabbas, qui a corrigé non seulement le texte arabe, mais aussi le grec, même si pour ce dernier est mentionné un autre correcteur (Ignace le Phytien).
4. Les explications en arabe par rapport au texte grec sont parfois plus développées lorsqu'il est question des bienfaits du pain béni de la Litie (l'Artos) et la colybe.

---

50 Charon, *Histoire des Patriarcats Melkites*, p. 80.
51 Charon, *Histoire des Patriarcats Melkites*, p. 96a.
52 Charon, *Histoire des Patriarcats Melkites*, p. 96a

5. Le texte grec était utilisé par les prêtres arabes car il rappelait leur lien avec Byzance qui les définissait eux aussi tant du point de vue de l'identité que de la terminologie, ils étaient orthodoxes-byzantins, c'est-à-dire *al-rūm*.

6. Certaines situations indiquent des parties communes exclusivement entre le Hiératikon gréco-arabe de 1701 et la version roumaine d'Anthime de 1706, publiée à Ramnic. On peut supposer qu'Anthime l'Ibérien soit intervenu dans le texte grec (interventions reprises en arabe aussi), et ultérieurement qu'il ait introduit ces aspects dans la version roumaine de 1706.

7. Le texte grec de 1701 contient souvent des références monastiques, comme en témoigne l'édition vénitienne de 1691 et l'édition roumaine de 1706. Le texte arabe ne se réfère pas au « saint patron protecteur du monastère » ou à « ce monastère », mais parle du « saint de l'église respective » et « du saint lieu en question », ce qui montre l'intention d'une plus large réception du Hiératikon de 1701, le texte arabe allant parfois indépendamment du texte grec.

8. Le texte arabe de 1701, comme le grec, présente des erreurs de graphie, inévitables quand on sait en quelles circonstances difficiles fut édité le livre.

9. L'analyse comparative des textes des éditions 1691, 1701 et la version de Mélèce Karma (Vatopedi 1049) montre qu'Athanase n'a pas traduit lui-même la liturgie du grec en arabe, puisqu'elle était déjà traduite par Mélèce Karma. Certes, ces hiérarques antiochiens se sont efforcés d'aligner les offices divins célébrés sur les règles byzantines grecques, devenues accessibles à tous, notamment grâce aux nombreux livres grecs vénitiens. Comme nous l'avons vu, le patriarche Athanase a ajouté des explications supplémentaires et des prières là où il l'estima nécessaire.

10. Dans notre analyse, nous avons comparé le Hiératikon de 1701, revu et peut être corrigé par Athanase, à la liturgie gréco-arabe traduite par Mélèce Karma et conservée en manuscrit au monastère de Vatopedi, au Mont Athos. C'est ce dernier volume qu'avait également utilisé le patriarche Macaire III d'Antioche, lequel avait même apposé sa signature à la fin dudit volume, comme pour confirmer son contenu. Nous avons pu constater que Mélèce Karma est très proche du texte grec de la liturgie édité à Venise, de même que l'édition de 1701.

11. De prime abord, le texte arabe de 1701 est très proche de celui de l'édition arabe de Jassy, 1745, imprimée par le patriarche Sylvestre au monastère de Saint Sabas. Il y a des parties qui ne se retrouvent que dans les éditions 1701-Snagov (gréco-arabe), 1706-Ramnic (roumaine) et 1745-Jassy (arabe), notamment en ce qui concerne les formules de clôture des offices pour les jours de la semaine.

12. Le Hiératikon édité à Snagov en 1701 par Anthime l'Ibérien et par le patriarche Athanase Dabas eut les mêmes conséquences que la version roumaine

des liturgies éditées en 1706 : le remplacement de la langue syriaque par l'arabe, langue parlée par le peuple (pour les Roumains, ce fut le remplacement du slavon par le roumain).

13. L'édition gréco-arabe de 1701 représente un progrès dans la liturgique antiochienne arabophone ; tout comme la version roumaine d'Anthime l'Ibérien, cette édition de 1701 cherchait à uniformiser la pratique liturgique (afin que tous les prêtres officient de la même manière), ou plutôt imposer un modèle de célébration afin d'éviter les innovations en matière de culte et en même temps mettre à la portée des prêtres un texte qui puisse être bien compris par eux et par la masse des fidèles.

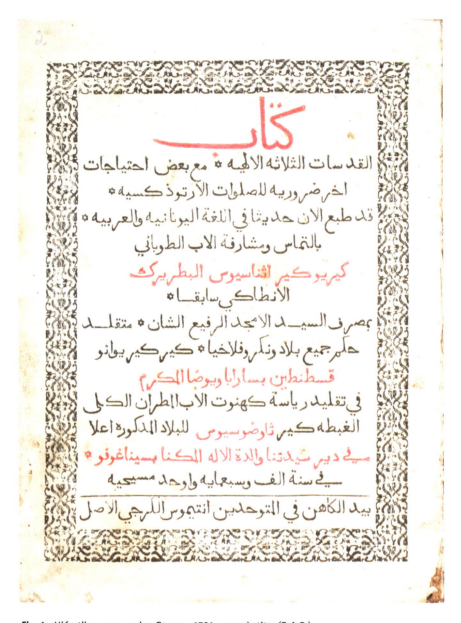

كتاب

القداسات الثلاثه الالهيه ٭ مع بعض احتياجات
اخر ضروريه للصلوات الارثوذكسيه ٭
قد طبع الان حديثا في اللغة اليونانييه والعربيه ٭
بالتماس ومشارفة الاب الطوباني

كيريوكير افناسيوس البطريرك
الانطاكي سابقـا ٭

بمصرف السيـد الامجد الرفيع الشان ٭ متقلـد
حاكم جميع بلاد ونكرو فلاخيا ٭ كيركير يوانو
قسطنطين بسارابا ويوضا المكرم
في تقليد رياسة كهنوت الاب المطران الكلي
الغبطه كير ثاوضوسيوس للبلاد المذكورة اعلا
سيفي دير سيدتنا والدة الاله المكنا بسيناغوفو ٭
سيفي سنة الف وسبعمايه واوحد مسيحيه

بيد الكاهن في التوحدين انتيموس الكرجي الاصل

Fig. 1: Hiératikon grec-arabe, Snagov, 1701, page de titre (B.A.R.).

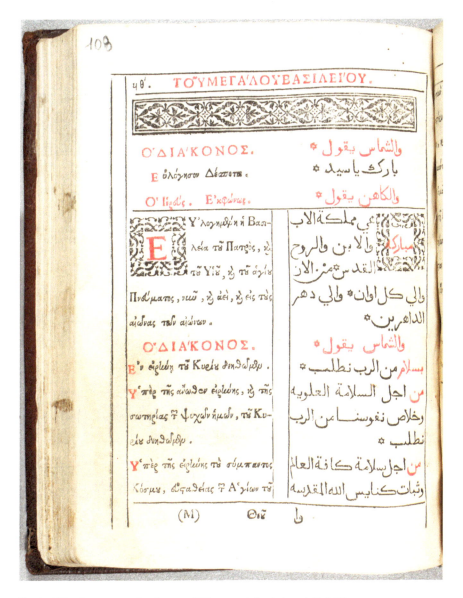

Fig. 2: Hiératikon grec-arabe, Snagov, 1701, exemplaire de type A (B.A.R.).

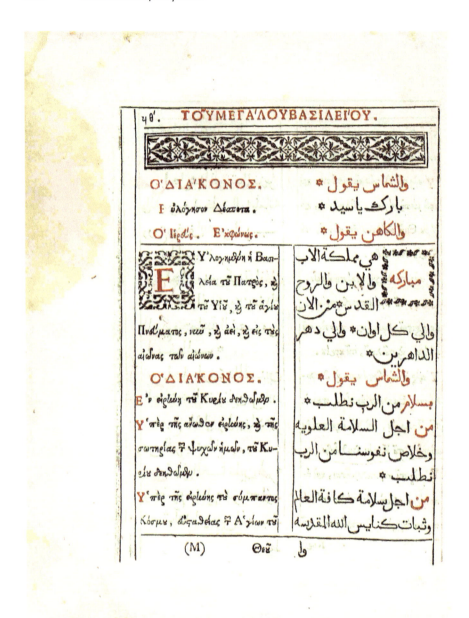

Fig. 3: Hiératikon grec-arabe, Snagov, 1701, exemplaire de type B, corrigé (B.A.R.).

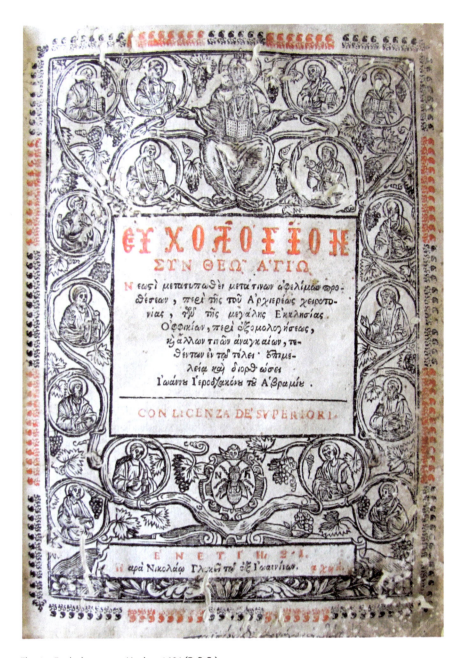

Fig. 4: Euchologe grec, Venise, 1691 (B.S.S.).

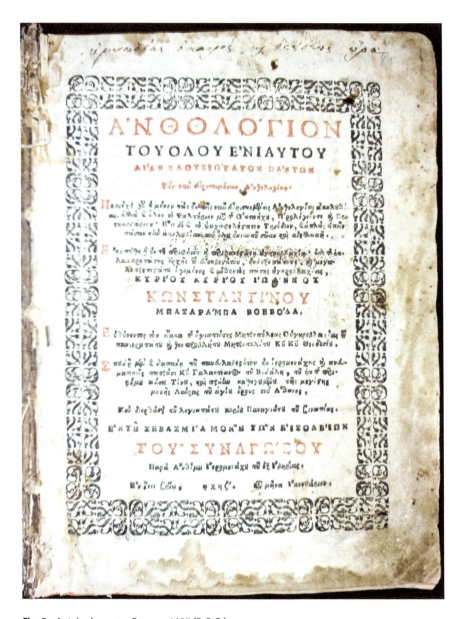

Fig. 5: Antologion grec, Snagov, 1697 (B.S.S.).

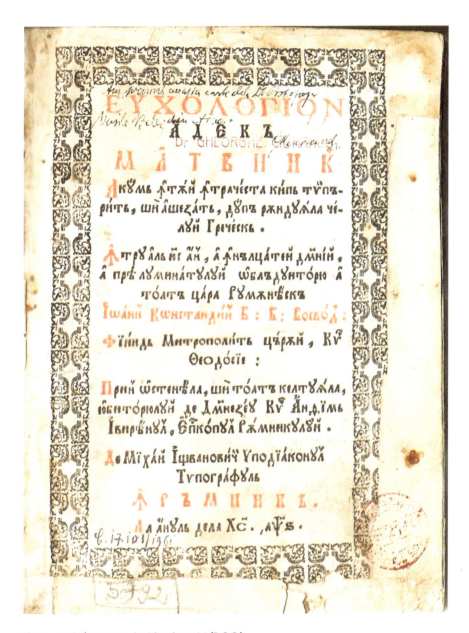

Fig. 6: Euchologe roumain, Râmnic, 1706 (B.S.S.).

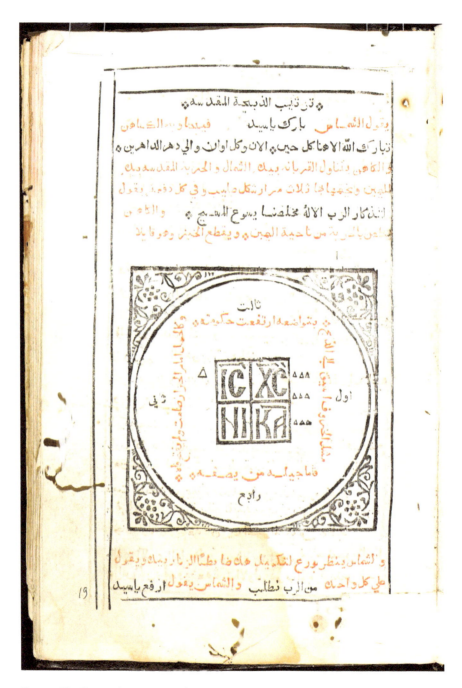

Fig. 7: Hiératikon arabe, Jassy, 1745 (Monastère de Balamand).

Bibliographie

Bădără, Doru. « Vademecum de istoria tiparului și cărții din Țara Românească și Moldova, 1508–1830 ». *Analele Brăilei*, 19, 2019, p. 245–284.

Bianu, Ioan, Nerva Hodoș. *Bibliografia Românească Veche. Vol. I (1508–1716)*. Bucarest : Stabilimentul grafic J.V. Socec, 1903.

Charon, Cyrille P. *Histoire des Patriarcats Melkites (Alexandrie, Antioche, Jérusalem) depuis le schisme monophysite du sixième siècle jusqu'à nos jours*, t. III. *Les institutions. Liturgie, Hiérarchie, Statistique, Organisation, Listes épiscopales*. Rome/Paris : Forzani et Cie, fasc. I-II, 1909–1911.

Chițulescu, Policarp (éd.). *Antim Ivireanul – Opera tipografică*. Bucarest : Editura Institutului Cultural Român, 2016.

Chițulescu, Policarp. « Etat de l'art des livres et objets sacrés ayant appartenu à Saint Anthime d'Ivir ». *Museikon*, 2, 2018, p. 105–116.

Chițulescu, Policarp. « Livres imprimés à Venise aux XVIIᵉ et aux XVIIIᵉ siècles avec la contribution des Pays Roumains ». Dans *Culture manuscrite et imprimée dans et pour l'Europe du Sud-Est*, éd. Archim. Policarp Chițulescu, Ioana Feodorov. Brăila : Editura Istros a Muzeului Brăilei "Carol I", 2020, p. 13–41.

Feodorov, Ioana. *Tipar pentru creștinii arabi. Antim Ivireanul, Atanasie Dabbas și Silvestru al Antiohiei*. Brăila: Editura Istros a Muzeului Brăilei "Carol I", 2016.

Feodorov, Ioana. « The Arabic Book of the Divine Liturgies Printed in 1745 in Iași by Patriarch Sylvester of Antioch ». *Scrinium*, 16, 2020, p. 158–176.

Feodorov, Ioana. *Arabic Printing for the Christians in Ottoman Lands. The East-European Connection*. Berlin/Boston: De Gruyter, 2023.

Frantsuzov, Serge A. « Pervaia arabografichnaia kniga, napechatannaia v mire islama, v sobranii Instituta vostochnykh rukopiseĭ RAN ». *Vestnik PSTGU. Seriia III: Filologiia*, 61. 2019, p. 104–122.

Nassif, Charbel. « La révision liturgique du métropolite melkite d'Alep Malâtyûs Karma et les réformes liturgiques dans les pays d'Europe de l'Est au XVIIᵉ siècle ». *Europe in Arabic Sources: "The Travels of Macarius", Patriarch of Antioch*, éd. Yulia Petrova, Ioana Feodorov. Kiev : A. Krymsky Institute of Oriental Studies of the NASU, 2016, p. 117–134.

Nassif, Charbel. « Le Liturgicon arabe de Vatopédi, (Mont Athos, Vatopédi 1049) ». *Chronos*, 42, 2021, p. 57–82.

Pancenko, Constantin A. *Arab Orthodox Christians under the Ottomans: 1516–1831*. Jordanville, NY: Holy Trinity Seminary Press, 2016.

Petrova, Yulia. « The Development of the Christian Vocabulary in Arabic ». *Romano-Arabica*, 20, 2020, p. 256–269.

Popescu, Radu. *Istoriile domnilor Țării Românești*. Constantin Grecescu (éd.). Bucarest: Editura științifică, 1959.

Fr Andrew Wade

A Preliminary Comparison of the *Horologion* in Sinai Arabic 232 (13th c.) with the 1702 Edition of Athanasios Dabbās and the Earlier Version of Meletios Karma

1. The Three (or Two) Versions of the Arabic Horologion under Discussion Here

The Arabic Horologion of Patriarch Athanasios Dabbās of Antioch, published in Romania in 1702 by St. Antim the Iberian is quite well known to scholars. Nevertheless, no studies have examined the Arabic translation used in this publication or investigated its provenance.[1] This article will shed light on this question in a completely neglected area of Christian Arabic studies: the Orthodox Arabic Horologion.

It has been widely supposed (based on Dabbās' statement at the beginning of his Horologion)[2] that the version published by Dabbās and St Antim in 1702 was based on the earlier text found in MS Vatican Borgia 178, which was submitted for publication by the Propaganda Fide by the bishop of Aleppo, Meletios ('Abd al-Karīm) Karma,[3] who had produced a renewed Arabic version of the Liturgikon in 1612, and of the Euchologion in 1630.

Meletios Karma[4] was born in 1572 in Hama in Syria. His biographer and disciple Makarios ibn al-Zaʿīm tells us that "Ever since his earliest infancy, Karma

---

1 There is only the passing statement that Dabbās used Karma's version for his publications in C.-M. Walbiner, " 'Und um Jesu Willen, schickt sie nicht ungebunden!' Die Bemühungen des Meletius Karma (1512–1635) um den Druck arabischer Bücher in Rom", in R. Ebied, H. Teule (eds.), *Studies on the Christian Arabic Heritage in Honour of Father Prof. Dr. Samir Khalil Samir S.I. at the Occasion of his Sixty-Fifth Birthday*, Leuven/Paris/Dudley, 2004, p. 175.

2 Page II.1: "In the name of God the One, the eternal (*al-abadī*), the transcendent, the eternal (*al-sarmadī*). The book of the Horologion, the statutory prayers at the seven times, translated from Greek (*rūmī*) to Arabic by the labour and toil, of the Patriarch Aftīmiyūs of Ḥamā (*al-Ḥamawī*) when he was bishop of the city of Aleppo beforehand".

3 A biographical account of Karma and his translations can be found in Walbiner, " 'Und um Jesu Willen'" and also in J. B. Darblade, P.B., "L'Euchologe arabe Melkite de Kyr Mélèce Karmî", *Proche-Orient Chrétien*, 6, 1956, p. 28–37. The article states "à suivre" at the end, but no second part was published. See also Ch. Nassif, "Autour de l'Euchologe melkite de Malatios Karmé († 1635)", *Proche-Orient Chrétien*, 68, 2018, p. 46–61.

4 The biographical information set forth here derives from the articles of Walbiner, " 'Und um Jesu Willen'", see note 1, and Darblade, "L'Euchologe arabe…", see note 2. Further information

---

∂ Open Access. © 2024, the author(s), published by De Gruyter. [CC] [BY-NC-ND] This work is licensed under the Creative Commons Attribution-NonCommercial-NoDerivatives 4.0 International License.
https://doi.org/10.1515/9783111060392-011

experienced love for the Holy Scriptures and preferred his study to the children's playground".[5] His spiritual formation was received in the Lavra of Saint Sabas in the Judaean desert, where he learned Greek. On comparing the recent Venetian editions of the Greek liturgical books and the Bible with the manuscripts in use in the churches of the Patriarchate of Antioch, he soon realized that the Arabic versions were corrupt and incomplete, as he mentioned later in his letter of May 1629 to the Propaganda Fide and in the various prefaces to the liturgical texts he subsequently revised. This was the beginning of a task that would occupy much of his time and efforts for the rest of his life. He acceded to the throne of metropolitan of Aleppo in 1612 and continued in that position for 22 years, but even earlier he had begun work on this project of revision of the liturgical books, pursuing the task with great dedication throughout that period.[6] Walbiner cites the following statement by Makarios: "He noticed that the heretics had sown their harmful weeds in certain books and he hastened to eliminate them. With great effort, he translated the Book of the Divine Liturgies, the Euchologion and the Horologion, as well as the complete Synaxarion and other books from Greek into Arabic and delighted the churches with them."[7]

Aleppo was the wealthiest and most populous diocese of the Patriarchate of Antioch. One of Meletios' predecessors, Metropolitan Gregorios ibn Fuḍayl (1549–1582) had also been an author and copyist, and had founded a library at the Metropolitanate of Aleppo, which was later used and extended by Karma.[8] During Karma's period as metropolitan of Aleppo, European missionaries of the Roman Catholic Church came to the Middle East and particularly to Aleppo, with its large Christian population, and their erudition greatly impressed many members of the local Orthodox community. Karma himself mentioned his positive impression of Tommaso da Novara[9] in the former's undated letter to the Pope of Rome and the College of Cardinals of the Propaganda Fide (not before 1621).

---

can be found in Nāwufīṭūs Idlibī (Neophytos Edelby), *Asāqifat al-Rūm al-Malikīyīn bi-Ḥalab fī al-'aṣr al-ḥadīth*, Aleppo, 1983, p. 3l–48, 52–55; J. Nasrallah, *Histoire du mouvement littéraire dans l'Eglise Melchite du Ve au XXe siècle*, vol. IV/I, Louvain, 1979, p. 70–76.

5 Lāwandiyūs Kilzī (ed.), "Ḥayāt al-baṭriyark Aftīmiyūs Karma al-Anṭākī al-Ḥamawī bi-qalam tilmīdhi-hi al-baṭriyark Makāriyūs al-Ḥalabī", *al-Masarra*, 4, 1913, p. 42.

6 Cf. Nasrallah, *Histoire*, p. 76-86; Idlibī, *Asāqifat al-Rūm al-Malikīyīn*, p. 48–52.

7 Kilzī, "Ḥayāt al-baṭriyark Aftīmiyūs Karma", p. 85–87.

8 On Gregorios Ibn Fuḍayl, see Idlibī, *Asāqifat al-Rūm al-Malikīyīn*, p. 1–22, especially p. 18–20; Nasrallah, *Histoire*, p. 246–247.

9 The Franciscan Tommaso Obicini (1585–1632), also known as Tommaso da Novara (his diocese of origin), was active in Syria as a missionary from 1612 to 1622, first in Aleppo and then as Guardian of Mount Zion and Custodian of the Holy Land in Jerusalem. He was devoted to Arabic and oriental

Soon after Karma's accession to the metropolitan throne of Aleppo, he took advantage of these contacts with the Western missionaries to start corresponding with the Vatican. The principal subject of his letters was a series of requests to send printed books, mostly in Greek, and to speak of his intention to revise and publish liturgical books and the Bible in Arabic.[10] After receiving encouragement from Pope Paul V Borghese (1550–1621), Karma sent his disciple and personal secretary, Protosyncellos Absalom, to Rome, accompanied by Tommaso da Novara,[11] to present his plans and requests. It appears that Absalom was very well received in Rome, where he stayed until mid-1622. He returned to Meletios with a number of publications in Latin and Greek, a present of money and the promise (made on June 3, 1622) that the Vatican would translate the Bible into Arabic and then publish it.[12] As we shall see, this promise encountered numerous obstacles, to Karma's disappointment. The question had already been discussed on May 16, 1622 by the cardinals of the Propaganda Fide, some of whom had raised the objection that the fourth instruction of the Index forbade the publication of the Bible in vernacular languages, although others countered this objection by pointing out that the peoples of the East did not understand Latin and that they should not be denied access to the Bible. No agreement could be reached, and it was decided to forward the question to a different congregation, although it was soon returned to Propaganda. An assembly was gathered on June 3, 1622 to examine the recent edition published in Leiden by Erpenius[13] along with other manuscripts from the Vatican and elsewhere.

Karma had different ideas about how to revise the Arabic text of the Bible and he asked the cardinals of Propaganda Fide and the pope to appoint Tommaso da Novara in charge of this project, stating that he was universally respected and competent in literary Arabic.[14]

In another undated letter, Karma asked to be sent a man conversant in Greek and Arabic theology to teach his flock and to undertake the translation of the Old

---

studies. After returning to Italy, he worked in favour of a revised version of the Arabic Bible and other liturgical books (see: G.-C. Bottini, "Tommaso Obicini [1585–1632] Custos of the Holy Land and Orientalist", in A. O'Mahony et al. (eds.), *The Christian Heritage in the Holy Land*, Jerusalem, 1995, p. 97–101; G. Graf, *Geschichte der christlichen arabischen Literatur*, vol. 4, Vatican City, 1951, p. 174–176).
10 On Karma's correspondence with the Vatican, see: Nasrallah, *Histoire*, p. 290; M. Jabbūr, Z. al-Khūrī, *Wathā'iq hāmma fī khidmat kanisatl-nā ul-Antākīya*, Beirut, 2000, p. 1–14, 16–19.
11 See note 9.
12 Idlibī, *Asāqifat al-Rūm al-Malikīyīn*, p. 44.
13 *Al-'Ahd al-jadīd*, ed. by T. Erpenius, Leiden, 1616.
14 Arabic text of the relevant passage from Karma's (undated) letter and German translation in Walbiner, "'Und um Jesu Willen'", p. 166.

and New Testaments together with Karma, suggesting that if no one of the kind were available in Rome, they could appoint the erudite Maronite priest in Nicosia on Cyprus, Caspar (al-Gharīb), who was competent in Arabic, Greek and Latin theology.[15] In this letter, Karma sets out his wishes in five points, which can be summarized as follows:[16]

1. Send Caspar from Cyrus to Aleppo.
2. Send with him the erudite Tommaso da Novara, who is respected by all.
3. Theology must be taught in Arabic and Greek in Aleppo, since no-one knows European languages.
4. Both Karma and Caspar are elderly, so the Bible translation is very urgent.
5. The translation must be done in Aleppo, since we can help here, and Arabic is our mother tongue. The result will then be sent to Rome.[17]

Unfortunately for Karma, the Propaganda had other ideas and decided to summon the Maronite scholar Gabriel Sionita[18] from Paris to take over the publication of the Arabic Bible in Rome, rather than in Aleppo. On October 30, 1623, the Propaganda decided that there were too many difficulties encountered in the various manuscripts of the Arabic Bible and resolved simply to translate from the Vulgate. Caspar told the Propaganda that he was too old and fragile to go to Aleppo and that the Greek Orthodox and the Maronites were averse to each other. On October 3, 1625, the Propaganda decided to set up a branch of the Carmelite mission in Aleppo to deal with Karma, which came into effect in 1627.

Undeterred by the tergiversation of Rome, Karma sent the Propaganda Fide another proposal in 1629 for the translation of the Bible into Arabic, stating that all the versions in use at present contain errors.[19] He therefore recommended that the pope buy Arabic manuscripts from Tripoli, Beirut, Damascus, Sinai, Jerusalem and Aleppo and submit them to a committee of six experts in Greek

---

15 Concerning Caspar al-Gharīb, also known as Gaspar Peregrinus, see F. al-Samarrānī, "Talāmidhat Qubrus fī al-madrasa al-mārūnīya", *al-Manāra*, 25/1–2, 1984, p. 188–189.

16 The full Arabic text of this passage and its German translation can be found in Walbiner, "'Und um Jesu Willen'", p. 167–168.

17 Letter of Meletios (Karma) to the College of Cardinals of Propaganda Fide, 4.10.1623, Archivio storico della Congregazione per l'evangelizzazione dei popoli o "de Propaganda Fide", Rome, Scritture Originali riferite nelle Congregazioni Generali (SOCG): *Lettere in Diverse Lingue dall'anno 1622 a 1629*, vol. 181, fol. 36v. The Arabic original is undated, but on fol. 34v there is an Italian summary of Karma's requests, dating the letter as 4 October 1623.

18 For the scientific and editorial activities of Gabriel Sionita, see: N. Gemayel, *Les échanges culturels entre les Maronites et l'Europe*, vol. 1, Beirut, 1984, p. 211–278, 322–734; P. Raphael, *Le rôle du Collège Maronite Romain dans l'orientalisme aux XVIIe et XVIIIe siècles*, Beirut, 1950, p. 73–85.

19 The full Arabic text of this passage and its German translation can be found in Walbiner, "'Und um Jesu Willen'", p. 169.

and Arabic, to be paid by the pope. He wanted nothing for himself, but again asked for Tommaso da Novara to be sent. Nevertheless, Rome decided that everything should take place in Rome. Faced with the intransigence of Rome for the Bible translation, Karma returned to the question of the liturgical books. According to Walbiner, Karma's revisions of the Menologion, Sticherarion and Liturgikon were made in 1612.[20] In October 1631, Karma informed Propaganda Fide that he had completed his translation of the Euchologion and the Horologion and asked the Congregation to have both books printed in Rome.[21] At their session of April 26, 1632, the College of Cardinals decided to request Karma's translations of the Euchologion and the Horologion with their old Greek originals, "in order to print both of them, according to his request". Of course, that never happened, and only the Euchologion was eventually printed in 1865 in Jerusalem.[22]

On May 1, 1634, Meletios Karma was enthroned as the patriarch of Antioch with the name of Euthymios II. As mentioned above, an abundant correspondence of Karma with the Congregation for the Propagation of the Faith has been preserved, for example, the letters of May 1629, December 1629, March 1631, October 1631 preserved in the Arch. Prop., *SOCG*, (The Propaganda Fide Historical Archives [Archivio Storico di Propaganda Fide]).[23] It appears that Karma planned to submit to the Roman Church, although this was never actually concluded. It is known that he sent his protosyncellos Pachomios,[24] who was given the patriarchal seal to subscribe to everything the Pope said in addition to the decree of Florence.[25]Pachomios travelled in the company of Isaac al-Shadrāwī, the Maronite metropolitan of Tripoli, who had studied in Rome at the Maronite College and

---

20 Walbiner, "'Und um Jesu Willen'", p. 170, referring to Nasrallah, *Histoire*, p. 80.

21 Letter from Meletios (Karma) to Cardinal (Gaspare) Borgia, mid-October 1631 (see: "Rasā'il qadīma muhimma li-l-baṭriyark al-Anṭākī Afthīmiyūs Karma al-Ḥamawī", ed. by Q. [al-Bāshā], *al-Risāla al-mukhalliṣīya*, 5, 1938, p. 315–316).

22 M. Abraṣ, "Tārīkh al-Afkhūlūjiyūn al-kabīr al-maṭbūʿ fī al-Quds al-ʿām 1865", *al-Masarra*, 84, 1998, p. 539, note 8.

23 *Acta Sacrae Congregationis* (1622–1938) in 311 volumes. The *Acta* are the minutes of the Congregazioni Generali (monthly meetings of Cardinals and other members of the Congregation: the reports of the Cardinal Ponente or of the Secretary and the resolution taken by the members. Thus, the *Acta* reflect the main Congregation's activities and decisions regarding its various duties and competences. Scritture Originali riferite nelle Congregazioni Generali (SOCG) Vol. 180, fol. 208r, 95r, 35v, and 75r (all in Arabic).

24 Pachomius al-Ṣāqizī (i.e., from Chios), d. 1645, later metropolitan of Ṣaydnāyā, see Walbiner, "'Und um Jesu Willen'", p. 171 and note 31.

25 Cf. *SOCG*, Vol. 395, fol. 295r and 296v; Vol. 180, fol. 39r and 40r.

was well acquainted with Vatican customs.[26] The patriarch did not expressly sign the official act of union, despite this condition being demanded by the College of Cardinals, possibly for fear of the Turks who would have considered this act as political allegiance with the Western enemy. However, Pachomios carried three letters of Karma addressed to the Pope and to the Congregation for the Propagation of the Faith for the printing of Arabic liturgical books.[27] The handwritten note on the flyleaf of Vatican Borgia 178 reads (Fig. 1, f. 1r): "*Horologion portato dal Monaco Pacomio inviato dal Patriarca Greco di Antiochia in tempo di Papa Vrbano. Questo era nella libraria del Collegio.*" Pachomios stayed eight months in Rome without obtaining his requests. The Roman see did not refuse to print these liturgical books, but made the question dependent on the scrutiny of the Greek Euchologion, which ended only by the mid-18th century, by which time the Uniate branch of the Melkites was already in union with Rome. Nevertheless, the abridged version of the Euthymios II/Meletios Euchologion was printed only in 1851 in Rome, while the complete Euchologion was printed in 1865 in Jerusalem, as noted above.[28] However, Karma's Horologion was never published and has not been studied until now.

Karma's letter accompanying his translations of the Euchologion and the Horologion begged for their publication in the most grovelling terms:

> From the poor servant Euthymios to our Lord, the exalted pope, and to the illuminated, holy Congregation and the Lords Cardinals, may God make your benevolence endure. Letter of request of the least of pupils and the greatest of friends, for our Lord Jesus Christ says in the Bible, 'Ask and it will be given to you. Seek and you will find. Knock, and it will be opened to you'.[29]

The letter makes several subsidiary requests: that the paper be white and thick, that the Arabic and Greek characters be not too small for elderly priests to read, that the vowel signs be omitted in order to avoid errors, that the red and black colors be respected in the text to avoid the rubrics being pronounced, that the word order of the Arabic be respected and not rearranged to correspond to the Greek syntax, that the books be bound before dispatch, with the Euchologion in

---

26 Concerning Isaac al-Shadrāwī, see N. al-Jūmayyil, "Jadwal bi-asmā' talāmidhat al-madrasa al-mārūnīya", *al-Manāra*, 25/1–2, 1984, p. 93–94.

27 Cf. SOCG, Vol. 180, fol. 41r, 42r and 43r.

28 Ch. Nassif, *L'euchologe melkite depuis Malatios Karmé (†1635) jusqu'à nos jours : Les enjeux des évolutions d'un livre liturgique*, unpublished Ph.D. thesis, Institut Catholique de Paris, Paris, 2017; Nassif, "Autour de l'euchologe melkite de Malatios Karmé (†1635)", *Proche-Orient Chrétien*, 68, Beirut, 2018, p. 46–61.

29 Matthew 7:7, Luke 11:9.

two volumes, with 1,000 copies of each of the resulting three volumes, along with other technical requests.[30] Not only were these requests ignored, but when Pachomios returned to Syria, Karma had already died, pleading for the publication of these liturgical books practically with his dying breath. His brother Thalja, the scribe who had copied the books, informed the Propaganda Fide of his brother's death,[31] but this letter too was ignored.

Although a different version of the Euchologion was eventually published two hundred years later, the Horologion never saw the light until Dabbās' edition, published by Saint Antim in Bucharest in 1702, and the manuscript has remained in the Vatican Library until the present day. In 1634 the Propaganda Fide had decided to translate both the Euchologion and the Horologion into Latin in order to check their content. It appears that even this remarkable project was never realized. This decision was accompanied by two conditions for the publication: a confession of the Roman Catholic faith by Patriarch Euthymios Karma (who was already dead) and the completion of the Vatican-directed revision of the Greek texts of these books. These conditions were communicated to Pachomios, who arrived in Damascus to find that Karma had been dead for over a year. It appears that Karma's successor, Patriarch Euthymios al-Ṣāqizī, did not follow up the matter.[32]

As we shall see, Karma's Horologion and Dabbās' published Horologion are practically identical. Dabbās' publication is clearly based on Karma's version, with very few corrections (and hypercorrections) and very minor variants. It is therefore probable that Dabbās had access to another manuscript of Karma's Horologion, since the one that was submitted to the Vatican remained unpublished and undisturbed in the Vatican Library. The manuscript used by Dabbās has not been located and may not be extant. It seems clear that Karma produced his version on the basis of the Greek liturgical books, recently published in Venice. The Horologion corresponds closely to the order of the services found in the Venetian editions. At the beginning of his Horologion, Karma writes:[33] "In the name of the one, eternal, transcendent, infinite God, and we ask for his help. The book of the Horologion, the statutory prayers at the seven times, translated from the

---

30 Meletios Karma, *Bayān ṭabʿ al-kutub: kayfa yakūn* (Memorandum to the Pope and to the Cardinals of the Propaganda Fide, ca. May 1634), Rome, Archivio storico della congregazione per l'evangelizzazione dei popoli o 'de propaganda Fide', Lettere di lingua straniera dall'Anno 1631 sino al 1645, vol. 180, fol. 41 ("Rasāʾil qadīma", p. 319–320, new folio number 30; facsimile in Idlibī, *Asāqifat al-Rūm al-Malikīyīn*, p. 50).
31 Letter of Thalja (Karma) to Pope Urban XIII (ca. 1635), ("Rasāʾil qadīma", p. 322–323; cf. also M. Jabbūr, Z. al-Khūrī, *Wathāʾiq hāmma fī khidmat kanīsati-nā al-Anṭākīya*, p. 20–21).
32 Abraṣ, "Tārīkh al-Afkhūlūjiyūn", p. 534–548; 1094–1107.
33 Folio 3 (the text begins on page 3 of the Vatican Apostolic Library photographs).

Greek (*rūmī*) to Arabic by the labor and toil of the wretched Meletios, bishop of Aleppo" (Fig. 2, f. 1v).

In the Horologion contained in Sinai Arabic 232 the order of the services is different: Karma follows the Greek printed books and begins with the Midnight Office, whereas Sinai Ar. 232 begins with Matins, as did the Studite Horologion. However, this 13th century manuscript presents a Melkite text originating from Alexandria in Egypt.[34]

Before examining certain texts in parallel from these three versions, we can briefly present the three Horologia. Dabbās' Horologion is a handsome edition printed specially by Saint Antim in 1702. The Arabic text contains a few short passages in Greek in the Horologion section, which generally correspond to the same phenomenon in Karma's Horologion. The book, in black and red type, has a preface in Greek and Arabic, pp. I.1–21, and then the text of the Horologion, covering 732 pages. Karma's Horologion is contained in Vatican Borgia 178, a beautiful manuscript in fine calligraphy, in black and red ink, with no preface other than the note quoted above, covering 598 pages and dated in a brief but florid colophon in Ottoman style *taʿlīq* script on May 8, 7132 "of Adam" by the scribe Thalja, who was the brother of Meletios and who copied several other translations by Meletios which bear similar colophons (Fig. 3, f. 298v).[35] The date 7132 of Adam would correspond to 1624 AD.[36] Sinai Arabic 232 is a 13th century manuscript in black and red ink, with no colophon, containing 397 paper folios measuring 13.5×9 cm. and comprising a Psalter, a partial lectionary, the Horologion and an extensive supplement. The Horologion is contained on ff. 206v–333v.[37]

---

34 See: A. Wade, "L'Horologion du Sinaï Arabe 232 (13ème s.), témoin d'une fusion pluriculturelle", in A. Lossky, G. Sekulovski (eds.), *Traditions recomposées : liturgie et doctrine en harmonie ou en tension, 63e Semaine d'études liturgiques, Paris, Institut Saint-Serge, 21–24 juin 2016*, Münster, 2017, p. 111–124; Wade, "Individual Prayer in the Monastic Cell between Alexandria and Mount Sinai in the 13th Century: the Hours in Sin. Ar. 232", in A. Lossky, G. Sekulovski, Th. Pott (eds.), *Liturgie et religiosité. 64e Semaine d'études liturgiques, Paris, Institut Saint-Serge, juin 2017*, Münster, 2017; Wade, "The Enigmatic Horologion Contained in Sinai Ar. 232", in M. Lüstraeten, B. Butcher, S. Hawkes-Teeples (eds.), *LET US BE ATTENTIVE! Proceedings of the Seventh International Congress of the Society of Oriental Liturgy*, Münster, 2020, p. 285–305; Wade, "Byzantinised or Alexandrianised – or Both? Vespers in the 13th c. Melkite Alexandrian Arabic Horologion Sinai Arabic 232", *MDPI Religions*, 13 (7), 2022, 607 (https://doi.org/10.3390/rel13070607).
35 See Rami Wakim's chapter in the present volume.
36 Cf. Darblade, "L'Euchologe arabe Melkite", who on p. 32 states that Meletios began work on this Horologion in 1630.
37 The manuscript can be consulted at https://www.loc.gov/item/0027938457A-ms/ of the Library of Congress (photographs made in 1950) (accessed December 16, 2022).

The limits of this presentation make it impossible to compare the whole of these three Horologia. However, we can select some passages that will show how close, but not absolutely identical, Dabbās' text is to that of Karma, and then compare them to Sin. Ar. 232. There are dozens of other Horologia online and in various libraries, including six early versions (12th–13th centuries) on Sinai. Unfortunately, none of these other manuscripts have been studied, and the field is too vast to attempt even a simple overview here.

2. The Initial Prayers

As has been mentioned, Dabbās, following Karma, who follows the Greek printed editions of Venice, begins the Horologion with the Midnight Office, giving the initial prayers in full. Sin. Ar. 232 has the Midnight Office as the final office of the Horologion. The initial prayers are given in full at Matins, at the beginning of the Horologion. The prayer "O heavenly King..." is absent in the initial prayers, but is found elsewhere in the Horologion, thus permitting comparison of the translations.

Tab. 1: Beginning of Midnight Office, comparison.

AD (Dabbās)	MK (Karma)
[1] *Prayer of midnight.* *The priest begins, saying* Blessed is God our God in every time, from now and to all times and to the age of the ages Amen. *And if there were no priest, you say* By the prayers of our holy fathers (*ābāyi-nā*), o Lord Jesus Christ our God, have mercy on us Amen. *And you say* Glory to you, O // [2] our God, glory to you *only and O* heavenly king, the Consoler, the Spirit of truth present in every place and region (N.B. *wa-ṣuqʾ*), filling everything, treasury of good things and supplier (*rāziq*) of life, come and abide among us and purify us of all defilement, and save, o Good One, our souls. *And you say three times* (*mirār*) Holy is God, holy is the mighty one, holy is the one that does not die, have mercy on us *with three prostrations* (*maṭānīyāt*) if it is	[1v] *The first of that is the prayer of midnight.* (Fig. 2) *The priest begins, saying* Blessed is God our God in every time, from now and to all times and to the age of the ages Amen. *And if there* were *no priest, you say* By the prayers of our holy fathers (*abahāti-nā*), o Lord Jesus Christ our God, have mercy on us Amen. *And you say* Glory to you, O our God, glory to you. O heavenly king, the Consoler, the Spirit of truth, present in every place and region (N.B. *wa-ṣuqʾ*), filling everything, treasury of good things and supplier (*rāziq*) of life, come and abide among us and purify us of all defilement, and save, o Good One, to [sic!] our souls. *And you say three times* (*mirār*) Holy is God, holy is the mighty one, holy is the one that does not die, have mercy on us *with three prostrations* (*maṭānīyāt*) if it is Alleluia // [2r] (Fig. 4), *and you say,* Glory to the Father and the Son and the Holy Spirit

Tab. 1: Beginning of Midnight Office, comparison (continued).

AD (Dabbās)	MK (Karma)
Alleluia,[38] *and you say* Glory to the Father and the Son and the Holy Spirit, from now and to all times and to[39] the age of the ages Amen. *O holy Trinity, have mercy on us, O Lord, forgive our sins, o Master, turn away from our wickedness, o holy one, visit (ittali') and heal our illnesses for the sake of your name. And you say three times (mirār)* O Lord, have mercy *Duksā kā nīn* Our Father (*Abūnā* !)[40] who are in the heavens, may your name be sanctified, may your kingdom come (*tātī*)[41], may your will be (*takūn*)[42], as in the heaven, thus upon[43] the earth, Give us (*a'tī-nā* !)[44] our substantial (*jawharī*) bread sufficient for our day, and forgive us our debts and our sins, as we forgive him who has done evil to us, and do not make us enter into the temptations (*al-tajārīb* !),[45] but deliver us (*najjī-nā* !)[46] from the evil one Amen. *And the priest says* Ὅτι σοῦ ἐστὶν *and you say twelve times (sawt)* // [3] O Lord, have mercy *Duksā kā nīn and three times (mirār)* Come let us prostrate and bow down to Christ our King and our God,	from now and to[47] all times and to the age of the ages Amen. *And you say,* O holy Trinity, have mercy on us. O Lord, forgive our sins. O Master, turn away from our wickedness. O holy one, visit (*ittali'*) and heal our illnesses for the sake of your name. *And you say three times* Kīriyālaysun [sic] *Duksā kā nīn and you say* Our Father (*Abūnā* !) who are in the heavens, may your name be sanctified may your kingdom come (*tātī*),[48] may your will be (*takūn*), as in the heaven, thus upon[49] the earth. Give us (*a'tī-nā* !)[50] our substantial (*jawharī*) bread sufficient for our day. And forgive us our debts and our sins. As we forgive him who has done evil to us. And do not make us enter into the temptations (*al-tajārīb* !). But deliver us (*najjī-nā* !) from the evil one. *And the priest says* Ὅτι [sic] *σοῦ and twelve times (sawt)* Kīriyālaysun *and you say Duksā kā nīn and three times (mirār)* Come let us prostrate and bow down to Christ our King and our God *three prostrations (matānīyāt).*

This initial comparison shows the identity of the texts, including unusual readings such as the addition of "region" (*wa-suq'*), and infrequently used plurals such as *mirār* in both texts instead of the more frequent form *marrāt*. Even the rubrics are identical, as is the superscription mentioning the author of the translation. The only variants worthy of note are the plural "our fathers", rendered in MK by *abahāti-nā* and in AD by *ābāyi-nā* (the latter with the customary omission

38 I.e., a fast day when "Alleluia" is sung at Matins instead of "God is the Lord".
39 *Ilá* written with the two diacritical points below the *alif maqsūra*.
40 Dialectal error (as in Sin. Ar. 232); the vocative should be *abā-nā*.
41 Kingdom (*malakūt*) is m., so the verb should be 3rd p. m. s. optative: *ya'ti*. Here it is 3rd p. f. s. indicative.
42 *Takūn*: indicative form instead of the optative *takun*.

of *hamza* in Christian texts), and the ungrammatical *li-nufūsi-nā* in MK corrected in AD to *nufūsa-nā*. Both texts give the incipit to the ecphonesis of the Lord's Prayer in Greek. MK has only the first two words, AD the first three. In the Lord's Prayer, the optatives or imperatives are nearly always rendered by the indicative. Both have the ungrammatical plural *al-tajārīb*. MK uses a little more Greek, transliterated into Arabic when it is not the priest's part.

These close similarities continue throughout the texts, so that we can state that AD is a faithful though very slightly revised re-edition of MK.

The initial prayers in Sin. Ar. 232 are found several times, and are given in full at the beginning of the Horologion (beginning of Matins):[51]

f. 206r is blank.

The Horologion starts on fol. 206v:

We write the Prayers of the Horologion of the Night and the Day
>X< Bless, O Lord
>X< Matins he says >X< three times[52] Holy God, Holy Mighty, Holy one who does not die, have mercy on us. *And he says* Glory to the Father and to the Son and to the Spirit of Holiness,[53] now and all times and to the age[54] of the ages. Amen. *And he says* O holy Trinity have mercy

---

43 *'alá*: see note 13.

44 Indicative instead of the imperative *a'ṭi-nā*.

45 *al-tajārīb*, ungrammatical plural form (instead of *al-tajārib*) of *tajriba*, temptation. The same is found in Sin. Ar. 232.

46 The imperative should be *najji-nā*.

47 *Ilā* written with the two diacritical points below the *alif maqṣūra*. No diacritical points at this point in AD, but they are present in AD in the next *ilā* but not it MK.

48 Kingdom (*malakūt*) is m., so the verb should be 3rd p. m. s. optative: *ya'ti*. Here it is 3rd p. f. s. indicative.

49 *'alā*: without diacritical points.

50 Correct imperative form *a'ṭi-nā*, hypercorrected to the indicative (dialectal imperative) form *a'ṭī-nā* in AD.

51 This section has been published in Wade, "The Enigmatic Horologion", p. 291.

52 *T[h]ilt[h]ah marrāt: tiltah marrāt* tor *thulāth marrāt* – the numbers are dialectal and the letter *thā* is systematically replaced dialectically by *tā*.

53 Gabriele Winkler kindly pointed out to me in her personal e-mail of 26 June 2018 that " 'Spirit of Holiness', is not a dialectal form for 'Holy Spirit', [...] but refers to the earliest Syriac form.' This apparently pre-Nicene (or pre-Constantinople I) Syriac formula is *rūḥā d-qudšā*.

54 *Sic*, usual form in Arab Orthodox liturgical texts.

on us,[55] forgive our sins, O Master, turn away from our iniquities,[56] O Holy One, visit[57] and heal our infirmities for the sake of[58] your name.

And he says Lord have mercy three times.

[207r] *And he says* Glory to the Father and to the Son and to the Spirit of Holiness, now and all times and to the age of the ages. Amen .... >< Our Father[59] who are in the heavens, may your name be sanctified, may your kingdom come,[60] may your will come about[61] as in the heaven, so on the earth.[62] Give us this day our daily bread[63] and forgive our transgressions as we also to him who did evil to us,[64] and do not cause us to enter into the temptations,[65] but deliver us from the evil one[66] >X<

It should be observed that there is no initial blessing other than "Bless, Master". There is no ecphonesis after the Lord's Prayer; these could be a sign of individual recitation rather than communal celebration.

The translation of "Glory to the Father [...] both now [...]" shows differences from MK/AD:

Sinai Arabic 232: *Al-majd li-l-ab wa-l-ibn wa-rūḥ al-qudus al-'ān wa-kull awān wa-ilá* [with two diacritical points] *dahr al-dāhirīn. Āmīn.*

MK & AD: *Al-majd li-l-ab wa-l-ibn wa-l-rūḥ al-qudus min al-'ān wa-ilá* (with two diacritical points) *kull awān wa-ilá* (with no diacritical points in MK but 2 in AD) *dahr al-dāhirīn. Āmīn.*

---

55 No "o Lord", which one would expect, probably a scribal omission.
56 SA232: *ātāmi-nā* (for *āthāmi-nā*); MK and AD: *sayyāti-nā*.
57 *iftaqid* ("lose, miss" but also: "inspect, examine"): MK/AD: *iṭṭali'*.
58 As is frequently the case in medieval, especially Christian, Arabic and even occasionally in Karma and Dabbās, *minajli* written all as one word (on account of the elimination of the *hamza*) instead of the more correct *min ajli*.
59 Dialectal error in Arabic: *yā abū-nā* ("o" + nominative), instead of the more correct accusative form *abā-nā* for the vocative. The same in MK and AD.
60 *Yātī* with no diacritical points under the first letter, permitting the reading *y*, which would be correct, rather than the incorrect *t* in MK and AD. The form is indicative rather than optative, as in MK and AD.
61 *takūn irādatu-ka*: the same indicative instead of optative as in MK and AD, but *irādatu-ka* (your will) instead of *mashī'atu-ka* (*mashiyatu-ka*), your will, as in MK/AD.
62 *mitl* [*mithl*] *mā fī al-samā*['] *wa-'alá* (with 2 dots) *al-arḍ.* MK/AD: *kamā fī al-samā*['] *kadhālika 'alá al-arḍ.*
63 *khubza-nā kafāfa-nā a'ṭi-nā* [sic] *al-yawm.* MK/AD: *a'ṭī-nā khubza-nā al-jawharī kafāt yawmi-nā.*
64 *wa-ṣfaḥ la-nā zallāti-nā mitlamā* [*mithla mā*] *wa-naḥnu li-man asā*['a] *ilay-nā.* MK/AD: *wa-ghfir la-nā dunūba-nā* [*dhunūba-nā*] *wa-khaṭāyā-nā kamā naghfir naḥnu li-man asā*['a] *ilay-nā.*
65 *al-tajārīb*, ungrammatical plural form (instead of *al-tajārib*) of *tajriba*, temptation. The same in MK and AD.
66 This last phrase is identical in SA232/MK/AD.

Comparison of the initial prayers (without "O heavenly King") shows that AD follows MK, with only very slight variations, but not SA232.

The prayer (or hymn) "O heavenly King" is found in Sinai Arabic 232 the place of the kontakion, after "Our Father" in the Third Hour:

[f. 240r]
And he says: Holy God and what follows it. *And he says:*
O heavenly King and the Comforter, the Spirit of truth, present in every place and every region,[67] filling everything, treasury of good things and provider (*rāziq*) of life, come and dwell in us and purify us from all filth, o good one, and save our souls.[68] *Dukṣā.*

A comparison of this version with MK/AD shows that the texts are identical. It appears that this version was already known and was incorporated into MK's version, whereas Karma (or a version he employed) revised all the other initial prayers, incorporating many hypercorrections.

3. The Psalms

A comparison of Psalm 50 LXX in MK and AD shows it is the same version. AD has introduced a hypercorrection in the verse "for I know my transgressions". MK actually writes the nunation in *li'annī 'ārifun bi-āthāmī*, whereas AD has *li'annī 'ārifā* (the *–ā* indicating an ungrammatical accusative nunation *-an!*) *bi-āthāmī*. Psalm 50 LXX is written out in full in the psalter that constitutes the first part of Sinai Arabic 232 and again during Matins on f. 212v. Although many expressions are the same, this is a different translation. Almost every verse shows differences, both major and minor. Further examination of the psalms in MK and AD has shown the versions are identical (there is another hypercorrection in AD in Psalm 118 LXX, *ṭūbā-hum alladhīna lā 'aybā* (!) *fī ṭarīqi-him*).

---

67 *suq'* in error for *ṣuq'* (!), but the same variant is found in AD and MK. The scribe of SA232 seems to have had a problem with this root, *ṣq'*, which has two main semantic fields, 'cold' and 'region'. In the canticle of the three children in Matins (fol. 218v), the scribe has written *al-saqī'* instead of *al-ṣaqī'* ("freezing"). It is true that if the scribe was writing from dictation, the sounds *s* and *ṣ* are similar, especially if the scribe is not familiar with these words.
68 The stichera of the Holy Spirit from the office of Pentecost is well known, with the variant also found in MK and AD. Cf. *Hōrologion to Mega*, Ekdosis 11, 1993, p. 4.

4. Other Important Texts

This brief presentation cannot give a full account of these three versions. However, it will be interesting to conclude with two important texts from Vespers.

4.1 The Vesperal Hymn Φῶς Ἱλαρόν

Sinai Arabic 232, f. 279v:

> *and he says* O Gladsome Light, the glory of the heavenly Father who does not die, the holy, good Jesus Christ! When comes the setting of the sun, let us see the light of the evening. We praise the Father and the Son and the Spirit of holiness, God, who is worthy at all times to be praised by just voices, O Son of God, giver of lasting life, on account of you the world glorifies you.[69]

MK f. 68v (Fig. 5) = AD p. II.121.
The text is quite different: *Ayyuhā al-nūr al-bahī al-mumajjad al-quddūs al-āb alladhī lā yamūt al-samāwī, ayyuhā al-quddūs al-maghbūṭ Yasūʿ al-Masīḥ*, "O Gladsome Light, the Father who does not die, the heavenly one; O holy, beatific Jesus Christ!"

This translation wrongly ascribes the initial vocative to the Father, whereas in the Greek original it is addressed to Christ and the Father is in the genitive. Here Sinai Arabic 232 is closer to the Greek: *Ayyuhā al-ḍaw[ʾ] al-bahī al-quddūs, majd al-ab al-samāwī alladhī lā yamūt, al-quddūs, al-ṭayyib Yasūʿ al-Masīḥ*.

4.2 The Vesperal Prayer: Make Us Worthy, O Lord

MK p. 138 = AD p. II.122 Once again, comparison shows that MK and AD are identical (including grammatical errors such as *takūn* for *takun*) and Sinai Arabic 232 (f. 280v) presents many differences.

---

[69] Cf. *Hōrologion to Mega*, p.150. This is the classic Vespers hymn *Phōs Hilaron*. Note the numerous liberties in the Arabic translation: "holy" refers to "light", rather than to "glory"; "comes" refers to the setting of the sun rather than to "us"; and the Greek says literally: "having come to the setting of the sun [and] having seen the light of the evening, we sing the Father, the Son and the Holy Spirit, God. You are worthy in all times to be sung by holy voices, O Son of God, giver of life; for this, the world glorifies you". The present state of research appears to show there is no "received" Arabic text of this hymn.

Tab. 2: English translation of MK/AD and Sinai Arabic 232.

Make us able, O Lord, for this evening. And without sin keep us. You are blessed, O Lord, the God of our fathers, and praised and glorified is your name for ever, amen. May, O Lord, your mercy be[70] upon us as we have hoped in you. Blessed are you, O Lord,[71] teach me your commandments. Blessed are you, O master, make me understand your statutes. Blessed are you, O holy one, illumine us by your justice. O Lord, your mercy is forever, and do not ignore the works of your hands. To you appertains glory, to you behooves praise, to you belongs honor and worship, O Father and the Son and the Holy Spirit, from now and to all times and to the age of the ages, amen.	Make us able, O Lord, in this evening to keep ourselves not sinning, because you are blessed, O Lord, the God of our fathers, and praised and glorified is your name for ever, amen. May, O Lord, your mercy be upon us as we have hoped in you. You have been blessed, O Lord, teach me your statutes. You have been blessed, you O master, enlighten me by your statutes. Blessed are you, O holy one, illumine me by your statutes. O Lord, your mercy is lasting for ever, O Lord, do not reject the works of your hands. To you behooves praise, to you behoves lauding, to you belongs rightly glory, to the Father and the Son and the Spirit of holiness, now and at all times and to the age of the ages, amen.[72]

As stated at the outset, the purpose of this presentation has been to compare the Arabic versions of the Horologia of MK, AD and Sinai Arabic 232. Our initial examination has shown that AD depends directly on MK, with only very slight revisions, whereas Sinai Arabic 232 has in general a completely different text, apart from the fact that it corresponds to an earlier stage of the rite with many Alexandrian elements. However, we have discovered that the prayer (hymn) "O heavenly King" to the Holy Spirit is identical in all three versions, including one surprising variant (*wa-ṣuqʿ*).

5. Other Sections of These Texts

We should point out that all three versions include other sections that require detailed study. As indicated above, Sinai Arabic 232 includes a Psalter, a partial lectionary, the Horologion and an extensive supplement containing prayers. The section after the Psalter and the final supplement in particular, which contains a

---

70 *Takūn* (indicative) instead of *takun* (optative).
71 "o Lord" has been added above the line following the scribe's omission in MK.
72 Cf. *Hōrologion to Mega*, p.153.

great deal of liturgical material, still await translation and analysis. These form part of my future projects.

In MK, a detailed Menologion follows the Horologion, beginning on p. 178, giving liturgical instructions and troparia and kontakia for every day. Then, on p. 481 we have the "service" of the Akathistos hymn to the Mother of God. On p. 513 we have the Canon to the Lord Jesus Christ. The Paraclisis Canon to the Mother of God begins on p. 523. On p. 538 we have the Canon of Supplication to the Guardian Angel. On p. 553 we find the Canon to be sung to the Heavenly Powers. On p. 563 we have the Order to be recited before receiving Communion, continuing on p. 591 with the Thanksgiving Prayers after Communion.

In AD, on p. II.169 we have the Menologion in two columns, Greek and Arabic. On p. II.482 we have a section of Troparia and Kontakia of the Triodion, in two columns, Greek and Arabic, and then the Paschal Hours, starting on p. II.511, also bilingual, continuing through the Pentecostarion. These are followed on p. II.529 by the bilingual troparia of the resurrection, and on p. II.545 by the troparia for the dead. On p. II.550 we have the theotokia for the whole year, in Arabic only, and then, on p. II.572 the weekday troparia. On p. II.578 we have the bilingual order of the Akathistos Hymn to the Mother of God, although the Hymn itself is given only in Arabic. On p. II. 608 we have the Canon to "Sweet Jesus". On p. II.616 we have the bilingual Paraclisis canon to the Mother of God (the Gospel is given in Arabic only on p. II.629). There follows the Canon of Supplication to the Guardian Angel, in Arabic, starting on p. II.640 and that to the Heavenly Powers, in Arabic on p. II.652. The Order of Communion begins, in Arabic, on p. II.560, continuing with the Thanksgiving Prayers on p. II.687. The Paschalia are set forth on pp. II.690-731. The final page, II.732 is the extensive colophon, in which the editor asked forgiveness for any shortcomings and errors because "I am foreign to the Arabic language". It was printed "in Bucharest in Ungro-Wallachia by Antim the priest-monk, Georgian by origin, in June 1702".

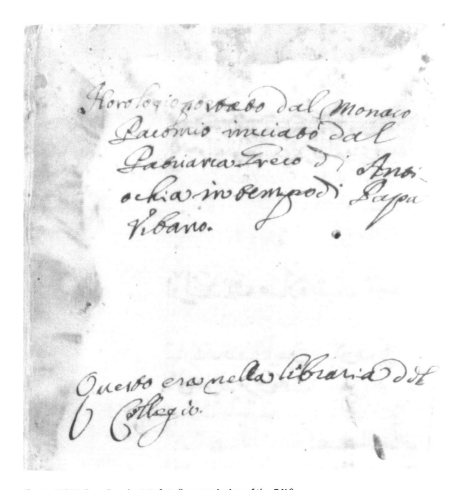

Fig. 1: MS Vatican Borgia 178, f. 1r (by permission of the BAV).

بسم الله الواحد الأبدي الازلي الذي مبدي وبه نستعين

كتاب ورتب الوجعون الصلوات

المفروضة في السبعة اوقات

اخرجه من الرومي بكر ويعب

الحقير ملاتيوس مطران حلب

اول ذلك صلاة نصف الليل

يبدا الكاهن قائلاً

تبارك الله الاهنا كل حين من الان والى كل اوات

والى دهر الداهرين امين وادم لمكن ما من يقول

بصلوات بهاتنا القديسين ايها الرب يسوع المسيح

الاها ارحمنا امين ويقول المجدلك يا الاها المجدلك

فقط ويقول ايها الملك السماوي المعزي روح الحق

الحاضر في كل مكان وصفع المالي الكل كنز الصالحا

ورازق الحياه هلم واسكن فينا وطهرنا من كل دنس

وخلص ايها الصالح لنفوسنا ويقول ثلاثا قدوس الله

قدوس القوي قدوس الذي لا يموت ارحمنا ثلاث مطانا

اد١

Fig. 2: MS Vatican Borgia 178, f. 1v (by permission of the BAV).

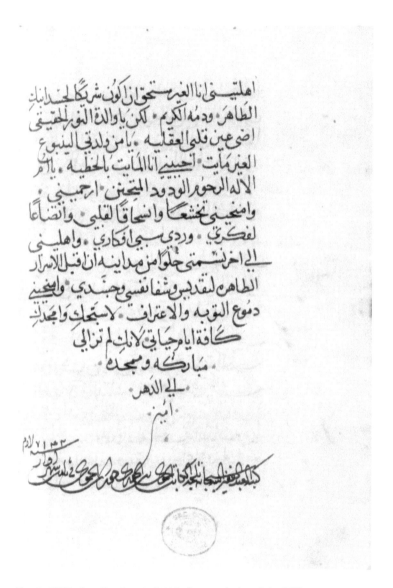

Fig. 3: MS Vatican Borgia 178, f. 298v (by permission of the BAV).

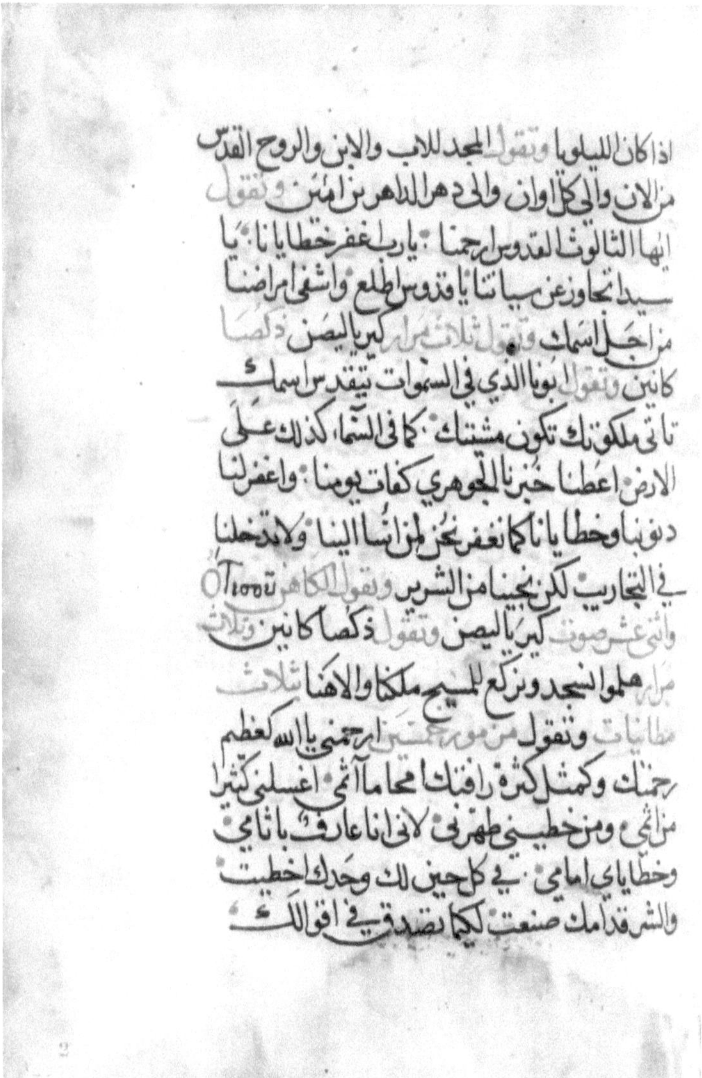

اذا كان الليلو يا وتقول المجد للاب والابن والروح القدس
من الان والى كل اوان والى دهر الداهرين امين وتقول
ايها الثالوث المدوس ارحمنا · يا رب اغفر خطايانا · يا
سيدنا تجاوز عن سياتنا يا قدوس اطلع واشفى امراضنا
من اجل اسمك وتقول ثلاث مرار كير باليصن ذلك ا
كائنين وتقول ابو يا الذي في السموات ليتقدس اسمك
تاتي ملكوتك تكون مشيتك · كما في السما، كذلك على
الارض اعطنا خبزنا الجوهري كفاف يومنا · واغفر لنا
ذنو بنا وخطايانا كما نغفر نحن لمن اسا الينا ولا تدخلنا
في التجارب لكن نجينا من الشرير وتقول الكاهن
وانتى عشرى صوف كير باليصن وتقول ذكصا كائنين و
مرار هلموا نسجد ونركع للمسيح ملكنا والاهنا ثلاث
طانيات وتقول من موسى ارحمنى يا الله كعظم
رحمتك وكمثل كثرة رافتك امحا ما آثمى اغسلنى كثيرا
من اثمى ومن خطيتى طهرنى لانى انا عارف باثامى
وخطاياى امامى · في كل حين لك وحدك اخطيت
والشر قدامك صنعت لكيما تصدق في اقوالك

Fig. 4: MS Vatican Borgia 178, f. 2r (by permission of the BAV).

لا نرى من الرب بالجمه · ومنه النجاه الكثير · وهو ينجي الابـ
من كل ثامه سبح الرب يا جميع الامم وامدحوه
يا سائر الشعوب لان قد قويته رحمته علينا وحق الرب
يدوم الى الدهر · ذكصاكابين ايها النور الابهى المجد
القدوس الاب الذي لا يموت السماوي · ايها القدوس
المنبوط يسوع المسيح · حين ناتي عند غروب الشمس
نظر بوز للسا · وتسبح الاب والابن والروح
القدس الا له المسجى في سائر الاوقات · ان ترى
باصوات بات · يا ابن السا المعطي للحياه الذي ترى
اجلك العالم لك يمجد وتقول البر ككمن

ليلة الاحد

الرب قد ملك · والجمال لبس لبس الرب القوه وتمنطق
بها سيبقى لانه ثبت المسكونه ليلا تتزعزع ·

ليلة الاثنين

ها منذا الان باركوا الرب يا كافة عبيد الرب سبحن
الواقفون في بيت الرب · وفي ديار بيت الاهنا ·

ليلة الثلاثا

الرب

Fig. 5: MS Vatican Borgia 178, f. 68v (by permission of the BAV).

Bibliography

Abraṣ, Mīkhā'īl. "Tārīkh al-Afkhūlūjiyūn al-kabīr al-maṭbū' fī al-Quds al-'ām 1865". *Al-Masarra*, 84, 1998, p. 534–548; 1094–1107.

Acta Sacrae Congregationis (1622–1938) in 311 volumes. Scritture Originali riferite nelle Congregazioni Generali (SOCG), Vol. 180, fols 35v, 39r and 40r, 41r, 42r and 43r, 75r, 95r, 208r, Vol. 395, fols 295r and 296v.

Al-'Ahd al-jadīd, ed. by Thomas Erpenius. Leiden: Typographia Erpeniana Linguarum Orientalium, 1616.

[al-Bāshā], Qusṭanṭīn (ed.), "Rasā'il qadīma muhimma li-l-baṭriyark al-Anṭākī Afthīmiyūs Karma al-Ḥamawī. *Al-Risāla al-mukhalliṣīya*, 5, 1938, p. 312–325.

Bottini, Giovanni-Claudio. "Tommaso Obicini [1585–1632] Custos of the Holy Land and Orientalist". In Anthony O'Mahony et al. (eds.), *The Christian Heritage in the Holy Land*. London: Scorpion Cavendish, 1995, p. 97–101.

Congregatio de Propaganda Fide, Acta Sacrae Congregationis (1622–1938) in 311 volumes (archives), Rome.

Darblade, Jean-Baptiste. "L'Euchologe arabe melkite de Kyr Mélèce Karmî". *Proche-Orient Chrétien*, 6, 1956, p. 29–36.

Gemayel, Nasser. *Les échanges culturels entre les Maronites et l'Europe*, vol. 1. Beirut: Impr. Y. et Ph. Gemayel, 1984.

Graf, Georg. *Geschichte der christlichen arabischen Literatur*, vol. 4. Vatican City: Biblioteca Apostolica Vaticana, 195l.

Horologion, ed. by Athanasios Dabbās, Aleppo, 1706.

Horologion (in Arabic), MS Sinai Arabic 232 (13th c.), Library of the Monastery of Saint Catherine, Sinai. The manuscript can be consulted at https://www.loc.gov/item/0027938457A-ms/ of the Library of Congress (photographs made in 1950).

Hōrologion to Mega, Ekdosis 11. Athens: Ekdosis tēs Apostolikēs Diakonias tēs Ekklēsias tēs Hellados, 1993.

Idlibī, Nāwufīṭūs (Neophytos Edelby). *Asāqifat al-Rūm al-Malikīyīn bi-Ḥalab fī al-'aṣr al-ḥadīth*. Aleppo: Maṭba'at al-Iḥsān, 1983.

Jabbūr, Makāriys, Ziyād Tawfīq al-Khūrī. *Wathā'iq hāmma fī khidmat kanīsati-nā al-Anṭākīya*. Beirut: Ta'āwunīyat al-Nūr, 2000.

al-Jūmayyil, Nāṣir. "Jadwal bi-asmā' talāmidhat al-madrasa al-mārūnīya". In *al-Manāra*, 25/l–2, 1984, p. 91–112.

Karma, Meletios. Arabic Horologion of Meletios Karma copied by his brother Thalja, 1621. MS Vatican Borgia 178, Biblioteca Apostolica Vaticana.

Karma, Meletios, Letter (1623) to the College of Cardinals of Propaganda Fide, 4.10.1623, Archivio storico della Congregazione per l'evangelizzazione dei popoli o "de Propaganda Fide", Rome, Scritture Originali riferite nelle Congregazioni Generali (SOCG): *Lettere in Diverse Lingue dall'anno 1622 a 1629*, vol. 181, fol. 36v.

Karma, Meletios, Letter to Cardinal (Gaspare) Borgia, mid October 1631 (see: Qusṭanṭīn [al-Bāshā] [Ed.], "Rasā'il qadīma muhimma li-l-baṭriyark al-Anṭākī Afthīmiyūs Karma al-Ḥamawī". In *al-Risāla al-mukhalliṣīya* 5 [1938], p. 315–316.

Karma, Meletios. *Bayān ṭab' al-kutub: kayfa yakūn* (Memorandum to the Pope and to the Cardinals of the Propaganda Fide, ca. May 1634), Rome, Archivio storico della congregazione per l'evangelizzazione dei popoli o 'de propaganda Fide', Lettere di lingua straniera dall'Anno l63l sino al 1645, vol. 180, fol. 4l.

Karma, Thalja. Letter to Pope Urban XIII (ca. 1635).

Kilzī, Lāwandiyūs (ed.). "Ḥayāt al-baṭriyark Aftīmiyūs Karma al-Anṭākī al-Ḥamawī bi-qalam tilmīdhi-hi al-baṭriyark Makāriyūs al-Ḥalabī". *al-Masarra* 4, 1913, p. 41–47, 81–89, 135–144.

Nasrallah, Joseph. *Histoire du mouvement littéraire dans l'Église Melchite du Vᵉ au XXᵉ siècle*, vol. IV/I. Louvain: Peeters, 1979.

Nassif, Charbel. *L'euchologe melkite depuis Malatios Karmé (†1635) jusqu'à nos jours: Les enjeux des évolutions d'un livre liturgique*. Unpublished Ph.D. thesis, Institut Catholique de Paris: Paris, 2017.

Nassif, Charbel. "Autour de l'Euchologe melkite de Malatios Karmé († 1635)". *Proche-Orient Chrétien*, 68, 2018, p. 46–61.

Raphael, Pierre. *Le rôle du Collège Maronite Romain dans l'orientalisme aux XVIIᵉ et XVIIIᵉ siècles*. Beirut: Université Saint Joseph, 1950.

al-Samarrānī, Fīlīb. "Talāmidhat Qubrus fī al-madrasa al-mārūnīya". *al-Manāra* 25/1–2, 1984, p. 187–202.

Wade, Andrew. "L'Horologion du Sinaï Arabe 232 (13ème s.), témoin d'une fusion pluriculturelle". In André Lossky, Goran Sekulovski (eds.), *Traditions recomposées : liturgie et doctrine en harmonie ou en tension, 63ᵉ Semaine d'études liturgiques, Paris, Institut Saint-Serge, 21–24 juin 2016*. Münster: Aschendorff Verlag, 2017, p. 111–124.

Wade, Andrew. "Individual Prayer in the Monastic Cell between Alexandria and Mount Sinai in the 13th Century: the Hours in Sin. Ar. 232". In André Lossky, Goran Sekulovski, Thomas Pott (eds.), *Liturgie et religiosité. 64ᵉ Semaine d'études liturgiques, Paris, Institut Saint-Serge, juin 2017*. Münster: Aschendorff Verlag, 2017, p. 353–374.

Wade, Andrew. "The Enigmatic Horologion Contained in Sinai Ar. 232". In Lüstraeten, Martin, Brian Butcher, Steven Hawkes-Teeples (eds.), *LET US BE ATTENTIVE! Proceedings of the Seventh International Congress of the Society of Oriental Liturgy*. Münster: Aschendorff Verlag, 2020, p. 285–305.

Wade, Andrew. "Byzantinised or Alexandrianised – or Both? Vespers in the 13th c. Melkite Alexandrian Arabic Horologion Sinai Arabic 232", *MDPI Religions*, 13/7, 2022, 607, p. 1–11 (https://doi.org/10.3390/rel13070607, 2022).

Walbiner, Carsten-Michael, " 'Und um Jesu Willen, schickt sie nicht ungebunden!' Die Bemühungen des Meletius Karma (1512–1635) um den Druck arabischer Bücher in Rom". In Rifaat Ebied, Herman Teule (eds.), *Studies on the Christian Arabic Heritage in Honour of Father Prof. Dr. Samir Khalil Samir S.I. at the Occasion of his Sixty-Fifth Birthday*. Louvain/Paris/Dudley: Peeters, 2004, p. 163–175.

Yulia Petrova

The Prefaces of the Christian Arabic Books Printed in Wallachia and Syria in the Early 18th Century

Dedications, prefaces, and afterwords are the constituent book elements established by the publishing tradition. They are conceived to present the book to a certain circle of readers and have specific functions. The dedication is characterized by an expression of gratitude to the persons who contributed to the publication of the book, the preface prepares the readers for perception of the book, focusing on its main idea and practical purpose and the afterword gives additional comments on the text and the history of its publication. At the initial stage of the development of printing, the genre features of these component parts of the book were not yet clearly formed.[1]

A separate and very numerous group among the texts included in early Eastern European editions is represented by prefaces. Usually, participants in and eyewitnesses of the printing process tell about the emergence of a particular printing house, mention the details of the work accompanying the publication of the book (e.g., translation of the text or its revision based on the original), list the names of participants in the printing process, give instructions to the readers on using the book, etc.

The study of the constituent elements of the first books printed by the Arab Christians makes it possible to trace the process of their editorial activity, the formation of book design, the development of structural and content features of prefaces and afterwords, their style and genre and the language peculiarities of a certain epoch and environment. All this makes these texts important objects for a separate study covering various aspects of them.

---

1 O. Kurhanova, "Prysviaty, peredmovy ta pisliamovy do ukraïns'kykh kyrylychnykh starodrukiv: problemy ta perspektyvy naukovo-bibliohrafichnoho obliku", *Bibliotechnyĭ Merkuriĭ*, 2(22), 2019, p. 94.

This research is part of a project that has received funding from the European Research Council (ERC) under the European Union's Horizon 2020 research and innovation programme (grant agreement No 883219-AdG-2019 – Project TYPARABIC).

∂ Open Access. © 2024, the author(s), published by De Gruyter. [CC BY-NC-ND] This work is licensed under the Creative Commons Attribution-NonCommercial-NoDerivatives 4.0 International License. https://doi.org/10.1515/9783111060392-012

1. Object of this Study

As is known, book printing emerged among Christian Arabs due to cooperation between the state and Church officials of the Danubian principalities – Wallachia and Moldavia – and the Christian East. In March 1700, the former patriarch of Antioch, at that time the metropolitan of Aleppo Athanasios III (Dabbās), having arrived at the court of the prominent Orthodox benefactor, the prince of Wallachia Constantin Brâncoveanu, asked him to help print liturgical books for the Church of Antioch, which was in a difficult situation. The Arabic letters were made by Antim, hegumen of Snagov Monastery, and later metropolitan of Ungrovlahia, a Georgian by origin (known in the Orthodox Church as the Hieromartyr Antim the Iberian, commemorated on September 27). Soon, the first two editions with parallel texts in Greek and Arabic were published: in 1701, a Liturgikon (Book of Divine Services) was printed in the Snagov monastery near Bucharest, and in 1702, a Horologion (Book of Hours) was printed in Bucharest.[2] Returning to Aleppo in 1705, Athanasios set up in his metropolitan residence the first printing press in the Middle East that used the Arabic script. It existed until 1711 and issued ten titles in Arabic, mostly without parallel Greek texts. Some of them were reprinted, and the total number of editions of the Aleppo printing press reached twelve books, including reprints. The list of the titles in an abridged form can be presented as follows:

1. Psalter (1706)
2. Tetraevangelion (book of the Four Gospels) (1706)
3. Lectionary (1706)
4. Chosen Pearls from the Homilies of St. John Chrysostom (1707)
5. Epistle book (1707)
6. Tetraevangelion sponsored by Ivan Mazepa (1708) – reprint of the 1706 edition
7. Tetraevangelion sponsored by Daniel Apostol (1708) – reprint of the 1706 edition
8. Prophetologion (1708)
9. Psalter (1709) – reprint of the 1706 edition
10. Homilies of Patriarch Athanasios of Jerusalem (1711)
11. Octoechos (1711)
12. Brief Epistle on Repentance and Confession (1711).[3]

---

[2] For details on these books see P. Chițulescu (ed.), *Antim Ivireanul: opera tipografică*, Bucharest, 2016, p. 88–96, 106–110.

[3] For details on the list of these books, see the recent and the most comprehensive study: I. Feodorov, *Arabic Printing for the Christians in Ottoman Lands. The East-European Connection*, Berlin/Boston, 2023, p. 255–285.

At the time of preparing this paper, nine editions from this list are available to us (either copies of books from the Library of the Romanian Academy or scanned texts of the original editions), in addition to copies of both books published in Wallachia – i.e., eleven books out of the 14 editions published by Athanasios Dabbās. By genre, these are primarily liturgical books (12 titles from the general list); there are two collections of homilies and one didactic treatise as well.

2. Prefaces as a Historical Source

The main source for the history of the emergence and development of Arabic printing is the prefaces of the first printed books. From a historical point of view, the most valuable are the prefaces in the first three editions that were published by the efforts of Athanasios Dabbās – the Liturgikon (1701), the Horologion (1702), and the Psalter (1706). Each of these editions has two prefaces, the first of which is addressed to the benefactor, Constantin Brâncoveanu, and the second– to the clergy of the Church of Antioch. These texts are signed by Dabbās, who used to sign his name in Arabic as "Athanasios, by the mercy of the Most High God, previously patriarch of Antioch and All the East" (*Athanāsiyūs bi-raḥmat Allāh ta'ālá al-baṭriyark al-Anṭākī wa-sā'ir al-Mashriq sābiqan*). However, the second preface in the Psalter is not signed by Dabbās, and his words are introduced by another person (this method is typical for most prefaces of the further editions). In the first two books, both prefaces are written in Arabic and Greek. The title page is presented only in Arabic, although both books have a dedication in Greek addressed to Brâncoveanu and signed by his court physician Ioannes Comnenos.

In terms of structure, content and style, the prefaces in the mentioned three editions are noticeably different from the rest of the accompanying texts in the books printed by Dabbās. In the first three editions, his authorship is also clearly observable (the exception is the second preface of the Psalter, written in a quite different style). Obviously, this is explained by the fact that in Wallachia Dabbās had to supervise the printing process and compose the prefaces personally. There were no connoisseurs of Arabic either among his attendants or among the locals, as he himself testifies in the second preface of the Liturgikon: "... and our Modesty made efforts in conducting and supervising the work, as the printers did not know Arabic" (*wa-bi-ijtihād ḥaqārati-nā wa-mushārafati-nā wa-muwāḍabati-nā*[4] *li-l-'amal li-ajl 'adam ma'rifat al-ṣunnā' bi-l-lugha al 'arabīya*). Unlike Aleppo, there was no assistant in Wallachia to act as a proofreader of the Arabic text.

---

4 Corr., *muwāẓabati-nā*.

This is confirmed by the fact that in the prefaces of both Wallachian books, the number of obvious misprints (not to be confused with the orthographic features of Middle Arabic) is noticeably higher than in the rest of Dabbās's editions. This can be presented as follows:

Tab. 1: Misprints in the Prefaces of the Editions of Athanasios Dabbās.

Edition	Number of misprints	Example	Correct variant
Liturgikon (1701)	16	واوحد	وواحد "and one"
Horologion (1702)	10	واتتضرع	واتضرع "and I beg"
Psalter (1706)	2	والانغام	والاغنام "and the sheep"
Tetraevangelion (1706)	2	الكى قدسه	الكلي قدسه "All-Holy"
Lectionary (1706)	2		
Chosen Pearls (1707)	–		
Gospel of Mazepa (1708)	1	اللاهيين	الالهيين "Divine"
Homilies of Athanasios (1711)	2	دوسيتوس	دوسيتيوس "Dositheos"
Octoechos (1711)	–		
Epistle on repentance (1711)	–		

Analyzing the structure and content of the prefaces in the editions of Dabbās, we can distinguish in them the following main components: a) narrative, b) praise, 3) sermon, 4) commentaries on the edition. They are presented in various proportions in different prefaces. As mentioned before, the prefaces of the first three editions are the richest in terms of factual material, which makes them different from the rest of the editions, and this especially applies to the prefaces of the first printed book, the Snagov Liturgikon.

Based on the fact that the narrative implies a sequential presentation of information about certain interconnected events, of great interest is the historical data contained in the prefaces that makes them an important historical source. In this regard, the following thematic lines can be noted in the first three editions of Dabbās:

1) *Acquaintance and cooperation of Athanasios Dabbās with Constantin Brân-coveanu.* In the first preface of the Liturgikon, Dabbās tells about his arrival in Wallachia "from the ends of the earth" (*min aqṣā al-maskūna*) in order to meet the outstanding Christian ruler, about whose virtues he had heard a lot and from whom he wanted to ask for help in establishing Arabic printing. According to the author's testimony, the prince himself, by divine inspiration (*bi-ilhām*

ilāhī), asked about the needs of the Church of Antioch regarding the availability of books, and then the former patriarch dared to ask for financial assistance, to which he immediately received a positive response.

Some publications mention that Athanasios Dabbās became the confessor of Constantin Brâncoveanu.[5] Indeed, at the beginning of the first preface in Liturgikon and Horologion, the Antiochian metropolitan calls his benefactor "our beloved spiritual son" (*waladu-nā al-rūḥānī al-ḥabīb*). However, the same expression is present in his address to the Ukrainian Hetman Ivan Mazepa in the preface of the Four Gospels book published at the latter's expense in 1708. Let us compare both addresses:

الي الجناب العالي المكرم والديوان السامى المفخم، السيد الامجد يواني قسطنطين فاصارافا برنكوفان ويوضة ساير
بلاد انكروفلاخيا المعظم، ولدنا الروحاني الحبيب، نعمة لك من الاله الاب الضابط الكل، وسيدنا يسوع المسيح
والروح القدس المعزي

To the highly revered and the most glorious lord, Ioan Constantin Basarab Brâncoveanu, the great voivod of the whole Ungrovlahia, our beloved spiritual son – grace be to you from God the Father the Almighty, from our Lord Jesus Christ and from the Holy Spirit, the Comforter....

الي حضرة ذي الجناب الرفيع المكرم، والديوان السامي المفخم، الهمام النبيل، والسيد الامجد والشريف الجليل،
جتمان بلاد الروسية الصغرى الزهيه، وريس طغمات العظمة الملوكيه، زابوراغا وحامل الصليب كافالير القديس
المجيد اندراوس الرسول، يواني مازابه، ولدنا الروحاني الحبيب، النعمه لك والبركه من الاله الاب وسيدنا يسوع
المسيح، والروح القدس المعزي

To the highly revered, noble and the most glorious lord, the Hetman of the flourishing Little Rus', voivod of the imperial Zaporozhian host, the holder of the Cross and Chevalier of the Order of the Holy Apostle Andrew, Ivan Mazepa, our beloved spiritual son – grace and blessing be to you from God the Father, from our Lord Jesus Christ and from the Holy Spirit, the Comforter....

The structure of both addresses is very similar: the title is followed by the expression "our beloved spiritual son" and the blessing of the addressee. The Hetman Mazepa never personally met Athanasios Dabbās (the latter received his donations for the needs of the Aleppo printing press through his representative, the protosyncellos Leontios, who traveled to Moscow via the territory of Ukraine).[6] Then why is such an expression used here? The fact is that in Arabic Christian language usage, this expression should be interpreted more broadly, taking into

---

5 Chiṭulescu, *Antim Ivireanul*, p. 19; I. Feodorov, *Arabic Printing for the Christians in Ottoman Lands*, p. 139.
6 K. Panchenko, *Blizhnevostochnoe pravoslavie pod osmanskim vladychestvom: pervye tri stoletiia. 1516–1831*, Moscow, 2012, p. 405.

account the ecclesiastical and diplomatic context. It is about the succession of Eastern European Orthodox Christianity from the Apostolic Churches of the East and about the historical spiritual connection between them. No wonder that in the preface of the Liturgikon addressed to the Wallachian prince, Dabbās reminds him of the historical role of the Church of Antioch as the one where the disciples of Christ were first called Christians (this fact has always had and still has a special significance in the historical memory of the Christians of Syria and Lebanon). In the Greek version of the preface of the Liturgikon, the respective phrase looks a little differently: "the beloved son of our Modesty in the Holy Spirit" (Τὸν ἐν ἁγίῳ Πνεύματι Υἰὸν Ἀγαπητὸν τῆς ἡμῶν Μετριότητος). Therefore, in a narrower sense, this expression may be understood as a hint of prayers for the addressee, and it should not be interpreted literally.

2) *The difficult situation of the Church of Antioch in that period.* In his prefaces, Dabbās reports on the poverty of Arabic-speaking Orthodox Christians who "languish in the humiliation of captivity and oppression" (*al-maḍnūkīn taḥta dhull al-asr wa-l-qahr*). He emphasizes several times the fact that handwritten liturgical books are not available to the clergy, so the priests do not have the opportunity to perform their daily liturgical duties. At the same time, in the first preface of the Liturgikon, the former patriarch reminds that it was in Antioch that the disciples of Christ first began to be called Christians, therefore giving alms to the ancient Apostolic See seems to him to be a completely fair gesture on the part of the generous benefactor.

3) *Technical details and the role of Antim in the initiation of Arabic printing.* From the testimony of Dabbās, we learn that the idea of publishing the liturgical texts in Wallachia in two languages belongs to Constantin Brâncoveanu, who learned from his guest about the functioning of both languages in the practice of the Church of Antioch at that time. By order of the prince, Antim – then hegumen of Snagov Monastery – prepared the Arabic letters. About Antim, who became the first printer for the Arab East, Dabbās mentions once in the second preface of the Liturgikon, calling him "the master of printing, hieromonk father[7] Kyr Antim" (*mu'allim al-ṭab' al-kāhin fī al-mutawaḥḥidīn bābā Kīr Antīmūs*). However, his name is mentioned several times in both Wallachian books, starting with the title page where a signature typical for the books printed by Antim is added under the title: "By the hand of the hieromonk Antim who is originally from Georgia" (*bi-yad al-kāhin fī al-mutawaḥḥidīn Antīmūs al-kurjī al-aṣl*). Also, in both books there is a publisher's afterword by Antim printed only in Arabic (apparently translated

---

7 *Bābā* < Gr. παπάς "priest".

by Dabbās), in which the printer addresses the users of the book (the texts are presented below, in the afterwords section).

As mentioned above, the printing process in Wallachia took place under the supervision of Dabbās himself. Having established a printing press in his metropolitan residence in the city of Aleppo, Dabbās sent a copy of the first printed book – the Psalter – to his benefactor. Unfortunately, the names of his collaborators and assistants in the process of printing in Aleppo are not mentioned in his prefaces.[8]

4) *Practical use of the printed books.* The liturgical books were intended primarily for the clergy of the Church of Antioch, who did not have even handwritten books. However, as Dabbās emphasizes in the first preface of the Liturgikon, given the presence of parallel Greek texts, the books could also be used by the Greek priests (*kahanat abnā' al-rūm*). The Wallachian prince ordered the entire edition of the books to be given for free to the "devout Arab priests" (*li-kahanat abnā' al-'arab al-wari'īn*),[9] "for the salvation of his soul and the remembrance of the souls of his parents" (*'an khalāṣ nafsi-hi wa-li-ajl tidkār wa-niyāḥ nufūs wāliday-hi*). Dabbās obliged the Antiochian priests to commemorate their benefactor at every liturgy together with his family and subordinates and to pray for the strengthening of his throne.

Historical information in the first book, the Liturgikon, occupies at least half of the volume of the prefaces. But in the subsequent books, we can observe a tendency towards its decreasing in favor of other genres, namely praise and sermon. This is especially noticeable starting with the preface of the book of the Four Gospels (1706), where concrete historical information is virtually absent.

---

8 This strange neglect can be compared with the practice of the printing house of the Kyiv Pechersk Lavra. In the old prints of the latter, the persons who worked at the correction of texts were often mentioned and even characterized and the secondary workers engaged in typesetting, printing, production of drawings and engravings were listed (see Kh. Titov, *Materialy dlia istoriï knyzhkovoï spravy na Ukraïni v XVI–XVIII v.v.: vsezbirka peredmov do ukraïns'kykh starodrukiv*, Kyiv, 1924, p. 4).

9 Litt.: "sons of the Arabs", "sons of the Greeks" (ethnonyms were often denoted in this way in Arabic Christian texts of the 17th and 18th centuries). If we turn to such an important source of the 17th century as Paul of Aleppo's *Journal*, it can be seen that he uses the expression *awlād al-rūm* to denote the ethnonym "Greeks". The word *rūm* taken separately in the post-Byzantine era indicated religious identification, i.e., belonging to the Orthodox Church. Apparently, the term *awlād al-rūm* is related to the Ottoman tradition of ethnonyms (Turk. *veled-i rum* "son of the Greeks", *veled-i boğdan* "son of the Moldavians", etc.).

An exception is the book of homilies of the Patriarch Athanasios of Jerusalem (1711). Its preface differs in its content and style from the rest of the Aleppo editions, so it is worthwhile to consider it in detail.

This book contains one preface written by the Patriarch Chrysanthus of Jerusalem (1707–1731) and addressed to "the Orthodox clergy… and all the blessed Arab Christians" (*jamā'at al-iklīrus al-urtūduksīyīn… wa-kāffat al-masīḥīyīn abnā' al-'arab al-mubārakīn*), probably of both Patriarchates of Antioch and Jerusalem. The author tells about his uncle, the previous patriarch of Jerusalem Dositheos II Notaras (1669–1707), who was his tutor and mentor since childhood (*murabbī-nā wa-murshidu-nā mundhu al-ṭufūlīya*). He depicts for the reader the image of an exemplary bishop, a tireless fighter against heresies and enlightener of his flock, whose example inspired him to continue this work. It is in this context that the edition of the book is mentioned, and the patriarch tells about it as follows:

لما مضينا الي المحل الذي ايتمنا عليه وحصلنا في مدينة اورشليم الشريفه ... وجدنا هذا الكتاب الرفيع المحل المشتمل علي اقوال خلاصبه نافعه للنفس، تتلا علي مدار السنه في الحدود والاعياد، وهو منتمي لاتاناسيوس بطريرك اورشليم الذي وان كنا لم نستطيع¹⁰ من ترادف المهمات الزايده واللوازم الضرورية المترادفه علي كرسينا الرسولي انه نفحص عنه متي وفي اي زمان كان، وان نطلع علي كيفية سيرته لكي نوضح ذلك للدين يقفون علي مجموعه هدا، لكننا عرفنا يقينًا من المطلعين علي هده اللغه ضرورية هدا السفر الشريف ونفعه، وخاصة من بطركي مدينة الله العظمي الجليلين الكليين الطوبا اي كير كيرللس المتقلد البطركيه برحمة الله تعالي، وكير اتاناسيوس البطريرك السابق الفايق الغبطه، اخوينا الحبيبين بروح القدس ... بما انهما متعمقان في فقه اللغة العربيه

> When we went to the place where we were appointed and reached the holy city of Jerusalem, … we found this very valuable book that contains salvific words, useful for the soul, that are read throughout the year on Sundays and feast days. They belong to Athanasios, patriarch of Jerusalem. Because of endless responsibilities and many urgent affairs related to our Apostolic See, we could not inquire about him to learn when he lived and about his life, so that we could tell it to those who would read this collection. But we learned for sure from those who know this [Arabic] language about the necessity and benefit of this noble book, namely from Their Beatitudes, the venerable patriarchs of the Great City of God [Antioch], Kyr Cyril, by the mercy of God the current patriarch, and His Beatitude Kyr Athanasios, the former patriarch, our beloved brothers in the Holy Spirit…, profound connoisseurs of Arabic philology.

The preface of the book does not contain a clear indication of the author. As can be seen from the quote above, the Patriarch Chrysanthus of Jerusalem failed to find information about his predecessor whose homilies he presented to the readers. J. Nasrallah attributed these homilies to Athanasius IV (1452–1460),[11]

---

10 *Sic.* Corr., نستطيع.

11 J. Nasrallah, *Histoire du mouvement littéraire dans l'Église melchite du Ve au XXe siècle*, vol. III, tome 2, Louvain/Paris, 1981, p. 52–55.

and this authorship is indicated in some recent brief descriptions of the book.[12] Athanasios IV occupied his see in a difficult historical period, namely during and after the fall of the Byzantine Empire, and little is known about him; in particular, there exists evidence for his relations with the Ottoman authorities regarding the restoration of the Patriarchal See in Jerusalem.[13] There is no data on the literary heritage of this patriarch (however, this also applies to the previous patriarchs of Jerusalem with the same name).[14] Earlier, L. Cheikho with a reference to M. le Quien[15] noted that the author of the published homilies probably was Athanasios II who became patriarch of Jerusalem around 1180[16] (according to the contemporary data, he occupied this See in the period between 1223/1224–1236 or 1231–1244). This view is supported by J. Pahlitzsch who carried out a textological study of the homilies[17] and published a German translation of one of them.[18] Therefore, the issue of authorship still needs further research.[19]

Another important issue is the authorship of the translation of this collection. The available publications mention Athanasios Dabbās as a translator.[20] His role in the book of homilies is mentioned twice: firstly, the patriarch Chrysanthos reports that he learned about the existence of these homilies and, in general, about their author from "the profound connoisseurs of Arabic philology" (*muta'ammiqān fī fiqh al-lugha al-'arabīya*), in particular from the patriarchs of Antioch Athanasios and Cyril. This means that the text reached him only in Arabic version and the Greek original was not available to him (at the moment,

---

12 Feodorov, *Arabic Printing for the Christians in Ottoman Lands*, p. 276; *Knyha Chesnoho Neporochnoho IEvanheliia, Svityl'nyka, shcho siaie ĭ osvitliuie*, ed. and foreword by I. Ostash, Kyiv, 2021, p. 27.

13 "Afanasiĭ IV", *Pravoslavnaia ėntsiklopediia* IV, Moscow, 2002, p. 52.

14 G. Graf, *Geschichte der christlichen arabischen Literatur*, II, Vatican City, 1947, p. 87.

15 M. le Quien, *Oriens Christianus in quatuor patriarchatus digestus: quo exhibentur ecclesiae, patriarchae caeterique praesules totius orientis. Tomus tertius*, Paris, 1740, p. 503.

16 L. Shaykhū, *Tārīkh fann al-ṭibā'a fī al-Mashriq*, Beirut, 1995, p. 35.

17 J. Pahlitzsch, "*Al-muwā'iẓ allatī hiyā bi-rasm dawr al-sana kullihā al-ḥudūd wa-l-a'yād ma'an min qawl al-qiddīs Athānāsiyūs baṭriyark Ûrshalīm*, 'The Sermons for the Cycle of the Year and All Sundays and Feast Days Together as Delivered by the Holy Athanasius, Patriarch of Jerusalem'", in D. Thomas, A. Mallett (eds.), *Christian-Muslim Relations. A Bibliographical History. Vol. 4 (1200–1350)*, Leiden/Boston, 2012, p. 328.

18 J. Pahlitzsch, "Graeci und Suriani im Palästina der Kreuzfahrerzeit. Beiträge und Quellen zur Geschichte des griechisch-orthodoxen Patriarchats von Jerusalem", *Berliner historische Studien*, 33, 2001, p. 270–289.

19 I am grateful to Samuel Noble for pointing out the bibliography concerning this book of homilies.

20 Feodorov, *Arabic Printing for the Christians in Ottoman Lands*, p. 276; *Knyha Chesnoho Neporochnoho IEvanheliia*, p. 27.

there is no known extant Greek version of these homilies). Secondly, more details about Dabbās's contribution to the edition of the homilies are indicated in the publisher's note placed immediately after the preface. It says that Dabbās edited the Arabic text after he had found significant distortions in the manuscript versions that had appeared over time due to differences in the approaches of copyists (*ma'a tamādī al-ayyām wa-takhāluf 'uqūl al-nāsikhīn*). It is mentioned also that Dabbās made structural corrections that he considered necessary, resulting in a "book without distortions" (*fa-ḥaṣala muṣḥaf^{an} 'arī min al-taḥrīf*). Therefore, Dabbās acted only as an editor of the existing Arabic text which, obviously, had appeared quite a long time earlier, was popular and was copied many times. J. Pahlitzsch argues that the homilies were translated from Greek more or less at the time they were given, but his only argument for this is the presence of Greek loanwords.[21] Therefore, the history of the translation of this mysterious collection also remains to be clarified and a close philological study is necessary to determine whether it is a translation.

According to the preface, the book of homilies was printed in Aleppo at the expense of the Brotherhood of the Holy Sepulchre and with the donations of Christians (*min ṣadaqāt al-masīḥīyīn*). The whole edition was to be distributed for free among the churches of Arab Orthodox Christians (*kanā'is abnā' al-'arab al-urtūduksīyīn*), probably of both patriarchates. At the end of his preface, the Patriarch Chrysanthus strongly recommends reading the proposed homilies in the places where the Christians gather (*yaqrū-hum[22] fī maḥall ijtimā'i-him*), apparently considering them a model of the art of homiletics.

Another edition which by its genre belongs to the literature of a didactic nature is the *Short treatise[23] on the way of repentance and confession and on what is necessary for the one who confesses and the confessor* (*Risāla wajīza tūḍiḥu kayfīyat al-tawba wa-l-i'tirāf wa-fī-mā yalzamu al-mu'tarif wa-l-mu'arrif*) printed in Aleppo in 1711. The book has a short preface that contains some information about it. Athanasios Dabbās is mentioned as its author (p. 4); he addresses his speech to both the believers and confessors, without dividing the preface into two parts. In his preface (p. 5–6) the author names this composition *The String of Well-Strung Pearls or the True Mystery of Repentance and Confession* (*Silk al-durr al-naẓīm fī sirr al-tawba wa-l-i'tirāf al-qawīm*) and states that it contains three parts: a) about repentance in general; b) about the mystery of repentance; c) a manual for confessors (p. 6). Prompted by paternal zeal, he compiled a handbook

---

21 Pahlitzsch, "*Al-muwā'iẓ*", p. 328.
22 Corr., *yaqra'ū-hum*.
23 Litt.: "epistle".

for Christians who had cooled to repentance, on the basis of the "gardens of the teachers' books" (*riyāḍ kutub al-mu'allimīn*). Further acquaintance with the book shows that the sources were both biblical texts and excerpts from classic works of the Holy Fathers (John Chrysostom, John of Damascus, etc.), as well as later Orthodox authors – e.g., the treatise the *Salvation of Sinners* (*Khalāṣ al-khuṭāt*) by Agapios Landos († ca. 1671) who is mentioned as a saint (*al-qiddīs Aghābiyūs*) (p. 49).[24]

The preface does not mention any sponsor or other contributor to this edition. Ioana Feodorov draws attention to the fact that this book was the last to come out of the Aleppo printing press. It was the period when the latter was facing severe financial difficulties, and for this reason Dabbās published this book at his own expense, probably spending all his resources on it. After that, the Aleppo printing press closed down.[25]

In addition to prefaces, historical information can be found on the title pages of the books. In the first two editions of Dabbās, the title page is designed in the most representative way and contains such components as the title of the book, the language of the publication, the editor, the sponsor, the bishop at the time, the place and year of publication and the printer-executor. The title pages of the rest of the editions are somewhat more modest. However, the books that appeared through the help of a sponsor necessarily mention this fact on the title page (this is the case of the book of the Four Gospels sponsored by the Hetman Mazepa and the book of homilies of the Patriarch Athanasios of Jerusalem).

---

24 It is worth noting that this work was extremely popular among Greek-speaking Orthodox Christians in the 17th century. It also consisted of three parts, including chapters on different types of sins and confession (see C. Walbiner, "'Popular'" Greek Literature on the Move: the Translation of Several Works of Agapios Landos of Crete into Arabic in the 17th Century", *Revue des études sud-est européennes*, 51 [1–4], 2013, p. 149).

25 I. Feodorov, "Recent Findings Regarding the Early Arabic Printing in the Eastern Ottoman Provinces", *Revue des études sud-est européennes*, 58, 2020, p. 93.

Tab. 2: The structure of the title pages of the editions of Dabbās can be presented as follows:[26]

	Title	Language	Editor	Sponsor	Bishop	Place	Year	Printer
Liturgikon (1701)	+	+	+	+	+	+	+	+
Horologion (1702)	+	+	+	+	+	+	+	+
Psalter (1706)	+	-	-	-	-	+	+	-
Tetraevangelion (1706)	+	-	-	-	-	+	+	-
Lectionary (1706)	+	-	-	-	-	+	+	-
Epistle book (1707)	+	-	-	-	-	+	+	-
Gospel of Mazepa (1708)	+	-	-	+	-	-	+	-
Homilies of Athanasios (1711)	+	-	-	+	-	+	+	-
Octoechos (1711)	+	-	+	-	-	+	+	-
Epistle on repentance (1711)	+	-	-	-	-	-	-	-

3. Prefaces as a Panegyric

As mentioned before, the personal authorship of Athanasios Dabbās is clearly observed in the prefaces of both Wallachian books and the first preface of the third book, the Aleppan Psalter. By composing these texts, he wanted to express his gratitude to his benefactor, Constantin Brâncoveanu. All five prefaces (both texts in the Wallachian editions and the first one in the Psalter) contain a solemn encomium of the prince, after praising God at the beginning of the text, according to the tradition. It should be noted that the panegyric prefaces, dedicated to political leaders and churchmen, became widespread in Eastern European books of that era. Many prefaces were dedicated to those who financially supported printing as a relevant problem for those times and contributed to its development. The authors of the prefaces and dedications emphasized the nobility of the addressee

---

26 The book of sermons of St. John Chrysostom (1707) is not included in the table, because its scanned copy from the Vatican Library available to us (R.G.Oriente.II.121) has no title page.

and his fidelity to the faith of his ancestors; in particular, he was praised for his charity for the benefit of education and the Church.[27]

Therefore, it is not surprising that Athanasios Dabbās wrote a significant part of his prefaces in the style of the Christian panegyric of that epoch. He lauded the Wallachian prince for building churches and monasteries, for enlightening his compatriots, for his generous donations to other Orthodox churches, as well as for his personal piety. Constantin Brâncoveanu is compared by Dabbās with Constantine the Great, King Solomon, the Prophet David, the Prophet Moses, Judah Maccabee, the Holy Apostles and St. John Chrysostom. In a manner similar to the European panegyric sermons of that epoch, Dabbās tries to represent a social ideal of a ruler of his time and his milieu. He goes as far as to state that there is no one at that time equal to Constantin Brâncoveanu in virtue and concern for the Orthodox Church (*lam najid fī zamāni-nā hādhā aḥad yuḍāhī manāqiba-kum al-ḥamīda fī al-i'tinā wa-l-ihtimām fī al-umūr al-lā'iqa al-kanā'isīya*). In the preface to the Horologion, he even proposes the following analogy:

كما يقال عن يوحنا الذهبي الفم، انه لو لم يكن في ذلك الزمان لكان حصل للايمان القويم تزعزع واضطراب عظيم، حتي انه كان يلزم الامر ان يحضر سيدنا المسيح الي العالم مرة ثانيه، لكي يتبت ايضا دفعة اخره بشارة الانجيل والاعتراف بالايمان الصحيح، فعلي هذا المثال في زماننا هذا ... اظهرت العناية الالهيه الوافرة الحكمه لذاتكم الشريفه الفايقه في حسن التدبير والفكر الثاقب

> They say that if John Chrysostom had not lived in his time, the Orthodox faith would have been shaken so much that it would have been necessary for our Lord Jesus Christ to come again to the world to confirm the Gospel and the true creed. Likewise in our time... the most wise Divine Providence showed your noble person, the most sage ruler with a penetrating mind...

At the end of each preface, the Antiochian hierarch expresses his prayers and good wishes to his benefactor. He asks God to give him prosperity and strengthen his throne, to preserve him and the members of his family and to grant him eternal life among the saints.

Looking at the second preface in the 1706 Aleppo Psalter, we encounter a text obviously composed by another person. The content and style of the prefaces in the books printed in Aleppo demonstrate significant changes. Dabbās's words are retold by an anonymous writer with poetic talent who introduces his speech after a typical phrase: "And then, the most holy father says" (*wa-ba'd fa-yaqūlu al-ab al-aqdas*), or "And then, the venerable father says" (*wa-ba'd fa-yaqūlu al-ab*

---

27 I. Chepiha, "Peredmovy ĭ pisliamovy do ukraïns'kykh starodrukiv iak dzherelo vyvchennia istoriï ukraïns'koï literaturnoï movy", *Movoznavstvo*, 5, 1988, p. 20–21.

al-mukarram), etc., followed by many colorful epithets accompanying Dabbās's name. Thus, in these texts Dabbās himself is praised.

We can observe the following structure of the panegyric component in the prefaces of the Aleppo editions:

a) *Praise to God:* it is found at the beginning of the prefaces (after the traditional Christian *basmala*)[28] that start usually with the words "Praise to God who..." (*al-ḥamdu lillāh allādhī...*), followed by the author's contemplation of God's providence, His creation of the world and humankind, His wisdom in ruling the universe, etc. It is worth noting that the editions printed with the assistance of sponsors do not contain such an incipit: in the book of the Four Gospels printed at the expense of Mazepa, the text begins with an address to the sponsor followed by a sermon on the rulers' attitude towards the worldly glory, while the book of the homilies of Athanasios presents the patriarch Chrysanthus's address to the clergy and the flock followed immediately by a didactic text.

b) *Praise of the editor:* before introducing the name of Athanasios Dabbās, the anonymous author accompanies it with a number of titles or epithets, mentioning some of his praiseworthy deeds. The Antiochian hierarch is likened to the prophets Moses, Aaron, Elijah, David, Solomon, Abraham, Joseph, as well as to the Holy Apostles, the Four Evangelists and St. Athanasios the Great.

c) *Praise of the book:* it is expressed with reference to Dabbās's words in the form of the 1st person. The editor (Dabbās) explains his decision to print the book presented in the edition, emphasizing its importance for the services of the Church or for the spiritual life of Christians. Some of the prefaces are composed as a panegyric dedicated completely to the glorification of the book; this is the case of Tetraevangelion, Lectionary and the *Chosen Pearls of St. John Chrysostom.*

Another component found in old prints, similar in content and structure to panegyric texts, are prefaces-dedications. According to the tradition, dedications in honor of patrons, sponsors and church hierarchs were often accompanied by the coats of arms of these persons, which were an important element of book design.[29] In the editions of Dabbās available to us, this type of dedication is included in both Wallachian books (in honor of Constantin Brâncoveanu), as well as in the second edition of the book of the Four Gospels sponsored by Mazepa; they are traditionally placed behind the coat of arms. In the Wallachian editions – the Liturgikon and the Horologion – the dedications to Brâncoveanu

---

28 "In the name of the Father, and of the Son and of the Holy Spirit, one God" (*Bi-smi l-Āb wa-l-Ibn wa-l-Rūḥ al-Qudus al-Ilāh al-wāḥid*).

29 IA. Isaievych, *Ukraïns'ke knyhovydannia: vytoky, rozvytok, problemy*, Lviv, 2002, p. 325.

are written only in Greek; the author is Ioannes Comnenos, the court physician of the Wallachian prince.

The dedication to Mazepa has Greek and Arabic versions. The Greek text is designed in the form of two epigrams, and the Arabic one, respectively, as a question (*su'āl*) and answer (*jawāb*); both texts are similar in content. The beginning of the dedication differs: the Greek text is more "historical". It contains an address to the sponsor with his extended title and is designed as a subtitle in the form of a colophon, while the Arabic one is composed in the form of four rhymed verses and is a panegyric. Both texts are signed on behalf of the clergy and laity of the Church of Antioch, which in the Greek version are literally called "the faithful of both ranks from Arabia" (Οἱ ἐν Ἀραβίᾳ εὐσεβεῖς ἀμφοτέρων τῶν τάξεων), and in Arabic – "the Orthodox clergy and laity living in Arab countries" (*ṭughmat al-kahana wa-l-'awāmm al-mustaqīmī al-ra'y qāṭinī al-bilād al-'arabīya*). Unfortunately, the real author of the dedications in this edition remains unknown.

Another text which can be considered a kind of dedication is found in the book of homilies of Athanasios. This is a *qasida* of thirteen verses (*bayts*) placed after the image of the Church of the Resurrection in Jerusalem. It praises the book offered to the readers and its author in a very elaborate style. The composer of these verses is not mentioned either.

4. Prefaces as Sermons

Prefaces in old prints of religious content are traditionally viewed as examples of independent prose works where the sermon genre is often dominant. In the European culture of the 17th century, the Baroque style of preaching, which went beyond the traditional type of homilies (the interpretation of the Gospel), spread. The greater part of the homilies became a panegyric sermon focused on the glorification of outstanding people – primarily contemporaries, as well as characters from Christian history.[30] Preachers of the 17th and 18th centuries willingly turned to world history, the Bible and mythology, projecting these images and examples on modernity.

The analyzed prefaces of the editions of Athanasios Dabbās also largely represent the genre of sermon, closely intertwined with panegyric. In this genre, there are many quotations from the Holy Scriptures, references to biblical images and events and even to historical figures. Thus, Dabbās begins his first preface addressed to Constantin Brâncoveanu (Liturgikon, 1701) by mentioning Alexan-

---

30 O. Zelins'ka, *Ukraïns'ka barokova propovid': movnyĭ svit i kul'turni vytoky*, Kyiv, 2013, p. 32, 35.

der the Great, with instruction on how rulers should use the power and authority granted to them by God – not for bloodshed and conquests, but in order to gain praise from people and God through their good deeds. In the preface of the Horologion, before proceeding to the praise of his benefactor, the author presents his meditations on the wisdom of God who rules the world. In the second preface, he proceeds to describe the two types of rulers, the good ("right") (*ahl al-yamīn*) and the evil ("left") (*ahl al-yasār*), who are the instruments of God's providence for every people in every age. He uses this method to move on to praising the Wallachian prince as the most pious ruler of his era appointed by God.

Special attention in the preaching component is given to the topic of almsgiving, in the context of the sponsors' donations for Arabic printing. Dabbās repeatedly refers to biblical images and quotes, emphasizing that charity for the needs of Christians – the brothers in faith – and for the sake of God's churches has a special value before God. The entire preface of the Four Gospels book sponsored by Mazepa was composed by the author (who arranged the words of Dabbās in the appropriate stylistic form) as a sermon – initially about a pious life which is a source of true bliss and happiness (*al-ghibṭa al-ḥaqīqīya wa-l-sa'āda*), then about good deeds for the benefit of the neighbor, which is the embodiment of God's commandment "to love your neighbor as yourself"[31] (*an tuḥibba qarība-ka ka-dhāti-ka*).

The genre of sermon in the European tradition of those times required an elevated rhetorical style, emotional presentation, effective poetic figures, plays on words, comparisons, hyperbole, complicated metaphors, allegory of symbols, bright epithets and reminiscences from ancient mythology and literature.[32] Pretentious prefaces in verse were popular in Europe until the first quarter of the 18th century.[33] The Arabic Christian literary tradition, in its turn, was influenced by the environment in which its representatives lived for centuries, and this influence was observable until the 19th century. The scholar Ahatanhel Krymsky describes in detail how Arab Christian authors tried to imitate examples of classical Arabic literature, in particular poetry, so that a hypercritical Muslim reader could see that the classical Arabic tradition was not alien to the Christian authors.[34] As is the case of the Baroque style, a characteristic feature of the Arabic tradition was the domination of verbal ornamentation, i.e., the form and

---

31 Matthew 22: 39.
32 Zelins'ka, *Ukraïns'ka barokova propovid'*, p. 35.
33 Kurhanova, "Prysviaty, peredmovy ta pisliamovy", p. 103.
34 A. Krymskiĭ, *Istoriia novoĭ arabskoĭ literatury: XIX – nachalo XX veka*, Moscow, 1971, p. 389.

the means of decorating the language were put first, while the content was given secondary importance.

The clear influence of the Arabic classical literary tradition is observed starting from the second preface of the 1706 Psalter, which is noticeably different from the previous prefaces written by Dabbās mostly as narrative texts. Almost all the prefaces of Dabbās's editions printed in Aleppo were composed in the form of rhymed prose (*saj'*) which was viewed as an ideal by the Arab authors. An exception is the preface by the Patriarch Chrysanthus in the book of homilies of Athanasios, which may have been written originally in Greek; as already noted, it contains much more narrative and concrete information than the other Aleppo editions.

All the prefaces, including the Wallachian editions, are full of metaphors, similes and hyperboles. In the Liturgikon, Dabbās likens his visit to Constantin Brâncoveanu to the arrival of the Queen of Sheba to Solomon (*ka-mithli-mā atat qadīman malikat al-Tayman min aqṣā al-maskūna li-tu'āyin ḥikmat Sulaymān*). According to Dabbās, the joy of Arabic-speaking Christians at the charitable assistance of the Wallachian prince exceeded the joy of the Christians in the Roman Empire when Constantine the Great freed them from the pagans' persecution (first preface of the 1706 Psalter).

The combination of metaphors and similes with rhymed prose can be demonstrated by two panegyric fragments which the author uses to introduce the words of Dabbās, comparing him to a number of biblical personalities in certain qualities. Here we can see a characteristic stylistic technique, namely stringing together a number of homogeneous elements of the sentence, which makes the text more solemn:

The second preface of the Psalter (1706):

فيقول الاب الاقدس والانا الانفس المضاهى موسى بدعوته، وهرون اب الاحبار بجريته، والياس بنسكه وغيرته، وداود باتضاعهِ ووداعته، وسليمن بتدبيره وحكمته، اعنى به اب الابا، وريس الروسا كيريو اتناسيوس البطريرك الانطاكي المعظم، والسيد الجليل المفخم، الذى اسعد دمشق حيث كان سليلها، وشرف حلب الشهبا حين صار نزيلها

> This is what the holy father and the most precious vessel says, [he who is] similar to Moses in his calling, to the high priest Aaron in his courage, to Elijah in his asceticism and zeal, to David in his humility and meekness, to Solomon in his wise rule – namely, the father of fathers and bishop of bishops, Kyr Kyr Athanasios, the great patriarch of Antioch, the honored and revered master, who made Damascus happy as he was born in it, and honored Aleppo where he settled...

Four Gospels book (1706):

فيقول الاب الجليل السامى، والهمام النبيل المتسامى، من تبوا السدة البطرسيه، وزين كرسى الابرشية الانطاكيه، المضاهى بتدبيره وتعليمه محفل الرسل السليحيه، والمساوم بانداره وارشاده السادة الانجيليه، اعنى به اب الابا السعيد، وريس الروسا المجيد، كيريو كيريو كير اتناسيوس البطريرك الانطاكى المفخم، والسيد النبيل المعظم، من شرف مدينة دمشق حين كان من بنيها، وانار حلب الشهبا اذ غدا راعيها ... من ضارع سميه بعلمه وعمله، وشابه ابرهيم بسخايه وكرمه، وماثل الحكيم بدقة عقله، وساوق يوسف الزكى بعفته وحزمه...

> This is what the revered, honorable and noble father says, [he who] who occupied the See of [the Apostle] Peter[35] and embellished [by his presence] the Antiochian Patriarchate, who is similar in his [wise] rule and knowledge to the Apostles, in his preaching and teaching to the Evangelists – namely, the blessed father of fathers and the glorious bishop of bishops, Kyr Kyr Athanasios, the revered patriarch of Antioch, the great noble master, who honored Damascus where he was born, and illuminated Aleppo when he became shepherd over it, ... who resembles his namesake[36] in his erudition and work, Abraham – in his generosity and hospitality, the wise [Solomon] – in his sharp mind, Joseph the All-Comely – in his virtue and resoluteness...

In the rhymed prefaces of the Aleppo editions there is a noticeable tendency toward a more complicated weaving of words with each subsequent book. The same applies to the magnificence of the epithets attached to the name of Athanasios Dabbās, who in the 1711 Octoechos is called "miracle of the miracles of his time" (u'jūbat 'ajā'ib al-'aṣr).

The Aleppan prefaces are abound in rare words and expressions as well, because "sophisticated" stylistics supposed the use of such vocabulary, e.g., ṣawādī "thirst", daydan "custom", 'asjad "gold" (Chosen Pearls, 1707). In some cases, the author was forced to choose artificial combinations in order to satisfy the demands of the rhymed prose, as was typical for Arab authors of those times. In addition, we can observe the use of words and expressions typical of Muslim culture that influenced the Arab Christians' vocabulary to a certain extent, e.g., tanzīl "[divine] revelation", al-rusul al-ḥawārīyūn "the Apostles", Ilāh al-'ālamīn "the Lord of all worlds", yawm al-ḥashr "Judgment Day" (Tetraevangelion, 1706).

---

35 A figurative name of the Church of Antioch as the one whose founders and patrons were the Apostles Peter and Paul. Athanasios III Dabbās occupied the See of Antioch twice, in 1686–1694 and 1720–1724. During the existence of the Aleppo printing press, he was the archbishop of Cyprus (appointed in 1705). Nevertheless, this fact is never mentioned in the prefaces of the books printed in Aleppo, and the title of the patriarch of Antioch is attached exclusively to the name of Athanasios Dabbās.

36 St. Athanasios the Great is meant.

5. Comments on the Edition

In most prefaces of the books printed by Athanasios Dabbās, we find some details about the edition itself. Firstly, the Antiochian hierarch mentions the motive that forced him to choose a certain book to be printed. These could be the following reasons: a) the urgent need for the book in liturgical use (the Liturgikon, Horologion); b) the didactic value of the book and the need for its availability to all Christians (the Psalter, the book of the Four Gospels, the homilies of Athanasios, the treatise on repentance); c) the need to correct and standardize the text that was distorted because of numerous manuscript versions that had circulated over a long period of time (the Octoechos). The latter fact is often mentioned as the main motive for printing a certain book. The presence of many deviations forced Dabbās to revise the texts by himself and collate them with the Greek original. His efforts to correct a given text are necessarily indicated in the preface; often this fragment is introduced with a phrase such as "And then I was prompted by divine zeal..." (*fa-ḥarrakat-nī ḥīna'idh al-ghīra al-ilāhīya*). In particular, he personally revised the Psalter, where he corrected the Arabic grammar (*qad aṣlaḥnā i'rāb hādhā al-mazāmīr... iṣlāḥan mutawassiṭan*), and the book of the Four Gospels, which was carefully ("phrase by phrase") checked with the Greek original and its grammar was corrected "word by word" (*ḥarrartu-hu 'alá al-lugha al-yūnānīya... jumlatan fa-jumla, wa-aṣlaḥtu i'rāba-hu lafẓatan fa-lafẓa*).

The prefaces also contain evidence of the translation of some books from Greek by Dabbās himself. This is the case of the homilies of St. John Chrysostom and the Octoechos. The latter was translated by him anew, because of the high degree of distortion in earlier versions available to him. Dabbās (via the author of the rhymed preface who used bright metaphors) reported that it was useless to correct the existing Arabic text of Octoechos, since "every fragment was full of misbelief and blasphemy" (*wa-idhā bi-kulli qiṭ'a min-hu qad ushḥinat min al-ḍalāla wa-l-tajdīf*). He complained about the presence of theological errors in Church books due to the ignorance of the scribes and that "godlessness roamed about them like a stray, skittish horse" (*mariḥa al-ilḥād bi-hā... maraḥ al-jawād al-jamūḥ al-sharūd*). Dabbās assured the readers of the correspondence of his translation to the original and of its compliance with all the grammatical rules of Classical Arabic. The Antiochian hierarch wanted to introduce the revised version of Octoechos into liturgical practice, so at the end of the preface he placed a strict order that no one has the right to correct a single letter, otherwise he is to be excommunicated from the Church (*wa-man ta'addā dhālika fa-l-yakun mafrūzan min al-bī'a al-ḥaqīqīya*).

In the prefaces of old Eastern European prints, readers were traditionally given instructions on how to use the book. There was sometimes information about conventional signs that publishers introduced in their editions.[37] In the editions of Dabbās available to us, some information of this kind is found as well:

a) In the first edition of the Psalter (1706), we encounter an attempt to introduce a question mark into the Arabic punctuation system (it was supposed to correspond to the Greek question mark, indicated as a semicolon). At the end of the second preface, the editor informs the reader: "And when you see at the beginning of the phrase a cross, you should read this phrase as interrogative, that is, a kind of question, up to the dot that follows it" (*wa-matá ra'ayta fī awwal al-jumla ṣalīban, iqra' tilka al-jumla istifhāmīya ay bi-naw' al-su'āl ilá 'inda l-maḥaṭṭ allādhī yalī-hā*). An example of such a question mark can be seen at the beginning of Psalm 2 (p. 3), where a symbol in the form of a cross is placed before the text: "Why do the nations rage and the peoples plot in vain?" (⁛ *Limādhā irtajjat al-umam wa-l-shu'ūb haddat bi-l-bāṭil*);

b) The edition of Octoechos contains a list of misprints (*waḍ'u iṣlāḥ al-ghalaṭ allādhī yūjadu fī hādhā al-kitāb*) which is placed after the preface rather than at the end of the book. The *Corrigenda* in two columns occupies five pages and a half and contains 238 items; it mentions the page number (*al-'adad*) and the line number (*al-saṭr*), incorrect (*al-ghalaṭ*) and correct (*al-iṣlāḥ*) variants;

c) Immediately after the *Corrigenda* in the Octoechos, an interesting linguistic note follows:

اعلم انه قد يوجد في هدا الكتاب ما يشتبه علي القاري الجهول تصحيحه كالحيوه والصلوة فان صحة املاهم كما هم بالواو اما لفظهم فبالالف فتقول الحياه والصلاة وايضًا الهنا خلوا من الف بعد اللام فلا تلفظ الا الاهنا بالف اما ما وجد فيه كالدال موضع الذال والتا موضع الثا فلا يعتبر لان الطبع لا يقوم الا بالضروري

> Know that some things in this book may seem to an ignorant reader as those that need to be corrected, e.g., [the words] *al-ḥaywa* and *al-ṣalwa*. Their correct spelling is this, with the letter *wāw*, but they are pronounced with *alif*, i.e., you should say *al-ḥayāt* and *al-ṣalāt*. Also, [the word] *Ilahu-nā* has no *alif* after *lām*, but it is pronounced only as *Ilāhu-nā*, with *alif*. Regarding things such *dāl* instead of *dhāl* and *tā* instead of *thā*, they are not to be considered, since when printing, only what is necessary is taken into account.

This comment indicates that at the beginning of the 18th century the orthographic forms *ḥaywa* ("life") and *ṣalwa* ("prayer") were already perceived as archaic and functioned alongside the modern forms *ḥayāt* and *ṣalāt*. The editor also commented on some orthographic features that were characteristic of the Arabic Christian manuscript tradition. In particular, the word *Ilāh* ("Lord") was often written with *alif*, although according to tradition the long vowel in it is not indicated by the letter; instead of the usual *alif* the optional diacritic is used, *alif*

---

37 Titov, *Materialy dlia istoriï knyzhkovoï spravy na Ukraïni*, p. 5.

khanjarīya (a historical remnant from Quranic orthography). The use of the dental variants *tā* and *dāl* instead of the interdental consonants *thā* and *dhāl* was one of the most typical graphic features of Christian Middle Arabic. As we can see, the attitude of the editor of the first printed books to this feature was not critical and in all editions of Dabbās a variation of both graphemes is observable.

Usually, prefaces, dedications and afterwords in the old prints were viewed as structurally separate parts of the book; they had no pagination and were not included in the table of contents (therefore, in contemporary bibliographic descriptions they are considered separate objects for accounting[38]). This is characteristic of Dabbās' editions as well – where the pagination is present, it starts with the main text of the book.

6. Afterwords in the Editions of Athanasios Dabbās

In addition to prefaces, many old European prints included afterwords which reported the start and end time of printing, additional indexes, misprints, and instructions for using the book. Most often, thanksgiving to God for the successfully completed work, requests for a lenient attitude towards the infirmities of the printer and apologies for mistakes were expressed.[39] Similar elements are also found in the editions of Dabbās. A typical example of the editor's afterword is a note composed by Antim the Iberian, printed only in Arabic in both Wallachian editions. The texts of this appeal are not identical, and they look as follows:

Address of Antim in the Liturgikon (placed after the second preface of Dabbās):

ايها الابا والاخوه بالمسيح الذين تباشروا قراءة هذا القنداق الشريف، اتوسل اليكم انا الفقير صانع هذا الطبع، ان
تسامحوني لاجل ما يوجد فيه من الغلط والنقص، ولاجل التنوين والتشديد من حيث لم يمكنا عملهم في هذا الوقت،
لاجل صعوبة اللغه وعدم معرفتنا لها من قبل، لان كما قيل كل ابتدا صعب، فاغفروا لي من اجل الرب، القايل
اتركوا يترك لكم لان الكمال هو لله، الذي له المجد الي الابد، امين

O, fathers and brethren in Christ, who start to read this noble Liturgikon! I, the humble printer of this book, beg you to forgive me for mistakes and defects found in it, and for the *tanwīn*s and *tashdīd*s which I was unable to insert this time, because of the difficulties of the [Arabic] language which I had not studied before. As they say, every beginning is difficult. So, forgive me for the sake of the Lord who said: "Forgive, and you shall be forgiven," because perfection belongs only to God. Praise to Him forever! Amen.

---

38 Kurhanova, "Prysviaty, peredmovy ta pisliamovy", p. 98.
39 Titov, *Materialy dlia istoriï knyzhkovoï spravy na Ukraïni*, p. 6.

Address of Antim in the Horologion (p. 732):

ايها الاخوه المكرمين الذين تطالعوا في هذا الكتاب المبارك، اسالكم واتتضرع[40] اليكم انا الفقير صانع هذا الطبع ان
تسامحوني عن جميع ما صدر فيه من الغلط وعدم التقويم، بما اني غريب من اللغة العربيه وكانسان مذنب ومخطي،
لان ليس احد كامل الا الله وحده، فاقبلوا نشاطي وعذري مثل ما قبل ربنا فلسين الارمله، وان يسر الله مرة اخره
في طبع كتاب اخر سوف نعمل اجتهاد اكثر وحرص ازيد، بمقدار ما يساعدنا ربنا الذي له المجد الي الابد، ولا زلتم
في نعمته ورحمته امين

> "O, honorable brethren who will read this blessed book! I, the humble printer of this book, ask and beg you to forgive me for all the mistakes and inaccuracies that occurred in it, because the Arabic language is foreign for me and I am a guilty sinner as a man, and because perfection belongs only to God. So, accept my work and my apology as our Lord accepted the widow's mite. If God helps us again print another book, we shall make more efforts with more eagerness, as much as Lord allows us. Praise to Him forever! May His grace and His mercy remain upon you. Amen".

In addition, at the end of the Liturgikon (p. 253) there is an afterword in Greek in the form of a colophon, informing about the end of the printing of the book in the Snagov monastery in January 1701, with a mention of the patron (Constantin Brâncoveanu), the printer (Antim), and the editor of the Greek text (hieromonk Ignatius Phitianos from Chaldia).[41] Below three *bayt*s in Arabic in honor of the printer are added:

نجز طبع هذا القنداق الشريف الكريم   بموازرة رب كافة البريا[42] العظيم الرحيم

ســـنة الف وواحـــد وسـبعمايه   في شـــهر كانـــون الثـاني مســـيحيه

بيد كـــير انتيمـــوس الاســـتاد   بمنـــة رب ســـاير العبـــاد

> The printing of this noble Liturgikon was finished, with the help of the Lord of all creation, the Great and Merciful, in the Christian year one thousand seven hundred and one, in January, by the hand of the master Kyr Antim, by the mercy of God of humankind.

In the Horologion, the afterword of Antim is followed by a note in the form of a colophon:

طبع في بكورشت المحميه من بلاد انكروفلاخيا من انتيموس الكاهن المتوحد الكرجي الاصل   في سنة الف
وسبعمايه واتنين مسيحيه في شهر حزيران المبارك، ثم الكتاب بمنة رب العباد

> Printed in the God-protected Bucharest of Ungrovlahia by Antim, the hieromonk of Georgian origin, in the Christian year one thousand seven hundred and two, in the blessed month of June. The book is completed by the mercy of God of humankind.

---

40 *Sic.* Corr., واتضرع.

41 For the full text of the afterword, see Chițulescu, *Antim Ivireanul*, p. 90.

42 *Sic.* Corr., البرايا.

Another important editorial note, similar in function to the afterword, is the above-mentioned comment on the role of Dabbās in revising the book of homilies of the patriarch Athanasios of Jerusalem, which is placed immediately after the preface. The editor emotionally appeals to his readers with a request to fully trust the corrected text, since the printed book, unlike the manuscript versions (which are full of errors), is "perfectly revised" (*muḥkam al-inshā'*).

The ending notes in the rest of the books are very short. They are placed at the end of the book and consist of a single phrase indicating the year and place of publication, e.g.: "Recently printed in God-protected Aleppo in the Christian year 1706" (*ṭubi'a ḥadīthan bi-maḥrūsat Ḥalab al-maḥmīya sanat 1706 masīḥīya*) (Four Gospels book, 1706). Thanksgiving to God for the completion of the book is contained at the end of the treatise on repentance in the form of a colophon: "Eternal praise and permanent thanks to our Lord. Amen." (*fa-li-Rabbi-nā al-ḥamd al-sarmad wa-l-shukr al-mu'abbad. Amīn*).

Thus, the prefaces of the Christian Arabic books printed in Wallachia and Syria by Athanasios Dabbās represent separate constituent elements of these editions. In terms of their content and style, they most closely resemble a panegyric sermon. They give an idea of the formation of book culture and literary style among the Arab Christians in the context of the common Orthodox tradition, when the most characteristic features of the latter were complemented by manifestations of local influences. As can be observed from the examples analyzed, the literary ideal for Arab Christian authors when addressing their patrons and readers at the beginning of the 18th century was a solemn and pathetic style intertwined with rhymed prose (*saj'*). It is not entirely correct to consider Dabbās the real author of the rhymed prefaces of the Aleppo editions. On his order, these texts were composed someone who had poetic talent and mastered Classical Arabic at a very high level. Since the name of this figure of Arabic Orthodox culture of the beginning of the 18th century remains unknown to us, there have been suggestions that it could be the deacon 'Abdallāh Zākhir or even Gabriel (Germanos) Farḥāt, the future Maronite metropolitan of Aleppo. Further research can shed some light on this issue, as well as on the following stages of the development of the book culture of Arab Christians, already in quite different socio-confessional conditions.

Bibliography

"Afanasiĭ IV". *Pravoslavnaia ėntsiklopediia*, vol. IV. Moscow: Tserkovno-nauchnyĭ tsentr "Pravoslavnaia ėntsiklopediia", 2002, p. 52.

Chepiha, Inna P. "Peredmovy ĭ pisliamovy do ukraïns'kykh starodrukiv iak dzherelo vyvchennia istoriï ukraïns'koï literaturnoï movy". *Movoznavstvo* 5, 1988, p. 16–25.

Chiţulescu, Policarp (ed.). *Antim Ivireanul: opera tipografică*. Bucharest: Editura Institutului Cultural Român, 2016.

Feodorov, Ioana. "Recent Findings Regarding the Early Arabic Printing in the Eastern Ottoman Provinces". *Revue des études sud-est européennes* 58, 2020, p. 91–105.

Feodorov, Ioana. *Arabic Printing for the Christians in Ottoman Lands*. Berlin/Boston: De Gruyter, 2023.

Graf, Georg. *Geschichte der christlichen arabischen Literatur*, II. Città del Vaticano: Biblioteca Apostolica Vaticana, 1947.

Isaievych, Iaroslav. *Ukraïns'ke knyhovydannia: vytoky, rozvytok, problemy*. Lviv: Instytut ukraïnoznavstva im. I. Kryp'iakevycha NANU, 2002.

Knyha Chesnoho Neporochnoho IEvanheliia, Svityl'nyka, shcho siaie ǐ osvitliuie, ed. and foreword by I. Ostash. Kyiv: Fond pam'iati Blazhennishoho Mytropolyta Volodymyra, 2021.

Krymskiǐ, Agatangel E. *Istoriia novoǐ arabskoǐ literatury: XIX – nachalo XX veka*. Moscow: Glavnaia redaktsiia vostochnoǐ literatury, 1971.

Kurhanova, Olena IU. "Prysviaty, peredmovy ta pisliamovy do ukraïns'kykh kyrylychnykh starodrukiv: problemy ta perspektyvy naukovo-bibliohrafichnoho obliku". *Bibliotechnyǐ Merkuriǐ* 2(22), 2019, p. 94–108.

Le Quien, Michaelis R. P. F. *Oriens Christianus, in quatuor patriarchatus digestus: quo exhibentur ecclesiae, patriarchae caeterique praesules totius orientis. Tomus tertius*. Paris: Ex Typographia Regia, 1740.

Nasrallah, Joseph. *Histoire du mouvement littéraire dans l'Église melchite du Ve au XXe siècle*, vol. III, tome 2. Leuven: Peeters/Paris: Chez l'auteur, 1981.

Pahlitzsch, Johannes. "Graeci und Suriani im Palästina der Kreuzfahrerzeit. Beiträge und Quellen zur Geschichte des griechisch-orthodoxen Patriarchats von Jerusalem". *Berliner historische Studien* 33, 2001, p. 270–289.

Pahlitzsch, Johannes. "*Al-muwā'iẓ allatī hiyā bi-rasm dawr al-sana kullihā al-ḥudūd wa-l-a'yād ma'an min qawl al-qiddīs Athānāsiyūs baṭriyark Ūrshalīm*, 'The Sermons for the Cycle of the Year and All Sundays and Feast Days Together as Delivered by the Holy Athanasius, Patriarch of Jerusalem'". *Christian-Muslim Relations. A Bibliographical History. Vol. 4 (1200–1350)*, edited by David Thomas, Alex Mallett. Leiden/Boston: Brill, 2012, p. 328–330.

Panchenko, Konstantin A. *Blizhnevostochnoe pravoslavie pod osmanskim vladychestvom: pervye tri stoletiia. 1516–1831*. Moscow: Indrik, 2012.

Shaykhū, Luwīs. *Tārīkh fann al-ṭibā'a fī al-Mashriq*. Beirut: Dār al-Mashriq, 1995.

Titov, Khvedir. *Materialy dlia istoriï knyzhkovoï spravy na Ukraïni v XVI–XVIII v.v.: vsezbirka peredmov do ukraïns'kykh starodrukiv*. Kyiv: Drukarnia Ukraïns'koï Akademiï nauk, 1924.

Walbiner, Carsten. " 'Popular' Greek Literature on the Move: The Translation of Several Works of Agapios Landos of Crete into Arabic in the 17th Century". *Revue des études sud-est européennes*, 51 (1–4), 2013, p. 147–157.

Zelins'ka, Oksana IU. *Ukraïns'ka barokova propovid': movnyǐ svit i kul'turni vytoky*. Kyiv: Vudavnychyǐ dim Dmytra Burago, 2013.

Fr Rami Wakim
Patriarch Athanasios III Dabbās' Gospel. Origin and Characteristics

Studying the history of the Arabic Gospel is a difficult task due to the complexity, variety and length of the translations and copying labor completed over the years. Orthodox Christians were split into three groups in the 15th century: those living in independent nations, those living under Muslim rule, and those residing in areas governed by Western Christians. Venice developed into a significant printing hub in Europe and had a significant role in the printing of Greek religious literature. The first printed book in Church Slavonic was produced in Krakow and the first South Slavonic book was produced in Cetinje in the 15th century, marking the beginning of printing for the Orthodox.

While the first Arabic press was created in Aleppo in 1706, the first Muslim-owned printing press in the Ottoman Empire was established in Istanbul in 1727. Other Orthodox nations, such as Russia, Romania and Greece, established printing presses in the 18th and 19th centuries. Production and distribution of Orthodox religious materials increased as a result of the development of these presses.[1] The publication of Patriarch Athanasios Dabbās' Arabic translation of the Gospels under two forms, the Tetraevangelion and the liturgical version, stands as a significant moment in the history of Arabic translations and publications of the Gospels. Dabbās' work was driven by the challenges faced by the Christian community in the Patriarchate of Antioch, including a shortage of educated clergy, the arrival of Counter-Reformation Latin missionaries, and the need for a unified Arabic version of the Gospel. To address these challenges, Dabbās established a printing press in Aleppo and produced a number of translated religious texts, including the Tetraevangelion and the Gospel for liturgical use. In his translations, Dabbās made a number of revisions and corrections to the text, including altering verb conjugations and distinguishing between the subject and object of phrases. He also made stylistic choices in word selection, sometimes replacing words used in earlier translations with synonyms.

---

1 See H. Kilpatrick, "From Venice to Aleppo: Early Printing of Scripture in the Orthodox World", *Chronos*, 30, 2014, p. 34–48.

This research is part of a project that has received funding from the European Research Council (ERC) under the European Union's Horizon 2020 research and innovation programme (grant agreement No 883219-AdG-2019 – Project TYPARABIC).

∂ Open Access. © 2024, the author(s), published by De Gruyter. [CC] [BY-NC-ND] This work is licensed under the Creative Commons Attribution-NonCommercial-NoDerivatives 4.0 International License.
https://doi.org/10.1515/9783111060392-013

In order to fully appreciate the significance of Patriarch Athanasios Dabbās' contribution to the Arabic translation of the Gospel, it is necessary to understand the origins of his work. The source of Dabbās' translation remains, however, a mystery to this day. It is known that Dabbās did not create a new translation, but rather revised an existing one. In the introduction to his both Gospels, he states that he edited the entire text based on the original Greek and made changes to its syntax. It is unclear which specific translation Dabbās used and whether he had any issues with it. Additionally, it is not known if he had access to only one translation or multiple versions, or if he built upon an already established translation or created a completely new approach. Understanding the answers to these questions would provide valuable context for the literary analysis of Dabbās' work and shed light on the value of the adaptations he made.

This paper aims to identify the source of Dabbās' Gospel and examine its connection to the revival of the Orthodox community in the Patriarchate of Antioch in the 17th century. It also aims to examine the types of amendments made by Dabbās and the impact of his translations on the Christian community in Antioch, as well as the lasting legacy of his work.

1. Patriarch Athanasios III Dabbās (1647–1724) in Line with the 17th-Century Orthodox Revival

In the 17th century, the Orthodox Christian community in the Patriarchate of Antioch faced numerous challenges as it lived under Ottoman rule. These challenges included poverty, oppressive rules imposed by the empire, political power struggles within the empire, a shortage of educated clergy, the arrival of Counter-Reformation Latin missionaries and the presence of European consulates leading to outside interference in its internal affairs. The Orthodox patriarchs of Antioch had to work hard to ensure the survival of their community. One of the challenges they faced was the shift in liturgical language from Greek and Syriac to Arabic, a process that took place over several centuries. Arabic began to be used in apologetic writings in the 8th century, and gradually spread through scripture passages, hagiographies, and liturgical rubrics.[2] After the Crusades ended, the Arabization of society intensified leading Christians to seek complete transla-

---

2 For the Melkite liturgy before the 17th century see C. Charon, *Histoire des patriarcats melkites Alexandrie, Antioche, Jérusalem depuis le schisme monophysite du sixième siècle jusqu'à nos jours*, vol. 3, Rome, 1911, p. 24–46; C. Korolevskij, *Le rite byzantin dans les patriarcats melkites Alexandrie, Antioche, Jérusalem adoption, versions, éditions, pratique, particularités*, Rome, 1908,

tions of the Bible. From the 16th century onwards, Arabic began to replace Syriac in the liturgy until it completely supplanted it in the 17th century.[3] This change also created a new challenge: ensuring a unified version of the Gospel. The invention of the printing press in the 15th century led to a focus on adapting and standardizing official translations of religious texts among Antiochian prelates. One notable effort in this direction was led by Metropolitan Meletios Karma, who later became patriarch of Antioch as Aftīmiyūs II (1634–1635).

Metropolitan Meletios Karma was an influential figure who had been trained at Saint Saba's Monastery near Jerusalem before returning to his city of Hamah and later being sent to Aleppo as a preacher. In 1612, he became metropolitan of Aleppo with the goal of educating his clergy and providing them with printed books. Karma was very persuasive and successfully justified his work twice before the Ecumenical Patriarch, despite internal Antiochian conflicts and rivalries.[4] He also convinced Rome that an Arabic translation of the entire Bible was necessary. He began working on the translation and even sent a specimen to Rome, but it was rejected.[5] Karma believed that the only solution to unify the translation was to revise it against the Greek text, due to the significant variations present in the Arabic translations derived from different Hebrew, Syriac, Greek, Armenian, and Coptic manuscripts. His concept of an Arabic Bible involved printing the entire scripture in two columns, with one column in Greek and the other in Arabic.[6] Karma also took on the task of revising and completing translations of liturgical books. In the year following his enthronement as metropolitan, he revised the Liturgikon and the Typikon. In 1630, he finished the Horologion and the Eucholo-

p. 27–52; J. Nasrallah, *Histoire du mouvement littéraire dans l'Église melchite*, Paris II.2, p. 182–186; III. 1, p. 359–386; III.2, p. 146–172; IV.1, p. 256–273.

3 On liturgical language in mediaeval time Melkite Church, see S. Griffith, "From Aramaic to Arabic: The Languages of the Monasteries of Palestine in the Byzantine and Early Islamic Period", *Dumbarton Oaks Papers*, 51, 1997, p. 11–31; C. Cannuyer, "Langues usuelles et liturgiques des melkites au XIIIe s.", *Oriens Christianus*, 70, 1986, p. 110–117; K. Leeming, "The Adoption of Arabic as a Liturgical Language by the Palestinian Melkites", *Aram*, 15, 2003, p. 239–246.

4 L. Kilzī, "Ḥayāt al-baṭriyark Aftīmiyūs Karma al-Anṭākī al-ḥamawī bi-qalam tilmīdhi-hi al-baṭriyark Makāriyūs al-ḥalabī", *al-Masarra*, 1913, p. 41–47, 81–89, 135–144.

5 Kilpatrick, "Meletios Karmêh's specimen translation of Genesis I-V", in L. Stefan, B. Sara (eds.), *Translating the Bible into Arabic: Historical, Text-Critical and Literary Aspects*, Würzburg, 2012, p. 61–73.

6 See E. Dannaoui, "From Multiplicity to Unification of the Arabic Biblical Text: a Reading of the Rūm Orthodox Projects for the Arabization and Printing of the Gospels during the Ottoman Period", in D. Bertaina et al. (eds.), *Heirs of the Apostles: Studies on Arabic Christianity in Honor of Sidney H. Griffith*, Leiden, 2018, p. 25–27.

gion. With the help of his brother Thalja, he also revised the Synaxarion and the Menaion.[7]

Makarios III al-Za'īm was similarly a significant figure in the revival of the Melkite Church and had a large literary output. He was one of the greatest patriarchs of the Melkite Church. Za'īm was born in Aleppo at the end of the 16th century to a priestly family; both his father and grandfather were priests. He was a married priest and had a son named Paul. After the death of his wife, he spent seven years at Saint Saba's Monastery (1627–1634). Patriarch Aftīmiyūs III made him metropolitan of Aleppo in 1635, and he became patriarch of Antioch in 1648, while his son Paul became archdeacon and his personal biographer.

During his tenure, Patriarch Makarios III strengthened his connections with Catholic missionaries.[8] He also took two trips to Orthodox countries in Southeast and Eastern Europe, such as Istanbul, Georgia, Wallachia, Moldavia, Ukraine, and Russia, in the years 1652–1659 and 1666–1668.[9] The purpose of the first trip was to raise funds to pay off the debts of the patriarchate, while the second trip was made at the invitation of Tsar Alexis to participate in the trial of the Patriarch Nikon. The most important source of information on Makarios III's life is his son's diary.[10] Makarios III also attempted to work with the Propaganda Fide to produce liturgical books, but he was unable to achieve this goal before his death in 1672.

With the help of his son, the Archdeacon Paul, the Patriarch Makarios III left a significant legacy through his books, which mainly consisted of translations and compilations of Greek writings by canonists, liturgists, and patristic authors. One of his important contributions was collecting and synthesizing all available information on the history and heritage of the Melkite Church.[11]

The third key figure in Antioch is Patriarch Athanasios III Dabbās. He was born in 1647 in Damascus and studied under the Jesuits before going to Saint

---

7 Nasrallah, *Histoire du mouvement littéraire* IV.1, p. 214–217; Ch. Nassif, "Autour de l'euchologe melkite de Malatios Karmé", *Proche Orient Chrétien*, 98, 2018, p. 46–61; A. Raheb, *Conception de l'union dans le patriarcat orthodoxe d'Antioche (1622–1672)*, Rome, 1981, p. 45–82.

8 See V. Tchentsova, "Le patriarche d'Antioche Macaire III Ibn Al-Za'īm et la chrétienté latine", in M.-H. Blanchet, F. Gabriel (eds.), *Réduire le schisme ? ecclésiologies et politiques de l'Union entre Orient et Occident (XIIIᵉ–XVIIIᵉ siècles)*, Paris, p. 313–335.

9 C.-M. Walbiner, "Macarius Ibn al-Za'īm and the Beginnings of an Orthodox Church Historiography in Bilād al-Shām", *Le rôle des historiens orthodoxes dans l'historiographie*, Al-Balamand, 2010, p. 11–27.

10 See I. Feodorov (ed.), *Makāryūs III Ibn al-Za'īm et Paul d'Alep : relations entre les peuples de l'Europe Orientale et les chrétiens arabes au XVIIᵉ siècle : actes du Ier colloque international le 16 septembre 2011*, Bucharest, 2012.

11 See Nasrallah, *Histoire du mouvement littéraire* IV.1, p. 87–127.

Sabba's Monastery. He was appointed patriarch of Antioch in 1685, but faced conflict with Patriarch Kirillus V Za'īm. In 1694, an agreement was reached and Athanasios became metropolitan of Aleppo, where he devoted himself to continuing the work of translating and publishing liturgical books and the Gospels in continuation of the work done by his predecessors. Athanasios also visited Eastern Europe and developed a close friendship with Prince Constantin Brâncoveanu of Wallachia, who provided support for the printing of the Liturgicon in 1701 at Snagov and the Horologion in 1702 at Bucharest,[12] with the help of Antim the Iberian, a Georgian theologian and skilled printer who later became the metropolitan of Ungro-Wallachia (1708–1716).[13]

In 1704, Athanasios Dabbās returned to Aleppo, bringing with him the typographic tools used for the printing of the first two books from Wallachia. He set up a new printing press in his residence in Aleppo, which operated from 1706 to 1711, and produced eleven religious books, considered to be the first Arabic books printed in an Arab country. These included a Psalter, the Paraclisis, a collection of selected texts from John Chrysostom, a collection of homilies by Athanasios of Jerusalem, and the Gospels in two forms: the Tetraevangelion and the Gospels for liturgical use (lectionary arrangement), with or without commentaries.[14]

2. The Different Versions of the Gospel and Dabbās' Intention

In 1706, Dabbās printed the Tetraevangelion (Four Gospels) under the title *Kitāb al-Injīl al-sharīf al-ṭāhir wa-l-miṣbāḥ al-munīr al-zāhir* (*The Book of the Noble, Pure Gospel and the Bright, Illuminating Lamp*), beginning with the Gospel of Matthew, which includes indications for liturgical use and an index of the Gospels to be read during the liturgical year. In the same year, he also printed the four Gospels arranged for liturgical use, commonly known as a lectionary, beginning with the Gospel of John, read at the Pascal liturgy, and featuring gospel passages to be read during various liturgical events. As is customary for many lectionaries, Dabbās included a commentary from older lectionaries after the gospel readings

---

12 Feodorov, "The Romanian Contribution to Arabic Printing ", in E. Siupiur, Z. Mihail (eds.), *Impact de l'imprimerie et rayonnement intellectuel des Pays Roumains*, Bucharest, 2009, p. 41–61. Also V. Cândea, "Dès 1701 : Dialogue roumano-libanais par le livre et l'imprimerie ", dans C. Aboussouan (ed.), *Le livre et le Liban jusqu'à 1900*, Paris, 1982, p. 283–294.
13 P. Chiţulescu, D. Bădără, *Antim Ivireanul. Opera tipografică*, Bucharest, 2016.
14 I. Feodorov, "Livres arabes chrétiens imprimés avec l'aide des principautés roumaines au début du XVIIIe siècle. Un répertoire commenté", *Chronos*, 34, 2016, p. 7–49.

for Sundays and important feasts.[15] This liturgical Gospel has the same title as the four Gospels, which has sometimes caused confusion in cataloguing these two books. To further complicate matters, Dabbās inserted the same introduction to both books. The shared introduction begins with an expression of thanksgiving to God for the creation of men and endowing them with a rational speaking soul, for giving them correct catholic faith, for the revelation of his mysteries, for the gift of the Orthodox Church, for divine adoption through the second birth, for the renovation by the spirit, and for the inheritance of His kingdom. The introduction then proceeds to recite praises about Patriarch Athanasios, listing a long series of complimentary attributes likely written by an assistant.[16] In the third part, Patriarch Athanasios takes back the discourse and shows insistence on the importance and duty of every believer to have the Gospel, as it is God's revelation on the way of perfection and virtue, regardless of whether the reader is married or single, a monk or clergy. He then states that the point of printing the Gospel is to make it easier for people to possess after he edited the text based on the Greek text and amended its syntax. In addition to the liturgical arrangement of the Gospels, the Lectionary features depictions of the four Evangelists before the reading of each Gospel and states, at the beginning of the book, that it is arranged for Church use, beginning with the Gospel of John (Fig. 1).

The same year, 1706, the Psalter was printed with the coat of arms of Prince Brâncoveanu on the first page. As a result, it has become common to associate the printing of the Gospels with funding from Brâncoveanu, even though neither the Tetraevangelion nor the Lectionary shows a direct link with him. It is probable that Dabbās refrained from showing links with Brâncoveanu so as not to upset the Ottoman authorities. The factors that contributed to the cessation of Orthodox publishing in the Arab world in the early 18th century are not fully understood. It is likely that financial issues played a role, as the books were distributed for free by Patriarch Athanasios III, who had to seek support from wealthy Orthodox individuals and organizations abroad. He also sent envoys to Tsar Peter I in 1707 and 1714, but the outcomes of these missions are not known.[17] In 1708, Dabbās reproduced the Tetraevangelion using funds provided by the Cossack Hetman Ivan Mazepa, who was a wealthy benefactor of Eastern Orthodox communities.

---

15 See S. Frantsouzoff, "Le premier lectionnaire arabe orthodoxe imprimé", in C. Manolache (ed.), *Istorie și cultură: in honorem academician Andrei Eșanu*, Chișinău, 2018, p. 461.
16 The author highlights, among many other attributes, his Damascene origin and the fact that he became metropolitan of Aleppo thus alluding to the historic rivalry between Damascus and Aleppo which caused, with other factors, the many schisms in the Antiochian Patriarchate leading to the creation of the dual hierarchy in 1724.
17 See Kilpatrick, "From Venice to Aleppo", p. 52–53.

This edition contained Mazepa's coat of arms and a different foreword dedicated to him, with verses in Greek and Arabic full of praise. The second edition of 1708 is the same as the 1706 edition, with only the date changed by hand from 1706 to 1708 (Fig. 2). It is quite probable that Dabbās had more printings of the Tetraevangelion but needed funds to bind them.[18]

In 1708, Dabbās received funds from the military leader Daniel Apostol (1654–1734), who was born into a Cossack family and initially fought alongside Hetman Ivan Mazepa against Peter I of Russia, but later switched sides and fought for Russia. The Gospel funded by Apostol was a liturgical Lectionary with commentary, starting with the Gospel of John, which was read on Pascha. The Gospel features Apostol's coat of arms at the beginning, followed by a short poem praising his donation for the suffering Orthodox in the Arab region. The rest of the structure is the same as the 1706 Lectionary (Fig. 2).[19] The Gospels of 1708, funded by both Mazepa and Apostol, demonstrate Dabbās' exceptional efforts to publish Gospel books and highlight the strong bond between the Orthodox world, Antioch, and Ukraine.

By providing uniform texts for the prayers said in the churches under the patriarchate, Patriarch Dabbās aimed to enhance the liturgical life of the faithful. Also, he printed hundreds of copies and distributed them widely in an effort to encourage people to read the Gospel and other theological texts. Every believer, according to Dabbās, should have a copy of the Gospel because it may be used as a weapon to counter unusual and erroneous doctrine. Were his actions influenced by the Reformation? It is a strong probability[20] but Dabbās' main motivation for this work was the pastoral and liturgical needs of his flock. The publication of two books of the Gospels, which standardized an Arabic translation of the Gospels and made it available to clergy and educated laypeople, was a significant achievement in Dabbās' activity and a highlight of the Melkite revival of the 17th century.

---

18 This view is also present in the analysis of Ihor Ostash. See Īhūr Ūstāsh, *Kitāb al-Injīl al-sharīf al-ṭāhir wa-l-miṣbāḥ al-munīr al-zāhir* [Introduction + facsimile], Kyiv, 2021, p. 40.

19 There are two copies of this Gospel: one preserved in Russia at the Central State Archive of Old Documents (RGADA/БMCT / inventory No. 2927) and a second one in Jerusalem. For a detailed description of both books see D. Morozov, "Arabskoe Evangelie Daniila Apostola", *Arkhiv russkoĭ istorii*, 2, 1992, p. 192–203; Morozov, "Vifleemskiĭ ėkzempliar arabskogo Evangeliia Daniila Apostola", *Arkhiv russkoĭ istorii*, 8, 2007, p. 645–651.

20 C. Walbiner believed that Dabbās was influenced by Protestant practice that he learned of in Wallachia. See Walbiner, "Melkite (Greek Orthodox) Approaches to the Bible at the Time of the Community's Cultural Reawakening", in S. Binay, S. Leder (eds.), *Translating the Bible into Arabic: Historical, Text-Critical, and Literary Aspect*, Beirut, 2012, p. 60–61.

3. The Origin of the Arabic Text

Determining the Arabic source of Dabbās' Gospel can be a complex task because of the multiple versions in use during that period. Hikmat Kashouh, in his book "The Arabic Versions of the Gospel", identifies fourteen different families of manuscripts, each containing hundreds of copies with small or large differences between them. Carsten Walbiner, following the research of Graf, believes that Dabbās used the Alexandrian Vulgate, a version familiar to readers of his time,[21] a view supported by Kashouh's work on Arabic Gospel families and by Elie Dannaoui.[22] Kashouh's studies did not include manuscripts from monasteries in Lebanon,[23] leaving a gap in our understanding of the sources used by Dabbās.

To address a gap in knowledge, a survey of libraries in Lebanon and Syria was conducted, leading to the examination of hundreds of manuscripts in the libraries of monasteries. As far as the commentary is concerned, it was traced back to manuscripts from the 13th century. This research led to the discovery of a particular liturgical Gospel manuscript at the Library of the Melkite Greek Catholic Patriarchate in Damascus (Damascus, Greek Catholic Patriarchate 146). The manuscript was copied by two scribes: Thalja al-Ḥamawī and Yūsuf al-Muṣawwir (refer to Figures 3 and 4). A closer examination of the Arabic text and commentary in this Gospel reveal it to be the likely direct source for Dabbās' Gospel.[24] Thalja al-Ḥamawī, the brother of Patriarch Euthymios II Karma, was a significant figure in the Church, working closely with him and playing a role in renewal efforts. Thalja's copying activity was extensive, taking place between 1599 and 1649, as indicated by his surviving manuscripts.[25] Yūsuf al-Muṣawwir was a talented icon painter, copyist, translator and miniaturist belonging to a long line of painters

---

21 See Walbiner, "Melkite (Greek Orthodox) Approaches to the Bible", p. 59–60.

22 See H. Kashouh, *The Arabic Versions of the Gospel. The Manuscripts and Their Families*, Berlin, 2012, p. 205. Kashouh argues that what is known as the Alexandrian Vulgate is unlikely to have been translated from Coptic, as previously claimed by scholars. It might have been translated from Syriac and Greek, or from Syriac and later corrected against the Greek. It is still, amongst all other Arabic versions, the most copied and widespread (ibid., p. 329). See also Dannaoui, "From Multiplicity to Unification", p. 29.

23 See Kashouh, *The Arabic Versions of the Gospel*, p. 45.

24 The colophon reads: "Letter of the weak and attenuated servant, confessing his sins and repentant to his God, Ṭaljah, son of priest Ḥūrān al-Ḥamawī, in 7137 to Adam."

"حرف العبد الضعيف النحيف المعترف بذنبه التايب الى ربه تلجه بن الخوري حوران الحموي في ٧١٣٧ لادم"

25 See H. Ibrahim, "Talġat an-nāsiḫ fils du prêtre Ḥūrān al-ḥamawī", *Chronos*, 39, 2019. In the list of books copied by Thalja, Ibrahim does not speak of MS 146 of the Melkite Greek Catholic Patriarchate because it was not available to him at the time of his research.

that continued until the late 18th century.[26] He also translated many books from Greek to Arabic at the request of Patriarch Makarios al-Zaʿīm.[27]

4. The Edition

The realization of the long-awaited aspiration of Metropolitan Meletios to print the Arabic Gospel is indeed a large responsibility, one that Patriarch Dabbās did not take lightly. As examined before, he gives a lot of weight to this printed Gospel and makes it every Christian's duty not only to obtain a copy, but also to read it. Dabbās had also another concern: the liturgical services. The liturgical use of translations of the scriptures into Arabic was an important factor in the initial production and continuous copying of the earliest versions of the Gospels in Arabic. Most recent studies of Arabic Gospel manuscripts ignore this context and do not consider liturgical markings or exegetical remarks contained in rubrics or marginal glosses. This neglect is detrimental to our understanding of the translation, copying, and transmission of the scriptures in Arabic. The early Arabic translation of the Gospels from Greek, found in the Jerusalem family of manuscripts, is marked off with liturgical rubrics that assign pericopes to the appropriate days in the temporal cycle of the old Jerusalem liturgy just as Dabbās added to his Tetraevangelion.[28]

The Arabic translations were in many times translations of translation. Generally speaking, the translator's treatment of the Syriac Vorlage is somewhat loose and they sometimes misunderstood or missed allusions to other biblical passages.[29] In many cases, there were even unintentional additions. Thus we can understand why Patriarch Dabbās insisted on revising the text completely after the Greek one, an established conviction since the time of Karma.

---

26 The colophon reads: "written by the poor servant, confessing his sins and repentant to his Lord, the priest Yūsuf son of Antonius, in the end of March 7137 to Adam."

"كتبه العبد الفقير المعترف بذنبه التايب الى ربه الخوري يوسف بن انطونيوس في اخر شهر ادار سنة سبع الف مايه سبعه وتلتون لادم ٧١٣٧."

27 See Naceif, *l'œuvre du peintre alépin Youssef Al-Musawwer contribution à l'essor de la peinture religieuse melkite au XVIIe siècle*, Leiden (Forthcoming); Nassif, "Le peintre Youssef Al-Musawwer, fondateur de l'école d'Alep", in R. Ziadé (ed.), *Chrétiens d'Orient 2000 ans d'histoire*, Paris, 2017, p. 162–166.

28 S. Griffith, *The Bible in Arabic. The Scriptures of the People of the Book in the Language of Islam*, Princeton, 2013, p. 132–133.

29 Griffith, *The Bible in Arabic*, p. 138–139.

4.1 Edition of the Text

As we move to study the type of revision done by Patriarch Dabbās, we can state three types of editing exercises.

4.1.1 Choice of Words and Grammar

In the case of word choices, there are several examples. In *Luke* 24:12, the Gospel passage read on Tuesday of Bright Week, the source manuscript copied by Thalja: *Ammā Buṭrus fa-inna-hu qāma wa-maḍá ilá al-qabr* ("But Peter got up and left for the tomb"). Dabbās replaces *maḍá* (left) with *asraʻa* (ran) to make it more closely match the original Greek "ἔδραμεν" ("ran"). In another example, the change of words seems misplaced. In the evening Gospel passage for Pascha Sunday (*John* 20:19), as written by Thalja, we read: *Fī al-masā' fī dhālika al-yawm* ("On that evening, on that day"). Dabbās changes the word *al-masā* ("evening") to *ʻashīya* ("eve"), a word he uses throughout the liturgical Gospel to mean "evening". However, this particular choice creates confusion rather than improving the original text, as "ὀψίας" ("eve") means "the evening before the mentioned day".

Overall, it seems that Dabbās' choices in word selection were for the most part successful in accurately conveying the intended meaning of the original text.

Tab. 1: Choice of Words.

Thalja	Dabbās	Greek
اما بطرس فانه قام ومضى الى القبر But Peter rose and left to the tomb	اما بطرس فقام واسرع الى القبر But Peter rose and ran to the tomb	Ὁ δὲ Πέτρος ἀναστὰς ἔδραμεν ἐπὶ τὸ μνημεῖον (*Luke* 24:12)
في المسا في ذلك اليوم in the evening in that day	في عشيّة ذلك اليوم in the eve of that day	Οὔσης οὖν ὀψίας τῇ ἡμέρᾳ (*John* 20:19)

When examining the corrections made by Dabbās to the grammar of the text, it is common to see changes to the conjugation of verbs, such as in the examples provided in the table below. For example, the verb *kānū* (were) is changed to *kāna* (was). In other cases, Dabbās makes changes to distinguish the subject and the object by correcting the diacritic marks. For instance, in the third example in the table, Talgat uses *aḥad^{an}* as the object of the phrase "No one has ever seen God" (*John* 1:18). Dabbās corrects this and changes it to the subject *aḥad* (one). Overall, these corrections made by Dabbās to the grammar of the text serve to improve the clarity and accuracy of the translation.

Tab. 2: Grammar Corrections.

	Thalja	Dabbās
	كانوا التلاميذ	كان التلاميذ
	فرحوا التلاميذ	فرح التلاميذ
	الله لم يراه احدًا قط	الله لم يراه احد قط

4.1.2 Correcting the Text Following the Original Greek

In the second case of alterations made to the text, we see the most significant contribution of Patriarch Dabbās.[30] In many places, Thalja includes additional phrases from parallel passages in other Gospels while citing the Gospel of John. For instance, in the first example, Thalja includes the phrase "and feet" when citing *John* 20:20, but Dabbās removes this addition and restores the text to its original form: "he showed them his hands and side" (as read on Pascha Sunday night).

In the second example, taken from *John* 1:27, read on Monday of Bright Week, we see that Thalja has incorporated a phrase from Matthew 3:11 into the verse. In Thalja's version, we read: "the straps of whose sandals I am not worthy to untie. He baptizes with the Holy Spirit and fire." Dabbās removes this added phrase, resulting in the verse reading: "the straps of whose sandals I am not worthy to untie".

In the third example, we see that Thalja has added the phrase "Jesus rose from the dead" to *Luke* 24:36, which is read on the Feast of the Dormition. This phrase has no basis in the original Greek text,[31] and Dabbās not only removes it but also restores the verse to its original form: "as the disciples were still talking, Jesus stood in their midst and said to them, 'Peace be with you'." These examples demonstrate the significant role played by Patriarch Dabbās in correcting and standardizing the Arabic translations of the Gospel.

---

30 Many Greek New Testament texts were available in that period as testifies al-Zākhir ın hıs introduction to the Epistles. We cannot determine which version Dabbās used. For the sake of comparison, the byzantine version available on http://myriobiblos.gr/ was referenced in the current research.
31 This addition still exists in the Liturgical Gospel in use in the Melkite Greek Catholic Church.

Tab. 3: Comparison of the Arabic Text with the Greek Text.

Thalja	Dabbās	Greek
ارا هم يديه ورجليه وجنبه	ارا هم يديه وجنبه	ἔδειξεν καὶ τὰς χεῖρας καὶ τὴν πλευρὰν αὐτοῖς (John 20:20)
الذي لست مستحق ان احل سيور حدايه. وهو يعمدكم الروح القدس والنار. هذا كان في بيت عنيا عبر الاردن	الذي لست انا مستحق ان احل سيور حدايه. هذا كان في بيت عنيا عبر الاردن	οὗ ἐγὼ οὐκ εἰμὶ ἄξιος ἵνα λύσω αὐτοῦ τὸν ἱμάντα τοῦ ὑποδήματος. Ταῦτα ἐν Βηθανίᾳ ἐγένετο πέραν τοῦ Ἰορδάνου (John 1:27-28)
في ذلك الزمان قام يسوع من الموتي ووقف في وسط تلاميذه وقال لهم السلام لكم	في ذلك الزمان بينما التلاميذ يتكلمون وادا بيسوع وقف في وسطهم وقال لهم السلام لكم	Ταῦτα δὲ αὐτῶν λαλούντων αὐτὸς ὁ Ἰησοῦς ἔστη ἐν μέσῳ αὐτῶν καὶ λέγει αὐτοῖς Εἰρήνη ὑμῖν (Luke 24:36)

4.1.3 Stylistic Choice of Words for Literary Purposes

In this case, Dabbās makes stylistic choices in word selection that do not closely follow the wording of the original Greek text. This may involve selecting words that convey a similar meaning but are not necessarily identical in wording to the Greek. These choices may be made for a variety of reasons, such as to improve the flow and readability of the text in Arabic or to make the text more accessible to the intended audience. It is important to note that while these stylistic choices may differ from the original Greek text, they should still accurately convey the intended meaning of the passage.

In some cases, Dabbās uses synonyms to replace words used in Thalja's copy. These synonym choices may be justified due to the evolution of the Arabic language or the influence of other Arabic translations that may have been available to Dabbās and his team. For example, in one verse, Dabbās translates the same verb "βάλω" as aḍa'u ("I put") and then as aj'alu ("I place"), while in Thalja's version, the verb is translated as aj'alu ("I place") twice.

In another example, a verse from *Luke* 2:25, read at Matins on the Presentation of Our Lord in the Temple, Dabbās translates the participle "κεχρηματισμένον" as ujība ("was answered"), implying that the request or hope to see the consolation of Israel was answered, while in Thalja's version, the word is translated as mūḥā 'alay-hi ("was revealed unto him"). These examples demonstrate the use of synonyms in Dabbās' translations to convey similar meanings but with different word choices.

Tab. 4: Stylistic Choices Different from the Original Greek.

Thalja	Dabbās	Greek
واجعل اصبعي في رسم المسامير، واجعل يدي في جنبه لست اومن	واضع اصبعي في رسم المسامير، واجعل يدي في جنبه لست اومن	καὶ βάλω τὸν δάκτυλόν μου εἰς τὸν τόπον τῶν ἥλων καὶ βάλω μου τὴν χεῖρα εἰς τὴν πλευρὰν αὐτοῦ, οὐ μὴ πιστεύσω (*John* 20:25)
كان انسان في اورشليم اسمه سمعان وكان رجل بارا تقيا يرجوا العزا لاسراييل. وروح القدس كانت عليه. وكان موحى عليه من الروح القدس انه لا يرى الموت حتى يعاين المسيح الرب	كان انسان في اورشليم اسمه سمعان. وكان رجلا بارا تقيا يرجوا تعزية اسراييل. وروح القدس كانت عليه. وكان قد اجيب من الروح القدس انه لا يرى الموت حتى يعاين مسيح الرب	ἦν ἄνθρωπος ἐν Ἰερουσαλὴμ ᾧ ὄνομα Συμεών καὶ ὁ ἄνθρωπος οὗτος δίκαιος καὶ εὐλαβὴς προσδεχόμενος παράκλησιν τοῦ Ἰσραὴλ καὶ πνεῦμα ἅγιον ἦν ἐπ᾽ αὐτόν· καὶ ἦν αὐτῷ κεχρηματισμένον ὑπὸ τοῦ Πνεύματος τοῦ Ἁγίου μὴ ἰδεῖν θάνατον πρὶν ἢ ἂν ἴδῃ τὸν Χριστὸν Κυρίου (*Luke* 2:25-26)

4.2 Edition of the Commentary

Biblical commentary was a significant concern for Arabic-speaking Christian scholars in the early Islamic period, particularly in East Syrian (Nestorian) communities where the tradition had flourished in Syriac. It was a key way to transmit the Church's distinctive doctrines and was often presented in the form of a commentary on selected scriptural passages, definitions of philosophical terms, and explanations of theological formulae. In the West Syrian tradition, scholars such as Dionysius bar Salibi and Bar Hebraeus produced scripture commentary in Islamic times. Several other Arab Christian authors also wrote commentaries on individual books of the Bible, including two on the Book of Revelation by 13th century Arabophone Copts.[32] Translations of patristic commentaries of the New Testament, especially those by John Chrysostom, were also popular. The commentary that we find in Dabbās' Lectionary can be traced back to the 13th century because it was included in manuscript Balamand 77 (compare Figure 5 to Figure 6). The same commentary can also be found in most Gospels arranged for Liturgical use, with minor changes.[33] Dabbās' commentary differs in only a few places from the one we find in the Lectionary copied by Thalja al-Ḥamawī

---

32 See Griffith, *The Bible in Arabic*, p. 149–152.
33 See MS Homs, Church of Saint Elian 12.

and Yūsuf al-Muṣawwir. Mainly, his edition is visible in two areas: homogenizing biblical quotes with his Arabic text and correcting the grammar. When all taken into account, the reader can see that Dabbās' edition of the commentary remains limited in comparison with the work applied to the Gospels.

To conclude, it is clear that Patriarch Athanasios III Dabbās was a significant figure in the Orthodox community of Antioch at the end of the 17th and beginning of the 18th centuries. He attempted to unify, correct and purify the text with the publication of the Tetraevangelion and the liturgical version of the Gospel, making it available for liturgical services, for the clergy's education, and for the general public. The desire to publish the Gospel was a long-standing aspiration, crucial for reinforcing the community's commitment to Scripture and standardizing an official Arabic translation.

Unfortunately, tensions between the Orthodox and Catholic factions within the Patriarchate of Antioch led to a schism in 1724, which greatly impacted the publication of books. The split resulted in the cessation of publishing and hindered the literary movement led by the Antiochian patriarchs. The division led to a dual hierarchy of Orthodox Antiochians and Antiochians aligned with Rome, causing an increase in polemical and apologetic literature. On the Catholic side, 'Abdallāh al-Zākhir, one of Dabbās' assistants, continued the printing work at the Monastery of Saint John the Baptist in Shuwayr, Mount Lebanon, and reissued the Lectionary, but without the commentary, which he claimed was not present in Greek books and had been added over time by copyists who made many mistakes. Orthodox printing briefly resumed in the mid-18th century when the Beirut community established a press in the Monastery of St. George, but only produced three liturgical books between 1751 and 1753. In many libraries of Orthodox monasteries and dioceses, al-Zākhir's Gospel could be found, suggesting that it may have been used by the Orthodox community until the appearance of the Orthodox Gospel in 1863 in Jerusalem, printed under the Patriarch Cyril II (1792–1877).

Despite the difficulties of his time, Patriarch Athanasios III Dabbās' work remains a significant contribution to the Arabic translation of the Gospel and the Orthodox community of Antioch. His efforts paved the way for a standardized version of scripture and made it available to a wider audience. The 17th century was a trying time for the Orthodox community of Antioch, with religious, political, and cultural tensions reflecting the broader situation in the Middle East. Nevertheless, Patriarch Athanasios III Dabbās persisted and left a lasting legacy, preserving and transmitting the Gospel for future generations.

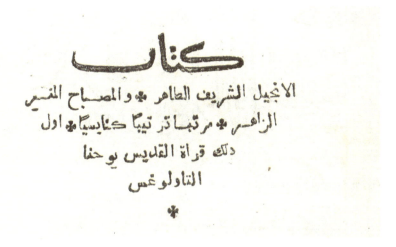

Fig. 1: *Book of the Noble, Pure Gospel and the Bright, Illuminating Lamp, Arranged for Church Use*, 1706, Aleppo (B.A.R.).

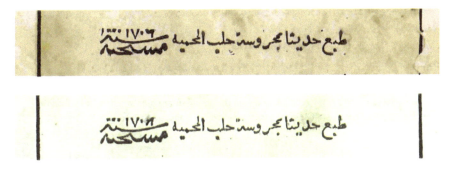

Fig. 2: Alteration of the dates in the two editions of the Tetraevangelion (idem).

Fig. 3: Colophon of Thalja al-Ḥamawī.

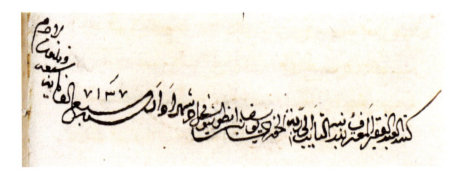

Fig. 4: Colophon of Yūsuf al-Muṣawwir.

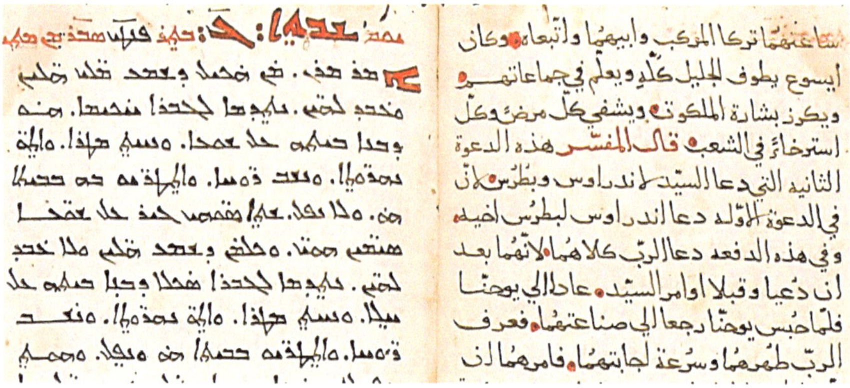

Fig. 5: MS Balamand 77, 13th century, showing the commentary following the *Gospel of the 2nd Sunday after Pentecost* (by permission Monastery of Balamand Library).

بيشارة الملكوت * ويشفي كل مرض واسترخا في الشعب قال المفسر
هذه الدعوة الثانيه التي دعا سيدنا يسوع المسيح لاندراوس وبطرس
لان الدعوة الاولي دعا اندراوس لبطرس اخيه * وفي هذه الدعوه
دعا الرب كلاهما * لانهما بعد ان دعيا وقبلا اوامر الرب السيد عاد
الي يوحنا * فلما حبس يوحنا رجعا الي صناعتهما * فعرف الرب
طهارتهما وسرعة اجابتهما * فامرهما ان يتبعاه ليحصل لهما عوض

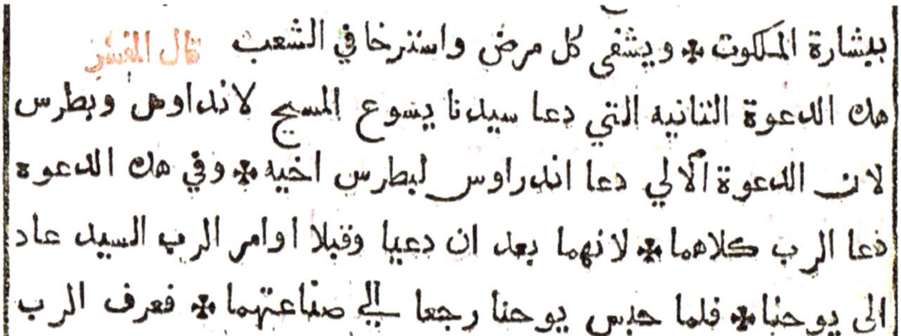

Fig. 6: Commentary present in the Liturgical Gospel of Dabbas following the *Gospel of the 2nd Sunday after Pentecost*, p. 83 (B.A.R.).

Bibliography

Cannuyer, Christian. "Langues usuelles et liturgiques des melkites au XIIIe siècle". *Oriens christianus*, 70, 1986, p. 110–117.

Cândea, Virgil. "Dès 1701 : Dialogue roumano-libanais par le livre et l'imprimerie". In C. Aboussouan (ed.), *Le livre et le Liban jusqu'à 1900*. Paris : Unesco, 1982, p. 283–294.

Charon, Cyrille. *Le rite byzantin dans les patriarcats melkites Alexandrie, Antioche, Jérusalem adoption, versions, éditions, pratique, particularités*. Rome: Typographie de la Propagande, 1908.

Charon, Cyrille. *Histoire des patriarcats melkites Alexandrie, Antioche, Jérusalem depuis le schisme monophysite du sixième siècle jusqu'à nos jours*, vol. III. Rome: Bretschneider, 1911.

Chiṭulescu, Policarp, Doru Bădără. *Antim Ivireanul. Opera tipografică*. Bucharest: Institutul Cultural Roman, 2016.

Dannaoui, Elie. "From Multiplicity to Unification of the Arabic Biblical Text: a Reading of the Rūm Orthodox Projects for the Arabization and Printing of the Gospels during the Ottoman Period". In David Bertaina, Sandra Toenies Keating, Mark N. Swanson, Alexander Treiger (eds.), *Heirs of the Apostles: Studies on Arabic Christianity in Honor of Sidney H. Griffith*. Leiden: Brill, 2018, p. 22–36.

Feodorov, Ioana. "The Romanian Contribution to Arabic Printing". In Elena Siupiur, Zamfira Mihail (eds.), *Impact de l'imprimerie et rayonnement intellectuel des Pays Roumains*. Bucharest: Editura Biblioteca Bucureștilor, 2009, p. 41–61.

Feodorov, Ioana (ed.). *Makāryūs III Ibn al-Zaʿīm et Paul d'Alep : relations entre les peuples de l'Europe Orientale et les chrétiens arabes au XVIIe siècle: actes du Ier colloque international le 16 septembre 2011*. Bucharest: Editura Academiei Române, 2012.

Feodorov, Ioana. "Livres arabes chrétiens imprimés avec l'aide des principautés roumaines au début du XVIIIe siècle. Un répertoire commenté". *Chronos*, 34, 2016, p. 7–49.

Frantsouzoff, Serge. "Le premier lectionnaire arabe orthodoxe imprimé". In C. Manolache (ed.), *Istorie și cultură: In honorem academician Andrei Eșanu*. Chișinău: Biblioteca Științifică, 2018, p. 459–486.

Griffith, Sidney. "From Aramaic to Arabic: The Languages of the Monasteries of Palestine in the Byzantine and Early Islamic Period". *Dumbarton Oaks Papers*, 51, 1997, p. 11–31.

Griffith, Sidney. *The Bible in Arabic. The Scriptures of the People of the Book in the Language of Islam*. Princeton: Princeton University Press, 2013.

Hikmat, Kashouh. *The Arabic Versions of the Gospel. The Manuscripts and Their Families*. Berlin: De Gruyter, 2012.

Ibrahim, Habib. "Talǧat an-nāsiḫ fils du prêtre Ḥūrān al-ḥamawī". *Chronos*, 39, 2019, p. 125–170.

Kilpatrick, Hilary. "Meletios Karmeh's specimen translation of Genesis I-V". In Leder Stefan, Binay Sara (eds.), *Translating the Bible into Arabic: Historical, Text-Critical and Literary Aspects*. Beirut: Orient-Institut, 2012, p. 61–73.

Kilpatrick, Hilary. "From Venice to Aleppo: Early Printing of Scripture in the Orthodox World". *Chronos*, 30, 2014, p. 33–61.

Kilzī, Lāwandiyūs. "Ḥayāt al-baṭriyark Aftīmiyūs Karma al-Anṭākī al-ḥamawī bi-qalam tilmīdhi-hi al-baṭriyark Makāriyūs al-ḥalabī". *al-Masarra* 4, 1913, p. 41–47, 81–89, 135–144.

Korolevskij, Cyrille. *Le rite byzantin dans les patriarcats melkites Alexandrie, Antioche, Jérusalem adoption, versions, éditions, pratique, particularités*. Rome: Typ. polyglotte de la S. congrégation de la Propagande, 1908.

Leeming, Kate. "The Adoption of Arabic as a Liturgical Language by the Palestinian Melkites". *Aram*, 15, 2003, p. 239–246.

Morozov, Dmitriĭ. "Arabskoe Evangelie Daniila Apostola". *Arkhiv russkoĭ istorii*, 2, 1992, p. 192–203.

Morozov, Dmitriĭ. "Vifleemskiĭ ėkzempliar arabskogo Evangeliia Daniila Apostola". *Arkhiv russkoĭ istorii*, 8, 2007, p. 645–651.

Nassif, Charbel. "Le peintre Youssef Al-Musawwer, fondateur de l'école d'Alep". In Raphaëlle Ziadé (ed.), *Chrétiens d'Orient 2000 ans d'histoire*. Paris: Gallimard, 2017, p. 162–166.

Nassif, Charbel. "Autour de l'euchologe melkite de Malatios Karmé". *Proche-Orient chrétien*, 98, 2018, p. 46–61.

Nasrallah, Jospeh. *Histoire du mouvement littéraire dans l'Église melchite*, vol. IV.1. Louvain: Peeters, 1979.

Raheb, Abdallah. *Conception de l'union dans le patriarcat orthodoxe d'Antioche (1622–1672)*. Rome: Pontificia Università Gregoriana, 1981.

Tchentsova, Vera. "Le patriarche d'Antioche Macaire III Ibn Al-Zaʿîm et la chrétienté latine". In M.-H. Blanchet, F. Gabriel (eds.), *Réduire le schisme ? ecclésiologies et politiques de l'Union entre Orient et Occident (XIIIᵉ–XVIIIᵉ siècles)*. Paris : Association des Amis du Centre d'histoire et civilisation de Byzance, 2013.

Ūstāsh, Īhūr. *Kitāb al-Injīl al-sharīf al-ṭāhir wa-l-miṣbāḥ al-munīr al-zāhir* [Introduction + facsimilé]. Kyiv: Fond pam'iati Blazhennishoho Mytropolyta Volodymyra, 2021.

Walbiner, Carsten. "Macarius Ibn al-Zaʿīm and the Beginnings of an Orthodox Church Historiography in Bilād al-Shām". In *Le rôle des historiens orthodoxes dans l'historiographie*, Lebanon: al-Balamand, 2010, p. 11–28.

Walbiner, Carsten. "Melkite (Greek Orthodox) Approaches to the Bible at the Time of the Community's Cultural Reawakening". In Sara Binay, Stefan Leder (eds.), *Translating the Bible into Arabic: Historical, Text-Critical, and Literary Aspect*. Beirut: Orient-Institut, 2012, p. 53–61.

Habib Ibrahim

Makarios ibn al-Zaʿīm's *Book of the Wheel*

1. Identifying Makarios ibn al-Zaʿīm's *Book of the Wheel*

During my visit to Oxford on a mission for the ERC Project TYPARABIC, I had an opportunity to visit several local libraries and consult some rare books and manuscripts. It helped me find new information for my project on the contributions of Meletios Karma[1] and his brother Talǧah. It is important to have an overview of the Christian literary activity in 17th century Aleppo that led to the establishment of the printing press by Athanasius Dabbas.

The *Fihrist* online catalogue describes manuscripts Huntington 27–30 from the Bodleian Library as "1 copy of Revision of the *Synaxarion* by Meletios Karma al-Ḥamawī (1572−1635)", in 4 volumes, with details such as "composed 1612" and "origin 1638 CE" provided.[2]

The original information undoubtedly comes from Joannes Uri's catalogue.[3] Uri notes that Huntington 27 is dated 7146 AM (1638 CE) and is composed of 190 folios. It is the first of four tomes of a martyrologion containing twenty-seven lives of saints from a book entitled *al-Dūlāb* or the *Book of the Wheel*. The author is said to be Meletios, metropolitan of Aleppo. Manuscripts Huntington 28-30 are all copied by the same hand as Huntington 27 (compare Fig. 1 and 3). They have, respectively 154, 212 and 300 folios, which contain the lives of ten, seventeen and nineteen saints in each volume. Uri believes that there is no reason not to consider Huntington 30 as part of this work even if it shows some peculiarities that I

---

[1] Metropolitan of Aleppo (1612–1634), subsequently known as Euthymius Karma, patriarch of Antioch (1634–1635).
[2] https://www.fihrist.org.uk/catalog/manuscript_11114. The Byzantine Synaxarion was translated into Arabic before 1084. The Arabic version is called the Melkite Synaxarion. In the year 1612, Meletios Karma compared it and made it conform with the Greek Printed version of Venice (1591–1603). This version is called by the author of the *Fihrist* "Revision of the Synaxarion by Meletius Karma". On the Melkite Synaxarion, see J.-M. Sauget, *Premières recherches sur l'origine et les caractéristiques des synaxaires Melkites : XIe – XVIIe siècles*, Brussels, 1969.
[3] J. Uri, *Bibliothecae Bodleianae codicum manuscriptorum. Orientalium... catalogus, Pars prima*, Oxford, 1787, p. 29–46.

This research is part of a project that has received funding from the European Research Council (ERC) under the European Union's Horizon 2020 research and innovation programme (grant agreement No 883219-AdG-2019 – Project TYPARABIC).

∂ Open Access. © 2024, the author(s), published by De Gruyter. [(cc) BY-NC-ND] This work is licensed under the Creative Commons Attribution-NonCommercial-NoDerivatives 4.0 International License.
https://doi.org/10.1515/9783111060392-014

shall discuss later. In this description, Uri does not say precisely which Meletios is in question, whether Karma or Ibn al-Zaʻīm.

The attribution of the manuscripts to Karma comes from Pusey's catalogue and is probably due to Nicoll, as indicated in the *Fihrist*. Page 566 of Pusey's catalogue, which has the *addenda* to manuscripts Huntington 27–30 (Urii Codd. Chr. 92–95), contains a note pointing to page 469, footnote b, where more information is to be found about these manuscripts and their author.[4] Page 469, together with page 468, mainly deals with the revision of the *Horologion* of Meletios Karma. Meanwhile, in footnote b Nicoll identifies the same Meletios Karma with the author of the three manuscripts preserved in the Bodleian Library (Hunt. 27–29. Urii Codd. Christ. 92–95). He adds that Hunt. 30 should be numbered with these, which can only be inferred from the copyist's hand, as there is no title. In all cases, the months of September and October are absent from the manuscript.

Nicoll challenges Uri's understanding of Meletios' title: *Kitāb qiṣaṣ al-qiddīsīn al-'abrār wa-waṣf istishhād al-shuhadā' al-aṭhār wa-huwa min jumlat al-kitāb al-mukannā bi-l-dūlāb* (= "The book of the lives of the righteous saints and the description of the pure martyrs' martyrdom, and it is from a book called *al-Dūlāb*"). Uri's thesis is that Meletios selected his hagiographical material from a book called *al-Dūlāb*. According to Nicoll, *al-Dūlāb* is the title Meletios gave to his work, and the four manuscripts form parts of it.

Nicoll is undeniably confused about the identity of *al-Dūlāb*'s author due to the book's similarity with Karma's *Synaxarion*. The name of al-Dūlāb's author is Meletios and he is bishop of Aleppo, which was indeed Karma's name when he was bishop of Aleppo. Both works are dedicated to the lives and passions of saints and martyrs. Both authors express the pain they suffered in order to correct their texts and complete them. Despite these similarities, there is no doubt that the work in question is not that of Karma but was, as indicated by Graf and Nasrallah, created by Makarios ibn al-Zaʻīm.[5] It is documented in some copies of Karma's revision that he completed his work in Aleppo in 1612 CE.[6] On the contrary, our author unequivocally states that he composed his work in the year 1638 CE, a few years after Karma's death.

It is also evident that the work is not the same either. Still, in the title and preface (Fig. 1–2), we find two major distinctive points. Firstly, Karma's work is entitled *Kitāb*

---

4 E. B. Pusey, *Bibliothecae Bodleianae codicum manuscriptorum Orientalium catalogi. Partis secundae volumen secundum, arabicos complectens*, Oxford, 1835, p. 566.
5 Graf, *GCAL* I, p. 496 ; III, p. 104; J. Nasrallah, *Histoire du mouvement littéraire dans l'Eglise melchite du Vᵉ au XXᵉ siècle*, vol. IV : Période ottomane 1516–1900, tome 1 : 1516–1724, Louvain/Paris, 1979, p. 108.
6 MS Balamand 152 (1667?), fol. 5r; MS Séminaire Sainte Anne, Jerusalem, 1654, fol. 1r.

al-Sinaksār (Book of the Synaxarion).[7] In contrast, the work in question is entitled *Kitāb al-Dūlāb* (Book of the Wheel). At this point, it is important to note that Graf identifies it wrongly as a new revision of the Synaxarion, and Nasrallah is incorrect in assuming that the title "Book of the Wheel" is another name for the Synaxarion. As we shall see later, in this particular case *al-Dūlāb* refers to a Menologion.[8]

The identity of the author is better revealed by a volume of Meletios' *Wheel* preserved not in the Bodleian Collection, but in the Greek Orthodox Patriarchate in Damascus, manuscript 167 (Fig. 4).[9] The scribe of this manuscript calls the author Meletios the second, bishop of Aleppo, distinguishing Meletios I Karma from Meletios II Ibn al- Za'īm.

Thus, there is no doubt that the author of this work, *al-Dūlāb*, which is a Menologion in the modern sense,[10] is the famous Makarios ibn al-Za'īm, metropolitan of Aleppo (1635–1647), then patriarch of Antioch (1647–1672). However, its nature and content should be corrected in both Graf and Nasrallah, and should be considered along with *Kitāb al-naḥla* (Book of the Bee), *Kitāb al-rumūz* (*Book of the Symbols*), *Majmū' laṭīf* (*Delightful Collection*), *Majmū' mubārak* (*Blessed Collection*), one of most important works of our author. [11]

Like his predecessor, Ibn al-Za'īm had an interest in the lives of saints. In his work entitled *Book of the Saints from our Land*, he collected stories of the saints of the Antiochian Church from the Arabic translation of the Synaxarion.[12] He used the service of the Feast of All-Saints (the first Sunday after the Pentecost) and probably sources like the *Annales* of Sa'īd ibn al-Baṭrīq to gather the names of bishops who participated in ecumenical councils and local synods. He added the names of honorable ecclesiastical authors that he considered saints, such as Theodor Balsamon, George the Younger, Paul of Sidon, Gerasimus, Nikon of the Black Mountain, 'Abdallah ibn al-Faḍl al-Anṭākī, and ten hymnographers. The same collection contains the

---

7 The complete title is:

كتاب السنكسار يتضمن أخبار الرسل والأنبياء وقصص النساك والزهاد والعباد والأبرار والاابرار وأصناف ما جرى على الشهداء
والشهيدات وكافة المجاهدين والمعترفين بالمسيح في ساير الأقطار يقرىء كل يوم على مدار ايام السنة ذكر من انتقل منهم
في ذلك اليوم من أول شهر أيلول المفهوم إلى آخر شهر آب المعلوم ومن أحد الفريسي والعشار والى يوم اثنين العنصره
الذي يليه صوم الرسل الاطهار.

8 Nasrallah, *HMLEM*, IV.1, p. 108.
9 Nasrallah provided the old call number 1611.
10 Scholars have established the definition of and the distinction between Synaxarion, Menaion and Menologion. See J. Noret, "Ménologes, synaxaires, ménées. Essai de clarification d'une terminologie", *Analecta Bollandiana*, 86, 1968, p. 21–24.
11 For a general idea of the works of Ibn Za'īm, see Nasrallah, *HMLEM* IV.1, p. 90–126.
12 This collection is preserved in the MS British Library Add. 9965 and MS Saint-Sauveur A.C. 1052.

stories of various saints that Makarios seems to have translated during his travels. These are the *Lives* of Saints Nikita, Ananias, Valasios (Blasius), bishop of Sebastia; the autobiography of Clement or his *Letter to James the Apostle*; the *Martyrdom of Clement*, copied by Makarios at Sinope, on December 22, 7167 (1659 CE); *The Life of Amphilochius of Iconium* written by Makarios on December 23, 7167; the *Story of the Third Finding of Saint John the Baptist's Head*; the *Life of Saint Akindynos and his Companions*; Excerpts from the *Life of Simon Stylite* attributed to Anthony; the *Miracle of Gregory the Theologian*, copied by Makarios at Sinope, on February 8, 7167.

Some of Makarios's important translations of hagiographical material are preserved in *al-Kitāb al-ṣayfī*. This title reflects the Greek name of the original work *Kalokairinē* (for summer) by Agapius Landos († before 1664).[13] It is preserved in the manuscript *Dayr al-Shīr 600bis*. It has sixteen lives of saints: *Story of the Seven Sleepers of Ephesus*; *Martyrdom of Christophorus*; *Life of Eythymius the Athonite*; *Martyrdom of Basiliscus*; *Life of David of Thessaloniki*; *Sampson the Hospitable*; *Acts of the Apostles Peter and Paul*; *Life of Athanasius the Athonite*; *Martyrdom of Pancras*; *Life of Michael Maleinos*; *Life of Irene of Chrysovalantou*; *Martyrdom of Callinicus*; *Life of Moses the Ethiopian*; *Life of Theodora of Thessaloniki*; *Story of the Mandylion*; *Martyrdom of Julian the Egyptian*.

A manuscript from the Greek Orthodox Patriarchate of Damascus used to have these sixteen texts together with thirteen other works of mostly hagiographical content:[14] The *Martyrdom and Miracles of George*; *Passio and Miracles of Demetrius*; *Miracles of Nicholas*; *Martyrdom of Theodorus Stratelates*; *Life of Theophanu the Queen*; *Acts of the Apostle Andrew*; *Life of Athanasius of Alexandria*; *Martyrdom of Cyriace*; *Life of Paraskeve*;[15] *Martyrdom of Charalampus*.

---

13 On Makarios' translations of Agapios Landos, see C. Walbiner, " 'Popular' Greek Literature on the Move: the Translation of Several Works of Agapios Landos of Crete into Arabic in the 17th Century", *Revue des Études Sud-Est Européennes*, 51, 2013, p. 147–157.

14 In their *Histoire*, Nasrallah refer to old call numbers of the Greek Orthodox Patriarchate in Damascus. According to him, manuscript 1640 is a collection of twenty-nine lives of saints compiled by Makarios ibn al-Za'īm. R. El-Gemayel attempted to make the concordance between the call numbers provided by Nasrallah and the ones given in the catalog. He correctly identified 1640 with 226. However, I have checked the reproductions of manuscript 226 provided on vHMML. It seems that this manuscript was replaced by an abridged Synaxarion by Acacius monk of the Sinai. See Nasrallah, *HMLEM*, IV.1, p. 105–106; el-Gemayel, "Les manuscrits du patriarcat grec-orthodoxe de Damas dans l'Histoire de Joseph Nasrallah et Rachid Haddad", in Ž. Paša (ed.), *Between the Cross and the Crescent. Studies in Honor of Samir Khalil Samir, S.J., on the Occasion of His Eightieth Birthday*, coll. OCA 304, Rome, 2018, p. 248.

15 He translated the *Life of Paraskeve* from a Greek version. He also included it in the collection *Majmū' laṭīf*. It was published by I. Feodorov, "The Arabic Version of the Life of Saint Paraskevi the New by Makarios Az-Za'īm", in *Proceedings of the 20th Congress of the Union* Éuropéenne *des*

Makarios also reports in *Kitāb al-Naḥla* (*Book of the Bee*) that he found in Georgia a Greek version of the *Vita of Simeon Stylites the Younger* longer than the one preserved in Arabic.[16] He translated the missing parts and copied them into the book.

At this stage, it is important to highlight with C. Walbinar that hagiography served for Makarios as an important instrument to propagate a history-based Antiochian identity.[17] The establishment of *Kitāb al-Dulāb* falls clearly in the scope of this endeavor.

2. Some Notes on Ibn al-Zaʿīm's *Book of the Wheel*

Ibn al-Zaʿīm's interest in hagiography grew when he became bishop of Aleppo in 1635 CE. Wishing to provide believers with spiritual texts, he asked the bishops and priests of the Patriarchate of Antioch to let him know about copies of saints' lives. Soon he discovered the *Book of the Wheel* by Yūḥannā ʿAbd al-Masīḥ (11th c.), also called *Maʿīn al-ḥayāt al-markab al-sāʾir fī mīnāʾ al-najāt*.[18] This raises the question

---

Arabisants et Islamisants, Part One, The Arabist. Budapest Studies in Arabic, ed. K. Dévényi, Budapest, 2002, p. 69–80.

16 On the Arabic translation of the *Life of Simeon Stylites the Younger*, see Ibrahim, Makhoul, "Les débuts du renouveau intellectuel à Antioche au Xe s. Quatre hagiographies inédites traduites au Mont-Admirable", *Pecia. Le livre et l'écrit*, 18/2, 2015, p. 39–54, here 42–47.

17 C. M. Walbiner, "Macarius Ibn al-Zaʾim and the beginnings of an Orthodox church historiography in bilad al-Sham", in Université de Balamand (ed.), *Le rôle des historiens orthodoxes dans l'historiographie. Actes du colloque 11–14 Mars 2007, al-Balamand*, Balamand, [2010], p. 14-17. See also: C. M. Walbiner, "Preserving the Past and Enlightening the Present: Macarius B. al-Zaim and Medieval Melkite Literature", *Parole de l'Orient*, 34, 2009, p. 433–441.

18 Yūḥannā's *Maʿīn* is composed of nine volumes that cover the twelve months of the calendar. It is preserved in fourteen manuscripts at Sinai (Sinai ar. 395–403 and 405–409). Examination of these manuscripts has revealed that twelve of them belong to two copies of the *Maʿīn*, while the other two were copied separately at unknown dates. The first copy (Sinai ar. 398, 401, 403, 406, and 408) was completed in 1259 in Antioch, likely having the autograph of Yūḥannā as its archetype. This copy has lost the volumes covering the months of September, October, November, May and July. The second copy (Sinai ar. 395, 396, 397, 402, 405, 407, and 409) was copied from the first at Sinai between 1328 and 1334 for the use of the Church of the Syrians at the monastery. This copy has lost the volumes covering the months of October, December and January. Manuscripts 399 and 400 were probably meant to replace the lost or damaged manuscripts of the second copy, as they cover the months of December and January. In addition to the fourteen manuscripts, Sinai ar. 423 should be mentioned. It is an abridged version of the *Maʿīn* in which the scribe selects the texts of interest and abbreviates certain texts that he considers too lengthy (e.g., the *Acts of the Apostle John* by his disciple Prochorus). We note that some parts of the *Maʿīn* have not survived in any of the mentioned manuscripts: the beginning of September, October, the end of

of whether there was any full copy of this work other than in Sinai. In the preface of *Kitāb siyar wa-qiṣaṣ wa-akhbār baʿḍ al-rusul wa-l-shuhadāʾ wa-l-abrār* (*Lives, Narratives, and Stories of some Apostles, Martyrs and Righteous Men*), he states that he copied the whole manuscript from Saydnaya that had the lives of saints for September.[19] In the same source, he says that he found a very old copy of the synaxarion for November in the region of Homs. However, he does not mention a complete copy of the *Book of the Wheel* by Yūḥannā ʿAbd al-Masīḥ. This raises the question of whether it was during a visit to Sinai or through some monks living there that he became aware of the full set. The preface of Ibn al-Zaʿīm's *Book of the Wheel* makes it clear that the texts he put together were scattered in different places. However, this statement might apply only to the accounts that he did not find in Yūḥannā's main corpus. It appears that the process of surveying the manuscripts took approximately three years, and Makarios completed his revision of the texts in 1638 CE.

Ibn al-Zaʿīm's *Book of the Wheel* contains a total of seventy-three texts for seventy commemorative feasts. Three feasts have two texts each and four others have only synaxaria. Surprisingly, the number of accounts provided by Uri (as mentioned above) and reiterated by Nasrallah is incorrect.[20] This should be corrected as follows:

- Tome 1B (Bodleian, Hunt. 27) has only twelve texts and one synaxarion.
- Tome 2 (Bodleian, Hunt. 28) has eleven texts and one synaxarion.
- Tome 3 (Bodleian, Hunt. 29) has nineteen texts and two synaxaria.
- Tome 4 (Bodleian, Hunt. 30) has nineteen texts.
- Additionally, we should include tome 1A (Damascus, Orthodox Patriarchate 167) which has eight texts.

September: In the aforementioned preface to *Kitāb siyar wa-qiṣaṣ wa-akhbār*, Macarios says that he copied the whole manuscript of Saydnaya that has the *Lives of Saints* for September.[21] We do not know what the fate of this copy was.

October: We do not know if Ibn al-Zaʿīm ever composed this volume. Unlike September and November, he says nothing about it. However, his silence could be because there is nothing special to say about this particular volume.

January, and the beginning of February (except for the pieces preserved in the abridged version). Therefore, the number of these identifiable pieces is far from definitive. In an article published in 2018, I counted 227 pieces. After correcting some data, we now count 231 pieces, including 44 sermons for the feasts of the Lord and 187 hagiographical pieces commemorating the saints.

19 This preface was published in L. Kilzī, " ʿInāyat al-baṭriyark Makāriyūs al-rābiʿ Zaʿīm bi-jamʿ akhbār al-qiddīsīn", *al-Masarra*, 25, 1939, p. 620–621. Parts of it were reproduced in C. M. Walbiner, "Preserving the Past and Enlightening the Present", p. 434–435.

20 Nasrallah, *HMLEM*, IV.1, p. 108.

21 This preface was published in L. Kilzī, "ʿInāyat al-baṭriyark Makāriyūs", p. 620–621. Parts of it were reproduced in C. M. Walbiner, "Preserving the Past and Enlightening the Present", p. 434–435.

November: In the same source mentioned in connection with September, Macarios informs us that he discovered a very old copy of November in the region of Homs. He proceeded to make a copy of it and delivered it to the archbishopric. Today, two codices contain this month: Greek Orthodox Patriarchate 167 and Hunt. 27. These two manuscripts complement each other (the patriarchate's manuscript covers up to November 14, while Hunt. 27 contains the remainder), albeit they were transcribed by different scribes. Both include Macarios's preface in which he elucidates the reasons for assembling this collection. Given these circumstances, I believe that Macarios originally divided the month of November into two volumes from the outset. One plausible rationale for this division could be the practical consideration that this volume was too big.

December and January: For some unknown reason, the Lives and Martyrdom collected in this tome are not in liturgical calendar order. The commemoration of John the Merciful, celebrated on November 12th (tome 1A), was reintroduced in this volume.

February, March and April: They are preserved in one volume. Strangely, we find the author's preface at the beginning of March and April, but not in February, which is the first month of the volume. These months are brief because they cover the period of Lent during which it is rarely allowed to commemorate saints. For example, whenever the Feast of Saint George (April 23) occurs during Lent, it is celebrated on May 6.

May: As for October, we do not know if Ibn al-Zaʿīm ever composed this volume.

June and July: They are preserved in one volume since June has a few commemorations.

August: Having access to only one life, he added it as an annex to July.

I summarize these facts in the following table:

Tab. 1: Manuscripts of the *Book of the Wheel* and their Content.

Tome	I	II	IIIA	IIIB	IV-(V)	VI			VII	VIII-(IX)		
Month	Sept	Oct	Nov		Dec-Jan[22]	Feb	Mar	Apr	May	Jun	Jul	Aug
Manuscript	Lost?	N/A	P	Hunt. 27	Hunt. 30	Hunt. 28			N/A	Hunt. 29		

---

22 Even though this volume only has saints for December and January – the exception is the Life of John the Merciful, which is clearly misplaced –, they are not in chronological order according to the liturgical calendar.

3. Relation between Yūḥannā 'Abd al-Masīḥ's and Ibn al-Za'īm's Menologia

There is no doubt Ibn al-Za'īm had access and used Yūḥannā 'Abd al-Masīḥ's *al-Dulāb*. Firstly, he gives his work an identical title to *al-Dulāb*. Secondly, as in Yūḥannā 'Abd al-Masīḥ's Menologion, the month of November is covered by two volumes,[23] February, March and April are covered by a single volume, as are the months of June and July. While we might consider the first evidence as a simple coincidence, the second is undoubtedly not.

As previously mentioned, Ibn al-Za'īm copied the entire manuscript in Saydnaya, which contained the lives of saints for September. Additionally, he discovered a very old manuscript in the village of Qatina in Homs, which contained the stories of the saints for November. Makarios provides more details about this particular manuscript, noting that it was copied while the city of Antioch was still under Christian control. This likely refers to a date earlier than the city's destruction by Baybars in 1268 CE. As Alexander Treiger and I have shown in our publications, volume III, covering November and copied in Antioch in 1258, has been lost.[24] Could the manuscript found by Makarios be the lost third tome of the 1258 copy of *al-Dulāb*? I attempted to locate this manuscript among the numerous manuscripts preserved in the Orthodox patriarchal and bishopric residences, as well as monasteries. Unfortunately, the existing catalogues of these collections did not yield significant results, and regrettably, this initial attempt did not succeed in locating the manuscript. Regarding the volume for September, I was similarly unable to locate either the archetype Makarios possessed or the copy he produced.

Another argument is that out of the sixty-nine stories and lives from Makarios' work, only six are not found in Yūḥannā's text (namely, numbers 5, 32, 35, 41, 48 and 49). Nineteen texts are preserved with minor differences, while approximately twenty texts were rewritten (recensions). The only other known collection of hagiographical texts that shares such a significant number of common names with Yūḥannā's work is the bipartite manuscript from the British Library Add. 26117/Or. 5019 (circa 11th century), with forty-two saints appearing in both texts.

---

23 With a slight difference, however; the cut is after John Chrysostom (November 13) in Yūḥannā's, but after the Apostle Philip (November 14) in Makarios'.
24 A. Treiger, "SINAITICA (1): The Antiochian Menologion, Compiled by Hieromonk Yūḥannā 'Abd al-Masīḥ (First Half of the 13th Century)", *Khristianskiĭ Vostok*, 8, 2017, p. 216–217; H. Ibrahim, "Liste des vies de saints et des homélies conservées dans les ms. Sinaï arabe 395–403, 405–407, 409 et 423", *Chronos*, 38, 2018, p. 49.

However, the London collection is not divided into months, and most of the texts are of different versions. In a previous study, I demonstrated the originality of the versions presented by Yūḥannā and the possibility that he used an archetype of the London manuscript as the basis for his works. I have also demonstrated that Yūḥannā's works were not widely disseminated, with only a few rare copies found in Sinai containing a very limited number of his texts.[25] It is noteworthy that all these exceedingly rare stories are preserved in Makarios' work, such as the stories of Photine (February 26)[26] and Benedict (March 14).

I have a fourth and last undeniable piece of evidence that Makarios had a direct connection with Yūḥannā's work. Within Makarios's work, two texts commemorate Gurias, Samona and Habib. The first text pertains to their martyrdom, while the second focuses on their miracles. Although the story of their martyrdom was entirely rewritten, the account of their miracles underwent only minor changes. To our delight, Makarios inadvertently retained important information in the title, indicating that the account was translated by "*al-rāhib anbā Yūḥannā al-qass*", the same way Yūḥannā identifies himself in his work.[27]

At this point, I should draw attention to the relationship between Makarios and Yūḥannā's *Book of the Wheel* and Sinai Arabic 540. The comparison between the three reveals a lost piece of Yūḥannā's work.

Sinai Arabic 540 is dated ca. 12th c. It is mainly composed of hagiographical texts: 1- *Miracle of Gurias, Samonas and Habib* (Beginning missing, 1r–4v); 2- *Martyrdom of Babilas, Patriarch of Antioch* (4v–24r); Martyrdom of Ananias (24r–32v); *Life and Martyrdom of Cosmas and Damian* (33r–40r and 40v–104v); *First and Second Letters of Abgar* and the answers of Jesus, and *Acts of Thaddeus* (105r–160v);[28] *Life of Barlaam of the Black Mountain* (161r–218r); *Life of Alexius the man of God* (219r–232r); Anastasius' *Commentary on Psalm* 6 (232v–265r); *Story of the Finding of the Cross* (265r–270v, end missing).

---

25 H. Ibrahim, "Un moine métaphraste à Antioche : Yūḥannā 'Abd al-Masīḥ († 11ᵉ siècle)", in R. Ceulemans, D. Oltean (eds.), *Foreign Monks in Byzantium: Migration Trends and Integration Policies in Religious Context*, Orientalia Lovaniensia Analecta / Bibliothèque de Byzantion, Leuven (forthcoming).

26 Graf only mentions two manuscripts: Sinai Ar. 403 (Yūḥannā's) and Sbath 411, copied in 1654, undoubtedly from Makarios' version. See Graf, *GCAL* I, p. 521–522.

27 See Treiger, SINAITICA (1), p. 234–236, also p. 215, 217, n. 8, 233.

28 While the *Letters of Abgar* and answers of Jesus are read on August 16, the *Acts and Martyrdom of Thaddeus* are separately read on June 19 in Yūḥannā's *Book of the Wheel*.

This manuscript seems to have at least two sources: while the first part is copied from Yūḥannā's work, the second part is from an unknown source.[29] The version of the *Miracle of Gurias, Samonas, and Habib*, as well as the story of Ananias, is the same as Yūḥannā's. As for the account of Babylas, the style resembles Yuhanna's texts written in *saj'* (eg. Charbel and Bebaia's *Life*). It seems that the author of the text, probably Yūḥannā, had already prepared the text to be written in *saj'* but did not complete his project.[30] I suggest that this is one of the lost texts of Yūḥannā's *Book of the Wheel*. It would be inexplicable, though, why the scribe of the abridged version omitted the important patriarch and martyr of Antioch, Babilas.

Regarding the accounts of Cosmas and Damian, it appears that the original text by Yūḥannā may have been lost because the first folios of the manuscript are missing. The abridged version of the *Book of the Wheel* contains a version that differs from both texts preserved in Sinai Ar. 540. Fortunately, Makarios' work has preserved the same version of the second account of Sinai Ar. 540. As mentioned earlier, both Makarios' work and Sinai Ar. 540 share the same version of the miracle of Gurias, Samonas and Habib.[31] Therefore, there are two possibilities: Makarios copied these two works either from Yūḥannā or Sinai Ar. 540.

In Sinai Ar. 540, the three hagiographical texts that follow, the letters to Abgar together with the *Acts of Thaddeus* and the accounts of Barlaam and Alexius, are preserved in a different version from Yūḥannā's work. The last two are also preserved in Makarios but in different versions from both Yūḥannā and Sinai Ar. 540. They seem, however, more like recensions from Yūḥannā.

Considering these factors, there is a limited chance that Makarios had access to Sinai Ar. 540. Instead, he likely copied, as he did with most of his accounts, from Yūḥannā's work. Thus, I believe that the version of Cosmas and Damian preserved in both Sinai Ar. 540 and Makarios' work originates from Yūḥannā's

---

29 Sinai Arabic 535 and 540 have Anastasius' *Commentary on Psalm 6* (232v–265r) and the *Finding of the Cross* (265r–270v, end missing) in common. Do they have the same archetype or did 535 copied from 540? This is a question to be investigated in the future.

30 Folio 6r:

فاذ علم بحيلة المغتصب واضماره فيها

جمع في الهيكل جماعة المؤمنين التي يتم امتلاؤه بها

وحثّهم على الانتصار بك الشرائع ممن يغتصبها

واستغاث بالاقتدار الإلهي لنجدته بطلبات وصلوات واصلها

31 Unfortunately, I cannot verify if this was the case for the accounts of Babylas (Sept. 4) and Ananias (Oct. 1) because I did not find any manuscript for September and October among Makarios' works.

Book of the Wheel. Consequently, this should be considered one of the lost pieces of that book.

On the other hand, Makarios seems not to have had access to the text for August of Yūḥannā's work. His version only has the story of Adrian and Nathalia. We can argue for two reasons that Makarios is using another source for this vita: first, the version he is copying is different; second, this story is easily accessible through other manuscripts.

It becomes evident that Makarios undoubtedly used Yūḥannā's *Book of the Wheel*, though he did not have access to all the volumes covering the twelve months. His work should therefore be considered while preparing the edition of Yūḥannā's *Book of the Wheel.* His text could be used with caution in some vitae to fill gaps that are due to the bad condition of preservation of the Sinai manuscripts.

4. Description of the Content of Ibn al-Zaʿīm's *Book of the Wheel*

The *Book of the Wheel* as preserved has a preface and seventy commemorative feasts, four of them synaxaria (short notices). If a saint has a vita and a martyrdom, I have gathered them under one number in the list of content below. Some saints are commemorated on another day in Yūḥannā's *Book of the Wheel.* I added this information in a footnote.

The preface is repeated five times at the beginning of both volumes for November, and the beginning of March, April and June of Tome II. It is inexplicably missing at the beginning of February, the first month of this tome. Thereafter, I provide the preface with an English translation as well as the list of the commemorations of the *Book of the Wheel.* The months of December and January are to be found at the end of the list because this volume is not organized according to the liturgical calendar like the others. Otherwise, I would have needed to separate the lives of January from those of February and create a new order for the whole manuscript.

In the list below, I will clarify whether the version of a life or a passion provided by Makarios is the same as, different from, or a recension (revised or edited version) of that of Yuḥannā ʿAbd al-Masīḥ.

Some parts of Yuḥannā ʿAbd al-Masīḥ's *Book of the Wheel* are lost in the earliest copies: September 1–20, October, November 1–5,[32] and January 16–31. They

---

32 November 5 seems to have two commemorations: Galaction and Episteme, and Agathangelus. While the first is completely lost, four folios survive from the second.

are partially preserved in the seventeenth abridged version.[33] However, I suspect that some of them are not genuine but were added by the scribe (nr 31, 66, 72, and 73).[34] If any of Makarios' texts are only preserved in the abridged version, I will specify that the text in question is compared to "*al-Dūlāb* abridged".

5. Preface

We shall begin with the help of God and His gracious guidance to write the book of the stories of the righteous saints and the narratives of the martyrdom of the pure martyrs. This is a selection from the book known as *al-Dūlāb*, which was carefully collected and edited with diligence by the humble Meletios, the bishop of the city of Aleppo.	نبتدئ بعون الله تعالى وحسن توفيقه نكتب كتاب قصص القديسين الابرار ووصف استشهاد الشهداء الأطهار وهو من جملة الكتاب المكنى بالدولاب مما اعتنى بجمعه وتحريره بجدف ونصب الحقير ملاتيوس مطران مدينة حلب
Praise be to God, who has blessed us with the light of upright and truthful faith, and has saved us from the depths of blasphemy and the misguidance of heretics. Thanks to Him continuously during the day and night.	المجد لله الذي جاد علينا بضياء الأمانة المستقيمة الصادقة وأنقذنا من وهاد الكفر وضلالة أرباب البدع والأراطقة له الشكر على الاستمرار في ساعات الليل والنهار
That said, God's truthful and authentic books illuminate the mind, intellect and senses, and cleanse the inner eye from the darkness of disbelief and confusion. Especially, the stories and accounts of the saints because they purify the soul and expose its blemishes, as claimed by our father, the chosen Saint John the Golden-Mouthed, for he said in some of his noble sayings and blessed teachings that the accounts of the saints and the righteous who have passed are like a clear mirror for the souls of believers who come after. When they contemplate the lives of those saints, observe their ways, witness their virtuous appearance, and recognize their ugly image, they may aspire at some point to emulate them and strive to attain their virtues.	أما بعد فإن كتب الله الصحيحة الصادقة تنير الذهن والعقل والحواس وتكشف عن بصائر القلوب ظلمة الكفر والالتباس ولا سيما أخبار وقصص القديسين فإن بها طهارة النفس وقباحتها تستبين كما زعم أبينا القديس الفيلسوف المنتخب وهو النبيل في القديسين يوحنا فم الذهب لأنه يقول في بعض أقاويله الشريفة وتعاليمه الطاهرة المنيفة إن أخبار القديسين والصديقين السالفين تشبه مرآة صاف صقالها لنفوس المؤمنين المستأنفين لأنهم إذا تأملوا سيرة أولائك القديسين وعاينوا هم طريقتهم وشاهدوا حسن شكل أولائك ورمقوا هم قبح صورتهم ربما نهضوا في وقت من الأوقات إلى الاقتداء بهم والتشبه بفضيلتهم

33 I have published this abridged version: Yuḥannā ʿAbd al-Masīḥ († 11ᵉ s.), '*Maʿīn al-ḥayāt al-Markab al-sāʾir fī mīnāʾ al-naǧāt*', *autrement connu comme al-Dūlāb*, 2 vols., Beirut, 2020–2021.
34 Check these numbers in Ibrahim, "Liste des vies", p. 59, 68–70.

However, when the nations conquered us and brought us harm and affliction, trials and tribulations befell us one after another, and difficulties and calamities overwhelmed us. At that time, we had neither the interest nor the means to preserve books. They were marginalized like something of no interest, and most of the books were lost, consumed by flames month after month, age after age, year after year. The accounts of the saints were nearly forgotten.	فلما استولت الأمم علينا وأوصلوا الأذى والأضرار إلينا ترادفت علينا أمواج التجارب والامتحانات وتراكمت علينا وغمرتنا سحابة الشدائد والآفات لم يكن حينئذ عندنا بالكتب اهتمام ولا عناية لكنها صارت مطروحة مقصاة إلى الغاية بمنزلة فضلة زائدة ليس بها منفعة ولا فائدة فاحترقت أكثر الكتب على ممر الشهور والدهور والأعوام وبقيت أخبار القديسين غير متعارفة على الدوام
So, I, the humble Meletios, when I realized this, resolved to cast away laziness and failure, discard the cloak of weariness and boredom, and dedicate myself to gathering and compiling these accounts from various places. I endeavored to organize and edit them for the benefit of the people, dividing them into several books, with diligence and dedication. At that time, I was metropolitan of the city of Aleppo. I composed this work in the year 1638 CE, equivalent to 1047 Hijri.	فلما رمقت ذلك أنا الحقير ملاتيوس طرحت عني الكسل والفشل وخلعت سربال الضجر والملل وأجهدت نفسي في جمعها وتحصيلها من البلاد وبالغت حسب مقدرتي في ضبطها وتحريرها للعباد وقسمتها في عدة كتب بجد ونصب وأنا يومئذ مطران بمدينة حلب وحررتها بتاريخ سنة ألف وستمائة ثمانية وثلاثين مسيحية آمين. الموافق ألف سبعة وأربعين للهجرة الإسلامية

6. Tome 1A

November (Damascus, Orthodox Patriarchate 167)

1. F. 3r–7v: Cosmas and Damianus (November 1), different from the one in the abridged *al-Dūlāb*.
2. F. 8r–15v: Galaction and Epistime (November 5), same as in the abridged *al-Dūlāb*.
3. F. 15v–22r: Agathangelus (November 5), recension.
4. a. F. 22v–31v: Martyrdom of Menas (November 11), different version.
    b. F. 31v–33v: Miracles of Menas, different from *al-Dūlāb*, probably a recension.
5. F. 34r–73v: John the Merciful (November 12), same version.
6. F. 74r–237v: John Chrysostom (November 13), recension.
7. F. 238r–243v: Philip the Apostle (November 14), different version.

7. Tome 1B

November (Bodleian, Hunt. 27)

8. a. F. 3r–21r: Gurias, Samona and Habib (November 15).

In the title, we read that it was translated by the monk Abba Yūḥannā the priest. However, the text is not the same as the one we find in *al-Dūlāb*. It seems to be a recension of Yūḥannā 'Abd al-Masīḥ.

b. F. 21v–29r: Miracle of Gurias, Samonas and Habib with the daughter of the widow, same version.

9. F. 33v–60r: Gregory of Neocesarea (November 17).

The scribe writes the date November 17, then leaves seven blank pages and starts his text on folio 33. The text is longer than the one in *al-Dūlāb*.

10. F. 60v–67v: Romanus (November 18), different version or recension.
11. F. 68r: Plato (November 18), synaxarion only.
12. F. 68r–71r: Barlaam (November 19; usually 16), same version.
13. F. 71v–77r: Amphilochius (November 23), same version.
14. F. 77v–133v: Gregory of Agrigento [November 24], same version.
15. F. 134r–145r Clement of Rome (November 24), same version.

In the end, we find the Synaxarion that tells the martyrdom of Clement.

16. F. 145v–154v: Peter of Alexandria (November 24),[35] different version.
17. F. 155r–167r: Catherina (November 25), same version.
18. F. 167v–179r: Mercurius [November 25], different version.
19. F. 179v–190r: Jacob (November 27), recension; same as Vatican, Sbath 26.

8. Tome 2

February (Bodleian, Hunt. 28)
20. F. 2r–14v: Julian of Homs (February 6), different version.
21. F. 15r–24r: Martinian (February 13), a recension.
22. F. 24v: Porphyrius (February 26), synaxarion only.
23. F. 25r–35r: Photine (February 26),[36] same version.
24. F. 35r–37r: Marana and Cyra (February 28), different version.

March
25. F. 38v–46v: Eudoxia (March 1), a recension.
26. F. 47r–54v: Forty Martyrs of Sebaste (March 9), different version.
27. F. 55r–86v: Benedictus (March 14), same version.
28. F. 87v–95v: Alexius (March 17), different version.

---

35 November 25 in *al-Dūlāb*.
36 March 20 in *al-Dūlāb*.

April

29. F. 97v–113r: Mary of Egypt attributed to Sophronius (April 1), different version.
30. a. F. 113v–125r: Martyrdom of George (April 23), different version, probably a recension.
    b. F. 125v–154v: Miracle of George, different version.

9. Tome 3

June

31. F. 3r–16r: Onuphrius (June 12), same version.
32. F. 16v–30r: Julian of Tarsus (June 21), not in Yūḥannā ʿAbd al-Masīḥ.
33. F. 30v–40r: Febronia (June25), recension.
34. F. 40v–52v: Peter and Paul [June 29], recension.
35. F. 53r–59v: Apostles (June 30), not in Yūḥannā ʿAbd al-Masīḥ.

July

36. F. 60r–70v: Procopius (July 8), different version.
37. F. 70v–77r: Cyricus and Julitta (July 15), different version (BHG 314?).
38. F. 77r–83v: Marina (July 17), different version, probably a recension.
39. F. 83v–94v: The Forty-Five Martyrs of Nicopolis (July 10!), different version, probably a recension.
40. F. 94v–95r: Dius and Macrina (July 19), synaxarion only.
41. F. 95v–131r: Theodore, metropolitan of Edessa (July 19), not in Yūḥannā ʿAbd al-Masīḥ.
42. F. 131v–137v: Barlaam [July 19], recension.
43. F. 138r–145v: the Prophet Elias (July 20), recension.
44. F. 145v–173v: Simon Salus and John (July 21), same version without the introduction.
45. F. 174r–180r: Christina (July 24), recension.
46. F. 180v: Synaxarion of July 25.
47. F. 180v–195r: Eupraxia (July 25), same version.
48. F. 195r–197r: Olympia (July 25), not in Yūḥannā ʿAbd al-Masīḥ.
49. F. 197r–198v: Hermolaus (July 26), not in Yūḥannā ʿAbd al-Masīḥ.
50. F. 198v–209v: Panteleimon (July 27), different version.

August

51. F. 210r–221r: Adrian and Nathalia (August 26), recension.

10. Tome 4 (Second?)

December-January

52. F. 2r–13r: Ignatius of Antioch (December 20), same version.
53. F. 13v–23r: Xenophon, his wife and their children (January 26), probably one of the lost pieces of Yūḥannā 'Abd al-Masīḥ.
54. F. 23v–36r: Martyrs of Raithu and Sinai (January 14), different version or recension.
55. F. 36v–59v: Eustratius (December 13), a different version.
56. F. 60r–93v: Basil the Great attributed to Ilarion [January 1], recension.
57. F. 94r–128v: Nicholas Thaumaturgus [December 6], the same version that we find in the abridged version of *al-Dūlāb* (1626 CE) which is not from Yūḥannā 'Abd al-Masīḥ. Probably a 17th c. version.
58. F. 129r–167r: John the Merciful [November 12], same version.
59. F. 167v–179r: John of Damascus (December 4), same version.
    It starts "on this same say" which means that the previous *Life* is commemorated on the same day, while referring to the *Life of Barbara* which was copied after.
60. F. 179r–187r: Barbara (December 4), different version.
61. F. 187v–191v: Tatiana (January 12), same version.
62. F. 192r–198r: John Calybite (January 15), recension.
63. F. 198v–216r: Spyridon (December 12), same version with modifications and sometimes abridged.
64. F. 216v–221v: Juliana (December 21), recension.
65. F. 222r–229r: Eugenia (December 24), different version (shorter) or recension.
66. F. 229v–267v: Sabas (December 5), recension.
67. F. 268r–293r: Clement and Agathangelus (January 23), probably one of the lost pieces of January.
68. F. 293r–301v: Melania (December 31), same version.
69. F. 302r–306v: Paul of Thebes (December 31?), a different version.
70. F. 307r–313v: James the hermit (January 28), probably one of the lost pieces of January.

11. Conclusions

In the 17th century, the bishops of Aleppo had an interest in hagiography. They considered the stories of saints to be spiritual material that should be at the disposal of the common reader. Meletios Karma reviewed the 11th century translation of the Synaxarion based on the Greek text printed in Venice toward the end of the 16th century. In this study, I have shown that Makarios reworked the *Book of the Wheel* by the 11th century author Yuḥannā 'Abd al-Masīḥ. Makarios did not have access to the complete nine volumes of Yuḥannā's original work. While the existence of a copy of the Synaxarion for September is attested to by Makarios, there is no way to verify that the texts for October and May have ever existed. It is noteworthy that October is also lost in the only copies of Yuḥannā's *Book of the Wheel* preserved in Sinai.

Furthermore, Makarios uses Yuḥannā's texts very differently. He copies some of them with nearly no changes, corrects others based on unknown sources, and discards others to add new accounts. The process of revision took nearly three years and Makarios completed this work very early in his career (1638 CE), at a time when he seems not yet to have discovered the works of Agapius Landos. What were his sources? Did he introduce his own ideas and popular accounts? These questions should be addressed in future studies of this newly uncovered work of Makarios ibn al-Za'īm while hoping to find more dispersed material from both Yuḥannā 'Abd al-Masīḥ's and Makarios' versions of the *Book of the Wheel*.

Appendix 1: List of Saints in Alphabetical Order

Adrian and Nathalia (August 26), n. 51

Agathangelus (November 5), n. 3

Alexius (March 17), n. 28

Amphilochius (November 23), n. 13

Apostles (June 30), n. 35

Barbara (December 4), n. 60

Barlaam (November 19; usually 16), n. 12

Barlaam of the Black Mountain [July 19], n. 42

Basil the Great [January 1], n. 56

Benedictus (March 14), n. 27

Catherina (November 25), n. 17

Christina (July 24), n. 45

Clement and Agathangelus (January 23), n. 67

Clement of Rome (November 24), n. 15

Cosmas and Damianus (November 1), n. 1

Cyra, see Marana and Cyra

Cyricus and Julitta (July 15), n. 37

Damianus, see Cosmas and Damianus

Dius and Macrina (July 19), n. 40

Elias, the Prophet (July 20), n. 43

Episteme, see Galaction and Episteme

Eudoxia (March 1), n. 25

Eugenia (December 24), n. 65

Eupraxia (July 25), n. 47

Eustratius (December 13), n. 55

Febronia (June25), n. 33

Galaction and Epistime (November 5), n. 2

George (April 23), n. 30

Gregory of Agrentis (date not indicated), n. 14

Gregory of Neocesarea (November 17), n. 9

Gurias, Samona and Habib (November 15), n. 8

Habib, see Gurias, Samona, Habib

Hermolaus (July 26), n. 49

Ignatius of Antioch (December 20), n. 52

Jacob (November 27), n. 19

James the Hermit (January 28), n. 70

John Calybite (January 15), n. 62

John Chrysostom (November 13), n. 6

John of Damascus (December 4), n. 59

John the Merciful (November 12), n. 5, 58

John, see Simon Salos and John

Julian of Homs (February 6), n. 20

Julian of Tarsus (June 21), n. 32

Juliana (December 21), n. 64

Julitta, see Cyricus and Julitta

Macrina, see Dius and Macrina

Marana and Cyra (February 28), n. 24

Appendix 2: Collation Sample of Yūḥannā's (1) and Makarios' (2) *Book of the Wheel*[37]

I shall provide a sample of collation of the beginning of the *Life of Photine*. I use Yūḥannā's text as the basis. I indicated in the apparatus Makarios' changes with "M".

١) في أيام نارون الملك على الروم نشأ على المسيحيين اضطهاد عظيم، وذلك ان بعد وفاة القديسين الرسولين بطرس وبولص الكثيرة سعادتهما الجزيلة مدحتهما بالشهادة الحميدة، تزايد البحث وكثر القبض على النصارى، ولا سيما على من كان لهما متلمذاً، من طريق انهم دعاة الى الحق ورسل الرب، وكانت فوتينه المغبوطة مع يوسى ابنها في مدينة قرطاجنة من بلد افريقية تنادي بالبشارة بابلغ المجاهرة، وكان ابنها الآخر الاكبر المسما فيقطر قد عظم شأنه وشاعت دربته في الحروب العظيمة المنسوبة الى الامة المعروفة بالغافرية التي تظافرت جيوشها على اهل رومية

نارون] M نارن؛ الملك] M ملك؛ على] om .M؛ ان] om .M؛ طريق] M اجل؛ دعاة] M يدعوا؛ ورسل] M وكانوا رسل؛ المغبوطة] M المغبوطة] om .M؛ بابلغ المجاهرة] M قدام كل الأمم؛ الاكبر] om .M؛ وشاعت دربته] M وكبر خبره؛ المنسوبة – جيوشها] M التي كانت على الاعدا

٢) وبعد ان ارسل الملك الى بلد ايطالية رئيسا لقواد جيوشه امره الملك ايضا بتعذيب جميع النصارى الذين في بلد ايطالية وهي الافرنجة فقال سافستيانوس الامير عند استماعه امر الملك لفيقطر رييس القواد، قد عرفتك مسيحيا وبالمسيح معترفا، واعرف هذا ايضا ان امك تلميذة للمسيح تابعة لبطرس هي ويوسى اخوك ابنها، فاطعني الآن واعمل ما قد امرك الملك به ليلا يصل الخطر الى نفسك. فقال له فقطر القديس، انا جندي لالاهنا

---

37 I provided a collation sample of the beginning of the *Life of Photine*. Yūḥannā's text is used as the basis. Macarios' changes are indicated with "M" in the apparatus.

ايسوع المسيح الملك العظيم الذي لا يموت ولست اطيع ملكا مايتا اذ كان ملكه وقتيًا زايلًا، وملك ربي ايسوع المسيح لا يموت ابديًا ومن يقيم في ملكه فقد ورث حياة مؤبدة. فقال له الامير اذ قد حصلت لجيوش الملك قايدًا فاقبل ما اشير به عليك، كقبولك مشورة صديق لك صدوق، وامتثل ما تقدم به الملك اليك، والذين تجدهم من النصارى فاستعرض نياتهم بحضرتك وعذبهم ان خالفوا طاعتك، واقبض على ما عندهم من الاموال التي جمعوها من مدنك وبلادك، فيحصل لك من الملك كرامات جسيمة وصلات عميمة، ويحل لك ما يمتلكونه ربحًا يخصك، وارسل الى امك واخيك واخيك رسالة بخطك مع اوثق غلمانك تامرهما الا يجاهروا بالتعليم للمسيحيين

ارسل] M ارسله؛ لقواد جيوشه] M على جنوده؛ جميع] M ساير؛ سافستيانوس] M om.؛ القواد] M الاجناد؛ قد عرفتك – هذا ايضا] M om.؛ للمسيح] M المسيح؛ قد] M om.؛ الملك] M om.؛ فقطر] M فيقطر؛ لالاهنا] M لالهنا؛ ايسوع] M يسوع؛ ابديًا] M ابدًا؛ يقيم] M قد ثبت؛ كقبولك] M كقولك؛ اليك] M وامرك؛ جسيمة وصلات عميمة] M جزيله ووهباة عظيمه؛ ما يمتلكونه] M كل مالهم؛ واخيك] M واخوك؛ الا يجاهروا] M ان يجتهدوا

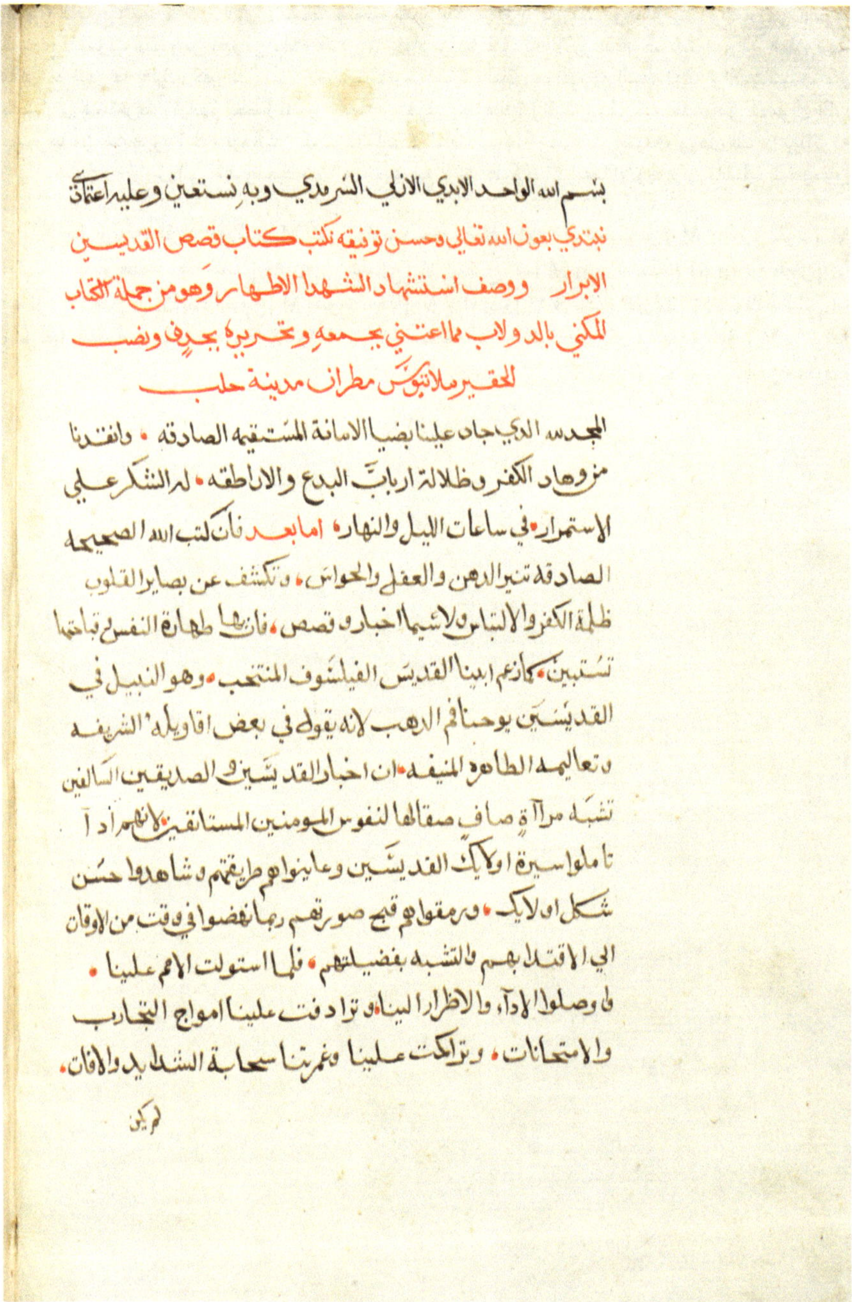
بسم الله الواحد الابدي الازلي السرمدي وبه نستعين وعليه اعتمادي
نبتدي بعون الله تعالى وحسن توفيقه نكتب كتاب قصص القديسين
الابرار ووصف استشهاد الشهدا الاطهار وهو من جملة الكتاب
المكني بالدولاب مما اعتني بجمعه وتحريره بحرف ونصب
الحقير مكاريوس مطران مدينة حلب
الحمد لله الذي جاد علينا بضيا الامانة المستقيمة الصادقة • وانقذنا
من وهاد الكفر وظلالة ارباب البدع والاراطقة • له الشكر على
الاستمرار • في ساعات الليل والنهار • اما بعد فان كتب الله الصحيحة
الصادقة تنير الذهن والعقل والحواس • وتكشف عن بصاير القلوب
ظلمة الكفر والالتباس ولاسيما اخبار وقصص • فان بها طهارة النفس وبها

Fig. 1: Makarios ibn al-Zaʿīm, Preface of the *Book of the Wheel* (beginning). The Bodleian Library, University of Oxford, MS Huntington 27, f. 1v.

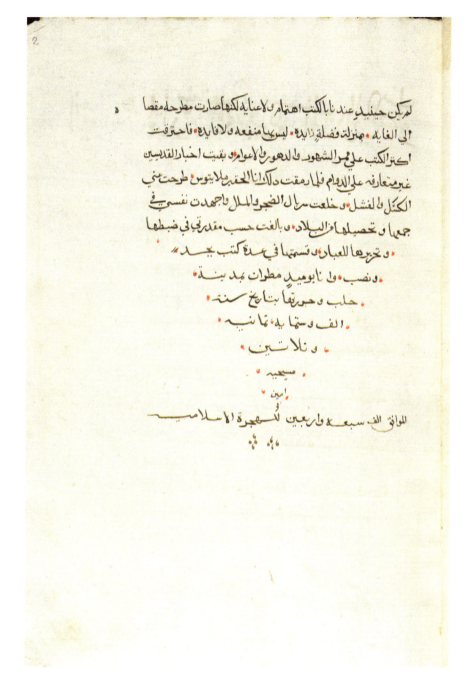

لم يكن حينئذٍ عند نا بالكتب اهتمام ولا عناية لكنها صارت مطرحه مقصا
الى الغايه • هنزلت وفضلة زايده • ليس بها منفعه ولا فايده • فاحترقت
اكثر الكتب على مر الشهود والدهور والاعوام و بقيت اخبار القديسين
غير متعارفه على الدوام فلما مقت ذلك انا الحقير ميلاتيوس طرحت عني
الكسل والفشل • و خلعت سربال الضجر والملل واجهدت نفسي في
جمعها و تحصيلها من البلاد • و بالغت حسب مقدرتي في ضبطها
• و تحريرها للعباره وقسمتها في عدة كتب جسد »
• و نصب • ول نا بو ميد مطران مدينة
• حلب و حوريها بتاريخ سنة
• الف و ستمايه • ثما نيه
• و ثلا ثين •
• مسيحيه •
• آمين •
الموافق الف سبعه واربعين للهجرة الاسلاميه
٪؞

Fig. 2: Makarios ibn al-Zaʿīm, Preface of the *Book of the Wheel* (end). The Bodleian Library, University of Oxford, MS Huntington 27, f. 2r.

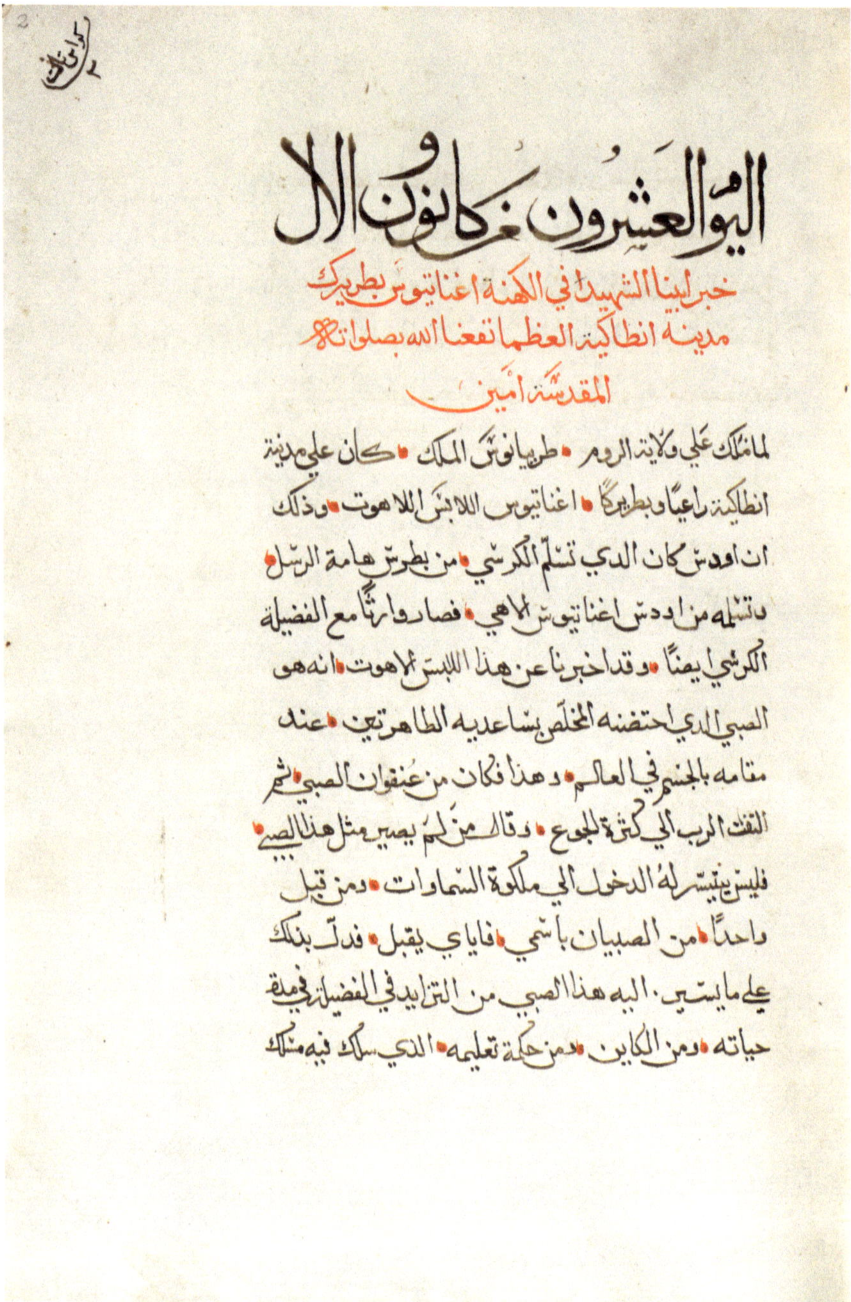

اليوم العشرون من كانون الاول

خبر ابينا الشهيد في الكهنة اغناطيوس بطريرك
مدينة انطاكية العظمى نفعنا الله بصلواته
المقدسة أمين

لما ملك على ولاية الروم ٠ طريانوش الملك ٠ كان على مدينة
انطاكية راعيًا وبطريركًا ٠ اغناطيوس اللابس اللاهوت ٠ وذلك
ان اودسى كان الذي تسلّم الكرسي ٠ من بطرس هامة الرسل
وتسلّمه من اودسى اغناطيوس الاهي ٠ فصار وارثًا مع الفضيلة
الكرسي ايضًا ٠ وقد اخبرنا عن هذا اللابس اللاهوت ٠ انه هو
الصبي الذي احتضنه المخلّص يساعديه الطاهرتين ٠ عند
مقامه بالجسم في العالم ٠ وهذا فكان من عنقود الصبي ثم
القت الرب الى كثرة الجوع ٠ وقال من لم يصير مثل هذا الصبي
فليس يتيسّر له الدخول الى ملكوت السماوات ٠ ومن قبل
واحدًا من الصبيان باسمي ٠ فاياي يقبل ٠ فدلّ بذلك
على ما يتبين ٠ اليه هذا الصبي من التزايد في الفضائل في جميع
حياته ٠ ومن الكائن ٠ ومن حكمة تعليمه الذي سلك فيه مثلك

Fig. 3: Makarios ibn al-Zaʿīm, *Book of the Wheel*: Tome 4. The Bodleian Library, University of Oxford, MS Huntington 30, f. 2r.

Fig. 4: Makarios ibn al-Zaʿīm, *Book of the Wheel*: Tome 1A. Damascus, Orthodox Patriarchate, MS 167, f. 1v.

Bibliography

El-Gemayel, Ronney. "Les manuscrits du patriarcat grec-orthodoxe de Damas dans l'Histoire de Joseph Nasrallah et Rachid Haddad ". In Željko Paša (ed.), *Between the Cross and the Crescent. Studies in Honor of Samir Khalil Samir, S.J. on the Occasion of His Eightieth Birthday* (Col. OCA 304). Rome: Pontificio Instituto Orientale, 2018, p. 248.

Feodorov, Ioana. "The Arabic Version of the Life of Saint Paraskevi the New by Makarios Az-Za'īm". In Kinga Dévényi (ed.), *Proceedings of the 20th Congress of the Union Européenne des Arabisants et Islamisants*, Part One, The Arabist. Budapest Studies in Arabic. Budapest: Eotvos Lorand University, Chair for Arabic Studies & Csoma de Koros Society, Section of Islamic Studies, 2002, p. 69–80.

Graf, Georg. *Geschichte der christlichen arabischen Literatur*, vol. I. Vatican City: Biblioteca Apostolica Vaticana, 1944.

Ibrahim, Habib, Mike Makhoul. "Les débuts du renouveau intellectuel à Antioche au Xe s. Quatre hagiographies inédites traduites au Mont-Admirable". *Pecia. Le livre et l'écrit*, 18, 2, 2015, p. 39–54.

Ibrahim, Habib. "Liste des vies de saints et des homélies conservées dans les ms. Sinaï arabe 395–403, 405–407, 409 et 423". *Chronos*, 38, 2018, p. 49.

Ibrahim, Habib. "Un moine métaphraste à Antioche : Yūḥannā 'Abd al-Masīḥ († 11e siècle)". In Reinhart Ceulemans, Daniel Oltean (eds.), *Foreign Monks in Byzantium: Migration Trends and Integration Policies in Religious Context* (col. Orientalia Lovaniensia Analecta / Bibliothèque de Byzantion). Leuven (forthcoming).

Kilzī, Lāwandiyūs. " 'Ināyat al-baṭriyark Makāriyūs al-rābi' Za'īm bi-jam' akhbār al-qiddīsīn. Muqaddimat makhṭūṭ maḥfūẓ fī maktabat dayr al-Shīr". *al-Masarra* 25, 1939, p. 619–623, 686–691.

Nasrallah, Joseph. *Histoire du mouvement littéraire dans l'Eglise melchite du Ve au XXe siècle*, vol. IV: Période ottomane 1516–1900, tome 1 : 1516–1724. Louvain: Peeters/Paris: Chez l'auteur, 1979.

Noret, Jacques. "Ménologes, synaxaires, ménées. Essai de clarification d'une terminologie". *Analecta Bollandiana*, 86, 1968, p. 21–24.

Pusey, Edward Bouverie. *Bibliothecae Bodleianae codicum manuscriptorum Orientalium catalogi*. Partis secundae volumen secundum, arabicos complectens. Oxford: E typographeo academico, 1835, p. 566.

Sauget, Joseph-Marie. *Premières recherches sur l'origine et les caractéristiques des synaxaires Melkites : XIe – XVIIe siècles* (col. Subsidia Hagiographica, 45). Brussels, 1969.

Treiger, Alexander. "SINAITICA (1): The Antiochian Menologion, Compiled by Hieromonk Yūḥannā 'Abd al-Masīḥ (First Half of the 13th Century)". *Khristianskīĭ Vostok*, 8, 2017, p. 216–217.

Uri, Joannes. *Bibliothecae Bodleianae codicum mss. Orientalium... catalogus. Pars prima.* Oxford: E typographeo clarendoniano, 1787, p. 29–46.

Walbiner, Carsten M. "Preserving the Past and Enlightening the Present: Macarius B. al-Zaim and Medieval Melkite Literature". *Parole de l'Orient*, 34, 2009, p. 433–441.

Walbiner, Carsten M. "Macarius Ibn al-Za'im and the beginnings of an Orthodox church historiography in bilad al-Sham". In Université de Balamand (ed.), *Le rôle des historiens orthodoxes dans l'historiographie. Actes du colloque 11–14 Mars 2007, al-Balamand* [Balamand], [2010], p. 11-28.

Walbiner, Carsten M. " 'Popular' Greek Literature on the Move: the Translation of Several Works of Agapios Landos of Crete into Arabic in the 17th Century". *Revue des Études Sud-Est Européennes*, 51, 2013, p. 147–157.

Yuḥannā ʿAbd al-Masīḥ († 11ᵉ s.). *'Maʿīn al-ḥayāt al-Markab al-sāʾir fī mīnāʾ al-naǧāt', autrement connu comme al-Dūlāb*, ed. by Habib Ibrahim, 2 vols. Beirut: CEDRAC, 2020–2021.

Contributors

Doru Bădără († 2022) was a graduate of the Faculty of History, University of Bucharest. From 1972, he worked as chief of the Department of Manuscripts and Rare Books of the "Carol I" Central University Library in Bucharest. He started his research on printing in 1980, with his Ph.D. thesis *Tiparul românesc la sfârșitul secolului al XVII-lea și începutul secolului al XVIII-lea* (*The Romanian Printing Press at the end of the 17th Century and the Beginning of the 18th Century*), published in 1998 (Editura Istros, Brăila), and continued with many articles and studies, recently collected in *Din istoria cărții și a tiparului românesc. Studii și materiale* (*History of the Romanian Book and Printing. Studies and Works*), published in 2019 (Editura Istros, Brăila). He was the editor-in-chief of the Romanian Magazine of Book History. In 2000, he received the "Dimitrie Onciul" Award of the Romanian Academy for his scientific discoveries regarding early printing in the Romanian Principalities. His expertise covered the entire area of printing in the Romanian lands, in Slavonic, Greek, and Romanian. He was an outstanding expert in the technical aspects of book-printing and binding.

Archim. Policarp Chițulescu, a Senior Member on the TYPARABIC project team, is a patriarchal counsellor and the director of the Library of the Holy Synod in Bucharest. He holds a Ph.D. in Theology – Christian Literature – and is an expert in early printed books and East-European presses. His main research fields are the history of printing, manuscripts, printed books, libraries, styles and practices of writing, the circulation of ideas, and cultural relations between the Romanian Principalities and Europe. His latest publications are *Viața monahală din Țara Românească la mijlocul secolului al XIX-lea* (*The Monastic Life in Wallachia in the mid-18th Century*), Bucharest, 2022, and *Cartea slavă din Biblioteca Sfântului Sinod – secolele XVI–XVIII* (*The Slavic Books in the Library of the Holy Synod*), Bucharest, 2020.

Hasan Çolak, a Senior Member on the TYPARABIC project team, is Associate Professor of Ottoman History at TOBB University of Economics and Technology in Ankara, Turkey. He completed his Ph.D. in 2013 with a dissertation on the interaction between the Eastern Patriarchates and the Ottoman central administration. His first monograph entitled *The Orthodox Church in the Early Modern Middle East* (2015), is based on his doctoral studies. In collaboration with Elif Bayraktar-Tellan, he published *The Orthodox Church as an Ottoman Institution* (2019) and founded the book series *Ecclesiastica Ottomanica*, both at the Isis Press in Istanbul.

Radu Dipratu, a Junior Researcher on the TYPARABIC project team, works as a historian at the Institute for South-East European Studies of the Romanian Academy in Bucharest. He completed his Ph.D. in 2017 at the Faculty of History, University of Bucharest, with a dissertation on the religious articles of Ottoman capitulations in the 17th century. His recent book, *Regulating Non-Muslim Communities in the Seventeenth-Century Ottoman Empire: Catholics and Capitulations* (Routledge, 2022), derives from this dissertation. His main areas of academic research are Ottoman diplomacy and the Catholic communities of the Ottoman Empire in the early modern era.

Ioana Feodorov, the Principal Investigator of the TYPARABIC Project, is a Senior Researcher with the Institute for South-East European Studies of the Romanian Academy in Bucharest. She was granted a Ph.D. in Philology from the University of Bucharest in 1999 for a thesis concerning *The Expression of Grading in Romanian and Arabic*, and a Dr. Habil. title in 2018. Her main fields of research are the Romanians' contribution to the beginnings of printing in Arabic type, Arabic texts that document the historical connections between Romanians and Arab Christians in the 16th–18th centuries, and cataloguing the Arabic manuscripts in Romanian collections. Among her publications are *Arabic Printing for the Christians in Ottoman Lands. The East-European Connection* (De Gruyter, 2023, in Open Access) and Dimitrie Cantemir, *Salvation of the Sage and Ruin of the Sinful World*, Arabic text and annotated English translation (Brill, 2016, with Yulia Petrova).

Habib Ibrahim, a Junior Researcher on the TYPARABIC project team, is an Assistant Researcher at CEDRAC – Université Saint Joseph, Beirut (Lebanon). He obtained his Ph.D. in 2016 from École Pratique des Hautes Études, Paris, for a thesis on John of Damascus in the Arabic tradition. His edition of several of John of Damascus's anti-Miaphysite and anti-Iconoclast treatises in Arabic will soon be published in the *Patrimoine arabe chrétien* collection. He is also a Research Associate with the *Religious Conflict and Mobility. Byzantium and the Greater Mediterranean, 700–900* project at the Eberhard Karls University of Tübingen, where he is researching the early Melkite canonical collection.

Taisiya Leber is a Research Fellow at the Department for Byzantine Studies, Gutenberg University of Mainz (Germany), from where she received her Ph.D. in 2018. At the same University, she is currently leading the postdoc project "The Beginnings of Book Printing in the Ottoman Empire: The Role of Printed Books in the Transmission of Byzantine and Post-Byzantine Heritage", funded by the DFG SPP Transottomanica: Osteuropäisch-osmanisch-persische Mobilitätsdy-namiken. She is one of the co-editors of *Knowledge on the Move in a Transotto-*

man Perspective. Dynamics of Intellectual Exchange from the Fifteenth to the Early Twentieth Century (V&R Unipress, 2021) and has authored several articles on book printing and print culture in the early modern Ottoman Empire.

Samuel Noble is a Senior Researcher on the TYPARABIC project team. He obtained his M.Phil. degree in 2009 from Yale University and a Ph.D. in 2022 from KU Leuven. His research focuses on the social and intellectual history of Arab Christians, particularly in the Patriarchate of Antioch. He is a co-editor of *The Orthodox Church in the Arab World (700-1700): An Anthology of Sources* (Cornell University Press, 2014), and *Arabic Christianity between the Ottoman Levant and Eastern Europe* (Brill, 2021), and co-translator from Russian of Constantin Panchenko's book *Arab Orthodox Christians under the Ottomans 1516–1831* (Holy Trinity Publications, 2016).

Ovidiu Olar is the Principal Investigator of the ERC project StG ORTHPOL hosted by the Austrian Academy of Sciences in Vienna. He obtained his Ph.D. in 2015 from École des Hautes Études en Sciences Sociales, Paris. He is the author of *La boutique de Théophile. Les relations du patriarche de Constantinople Kyrillos Loukaris (1570–1638) avec la Réforme* (Centre d'études byzantines, néo-helléniques et sud-est européennes – EHESS, 2019). His main research interests are the history of political ideas, cultural history, early modern adventurers, the religious reforms, and the confessional "Cold War" of the 17th century.

Yulia Petrova, a Senior Researcher on the TYPARABIC project team, is a Senior Researcher with the "A. Krymsky" Institute of Oriental Studies of the National Academy of Sciences of Ukraine in Kyiv. She obtained her Ph.D. in 2007 and is a specialist in Arabic Philology with the same Institute. Her current research interests focus on textual criticism, the edition and translation of Christian Arabic manuscripts, and the study of the Christian Arabic literary heritage. She has edited and translated into Russian the abridged Arabic manuscript copy of *The Travels of Macarius, Patriarch of Antioch* preserved in Kyiv (2015).

Orlin Sabev, a Senior Member on the TYPARABIC project team, is a Professor of History at the Institute for Balkan Studies and Centre of Thracian Studies of the Bulgarian Academy of Sciences in Sofia. In 2000, he obtained his Ph.D. degree with a doctoral thesis on the Ottoman education institutions of Bulgaria in the 15th–18th centuries and in 2015 he obtained a Dr. Habil. degree by defending a habilitation thesis on the educational policies of Robert College in Istanbul (1863–1933). He is the author of over 100 articles dedicated to Ottoman cultural and social history and Ottoman paleography. Among his most recent publications are *Spiritus Roberti: Shaping New Minds at Robert College in Late Ottoman Society*

(1863–1923) (Boğaziçi Üniversitesi Yayınevi, 2014) and *Waiting for Müteferrika: Glimpses of Ottoman Print Culture* (Academic Studies Press, 2018).

Vera Tchentsova, a Senior Member on the TYPARABIC project team, is a Professor at École Pratique des Hautes Études, Paris. She is also an associated member of the UMR 8167 "Orient et Méditerranée / Monde byzantin" in Paris. She received her Ph.D. from the Institute of General History of the Academy of Sciences of Russia, Moscow (1995), where she started to conduct research specializing in Byzantine history. Her interest in manuscripts and archival documents led her to join the research projects on unpublished materials concerning the relations of Russia with the Christian East in the 16th-18th centuries from the Muscovite depositories. Later she combined these studies with the research of documentary materials in foreign collections (Greece, Italy, Ukraine, and Romania), publishing on topics related to the contacts between Churches, diplomatic links assured by representatives of the Orthodox clergy, international politics in Eastern and South-Eastern Europe, the translation of the "Byzantine heritage" literature, post-Byzantine art, and its influence in East-European countries. She is the author of *Ikona Iverskoĭ Bogomateri* (*The Icon of Our Lady of Iviron*, Moscow, 2010), *Kievskaia mitropolia mezhdu Konstantinopolem i Moskvoj, 1686* (*The Metropolitan See of Kyiv between Constantinople and Moscow, 1686*, Kyiv, 2020), and of numerous articles on Church history.

Mihai Țipău, a Senior Member on the TYPARABIC project team, is a Senior Researcher with the Institute for South-East European Studies of the Romanian Academy. He holds a Ph.D. in Political Science (National and Capodistrian University of Athens, 2004) and a Ph.D. in History (University of Bucharest, 2005). His main fields of research are Byzantine and Post-Byzantine history and medieval and early modern Greek historical literature. Among his published works works are *Ορθόδοξη συνείδηση και εθνική ταυτότητα στα Βαλκάνια (1700–1821)* (*Orthodox Consciousness and National Identity in the Balkans (1700–1821)*), with a foreword by Paschalis M. Kitromilides (Thessaloniki, 2015), and *Identitate post-bizantină în sud-estul Europei. Mărturia scrierilor istorice greceşti* (*Post-Byzantine Identity in South-East Europe. The Evidence of the Greek Historical Writings*, Bucharest, 2013).

Fr Andrew Wade is an independent researcher, parish priest and Superior of the Orthodox Priory of Saint Mammas, Pistoia (Italy). An alumnus of the University of Cambridge (BA in 1974, MA in 1977), he completed his postgraduate studies in philosophy and theology in Italy (1974-1984). He held lectures at several universities in Italy, France, Moldova, Romania, and Russia, and he is the author of numerous articles on history, theology, and liturgy. Among the latest: "The Enigmatic

Horologion contained in Sinai Ar. 232", in M. Lüstraeten, B. Butcher, S. Hawkes-Teeples (eds.), *LET US BE ATTENTIVE! Proceedings of the Seventh International Congress of the Society of Oriental Liturgy*, Verlag Aschendorff, 2020, p. 285–305, and "Byzantinised or Alexandrianised – or Both? Vespers in the 13ᵗʰ c. Melkite Alexandrian Arabic Horologion Sinai Arabic 232", *MDPI Religions*, 13, 2022, 607.

Fr Rami Wakim is a Senior Researcher with the TYPARABIC team, a priest of the Melkite Greek Catholic Church and the Head of the Patriarchal Chancellery. He holds a Ph.D. in Patristic Theology from Centre Sèvres (Jesuit Faculties of Paris) for a thesis on Saint Maximus the Confessor's logocentric anthropology in *Ambiguum 41*. He is a senior lecturer at the University Saint-Joseph of Beirut (Lebanon) and is currently coordinating the edition and publication of the Lexicon of Practical Theology in Arabic. His main research fields are Late Antiquity, Byzantine history and theology, formation of the Christian doctrine, and inter-Christian relations. Selected publications: "la Mystagogie de Maxime le Confesseur : l'être ecclésial et l'unité à Dieu", in *Proche Orient Chrétien*, N°3, 2015, p. 235–253 ; " 'L'Église: vers une vision commune' : Réponse catholique" (1) et (2), translation, in *Proche Orient Chrétien*, N°69, 2019, p. 318–325, et N° 70, 2012, p. 150–191; "The Virgin Mary, a Model of Encounter: The Relevance of Qur'anic Mary to Christian-Muslim Dialogue", in *Mary, God-Bearer to a World in Need*, Maura Hearden & Virginia M. Kimball (ed.,), Wipf and Stock Publications, 2013, p. 110–125.

Carsten-Michael Walbiner works at the Research Center for the Christian Orient at the Catholic University of Eichstätt-Ingolstadt (Germany). He received his Ph.D. in 1995 from Leipzig University for a thesis on Makarios Ibn al-Zaʿim. His research interests gravitate around the history and literature of Arab Christianity in Ottoman times, on which he has written several dozen articles, including entries in the series of *Christian-Muslim Relations. A Bibliographical History* and *The Encyclopaedia of Islam THREE*, both published by Brill. Among his recent projects is the conception of a catalogue of the Christian Oriental manuscripts kept at Andechs monastery in Bavaria and a record of the yet uncatalogued Christian Arabic manuscripts conserved by the Custody of the Holy Land in Jerusalem.